Foreword

In my first two years as Chairman of Resource, the Council for Museums, Archives and Libraries, I have had the extraordinary pleasure of visiting a large number of museums, galleries and historical houses throughout the UK.

The variety and depth of collections on public display in the United Kingdom is unrivalled. We are the envy of Europe and yet most of us have little knowledge of this huge quantity and geographic spread of places and collections available to us.

Lord Evans of Temple Guiting
Photo Richard H Smith

I have been struck by both the quantity and quality of museums, galleries, houses and sites, extending from the great collections in our National Museums & Galleries to the fine collections of the Cecil Higgins Art Gallery in Bedford, to the glories of Hadrian's Wall, the delights of the collection at Harewood House and, at the other end of the country, Truro's Royal Cornwall Museum.

This publication draws together comprehensive listings information and maps that will contribute to raising the profile of many lesser known sites and institutions and provide greater detail to cover wider audiences.

The galleries, houses and museums listed here and the people that look after and interpret them for us are a vital part of our cultural well-being. It is these places and these things which inspire our creativity and sense of exploration. They provide us with experiences that can enrich, make sense of and change our lives. They can help ground our modern society in its history and traditions and help build a thriving cultural economy.

This slim volume has a great role to play, in widening our horizons, and widening the audiences who will enjoy and discover the heritage around us.

Matthew Evans
Chairman of Resource

Contents

	Page	Map
Foreword	3	
Introduction	6	
How to use	7	
Ireland Counties Map	8	
UK Counties Map	9	
UK Railways Network	10	
England	13	
Bath, Bristol & NE Somerset	13	12
Bedfordshire	20	19
Berkshire	20	19
Bristol	13	12
Buckinghamshire	20	19
Cambridgeshire	33	32
Cheshire	41	40
Cleveland	216	215
Cornwall	61	60
Cumbria	70	69
Derbyshire	78	77
Devon	88	87
Dorset	97	96
Durham	216	215
Essex	104	103
Gloucestershire	111	110
Hampshire	117	116
Herefordshire	134	133
Hertfordshire	20	19
Isle of Wight	117	116
Kent	140	139
Lancashire	151	150
Leicestershire	158	157
Lincolnshire & South Humberside	168	167
London - Central	175	173
London - Outer	195	194
Manchester	41	40
Merseyside	41	40
Norfolk	208	207
Northamptonshire	33	32

Contents

	Page	Map
England *(continued)*		
Northumberland	216	215
Nottinghamshire	158	157
Oxfordshire	231	230
Shropshire	238	237
Somerset	243	242
Staffordshire	78	77
Suffolk	248	247
Surrey	253	252
Sussex - East & West	258	257
Tyne & Wear	216	215
Warwickshire	270	269
West Midlands	270	269
Wiltshire	281	280
Worcestershire	134	133
Yorkshire & North Humberside	287	286
Scotland	313	
Edinburgh, Glasgow & Southern Scotland	313	312
Central, East & Northeast Scotland	341	340
Highlands & Islands	358	357
Wales	366	
South & Southwest Wales	366	365
Mid-Wales	377	376
North Wales	381	380
Ireland	390	
Northern Ireland	390	389
Dublin & Ireland	398	397
Isle of Man	412	
Channel Islands	414	
Index by Classification	417	
Index by Museum/Gallery Name	429	
Index by Town	441	

Introduction

Welcome to the 2002 edition of 'Collections in Museums & Galleries, Historic Houses & Sites'.

Many of the greatest treasures in the world are in British and Irish museums and art galleries. Also stately homes and historic country houses have superb collections of fine pictures, furniture and decorative art.

Local culture and history intrigues many of us and are accessible in museums in every part of the country. Contemporary and modern art are well served by numerous dedicated galleries.

We are indebted to curators, owners and their staff who have provided us with profiles and photographs of their wonderful and diverse collections from over 1700 museums, art galleries, historic houses and sites - and now many, including our national museums and art galleries, have free entry for everyone.

Our book caters for all ages and will assist you in finding whatever you are looking for. Refer to the three indexes at the back of the book to search by Name, Town or Classification. There are 29 different and specialist classifications ranging from Anthropology to Victoriana (listed on page 11).

In this our first edition it is inevitable that we have omitted some museums and galleries that you feel should be listed. Please email us on *editor@tomorrows.co.uk* or return the report form on page 448, and we will add them to the 2003 edition to be published in November 2002.

Davina Ludlow
Publisher

How to use

Finding the right Museum, Gallery, Historic House

We have divided the publication into England, Scotland, Wales, Ireland, Isle of Man and Channel Islands. Each section has its own colour coding. The maps on pages 8-9 detail the Areas/Counties for each Country, and the contents (pages 4-5) provide a page reference to each Area/County, where you will find a more detailed map showing Map References for museums etc listed within that Area/County. You should use these Map References to locate museums etc within the Town or Area that you wish to visit. Also refer to the quick reference indexes at the back which provide page references by Classification, Town and, if you are looking for a particular museum, by Name.

Sequence of Entries

The listings within each Area (i.e North Wales) or within each County (i.e Cumbria) are sequenced by Town Name. Multiple listings within the same town are shown in alphabetical name order.

Profiles

Each entry has a profile of its collection/s written by the Museum's Curator (or in some cases its owner).

Opening Times

The periods of the year, the days of the week and opening times (24 hour clock) are provided.

Key to Symbols

✍	Guided or Private Tours	☕	Café or Refreshments
♿	Disabled Access (Please check for exact details)	🍴	Restaurant
🎁	Gift Shop or Sales Point	🚗	Car Parking

Ireland Counties Map

UK Counties Map

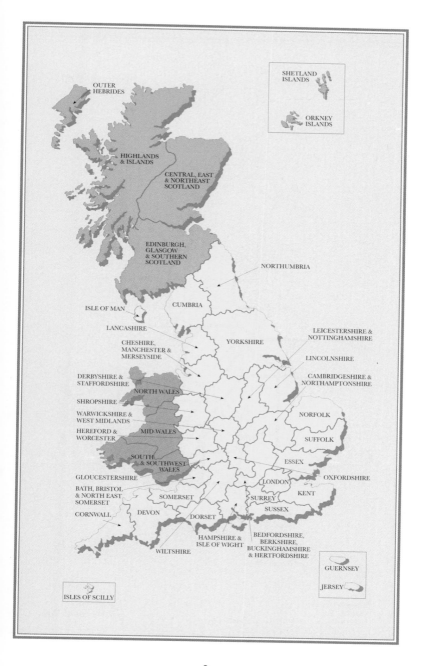

UK Railways Network

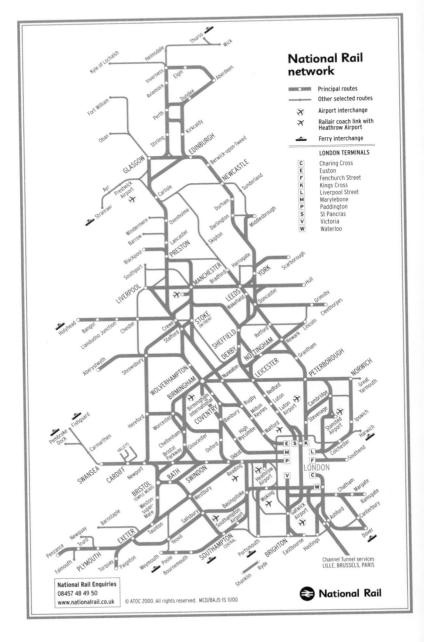

How to use

Admission Charges

Admission charges for England, Scotland, Wales, Northern Ireland, isle of Man and the Channel Islands are shown in British £, and for Ireland in Euros (€) which is now the monetary unit in Ireland.

Locations

Each listing has a brief description of its location as well as a Map Reference which is shown on the Map at the start of each Area/County.

Indexes

At the back of the book there are quick reference indexes by Classification (see key below), Museum/Gallery Name and Town Name.

Feedback

There is a Report Form on page 448 and this should be used to let us know about Museums etc that you visit (we value your comments, good or bad), also to advise us of any Collections that are not listed in our book that you feel should be listed. Feedback is essential for the integrity of our book.

Key to Classifications
see Classifications Index on page 417

Anthropology	Jewellery	Railway
Archaeological	Literature & Libraries	Religion
Arts, Crafts & Textiles	Maritime	Roman
China & Glass	Military & Defence	Science - Earth
Communications	Mills - Water & Wind	& Planetary
Egyptian	Multicultural	Sculpture
Fashion	Music & Theatre	Sporting History
Geology	Oriental	Toy & Childhood
Health & Medicine	Palaces	Transport
Horticultural	Police, Prisons & Dungeons	Victoriana

Bristol, the largest university city in the southwest of England with its beautiful cathedral, is a industrial and commercial centre with a long history of maritime adventure and commerce an housing a wealth of historic treasures.

The jewel of this lovely region is undoubtedly Bath, built on hills rising steeply from the River Avo This delightful city, a spa centre since Roman times, became a centre of fashion and manne during the eighteenth century. The tradition and history of this region is innovatively an fascinatingly revealed to the visitor through a wealth of fine galleries, museums and displays.

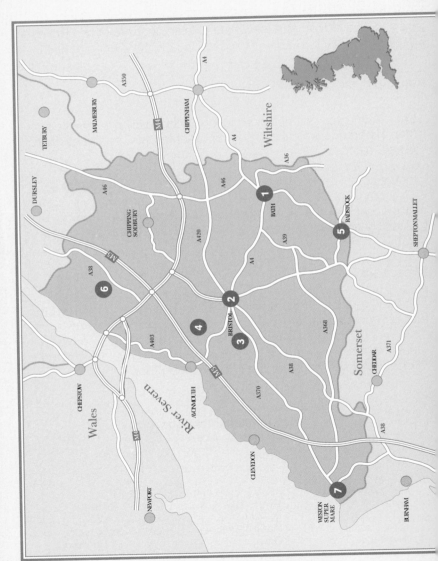

The Red Map References should be used to locate Museums etc on the pages that follow

Bath, Bristol & Northeast Somerset

American Museum in Britain

🐕 ☕ 🚌

Claverton Manor, Bath BA2 7BD   Tel: 01225 460503   Fax: 01225 480726
Email: amibbath@aol.com   Web: www.americanmuseum.org

The American Museum shows in a series of 18 period rooms how Americans lived between the late 17th and mid-19th centuries. There are galleries devoted to Folk Art and to an extensive textile collection. The grounds contain an arboretum of American trees and shrubs as well as a replica of part of the garden at Mount Vernon, George Washington's Virginia home.

Opening Times: 23 Mar to 3 Nov Tue to Sun 14:00-17:00. 23 Nov to 15 Dec Tue to Sun 13:00-16:00. Closed Mon.
Admission: Adult £6.00, Child £3.50, OAP £5.50.
Location: Two miles south east of City Centre.   Map Ref: 1

Conkey's Tavern

Bath Abbey Heritage Vaults

✍ ♿

13 Kingston Buildings, Bath BA1 1LT   Tel / Fax: 01225 422462
Email: laj@heritagevaults.fsnet.co.uk

A pageant of the Abbey's past from the 18th century to the present day in words and pictures, lights and sounds.

Opening Times: Daily 10:00-16:00, closed Xmas & New Year and Good Friday.
Admission: Adult £2.00, Child Free, OAP/Student £1.00.   Location: In the centre of Bath, alongside Bath Abbey.
Map Ref: 1

Bath Postal Museum

♿ 🐕 ☕

8 Broad Street, Bath BA1 5LJ   Tel / Fax: 01225 460333   Email: info@bathpostalmuseum.org
Web: www.bathpostalmuseum.org

We illustrate 4,000 years of communication from clay-mail to e-mail. This time-line includes exhibitions on the Romans and the Victorians, an essential ingredient in KS1 and KS2 curricula. Four computer games can demonstrate not only how the post was 'carried' then, but also during medieval times and the 1930's. A constantly playing video room; plus an international airmail room showing early aviation films and special exhibitions.

Opening Times: Mon to Fri 11:00-17:00.   Admission: Adult £2.90, Child/Concession £1.50, OAP £2.20.   Location: In town centre, one minute walk from General Post Office.   Map Ref: 1

Postboy 18th/19th century

Beckford's Tower & Museum

✍ 🐕

Lansdown Road, Bath BA1 9BH   Tel: 01225 422212/460705   Fax: 01225 481805
Email: beckford@bptrust.demon.co.uk   Web: www.bath-preservation-trust.org.uk

The recently restored Tower, built in 1827 for William Beckford, boasts a spiral staircase and elegant Belvedere offering panoramic views. It contains a museum collection, with paintings, prints, models and art objects, illustrating Beckford's life and interests.

Opening Times: Easter to end Oct Sat Sun & BH 10:30-17:00.   Admission: Adult £2.50, Child/OAP £2.00, Family £6.00.   Location: One and a half miles north from Bath centre on Lansdown Road towards the racecourse.
Map Ref: 1

Building of Bath Museum

✍ 🐕

Countess of Huntingdon's Chapel, The Vineyards, Bath BA1 5NA   Tel: 01225 333895
Fax: 01225 445473   Email: curator@bobm.fsnet.co.uk   www.bath-preservation-trust.org.uk

Situated in the beautiful Gothic chapel built in 1765 is the complete guide to how Georgian Bath was conceived and built. The exhibition is illustrated with a number of models, artefacts, paintings and touch screen computer.

Opening Times: 12 Feb to 31 Jun Tue to Sun & BH 10:30-17:00, 1 Jul to 31 Aug Daily, 1 Sep to 30 Nov Tue to Sun & BH. Closed 30 Nov to mid Feb.   Admission: Adult £4.00, Child £1.50, Concession £3.00.   Location: Short walk from Bath Town Centre on The Paragon which runs parellel with Lansdown and Walcot Street.
Map Ref: 1

Holburne Museum of Art

Great Pulteney Street, Bath BA2 4DB   Tel: 01225 466669   Fax: 01225 333121
Email: holburne@bath.ac.uk   Web: www.bath.ac.uk/holburne

The Holburne Museum of Art by Ray Williams

This jewel in Bath's crown was once the Georgian Sydney Hotel, whose glittering society Jane Austen watched from her house opposite. It displays the treasures collected by Sir William Holburne: superb English and continental silver, porcelain, maiolica, glass and Renaissance bronzes. The Picture Gallery contains works by Turner, Guardi, Stubbs and other artists plus portraits of Bath society by Thomas Gainsborough.

Opening Times: Mid Feb to Mid Dec Tue to Sat 10:00-17:00, Sun 14:30-17:30.   Admission: Adult £3.50, Child £1.50, OAP £3.00, Family £7.00, Residents of Bath & NE Somerset £2.50.   Location: Five minutes walk from town centre.   Map Ref: 1

Museum of Bath at Work

Campden Works, Julian Road, Bath BA1 2RH   Tel / Fax: 01225 318348
Email: mobaw@hotmail.co.uk   Web: www.bath-at-work.org.uk

Stories of working life in Bath, of Bath stone and building industry, Victorian ironmonters, mineral water factory and engineering works, furniture making and car factory. Temporary exhibitions.

Opening Times: Apr to Nov daily, Nov to Apr Sat & Sun 10:00-17:00. Admission: Adult £3.50, Concession £2.50, Family £10.00. Location: North of city centre, five minutes walk. Map Ref: 1

Museum of Costume

Assembly Rooms, Bennett Street, Bath BA1 2QH   Tel: 01225 477785
Fax: 01225 477743   Email: costume_bookings@bathnes.gov.uk
Web: www.museumofcostume.co.uk

18th Century Gallery

One of the most prestigious and extensive collections of its kind. Displays include over 150 dressed figures illustrating the changing styles in fashionable dress for men, women and children from the late 16th century to the present day. The modern collection contains work by many of the world's top designers. Free personal audio guides. Jubilee exhibition of dresses from Her Majesty The Queen's Collection until 3 Nov 2002.

Opening Times: Daily 10:00-16:30. Closed 25-26 Dec. Admission: Adult £5.00, Child £3.50, OAP £4.00, Family £14.00. Group rates and Saver tickets with Roman Baths are available.   Location: Ten minute walk from city centre, 15 minute walk from bus and railway stations.   Map Ref: 1

Gilt bronze statue of a standing monk with begging bowl

Museum of East Asian Art

12 Bennett Street, Bath BA1 2QL   Tel: 01225 464640
Fax: 01225 461718   Email: museum@east-asian-art.freeserve.co.uk   Web: www.east-asian-art.co.uk

A unique museum housing a fine collection of objects from all over East Asia, ranging in date from circa 5000 BC to the present day. The exquisite collection includes Chinese ceramics and metalware, Japanese lacquer and a range of south east Asian ceramics, as well as some outstanding examples of Chinese jade.

Opening Times: Tue to Sat 10:00-17:00, Sun 12:00-17:00, some BH. Closed Mon, Xmas & New Year. Admission: Adult £3.50, Child (under 12) £1.00, OAP £3.00. Location: Upper town area of city; just off The Circus. 20 minutes walk from railway/bus station.

Map Ref: 1

No 1 Royal Crescent

Bath BA1 2LR   Tel: 01225 338727   Fax: 01225 481850   Email: admin@bptrust.demon.co.uk
Web: www.bath-preservation-trust.org.uk

The Lady's Bedroom

A grand town house of the late 18th century accurately restored and furnished with authentic furniture, paintings and carpets. On the ground floor are the study and dining room and on the first floor a lady's bedroom and drawing room. In the basement is a period kitchen and a museum shop.

Opening Times: Mid-Feb to end Oct Tue to Sun 10:30-17:00, Nov Tue to Sun 10:30-16:00. Closed Good Friday, open BH and Bath Festival Mon. Admission: Adult £4.00, Child/Concession/Student £3.50, Family £10.00, Group £2.50.   Location: Central.   Map Ref: 1

Roman Baths

Pump Room, Stall Street, Bath BA1 1LZ   Tel: 01225 477785   Fax: 01225 477743
Email: romanbaths_bookings@bathnes.gov.uk   Web: www.romanbaths.co.uk

Great Bath, Roman Baths

The Roman Baths contain the remains of one of the greatest religious spas in the ancient world and a fine Roman museum. Bath's unique thermal springs rise at the heart of the site. It is the most popular visitor attraction in the West Country and is among the UK's major heritage sites. Free audio tours are available in seven languages.

Opening Times: Jan to Feb, Nov to Dec 09:30-16:30, Mar to Jun, Sep to Oct 09:00-17:00, Jul to Aug 09:00-21:00. Closed 25-26 Dec. Admission: Adult £8.00, Child £4.60, OAP £7.00, Family £20.50. Group rates and saver tickets with Museum of Costume are available.
Location: City centre.   Map Ref: 1

Sally Lunns House & Kitchen Museum

4 North Parade Passage, Bath BA1 1NX   Tel: 01225 461634

The oldest house in Bath, home of the world famous Sally Lunn Bun.

Opening Times: Mon to Sat 10:00-18:00, Sun 11:00-18:00.   Admission: Adult 30p, Child/OAP Free.   Location: One minute walk from railway station.   Map Ref: 1

Victoria Art Gallery

Bridge Street, Bath BA2 4AT   Tel: 01225 477233   Fax: 01225 477231
Email: victoria_enquiries@bathnes.gov.uk   Web: www.victoriagal.org.uk

The permanent collection at the Victoria Art Gallery

Bath and North East Somerset's art gallery, housing a substantial permanent collection in addition to major touring exhibitions. Paintings by Gainsborough, Turner and Sickert hang in the recently refurbished Upper Gallery and are described on free audio guides. Decorative arts newly on display include collections of pottery, porcelain, glass and watches.

Opening Times: Tue to Fri 10:00-17:30, Sat 10:00-17:00. Sun 14:00-17:00. Closed BH. Admission: Free.
Location: City centre.   Map Ref: 1

William Herschel Museum

19 New King Street, Bath BA1 2BL   Tel: 01225 311342/446865   Fax: 01225 446865
Email: curator12@hotmail.com   Web: www.bath-preservation-trust.org.uk

Home of 18th century astronomers William and Caroline Herschel. A charming Georgian townhouse furnished in the style of the period, includes workshop where Herschel made telescopes and discovered the planet Uranus in 1781. Collection of astronomical and musical instruments. 'Star Vault' attraction showing astronomy programmes. Delightful Georgian garden.

Opening Times: Mar to Oct Daily 14:00-17:00, Sat & Sun 11:00-17:00. Sat & Sun 11:00-17:00

only throughout the winter. Admission: Adult £3.50, Child £2.00, Family £7.50. Bath Pass Scheme & Bath Preservation Trust Museums Concession. Location: Six minutes walk from central bus and railway stations, near city centre. Map Ref: 1

BRISTOL

Arnolfini

🐾 🐕 📷 **ARNOLFINI**

16 Narrow Quay, Bristol BS1 4QA   Tel: 0117 929 9191   Fax: 0117 925 3876
Email: arnolfini@arnolfini.demon.co.uk   Web: www.arnolfini.demon.co.uk

Photo: Woodley and Quick

Arnolfini is one of Europe's leading centres for the contemporary arts with an international reputation for presenting new and innovative work. Arnolfini presents international developments and emerging trends in visual art through one-person and group exhibitions, commissions and projects. The Programme draws attention to important British artists at the early stage of their career and presents timely exhibitions by major international artists.

Opening Times: Exhibitions - Mon to Wed, Fri & Sat 10:00-19:00, Thu 10:00-21:00, Sun & BH Mon 12:00-19:00. Closed Xmas, New Year & Good Friday.

Admission: Free. Location: Located in the harbourside, near to the town centre, fifteen minute walk from Bristol Temple Meads Railway Station. Map Ref: 2

Ashton Court Visitor Centre

🐾 🐕 🚂

Ashton Court Estate, Long Ashton, Bristol BS41 9JN   Tel: 0117 963 9174   Fax: 0117 953 2143
Email: marionm_britton@bristol-city.co.uk

Visitor Centre has display of landscape makers and some exhibitions. Information point and small shop, situated in 850 acres of historic parklands with two deer parks and historic gardens.

Opening Times: Easter to end Sep Sat & Sun 10:30-17:30 plus some weekdays in Jul & Aug 13:00-16:30. Oct to Easter Sun only 11:00-16:00. Admission: Free. Location: Off A369 Bristol/Portishead Road. Map Ref: 3

At-Bristol Ltd

♿ 🐕 📷 🐾 🚂

Anchor Road, Harbourside, Bristol BS1 5DB   Tel: 0845 345 1235   Fax: 0117 915 7200
Email: information@at-bristol.org.uk   Web: www.at-bristol.org.uk

At-Bristol brings science, nature and art to life. It consists of Explore, an interactive science centre; Wildwalk, a journey through the history of life on Earth; and the IMAX Theatre, showing giant-screen films.

Opening Times: Daily 10:00-18:00. Admission: Adult from £6.50, Child from £4.50, Concession from £5.50. Location: On Bristol's harbourside in the city centre. Map Ref: 2

Blaise Castle House Museum

📷

Henbury Road, Henbury, Bristol BS10 7QS   Tel: 0117 9039818   Web: www.bristol-city.gov.uk/museums

Steeped in history and set in beautiful parkland, discover everyday objects from times past including kitchen and laundry equipment; sumptuous costume and accessories; a Victorian school room; Victorian baths; model trains, dolls and toy soldiers and more.

Opening Times: Apr to Oct Sat to Wed 10:00-17:00. Admission: Free.

Bristol City Museum & Art Gallery

📷 🐕 **Bristol Museums & Art Gallery**

Queens Road, Bristol BS8 1RL
Tel: 0117 922 3571   Fax: 0117 922 2047
Web: www.bristol-city.gov.uk/museums

Be amazed by countless, wonderful objects. Some of the treasures include: minerals and fossils; Egyptian galleries; Far Eastern art; wildlife galleries; archaeology; ceramics and glass; seven galleries of art. Temporary exhibitions and special events are held throughout the year.

Opening Times: Daily 10:00-17:00. Admission: Free.
Map Ref: 2

'La Belle Dame/Sans Merci' Frank Dicksee 1902

16

Bristol Industrial Museum

& ✦

Princes Wharf, Wapping Road, Bristol BS1 4RN   Tel: 0117 925 1470   Web: www.bristol-city.gov.uk/museums

*Tobacco and Aircraft - two of
Bristol's major industries*

Bringing the past to life. Discover loads of things to see and do. The Museum's exhibits based on Bristol's rich industrial past include: The story of the Port of Bristol's trading past and present; Bristol's involvement in transatlantic slave trade; Bristol-made cars, buses, bicycles and motorbikes; how printing and packaging was made; how the aircraft industry developed in the city, with real aircraft and engines.

Opening Times: Apr to Oct Sat to Wed 10:00-17:00. Nov to Mar Sat & Sun 10:00-17:00.   Admission: Free.

Map Ref: 2

British Empire & Commonwealth Museum

& ✦ ◖

Clock Tower Yard, Temple Meads, Bristol BS1 6QH   Tel: 0117 9254 980   Fax: 0117 9254 983   Email: staff@empiremuseum.co.uk   Web: www.empiremuseum.co.uk

The permanent galleries chart the history of the British Empire and Commonwealth. The galleries use material from the museum's vast collections ranging from uniforms and other costume to ethnographic material, photographs, film and oral history collections.

Opening Times: Closed until Autumn 2002, please phone for opening times.   Location: Near Templemeads Station, one minute walk from the station.

Map Ref: 2

Georgian House

7 Great George Street, Bristol BS1 5RR   Tel: 0117 921 1362   Web: www.bristol-city.gov.uk/museums

The Georgian House is an exquisite example of a town house of about 1790. The house is furnished to illustrate life both above and below stairs.

Opening Times: Apr to Oct Sat to Wed 10:00-17:00.   Admission: Free.

Map Ref: 2

Red Lodge

Park Row, Bristol BS1 5LJ   Tel: 0117 921 1360   Web: www.bristol-city.gov.uk/museums

Red Lodge is an Elizabethan house built around 1590, with the city's last surviving suite of 16th century rooms. There is also an impressive Tudor-style knot garden.

Opening Times: Apr to Oct Sat to Wed 10:00-17:00.   Admission: Free.

Map Ref: 2

SS Great Britain

✑ ✦ ◖ ⚓ **ss GREAT BRITAIN**

Great Western Dock, Gas Ferry Road, Bristol BS1 6TY   Tel: 0117 926 0680   Fax: 0117 925 5578   Email: enquiries@ss-great-britain.com   Web: www.sss-great-britain.com

The SS Great Britain, Brunel's masterpiece of ship design and engineering, is housed in the original 'Great Western Dock' in which she was built in 1843. The ship is the world's first great ocean liner - before she was built, long distance sea voyages that were made on wooden sailing ships were dangerous and unpredictable. Sea travel took a great leap forward when famous Victorian engineer Isambard Kingdom Brunel applied his

remarkable skill to the problem. The design of Brunel's SS Great Britain embodied so many innovative engineering ideas. She was the largest ship of her day and the first screw-propelled iron passenger liner; in fact the ship is really the forerunner of all modern ships. Admission also includes a visit to The Matthew - a replica of John Cabot's 15th century ship that sailed the Atlantic. Your ticket also includes the Maritime Heritage Centre, exhibiting a collection that portrays the history of shipbuilding in Bristol.

Opening Times: Apr to Oct 10:00-17:30, Nov to Mar 10:00-16:30.   Admission: Adult £6.25, Child/Student £3.75, OAP £5.25, Family (2 adults and 2 children) £16.50.

Map Ref: 2

Bath, Bristol & Northeast Somerset

Radstock Museum

The Market Hall, Waterloo Road, Radstock BA3 3ER   Tel: 01761 437722   Fax: 01761 420470
Web: www.radstockmuseum.co.uk

Local history museum depicting the lives of those who worked in the north Somerset coalfield. Where they lived, shopped and went to school. Also geology and local connections with Nelson and Wesley.

Opening Times: Tue to Fri, Sun & BH Mon 14:00-17:00, Sat 11:00-17:00. Closed Mon and all Dec & Jan.   Admission: Adult £3.00, Concession £2.00. Carers of disabled Free. Groups of 15 or more £2.00 per person.   Location: In centre of Radstock, one minute from bus stop.

Map Ref: 5

Thornbury & District Museum

c/o The Town Hall, 35 High Street, Thornbury BS35 2AR   Tel: 01454 857774
Email: enquiries@thornburymuseum.org.uk   Web: www.thornburymuseum.org.uk

Museum of the local and social history of Thornbury and the Lower Severn Vale.

Opening Times: Tue to Fri 13:00-16:00, Sat 10:00-16:00. Closed Sun, Mon & BH.
Admission: Free.   Location: In town centre next to Armstrong Hall.

Map Ref: 6

The Helicopter Museum

The Heliport, Locking Moor Road, Weston-super-Mare BS24 8PP   Tel: 01934 635227
Fax: 01934 645230   Email: office@helimuseum.fsnet.co.uk
Web: www.helicoptermuseum.co.uk

Britain's only helicopter museum is a fascinating place to visit with many rare and unique helicopters on display under cover. Group/school visits welcome by prior arrangement. Restoration hangar, adventure play area, open cockpit days and pleasure flights.

Opening Times: Apr to Oct Wed to Sun 10:00-18:00, Nov to Mar 10:00-16:00. Open daily during Easter and summer school holidays.   Admission: Adult £3.95, Child £2.75, OAP £3.25, Family (2 adults and 2 children) £11.00, Concessions for groups.   Location: Museum is on A368/A371, three miles from Weston-super-Mare seafront. Approx one and a half miles from junction 21 on M5.

Map Ref: 7

North Somerset Museum

Burlington Street, Weston-super-Mare BS23 1PR   Tel: 01934 621028   Fax: 01934 612526
Email: museum.service@n-somerset.gov.uk   Web: www.n-somerset.gov.uk/museum

Victorian museum featuring galleries of archaeology, social and natural history, The Seaside Gallery and the unique Clara's Cottage make up the static displays. Exhibitions, Peoples Collection, events and seminars make this a very popular attraction.

Opening Times: Mon to Sat 10:00-16:30.   Admission: Adult £3.50 Child £1.50 OAP £2.50
Family £8.00.   Location: Town centre, five minutes walk from all car parks.

Map Ref: 7

Bedfordshire, Berkshire, Buckinghamshire & Hertfordshire

ese four counties encapsulate much of the English way of life. At the very heart of the country
d surrounding the capital, the region was the culmination of ancient tracks and trade routes,
e Ridgeway and the Icknield Way, dating back to the Bronze Age. The Romans too in their turn
t their road building mark. In a country of magnificent medieval castles, this area being so close
the country's heart felt safe from invaders and as a consequence, what it lacks in military
chitecture it more than makes up for with its glorious domestic architecture.

e marks indelibly stamped on these four counties by their early occupants are thankfully well
corded in their splendid museums and heritage centres.

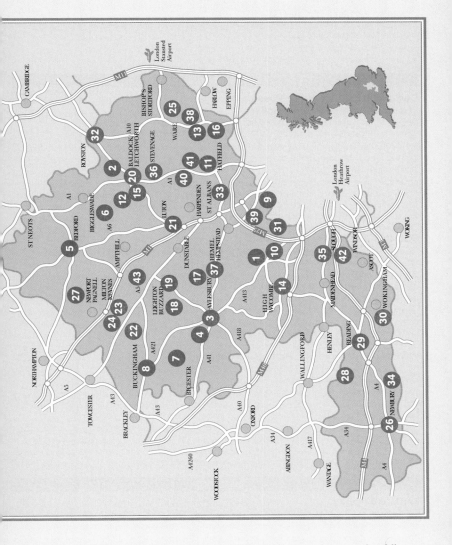

The Red Map References should be used to locate Museums etc on the pages that follow

Beds, Berks, Bucks & Herts

AMERSHAM *Bucks*

Amersham Museum

49 High Street, Amersham HP7 0DP   Tel: 01494 723700/725754   Fax: 01494 725754
Email: amersham_museum@hotmail.com   Web: www.amersham.org.uk

Museum of local history in part of a restored 15th century hall-house, thought to be the oldest building in the town, with its own herb garden. National Heritage Award 1993.

Opening Times: Easter to Oct Sat, Sun & BH 14:00-16:30, also Wed in Jun to Sep 14:00-16:30.
Admission: Adult £1.00, Child Free.   Location: In main High Street in Amersham Old Town, a short walk from the Market Hall.   Map Ref: 1

ASHWELL *Herts*

Ashwell Village Museum
Swan Street, Ashwell SG7 5NY   Tel: 01462 742956

Life in an English village from the Stone Age to the present day exhibited in a timber-framed building and modern galleries.

Opening Times: Sun and BH 14:30-17:00.   Admission: Adult £1.00, Child 25p.
Location: Near the church in the centre of the village.   Map Ref: 2

AYLESBURY *Bucks*

Buckinghamshire County Museum & The Roald Dahl Children's Gallery

Church Street, Aylesbury HP20 2QP   Tel: 01296 331441   Fax: 01296 334884
Email: museum@buckscc.gov.uk   Web: www.buckscc.gov.uk/museum

You really can awaken your senses at this award-winning museum with its innovative touchable displays, exciting programme of family exhibitions, and regular events and activities. Let your imagination run wild.

Opening Times: Mon to Sat 10:00-17:00, Sun 14:00-17:00. On school days the Dahl Gallery is reserved for school use only until 15:00.   Admission: Bucks County Museum - Free. Roald Dahl Children's Gallery: Adult £3.50, Child £2.75.   Location: In the old part of Aylesbury near the town centre, three minutes walk from bus station.   Map Ref: 3

Buckinghamshire Railway Centre

Quainton Road Station, Quainton, Aylesbury HP22 4BY   Tel: 01296 655450   Fax: 01296 655720   Web: www.bucksrailcentre.org.uk

A working steam railway museum with a large collection of vintage steam/diesel locomotives, carriages and wagons, and small relics. Steam train rides most weekends. Miniature railway, gift and bookshop, refreshment room.

Opening Times: Apr to Oct Tue to Sun 10:30-16:30. Steam trains on Sun & BH. Also Jun to Aug Wed.   Admission: Adult £4.50, Child/OAP £3.50, Under 5s Free.   Location: Off A41 Aylesbury to Bicester Road, seven miles north west of Aylesbury.   Map Ref: 4

Waddesdon Manor - The Rothschild Collection

Waddesdon, Aylesbury HP18 0JH   Tel: 01296 653226   Fax: 01296 653208
Web: www.waddesdon.org.uk

Waddesdon Manor (built 1874-89) is a magnificent French Renaissance-style chateau, housing The Rothschild Collection of art treasures, a superb cellar of Rothschild wines, and surrounded by spectacular grounds.

Opening Times: House: 27 Mar to 3 Nov Wed to Sun & BH Mon 11:00-16:00. Grounds: 27 Feb to 22 Dec Wed to Sun & BH Mon 10:00-17:00.   Admission: House & Grounds: Adult £10.00, Child £7.50, National Trust Members Free. Grounds only: Adult £3.00, Chld £1.50, National Trust Members Free.   Location: On A41 between Aylesbury and Bicester.   Map Ref: 4

BEDFORD

Bedford Museum
Castle Lane, Bedford MK40 3XD   Tel: 01234 353323   Fax: 01234 273401
Email: bmuseum@bedford.gov.uk   Web: www.bedfordmuseum.org

Embark on a fascinating journey through the human and natural history of North Bedfordshire. Go back in time to visit the delightful rural room sets and the Old School Museum.

Opening Times: Tue to Sat 11:00-17:00, Sun & BH Mon 14:00-17:00. Closed Good Friday, Xmas & New Year. Admission: Adult £2.10, Child/OAP/Concession Free. Annual ticket £8.40.
Location: Close to two town centre car parks and a short walk from Allhallows bus station and the Midland Road railway station. Map Ref: 5

Cecil Higgins Art Gallery
Castle Lane, Bedford MK40 3RP Tel: 01234 211222 Fax: 01234 327149
Email: chag@bedford.gov.uk Web: www.cecilhigginsartgallery.org

'Norham Castle, Summer's Morn' 1798
by J M W Turner

Entrance Hall, Victorian Mansion

Housed in an elegantly converted and extended Victorian mansion, the Gallery is home to one of the most outstanding fine and decorative art collections outside London. A remarkable collection of British and European watercolours from the 18th to the 20th centuries and international prints from Impressionism to the present. Ceramics and glass from the Renaissance to the 20th century, with particular focus on 18th century porcelain, Whitefriars glass and ceramics of the Art & Crafts movement. Authentically reconstructed Victorian room settings, including the William Burges Room, a complete Gothic experience. Thomas Lester lace collection and changing exhibitions, programme events, lectures and workshops for all ages.

Opening Times: Tue to Sat 11:00-17:00, Sun & BH Mon 14:00-17:00. Admission: Adult £2.10, Child/Concession Free.
Location: Centre of Bedford, just off the Embankment. Map Ref: 5

Elstow Moot Hall
Church End, Elstow, Bedford MK42 9XT Tel: 01234 266889 Fax: 01234 228531
Email: garyfuller1@ntlworld.com

Collection of furniture dating from the 17th century display of Bedfordshire lace and straw plait. Also John Bunyan book collection, many in foreign languages.

Opening Times: Apr to Sep 13:00-16:00 Tue to Thu, Sun and BH. Admission: Adult £1, Child/Concession 50p, Group - 30 Adults £20, 30 Child/Concession £10.
Location: Approximately three miles from Bedford Town Centre. Map Ref: 5

John Bunyan Museum
Bunyan Meeting Free Church, Mill Street, Bedford MK40 3EU Tel / Fax: 01234 213722

Walk through the life and times of the famous 17th century preacher, pastor and author of The Pilgrim's Progress. The collection includes copies of John Bunyan's most celebrated work in over 170 languages.

Opening Times: 5 Mar to 26 Oct Tue to Sat 11:00-16:00. Closed Good Friday.
Admission: Free Location: Near town centre, just off the High Street. Map Ref: 5

BIGGLESWADE *Beds*

Shuttleworth Collection
Old Warden Aerodrome, Biggleswade SG18 9EA Tel: 01767 627288

A collection of historic aeroplanes kept in flying condition housed in eight hangars in a quiet countryside setting on an established all-grass runway. Flying displays during summer months.

Opening Times: Daily Apr to Oct 10:00-17:00, Nov to Mar 10:00-16:00. Closed Xmas & New Year. Admission: Adult £6.00, Child Free. Flying Display Day £10.00, Event Day £7.50, Military Pageant Adult £15.00. Location: Three miles west of A1 at the Biggleswade roundabout, nearest railway station - Biggleswade. Map Ref: 6

BUCKINGHAM

Claydon House
Middle Claydon, Buckingham MK18 2EY

National Trust property with family museum containing mementoes of Florence Nightingale,

military uniforms, weapons, costume and musical instruments.

Opening Times: Apr to Oct Sat to Wed 13:00-17:00. Admission: Adult £4.40, Child £2.20, Family £11.00, Free to National Trust members. Location: Four and a half miles from Winslow, seven miles from Buckingham.

Map Ref: 7

The Old Gaol Museum

Market Hill, Buckingham MK18 1JX   Tel: 01280 823020

One of the first purpose bulit county gaols in England, now a museum proudly displaying aspects of historical Buckingham.

Opening Times: Mon to Sat 10:00-16:00. Admission: Adult £1.50, Child/Concession £1.00. Location: One minute walk from town centre car park.

Map Ref: 8

BUSHEY *Herts*

Bushey Museum & Art Gallery

Rudolph Road, Bushey WD23 3HW   Tel: 020 8420 4057   Fax: 020 8420 4923
Email: busmt@bushey.org.uk   Web: www.busheymuseum.org

An award-winning community museum telling the unique story of Bushey from the earliest times to the present day. Art galleries and special displays show two hundred years of art teaching and practice in Bushey from the early watercolours of the Monro Circle to the social realism and portraiture of the Herkomer Art School, to the animal painting of Lucy Kemp-Welch and Marguerite Frobisher Schools.

Opening Times: Thu to Sun 11:00-16:00. Admission: Free.
Location: Just off Bushey High Street.

Map Ref: 9

CHALFONT ST GILES *Bucks*

Chiltern Open Air Museum

Newland Park, Gorelands Lane, Chalfont St Giles HP8 4AD   Tel: 01494 871117/872163   Fax: 01494 872774
Email: coam@tesco.net   Web: www.coam.org.uk

Chiltern Open Air Museum consists of more than 30 historic buildings which were all rescued from demolition and are representative of the built heritage of the Chilterns. Visitors are able to roam the museum's 45 acre woodland and parkland site at their leisure and explore the buildings. Brick making, straw plaiting, candle making and rag rug making are just some of the hands-on activities that take place throughout the season .

Opening Times: 30 Mar to 27 Oct daily 10:00-17:00.
Admission: Adult £5.50, Child £3.00, Concession £4.50, Family (2 adult and 2 children) £15.00. Location: One mile off the A413 at Chalfont St Giles in Buckinghamshire.

Map Ref: 10

Walk into History at The Chiltern Open Air Museum

Milton's Cottage

Deanway, Chalfont St Giles HP8 4JH   Tel: 01494 872313   Email: pbirger@clara.net
Web: www.clara.net.pbirger

Probably the finest collection of Milton 17th century 1st editions in the world. Milton memorabilia and civil war artefacts. All housed in the 16th century grade I listed cottage to which he escaped from the plague in 1665.

Opening Times: 1 Mar to 31 Oct Tue to Sun 10:00-13:00 and 14:00-18:00. Closed Mon except BH. Admission: Adult £2.50, Child £1.00, Group (20+) £2.00. Location: Centre of village.

Map Ref: 10

HATFIELD *Herts*

Mill Green Museum & Mill

Mill Green, Hatfield AL9 5PD   Tel: 01707 271362   Email: museum@welhat.gov.uk
Web: www.welhat.gov.uk

An 18th century watermill, restored to working order, with a museum in the adjoining millers house complete with Victorian kitchen. The museum also features regular special exhibitions and events.

Opening Times: Tue to Fri 10:00-17:00 Sat, Sun & BH 14:00-17:00. Closed Mon.
Admission: Free. Location: In hamlet of Mill Green. One mile from Hatfield railway station.

Map Ref: 11

Stondon Museum

Station Road, Lower Stondon, Henlow SG16 6JN Tel: 01462 850339 Fax: 01462 850824
Email: enquiries@transportmuseum.co.uk Web: www.transportmuseum.co.uk

Largest private collection in the country, covering one hundred years of motoring, plus military vehicles, fire engines etc, even a full size replica of Captain Cook's ship, 'Endeavour'.

Opening Times: Daily 10:00-17:00. Closed Xmas & New Year. Admission: Adult £5.00, Child £2.50, OAP £4.00, Family £13.00. Group rates available, please pre-book. Location: Off A600 Hitchin - Bedford road, 4 miles from Hitchin.

Map Ref: 12

HERTFORD

Hertford Museum

18 Bull Plain, Hertford SG14 1DT Tel: 01992 582686 Fax: 01992 534797

Located in 17th century town house with attractive Jacobean style garden. Century old collections of local and social history, geology, archaeology, photographs and fine art, changing exhibitions, events and activity room for schools.

Opening Times: Tue to Sat 10:00-17:00. Admission: Free. Location: Town centre. Map Ref: 13

HIGH WYCOMBE *Bucks*

Hughenden Manor

Valley Road, High Wycombe HP14 4LA Tel: 01494 755573 Fax: 01494 474284

Home of Benjamin Disraeli from 1848 to 1881. Most of his furniture, pictures and books remain. A collection of personal memorabilia is also shown.

Opening Times: 3 Apr to 3 Nov Wed to Sun 13:00-17:00. Open Good Friday & BH.
Admission: Adult £4.40, Child £2.20, Family £11.00. Garden: Adult £1.50, Child 75p.
Location: One and a half miles north of High Wycombe on A4128.

Map Ref: 14

Wycombe Museum

Priory Avenue, High Wycombe HP13 6PX Tel: 01494 421895 Fax: 01494 421897
Email: enquiries@wycombemuseum.demon.co.uk Web: www.wycombe.gov.uk/museum

Friendly local museum set in 18th century house with attractive grounds. Modern displays include interactive exhibits and children's activities. Collections include historic Windsor chairs from the Chiltern's traditional furniture industry.

Opening Times: Mon to Sat 10:00-17:00 & Sun 14:00-17:00. Closed BH. Admission: Free.
Location: Five minute walk from High Street; ten minute walk from bus station, two minute walk from railway station.

Map Ref: 14

HITCHIN *Herts*

Hitchin Museum & Art Gallery

Paynes Park, Hitchin SG5 1EQ Tel: 01462 434476 Fax: 01462 431316
Email: caroline.frith@nhdc.gov.uk Web: www.north-herts.gov.uk

Hitchin Museum & Art Gallery

Hitchin Museum is housed in a beautiful Georgian town house build by George Kershaw in 1825, who ran a coaching service between the town and London. In this historical setting we tell the story of Hitchin's past through imaginative displays. Explore Hitchin's industrial and domestic life, contemplate the clothes people have worn for the last 170 years and fabulous art collection. Keepers of the Herts Yeomanry on permanent display.

Opening Times: Mon, Tue, Thur to Sat 10:00-17:00.
Closed Wed, Sun & BH. Admission: Free.
Location: 20 minute walk from Hitchin Railway Station situated next door to Hitchin Library, two minute walk from Market Place.

Map Ref: 15

Beds, Berks, Bucks & Herts

HODDESDON *Herts*

Lowewood Museum

High Street, Hoddesdon EN11 8BH   Tel: 01992 445596

Lowewood Museum is situated in a listed Georgian building. It houses a collection of photographs and memorabilia depicting town life in the 19th century, and changing temporary exhibitions.

Opening Times: Wed to Sat 10:00-16:00. Admission: Free. Location: Five minute walk from town centre, half a mile from Broxbourne Railway Station. Map Ref: 16

IVINGHOE *Bucks*

Ford End Watermill

Station Road, Ivinghoe   Tel: 01582 600391

The only working watermill in Buckinghamshire with its original machinery. Built in 1700s, has all the atmosphere of a small corn mill of the 1800s. Stone ground wholemeal flour for sale on milling days.

Opening Times: 1 Apr, 5, 6* & 12* May, 2 & 4* Jun, 7 & 14* Jul, 4 & 26* Aug, 1 Sep,all 14:30-17:30. * = milling days. Admission: Adult £1.20, Child 40p. Location: Three miles from Tring, six miles from Aylesbury, seven miles from Dunstable. Map Ref: 17

LEIGHTON BUZZARD *Beds*

Ascott House

Ascott Estate Office, Wing, Leighton Buzzard LU7 0PS   Tel: 01296 688242   Fax: 01296 681904   Email: paf@ascottestate.co.uk

Originally a half timbered Jacobean farmhouse, Ascott was bought in 1876 by the De Rothschild family and considerably transformed and enlarged. It now houses a quite exceptional collection of fine paintings, Oriental porcelain and English and French furniture.

Opening Times: House & Gardens: 2-30 Apr & 6 Aug to 13 Sep Daily except Mon 14:00-18:00. Gardens: 1 May to 31 Jul every Wed & last Sun in month 14:00-18:00.18 & 25 Sep.Sep. Admission: House & Gardens: Adult £5.60, Child £2.80. Gardens: Adult £4.00, Child £2.00 National Trust Members Free. Location: Half a mile east of Wing, two miles south west of Leighton Buzzard on A418. Map Ref: 18

Leighton Buzzard Railway

Pages Park Station, Billington Road, Leighton Buzzard LU7 4TN   Tel: 01525 373888 Fax: 01525 377814   Email: info@buzzrail.co.uk   Web: www.buzzrail.co.uk

A working passenger railway, using the line of the narrow-gauge Leighton Buzzard light railway, built in 1919 to carry sand trains. Displays of photographs and actual locomotives and rolling stock. Regular working displays.

Opening Times: Mar to Oct Sun & BH weekends, extra days Jul & Aug. Admission: Adult £5.00, Child £2.00, Under 2's Free, OAP £4.00. Location: On A4146 Hemel Hempstead road, near roundabout with A505 from Dunstable and A5. Map Ref: 19

LETCHWORTH *Herts*

First Garden City Heritage Museum

296 Norton Way South, Letchworth SG6 1SU   Tel: 01462 482710   Fax: 1462 486056 Email: fgchm@letchworth.com   Web: www.letchworth.com

This museum tells the story of Letchworth, the First Garden City and the history of the Garden City Movement. Permanent displays of paintings, photographs, arts and crafts style furniture are complemented by a fascinating temporary exhibition programme.

Opening Times: Mon to Sat 10:00-17:00. Admission: Non-Resident £1.00, Resident 50p, under 16 free. Location: Two minutes form town centre and multi-storey car park. Map Ref: 20

Museums, Galleries, Historic Houses & Sites

Please let us know of any collections that are not listed in this guide that you feel should be listed. E-mail us on *editor@tomorrows.co.uk* or return the Report Form on page 448

Beds, Berks, Bucks & Herts

Letchworth Museum & Art Gallery

The Broadway, Letchworth SG6 3PF   Tel: 01462 685647   Fax: 01462 481879
Email: letchworth.museum@north-herts.gov.uk   Web: www.north-herts.gov.uk

Manor Farm, Norton, oil on canvas, c.1912
(William Ratcliffe)

Letchworth Museum opened in 1914 to house the collections of the Letchworth Naturalists Society, but since then has expanded greatly. The attractive downstairs Natural History Gallery shows local wildlife in realistic settings, including the famous Letchworth black squirrel. The Archaeology Gallery upstairs displays fascinating Celtic and Roman collections, while the Art Gallery is home to a wide range of temporary exhibitions.

Opening Times: Mon to Sat 10:00-17:00. Closed Wed, Sun & BH. Admission: Free. Location: Near Broadway Cinema, next door to Letchworth Library, five minutes walk from B R Station.   Map Ref: 20

LUTON *Beds*

Luton Museum & Art Gallery

Wardown Park, Luton LU2 7HA   Tel: 01582 746722

French Needle lace Flounce c.1700

The collections present the story of the people of Luton from earliest times to the present century. Highlights include the spectacular hoard of Roman gold coins, wonderful Saxon jewellery, the nationally important lace collection and the straw plait and hat collections. The Bedfordshire and Hertfordshire Regimental Gallery has just been refurbished and other galleries are being updated during the course of 2002. This means that certain areas may be closed temporarily.

Opening Times: Tue to Sat 10:00-17:00, Sun 13:00-17:00. Admission: Free. Location: Situated in beautiful Wardown Park, one mile north of town centre, Bus 24 & 25. Follow brown tourism signs.   Map Ref: 21

Stockwood Craft Museum & Gardens & Mossman Collection

Stockwood Park, Farley Hill, Luton LU1 4BH   Tel: 01582 738714

The Favourite Omnibus c.1850 on display in the Museum Collection

The Craft Museum collections focus on the rural life, crafts and trades of Bedfordshire. In the Mossman Building, visitors can enjoy the largest collections of horse-drawn vehicles on public display in Britain. In addition, the Transport Gallery brings the story into the 20th century with vintage cars, bicycles and a model of Luton's trams.

Opening Times: Apr to Oct Tue to Sat 10:00-17:00, Sun 10:00-18:00. Nov to Mar Sat to Sun 10:00-15:45. Admission: Free. Location: In Stockwood Country Park, five minutes drive from junction 10 of the M1, Buses 1 & 4 from Park Square, town centre five minutes.   Map Ref: 21

MILTON KEYNES *Bucks*

Bletchley Park

The Mansion, Wilton Avenue, Bletchley, Milton Keynes MK3 6EB   Tel: 01908 640404
Fax: 01908 274381   Email: majenkins@bletchleypark.org.uk   Web: www.bletchleypark.org.uk

Bletchley Park, also known as 'Station X' was home to the famous codebreakers of the Second World War and the birthplace of modern computing and communications. Historic buildings, exhibitions and tours.

Opening Times: Mar to Dec Sat, Sun & BH 10:30-17:00. Admission: Adult £6.00, Child/Concession £5.00, Under 8's Free. Location: Two minute walk from Bletchley Railway Station.   Map Ref: 22

Milton Keynes Gallery

900 Midsummer Boulevard, Milton Keynes MK9 3QA   Tel: 01908 676900   Fax: 01908 558308
Email: mkgallery@mktgc.co.uk   Web: www.mkweb.co.uk/mkg

This successful new contemporary art gallery offers 8-10 solo and group exhibitions a year, presenting all media, including painting, sculpture, photography, printmaking and installation. There are regular talks, tours and weekend and holiday activities for children. Recorded information (01908) 558307.

Opening Times: Tue to Sat 10:00-17:00, Sun 11:00-17:00. Closed Mon & BH. Admission: Free. Location: City Centre.   Map Ref: 23

Milton Keynes Museum

Stacey Hill Farm, Southern Way, Wolverton, Milton Keynes MK12 5EJ   Tel: 01908 316222
Fax: 01908 319148   Email: mkmuseum@mkmuseum.org.uk   Web: www.mkmuseum.org.uk

Victorian/Edwardian room settings, schoolroom and nursery provide a link with times past. The Shopping Street is now open. In the Hall of Transport the restored Wolverton to Stony Stratford Tramcar provides an eye-catching centre piece. Jessie the shire horse can be seen working in the extensive grounds.

Opening Times: Easter to Oct Wed to Sun 12:30-16:30. Also BH Mon & Spring half term.
Admission: Adult £3.50, Concession £2.50, Family £8.00. Location: Five minutes by car from Milton Keynes Station or Wolverton Station.   Map Ref: 24

MUCH HADHAM *Herts*

Forge Museum & Victorian Cottage Garden

The Forge, High Street, Much Hadham SG10 6BS   Tel / Fax: 01279 843301
Email: christinaharrison@hotmail.com   Web: www.hertsmuseums.org.uk

The museum displays tell fascinating stories of how the crafts of blacksmithing and farriery have developed over the years, as well as smaller exhibits of local village life. There is a resident working blacksmith at the museum.

Opening Times: Mar to Dec Fri to Sun & BH 11:00-17:00. Jan & Feb by appointment.
Admission: Adult £1.00, Child/OAP 50p. Group rates available. Location: Situated on B1004 between Bishop's Stortford and Ware on Much Hadham High Street, opposite the village hall.
Map Ref: 25

NEWBURY *Berks*

West Berkshire Museum

The Wharf, Newbury RG14 5AS   Tel: 01635 30511   Fax: 01635 38535
Email: Heritage@westberks.gov.uk   Web: www.westberks.gov.uk

West Berkshire Museum

West Berkshire Museum is situated in two historic buildings in the heart of Newbury. The 17th century Cloth Hall and 18th century granary overlooking the Kennet & Avon Canal house fascinating displays of local history and archaeology, decorative arts, costume and rural crafts. There are galleries devoted to the Civil War, battles of 1643 and 1644 and the history of Greenham Common.

Opening Times: Apr to Sep Mon to Fri 10:00-17:00, Sat 10:00-16:30. Oct to Mar Mon to Sat 10:00-16:00. Closed Wed except school holidays. Admission: Free.
Location: Town centre, five minute walk from bus and railway station.   Map Ref: 26

OLNEY *Bucks*

Cowper Memorial Museum

Orchard Side, Market Place, Olney MK46 4AJ   Tel: 01234 711516   Fax: 0870 164 0662
Email: cnm@mkheritage.co.uk   Web: www.cowperandnewtonmuseum.org

Home of 18th century poet and letter-writer, William Cowper. Artefacts of Cowper and former slave trader, John Newton, author of 'Amazing Grace'. Period gardens. Collections of bobbin lace, dinosaur bones and local history.

Opening Times: 1 Mar to 23 Dec Tue to Sat 10:00-13:00-14:00-17:00. Also Sun in June, Jul & Aug 14:00-17:00, also BH 10:00-17:00. Closed Good Friday. Admission: Adult £3.00, Child £1.50, Concession £2.00, Family £7.50. Group/Tour rates available. Garden only £1.00. Location: In south east corner of Market Place in centre of Olney on A509. Five miles from junction 14 of M1.
Map Ref: 27

READING *Berks*

Basildon Park

Lower Basildon, Reading RG8 9NR   Tel: 0118 9843040   Fax: 0118 9841267
Email: tbdgen@smtp.ntrust.org.uk   Web: www.nationaltrust.org.uk/regions/thameschilterns

An 18th century Palladian mansion set in 400 acres of parkland, contains fine plasterwork, an important collection of furniture and paintings, a decorative shell room and Graham Sutherland's studies for the tapestry 'Christ in Glory'.

Opening Times: 23 Mar to 3 Nov Wed to Sun, BH Mon & Tue 4 Jun 12:00-17:30.
Admission: Adult £4.40, Child £2.20, Family £11.00.   Location: On A329 between Pangbourne and Streatley, one mile walk from Pangbourne Station.
Map Ref: 28

Museum of Reading

The Town Hall, Blagrave Street, Reading RG1 1QH   Tel: 0118 939 9800
Web: www.readingmuseum.org.uk

Excellent collections of archaeology including Roman Silchester, Reading Abbey, art and natural history. Now featuring 12 hands-on galleries.

Opening Times: Tue to Sat 10:00-16:00, Thu 10:00-19:00, Sun & BH Mon 11:00-16:00. Closed Mon.   Admission: Free.   Location: In town centre, two minutes from station.
Map Ref: 29

REME Museum of Technology

Isaac Newton Road, Arborfield Garrison, Reading RG2 9NJ   Tel / Fax: 0118 9763375
Email: reme-museum@gtnet.gov.uk   Web: www.rememuseum.org.uk

Reflective of the skills and training REME has employed since 1942. Displays include; avionics, aeronautical instruments, control equipment, optics, radar and radios. The museum exhibition hall displays 19 specialist vehicles, a helicopter and an education area.

Opening Times: Mon to Thu 09:00-16:30, Fri 09:00-16:00, Sun 11:00-16:00. Closed BH.
Admission: Adult £3.00, Child £2.00, OAP/Concession £2.50, Family £8.00, Group rates available, School visits please enquire and book in advance.   Location: Off Biggs Lane, three miles from Wokingham in Berkshire countryside.
Map Ref: 30

Rural History Centre (incorporating Museum of English Rural Life)

The University of Reading, Whiteknights, Reading RG6 6AG   Tel: 0118 9318661   Fax: 0118 9751264   Email: r.d.brigden@reading.ac.uk   Web: www.ruralhistory.org

A national collection with public displays relating to the farming, rural industries and country life of the last 200 years. The library and resident collections of photographs and archives may be viewed by appointment.

Opening Times: Tue to Sat 10:00-13:00 14:00-16;30. Closed Xmas & New Year.
Admission: Adult £1.00, Child/student Free, OAP/Concession 75p.   Location: Two miles south east from Reading Town Centre, on the University Campus.
Map Ref: 29

RICKMANSWORTH *Herts*

Three Rivers Museum of Local History

Basing House, 46 High Street, Rickmansworth WD3 1HP   Tel: 01923 775882
Email: ann@elgar.org

Small museum containing all aspects of local history in the Three Rivers area, with a focus on Rickmansworth. The collection includes artefacts, early photographs and archaeological finds. A new chronology board provides a concise historical record.

Opening Times: Mon to Fri 14:00-16:00, Sat 10:00-16:00. Closed Sun & BH.   Admission: Free.
Location: In High Street, between library and Watersmeet Theatre.
Map Ref: 31

Beds, Berks, Bucks & Herts

Royston & District Museum

Lower King Street, Royston SG8 5AL   Tel: 01763 242587

Local history and archaeology. Changing Exhibitions. Excellent ceramic collection covering late 19th and 20th century.

Opening Times: Wed, Thu & Sat 10:00-16:45. From 1 Sun in Mar to last Sun in Oct additional opening Sun & BH Mon 14:00-16:45. Closed Xmas & New Year. Admission: Free. Groups by appointment. Location: Five minutes from railway station, ten minutes from bus station. Car parking within two minutes.
Map Ref: 32

ST ALBANS *Herts*

Clock Tower

Market Place, St Albans AL1   Tel: 01727 751810   Fax: 01727 859919
Email: c.green@stalbans.gov.uk   Web: www.stalbansmuseums.org.uk

Built between 1403 and 1412 this four-staged tower is the only Medieval town belfry in England. Its fine bell has also survived almost 600 years of use.

Opening Times: Easter to Oct Sat, Sun & BH 10:30-17:00. Admission: 30p. Location: In town centre.
Map Ref: 33

De Havilland Aircraft Heritage Centre (inc the Mosquito Aircraft Museum)

PO Box 107, Salisbury Hall, London Colney, St Albans AL2 1EX   Tel: 01727 822051   Fax: 01727 826400   Web: www.hertsmuseums.org.uk

A secret wartime site waiting to be discovered by you. Home of the prototype Mosquito. On display there is a variety of De Havilland aircraft, ranging from Tiger Moth to modern military and civil jets including various sections. A working museum. Comprehensive collection of De Havilland engines and memorabilia.

De Havilland Aircraft Heritage Centre

Opening Times: First Sun in Mar to last Sun in Oct, Tue to Thu & Sat 14:00-17:00, Sun & BH 10:30-17:00. Admission: Adult £5.00, Child/OAP £3.00, Family £13.00. Groups by arrangement. Location: Junction 22 of M25, follow signs (near St Albans).
Map Ref: 33

Hypocaust

Verulamium Park, St Michaels, St Albans AL3 4SW   Tel: 01727 751810   Fax: 01727 859919
Email: d.thorold@stalbansmuseums.org.uk   Web: www.stalbansmuseums.org.uk

The hypocaust building presents in situ on original Roman mosaic and its underfloor heating system. It was once part of a large house.

Opening Times: Mon to Sat 10:00-17:00, Sun 14:00-17:00. Admission: Free. Location: In Verulamium Park, opposite Verulamium Museum.
Map Ref: 33

Kingsbury Watermill Museum

St Michaels Village, St Albans AL3 4SJ   Tel: 01727 853502

Elizabethan Watermill on three floors with working waterwheel. Fine display of milling machinery and comprehensive selection of 19th century dairy and farming implements. Pottery and gift shop.

Opening Times: Mon to Sat 10:00-18:00 Sun & BH 11:00-18:00. Winter closing time 17:00.
Admission: Adult £1.10, Child 60p, Concession 75p. Location: Ten minute walk from town centre.
Map Ref: 33

Museum of St Albans

Hatfield Road, St Albans AL1 3RR   Tel: 01727 819340   Fax: 01727 837472
Email: a.wheeler@stalbans.gov.uk   Web: www.stalbansmuseums.org.uk

The story of historic St Albans from the departure of the Romans to the present day. Also home to the Saloman Collection of craft tools. Regular exhibitions and wildlife garden.

Opening Times: Mon to Sat 10:00-17:00, Sun 14:00-17:00. Admission: Free. Location: Five minutes walk from town centre, ten minutes walk from railway station.
Map Ref: 33

The Roman Theatre of Verulamium

Bluehouse Hill, St Albans AL3 6AH   Tel: 01727 835035   Email: stalbans@strutlandparker.co.uk
Web: www.romantheatre.co.uk

The Roman Theatre of Verulamium was built in 140 AD as a theatre with a stage, rather than an amphitheatre, which is unique in Britain. The current ruins were found in 1847 but were not fully excavated until 1930-1935.

Opening Times: Daily all year - summer 10:00-17:00, winter 10:00-16:00. Admission: Adult £1.50, Child 50p, Concession £1.00, Under 5's Free. Location: On the western outskirts of St Albans, just off the A4147 and on the road known as Bluehouse Hill.   Map Ref: 33

Verulamium Museum

St Michaels, St Albans AL3 4SW   Tel: 01727 751810   Fax: 01727 859919
Email: a.coles@stalbans.gov.uk   Web: www.stalbansmuseums.org.uk

Discover the life and times of a major Roman city, set in attractive parkland. Nearby Roman theatre, walls, hypocaust. Demonstrations by Roman soldiers every second weekend of the month.

Opening Times: Mon to Sat 10:00-17:00, Sun 14:00-17:30. Admission: Adult £3.20 Child/ Concession £1.85 Family £8.05 Location: Ten minutes from St Albans City Centre Map Ref: 33

SILCHESTER Berks

Calleva Museum

Bramley Road, Silchester RG7 2LU   Tel: 0118 9700825

Calleva Museum is unmanned and gives a pictorial record of life in Roman times. The museum acts as an information point.

Opening Times: Daily 09:30 to Dusk. Admission: Free. Location: In the village of Silchester, Bramley Road.   Map Ref: 34

SLOUGH Berks

Slough Museum

278/286 High Street, Slough SL1 1NB   Tel / Fax: 01753 526422
Email: info@sloughmuseum.co.uk   Web: www.sloughmuseum.co.uk

Horlicks has been made in Slough since 1906

Slough has a unique and fascinating history stretching back thousands of years. The museum traces this history in its exhibition 'A Journey Through Time', telling the story of Slough from mammoths to the modern day. Work by local groups is on display in the temporary exhibition room and there are lots of special activities for schools, children and families.

Opening Times: Wed to Sat 11:30-16:00. Admission: Free. Location: Bottom of Slough High Street, ten minutes walk from train/bus station.   Map Ref: 35

STEVENAGE Herts

Stevenage Museum

St Georges Way, Stevenage SG1 1XX   Tel: 01438 218881   Fax: 01438 218882
Email: museum@stevenage.gov.uk   Web: www.stevenage.gov.uk/museum

The main galleries focus on the history of the town, from the Stone Age right up to the present day. Frequently changing exhibitions on a wide range of topics.

Opening Times: Mon to Sat 10:00-17:00. Closed BH. Admission: Free. Location: Three minutes walk from town centre.   Map Ref: 36

Walter Rothschild Zoological Museum

Akeman Street, Tring HP23 6AP   Tel: 020 7942 6171

This museum was once the private collection of Lionel Walter, second Baron Rothschild, and is now part of The Natural History Museum. It houses more than 4000 mounted specimens of animals in a unique Victorian setting.

Opening Times: Mon to Sat 10:00-17:00, Sun 14:00-17:00. Admission: Free. Location: Akeman Street.

Map Ref: 37

Ware Museum

The Priory Lodge, Ware SG12 9AL   Tel: 01920 487848

Objects of local and historical nature relevant to Ware. Main collections: Roman archaeology from Glaxo-Wellcome manufacturing site; malting industry; D Wickham & Co, railcar manufacturers.

Opening Times: Summer Sat 11:00-17:00, Sun & BH 14:00-17:00. Winter Sat 11:00-16:00, Sun & BH 14:00-16:00. Admission: Free.

Map Ref: 38

Watford Museum

194 High Street, Watford WD17 2DT   Tel: 01923 232297   Fax: 01923 224772
Email: museum@artsteam-watford.co.uk   Web: www.hertsmuseums.org.uk

Watford Museum tells the story of Watford and its people from the earliest times to the present. Special exhibitions on printing and brewing and regularly changing temporary exhibitions offer something for everyone.

Opening Times: Mon to Fri 10:00-17:00, Sat 10:00-13:00 14:00-17:00. Closed Sun & BH. Admission: Free. Location: Near town centre, five minute walk from Harlequin Shopping Centre.

Map Ref: 39

Shaw's Corner

Ayot St Lawrence, Welwyn AL6 9BX   Tel / Fax: 01438 820307
Email: shaws@smtp.ntrust.org.uk   Web: www.nationaltrust.org.uk/thameschilterns

An arts and crafts inspired house, home to playwright and socialist G Bernard Shaw for over 40 years. The rooms are much as he left them, a faithful reflection of pre-war furniture and decoration.

Opening Times: 27 Mar to 3 Nov Wed to Sun & BH Mon 13:00-17:00. Admission: Adult £3.60, Child £1.80, Free to National Trust members. Location: A1(M) junction 4, five miles Welwyn Garden City, five miles Harpenden.

Map Ref: 40

Welwyn Roman Baths

Welwyn By-pass, Welwyn   Tel: 01707 271362   Fax: 01707 272511
Email: museum@welhat.gov.uk   Web: www.welhat.gov.uk

A Roman bath house, part of a villa built 1,700 years ago. Ingeniously preserved in a vault under the A1(M), together with displays of material excavated from the villa.

Opening Times: Jan to Nov Sat, Sun & BH 14:00-17:00 School Holidays (exc. Dec) Mon to Sun 1400-17:00. Admission: Adult £1.00 Child/Concession free. Location: Situated under A1(M) at its junction with the A1000, just off the central roundabout of Welwyn by-pass. Approximately one mile from Welwyn North Station.

Map Ref: 41

Beds, Berks, Bucks & Herts

Museum of Eton Life

Eton College, Windsor SL4 6DW   Tel: 01753 671177   Fax: 01753 671265
Email: visits@etoncollege.org.uk   Web: www.etoncollege.com

School Yard, Eton College

The Museum of Eton illustrates the history and function of Eton College. There is a short video which depicts life and work of the school today. A visit to the Museum usually follows a guided tour of the College although it is open to visitors who do not take a tour.

Opening Times: 29 Mar to 17 Apr & 29 Jun to 4 Sep 10:30-16:30. 18 Apr to 28 Jun & 5 to 29 Sep 14:00-16:30.
Admission: Ordinary entrance £3.00, Guided tours £4.00.
Location: Fifteen minutes walk from Windsor.

Map Ref: 42

Woburn Abbey

Woburn MK17 9WA   Tel: 01525 290666   Fax: 01525 290271
Email: enquiries@woburnabbey.co.uk   Web: www.woburnabbey.co.uk

Woburn Abbey

Woburn Abbey has been home to the Dukes of Bedford for almost 450 years. Over the centuries the Russell family have, with their love of art, created one of the finest private collections in England. There are paintings by Van Dyck, Gainsborough, Reynolds and Velazquez. 21 views of Venice by Canaletto can be seen in the Venetian Room in the Private Apartments. The Vaults contain beautiful porcelain from France, Japan, Germany, England and China,   inc-uding the famous Sevres dinner   service given to the 4th Duchess by Louis XV. The 3,000 acre deer park contains nine species of deer and there are two gift shops, a pottery and an Antique Centre with 40 shops.

Racing Room at Woburn Abbey

Opening Times: 24 Mar to 29 Sep weekdays 11:00-16:00, weekends 11:00-17:00. Open 1 Jan to 23 Mar and 5 to 27 Oct weekends only.   Admission: Adult £8.00, OAP £7.00, Child £3.50. Group Adult £6.50, Group OAP £5.50, Group Child £2.75.   Location: Woburn Village one mile distance, Flitwick Railway Station five miles. No local transport available.

Map Ref: 43

Cambridgeshire & Northamptonshire

Cambridgeshire, which includes the Soke of Peterborough and the Isle of Ely, boasts a wealth historic sites and spectacular buildings. Northamptonshire, 'the county of spires and squires' primarily a farming county.

Both Cambridgeshire and Northamptonshire can be considered to be counties of personalit their stories carefully preserved in collections of memorabilia.

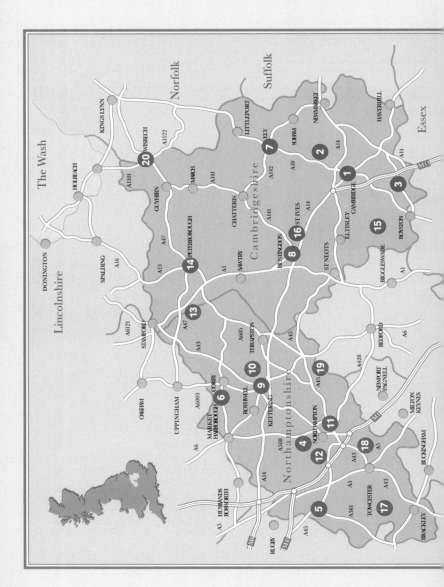

The Red Map References should be used to locate Museums etc on the pages that follow

Cambridgeshire & Northamptonshire

Cambridge & County Folk Museum

2/3 Castle Street, Cambridge CB3 0AQ   Tel: 01223 355159   Email: info@fokmuseum.org.uk
Web: www.folkmuseum.org.uk

The museum is housed in a superb late 15th century timber-framed building. The displays reflect the everyday life of the people of Cambridge and the surrounding county from 1700 to the present day.

Opening Times: Apr to Sep Mon to Sat 10:30-17:00, Sun 14:00-17:00. Oct to Mar Tue to Sat 10:30-17:00, Sun 14:00-17:00.   Admission: Adult £2.50, Child 75p, Concession £1.50.
Location: Near the town centre, a five minute walk from central shopping area and two minutes drive from M11.
                                                                                          Map Ref: 1

The Farmland Museum & Denny Abbey

Ely Road, Waterbeach, Cambridge CB5 9PQ   Tel / Fax: 01223 860988
Email: f.m.denny@tesco.net   Web: www.dennyfarmlandmuseum.org.uk

Find out about the Countess and fighting monks, country craftsmen and local farming in this peaceful setting. Visit the Medieval Abbey, 17th century stone barn and farmworker's cottage from the 1940s. Interactive exhibits for children and play and picnic areas.

Opening Times: Apr to Oct Daily 12:00-17:00.   Admission: Adult £3.60, Child £1.40, Concession £2.60, Family £8.50.   Location: Eight miles north of Cambridge on the A10.
                                                                                          Map Ref: 2

Fitzwilliam Museum

Trumpington Street, Cambridge CB2 1RB   Tel: 01223 332900   Fax: 01223 332923
Email: fitzmuseum-enquiries@lists.cam.ac.uk   Web: www.fitzmuseum.cam.ac.uk

Magnificent permanent collection including antiquities from Ancient Egypt, Greece and Rome, sculpture, furniture and paintings by artists such as Titian, Canaletto, Constable, Monet and Picasso. Guided tours, concerts, gallery tours and other events. Details on www.fitzmuseum.cam.ac.uk. For disabled access please phone 01223 332937 in advance.

The Fitzwilliam Museum Founder's Building

Opening Times: Tue to Sat 10:00-17:00, Sun 14;15-17:00, Easter Mon 1 Apr. Closed Mon & Good Friday, Xmas & New Year.   Admission: Free.   Location: Near town centre.
                                                                                          Map Ref: 1

Imperial War Museum Duxford

HMS BELFAST

Cambridge CB2 4QR   Tel: 01223 835000   Fax: 01223 837267
Web: www.iwm.org.uk

Duxford, part of the Imperial War Museum, is unique. A historic airfield built during the First World War and later a Battle of Britain fighter station, its preserved hangars and exhibition buildings today house some 200 aircraft, one of the finest collections of tanks and military vehicles in the country, dramatic land warfare exhibits and much more. The Royal Anglian Regiment Museum is also housed on this site.

Opening Times: 17 Mar to 27 Oct 10:00-18:00 (summer) 10:00-16:00 (winter). Closed Xmas.   Admission: Adult £8.00, Child (under 16) Free, OAP £6.00, Concession £4.00, Group (20+ adults) £6.00, OAP £4.00, Concession £3.00. Prices vary on Air Show days, Children under 12 must be accompanied by an adult.   Location: Off junction 10 on M11, nr Cambridge.   Map Ref: 3

Kettle's Yard

Castle Street, Cambridge CB3 0AQ   Tel: 01223 352124   Fax: 01223 324377
Email: mail@kettlesyard.cam.ac.uk   Web: www.kettlesyard.co.uk

Interior of Kettle's Yard

Kettle's Yard is a house with a permanent collection and a Gallery showing a changing programme of exhibitions. Founded by Jim Ede, once a curator at the Tate Gallery, it was intended as a 'refuge of peace and order, of the visual arts and music'. Works of art by Ben and Winifred Nicholson, Christopher Wood, Alfred Wallis, Barbara Hepworth, Constantin Brancusi and Henri Gaudier-Brzeska.

Opening Times: House: 30 Mar to 26 Aug Tue to Sun 13:30-16:30, 27 Aug to 29 Mar Tue to Sun 14:00-16:00. Gallery: Tue to Sun 11:30-17:00. Admission: Free. Location: Near town centre.   Map Ref: 1

Scott Polar Research Institute Museum

Lensfield, Cambridge CB2 1ER Tel: 01223 336540   Fax: 01223 336549
Web: www.spri.cam.ac.uk

Displays include materials from the Antarctic expeditions of Robert Falcon Scott and Sir Ernest Shackleton, and the Arctic expeditions of Sir John Franklin and others searching for the 19th century.

Opening Times: Tue to Sat 14:00-16:00. Admission: Free. Location: Ten minutes walk from railway station and central bus station.   Map Ref: 1

Sedgwick Museum of Geology

Dept of Earth Sciences, Downing Street, Cambridge CB2 3EQ   Tel: 01223 333456

Fossils and minerals, mounted skeletons, important local displays, historical material. Major new displays opening early summer 2002.

Opening Times: Mon to Fri 09:00-13:00 and 14:00-17:00, Sat 10:00-13:00. Closed Xmas and Easter. Admission: Free. Location: Near town centre, two minutes walk from bus station.
                    Map Ref: 1

University Museum of Archaeology & Anthropology

Downing Street, Cambridge CB2 3DZ   Tel: 01223 333516   Fax: 01223 333517
Email: cumaa@hermes.cam.ac.uk   Web: www.cumaa.archanth.cam.ac.uk

The collections and their associated photographic and archival material are of outstanding research and historical value; they cover the ethnography and pre-history of the world together with local archaeology. The museum is an important national resource in archaeology and anthropology.

Opening Times: Tue to Sat 14:00-16:30, closed Sun, Mon & BH. Admission: Free.
Location: City centre.   Map Ref: 1

Whipple Museum of the History of Science

Free School Lane, Cambridge CB2 3RH   Tel: 01223 330906   Fax: 01223 334554   Email: hps-whipple-museum@lists.cam.ac.uk   Web: www.hps.cam.ac.uk/whipple/

The main gallery of the Whipple Museum

The Whipple Museum is a pre-eminent collection of scientific instruments and models, dating from the Middle Ages to the present. Microscopes and telescopes, sundials, early slide rules, pocket electronic calculators, teaching and demonstration apparatus, as well as laboratory equipment are included in this outstanding collection. Part of the Department of History and Philosophy of Science, it plays an important role in the Department's teaching and research.

Opening Times: Mon to Fri 13:30-16:30. Closed Sat, Sun & BH. Please check beforehand as the Museum is not always open during the University vacations. Admission: Free. Location: In town centre.
                    Map Ref: 1

Cambridgeshire & Northamptonshire

CHAPEL BRAMPTON Northants

Northampton & Lamport Railway

Pitsford and Brampton Station, Pitsford Road, Chapel Brampton NN6 8BA   Tel: 01604 820327
Email: simon.crowl@ntlworld.com   Web: www.nrl.org.uk

The Northampton & Lamport Railway is a classic steam and heritage diesel operated railway set in the Northamptonshire countryside.

Opening Times: For current timetable information call (01604) 820327.   Location: Between Chapel Brampton and Pitsford, approximately five miles north of Northampton. Off the A508 north of Northampton.
Map Ref: 4

DAVENTRY Northants

Daventry Museum

The Moot Hall, Market Square, Daventry NN11 4BH   Tel: 01327 302463   Fax: 01327 706035

A local history museum featuring archaeology from Borough Hill Iron Age hill fort and other sites, the development of the market town of Daventry and the history of this part of rural Northamptonshire.

Opening Times: Oct to Mar Mon to Sat 10:00-14:00 & 14:30-15:30. Apr to Sep 10:00-14:00 & 14:30-16:30. Admission: Free. Location: In Market Square, free short and long stay car parks adjacent.
Map Ref: 5

EAST CARLTON Northants

East Carlton Steel Heritage Centre

East Carlton Park, East Carlton LE16 8YF   Tel: 01536 770977   Fax: 01536 770661

Set in 100 acres of beautiful parklands, with ponds, the largest Bold Lime tree in the country, walks and stunning views over the Welland Valley. Also in the grounds the lovely East Carlton Park Hall.

Opening Times: Winter daily 09:30-15:45, summer daily 09:30-17:00, weekends in summer, Sat 09:30-17:15, Sun 09:30-17:45. Admission: Free. Location: Signposted three miles from Corby on the A427.
Map Ref: 6

ELY Cambs

Ely Museum

The Old Gaol, Market Street, Ely CB7 4LS   Tel: 01353 666655   Fax: 01353 659259

The history centre for the Isle of Ely and The Fens. Displays include fossils, Roman remains, original gaol cells and regimental uniforms. Housed in the Bishop's Gaol.

Opening Times: Summer: Daily 10:30-17:30. Winter: Daily 10:30-16:30. Closed Xmas & New Year. Admission: Adult £2.00, Accompanied Child Free, Concession £1.25. Location: Corner of Market Street and Lynn Road, only 250 metres from Ely Cathedral.
Map Ref: 7

Oliver Cromwell's House

29 St Marys Street, Ely CB7 4HF   Tel: 01353 662062   Fax: 01353 668518
Email: tic@eastcambs.gov.uk   Web: www.eastcambs.gov.uk

Cromwell's family home from 1636. Period rooms, exhibitions and displays tell the story of Ely's most famous resident.

Opening Times: Summer Daily 10:00-17:30, winter Mon to Sat 10:00-17:00, Sun 11:00-16:00. Admission: Adult £3.50. Wide range of Concessions available. Location: In heart of conservation area, 300 yards from cathedral.
Map Ref: 7

Cambridgeshire & Northamptonshire

Stained Glass Museum

South Triforium, The Cathedral, Ely CB7 4DL   Tel: 01353 660347   Fax: 01353 665025
Email: stainedglass@lineone.net   Web: www.stainedglassmuseum.org

A unique museum with an exhibition of stained glass from 1240 to the present. The exhibition contains examples of stained glass from all over Britain and explains the history of the craft.

Opening Times: Mon to Fri 10:30-17:00, Sat 10:30-17:30 (winter 10:30-17:00), Sun 12:00-18:00 (winter 12:00-4:30). Closed Xmas & New Year and Good Friday.   Admission: Adult £3.50, Child (over 12)/Concession £2.50. Group rates available.   Location: In the centre of city, ten minute walk from the railway station.   Map Ref: 7

HUNTINGDON *Cambs*

Cromwell Museum

Grammar School Walk, Huntingdon PE29 3LF   Tel: 01480 375830   Fax: 01480 459563
Email: cromwellmuseum@cambridgeshire.gov.uk   Web: http://edweb.camcnty.gov.uk/cromwell

The collection includes many portraits, personal objects, books and documents, which illustrate the man, his family and his significance.

Opening Times: Apr to Oct Tue to Fri 11:00-13:00 14:00-17:00 Sat & Sun 11:00-13:00 14:00-16:00 Nov to Mar Tue to Fri 13:00-16:00 Sat 11:00-13:00 14:00-16:00 Sun 14:00-16:00.
Admission: Free.   Location: Centre of Huntingdon, opposite All Saints Church, next to the market place. Five minute walk from Central Bus Station, ten minute walk from railway station.
                                                                                        Map Ref: 8

KETTERING *Northants*

Alfred East Gallery

Sheep Street, Kettering NN16 0AN   Tel: 01536 534274   Web: www.kettering.gov.uk

Works by late 19th/early 20th century artists, including Sir Alfred East, Thomas Cooper Gotch and members of the Newlyn School, plus a collection of contemporary works made in conjunction with the contemporary art society.

Opening Times: Mon to Sat 09:30-17:00. Closed Sun & BH. Also Wed until 10:00am.
Admission: Free.   Location: In town centre, by library and Tourish Information Centre.
                                                                                        Map Ref: 9

Boughton House

Kettering NN14 1BJ   Tel: 01536 515731   Fax: 01536 417255
Email: lit@boughtonhouse.org.uk   Web: www.boughtonhouse.org.uk

Northamptonshire home of the Duke of Buccleuch and Queensberry, KT. A superb collection of paintings, furniture, tapestries, needlework, carpets, porcelain, arms and silver.

Opening Times: Aug to Sep, Park from 13:00-17:00, House from 14:00-16:30
Admission: House & Grounds: Adult £6.00, Child/OAP £5.00. Grounds only: Adult £1.50, Child/OAP £1.00.   Map Ref: 10

Manor House Museum

Sheep Street, Kettering NN16 0AN   Tel: 01536 534381   Fax: 01536 534370
Web: www.kettering.gov.uk

Collections reflecting the history of Kettering Borough from pre-historic times to the modern day.

Opening Times: Mon to Sat 09:30-17:00. Closed Sun & BH. Also Wed until 10:00am.
Admission: Free.   Location: In town centre, next to Tourist Information Centre.   Map Ref: 9

NORTHAMPTON

Abington Museum

Abington Park, Park Avenue South, Northampton NN1 5LW   Tel: 01604 631454   Fax: 01604 238720   Email: museums@northampton.gov.uk   Web: www.northampton.gov.uk/museums

Once a 15th century manor house, the museum includes Northamptonshire's military history - at home and abroad. Northampton life from the cradle to the grave. Also a 19th century fashion gallery.

Opening Times: Mar to Oct Tue to Sun 13:00-17:00, Nov to Feb Tue to Sun 13:00-16:00.
Admission: Free.   Location: Under ten minute journey from town centre, situated in Abington Park.   Map Ref: 11

Cambridgeshire & Northamptonshire

Althorp

The Stables, Althorp, Northampton NN7 4HQ
Tel: 01604 770107 Fax: 01604 772110
Email: mail@althorp.com Web: www.althorp.com

Next to the House lies the honey-coloured stable block, a truly breathtaking building that at one time accommodated up to 100 horses and 40 grooms. This is the setting for the Exhibition celebrating the life and work of Diana, Princess of Wales and honouring her memory after her death. The freshness and modernity of the facilities are a unique tribute to a woman who captivated the world in her all-too-brief existence.

Opening Times: 1 Jul to 30 Sep daily 10:00-17:00. Closed 31 Aug.
Admission: Pre-booked rates - Adult £10.50, Child £5.50 (under 5's free), OAP £8.50, Family (2 adults and 3 children) £26.50.

The Saloon, Althorp House

Location: Located seven miles west of Northampton.

Map Ref: 12

Northampton Central Museum & Art Gallery

Guildhall Road, Northampton NN1 1DP Tel: 01604 238548
Fax: 01604 238720 Email: museums@northampton.gov.uk
Web: northampton.gov.uk/museums

The Museum houses a collection of boots and shoes, the largest in the world. Also on display; Northampton's history, decorative arts - Oriental and British ceramics, Italian 15th to 18th century paintings and British art.

Opening Times: Mon to Sat 10:00-17:00, Sun 14:00-17:00.
Admission: Free. Location: Situated in town centre, five minute walk from bus station.

Map Ref: 11

Cloud and Rainbow' shoe 1979, designed by Thea Cadabra

PETERBOROUGH Cambs

Nene Valley Railway

Wansford Station, Stibbington, Peterborough PE8 6LR Tel: 01780 784444
Fax: 01780 784440 Web: www.nvr.org.uk

A large collection of British and continental locomotives and carriages are available for viewing on site, many of which are used to run the train service. For lovers of steam both young and old, visit Britain's International Steam Railway for a great day out. Travelling between Wansford and Peterborough the seven and a half mile of track passes through the heart of the picturesque 500 acre Ferry Meadows Country Park. There is a small museum and a second hand railway bookshop housed in a railway carriage at Wansford Station. Visit the restored Southern Railway Travelling Post Office carriage where letters and parcels can be sorted by visitors. NVR is the home of 'Thomas' the childrens favourite engine. Talking Timetable 01780 784404.

Thomas and Britannia at Nene Valley Railway

The golden age of steam come to life at Nene Valley Railway

Opening Times: Sun from Jan, weekends from Apr to Oct, Wed from May, plus other mid-week services in summer. Santa Specials end Nov and throughout Dec. Admission: Adult £10.00 (inc 1 child free), Child £4.00, OAP £6.00, Family (2 adults and 3 children) £20.00. Special fares apply for Santa Specials and Thomas. Location: Wansford Station, off southbound carriageway of A1 at Stibbington - west of Peterborough.

Map Ref: 13

Peterborough Museum & Art Gallery

Priestgate, Peterborough PE1 1LF
Tel: 01733 343329 Fax: 01733 341928
Email: museum@peterborough.gov.uk
Web: www.peterboroughheritage.org.uk

Exhibitions of the permanent collection covering the history and community of Peterborough. Collections include local archaeology, social history and geology. Unique collections of 'Sea Dinosaurs' and French Napoleonic prisoner of war ware. Changing historical and art exhibition programme, plus events and activities every weekend.

Opening Times: Sat 10:00-17:00, Sun & BH 12:00-16:00, Tue to Fri 12:00-17:00 (termtime) 10:00-17:00 (school holidays). Closed Mon, Xmas & New Year. Admission: Free. Small charge for some events or exhibitions. Location: City centre, just off Main Street, within five minutes walk of both railway and bus stations.

Spinning Jenny carved from bone by Napolaeonic prisoners of war at Norman Cross

Map Ref: 14

Peterborough Sculpture Trust

c/o 12 Burghley Road, Peterborough PE1 2QB   Tel: 01733 755545

Sculpture by major artists of the last 25 years, including Gormley and Caro.

Opening Times: Year round. Admission: Free. Location: Twenty minutes walk from city centre. The Sculpture Park is on either side of the one kilometre long Rowing Lake. Map Ref: 14

Railworld

Oundle Road, Peterborough PE2 9NR   Tel / Fax: 01733 344240   Web: www.railworld.net

Railworld's exhibition centre and museum highlights modern trains worldwide and environmental concerns. Railworld's model railway is impressive. Railworld also has 'Age of Steam' exhibits, flower beds and 'Stephenson' the cat!

Opening Times: Mar to Oct daily 11:00-16:00, Nov to Feb Mon to Fri 11:00-16:00. Xmas & New Year by appointment. Admission: Adult £2.50, Child £1.50, Concession £2.00, Family £6.50. Location: Near city centre, 15 minute walk from bus and railway station. Map Ref: 14

ROYSTON *Cambs*

Wimpole Hall & Home Farm

Wimpole Hall, Arrington, Royston SG8 0BW   Tel: 01223 207257   Fax: 01223 207838
Email: aweusr@smtp.ntrust.org.uk   Web: www.wimpole.org

The finest country house in Cambridgeshire, see over thirty rooms including the Library, plunge bath and basements. Enjoy walks around the landscaped park. Home Farm with a historical farmyard where you can see and feed some of our rare breeds of cattle, sheep, pigs and poultry. Also Pets Corner, Adventure Playground and Mini Tractors.

Opening Times: Hall: Mar to Nov Tue to Thu, Sat & Sun 13:00-17:00. Farm: Mar to Nov Tue to Thu, Sat & Sun 10:30-17:00. Nov to Mar Sat & Sun 11:00-16:00. Admission: Hall: Adult £6.20, Child £2.80. Farm: Adult £4.90, Child £2.80. Garden: Adult £2.50, Child Free. Estate: Adult £9.00, Child £4.50. Location: Eight miles

Wimpole Hall viewed across the parterre - Olga Damant / The National Trust

south west of Cambridge off A603. Junction 12 of M11. Map Ref: 15

ST IVES *Cambs*

Norris Museum

The Broadway, St Ives PE27 5BX   Tel: 01480 497314

History of Huntingdonshire: fossils and dinosaurs, archaeology, history, the Civil War, Fen skating, art gallery with regular special exhibitions.

Opening Times: May to Sep Mon to Fri 10:00-13:00 14:00-17:00, Sat 10:00-12:00 14:00-17:00, Sun 14:00-17:00. Oct to Mar Mon to Fri 10:00-13:00 14:00-16:00, Sat 10:00-12:00. Admission: Free. Location: West end of town centre, beside the river and near the parish church. Map Ref: 16

Cambridgeshire & Northamptonshire

Sulgrave Manor

Manor Road, Sulgrave, Banbury OX17 2SD   Tel: 01295 760205   Fax: 01295 768056
Email: sulgrave-manor@talk21.com   Web: www.stratford.co.uk/sulgrave

A Tudor manor house and gardens, the ancestral home of George Washington. Well known for the excellence of the guided tours and the quality of the special events.

Opening Times: Mar 29 to Oct 31 14:00-17:30. Closed Mon and Fri, except BH.
Admission: Adult £5.00, Child £2.50. Garden only £2.50.   Location: In the village of Sulgrave, seven miles from M40 junction 11.

Map Ref: 17

Canal Museum

Stoke Bruerne, Towcester NN12 7SE   Tel: 01604 862229   Fax: 01604 864199

An old cornmill housing a colourful collection depicting 200 years of inland waterways, situated in a rich historical site by the busy Grand Union Canal.

Opening Times: Easter to Oct daily 10:00-17:00, Oct to Easter Tue to Sun 10:00-16:00. Closed Xmas.   Location: Village four miles from junction 15 of M1.

Map Ref: 18

Irchester Narrow Gauge Railway Museum

Little Irchester Country Park, Wellingborough NN9   Tel: 01234 750469
Email: irchester@kingstonray.freeserve.co.uk   Web: www.ingrt.freeuk.com/

A narrow gauge railway museum, with operating locomotives. A total of four steam, four diesel and over 30 items of rolling stock.

Opening Times: Sun and BH, 10:00-17:00 (Winter 10:00-16:00).   Admission: Free.
Location: Irchester Country Park, one mile from Wellingborough.

Map Ref: 19

Wisbech & Fenland Museum

Museum Square, Wisbech PE13 1ES   Tel: 01945 583817   Fax: 01945 589050
Email: wisbechmuseum@beeb.net

A purpose built Victorian Museum, dating from 1847, with much of its original fittings and charm. Decorative art, ceramics, archaeology, natural history, geology, fossils, social history, egyptology, ethnography and numismatics. Exhibition on The Fenland, and Thomas Clarkson and his campaign to abolish slavery.

Opening Times: Summer Tue to Sat 10:00-17:00, winter Tue to Sat 10:00-16:00.   Location: At centre of town's Georgian Crescent, opposite Wisbech Castle and next to St Peter's Church.

Map Ref: 20

Chester, a port until silting-up forced it to relinquish its sea trade to its neighbour Liverpool, is city of great age, remarkable charm and some of the finest half-timbered buildings in the wor Manchester, despite dating back to the Roman era, is predominantly Victorian, and in Liverpo though the days of the great ocean going liners have gone, much of the associated architect remains.

Nearly 80 museums, galleries and historic houses combine to display the military, shipping a industrial history of this region.

The Red Map References should be used to locate Museums etc on the pages that follow

Cheshire, Manchester & Merseyside

Dunham Massey Hall, Park & Garden

The National Trust, Dunham Massey Hall, Altrincham WA14 4SJ   Tel: 0161 941 1025
Fax: 0161 929 7508   Email: mdmjxe@smtp.ntrust.org.uk

18th century house, with sumptuous Edwardian interiors, containing collections of Huguenot silver, paintings and walnut furniture. Extensive below stairs complex. Ancient formal parkland and large garden.

Opening Times: 23 Mar to 3 Nov. House: Sat to Wed 12:00-17:00. Garden: daily 11:00-17:00. Closed one hour earlier in Oct/Nov.   Admission: Adult (House & Garden) £5.50, (House or Garden) £3.50. National Trust Members Free.   Location: Three miles south west of Altrincham.
Map Ref: 1

Central Art Gallery

Old Street, Ashton-under-Lyne OL6 7SF   Tel: 0161 342 2650

The Central Art Gallery is on Old Street in Ashton-under-Lyne. The first floor of this fine Victorian Gothic building provides three excellent galleries. A varied programme of temporary exhibitions has been established featuring a wide range of work including paintings, sculptures and textiles from regional artists and touring exhibitions.

Opening Times: Tue, Wed & Fri 10:00-17:00 Thur 13:00-19:30 Sat 09:00-12:30 13:00-16:00.
Admission: Free.   Location: Five minutes walk to Ashton railway and bus station.   Map Ref: 2

Museum of the Manchesters: Social & Regimental History

Town Hall, Ashton-under-Lyne OL6 6DL   Tel: 0161 342 3078

Museum displays feature the experience of 'Women At War' and the 'Home Front', the trenches of the First World War and computer interactives. You can also enjoy the fine collection of weapons and uniform.

Opening Times: Mon to Sat 10:00-16:00.   Admission: Free.   Location: Two minute walk to Ashton-under-Lyne railway and bus stations.   Map Ref: 2

Portland Basin Museum

Portland Place, Ashton-under-Lyne OL7 0QA   Tel: 0161 343 2878   Fax: 0161 343 2869
Email: jo.edwards@mail.tameside.gov.uk   Web: www.tameside.gov.uk

Portland Basin Museum is the centre piece of the recently rebuilt Ashton Canal Warehouse, now looking much as it did in 1834 when it was first built. This historic building houses exciting displays, describing the social and industrial history of Tameside and its people.

Opening Times: Tue to Sun 10:00-17:00. Closed Mon except BH.   Admission: Free.   Map Ref: 2

Lady Lever Art Gallery

Port Sunlight Village, Lower Road, Bebington, Wirral CH62 5EQ   Tel: 0151 478 4136
Fax: 0151 478 4140   Web: www.ladyleverartgallery.org.uk

The jewel in the crown of the garden village of Port Sunlight, housing the magnificent personal collection of the first Lord Leverhulme. Built by the soap magnate and philanthropist in 1922, the gallery includes Pre-Raphaelites, paintings by Turner and Constable, 18th century furniture alongside ceramics, Wedgewood, sculpture, tapestries and Napoleonic memorabilia.

Opening Times: Mon to Sat 10:00-17:00, Sun 12:00-17:00. Closed 23-26 Dec & 1 Jan. Admission: Free.
Location: Signposted from A41 New Chester Road. Bebington railway station.
Map Ref: 3

Lady Lever Art Gallery

Port Sunlight Heritage Centre

95 Greendale Road, Port Sunlight, Bebington, Wirral CH62 4XE   Tel: 0151 644 6466
Fax: 0151 645 8973

Port Sunlight Heritage Centre explores the fascinating story about the village and its community. Old photographs and early film footage depict a quality of life for residents unimaginable in most

41

19th century industrial communities.

Opening Times: Mon to Fri 10:00-16:00, Sat & Sun (Apr to Oct) 10:00-16:00, (Nov to Mar) 11:00-16:00. Closed Xmas.   Admission: Small admission charge. Group discount.
Location: 20 minutes by road or rail from Chester and Liverpool.   Map Ref: 3

BIRKENHEAD *Merseyside*

Birkenhead Priory & St Marys Tower

Priory Street, Birkenhead CH41 5JH   Tel: 0151 666 1249

Scheduled ancient monument, site of monastery founded 1150; small museum on site and remains of St Mary's Parish Church - tower now dedicated to those lost on HMS Thetis in 1939.

Opening Times: Jan to Mar & Nov to Dec Tue to Sun 12:00-16:00, Apr to Oct Tue to Sun 13:00-17:00. Closed Mon except BH. Admission: Free. Location: Five minute walk from Woodside Ferry/Hamilton Square.   Map Ref: 4

Egerton Bridge

Shore Road, Birkenhead

Working Bascule Bridge on docks network affording views of docks and River Mersey. Film interpretation of history of docks.

Opening Times: Jan to Mar & Nov to Dec Sat & Sun 12:00-16:00, Apr to Oct Sat & Sun 13:00-17:00. School holidays Tue to Sun 13:00-17:00. Admission: Free. Location: Tram ride from Woodside Ferry.   Map Ref: 4

Shore Road Pumping Station

Hamilton Street, Birkenhead CH41 6DN   Tel: 0151 650 1182

Grasshopper Steam Engine built to extract water from railway tunnel under River Mersey. Audio visual presentation on history of tunnel and railway.

Opening Times: Jan to Mar, Nov & Dec Sat & Sun 12:00-16:00, Apr to Oct Sat & Sun 13:00-17:00. School Holidays Tue to Sun 13:00-17:00. Admission: Free. Location: One minute walk from Woodside Ferry/Hamilton Square.   Map Ref: 4

Williamson Art Gallery & Museum

Slatey Road, Birkenhead CH43 4UE   Tel: 0151 652 4177   Fax: 0151 670 0253

Large but unintimidating gallery and museum with excellent picture and maritime displays, and active exhibition programme.

Opening Times: Tue to Sun 10:00-17:00. Closed Mon except BH. Admission: Free.
Location: 20 minute walk from Birkenhead Park or Birkenhead Central Stations; five minute drive from town centre.   Map Ref: 4

Wirral Museum - Birkenhead Town Hall

Hamilton Street, Birkenhead CH41 5BR   Tel: 0151 666 4010

Refurbished Victorian Town Hall still being developed as local history museum and access point for archives service.

Opening Times: Tue to Sun 10:00-17:00. Closed Mon except BH. Admission: Free.
Location: One minute walk from Hamilton Square Station.   Map Ref: 4

Cheshire, Manchester & Merseyside

Bolton Museum, Art Gallery & Aquarium

Le Mans Crescent, Bolton BL1 1SE   Tel: 01204 332211   Fax: 01204 332241
Email: museums@bolton.gov.uk   Web: www.boltonmuseums.org.uk

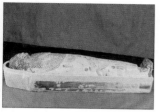

*Wooden coffin and carfonnage mummy case.
Egypt Dynasty XXII, c.900 BC*

Bolton Museum, Art Gallery and Aquarium is one of the largest regional art galleries in the North West, housing an impressive collection of fine and decorative art dating from the 18th to the 20th century. This includes watercolours and drawings, a prominent collection of modern British art prints, along with 20th century sculpture and contemporary ceramics. The Museum has recently purchased the Thomas Moran painting 'Nearing Camp on the Upper Colorado River' after a national campaign. The Museum has extensive collections of Egyptology, ethnography, natural, local and industrial history, with examples of machinery and working models. The Natural History department includes the Wildlife on your Doorstep Gallery and an award winning, interactive Wildlife Study Centre and dinosaurs. The art gallery has a constantly changing programme of events and exhibitions. The aquarium is heavily involved in conservation and has a highly specialised breeding programme. It features a wide variety of species of fish from around the world, some now extinct in their natural habitat. The education department plays a prominent and important role in the Museum's success and works closely with schools and other groups, particularly in subject areas included in the national curriculum.

Thomas Moran, Nearing Camp, Evening on the Upper Colorado River, 1882

Opening Times: Mon to Sat 10:00-17:00. Closed Sun & BH. Admission: Free. Location: Town centre, behind town hall, five minutes from train and bus stations.

Map Ref: 5

Bury Art Gallery & Museum

Moss Street, Bury BL9 0DR   Tel: 0161 253 5878   Fax: 0161 253 5915
Email: artgallery@bury.gov.uk   Web: www.bury.gov.uk/culture.htm

Spring Morning: Haverstock Hill, George Clausen

Discover world-famous paintings by Turner and Constable and sample the best of Victorian art. Love or hate the lively changing exhibitions of contemporary art. Stroll down 'Paradise Street' in the museum and remember. Don't miss the family-friendly 'Art Trolley' and hands-on activities - all this in a beautiful Edwardian building that's a work of art in itself.

Opening Times: Tue to Sat 10:00-17:00.
Admission: Free. Location: Bury Town Centre, two minute walk from bus/tram interchange.

Map Ref: 6

Fusiliers Museum (Lancashire)

Wellington Barracks, Bolton Road, Bury BL8 2PL   Tel / Fax: 0161 764 2208
Email: rrflhq@aol.com   Web: www.thefusiliers.org.uk

The museum contains uniforms, arms, medals, records, military art and regimental silver dating from 1688 to present day. Artefacts are also held of General Wolfe, Napoleon and General Robert Ross of Bladenburg.

Opening Times: Daily except Wed & Sun 09:30-16:30.   Admission: Adult £2.00, Child Free, OAP £1.00.   Location: One mile from town centre on the Bolton Bury Road (A58). Bus service from Bury Interchange/Metroline.

Map Ref: 6

Cheshire, Manchester & Merseyside

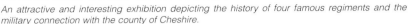

CHESTER *Cheshire*

Cheshire Military Museum

The Castle, Chester CH1 2DN   Tel / Fax: 01244 327617

An attractive and interesting exhibition depicting the history of four famous regiments and the military connection with the county of Cheshire.

Opening Times: Daily 10:00-17:00.   Location: From town centre, follow castle signs. We are left wing building of Greek Revival Castle buildings, next to the Crown Court.   Map Ref: 7

Dewa Roman Experience

Pierpoint Lane, Off Bridge Street, Chester CH1 1NL   Tel: 01244 343407

Walk through a reconstructed Roman street, discover the Roman remains in the on-site excavation and handle actual 'dig' finds.

Opening Times: Feb to Nov daily 09:00-17:00, Dec to Jan daily 10:00-16:00.   Admission: Adult £3.95, Child £2.25, Under 5's Free, Student/OAP £3.50, Family £11.00. Group rate £3.00 per person.   Location: In the city centre, one minute walk from the bus station.   Map Ref: 7

Face to face with yesterday

Grosvenor Museum

27 Grosvenor Street, Chester CH1 2DD
Tel: 01244 402008   Fax: 01244 347587
Email: s.rogers@chestercc.gov.uk
Web: www.chestercc.gov.uk/heritage/museum/home.html

The museum to visit for the 21st century family. Step-free access to ground floor. Fascinating audio-visual introduction to the city's history. Unique Roman cemetery with world-renowned tombstone collection. Paintings by local artists. Work from Chester's silversmiths. Period rooms in a townhouse. Cheshire's wildlife. Temporary exhibitions. Interactives. Keeper-guided video tours of first floor galleries. Computerised collections.

Opening Times: Mon to Sat 10:30-17:00, Sun 14:00-17:00.
Admission: Free. There is a charge for guided tours.
Location: Near town centre and drop-off point for open bus tours.
Map Ref: 7

ELLESMERE PORT *Cheshire*

Boat Museum

South Pier Road, Ellesmere Port CH65 4FW   Tel: 0151 355 5017   Fax: 0151 355 4079
Email: bookings@boatmuseum.freeserve.co.uk   Web: www.boatmuseum.org.uk

The Boat Museum is situated on the Shropshire Union Canal

Set within a historic dock complex, see the world's largest floating collection of canal craft. A video sets the scene while eight indoor exhibitions tell the history of canals. Together with four period cottages, power hall, blacksmiths forge, shop, cafe, free parking, disabled access, boat trips (seasonal)

Opening Times: Apr to Oct daily 10:00-17:00. Nov to Mar Sat to Wed 11:00-16:00. Closed Thu & Fri.
Admission: Adult £5.50, Child £3.70, Concession £4.30, Family £16.50. Group rates available.   Location: Just off J9 M53. Ten minute walk from railway station, 15 minute walk from central bus station.   Map Ref: 8

HEYWOOD *Gtr Man*

The Corgi Heritage Centre

53 York Street, Heywood OL10 4NR   Tel: 01706 365812   Fax: 01706 627811
Email: chris@corgi-heritage.co.uk

The Corgi Heritage Centre offers you the chance to discover the fascinating history of Corgi Toys. James Bond models, Chitty Chitty Bang Bang, Yellow Submarine are all on display.

Opening Times: Mon to Fri 09:00-17:30, Sat 09:00-17:00. Closed Sun.   Admission: Free.
Location: In the town centre, only one minute walk from the bus station.   Map Ref: 9

Cheshire, Manchester & Merseyside

Knutsford Heritage Centre

90A King Street, Knutsford WA16 6ED   Tel: 01565 650506   Email: Pat.heath@virgin.net

Permanent exhibition 'History of Knutsford' plus local history video 'Knutsford in Portrait'. Monthly changing exhibitions on themes of local history and interest.

Opening Times: Mon to Fri 13:30-16:00, Tue Apr to Oct 11:00-16:00, Sat 12:00-16:00, Sun 14:00-16:30.   Admission: Free.   Location: In town centre, five minute walk from bus and railway station.

Map Ref: 10

Tabley House Stately Home

Tabley House, Knutsford WA16 0HB   Tel: 01565 750151   Fax: 01565 653230
Email: inquiries@tableyhouse.co.uk   Web: www.tableyhouse.co.uk

The finest Palladian House in the north west, containing fascinating Leicester family memorabilia, furniture by Chippendale, Gillow and Bullock, and the first collection of English paintings ever made, shown in the State Rooms.

Opening Times: Apr to end Oct Thu, Fri, Sat, Sun and BH 14:00-17:00.   Admission: Adult £4.00, Child/Student £1.50.   Location: Rural, two and a half miles west of Knutsford (M6 J19)

Map Ref: 11

Tatton Park

Knutsford WA16 6QN   Tel: 01625 534400   Fax: 01625 534403
Email: tatton@cheshire.gov.uk   Web: www.tattonpark.org.uk

Magnificent grounds, superb gardens, lakes, a Neo-classical mansion and Tudor Old Hall make Tatton Park one of Englands's greatest country estates. Step into the enchanted gardens where you will find exotic trees and plants from all over the world. Visit the Mansion with its collection of art treasures and original furniture by Gillows of Lancaster. There is a working farm with rare breeds.

Music Room

Opening Times: Mansion: 13:00-16:00 (guided tours 12:00 & 12:15). Tudor Old Hall: Tue to Fri guided tours 15:00-16:00, Sat & Sun hourly from 12:00-16:00.
Admission: Per attraction: Adult £3.00, Child £2.00, Family £8.00. Saver Tickets (any two attractions) Adult £4.60, Child £2.60, Family £12.80.   Location: Three miles from Knutsford station.

Map Ref: 12

Turnpike Gallery

Civic Square, Leigh WN7 1EB   Tel: 01942 404469   Fax: 01942 404447
Email: turnpikegallery@wiganmbc.gov.uk   Web: www.wiganmbc.gov.uk

The gallery aims to show the best of contemporary art to the widest possible audience through exhibitions, projects, arts outreach and education. The exhibition programme consists of six/seven exhibitions per year, and aims to reflect the broad variety of current visual arts practice by regional, national and international artists. The gallery also accommodates an artist-in-residence.

Opening Times: Mon, Thu & Fri 09:30-17:30 Tue 10:00-17:30 Wed 09:30-17:00 Sat 10:00-15:00. Closed Sun & BH.   Admission: Free.   Location: In town centre, three minute walk from bus station.

Map Ref: 13

www.tomorrows.co.uk

Full information on our collection of travel guides and secure store

Cheshire, Manchester & Merseyside

LIVERPOOL *Merseyside*

Conservation Centre

Whitechapel, Liverpool L1 6HZ Tel: 0151 478 4999
Fax: 0151 478 4804
Web: www.conservationcentre.org.uk

The award-winning Conservation Centre is dedicated to the preservation of precious items, from ceramics and paintings to textiles and sculpture. It is the only centre of its kind to open its doors to the public revealing the fascinating techniques with its weekly studio tours.

Opening Times: Mon to Sat 10:00-17:00, Sun 12:00-17:00. Closed 23-26 Dec & 1 Jan. Admission: Free. Location: Lime Street Stn and Queen Square bus station - five minute walk. Map Ref: 14

Conservation Centre, Liverpool

Croxteth Hall & Country Park

Croxteth Hall Lane, West Derby, Liverpool L12 0HB Tel: 0151 228 5311 Fax: 0151 228 2817
Web: www.croxteth.uk

The Hall depicts the lifestyle of the Earl and family, where visitors can appreciate an Edwardian country house with character figures of the family and of the servants working below stairs. Over 100 paintings, family portraits and sporting pictures. No visit to the Earl's estate would be complete without also visiting the Victorian walled garden and home farm which contains rare breeds.

Opening Times: Apr to Oct 10:30-17:00.
Admission: Hall & Farm: Adult £2.00, Child/OAP £1.18.
Walled Garden: Adult £1.18, Child/OAP 67p.

Croxteth Hall

Location: Six miles from the city centre. Map Ref: 14

HM Customs & Excise National Museum

Albert Dock, Liverpool L3 4AQ Tel: 0151 478 4499 Fax: 0151 478 4590
Web: www.nmgm.org.uk

Enter into the intriguing world of customs and excise. This surprising museum demonstrates how the battle against smuggling is undertaken by sniffer dogs and customs officers, from uncovering endangered species to drugs and replica goods. Meet some of the museum's colourful characters, including Mother Redcap and our very own hero-hound, Sniffer.

Opening Times: Mon to Sun 10:00-17:00. Closed 23-26 Dec & 1 Jan. Admission: Free. Location: James Street Station ten minute walk. Map Ref: 14

Entrance to HM Customs & Excise National Museum

Liverpool Central Library

William Brown Street, Liverpool L3 8EW Tel: 0151 233 5845 Fax: 0151 233 5886
Email: refhuw.central.library@liverpool.co.uk Web: www.liverpool.gov.uk

Major public library service, with superb collection of rare illustrated books, fine bindings, craft printing etc. Permanent display in historic Picton Library, visitors may view other items from Hornby and Oak Collections by appointment.

Opening Times: Mon to Thu 09:00-20:00, Fri 09:00-19:00, Sat 09:00-17:00, Sun 12:00-16:00. Closed BH. Admission: Free. Location: Two minute walk from Lime Street main line and Merseyrail station. Close to Liverpool Museum and Walker Art Gallery. Map Ref: 14

Cheshire, Manchester & Merseyside

Lixerpool Museum

William Brown Street, Liverpool L3 8EN   Tel: 0151 478 4399   Fax: 0151 478 4322
Web: www.liverpoolmuseum.org.uk

Liverpool Museum

A popular family destination, exploring the secrets of the natural world and the mysteries of outer space. A truly world class museum with important and diverse collections covering archaeology, ethnology and the natural and physical science. Liverpool Museum is currently undergoing extensive building improvements and refurbishments. The project will see the museum double in size with new attractions like The Bug House and The Exploration Zone. Expected completion date - 2003.

Opening Times: Mon to Sat 10:00-17:00, Sun 12:00-17:00. Closed 23-26 Dec & 1 Jan. Admission: Free.
Location: Lime Street train station five minute walk.   Map Ref: 14

Merseyside Maritime Museum

Albert Dock, Liverpool L3 4AQ   Tel: 0151 478 4499   Fax: 0151 478 4590
Web: www.merseysidemaritimemuseum.org.uk

Merseyside Maritime Museum

Explore the diverse world of maritime history, from tales of the Titanic to the award-winning Transatlantic Slavery Gallery. There are ship models, paintings, street recreations and fascinating finds, as well as lots of family activities. In the summer, this popular venue also features 'ships and quaysides', including full-size historical vessels.

Opening Times: Mon to Sun 10:00-17:00. Closed 23-26 Dec & 1 Jan. Admission: Free. Location: James Street train and Paradise Street bus station - ten minute walk.   Map Ref: 14

Museum of Liverpool Life

Pier Head, Liverpool L3 1PZ   Tel: 0151 478 4080   Fax: 0151 478 4090
Web: www.museumofliverpoollife.org.uk

Museum of Liverpool Life

Liverpool is famous for its music, sporting history and its river. At the Museum of Liverpool Life, there's all this and more. From Brookside to the MP Bessie Braddock, from the King's Regiment to the Kop, the museum celebrates this vibrant city, its unique character and multicultural identity.

Opening Times: Mon to Sun 10:00-17:00. Closed 23-26 Dec & 1 Jan Admission: Free. Location: James Street train station and Paradise Street bus station - ten minute walk.   Map Ref: 14

Sudley House

Mossley Hill Road, Mossley Hill, Liverpool L18 8BX   Tel: 0151 724 3245
Web: www.sudleyhouse.org.uk

Sudley House

The former home of Victorian ship builder George Holt, housing his personal collection of 18th and 19th century British art. A charming gallery with works by Turner, Gainsborough, Lord Leighton and Holman Hunt. Many of the original Victorian features of the building survive, including tiles, ceramics, stained glass and wallpaper.

Opening Times: Mon to Sat 10:00-17:00, Sun 12:00-17:00. Closed 23-26 Dec & 1 Jan. Admission: Free.
Location: Mossley Hill train and bus stop ten minute walk.   Map Ref: 14

Tate Liverpool

Albert Dock, Liverpool L3 4BB   Tel: 0151 702 7400   Fax: 0151 702 7401
Email: liverpoolinfo@tate.org.uk   Web: www.tate.org.uk/liverpool/

Experience for free the national collection of modern art on three floors of galleries, all with stunning views across the historic Albert Dock and River Mersey. Temporary exhibitions featuring internationally renowned artists are shown in the top floor galleries.

Opening Times: Tue to Sun 10:00-17:50. Closed Mon (except BH), 24-26 Dec, 31 Dec & 1 Jan & Good Friday.   Admission: Free to Tate Collection; charges for special exhibitions   Location: Five minute walk from city centre, ten minute walk from Lime Street Station.   Map Ref: 14

Exterior of Tate Liverpool,
Photo Roger Sinek

University of Liverpool Art Gallery

3 Abercromby Square, Liverpool L69 3BX   Tel: 0151 794 2347/8   Fax: 0151 794 2343
Email: artgall@liv.ac.uk

Fine and decorative art from the University collections is displayed in an elegant Georgian house. Works by JMW Turner, Wright of Derby, Burne-Jones, Augustus John, Epstein, Freud and Frink.

Opening Times: Mon to Fri 12:00-16:00. Closed Aug BH & weekends.   Admission: Free.
Location: Ten minute walk from City Centre.   Map Ref: 14

The Walker

William Brown Street, Liverpool L3 8EL   Tel: 0151 478 4199   Fax: 0151 478 4190
Web: www.walkerartgallery.org.uk

The Walker Art Gallery houses an internationally important collection of art from the 14th to the 20th century. It is especially rich in European Old Masters, Victorian and Pre-Raphaelite pictures and modern British works. Outstanding works include Simone Martini's Christ Discovered in the Temple and masterpieces by Rubens, Rembrandt, Poussin, Gainsborough and Hogarth. There is an exciting exhibition programme, including Britain's premier painting biennial, the John Moores exhibition.

Opening Times: Mon to Sat 10:00-17:00, Sun 12:00-17:00. Closed 23-26 Dec & 1 Jan.   Admission: Free.   Location: Lime Street Railway Station and Queen Square bus station - five minute walk.   Map Ref: 14

MACCLESFIELD *Cheshire*

Jodrell Bank Science Centre

Lower Withington, Macclesfield SK11 9DL   Tel: 01477 5711339

On the flat plain of Cheshire, just outside Macclesfield stands an awe inspiring sight, the 76 metre Lovell Radio Telescope. Completed in the autumn of 1957, the telescope became an icon for the new dawn of 'the Space Age' because of its success in tracking the carrier rocket of the Earth's first artificial satellite, Sputnik 1. Today, the telescope is one of the foremost astronomical re-search instruments in the world. It is operated by the astronomers of the Jodrell Bank Observatory, a department of the University of Manchester. At the feet of the telescope stands the Visitor (Science) Centre of the Observatory. It contains many exhibitions on astronomy and space and in its 157 seat Planetarium, visitors can see the wonders of the Universe from the comfort of their seats. The 14 hectare Arboretum contains collections of a more earthly kind with over 2500 species of trees and shrubs forming natural habitats for a range of wildlife. A visit to Jodrell Bank is a fascinating mix of experiences for all.

Opening Times: 16 Mar to 27 Oct daily 10:30-17:30, 28 Oct to 15 Mar Tue to Sun 11:00-16:30.
Admission: Adult £4.90, Child £2.50, OAP £3.50, Under 4s Free (but not admitted to Planetarium).   Location: A535 between Holmes Chapel and Chelford, junction 18 of M6.
Map Ref: 15

Macclesfield Silk Museum

Heritage Centre, Roe Street, Macclesfield SK11 6UT   Tel: 01625 613210   Fax: 01625 617880
Web: www.silk-macclesfield.org

Tells the fascinating story of silk which links Macclesfield, once the centre of the English silk industry, with China and the Far East through an AV programme, costume, textiles and models.

Opening Times: Mon to Sat 11:00-17:00, Sun & BH 13:00-17:00. Closed Xmas & New Year and Good Friday.   Admission: Admission charge.   Location: In town centre - five minutes walk from bus and railway station.   Map Ref: 16

Paradise Mill

Park Lane, Macclesfield SK11 6TJ   Tel: 01625 618228   Web: www.silk-macclesfield.org

Working silk mill until 1981 and today the top floor is a living museum. Knowledgeable guides demonstrate the silk processes on the restored 26 hand jacquard silklooms and ancillary equipment. Room sets depict life in the 1930s.

Opening Times: Mar to Oct Tue to Sun 13:00-17:00. Nov to Feb Tue to Sat 13:00-16:00. Closed Xmas & New Year, Good Friday, Mon (except BH).   Admission: Admission charge.
Location: Town centre - five minutes walk from bus and railway stations.   Map Ref: 16

West Park Museum

Prestbury Road, Macclesfield   Tel: 01625 619831   Web: www.silk-macclesfield.org

Established in 1898 it houses a small but interesting collection of Egyptian antiquities, fine and decorative art and a gallery devoted to works of local born artist Charles Tunnicliffe.

Opening Times: Apr to Oct Tue to Sun & BH 13:30-16:30. Nov to Mar Tue to Sun 13:00-16:00. Closed Xmas & New Year, Good Friday.   Admission: Free.   Location: On outskirts of town located in public park.   Map Ref: 16

MANCHESTER

Gallery of Costume

Platt Hall, Rusholme, Manchester M14 5LL   Tel: 0161 224 5217

The Gallery of Costume is an elegant 18th century textile merchants house, housing Manchester's extraordinary collection of clothing and fashion accessories. The collection gives a fascinating insight into styles of dress from the 17th century to the present day.

Opening Times: Mar to Oct Tue to Sun 10:00-17:30, Nov to Feb Tue to Sun 10:00-16:00. Closed Mon (except BH). Admission: Free. Location: Platt Fields Park, Wilmslow Road, Rusholme, South Manchester.   Map Ref: 17

Heaton Hall

Heaton Park, Prestwich, Manchester M25 5SW   Tel: 0161 234 1456

Heaton Hall is a magnificent 18th century neo-classical country house set in 650 acres of rolling parkland. The Hall is now Grade I listed and its interiors have been beautifully restored to reflect late 18th and early 19th century life in Heaton.

Opening Times: 30 Mar to 29 Sep Thu to Sun & BH Mon. Times may very please phone 0161 235 8888 for details. Admission: Free. Location: In Heaton Park, off Middleton Road, near Prestwich north of the city centre.
Map Ref: 17

Imperial War Museum North

Trafford Wharf Road, Trafford Park, Manchester M17 1HH   Tel: 0870 220 3435
Fax: 0161 876 4319   Email: info@iwmnorth.org.uk   Web: www.iwm.org.uk

Imperial War Museum North copyright Len Grant

Opening in July 2002, Imperial War Museum North offers a new way of understanding war and conflict and the impact it has on all our lives. In the stunning aluminium-clad building - the first in the UK by international architect Daniel Libeskind - visitors will enjoy a multi-sensory experience expressing how war affects everything it touches. The Museum utilises the world-famous collections of the Imperial War Museum with a number of new display techniques. The Big Picture uses the sound and photography archive to immerse visitors in a spectacular audio-visual show using over 60 projectors. Interactors are on hand to discuss objects from the TimeStacks with visitors and the Timeline tells the story of the 20th century. 'Silos' pick out themes for further study - Women and War, Commonwealth, Legacy, Experience, Impressions and Science - and a number of iconic objects such as a Harrier Jump-Jet, a Trabant estate car and a T34 Tank are highlights in the breathtaking gallery. The Special Exhibition Gallery will show exhibitions on the themes of war and conflict, as well as the first show which looks at the building itself.

Child's toy teddy bear, made 1945

Opening Times: Daily 10:00-18:00. Admission: Free.
Location: Two miles from Manchester City Centre at the Quays,
Trafford Park.   Map Ref: 17

John Rylands University Library of Manchester

150 Deansgate, Manchester M3 3EH   Tel: 0161 834 5343   Fax: 0161 834 5574
Email: dmsshiel@fs1.li.man.ac.uk   Web: www.rylibweb.man.ac.uk/spcoll

The John Rylands Library is one of the finest examples of Neo-Gothic architecture in Europe, housing a spectacular collection of printed books, manuscripts and archives. Public library with regular exhibitions.

Opening Times: Mon to Fri 10:00-17:15, Sat 10:00-13:00. Closed Sun, BH, Xmas/New Year period, Easter weekend. Admission: Free (public tours each Wednesday 12:00 £1 a head).
Location: In town centre, few minutes walk from several train stations, metrolink stops (tram) and bus stops.   Map Ref: 17

The Lowry

Pier 8, Salford Quays, Manchester M5 2AZ   Tel: 0161 876 2020   Fax: 0161 876 2021
Email: info@thelowry.com   Web: www.thelowry.com

The Gallery

The Lowry features the work of LS Lowry, Salford's most famous son and one of the most popular of all English painters. Changing exhibitions explore the Lowry collection along with a wide range of contemporary and historical art from Britain and abroad. The Deck and The Promenade spaces have solo and group exhibitions by significant regional, national and international artists and photographers.

Opening Times: Sat 10:00-19:30 Sun to Wed 11:00-17:00
Thu & Fri 11:00-19:30. Please ring to check times as Galleries may close between exhibitions. Admission: Free. Location: In the heart of Salford Quays, five minutes walk from Broadway tram stop.   Map Ref: 17

Manchester Art Gallery

Moseley Street, Manchester M2 3JL   Tel: 0161 234 1456

Manchester Art Gallery re-opens in May 2002 after a £35 million transformation. The Gallery houses one of the UK's finest art collections in spectacular surroundings. Six centuries of British art, including some wonderful 19th century Pre-Raphaelite works, alongside fine examples of Dutch and Italian paintings. The Gallery is also renowned for its collection of decorative art. A lively special exhibitions programme showcases the best in British and international art and design.

Opening Times: Tue to Sun 10:00-17:00. Closed Mon (except BH).   Admission: Free.
Location: Manchester City Centre.   Map Ref: 17

Manchester Jewish Museum

190 Cheetham Hill Road, Manchester M8 8LW   Tel: 0161 834 9879
Fax: 0161 834 9801   Email: info@manchesterjewishmuseum.com
Web: www.manchesterjewishmuseum.com

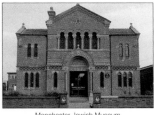

The Museum, set in a beautifully restored Grade II* listed synagogue building, tells the history of the Jewish community in Manchester and Salford over the past 250 years. Our education and outreach programme won the 1998 Sanford Award and is much in demand. The shop sells educational materials, books and gifts. Exhibition: until 11 August 2002 - 'The Art of Hebrew Script: Jewish Manuscipts and Ceremonial Objects'.

Manchester Jewish Museum

Opening Times: Mon to Thu 10:30-14:00, Sun 10:30-17:00. Closed Xmas, 28 Mar, 3 & 4 Apr, 8, 16, 22 & 29 Sep.   Admission: Adult £3.65, Concession £2.75, Family £8.95.   Location: Half a mile from Manchester Victoria and Metrolink Station.   Map Ref: 17

The Manchester Museum

The University of Manchester, Oxford Road, Manchester M13 9PL   Tel: 0161 275 2634
Fax: 0161 275 2676

The Manchester Museum has just undergone a major £19.5 million refurbishment which has created new galleries with hundreds of fascinating displays, a temporary exhibition programme, a new Discovery Centre with hands-on exhibits, a café, shop and disabled access to all areas. It amazing collections, containing six million items, provide a window on the world from Peru to Japan, from Egypt to North America.

Opening Times: Mon to Sat 10:00-17:00, Sun & BH 11:00-16:00. Please ring for Christmas opening.
Admission: Free.   Location: One mile south of Manchester City Centre on the campus of the University of Manchester.   Map Ref: 17

Museums, Galleries, Historic Houses & Sites

Please let us know of any collections that are not listed in this guide that you feel should be listed. E-mail us on *editor@tomorrows.co.uk* or return the Report Form on page 448

Manchester United Museum & Tour Centre

Sir Matt Busby Way, Old Trafford, Manchester M16 0RA   Tel: 0161 868 8631   Fax: 0161 868 8861   Email: tours@manutd.co.uk   Web: www.manutd.com

Ryan Giggs - one of our regular temporary exhibitions

Manchester United's new museum was opened by the legendary Pele in April 1998. Filling three floors of Old Trafford's massive North Stand, the museum outlines Manchester United's history from 1878 to the present day. Displays include the magnificent Trophy Room, the history of United, a special display on the Munich Air Disaster, kit and equipment, fans, the Legends Gallery and the new Treble Exhibition. There is also a changing programme of temporary exhibitions throughout the year. Explore the interactive Man-U-Net and find out about every player to have made a first team appearance

for the club. Take a virtual tour of Old Trafford and go behind the scenes at one of the world's most famous stadiums. Add your own distinctive style of commentary to match action as Martin Tyler gives you tips in our commentary booth. Visit our audio-visual theatre and see 'Backstage at The Theatre of Dreams'. Listen to United fans describing their experiences watching United in our Fanzone. Pop into our Legends Cafe for a quick snack or into the Red Cafe for something more substantial. After visiting the Museum, why not go on a tour and see the

Ruud van Nistelrooy - A British record transfer to United

pitch, sit in the dugout, enter the changing rooms and walk down the players' tunnel.

Opening Times: Daily 09:30-17:00, tours daily 09:40-16:30.   Admission: Museum - Adult £5.50, Child/OAP £3.75, Family £15.50. Museum & Tour - Adult £8.50, Child/OAP £5.75, Family £23.50, Under 5s Free.   Location: Five minute walk from Old Trafford Metro Station, which is accessible from Piccadilly Train Station in Manchester.   Map Ref: 17

The Museum of Science and Industry in Manchester

Liverpool Road, Castlefield, Manchester M3 4FP   Tel: 0161 832 2244/1830 24hr   Fax: 0161 833 1471   Email: marketing@msim.org.uk   Web: www.msim.org.uk

Based in the building of the world's oldest passenger railway station

The Museum of Science and Industry in Manchester is one of the world's biggest and most impressive science museums. Bursting with entertaining galleries and amazing exhibits, the Museum tells the compelling story of Manchester. Highlights include: historic locomotives and incredible aircraft, thunderous cotton machinery and huge steam mill engines, interactive exhibits and Special Exhibitions, including Dinosaurs - they're back! and Star Trek: Federation Science in 2002.

Opening Times: Daily 10:00-17:00. Closed 24-26 Dec. Admission: Free entry to permanent collections, charge for Special Exhibitions.   Location: City centre location, nearest railway station, Deansgate is five minutes walk. Nearest Metrolink station, G-Mex is five minutes walk.   Map Ref: 17

Museum of Transport - Greater Manchester

Boyle Street, Cheetham, Manchester M8 8UW   Tel: 0161 205 2122

Over 85 vehicles mainly buses relating to over a century of road public transport in Greater Manchester. Small exhibits and archives.

Opening Times: Wed, Sat, Sun & BH 10:00-17:00. Admission: Adult £3.00, Concession £1.75, Under 5s Free.   Location: One and a half miles north of Victoria Station, five minute walk from Woodlands Road Metrolink.

Map Ref: 17

Pankhurst Centre
60/62 Nelson Street, Chorlton on Medlock, Manchester M13 9WP Tel: 0161 273 5673
Fax: 0161 274 4979 Email: pankhurst@zetnet.co.uk

Living memorial to the Pankhursts and their activism to secure the right to vote for women. History of the women's suffragette movement. Parlour (reconstruction), museum, display about Sylvia Pankhurst.

Opening Times: Mon to Fri 10:00-16:00. Closed Sat, Sun & BH. Admission: Free.
Location: Near town centre, Eye Hospital and Manchester Royal Infirmary.
Map Ref: 17

Peoples History Museum
Bridge Street, Manchester M3 3ER Tel: 0161 839 6061 Fax: 0161 839 6027 Email: info@peopleshistorymuseum.org.uk
Web: www.peopleshistorymuseum.org.uk

People's History Museum

National Union of Railwaymen banner, Wakefield branch, about 1920

The People's History Museum is the only national museum in Britain dedicated to people's history, it celebrates the triumphs and struggles of everyday people. Watch the first Match of the Day, visit the Co-op shop, play your favourite vinyl on the jukebox and try your hand at sweated labour. The Head Office of the museum houses the Textile Conservation Centre which specializes in the conservation of banners in both the museums own collection nationally.

Opening Times: Tue to Sun 11:00-16:30. Closed Mon (except BH) & Good Fridays. Admission: Adult £1.00, Child/OAP/Student/Concession Free, Free to all on Fri.
Location: Easy walking distance from city centre. Gartside Street multi-storey car park next door. Ten minute walk from Deansgate Train Station.
Map Ref: 17

The Whitworth Art Gallery

The Whitworth Art Gallery

The University of Manchester, Oxford Road,
Manchester M15 6ER Tel: 0161 275 7450 Fax: 0161 275 7451
Email: whitworth@man.ac.uk Web: www.whitworth.man.ac.uk

'Sudden Shower at Ohashi Bridge' Utagawa Hiroshige 1797-1858

The Whitworth is home to internationally famous collections of British watercolours, textiles and wallpapers, as well as an impressive range of modern and historic prints, drawings, paintings and sculpture. An ever-changing and varied programme of temporary exhibitions also runs throughout the year.

Opening Times: Mon to Sat 10:00-17:00, Sun 14:00-17:00.
Admission: Free Location: Approx 1.5 miles south of Manchester City Centre, in Whitworth Park (Oxford Road), opposite Manchester Royal Infirmary.
Map Ref: 17

Wythenshawe Hall
Wythenshawe Park, Northenden, Manchester M23 0AB Tel: 0161 234 1456

Wythenshawe Hall is a striking half-timbered Tudor house with fine oak-panelled interiors, set in its own beautiful gardens. The Hall was the home of the Tatton family for nearly four hundred years and its long history includes a dramatic role in the events of the English Civil War. A visit to the Hall today gives a fascinating insight into the changing history of this part of Manchester.

Opening Times: 30 Mar to 29 Sep Thu to Sun & BH.
Times may vary please phone 0161 235 8888 for details.
Admission: Free.
Location: Five miles south of city centre in Wythenshawe Park, B5167.
Map Ref: 17

Cheshire, Manchester & Merseyside

NANTWICH *Cheshire*

Nantwich Museum
Pillory Street, Nantwich CW5 5BQ   Tel: 01270 627104   Email: nantwich.museum@virgin.net

A fascinating insight into the history of the ancient market town of Nantwich together with a cheese making room and a modern Millennium Gallery for temporary exhibition.

Opening Times: Apr to Sep Mon to Sat 10:30-16:30, Oct to Mar Tue to Sat 10:30-16:30.
Admission: Free.   Location: Near town centre.   Map Ref: 18

OLDHAM *Gtr Man*

Gallery Oldham

Greaves Street, Oldham OL1 1AL   Tel: 0161 911 4657   Fax: 0161 911 4669
Email: els.museum@oldham.gov.uk

This fine and decorative art collection of mainly British artists was first established by Victorian industrial philanthropists and now includes work by modern and contempory artists. Large collection of objects representing Oldham people's lives form the industrial era of cotton and engineering. Extensive natural history collection of mainly local plants, geology, insects and birds reflects historic local passion for scientific study.

Opening Times: Mon to Sat 10:00-17:00.
Admission: Free.   Location: In Oldham Town Centre behind library, two minutes from bus station, five minutes

Gallery Oldham open February 2002

from Oldham Mumps Station.   Map Ref: 19

Saddleworth Museum & Art Gallery

High Street, Uppermill, Oldham OL3 6HS   Tel: 01457 874093   Fax: 01457 870336
Email: museum-curator@saddleworth.net   Web: www.museum.saddleworth.net

Set in a beautiful location beside the Huddersfield narrow canal, Saddleworth Museum charts 3000 years of history in this ancient Yorkshire parish, set in the foothills of the Pennines.

Opening Times: Mar to Oct Mon to Sat 10:00-17:00, Sun 12:00-17:00. Nov to Feb Mon to Sun 13:00-16:00.   Admission: Adult £2.00, Child/OAP £1.00, Family £4.00.   Location: In the centre of Uppermill village, eight miles from Oldham on A670.   Map Ref: 20

PRESCOT *Merseyside*

Prescot Museum
34 Church Street, Prescot L34 3LA   Tel: 0151 430 7787

Collections on local history and history of horology. Exhibitions - An active special exhibition programme brings museum objects to life and hands-on exhibits, activities and events. Holiday activities for children.

Opening Times: Tue to Sat 10:00-13:00 and 14:00-17:00, Sun 14:00-17:00.   Admission: Free.
Location: Town centre.   Map Ref: 21

ROCHDALE *Gtr Man*

Rochdale Pioneers Museum or Toad Lane Museum

31 Toad Lane, Rochdale OL12 0NU   Tel: 01706 524920   Email: museum@co-op.ac.uk
Web: www.co-op.ac.uk/toad_lane.htm

The home of the worldwide co-operative movement. In 1844 the Rochdale Pioneers opened their store selling pure food at fair prices and honest weights and measures. See how your ancestors did their shopping.

Opening Times: Tue to Sat 10:00-16:00, Sun 14:00-16:00.   Admission: Adult £1.00,
OAP/Student 50p, Family £2.00.   Location: Situated in the Toad Lane Conservation Area at the rear of the Rochdale Exchange Shopping Precinct on Hunters Lane.   Map Ref: 22

RUNCORN *Cheshire*

Norton Priory Museum & Gardens

Tudor Road, Manor Park, Runcorn WA7 1SX   Tel: 01928 569895   Fax: 01928 589743
Email: info@nortonpriory.org   Web: www.nortonpriory.org

Cheshire, Manchester & Merseyside

Unique and beautiful site incorporating atmospheric museum, excavated Priory remains, sculpture trail, peaceful and relaxing two and a half acre walled garden and the awe inspiring St Christopher statue, now housed in its own gallery.

Opening Times: Apr to Oct Mon to Fri 12:00-17:00, Sat, Sun & BH 12:00-18:00. Nov to Mar daily 12:00-16:00. Closed Xmas & New Year. Admission: Adult £3.75, Concession £2.50, Family £9.80. Location: Less than 30 minutes by car from Chester, Liverpool and Manchester. Close to junction 11 of M56.

Map Ref: 23

ST HELENS *Merseyside*

The World of Glass
Chalon Way East, St Helens WA10 1BX   Tel: 08707 444 777   Fax: 01744 616 966
Email: info@worldofglass.com   Web: www.worldofglass.com

The World of Glass is constructed on a historic site, which incorporates a Grade II* listed Victorian glassmaking furnace. The centre also houses the Pilkington Glass Collection and St Helen's MBC Social History Collection.

Opening Times: Daily 10:00-17:00 except Mon. Closed Xmas & New Year. Admission: Adult £5.00, Child £3.60, Under 5s Free, Concession £3.60. Group rates available.
Location: Situated in the heart of St Helens, just a five minute walk from the bus and railway station. Excellent access by road from junction 7 on M62.

Map Ref: 24

SALFORD *Gtr Man*

Ordsall Hall Museum
332 Ordsall Lane, Salford M5 3AN   Tel: 0161 872 0251   Fax: 0161 872 4951
Email: admin@ordsallhall.org   Web: www.ordsallhall.org

Grade I listed Tudor Manor House with black and white timbers, and 600 years of history, including a part in the gunpowder plot. Educational visits, guided tours and temporary exhibitions.

Opening Times: Mon to Fri 10:00-16:00, Sun 13:00-16:00. Admission: Free. Location: Five minutes walk from Exchange Quay Metrolink.

Map Ref: 25

Salford Museum & Art Gallery
Peel Park, Crescent, Salford M5 4WU   Tel: 0161 736 2649   Fax: 0161 745 9490
Email: salford.museum@salford.gov.uk   Web: www.salfordmuseum.org

A traditional reconstructed Victorian Street with shops, workshops and houses - plus a Victorian Gallery. Most exhibitions here look forward rather than back, showcasing the work of both young British artists and international culture.

Opening Times: Mon to Fri 10:00-16:45, Sat & Sun 13:00-17:00. Admission: Free.
Location: Situated on the A6 near the Greater Manchester Motorway network, five minutes.

Map Ref: 25

SOUTHPORT *Merseyside*

Breton Dining Room by
Sir William Russell Flint (1880-1969)

Atkinson Art Gallery
Lord Street, Southport PR8 1DH   Tel: 01704 533133
Fax: 0151 934 2109   Web: www.seftonarts.co.uk

Permanent collection of nineteenth and twentieth century works, including LS Lowry, John Piper and Henry Moore. Temporary exhibition programme, including contemporary artists.

Opening Times: Mon to Wed & Fri 10:00-17:00, Thu & Sat 10:00-13:00. Closed BH. Admission: Free.
Location: In town centre, next to library.   Map Ref: 26

Botanic Gardens Museum
Churchtown, Southport PR9 7NB   Tel: 01704 227547   Fax: 01704 224112
Web: www.seftonarts.co.uk

Local history galleries, Victorian room with toy display and costume, natural history gallery. Temporary exhibition programme.

Opening Times: Tue to Fri 11:00-15:00, Sat & Sun 14:00-17:00, BH 12:00-16:00, closed following Fri. Admission: Free. Location: In Churchtown to north of Southport.   Map Ref: 26

Cheshire, Manchester & Merseyside

Astley Cheetham Art Gallery

Trinity Street, Stalybridge SK15 2BN   Tel: 0161 338 2708

Astley Cheetham Art Gallery originally operated as a lecture hall but developed into an art gallery when J F Cheetham bequeathed his collection of paintings to the town in 1932. The collection includes Italian paintings from the 14th and 15th centuries and works from British masters such as Cox and Burne-Jones.

Opening Times: Mon to Wed & Fri 10:00-12:30 13:00-17:00 Sat 09:00-12:30 13:00-17:00.
Admission: Free. Location: Two minutes from bus station.   Map Ref: 27

Bramall Hall

Bramall Park, Bramhall, Stockport SK7 3NX   Tel: 0161 485 3708   Web: www.stockport.gov.uk

Magnificent black and white timber-framed Tudor manor house with Victorian additions, set in 70 acres of beautiful parkland. Tour the beautiful period rooms and glimpse into the Hall's fascinating history spanning over six centuries.

Opening Times: Good Friday to Sep 13:00-17:00, Sun & BH 11:00-17:00. Oct to 1 Jan Tue to Sat 13:00-16:00 Sun & BH 11:00-16:00. 2 Jan to Good Friday Sat & Sun 13:00-16:00.
Admission: Park, Gardens & Shop - Free. Hall: Adult £3.95, Concession £2.50, Family £10.00.
      Map Ref: 28

Chadkirk Chapel

Vale Road, Chadkirk, near Romiley, Stockport   Tel: 0161 430 5611
Web: www.stockport.gov.uk

Chadkirk Chapel, beautifully restored, is set in the heart of Chadkirk Country Estate. With a fascinating history, it houses marvellous pieces of artwork, such as the popular 'East Window'.

Opening Times: Sat & Sun 13:00-17:00, winter 12:00-16:00. Admission: Free. Location: Set in the heart of Chadkirk Country Estate.   Map Ref: 29

Hat Works - The Museum of Hatting

Wellington Mill, Wellington Road South, Stockport SK3 0EU   Tel: 0161 355 7770   Fax: 0161 480 8735   Web: www.hatworks.org

The UK's only museum dedicated to the hatting industry and headwear. Guides reveal the art of hat making with working machinery. The gallery houses a fantastic collection of hats which date back to the 18th century.

Opening Times: Mon to Sat 10:00-17:00, Sun 11:00-17:00. Admission: Adult £3.95, Concession £2.50, Family £11.00. Free entry to top level, cafe, internet access and community room. Location: Centre of Stockport, five minute walk from bus and railway stations.   Map: 30

Lyme Park

Disley, Stockport SK12 2HA   Tel: 01663 762023   Fax: 01663 765035
Email: mlyrec@smtp.ntrust.org.uk   Web: www.nationaltrust.org.uk

Originally a Tudor house, Lyme was transformed by the Venetian architect Leoni into an Italianate palace. Some of the Elizabethan interiors survive and contrast dramatically with later rooms. The state rooms are adorned with Mortlake tapestries, Grinling Gibbons wood-carvings and an important collection of English clocks. The 17 acre Victorian garden boasts impressive bedding schemes, a sunken parterre, an Edwardian rose garden, Jekyll-style herbaceous borders, reflection lake, a ravine garden and Wyatt conservatory. The garden is surrounded by a medieval deer park of almost 1400 acres of moorland, woodland and parkland, containing an early 18th century hunting tower. Lyme appeared as 'Pemberley' in the BBC's recent adaptation of the Jane Austen novel Pride and Prejudice.

Opening Times: House: 29 Mar to 30 Oct Fri to Tue 13:00-17:00. BH Mon & Tue 4 Jun 11:00-17:00. For other opening times please contact us. Admission: House & Garden: Adult £5.50, Family £12.00. House: £4.00, Garden: £2.50. Location: Entrance on A6, six and a half miles south east of Stockport, nine miles north west of Buxton. Disley Station half a mile from park entrance.

Map Ref: 31

Stockport Air Raid Shelter Tours

61 Chestergate, Stockport SK1 1NE Tel: 0161 474 1940 Web: www.stockport.gov.uk

The unique Stockport Air Raid Shelters have been carved into the natural sandstone cliffs in Stockport Town Centre. Boarded up after the war and rediscovered five years ago, they are now imaginatively restored with the use of light, sound and objects.

Opening Times: Mon to Sat 11:00-17:00, Sun 13:00-17:00. Admission: Adult £3.50, Adult Leisure Key £2.25, Child £2.25, Child Leisure Key £1.25, Concession £2.75, Family £10.00. Location: Located in the centre of Stockport - five minute walk from nearest bus and railway station.

Map Ref: 30

Stockport Art Gallery & War Memorial

Wellington Road South, Stockport SK3 8AB Tel: 0161 474 4453 Fax: 0161 480 4960 Email: stockport.art.gallery@stockport.gov.uk

Three galleries showing a changing programme of exhibitions of local, regional and national significance. Small permanent collection of 19th and 20th century works and local community based exhibitions and events.

Opening Times: Mon to Fri 11:00-17:00, Sat 10:00-17:00. Closed Wed & Sun. Admission: Free. Location: Next door to Stockport College. One minute from railway station, five minutes from bus station on A6.

Map Ref: 30

Stockport Museum

Vernon Park, Turncroft Lane, Stockport SK1 4AR Tel: 0161 474 4460 Web: www.stockport.gov.uk

Set in beautiful surroundings of Vernon Park, Stockport Museum houses a fascinating collection of objects dating back to the Stone Ages and is home to 'One Round Hill' - the story of the history of Stockport.

Opening Times: Apr to Oct daily 13:00-17:00, winter months Sat & Sun 13:00-17:00. Admission: Free. Location: Located in the glorious Vernon Park, five minute drive from Stockport.

Map Ref: 30

TURTON *Gtr Man*

Turton Tower

Tower Drive, Chapeltown Road, Turton BL7 0HG Tel: 01204 852203 Fax: 01204 853759 Email: turtontower.lcc@btinternet.com Web: www.bringinghistoryalive.co.uk

A distinctive English country house with period rooms displaying a magnificent collection of decorative woodwork, paintings and furniture, including items loaned from the Victoria and Albert Museum.

Opening Times: Feb to Nov. Admission: Adult £3.00, Child/Concessions £1.50, Family £8.00. Location: Rural location, nearest railway station one and a half miles - Bromley Cross. Buses stop outside.

Map Ref: 32

Cheshire, Manchester & Merseyside

WARRINGTON *Cheshire*

Warrington Museum & Art Gallery   ♿ ✦

Bold Street, Warrington WA1 1JG   Tel: 01925 442392   Fax: 01925 442399
Email: museum@warrington.gov.uk   Web: www.warrington.gov.uk/museum

Warrington Museum & Art Gallery combines a Victorian 'cabinet of curiosities' charm with state-of-the-art temporary exhibition galleries. Displays feature a wealth of material on the natural world, local history, fine art and treasures from ancient civilisations and distant continents. Many galleries feature free hands-on activities for younger visitors. Lively temporary exhibition programme - ring for details.

Opening Times: Mon to Fri 10:00-17:30, Sat 10:00-17:00. Closed Sun & BH. Admission: Free. Location: Town centre location, five minute walk from Bank Quay station.

The Earth's History Gallery

Map Ref: 33

WIDNES *Cheshire*

Catalyst   ♻ ♿ ✦ ☕ 🚌

Gossage Building, Mersey Road, Widnes WA8 0DF   Tel: 0151 420 1121   Fax: 0151 495 2030
Email: info@catalyst.org.uk   Web: www.catalyst.org.uk

Catalyst has hands-on exhibits relating to chemistry and the everyday products of the chemical industry. Winner of 13 major awards; history, science and technology. Science fuses with fun at Catalyst.

Opening Times: Tue to Fri 10:00-17:00, Sat & Sun 11:00-17:00, BH Mon & Mon in school holidays. Closed Xmas & New Year. Admission: Adult £4.65, Child £3.40, Concession £3.95, Family £13.95. Group rates available. Location: Widnes, Junction 12 of M56, junction 7 of M62, nearest railway station Widnes.

Map Ref: 34

WIGAN *Gtr Man*

History Shop   ♿ ✦

Library Street, Wigan WN1 1NU   Tel: 01942 828128   Fax: 01942 827645
Email: heritage@wiganmbc.gov.uk   Web: www.wiganmbc.gov.uk

Wigan Heritage Flagship venue - Museum, local history, study centre and genealogy study centre. Displays feature social and industrial heritage of Wigan. Local history and genealogy for the greater Wigan area.

Opening Times: Mon 10:00-19:00, Tue to Fri 10:00-17:00, Sat 10:00-13:00. Closed Sun & BH. Admission: Free. Location: Town centre, five minute walk from railway and bus stations.

Map Ref: 35

Wigan Pier   ♿ ✦ ☕ 🚌

Trencherfield Mill, Wigan WN3 4EF   Tel: 01942 323666   Fax: 01942 701927
Email: wiganpier@wiganmbc.gov.uk   Web: www.wiganpier.net

The Wigan Pier Experience set on the Leeds-Liverpool Canal

Opie's Museum of Memories at the Wigan Pier Experience. The Robert Opie collection had been assembled to reflect the remarkable story of domestic life in Britain since the industrial revolution. By displaying the actual products, brands, posters, magazines, toys, televisions and royal souvenirs of each era, along with the advertisements and images that reflect fashion and design, it is possible to gain a sense of ever changing culture and lifestyle through which our parents and grandparents lived. The Museum of Memories not only tells the incredible story of our consumer society but also revives our own memories, placing us in the context of history, of which we are all part of. The Way We Were

Let us take you back in time at the Wigan Pier Experience

Cheshire, Manchester & Merseyside

Heritage Centre takes you back to the strict days of Victorian Britain, experience the hardship, social lives and in some instances the entertaining times of people of Wigan in 1900. See for example what they did on holiday during 'wakes week', walk through our mine, witness the maypole colliery diaster. Visitors never forget our Victorian schoolroom - you will meet the schoolmaster and participate in choir practice, you may even be the bell monitor or 'lice' inspector. At Wigan Pier Experience we will provide you and your family with the opportunity to take a journey through yesteryear.

Opening Times: Mon to Thu 10:00-17:00, Sat & Sun 11:00-17:00. Closed Fri, 25-26 Dec & New Year's Day. Admission: Adult £7.50, Child £5.95, Concession £5.95, Group 20+ £4.95. Location: Signposted from all major road networks. Near town centre, five minute walk from Wigan Train Station.

Map Ref: 35

WILMSLOW *Cheshire*

Quarry Bank Mill, Styal

Quarry Bank Mill & Styal Estate

Styal, Wilmslow SK9 4LA   Tel: 01625 527468   Fax: 01625 539267
Email: msyrec@smtp.ntrust.org.uk
Web: www.quarrybankmill.org.uk

Working water powered cotton mill, with its estate village, farm and woodland. See a Spinning Jenny, a mule, and Lancashire looms in action. Original Apprentice House and garden - see how pauper children were fed, worked and slept. Purchase unique Styal Calico from the shop.

Opening Times: Easter to Sep daily 10:30-17:30, Oct to Mar Tue to Sun 10:30-17:00. Admission: Mill: Adult £5.00, Concession £3.40. Mill & Apprentice House: Adult £6.50, Concession £3.70. Free to National Trust Members. Location: Ten minutes drive from Wilmslow and Manchester Airport.

Map Ref: 36

Cornwall is truly a county of romance with its tales of King Arthur who legend has it was born Tintagel. The River Tamar, in separating the county from the rest of England, successful preserves the distinct Cornish character.

Museums and Galleries admirably record Cornwall's social history, its association with the se smuggling and piracy, its magnetic appeal to artists, its mining past and mineral collections ar its living plant collection.

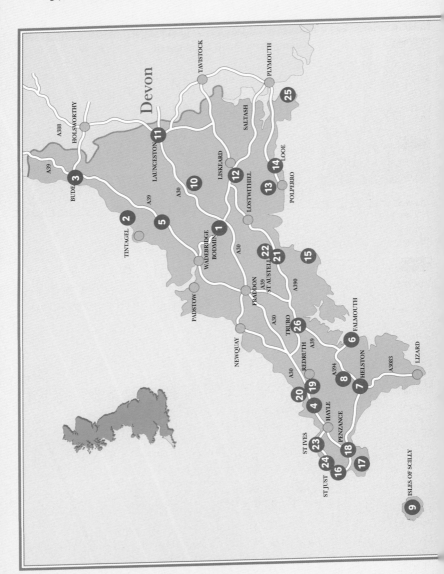

The Red Map References should be used to locate Museums etc on the pages that follow

Cornwall & Isles of Scilly

BODMIN

Bodmin Town Museum

Mount Folly, Bodmin PL31 2HQ   Tel: 01208 77067   Fax: 01208 79268
Email: bodmin.museum@ukonline.co.uk

Local history museum with exhibits and text from medieval times to the 1950's, featuring Bodmin Moor, agriculture, law and order, trades and occupations, transport, Victorian domestic life and costume, World Wars I & II.

Opening Times: Apr to Sep Daily 10:30-16:30, Oct 11:30-15:30. Closed Sun & BH.
Admission: Free.   Location: Town centre, two minute walk from car parks.   Map Ref: 1

Duke of Cornwalls Light Infantry Regimental Museum
(Military Museum Bodmin)

The Keep, Bodmin PL31 1EG   Tel / Fax: 01208 72810   Email: dclimus@talk21.com

Covers military history from the capture of Gibraltar in 1704 up to World War II. Fascinating displays of weapons, pictures, uniforms and documents - including General George Washington's Bible 'taken' by the Regiment in 1777.

Opening Times: Mon to Fri (and Sun in Jul & Aug) 09:00-17:00.   Admission: Adult £2.00, Child 50p.   Location: Bodmin.   Map Ref: 1

BOSCASTLE

The Museum of Witchcraft

The Harbour, Boscastle PL35 0AE   Tel: 01840 250111   Email: museumwitchcraft@aol.com
Web: www.museumofwitchcraft.com

The world's largest collection of Witchcraft related artefacts. This unique museum (now 50 years old) is one of the most popular in Cornwall.

Opening Times: Easter to Halloween Mon to Sat 10:30-18:00, Sun 11:30-18:00.
Admission: Adult £2.00, Child/OAP £1.00.   Location: Boscastle Harbour.   Map Ref: 2

BUDE

Bude-Stratton Museum

Lower Wharf, Bude EX23 8LG   Tel / Fax: 01288 353576   Email: theclerk@bude-stratton.gov.uk
Web: www.bude-stratton.gov.uk

Old photographs, models and an audio-visual presentation tell the story of the canal and the ships that used it.

Opening Times: Good Friday to Sep Daily 11:00-17:00.   Admission: Adult 50p, Child Free, OAP 25p.   Location: On Bude's canalside.   Map Ref: 3

CAMBORNE

Camborne Public Library & Museum

The Cross, Camborne TR14 8HA   Tel: 01209 713544
Email: enquiries@helstonmuseum.org.uk

A history of Camborne and the immediate area. Trades inventions, archaeology, mining, Roman villa.

Opening Times: Mon & Wed to Fri 15:00-17:00, Sat 10:00-12:00. Closed Sun & Tue.
Admission: Free.   Location: Town centre location, above the public library.   Map Ref: 4

Trevithick Cottage

Penponds, Camborne TR14 0QG   Tel: 01209 612154   Fax: 01209 612142

Home of the famous Cornish engineer, Richard Trevithick. Now a private house owned by the National Trust, but one room contains portraits and memorabilia.

Opening Times: Apr to Oct Wed 14:00-17:00.   Admission: Donations of £1.00 invited.
Location: Take Barriper Road after leaving Camborne towards Helston. Turn right into Penponds at the School, cottage is first on right.   Map Ref: 4

Cornwall & Isles of Scilly

CAMELFORD

British Cycling Museum

The Old Station, Camelford PL32 9TZ   Tel / Fax: 01840 212811   Web: www.chycor.co.uk/

The British Cycling Museum is the largest and foremost display of cycling history from 1818 to present day with over 400 various machines and the largest display of cycling memorabilia on show.

Opening Times: Sun to Thu 10:00-17:00. Admission: Adult £2.50, Child £1.50.
Location: One mile north of Camelford on B3266.

Map Ref: 5

North Cornwall Museum & Gallery

The Clease, Camelford PL32 9PL   Tel / Fax: 01840 212954
Email: camelfordtlc@eurobell.co.uk

The museum shows many aspects of life in North Cornwall from 50-100 years ago. The gallery has monthly changing exhibitions by artists and craftsmen.

Opening Times: Apr to Sep Mon to Sat 10:00-17:00. Closed Sun. Admission: Adult £1.50, Child £1.00, OAP/Concession £1.25.   Location: Just off the A33 in Camelford at southern end of town, opposite free car park.

Map Ref: 5

FALMOUTH

Falmouth Art Gallery

Muncipal Buildings, The Moor, Falmouth TR11 2RT   Tel: 01326 313863   Fax: 01326 318608   Email: info@falmouthartgallery.com   Web: www.falmouthartgallery.com

John T Richardson, The Bar Pool, Falmouth signed and dated 1912, oil on canvas

Falmouth Art Gallery is one of the leading art galleries in the South West. Its permanent collection features works by major British artists including Sir Frank Brangwyn, Sir Edward Coley Burne-Jones, Sir Alfred Munnings, Henry Scott Tuke and Dame Laura Knight. The gallery's most famous work is 'The Lady of Shallot' by John William Waterhouse, which is known throughout the world. The gallery also puts on a varied temporary exhibitions programme, showing major one person shows, touring and mixed themed exhibitions.

Self portrait by Julian Dyson, March 2000, acrylic

Opening Times: Mon to Sat 10:00-17:00. Admission: Free.
Location: On the Moor, above the library.

Map Ref: 6

National Maritime Museum Cornwall

NATIONAL MARITIME MUSEUM CORNWALL

Discovery Quay, Falmouth TR11 3QY Tel: 01326 313388   Fax: 01326 317878   Email: enquiries@nmmc.co.uk   Web: www.nmmc.co.uk

Aerial Shot of the Museum Building, Summer 2001

Opening in June 2002, National Maritime Museum Cornwall is a brand new state-of-the-art museum set in a landmark new building on Falmouth's waterfront. It offers you an outstanding experience whatever your age or interest. Enjoy a wide range of interactive displays and demonstrations, explore Cornwall's unique maritime heritage and discover an unrivalled range of boats - including many in active use on the water.

Opening Times: Daily from 22 Jun 2002. 10:00-18:00 from opening to end Aug, otherwise 10:00-17:00. Closed 6 to 31 Jan 2003. Admission: Adult approx £5.90.

Location: On Waterfront, near town centre, five minutes walk from train station.

Map Ref: 6

Cornwall & Isles of Scilly

Pendennis Castle
Falmouth TR11 4LP Tel: 01326 316594

Pendennis Castle formed part of a chain of castles built by Henry VIII along the south coast as protection against attack from France. Pendennis has been adapted over the years to meet changing defence requirements. The collection provides a survey of coastal defence cannon from the 18th to 20th centuries.

Opening Times: Apr to Sep daily 10:00-18:00, Oct daily 10:00-17:00, Nov to Mar daily 10:00-16:00. Closed Xmas & New Year. Admission: Adult £3.80, Child £1.90, Concession £2.90. Location: On Pendennis Head, Cornwall, one mile south east of Falmouth. Map Ref: 6

HELSTON

Flambards Victorian Village & Gardens
Culdrose Manor, Helston TR13 0QA Tel: 01326 573404 Fax: 01326 573344
Email: info@flambards.co.uk Web: www.flambards.co.uk

Over 50 life size Victorian shops, homes and traders set in cobbled streets with carriages and fashions. Audio tour availble for hire. Adult and childrens rides from the gentle to the daring, live entertainment, shows and amusements all set in award winning gardens. One of Britain's top ten all weather family attractions.

Opening Times: Easter to End Oct 10:30-17:00, extended opening to 18:00 in Aug. Closed some Mon & Fri in low season. Location: Half a mile from Helston on A3083 Lizard Road. Map Ref: 7

Flambards Victorian Village

Helston Folk Museum
Market Place, Helston TR13 8TH Tel: 01326 564027 Fax: 01326 569714
Email: enquiries@helstonmuseum.org.uk Web: www.helstonmuseum.org.uk

A community focus on the lives and history of the people of Helston and the Lizard area, and a heritage hub for Cornish tradition in west Cornwall. Mezzanine Art Gallery - temporary exhibition programme.

Opening Times: Mon to Sat 10:00-7:00. Closed Sun & BH. Admission: Adult £2.00 (Free on Sat), Under 16s and local Kerrier residents Free. Location: Town centre, situated behind the Guildhall. Map Ref: 7

Poldark Mine & Heritage Complex
Poldark Mine, Wendron, Helston TR13 0ER Tel: 01326 573173 Fax: 01326 563166

18th century tin mine and museum explaining early tin recovery and the fascinating story of the Cornish overseas. Set in attractive surroundings complete with craft workshops and family entertainments.

Opening Times: Easter to 1 Nov daily 10:00-18:00, last mine tour 16:00. Admission: Site: Free, Tour: Adult £5.75, Child £3.75, Family £15.50. Location: Two miles from Helston on the B3297. Map Ref: 8

ISLES OF SCILLY

Isles of Scilly Museum
Church Street, St Mary's, Isles of Scilly TR21 0JT Tel / Fax: 01720 422337
Email: IOS.museum@talk21.com Web: www.aboutbritain.com/isleofscillymuseum.htm

Collections feature local history and archaeology, particularly ships and the sea. Extensive exhibitions on shipwrecks, birds and local flora. Exhibitions on special topics during summer.

Opening Times: Easter to Oct daily 10:00-12:00 13:30-16:30. Also 19:30-21:00 (weekdays) Whitsun to Sep. Winter Wed 14:00-16:00. Admission: Adult £1.00, Child 50p. Location: In Church Street, Hugh Town ten minute walk from harbour. Map Ref: 9

Cornwall & Isles of Scilly

Daphne Du Maurier's Smugglers at Jamaica Inn

Jamaica Inn Courtyard, Bolventor, Launceston PL15 7TS   Tel: 01566 86025

Tableaux in light and sound from the book 'Jamaica Inn.' Some history of the Du Maurier family and smuggling history, ancient and modern.

Opening Times: Daily Easter to Oct 10:00-17:00, high season 10:00-19:00. Admission: Adult £2.50, Child/OAP £2.00. Group rates available. Location: In the village of Bolventor. Half way between Launceston and Bodmin, short distance from A30.   Map Ref: 10

Launceston Steam Museum

St Thomas'Hill, Launceston PL15 8DA   Tel: 01566 775665

The museum contains vintage cars, motorcycles and steam rollers, with collection of railway signs and notices. A powered 1905 Robey Steam Engine is on show.

Opening Times: Jun Sun to Wed; Jul to Sep Sun to Fri; Oct half term week except Sat; Good Friday for 8 days 10:30-16:30. Admission: Free when visiting Launceston Steam Railway. Location: Located at Launceston Steam Railway, Newport, 1 mile from town centre. Map Ref: 11

Lawrence House Museum

9 Castle Street, Launceston PL15 8BA   Tel: 01566 773277/773693   Fax: 01566 773693

Lawrence House is a Georgian property housing a registered local history museum. With artefacts from the bronze age up to the present day.

Opening Times: Apr to Sep Mon to Fri 10:30-16:30. Closed Sat & Sun. Admission: Free. Location: Castle Street, three minutes walk from town centre.   Map Ref: 10

Potters Museum of Curiosity

Jamaica Inn Courtyard, Bolventor, Launceston PL15 7TS   Tel / Fax: 01566 86838

Unique collection established in 1861 by founder Walter Potter of Victorian taxidermy and weird and wonderful curiosities from all over the world, includes weapons, toys, fossils, smoking memorabilia, etc.

Opening Times: Daily Nov, Dec, Feb & Mar 11:00-16:00, Apr to Jun & Sep 10:00-17:00, Jul & Aug 10:00-19:00. Admission: Adult £2.50, Child/OAP £2.00, Family £6.95, Groups £1.50. Location: Just off A30, halfway between Launceston and Bodmin.   Map Ref: 11

John Southern Wildlife Art Gallery

Dobwalls, Liskeard PL14 6HB   Tel: 01579 320325   Fax: 01579 321345

Original watercolours and limited edition prints by Steven Townsend - Artist of the Year 1999. Also the largest and most comprehensive permanent display of limited edition prints by Carl Brenders in the UK, supported by the work of Robert Bateman, Antony Gibbs, Matthew Hillier, Terry Isaac and Daniel Smith.

Opening Times: Daily 10:30-16:00. Closed Xmas & New Year. Admission: Free. Location: Adjacent to Dobwalls Adventure Park.   Map Ref: 12

The Old Guildhall Museum

c/o The East Looe Town Trust, The Guildhall, Fore Street, East Looe PL13 1BP   Tel: 01503 263709   Fax: 01503 265674

The museum is housed in a 15th century listed building which retains the old magistrates benches, cells and stocks. Models of boats, local history, smuggling, lifeboat logs, fishing, minerals and porcelain.

Opening Times: Easter week, then Sun to Fri 11:30-16:30 end of May to Sep including BH Sat. Admission: Adult £1.50, Child 50p. Special rates for school parties. Location: Near town centre and the beach.   Map Ref: 14

Cornwall & Isles of Scilly

Mevagissey Folk Museum

East Quay, Mevagissey PL26 6PP   Tel: 01726 843568   Email: ronforder@talk21.com

Located in an 18th century boat builders (1745) with the original lathe insitu. Three floors of artefacts with one of the best collection of photos taken throughout the last century. Twice voted the best small museum in Cornwall.

Opening Times: Good Friday to end Oct Mon to Fri 11:00-17:00, Sat & Sun 10:00-16:00.
Admission: Adult £1.00, Child 50p.   Location: Town Quay.   Map Ref: 15

Geevor Tin Mine

Pendeen, Penzance TR19 7EW   Tel: 01736 788662   Fax: 01736 786059
Email: pch@geevor.com

Mining museum, largest preserved mining site in UK. Guided underground tour, spectacular coastal setting. Support for educational/study groups.

Opening Times: Apr to Sep 10:00-17:00, Nov to Feb 10:00-16:00. Closed Sat (unless a BH) & Sun in winter season.   Admission: Adult £6.00, Student £3.50, OAP £5.50, Family £16.00.
Location: In Pendeen, on B3066 road from St Ives to Lands End, six miles from Penzance (bus/railway station).   Map Ref: 16

Museum of Submarine Telegraphy

Porthcurno, Penzance TR19 6JX   Tel / Fax: 01736 810966

The submarine cable that landed on Porthcurno beach in 1870 was the start of a world spanning telegraph system that led to Porthcurno becoming the largest cable station in the world.

Opening Times: Up to 25 Mar & 3 Nov to Mar 2003 Sun & Mon 10:00-16:00, 25 Mar to 3 Nov Sun to Fri & BH Sat 10:00-17:00, Jul & Aug Sun to Sat 10:00-17:00. Closed Xmas & NY.
Admission: Adult £4.00, Concession £3.50, Student £2.50, Family £10.50.   Location: At Porthcurno, take A30 from Penzance towards Land's End.   Map Ref: 17

Newlyn Art Gallery

New Road, Newlyn, Penzance TR18 5PZ   Tel: 01736 363715   Fax: 01736
331578   Email: newlyn@newlynartgallery.freeserve.co.uk
Web: www.newlynartgallery.co.uk

NEWLYN
ART GALLERY

Newlyn Art Gallery showing the Newlyn Society of Artists Critic's Choice - 2001

Newlyn Art Gallery is one of the South West's leading contemporary art organisations, showing work by local, national and international artists. As an educational charity the gallery's education programme encourages a better understanding and enjoyment of the work on show. The programme includes talks, discussion sessions, workshops and projects for the widest cross section of the community as possible.

Opening Times: Mon to Sat 10:00-17:00 (including BH).
Admission: Free.   Map Ref: 18

Pendeen Lighthouse

Pendeen, Penzance TR19 7ED   Tel: 01736 788418   Fax: 01736 786059

Built in 1900, this dramatically positioned lighthouse is open with its Engine Room containing the last surviving 12 inch siren in England.

Opening Times: 29 Mar to 4 Apr, 3 to 9 May, 26 to 31 May, Jul & Aug Sun to Sat 11:00-17:00.
Admission: Adult £2.00, Concession £1.50, Student £1.00, Family £5.00.   Location: Signed from B3306 St Just to St Ives road in Pendeen village.   Map Ref: 16

Penlee House Gallery & Museum

PENLEE HOUSE
Gallery & Museum

Penlee Park, Morrab Road, Penzance TR18 4HE   Tel: 01736 363625
Fax: 01736 361312   Email: info@penlee-house.demon.co.uk   Web: www.penleehouse.org.uk

Penlee House Gallery & Museum, Penzance, is an elegant gallery set within a Victorian house and park. Changing exhibitions mainly feature famous 'Newlyn School' artists (1880-1930), including Stanhope and Elizabeth Forbes, Walter Langley, Harold Harvey and 'Lamorna' Birch. The museum features 5,000 years of the history of Penwith. There is an excellent café and shop .

Opening Times: May to Sep Mon to Sat 10:00-17:00, Oct to Apr Mon to Sat 10:30-16:30. Admission: Adult £2.00, Child Free, Concession £1.00. Location: Situated in Penlee Park, a short walk from town centre and seafront.

Map Ref: 18

Exterior of Penlee House

The Pilchard Works

Tolcarne, Newlyn, Penzance TR18 5QH   Tel: 01736 332112   Fax: 01736 332442
Email: nick@pilchardworks.co.uk   Web: www.pilchardworks.co.uk

Text, photographs and artefacts combine in this 'working museum'. Sole producers of salted, pressed pilchards using traditional methods. Visitors can taste the product, draw their own stencils and talk to production staff.

Opening Times: Apr to Oct Mon to Fri 10:00-18:00. Admission: Adult £3.25, Child £1.95, OAP £2.95, Family £10.00. Location: 50 yards upstream from Newlyn Bridge.

Map Ref: 18

Trinity House National Lighthouse Centre

The Former Buoy Store, Wharf Road, Penzance TR18 4BN   Tel: 01736 360077

The job of lighthouse keeper has gone, but items once found in daily use including lamps, clocks, engines, uniforms, fog signals, furniture and some major optics removed from lighthouses, form this collection.

Opening Times: Apr to Oct daily 10:30-16:30. Admission: Adult £3.00, Child £1.00, OAP/Student £2.00, Family £6.00. Location: Penzance Harbourside - five minute walk from main car parks.

Map Ref: 18

REDRUTH

Camborne School of Mines Geological Museum & Art Gallery

University of Exeter, Redruth TR15 3SE   Tel: 01209 714866   Fax: 01209 716977
Email: scamm@csm.ex.ac.uk   Web: www.geo-server.ex.ac.uk

The museum features an extensive collection of rocks which is continuously updated by international geological research at CSM. There are also displays on the history and future of mining in Cornwall.

Opening Times: Mon to Fri 10:00-16:00. Admission: Free. Location: Next to Camborne Pool, Redruth College, 20 minutes walk from Camborne or Redruth station.

Map Ref: 19

Cornish Mines & Engines & Cornwall Industrial Discovery Centre

Poo1, Redruth TR15 3NP   Tel / Fax: 01209 315027

The gateway to Cornwall's industrial past: including the Discovery Centre with a stunning audio visual presentation; Taylor's 1892 90" single cylinder pumping engine; Michell's 1887 winding or 'whim' engine.

Opening Times: Jan to Mar Fri 11:00-16:00, 25 Mar to 3 Nov Sun To Fri 11:00-17:00, Aug Sun to Sat 11:00-17:00, Nov to Mar by arrangement (01209 210900). Admission: Adult £5.00, Concession £4.60, Student £3.00, Family £13.00. Location: At Pool, two miles west of Redruth on both sides of A3047.

Map Ref: 19

Tolgus Tin

c/o Cornish Gold Site, Portreath Road, Redruth TR16 4HN   Tel: 01209 215185   Fax: 01209 219786

One of two tin streaming works in Cornwall, contains Cornish stamps driven by waterwheel and one of the last round frames.

Cornwall & Isles of Scilly

Opening Times: Jan to Mar Sun 10:30-16:00, Mon to Wed 09:30-17:00, Apr to Oct Sun & BH Sat 10:30-16:00, Mon to Fri 09:30-17:00, Nov to Mar Sun to Wed 10:00-16:00.
Admission: Adult £2.25, Concession £1.75, Student £1.50, Family £6.50. Location: From A30 take B3300 to Portreath. On the site of the Cornish Goldcentre.
Map Ref: 20

ST AUSTELL

The China Clay Museum, Wheal Martyn
Carthew, Wheal Martyn, St Austell PL26 8XG   Tel / Fax: 01726 850362

Site museum of the china clay industry. Comprises industrial and social history items. Photographic and archive collections. Features two water wheels, sand and mica drags, settling pits, pan kiln, transport etc.

Opening Times: Apr to Oct daily 10:00-17:00, Nov to Mar Tue to Thu 11:00-16:00.
Admission: Adult £5.00, Child £3.00, OAP £4.60, Family £13.00. Group rates available.
Location: Two miles north of St Austell B3274.
Map Ref: 21

Eden Project
Bodelva, St Austell PL24 2SG   Tel: 01726 811900   Fax: 01726 811912
Web: www.edenproject.com

An unforgettable experience in a breathtaking epic location. Eden is a gateway into the fascinating world of plants and people and a vibrant reminder of how we need each other for our mutual survival. Its home is a dramatic global garden the size of thirty football pitches, nestling like a lost world in a crater overlooking St Austell Bay. One of its giant conservatories is a majestic rainforest cathedral, the other is host to the fruits of the Mediterranean and the flowers of South Africa and California. Outside in the landscaped grounds you will find tea and lavender, sunflowers and hemp. It is a place to tell a hundred plant stories from cocoa and coffee to bananas and rubber. From plants and medicine to plants in construction, from paper and wine and from perfume to brewing. Wherever you are in the world you will instantly recognise this spectacular place with its stunning architecture and breathtaking living plant collection as the Eden Project, Cornwall, UK.

Opening Times: Mar to Oct daily 10:00-18:00, Nov to Feb daily 10:00-16:30. Closed Xmas.   Admission: Adult £9.80, Child £4.00, OAP £7.50, Family £23.00.
Location: Near St Austell. Follow brown tourism signs from A390, A30 and A391.   Map Ref: 22

ST IVES

Penwith Galleries
Back Road West, St Ives TR26 1NL   Tel: 01736 795579

Mixed exhibitions and one man shows all year.

Opening Times: Tue to Sat 10:00-13:00 14:30-17:00.   Admission: Adult 50p.   Location: Near town centre.
Map Ref: 23

St Ives Museum
Wheal Dream, St Ives TR26 1PR   Tel: 01736 796005

A 'real' museum, in which every facet of St Ives' fascinating history is represented in its many collections, from which old and young can glean and learn of the past. These include: art, blacksmith, boat building, Cornish kitchen, crysede, farming, fire brigade, fishing, geology, Hain Steamship Company, lifeboat, lighthouses, mining, photographs, police, railway, shipwrecks, toys, Victorian clothes, wartime memorabilia.

Opening Times: 25 Mar to 6 Apr (excluding Good Friday), 22 Apr to 2 Nov Mon to Fri 10:00-17:00, Sat 10:00-16:00. Closed Sun.
Location: Near harbour quay.
Map Ref: 23

A glimpse of what awaits you

St Ives Society of Artists

Norway Gallery, Old Mariners Church, Norway Sq, St Ives TR26 1NA   Tel: 01736 795582
Fax: 01736 731823   Email: gallery@stivessocietyofartists.com
Web: www.stivessocietyofartists.com

Art works in this gallery are largely traditional and representational. Members submit new work each year for inclusion in the Exhibition. Paintings sold are replaced by others, therefore the Exhibition is continuous but changing.

Opening Times: Mid Mar to early Nov Mon to Sat & BH Sun 10:00-16:30.   Admission: Adult 25p, Child Free.   Location: Close to harbour - behind The Sloop Inn car park. In the Old Mariners Church.
Map Ref: 23

Tate St Ives

Porthmeor Beach, St Ives TR26 1TG   Tel: 01736 796226   Fax: 01736 794480   Web: www.tate.org.uk

Tate St Ives opened in 1993 and offers a unique introduction to modern art, where paintings and sculpture can be seen in the surroundings which inspired many of them. The gallery presents changing displays from the Tate Collection focusing on the post-war modern movement for which St Ives is famous. Tate St Ives also manages the

Alfred Wallis, The Blue Ship c. 1934

Barbara Hepworth Museum and Sculpture Garden in St Ives, which offers a remarkable insight into the work and outlook of one of Britain's most important 20th century sculptors.

Opening Times: Mar to Oct daily 10:00-17:30, Nov to Feb Tue to Sun 10:00-16:30.   Admission: Adult £3.95, Child Free, Concession £2.50, OAP Free.
Location: Situated by Porthmeor Beach close to town centre.

Barbara Hepworth, Sea Form (Porthmeor) 1958
Map Ref: 24

TORPOINT

Mount Edgcumbe House & Country Park

Mount Edgcumbe House, Cremyll, Torpoint PL10 1HZ   Tel: 01752 822236

Sir Richard Edgcumbe of Cotehele built a new home in his deer park at Mount Edgcumbe in 1547-53. It is now beautifully furnished with family possessions, including paintings by Sir Joshua Reynolds, Gerard Edema and William van der Velde, Irish bronze age horns, 16th century tapestries and 18th century Chinese and Plymouth porcelain. Exhibitions include April to June - Lenckewicz prints. August to September Robin Armstrong Wildlife Artist.

Mount Edgcumbe House, Cornwall

Opening Times: 29 Mar to 29 Sep Wed to Sun & BH 11:00-16:30.   Admission: Adult £4.50, Child £2.25, Concession £3.50. Group advanced booking (min 10) £3.50.   Location: Across the river from Plymouth by passenger ferry (10 mins). By car - Torpoint Ferry or Tamar Bridge (A374, B3247 follow brown signs).
Map Ref: 25

TRURO

Royal Cornwall Museum

River Street, Truro TR1 2SJ   Tel: 01872 272205   Fax: 01872 240514   Email: enquiries@royal-cornwall-museum.freeserve.co.uk   Web: www.royalcornwallmuseum.org.uk

Nationally important collection of Cornish minerals, Cornish archaeology and local history, paintings, ceramics, Greek, Roman and Egyptian archaeology, and a regular temporary exhibition programme. Many activities for children and families, especially in holidays.

Opening Times: Mon to Sat 10:00-17:00, closed Sun and BH.   Admission: Adult £3.00, Child free, OAP/Student £2.00.   Location: Near town centre on A390 past the railway stn.   Map Ref: 26

Cumbria

many, Cumbria is synonymous with the Lake District, with its amazing variety of scenery
tained within a relatively small area. South Cumbria, sandwiched between the Lake District
the Yorkshire Dales has its history recorded in the art and literature of William Turner and John
kin. On the west coast a succession of ports once exported coal and in the north the county
n, Carlisle, stands guard over the flat lands leading to the Scottish boarder, its castle for
turies a bastion against the marauding Scots.

bria lays claim to some outstanding museums including collections of its literary, artistic,
ting and military history.

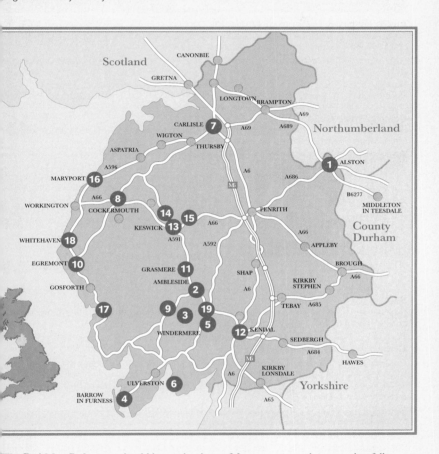

The Red Map References should be used to locate Museums etc on the pages that follow

Cumbria

ALSTON

South Tynedale Railway   ⚷ ● ▭ ♿

The Railway Station, Alston CA9 3JB   Tel: 01434 381696   Web: www.strps.org.uk

A narrow gauge railway built on the former Haltwhistle - Alston standard gauge branch line. The trains are hauled by preserved steam and diesel locomotives from the UK and abroad.

Opening Times: Weekends Apr to Oct. Daily in summer peak season. Tel (01434) 382828 for talking timetable.   Location: Alston Station is off A686 Hexham - Penrith road, north of Alston Town Centre. Follow brown tourist signs on roads to Alston.   Map Ref: 1

AMBLESIDE

Armitt Library & Museum of Ambleside   ⟲ ⚷ ●

Rydal Road, Ambleside LA22 9BL   Tel: 015394 31212   Fax: 015394 31313
Email: mail@armitttrust.fsbusiness.co.uk   Web: www.armitt.com

2000 years of local history from Romans to Beatrix Potter's watercolours (largest collection in Britain).

Opening Times: Daily 10:00-17:00. Closed Xmas & Boxing Day.   Admission: Adult £2.50, Concession £1.80, Family £5.60.   Location: 2 mins from Tourist Information Centre.   Map Ref: 2

Beatrix Potter Gallery   ❦

Main Street, Hawkshead, Ambleside LA22 0NS   Tel: 01534 36355   Fax: 01534 36187
Email: rhabpg@smtp.ntrust.org.uk   Web: www.nationaltrust.org.uk

A unique collection of Beatrix Potter's work. The gallery has the largest collection of her published work, including most of the original watercolour illustrations and manuscripts from the 'Peter Rabbit' series of little books. Annually, a selection of Potter's work is displayed in the gallery, which were formerly the offices of her husband's solicitors' practice and is set within the picturesque village of Hawkshead.

Opening Times: 24 Mar to 31 Oct Sun to Thu 10:30-16:00.   Admission: Adult £3.00, Child £1.50, Family £7.50   Location: Main Street - Hawkshead, close to car park.   Map Ref: 3

Beatrix Potter Gallery

Hill Top   ⚷ ▭

Near Sawrey, Hawkshead, Ambleside LA22 0LF   Tel: 015394 36269   Fax: 015394 36187
Email: rpmht@smtp.ntrust.org.uk   Web: www.nationaltrust.org.uk

Beatrix Potter wrote many of her famous children's stories in this little 17th century house and it has been kept exactly as she left it, complete with her furniture and china.

Opening Times: 31 Mar to 31 Oct daily except Thur & Fri (open Good Friday). Mar to May 11:00-16:00, Jun to Aug 10:30-17:00, Sep to Oct 11:00-16:30.   Admission: Adult £4.00, Child £2.00, Family £9.75.   Location: Two miles south of Hawkshead, in hamlet of Near Sawrey, behind the Tower Bank Arms.   Map Ref: 3

BARROW-IN-FURNESS

The Dock Museum   ⟲ ⚷ ● ▭ ♿

North Road, Barrow-in-Furness LA14 2PW   Tel: 01229 894444   Fax: 01229 811361
Email: rlitten@barrowbc.gov.uk   Web: www.dockmuseum.org.uk

Spectacular new permanent exhibition 'Shipbuilders To The World'; fine collection of ship models, social and industrial history and fine art gallery. The waterfront site has an adventure playground and walkways linked to Cumbria's Coastal Way.

Opening Times: Apr to Oct Tue to Fri 10:00-17:00, Sat & Sun 11:00-17:00. Nov to Mar Wed to Fri 10:30-16:00, Sat & Sun 11:00-16:30.   Admission: Free.   Location: One mile from town centre; 15 minute walk from railway station.   Map Ref: 4

The Dock Museum has a fully landscaped waterfront site

Cumbria

Furness Abbey

Barrow-in-Furness LA13 0TJ   Tel: 01229 823420

Furness Abbey was once the richest Cistercian abbey in England. The remains of the earlier monastery can still be seen. The museum contains an exhibition and a wealth of stonework from the abbey.

Opening Times: Apr to Sep daily 10:00-18:00, Oct daily 10:00-17:00, Nov to Mar Wed to Sun 10:00-13:00 14:00-16:00. Closed Xmas & New Year. Admission: Adult £2.70, Child £1.40, Concession £2.00. Location: One and a half miles north of Barrow-in-Furness, on minor road off A590.

Map Ref: 4

BOWNESS-ON-WINDERMERE

Blackwell - The Arts & Crafts House

Bowness-on-Windermere LA23 3JR   Tel: 015394 46139   Fax: 015394 88486
Email: info@blackwell.org.uk   Web: www.blackwell.org.uk

Designed by MH Baillie Scott as a holiday home, Blackwell has survived intact with many original details - stained glass windows, carved oak panelling, iron work, stone carving and decorative plasterwork. Changing exhibitions.

Opening Times: Feb to Dec daily 10:00-17:00. Winter closing 16:00. Admission: Adult £4.50, Child £2.50, Family £12.00. Location: On B5360, one and a half miles south of Bowness-on-Windermere.

Map Ref: 5

CARK-IN-CARTMEL

Lakeland Motor Museum

Holker Hall and Gardens, Cark-in-Cartmel LA11 7PL   Tel / Fax: 015395 58509

A nostalgic reminder of transport and horticultural bygones appealing to all ages and offering a truly astonishing insight into our forefathers' inventiveness and dexterity. Over 20,000 exhibits including The Campbell Legend Bluebird Exhibition.

Opening Times: Apr to Oct Sun to Fri 10:30-16:45. Admission: Motor museum and gardens: Adult £6.50, Child £3.95. Location: On B5278 near Grange-over-Sands.

Map Ref: 6

CARLISLE

Carlisle Cathedral Treasury Museum

Carlisle Cathedral, Castle Street, Carlisle CA3 8TZ   Tel: 01228 548151   Fax: 01228 547049
Email: office@carlislecathedral.org.uk   Web: www.carlislecathedral.org.uk

A display of Cathedral and Diocesan silver and treasures, illustrating the story of Christians in Cumbria through the centuries.

Opening Times: Daily 08:30-16:30. Admission: Free. Donation of £2.00 invited. Location: In town centre, ten minutes walk from main railway station and bus station.

Map Ref: 7

Guildhall Museum

Greenmarket, Carlisle   Tel: 01228 534781   Fax: 01228 810249
Email: enquiries@tullie-house.co.uk   Web: www.tulliehouse.co.uk

The Guildhall is a half timbered house on the corner of the Greenmarket and Fisher Street. It was given to the city by Richard De Redeness and was long used as the meeting place of the town's eight medieval Trade Guilds. Four of the Guilds survive today and continue to meet annually in the building on Ascension Day.

Opening Times: Apr to Oct Tue to Sun 12:00-16:30. Closed Mon except BH. Admission: Free.
Location: Located in the city's pedestrianised area at the southern end of Fisher Street, close to Carlisle Visitor Centre.

Guildhall Museum

Map Ref: 7

Gateway, Carlisle Castle c.1835

Museum of the Border Regiment & Kings Own Royal Border Regiment

Queen Marys Tower, The Castle, Carlisle CA3 8UR
Tel: 01228 532774   Fax: 01228 521275
Email: RHQ@kingsownborder.demon.co.uk
Web: www.armymuseums.org.uk

The Museum relates the history of Cumbria's County Infantry Regiment, local Militia and Volunteer units from 1702 to the present day and is located in Carlisle Castle, a superb medieval fortress founded in 1092, which has been the home of the Regiment since 1873. The displays on two floors include uniforms, weapons, equipment, medals, silver, pictures, memorabilia and much more.

Opening Times: Apr to Sep Mon to Sun 09:30-18:00, Oct Mon to Sun 10:00-17:00, Nov to Mar Mon to Sun 10:00-16:00. Closed Xmas & New Year. Admission: Included in entry charge to castle - Adult £3.20, Child £1.60, Concession £2.40. Location: North side of City Centre, ten minutes from railway station. Adjacent car-park Devonshire Walk on the west side of the Castle, disabled parking in the Castle.   Map Ref: 7

The Bishops Stone,
Border Reiver Pathway

Tullie House Museum & Art Gallery

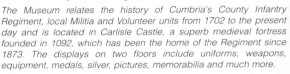

Castle Street, Carlisle CA3 8TP   Tel: 01228 534781   Fax: 01228 810249   Email: enquiries@tullie-house.co.uk   Web: www.tulliehouse.co.uk

Tullie House combines the features of historic house and modern Museum. Old Tullie House is a 17th century town house of character, with a fine classical façade overlooking a herb garden. Inside are some early features - including Jacobean staircase and panelled Drawing Room. The latter displays key artworks by the Pre-Raphaelites; other rooms feature portraits and fine paintings and a childhood gallery. The modern Border Galleries show Carlisle's exciting history and wildlife.

Railway Area, Border Gallery

There is a wealth of objects from prehistoric and Roman times (complete with reconstruction of Hadrian's Wall). Inter-actives include Roman writing and artillery. The spectacular Reivers audio-visual presentation brings to life the lawless Borders of the Middle Ages; the railway story is told by the 'station announcer'. Local wildlife - complete with badger sett - is seen under a domed ceiling with changing light and sound. The New Rotunda viewing platform affords striking views of Carlisle Castle and opened in 2001 with the excitingly different Millennium Gallery. This celebrates unique aspects of Carlisle's collections and includes a stunning display of minerals from Cumbria/N Pennines, set on cast glass; rare archaeology (with transforming 'Peppers Ghost' interactive); local paintings and costume. The walls feature Carlisle building styles and also tell stories.

Opening Times: Nov to Mar Mon to Sat 10:00-16:00, Sun 12:00-16:00. Apr to Oct Mon to Sat 10:00-17:00, Sun 12:00-17:00 Closed Xmas. Admission: Adult £5.00, Child £2.50, Concession £3.50, Family £14.00.   Map Ref: 7

COCKERMOUTH

Cumberland Toy & Model Museum

Banks Court, Market Place, Cockermouth CA13 9NG   Tel: 01900 827606
Email: rodmoore42@hotmail.com   Web: www.toyandmodelmuseum.gbr.cc

This national award winning museum has many visitor operated exhibits including Hornby Trains, Scalextric Cars and Lego. Come and re-live your childhood.

Opening Times: Feb to Nov 10:00-17:00. Dec to Jan times vary, please phone.
Admission: Adult £3.00, Child £1.50, OAP £2.60, Group rates for parties of 10+.
Location: Market Place. Follow signs from car parks.   Map Ref: 8

Cumbria

Brantwood

🦽 🌐 💿 🌕 🚜

Coniston LA21 8AD   Tel: 015394 41396   Fax: 015394 41263
Email: enquiries@brantwood.org.uk   Web: www.brantwood.org.uk

The former home of John Ruskin, Brantwood presents and explores the various themes that interested him throughout his life - art, the environment, geology, architecture and society.

Opening Times: Mid Mar to mid Nov daily 11:00-17:30, mid Nov to mid Mar Wed to Sun 11:00-16:30. Admission: Adult £4.50, Child £1.00, Student £3.00, Family £10.00. Garden only £2.00.
Location: On the east side of Coniston Water, two and a half miles from the village of Coniston.
Map Ref: 9

The Ruskin Museum

📖 🦽 🌐 🚜

Yewdale Road, Coniston LA21 8DU   Tel: 015394 41164   Fax: 015394 41132
Email: vmj@ruskinmuseum.com   Web: www.ruskinmuseum.com

Sunset at Herne Hill through the smoke of London, 1886 watercolour

The Ruskin Museum, Coniston's award-winning 'cabinet of curiosities' introduces a local story as old as the hills which copper-bottomed the fleet and slate-roofed the world; celebrates the life, art and radical ideas of John Ruskin, 'one of those rare men who think with their hearts'; honours heroic Speed Ace Donald Campbell and Bluebird.

Opening Times: Easter/1 Apr to Oct daily 10:00-17:30, Nov to Mar Wed to Sun 10:30-15:30. Admission: Adult £3.50, Child £1.75, Family £9.00. Group rates available.
Location: Near village centre, on Yewdale Road, three minute walk from main car park and Tourist Information Centre.
Map Ref: 9

Florence Mine Heritage Centre

📖 🦽 🌐 💿 🚜

Egremont CA22 2NR   Tel / Fax: 01946 820683   Email: info@florencemine.com
Web: www.florencemine.com

Geological and fossil collections, site of special scientific interest.

Opening Times: Apr to Oct daily 10:00-16:00. Admission: Underground Tour & Museum: Adult £6.50, Child/OAP £4.50. Group rates available. Location: Near Egremont Town Centre, ten minute walk. Bus stops two minutes away.
Map Ref: 10

Dove Cottage & the Wordsworth Museum

📖 🌐 ☕ 🌕 🚜   *The Wordsworth Trust*
Centre for British Romanticism

The Wordsworth Trust, Dove Cottage, Grasmere LA22 9SH   Tel: 015394 35544/8   Fax: 015394 35748   Email: enquiries@wordsworth.org.uk
Web: www.wordsworth.org.uk

Dove Cottage - home to Wordsworth when he wrote his greatest poetry

Dove Cottage was the poet, William Wordsworth's home from 1799-1808. Visitors are offered guided tours of this atmospheric cottage. The award-winning museum displays the Wordsworth Trust's unique collections of manuscripts, books and paintings interpreting the life and work of William Wordsworth, his family and circle. There is a major special exhibition every year.

Opening Times: Daily 09:30-17:30. Closed Xmas and last three weeks of Jan and first week of Feb.
Admission: Adult £5.00, Child £2.50, Groups £4.40 per person. Museum only: Adult £2.50, Child £1.25.
Location: South of Grasmere village, on the main A591 Kendal to Keswick road.   Map Ref: 11

KENDAL

Abbot Hall Art Gallery

Abbot Hall, Kendal LA9 5AL   Tel: 01539 722464   Fax: 01539 722494
Email: info@abbothall.org.uk   Web: www.abbothall.org.uk

A fine Georgian house containing a growing collection of modern art. The ground floor rooms contain furniture by Gillows of Lancaster and painting by Kendal born artist George Romney. Changing exhibitions.

Opening Times: Feb to Dec Mon to Sat 10:30-17:00. Winter closing 16:00.   Admission: Adult £3.50, Child £1.75, Family £9.00.   Location: Junction 36 of M6, Kendal is ten minutes drive. Nearest station: Oxenholme.   Map Ref: 12

Kendal Museum

Station Road, Kendal LA9 6BT   Tel: 01539 721374   Fax: 01539 737976
Email: info@kendalmuseum.org.uk   Web: www.kendalmuseum.org.uk

Displays of archaeology and natural history, both local and global. With examples of lakeland flora and fauna, the museum charts developments from pre-historic times through Roman, Medieval and Victorian and into the 21st century.

Opening Times: Feb to Dec Mon to Sat 10:30-17:00. Winter closing 16:00.   Location: Junction 36 on M6, ten minutes drive. Nearest station: Kendal.   Map Ref: 12

Museum of Lakeland Life

Abbot Hall, Kendal LA9 5AL   Tel: 01539 722464   Fax: 01539 722494
Email: info@lakelandmuseum.org.uk   Web: www.lakelandmuseum.org.uk

Real objects and displays tell the story of Cumbria's history - from the age of 18th century Yeoman farmers, through Georgian and Victorian periods and into living memory.

Opening Times: Feb to Dec daily 10:30-17:00. Winter closing 16:00.   Admission: Adult £3.50, Child £1.75, Family £9.00.   Location: Junction 36 of M6, ten minutes drive to Kendal. Nearest station: Oxenholme.   Map Ref: 12

KESWICK

Cars of The Stars Motor Museum

Standish Street, Keswick CA12 5HH   Tel: 0176787 73757   Fax: 0176787 72090
Web: www.carsofthestars.com

Delorean - Back to the Future

This world famous museum features vehicles from television and film, including Chitty Chitty Bang Bang, Batmobiles, Herbie, A-Team van, Del Boy's yellow Reliant, FAB 1, Back to the Future, James Bond's Aston Martin and many more. A souvenir shop and famous autographs. Definitely not to be missed!

Opening Times: Easter to end Nov daily 10:00-17:00. Also open Feb half term and weekends in Dec. Admission: Adult £3.00, Child £2.00. Discount of 10% on parties of 20+.   Location: In town centre. 100 yards from car park, five minutes walk from bus station.   Map Ref: 13

Cumberland Pencil Museum

Southey Works, Greta Bridge, Keswick CA12 5NG   Tel: 017687 73626   Fax: 017687 74679
Email: museum@acco-uk.co.uk   Web: www.pencils.co.uk/

The pencil story; from the discovery of graphite to the present day method of pencil manufacture. Told through exhibitions and a video presentation. Including a techniques video, world's longest pencil, gift shop.

Opening Times: 09:30-16:00. Closed Xmas & New Year.   Admission: Adult £2.50, Child/OAP £1.25, Family £6.25.   Location: 300 yards west of town centre.   Map Ref: 13

www.tomorrows.co.uk

Full information on our collection of travel guides and secure store

Keswick Museum & Art Gallery

Fitz Park, Station Road, Keswick CA12 4NF   Tel: 017687 73263   Fax: 017687 80390
Email: keswick.museum@allerdale.gov.uk   Web: www.allerdale.gov.uk

Keswick's Victorian museum is full of surprises; the amazing musical stones played by Royal Command, the 500 year old cat and a stunning collection of crystals. Art exhibitions monthly.

Opening Times: Good Friday to 31 Oct daily 10:00-16:00.   Admission: Adult £1.00, Child/Concession 50p, Groups 10% discount on 10 or more.   Location: In Fitz Park, on Station Road, five minutes walk from town centre, follow brown and white signs for 'Museum & Art Gallery'.

Map Ref: 13

Mirehouse

Underskiddaw, Keswick CA12 4QE   Tel / Fax: 017687 72287
Email: info@mireho.freeserve.co.uk

Living family home which has passed by descent for three hundred years. Remarkable group of 19th century friendships illustrated by manuscripts and portraits: Tennyson, Wordsworth, Southey, Carlyle, Fitzgerald, Constable. Also Francis Bacon collection from his biographer James Spedding.

Opening Times: Gardens & Tearoom: Apr to Oct daily 10:00-17:30. House: Apr to Oct Sun & Wed 14:00-17:00 (last entry 16:30), also Fri in Aug. Groups by appt throughout year
Admission: Gardens & Lakeside Walk: Adult £2.00, Child £1.00. House & Gardens: Adult £4.00, Child £2.00.   Location: Three and a half miles north of Keswick on A591. Excellent rural bus service.

Map Ref: 14

Threlkeld Quarry & Mining Museum

Threlkeld Quarry, Threlkeld, Keswick CA12 4TT   Tel: 017687 79747
Email: coppermaid@aol.com   Web: www.golakes.co.uk   www.earthlines.com

The finest mining museum in the north of England - realistic mine tour of 45 minutes pure history and adventure. Excavators and locomotives, we have the 'lot'.

Opening Times: Mar to Oct daily 10:00-17:00.   Admission: Museum: Adult £2.50. Mine Tour: £3.00.   Location: Keswick - four miles on A66 Penrith/Keswick Road.

Map Ref: 15

MARYPORT

The Senhouse Roman Museum

Sea Brows, Maryport CA15 6JD   Tel / Fax: 01900 816168
Email: romans@senhouse.freeserve.co.uk

The museum houses the Netherhall Collection, one of the largest collections of Roman altars from a single site in Britain. Also many fine religious sculptures, including the mysterious 'Serpent Stone'.

Opening Times: Apr to end Jun Tue, Thu, Fri to Sun 10:00-17:00, Jul to end Oct daily 10:00-17:00. Nov to end Mar Fri to Sun 10:30-16:00.   Admission: Adult £2.00, Child 75p. Group rates available.   Location: Set on low lying cliffs overlooking Maryport harbour.

Map Ref: 16

RAVENGLASS

Muncaster Castle Gardens & Owl Centre

Muncaster Castle, Ravenglass CA18 1RQ   Tel: 01229 717614   Fax: 01229 717010
Email: info@muncastercastle.co.uk   Web: www.muncastercastle.co.uk

Home to the Pennington family for 800 years. Muncaster is a genuine treasure trove of art and antiques including Henry VI's drinking bowl. The rich furnishings and decor include some fine Elizabethan furniture and embroidery. A walk through the castle brings you seven centuries of glorious history including portraits by famous artists and beautiful tapestries.

Opening Times: Mar to Nov daily 10:30-18:00. Castle open Sun to Fri 12:00-17:00. Admission: Adult £7.50, Child £5.00, Family £20.00. Location: One mile south of Ravenglass on the A595.

Map Ref: 17

Ravenglass Railway Museum

Ravenglass & Eskdale Railway, Ravenglass CA18 1SW   Tel: 01229 717171   Fax: 01229 717011   Email: rer@netcomuk.co.uk   Web: www.ravenglass-railway.co.uk

The story of La'al Ratty, the world's smallest public railway, from its origins 125 years ago - with diagrams, models, audio-visual, photo displays and historic trains.

Opening Times: Mar to Nov Daily 10:00-17:00.   Admission: Free.   Location: Ravenglass Station.   Map Ref: 17

WHITEHAVEN

The Beacon

West Strand, Whitehaven CA28 7LY   Tel: 01946 592302   Fax: 01946 599025
Email: thebeacon@copelandbc.gov.uk   Web: copelandbc.gov.uk

Home to Whitehaven's museum, The Beacon also offers the world's first Met Office Weather Gallery and an attractive programme of exhibitions throughout the year.

Opening Times: Easter to Oct Tue to Sun 10:00-17:30. Nov to Mar 10:00-16:30. School & BH open Mon.   Admission: Adult £4.00, Child/Concession £2.65, OAP £3.30, Family £12. Group rates available.   Location: On harbourside.   Map Ref: 18

WINDERMERE

Windermere Steamboat Centre

Rayrigg Road, Windermere LA23 1BN   Tel: 015394 45565   Fax: 015394 48769
Email: diana.matthews@talk21.com   Web: www.steamboat.co.uk

Large collection of Victorian/Edwardian launches and motor boats in spectacular lakeside setting. Cruises on steam launches. Swallows & Amazons exhibition. 'Model Boats - You Too Can Do It!' exhibition.

Opening Times: 16 Mar to 27 Oct daily 10:00-17:00.   Admission: Adult £3.50, Child £2.00, Family £8.50. Group rates available.   Location: Half a mile north of Bowness-on-Windermere on A592.   Map Ref: 19

…erby, famous for its Royal Crown Derby porcelain as well as its Rolls-Royce engines, has a fine …thedral and despite its industrial heart fine scenery is never far away. Staffordshire too offers …ite remarkable contrasts. Within a short distance of the busy county town of Stafford lies …annock Chase, over 20,000 acres of glorious heath and woodland.

…ere was the cradle of the Industrial Revolution and the creative expertise and heritage of these …o counties is clearly reflected in their fine museums and art galleries and from mills, and mining … potteries and brewing.

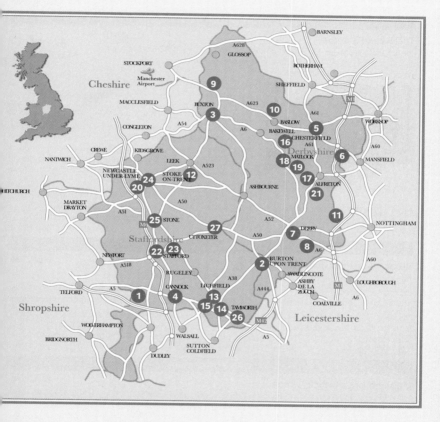

The Red Map References should be used to locate Museums etc on the pages that follow

Derbyshire & Staffordshire

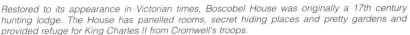

BISHOP'S WOOD *Staffs*

Boscobel House

Brewood, Bishop's Wood ST19 9AR   Tel: 01902 850244

Restored to its appearance in Victorian times, Boscobel House was originally a 17th century hunting lodge. The House has panelled rooms, secret hiding places and pretty gardens and provided refuge for King Charles II from Cromwell's troops.

Opening Times: Apr to Sep daily 10:00-18:00, Oct daily 10:00-17:00, Nov Wed to Sun 10:00-16:00, 1 to 16 Dec Sat & Sun 10:00-16:00. Closed Xmas & 1 Jan to 28 Mar.   Admission: Adult £4.40, Child £2.20, Concession £3.30, Family £11.00.   Location: On minor road from A41 to A5, eight miles north west of Wolverhampton.   Map Ref: 1

BURTON UPON TRENT *Staffs*

The Bass Museum

Horninglow Street, Burton upon Trent DE14 1YQ   Tel: 01283 511000
Fax: 01283 513509   Email: darren.robinson@brewers.bass.com
Web: www.bass-museum.com

The multi-media collection encompasses the history of British brewing, of Bass and of Burton-upon-Trent. There are three major galleries covering the brewing process, the Bass Company Story and local history, and history of transport. The Bass Museum is the home of the famous Bass Shire Horses, and there is a collection of vintage horse-drawn drays and vehicles. The brewery railway system is illustrated by an inter-active model of Burton in 1921. Programme of temporary exhibitions and special events throughout the year.

Opening Times: Daily 10:00-17:00. Closed Xmas & New Year.   Admission: Adult £4.95, Child £2.50, Under 5s Free, OAP £3.50, Family £15.00.
Location: Five minutes walk from main town shopping area, 15 minutes from railway station.
Map Ref: 2

BUXTON *Derbys*

Buxton Museum & Art Gallery

Terrace Road, Buxton SK17 6DA   Tel: 01298 24658   Fax: 01629 585345

Explore the wonders of the Peak through seven time zones revealing the geology, archaeology and history of the Peak District. Enjoy our busy programme of temporary art and craft exhibition.

Opening Times: Tue to Fri 09:30-17:30, Sat 09:30-17:00. Also from Easter to 30 Sep Sun & BH Mon 10:30-17:00. Closed Mon.   Admission: Downstairs: Free. Upstairs: Adult £1.00, Concession 50p, Family £2.00.   Location: Near Town Hall, ten minutes from train station.
Map Ref: 3

CANNOCK *Staffs*

Museum of Cannock Chase

Valley Road, Hednesford, Cannock WS12 5TD   Tel: 01543 877666   Fax: 01543 428272
Email: museum@cannockchasedc.gov.uk   Web: www.museumofcannockchase.co.uk

Small museum occupying ex-colliery site. Illustrates history of Cannock Chase from Medieval hunting forest to coalfield community. Collections comprise social history, domestic and industrial artefacts.

Opening Times: Easter to Sep daily 11:00-17:00. Oct to Easter Mon to Fri 11:00-16:00.
Admission: Free except for guided parties.   Location: Near Hednesford centre on A460 to Rugeley, ten minutes from station.   Map Ref: 4

CHESTERFIELD *Derbys*

Chesterfield Museum & Art Gallery

St Marys Gate, Chesterfield S41 7TD   Tel: 01246 345727

Taking the 'Story of Chesterfield' as its theme the museum shows how the town has become the place it is today, by looking at different aspects of its history.

Opening Times: Mon, Tue, Thu, Fri, Sat 10:00-16:00. Closed Wed & Sat and Xmas & New Year.
Admission: Free.   Location: The museum is located on St Mary's Gate close to the parish church (crooked spire), easy walking distance of car parks and railway stations.   Map Ref: 5

Derbyshire & Staffordshire

Hardwick Hall, Gardens & Park

Doe Lea, Chesterfield S44 5QJ   Tel: 01246 850430   Fax: 01246 854200
Email: ehwcct@smtp.ntrust.org.uk

The Long Gallery containing the famous Gideon Tapestries

Set high on a hill in North East Derbyshire, spectacular 405 year old Hardwick, the home of Bess of Hardwick. One of the greatist Elizabethan houses, surviving almost unchanged to date. The Hall contains one of Europe's best collections of furniture, embroideries and tapestries. Surrounded by four walled courtyards, aromatic garden and famous herb garden. Enjoy great walks around the ponds.

Opening Times: 27 Mar to 27 Oct Hall: Wed, Thu, Sat, Sun, BH Mon & Good Friday 12:30-17:00. Garden: daily except Tue 11:00-17:30. Admission: Adult £6.40, Child £3.20, Family £16.00, National Trust Members Free. Location: Near junction 29 on the M1, follow with Brown Tourist Signs.

Map Ref: 6

Peacock Heritage Centre

Low Pavement, Chesterfield S40 1PB   Tel: 01246 345777/8   Fax: 01246 345770
Email: tourism@chesterfieldbc.gov.uk

Changing programme of exhibitions of art, photography, crafts etc by local societies and individuals. Housed on first floor of a 16th century building. Tourist Information Centre on ground floor.

Opening Times: Mon to Sat 11:00-16:00. Closed Sun. Due to close to the public in October 2002. Admission: Free. Location: Town centre, five to ten minute walk from railway station.

Map Ref: 5

DERBY

Derby Industrial Museum

The Silk Mill, Silk Mill Lane, off Full Street, Derby DE1 3AF   Tel: 01332 255308   Fax: 01332 716670   Web: www.derby.gov.uk/museums

The museum is housed in Derby's historic Silk Mill. Built circa 1720 as one of Britain's first factories. Displays feature local industries, including railway engineering and Rolls Royce aero engines.

Opening Times: Mon 11:00-17:00 Tue to Sat 10:00-17:00 Sun & BH 14:00-17:00. Closed Xmas & New Year break. Admission: Free. Location: Beside the River Derwent, five minutes walk from bus station, 15 minutes walk from railway station.

Map Ref: 7

Derby Museum & Art Gallery

The Strand, Derby DE1 1BS   Tel: 01332 716659   Fax: 01332 716670
Web: www.derby.gov.uk/museums

The Ceramics Gallery

The museum houses internationally important collections of Derby porcelain and major paintings by Joseph Wright of Derby (1734-97). Derbyshire wildlife and geology feature in a splendid series of natural settings and hands-on exhibits. Other galleries are devoted to local regiments, local archaeology, Bonnie Prince Charlie's visit to Derby during the 1745 uprising, and to exciting temporary exhibitions.

Opening Times: Mon 11:00-17:00 Tue to Sat 10:00-17:00 Sun & BH 14:00-17:00. Closed Xmas & New Year break.

Admission: Free. Location: In city centre, ten minutes walk from bus station, 15 minutes walk from railway station.

Map Ref: 7

Donington Grand Prix Collection

Donington Park, Castle Donington, Derby DE74 2RP   Tel: 01332 811027
Fax: 01332 812829   Email: enquiries@doningtoncollection.co.uk
Web: www.doningtoncollection.com

The Mclaren Hall, featuring the World's largest collection of McLaren F1 Cars

Take a lap around the Donington Grand Prix Collection, which is the world's largest collection of Grand Prix racing cars. Featuring over 130 cars within five halls and described by a number of visitors as 'a gold mine to motor racing heritage'. The collection features the world's largest collection of McLaren Formula One cars on public display and also cars such as Ferrari, Jordan, Williams, BRM and Vanwalls. Driven by such famous names as Senna, Nuvolari, Moss, Hill and Fangio. Also there are drivers' helmets and memorabilia covering every wall within the collection.

1955 Lancia D50 Ferrari - the newest arrival within the collection

Opening Times: Daily 10:00-17:00, last admission 16:00.
Admission: Adult £7.00, Child £2.50, Student/OAP £5.00, Family (2 adults and 3 children) £14.00, Group discount available.   Location: Two miles from junction 23A M1/M42.

Map Ref: 8

Pickfords House Museum

41 Friar Gate, Derby DE1 1DA   Tel: 01332 255363   Fax: 01332 716670
Web: www.derby.gov.uk/museums

A fine Georgian town house built in 1770 by local architect, Joseph Pickford, as his home. Displays include period rooms circa 1800, historic costume and an 18th century style garden.

Opening Times: Mon 11:00-17:00 Tue to Sat 10:00-17:00 Sun & BH 14:00-17:00. Closed Xmas & New Year break.   Admission: Free.   Location: 15 minutes from railway station by foot, ten minutes walk from bus station.

Map Ref: 7

Regimental Museum of the 9th/12th Royal Lancers (Prince of Wales's)

City Museum & Art Gallery, The Strand, Derby DE1 1BS   Tel: 01332 716656
Fax: 01332 716670

Information panels, audio system and items relating to the history of the Regiment and its predecessors from 1715 to Bosnia. Displays include a reconstruction stable. 9th/12th Lancers archives and photos are available by appointment.

Opening Times: Mon 11:00-17:00, Tue to Sat 10:00-17:00, Sun 14:00-17:00.   Admission: Free.
Location: Town centre, 15 minute walk from railway station.

Map Ref: 7

Royal Crown Derby Visitor Centre

194 Osmaston Road, Derby DE23 8JZ   Tel: 01332 712800   Fax: 01332 712899
Web: www.royal-crown-derby.co.uk

Superb collection of Royal Crown Derby porcelain from earliest origins circa 1750 to present day. Highlights include Raven Room Collection incorporating works of most renowned artists. Also Factory Tours and Demonstrations.

Opening Times: Mon to Sat 09:30-17:00, Sun 10:00-16:30. Closed Xmas.   Admission: Factory Tour including Visitor Centre Adult £4.75, Visitor Centre Adult £2.95, Concession £2.75.
Location: One mile outside Derby Town Centre.

Map Ref: 7

HIGH PEAK *Derbys*

New Mills Heritage & Information Centre

Rock Mill Lane, New Mills, High Peak SK22 3BN   Tel / Fax: 01663 746904
Web: www.newmills.org.uk

Tells the story of 'New Mills'. Describes the formation of the Torrs Gorge, the pre-industrial history including Domesday and the royal forest of Peak, the 'New Mill', and the growth of communications, coal mining, and the textile industry.

Derbyshire & Staffordshire

Opening Times: Tue to Fri 11:00-16:00, Sat & Sun 10:30-16:30 (16:00 winter). Closed Mon (except BH). Admission: Free. Location: In town centre, next to the bus station, only one minute walk from the Central railway station. Convenient for Millenium Walkway. Map Ref: 9

HOPE VALLEY Derbys

Eyam Museum

Hawkhill Road, Eyam, Hope Valley S32 5QP Tel: 01433 631371 Fax: 01433 630777
Web: www.cressbrook.co.uk/eyam/museum

The display covers the 1665/6 outbreak of bubonic plague in Eyam. The collection includes local documents, fossils and minerals, archaeological material and many local photographs.

Opening Times: 26 Mar to 3 Nov Tue to Sun & BH 10:00-16:30. Admission: Adult £1.50, Child/Concession £1.00, Family £4.25. Location: Opposite main car park in Hawkhill Road, Eyam. Map Ref: 10

ILKESTON Derbys

Erewash Museum

High Street, Ilkeston DE7 5JA Tel: 0115 907 1141 Fax: 0115 932 9264
Email: museum@erewash.gov.uk Web: www.erewash.gov.uk

Local and social history collections plus regular events and exhibitions. Suitable for all ages.

Opening Times: Feb to Dec Tue, Thu, Fri, Sat & BH 10:00-16:00. Admission: Free. Location: Near town centre. Map Ref: 11

LEEK Staffs

Cheddleton Flint Mill

Leek Road, Cheddleton, Leek ST13 7HL Tel: 01782 502907
Web: www.ex.ac.uk/~akoutram/cheddleton-mill/index.htm

Two water mills, complete with wheels. Shows the process of grinding flint for the pottery industry. Panels tell the story of the materials used in pottery manufacture. Allow an hour.

Opening Times: Sat & Sun 13:00-17:00. Open most weekdays 10:30-17:00. Closed Xmas & New Year. Admission: Free, but donations most welcome. Location: Cheddleton village on A520, three miles south of Leek. Map Ref: 12

LICHFIELD Staffs

Lichfield Heritage Centre

Market Square, Lichfield WS13 6LG Tel: 01543 256611 Fax: 01543 414749
Email: heritage@lichfield.gov.uk Web: www.lichfieldheritage.org.uk

The new permanent home of the Staffordshire Millennium Tapestries. Climb the spire. Wonderful new exhibition opens Easter weekend 2002 'Lichfield Through The Ages', Treasury Room, audio visuals etc.

Opening Times: Mon to Sat 10:00-17:00 Sun 10:30-17:00. Closed 25-26 Dec & New Year.
Admission: Adult £3.00, Concession £2.00, Booked Groups £2.00, Spire £1.00.
Location: Inside Church building on main Market Square in town centre. Map Ref: 13

Samuel Johnson Birthplace Museum

Breadmarket Street, Lichfield WS13 6LG Tel: 01543 264972 Fax: 01543 414779
Email: sjmuseum@lichfield.gov.uk Web: www.lichfield.gov.uk/sjmuseum

The birthplace of Dr Samuel Johnson now houses a splendid museum dedicated to the life, work and personality of one of England's greatest writers and most fascinating characters.

Opening Times: Apr to Sep daily 10:30-16:30. Oct to Mar daily 12:00-16:30. Admission: Adult £2.20, Child/Concession £1.30, Family £5.80. Location: City centre, location overlooking Market Place. Map Ref: 13

Staffordshire Regiment Museum

Whittington Barracks, Lichfield WS14 9PY Tel: 0121 311 3229 Fax: 0121 311 3205
Email: museum@rhqstaffords.fsnet.co.uk Web: www.armymuseums.org.uk

History of the Regiment and its forebears since 1705. Good collections of medals (including British & Victoria Cross sets), uniforms and weapons. Hands on area and quizzes for children. 100 metres of outdoor World War I trench, two World War II Anderson shelters. Key stage 2 and 3 education, archive (booking only).

Opening Times: Year round Tue to Fri 10:00-16:30. Apr to Oct Sat, Sun & BH 12:30-16:30. Closed Xmas & New Year. Admission: Adult £2.00, Concession £1.00, Under 5s Free, Family £5.00, Group £1.00. Members of MOD (Army), Regimental Association Free. Location: On A51 between Lichfield and Tamworth. Between main barracks and golf club. Map Ref: 14

Wall Roman Site & Museum (Letocetum)
Watling Street, Wall, Lichfield WS14 0AW   Tel: 01543 480768

Wall was once a staging-post on Watling Street, with a bath house and guest house where travellers could stay overnight. The museum houses a display of Romano-British finds from the site including pottery, jewellery, coins and metalwork.

Opening Times: Apr to Sep daily 11:00-17:00. Admission: Adult £2.40, Child £1.20, Concession £1.80. National Trust members Free. Location: Off A5 at Wall near Lichfield.
Map Ref: 15

MATLOCK *Derbys*

Caudwell's Mill & Craft Centre
Rowsley, Matlock DE4 2EB   Tel / Fax: 01629 734374   Web: www.caudwellsmill.museum.com

The only complete Victorian water turbine-powered roller flour mill in the country. Powered by the River Wye, four floors of fascinating machinery demonstrate how wheat was turned into flour.

Opening Times: Apr to Oct daily 10:00-17:30 Nov to Mar Sat & Sun 10:00-16:30.
Admission: Adult £3.00, Child £1.50, OAP £2.50. Location: In Rowsley village on the main A6 between Matlock and Bakewell. On bus routes with stops immediately outside the mill.
Map Ref: 16

Crich Tramway Village
Crich, Matlock DE4 5DP   Tel: 01773 852565   Fax: 01773 852326   Email: info@tramway.co.uk
Web: www.tramway.co.uk

Derbyshire's award-winning family attraction where you can enjoy unlimited tram rides in a recreated village street, plus play areas, shops, tearooms and lots, lots more. A relaxing day out for all the family!

Opening Times: Sun from 9 Feb, 23 Mar to 3 Nov Daily. Sat & Sun until 22 Dec. Admission: Adult £7, Child £3.50, OAP £6.00, Family £19.00. Location: Six miles from Matlock, eight miles from junction 28 on M1.
Map Ref: 17

Peak District Mining Museum & Temple Mine
The Pavilion, Matlock Bath, Matlock DE4 3NR   Tel: 01629 583834
Email: mail@peakmines.co.uk   Web: www.peakmines.co.uk

Depicting mining in Derbyshire since Roman times, Wills founder engine, Howie mineral collection, rag and chain pump, informative displays. Temple mine shows insight into mineral mining with spacious well lit tunnels.

Opening Times: Apr to Oct daily 10:00-17:00, Nov to Mar daily 11:00-15:00. Closed Xmas. Admission: Museum or Mine: Adult £2.50, Child/OAP £1.50, Family £6.00. Joint Ticket: Adult £4.00, Child/OAP £2.50, Family £9.00. Group rates available. Location: Adjacent A6 Matlock Bath.
Map Ref: 18

Sir Richard Arkwrights Cromford Mill
Cromford Mill, Mill Lane, Cromford, Matlock DE4 3RQ   Tel / Fax: 01629 823256

Visit the world's first successful water powered cotton spinning mill. Tours available daily and exhibitions. Part of the Derwent Valley Mills, under application for inscription on the World Heritage List.

Opening Times: Daily 9:00-17:00. Closed Xmas. Admission: No charge to the site. Tours - Adult £2.00, Concession £1.50. Location: Off the A6 Derby to Buxton Road, located on the outside of the village of Cromford.
Map Ref: 19

Borough Museum & Art Gallery

Brampton Park, Newcastle-under-Lyme ST5 0QP Tel: 01782 619705 Fax: 01782 626857 Email: nulmuseum@newcastle-staffs.gov.uk Web: www.newcastle-staffs.gov.uk/museum.htm

Newcastle's long history can be traced through the Roman period, its medieval castle, Royal Charters and industries. All of these and more are represented in the museum's permanent displays. The art gallery includes local artists, travelling exhibitions and a frequently changing programme of exhibitions, which means that there is always something new to see in both the main art gallery and the small gallery.

Chemist, Victorian Street Scene

Opening Times: Mon to Sat 10:00-17:30, Sun 14:00-17:30. Admission: Free. Location: In Brampton Park on Brampton Road (A527), just 1/2 mile from Newcastle Town Centre and three miles from junction 15 of the M6. Map Ref: 20

Midland Railway Centre

Butterley Station, Ripley DE5 3QZ Tel: 01773 747674 Fax: 01773 510721 Email: info@midlandrailwaycentre.co.uk

Large collection of railway locomotives and rolling stock. Operating standard gauge railway (three and a half miles) and narrow gauge railway (one mile). Farm Park, Country Park, Demonstration Signal Box, Victorian Railwayman's Church and much more.

'Midday Midlander' Sunday lunch train departs from Butterley Station

Opening Times: Daily 10:00-16:00. Trains run weekends throughout the year, Wed Apr to Oct & school holidays. Admission: Adult £7.95 (2 children free with 1 adult), OAP £6.50. Location: On B6179, one mile north of Ripley, signposted from A38. Map Ref: 21

The Princess Royal Class Locomotive Trust

West Shed, Midland Railway Centre, Swanwick Junction, Ripley DE5 3QZ Tel: 01773 747471 Fax: 01335 346546

Steam locomotives on display together with historical 21" gauge locos and small exhibits museum. No 46203 'Princess Margaret Rose', No 6233 'Duchess of Sutherland', 80098 & 80080 British railway standard tank locos workshops, museum, display in 'The West Shed'.

The Duchess of Sutherland

Opening Times: Daily 10:30-16:30. Admission: Free. Location: Adjacent to Swanwick Junction, Midland Railway Centre. Map Ref: 21

Ripley Castle

Ripley HG3 3AY Tel: 01423 770152 Fax: 01423 771745 Email: enquiries@ripleycastle.co.uk Web: www.ripleycastle.co.uk

Ripley Castle stands at the heart of a delightful estate village with lakes, deer park and Victorian walled garden.

Opening Times: Sep to May Tue, Thu, Sat, Sun 10:30-15:00. Jun to Aug daily. Admission: Adult £5.50, Child £3.00, OAP £4.50. Location: A61 north of Harrogate (three miles). Map Ref: 21

Ancient High House

Greendale Street, Stafford ST16 2JA   Tel: 01785 619131
Fax: 01785 619132   Web: www.staffordbc.gov.uk

The Ancient High House is the largest timber-framed Elizabethan town house in England. The house contains an extensive collection of period furniture and it is also the home of the Museum of the Staffordshire Yeomanry.

Opening Times: Mon to Sat 10:00-17:00.   Location: In the town centre.   Map Ref: 22

Front elevation of Ancient High House (built 1595)

Shire Hall Gallery

Market Square, Stafford ST16 2LD   Tel: 01785 278345

Paintings, prints by Staffordshire artists. Contemporary jewellery.

Opening Times: Mon to Sat 09:30-17:00. Closed Sun & BH.   Admission: Free.
Location: Centre of town, next to Guildhall Shopping Centre.   Map Ref: 22

Shugborough Estate

Millford, Stafford ST17 0XB   Tel: 01889 881388   Fax: 01889 881323
Email: shugborough.promotions@staffordshire.gov.uk
Web: www.staffordshire.gov.uk/shugborough

Shugborough is the ancestral home of the fifth Earl of Lichfield, who as Patrick Lichfield is known worldwide as a leading photographer. The 18th century Mansion House contains a fine collection of ceramics, silver, paintings and French furniture. Part of the house continues to be lived in by the Earl and his family.

Visitors can enjoy the 18 acre Grade 1 listed historic garden and a unique collection of neo-classical monuments by James 'Athenian' Stuart. Other attractions include the original servants' quarters. The working laundry, kitchens, brewhouse and coach houses have all been lovingly restored. Costumed guides can show how the servants lived and worked over 100 years ago. Shugborough Park Farm is a Georgian farmstead that features an agricultural museum, working corn mill and rare breeds centre. The livestock are all historic breeds and in the farmhouse visitors can see brick bread ovens in operation and butter and cheese making in the dairy. The annual programme of events ranges from seasonal craft fairs to the delights of candlelit evenings, a Victorian street market of

Cherubs in The Rose Garden

spectacular firework displays. Teachers will be pleased to note that there is an extensive educational programme available for children of all ages with an attractive selection of adult tours and demonstrations. There is something for everyone on the Shugborough Estate.

Opening Times: Mar to Oct Tue to Sun 11:00-17:00. Open BH Mon.   Admission: Telephone (01889) 881388 for details.   Location: Three miles from Stafford.   Map Ref: 23

Derbyshire & Staffordshire

Stafford Castle Visitor Centre

Newport Road, Stafford ST16 1DJ   Tel: 01785 257698
Web: www.staffordbc.gov.uk

stafford castle

Try on armour and costume, see finds from the archaeological dig at Stafford Castle, watch a video describing the history of the site. Visit the ruined remains of this motte and bailey castle.

Opening Times: Apr to Oct Tue to Sun & BH Mon 10:00-17:00. Nov to Mar Tue to Sun & BH Mon 10:00-16:00.
Location: Five minutes by car from the town centre.

Stafford Castle

Map Ref: 22

STOKE-ON-TRENT Staffs

Ford Green Hall

Ford Green Road, Smallthorne, Stoke-on-Trent ST6 1NG   Tel: 01782 233195

17th century timber-framed Yeoman farmhouse complete with period herb garden. The hall is furnished with textiles, ceramics and furniture. Events programme throughout the year including children's activities every holiday. The hall is licensed for weddings, and children's parties are available. Changing displays and touring exhibitions. Family friendly with interactives for children. Disabled access to ground floor. Situated next to a nature reserve.

Opening Times: Sun to Thu 13:00-17:00.   Admission: Adult £1.50, Concession £1.00.
Location: Ten minutes from Hanley (city centre).

Map Ref: 24

Gladstone Pottery Museum

Uttoxeter Road, Longton, Stoke-on-Trent ST3 1PQ   Tel: 01782 311378/319232

Last remaining Victorian Pottery Factory complete with traditional bottle ovens. Live demonstrations and audio-visual tours show visitors the skills of the Potteries. The museum also has the new Flushed with Pride - Story of the Toilet exhibition, which contains the most comprehensive collection of historic toilets in the world. Gladstone also has the nationally recognised collection of decorated tiles now redisplayed in our new Tile Gallery.

Opening Times: Daily 10:00-17:00.   Admission: Adult £4.95, Child £3.50, Concession/OAP £3.95.   Location: Longton, Stoke-on-Trent. Two minutes off A50, ten minutes junction 15 of the M6.

Gladstone Pottery Museum Yard

Map Ref: 24

The Potteries Museum & Art Gallery

The POTTERIES museum art gallery

Bethesda Street, Hanley, Stoke-on-Trent ST1 3DW   Tel: 01782 232323

Welcome to the home of the world's finest collection of Staffordshire ceramics. We also own the most comprehensive collection of 20th century studio and industrial pottery. With over 650,000 objects, The Potteries Museum & Art Gallery collections are designated of national and international importance. Discover the story of Stoke-on-Trent's people, products and landscapes through imaginative displays of local history, archaeology, geology and wildlife. Explore the rich collections of paintings, prints, drawings, costume and glass in the Art Gallery and Changing Fashions displays. From ancient Roman pots to a Mark XVI Spitfire; from a Staffordshire Wallaby to our famous slipware owl jug; from a Rodin bronze to a popular dolls' house - there is something here for everyone! Enjoy hands-on exhibits, touch-screen computers and a lively programme of holiday activities, talks, tours and workshops. Expert opinion is available through our public enquiry service.

Opening Times: Mar to Oct Mon to Sat 10:00-17:00, Sun 14:00-17:00. Nov to Feb Mon To Sat 10:00-16:00, Sun 13:00-16:00. Admission: Free. Location: In the City Centre, within the cultural quarter, one mile from railway station, four miles from junction 15, M6. Map Ref: 24

Spode Museum & Visitor Centre

Church Street, Stoke-on-Trent ST4 1BX Tel: 01782 744011 Fax: 01782 572526

Museum Gallery part of Visitor Centre housing a selection of items produced by Spode from 1770 up to the present day. Contact the Visitor Centre for special exhibitions and more details.

Opening Times: Jan to Dec Mon to Sat 09:00-17:00, Sun 10:00-16:00. Closed 25-26 Dec, New Years Day and 3-4 Jun. Admission: Adult £2.75, Child/OAP £2.25, Under 5s Free. Location: Town centre, ten minute walk from Stoke-on-Trent railway station. Map Ref: 24

STONE *Staffs*

Izaak Walton's Cottage

Worston Lane, Shallowford, Stone ST15 0PA Tel: 01785 760278/619619 Fax: 01785 760278 Web: www.staffordbc.gov.uk

The Cottage is set in picturesque gardens

Izaak Walton, author of 'The Compleat Angler' once owned this charming cottage. There is an Anglers Museum in this 16th century half timbered building, and the splendid rose and herb gardens are a delight to visit.

Opening Times: Apr to Oct Wed to Sun 13:00-16:00. Location: Ten minutes by car from Stafford. Map Ref: 25

TAMWORTH *Staffs*

Tamworth Castle & Museum Service

The Holloway, Ladybank, Tamworth B79 7NA Tel: 01827 709626 Fax: 01827 709630 Email: heritage@tamworth.gov.uk Web: www.tamworth.gov.uk/tamworthleisure

Dramatic Norman castle with later additions houses furnished room displays plus 'Tamworth Story' and Norman exhibitions. Reputedly haunted by two lady ghosts, clothes to try on, rubbings and two free quizzes, there's lots to interest children.

Opening Times: Mar to Oct Mon to Fri 10:00-17:30, Sun 12:00-17:30. Please check opening times in Nov, Dec, Jan and early Feb. Admission: Adult £4.30, Child £2.20, OAP £2.20, Family £11.90. Location: In town centre, five minute walk from central bus stops, ten minutes from the railway station. Map Ref: 26

UTTOXETER *Staffs*

Uttoxeter Heritage Centre

34/36 Carter Street, Uttoxeter ST14 8EU Tel: 01889 567176 Fax: 01889 568426

Local history collection, (largely documents and photos) housed in 17th century part timber-framed building. Fixed and changing displays highlight elements of the history of Uttoxeter. Courtyard garden with display on Victorian wash days.

Opening Times: Jan to Dec Mon to Wed, Fri & Sat 10:00-16:00. Closed BH. Admission: Free. Groups wishing a guided tour £2.00 each. Location: Near town centre, three minutes walk from High Street. Map Ref: 27

Devon

von is a county of great seafarers. It was from the fine natural harbour of Plymouth that the grim Fathers sailed to the New World, and it was from here that Sir Francis Drake and Sir John wkins sailed to confront the mighty Spanish Armada. Between the coasts the county is minated by lofty brooding Dartmoor and the north of the county includes a part of Exmoor ere moorland meets the sea. Exeter, the county town has a magnificent Norman cathedral lding the remarkable Anglo-Saxon Exeter book.

von's many excellent museums, mills and historic houses cover all aspects of the regions aritime history, its local industries and social history including 'Dartmoor Life'.

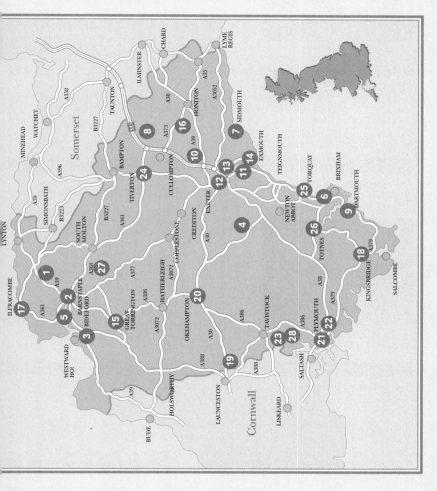

The Red Map References should be used to locate Museums etc on the pages that follow

Devon

Arlington Court
Arlington, Barnstaple EX31 4LP   Tel: 01271 850296

Arlington Court, a National Trust mansion situated in peaceful gardens surrounded by parklands and woods and miles of walks. Previously owned by Rosalie Chichester, the house is full of fascinating collections. The working stables have horses, carriages driving school and the Trust's carriage collection.

Opening Times: 23 Mar to 3 Nov daily except Tue 10:30-17:00. Admission: Adult £5.60, Child £2.60, Groups £4.80. Location: On A39, eight miles north of Barnstaple.
Map Ref: 1

Arlington Court North Devon

Museum of Barnstaple & North Devon
The Square, Barnstaple EX32 8LN   Tel: 01271 346747

Story of North Devon from pre-history to 1930's. Tarka Centre depicting river life and woodland life. Undersea room with replica mammals and fish around North Devon coast. Temporary exhibitions, seven centuries of pottery.

Opening Times: Tue to Sat 10:00-16:30. Closed Sun, Mon & BH. Admission: Free.
Location: By the Long Bridge and Clock Tower.
Map Ref: 2

The Burton Art Gallery & Museum
Kingsley Road, Bideford EX39 2QQ   Tel: 01237 471455   Fax: 01237 473813   Web: www.burtonartgallery.co.uk

MUSEUM Art GALLERY

North Devon Slipware, model of Bideford Long Bridge 1280-1925, Delft ware, Napoleonic bone ship models, history of Bideford personalities. Paintings by Hubert Coop, Clausen, Fisher, E Aubrey Hunt, Reynolds, Ackland/Edwards collection etc plus contemporary national and local artists. Craft Gallery displays work by regional craft artists, Devon Guild members, including solo exhibitions.

Opening Times: Easter to end Oct Tue to Sat 10:00-17:00, Sun 14:00-17:00. Nov to Easter Tue to Sat 10:00-16:00 Sun 14:00-16:00. Open BH. Admission: Free. Some special exhibitions Adult £1.00, Concession 50p. Location: Near town centre, opposite coach park.
Map Ref: 3

Devon Guild of Craftsmen
Riverside Mill, Bovey Tracey TQ13 9AF   Tel: 01626 832223   Fax: 01626 834220
Email: devonguild@crafts.org.uk   Web: www.crafts.org.uk

The South West's leading gallery and craft showrooms with work selected from around 240 designer/makers. Top touring and themed shows in Grade II listed Riverside Mill.

Opening Times: Daily 10:00-17:30. Closed Xmas Day & New Years Day. Admission: Free admission to all exhibitions and facilities. Location: In the centre of Bovey Tracey, only two miles off A38, Exeter to Plymouth road.
Map Ref: 4

Braunton & District Museum
The Bakehouse Centre, Caen Street, Braunton EX33 1AA   Tel: 01271 816688
Email: braunton@devonmuseums.net   Web: www.devonmuseums.net/braunton

Local history including, Velator once a sea port, with model ships etc. Braunton Great Field, one of two left in the country (strip farming), Braunton pottery and basket factory etc.

Opening Times: Mon to Sat & BH 10:00-16:00 & 6 Sun in summer school holidays. Closed Xmas. Admission: Free. Location: Next to main car park centre of village.
Map Ref: 5

BRIXHAM

Brixham Heritage Museum & History Society

Bolton Cross, Brixham TQ5 8LZ   Tel: 01803 856267   Email: mail@brixhamheritage.org.uk
Web: www.brixhamheritage.org.uk

The museum exhibits Brixham's heritage: the fishing industry, Reverend Lyte (Abide With Me), Victorian Life, World War II, interactive displays, model of former town railway, Napoleonic forts at Berry Head with exhibits of museum's archeological 'digs'.

Opening Times: Mid Feb to Easter 10:00-13:00. Easter to end Oct Mon to Fri 10:00-17:00, Sat 10:00-13:00.   Admission: Adult £1.50, Child 50p, OAP £1.00, Family £3.50.   Location: Near town centre, one minute walk from central bus station.

Map Ref: 6

The Golden Hind Museum Ship

The Quay, Brixham Harbour, Brixham TQ5 8AW   Tel: 01803 856223
Email: postmaster@goldenhind.co.uk   Web: www.goldenhind.co.uk

Drake's incredible voyage of 1577 aboard this full sized replica. The ship gives a fascinating insight into life aboard in the 16th century. Registered for civil weddings.

Opening Times: Mar to Oct daily 10:00-16:00, Jul to Aug 09:00-22:00.   Admission: Adult £2.00, Child/OAP £1.50.   Location: Brixham Habour.

Map Ref: 6

BUDLEIGH SALTERTON

Bicton Park Countryside Museum

East Budleigh, Budleigh Salterton EX9 7BJ   Tel: 01395 568465   Fax: 01395 568374
Email: info@bictongardens.co.uk   Web: www.bictongardens.co.uk

Bicton Park is a magical blend of 18th century tranquillity and modern-day facilities for all the family. The magnificently landscaped grounds provide a kaleidoscope of colour through the seasons. Fragrant borders, manicured lawns, majestic woodlands, reflective lakes and rippling streams form a scene of peaceful grandeur that has existed for almost 300 years. The Grade I listed gardens originated in the 1730s when the Italian Garden was laid out in the formal style of Versailles designer Andre le Notre. Outstanding among the glasshouses is the high-domed 19th century Palm House, several years older than the palm house at Kew, it has been fully restored as a home for tropical and subtropical plants, including Bicton's own orchid. A tour of the 63 acre park, either on foot or aboard the narrow-gauge Bicton Woodland Railway, reveals many fascinating features. There is a Secret Garden near the quaint old Hermitage summerhouse, some amazing seashells in the American Garden's Shell House, and a large collection of agricultural and horticultural implements, including traction engines, in the Countryside Museum. Drought tolerant plants bloom in the sunny Mediterranean Garden, while shade-lovers flourish in the Stream Garden. Rare conifer trees grow in the Pinetum, near which there are play areas for children.

Opening Times: Summer 10:00-17:00, winter 10:00-17:00. Closed Xmas Day.
Admission: Adult £4.75, Child £2.75, Concession £3.75, Family £12.75.

Map Ref: 7

Otterton Mill Centre & Working Museum

Budleigh Salterton EX9 7HG   Tel / Fax: 01395 568521   Email: ottertonmill@ukonline.co.uk
Web: www.ottertonmill.co.uk

A working watermill dating back to before the Norman Conquest. Bakery and restaurant with home baking. Crafts, exhibitions, events, courses in environmental and art topics.

Opening Times: Daily Mar to Oct 10:30-17:30, Nov to Mar 11:00-16:00.   Admission: Adult £2.00, Child 75p. Group rates: Adult £1.00, Child 70p.   Location: 15 minutes from the M5, one and a half miles from Budleigh Salterton.

Map Ref: 7

Museums, Galleries, Historic Houses & Sites

Please let us know of any collections that are not listed in this guide that you feel should be listed. E-mail us on *editor@tomorrows.co.uk*
or return the Report Form on page 448

Devon

CULLOMPTON

Coldharbour Mill Working Wool Museum

Coldharbour Mill, Uffculme, Cullompton EX15 3EE   Tel: 01884 840960   Fax: 01884 840858
Email: info@coldharbourmill.org.uk   Web: www.coldharbourmill.org.uk

Tells the story of the men, women and children who worked at the Victorian mill. The museum houses an impressive array of working spinning and weaving machines, two steam engines restored to their former glory. It is also home to the giant 'New World Tapestry'.

Opening Times: Apr to Oct daily 10:30-17:00, Nov to March Mon to Fri please telephone for details.   Admission: Adult £5.50, Child £2.50, Family £15.00.   Location: Five minutes drive off junction 27 of M5, in village of Uffculme.   Map Ref: 8

DARTMOUTH

Dartmouth Museum

The Butterwalk, Duke Street, Dartmouth TQ6 9PZ   Tel: 01803 832923
Email: curator@dartmouthmuseum.org.uk   Web: www.devonmuseum.net/dartmouth

Local history and maritime museum set in old merchants' house (1640).

Opening Times: Mar to Oct Mon to Sat 11:00-16:30. Nov to Feb Mon to Sat 12:00-15:00.
Admission: Adult £1.50, Child 50p, OAP £1.00.   Location: In the town centre.   Map Ref: 9

EXETER

Killerton House

Broadclyst, Exeter EX5 3LE   Tel: 01392 881345

Elegant 18th century house with costume collection. Exhibition on Lace 2002. 18 acre garden with original plantings from the plant hunters, laid out by Veitch, woodland and open parkland.

Opening Times: 9 Mar to 2 Sep 11:00-17:00. Closed Tue (Mon & Tue in Mar). Aug daily 11:00-17:00.   Admission: House & Garden: Adult £5.40, Child £2.70. Garden: Adult £3.90, Child £1.95. National Trust Members Free.   Location: Six miles from Exeter off B3181.   Map Ref: 10

Powderham Castle

Kenton, Exeter EX6 8LQ   Tel: 01626 890243   Fax: 01626 890729
Email: castle@powderham.co.uk   Web: www.powderham.co.uk

Powderham Castle

Family home of the Earl of Devon. Castle dates back to 1391 and has been in the family for over 600 years. Magnificent state rooms, 17th and 18th century fine furniture, china, paintings. Guided tours throughout the day. Beautiful location in ancient deer park overlooking the Exe Estuary, with tranquil gardens and woodland walks to enjoy.

Opening Times: 26 Mar to 3 Nov Sun to Fri 10:00-17:30.
Admission: Adult £6.45, Child £2.95, OAP £5.95.
Location: Kenton village on A379, eight miles outside Exeter.   Map Ref: 11

Royal Albert Memorial Museum

Queen Street, Exeter EX4 3RX   Tel: 01392 665858

From archaeology to zoology this fine building holds outstanding collections of local and national importance and presents a range of exciting displays. Archaeology and Local History Galleries present finds from c.500,000 years ago to the end of the Middle Ages, including a Roman mosaic a reproduction of a Roman bathhouse.

Superlatives abound in the Natural History displays, animals from all around the globe including the largest and tallest land mammals - elephant and giraffe - as well as exotic birds and butterflies, sea urchins, starfish and whales. The effect Geology has had on the landscape and people of Devon is explored in the Geology at Work Gallery. Three galleries

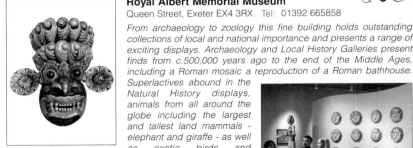

of world cultures present thousands of amazing objects from all around the globe including exceptional Pacific and North West Coast material from the early voyages of Captain Cook. The museum also presents regular themed exhibitions of works from the Fine Art collection. The Museum shop stocks fascinating items from all over the world and the friendly, licensed cafe serves snacks, simple meals and a delicious selection of cakes and biscuits.

Opening Times: Mon to Sat 10:00-17:00. Closed BH. Admission: Free. Location: In Queen Street, just off high street in Exeter City Centre. Central Station is 100m away. St David's Station is ten minutes walk or short bus/taxi ride. Map Ref: 12

Topsham Museum

25 The Strand, Topsham, Exeter EX3 0AX Tel: 01392 873244 Email: museum@topsham.org
Web: www.devonmuseums.net/topsham

Museum situated in 17th century furnished house overlooking Exe Estuary. Exhibits include history of maritime and wildlife around Topsham with multi-media presentations. 2002 Exhibition - Topsham Ships & Shipbuilding.

Opening Times: Apr to Oct Mon, Wed, Sat & Sun 14:00-17:00. Admission: Free. Membership subscription £5.00 annually. Location: 300 yards from Topsham Quay - terminus of the 'T' bus from centre of Exeter. Map Ref: 13

EXMOUTH

World of Country Life

Sandy Bay, Exmouth EX8 5BU Tel: 01395 274533 Fax: 01395 273457
Email: worldofcountrylife@hotmail.com Web: www.worldofcountrylife.co.uk

Vintage vehicles, motorcycle collection, steam engines, vintage farm machinery, Victorian street, working models, play areas, farm animals, pets centre, owl displays, safari deer train, quad bikes, crazy golf.

Opening Times: Easter to end Oct daily 10:00-17:00. Admission: Adult £6.00, Child £5.00, OAP £5.00, Family £20.00. Location: Just ten miles from junction 30 on M5. Follow A376 Exmouth/Sandy Bay. Map Ref: 14

GREAT TORRINGTON

Dartington Crystal

Linden Close, Great Torrington EX38 7AN
Tel: 01805 626242 Fax: 01805 626263

Dartington Crystal is internationally famous for beautiful, handmade, contemporary glassware and is dedicated to innovative designs. Visitors to the factory site will be fascinated to watch the highly skilled craftsmen and to discover the history of glass and unique Dartington Story in the popular Visitor Centre. Finally, be tempted by the dazzling collection of glass for sale (the biggest glass shop in the country), many seconds at fantastic prices!

Opening Times: 09:30-16:00. Factory tour closed weekends and BH. Admission: Adult £3.95, Child £1.50, OAP £2.95, Family £10.00. Location: In centre of Torrington. Turn off A386, opposite church, down School Lane 500 metres. Map Ref: 15

Torrington Museum & Archive

Town Hall Building, The Square, Great Torrington EX38 8HN Tel: 01805 624324

Local bygones, local industries and personalities, 17th to 20th century portrait collection, extensive family archive, domestic and agricultural equipment, features on Thomas Fowler (inventor of Thermosyphon and calculator) and Keble Martin of Concise British Flora fame.

Opening Times: May to Sep daily 11:00-16:00, Sat 11:00-13:30. Admission: Free. Location: In Town Hall building, The Square. Map Ref: 15

HONITON

Allhallows Museum of Lace & Antiquities

High Street, Honiton EX14 1PG Tel: 01404 44966 Fax: 01404 46591
Email: dyateshoniton@email.msn.com Web: www.honitonlace.com

The museum's world famous collection of Honiton lace is displayed in a former mediaeval chapel.

Devon

There are interesting relics of the town's past including pottery, fossils and souvenirs of the Rotten Borough.

Opening Times: Easter to Sept Mon to Fri 10:00-17:00, Oct 10:00-16:00, Sat 10:00-13:30.
Admission: Adult £2.00, Child 50p, OAP £1.50. Location: Town Centre next to St Paul's
Church. Map Ref: 16

ILFRACOMBE

South American Pottery explored by
M G Palmer, first curator

Ilfracombe Museum

Runnymede Gardens, Wilder Road, Ilfracombe EX34 8AF
Tel: 01271 863541   Email: ilfracombe@devonmuseums.net
Web: www.devonmuseums.net

A fascinating collection started in 1932 by Mervyn G Palmer who collected in South America for the British Museum. Be amazed by the variety of displays, some slightly old fashioned but popular; Granny's attic, childhood memories, butterflies, beetles, bats, ethnography, Lundy Island, ship to shore radio, yesterday's domestic luxuries, Victorian costume and trinkets, Ilfracombe railway and paddle steamer history and lots more.

Opening Times: Apr to Oct 10:00-17:00 daily, Nov to Mar 10:00-13:00 Mon to Fri. Admission: Adults £1.50, Child 50p, OAP/Concessions £1.00. Location: Next to Landmark Theatre on Sea front. Map Ref: 17

KINGSBRIDGE

Cookworthy Museum

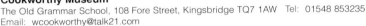

The Old Grammar School, 108 Fore Street, Kingsbridge TQ7 1AW   Tel: 01548 853235
Email: wcookworthy@talk21.com

Discover the story of Kingsbridge in our 17th century school room, complete walk in Victorian kitchen, Edwardian pharmacy, large farm gallery in walled garden. With everything from costumes to carts this lively museum provides something for all the family.

Opening Times: 25 Mar to Sep Mon to Sat 10:00-17:00, Oct 10:00-16:00. Local Heritage Resource Centre open throughout the year. Admission: Adult £2.00, Child 90p, OAP £1.50, Family £5.00, Group £1.50 per person, child 45p. Location: 100 metres up Fore Street from Cookworthy Road car park. Map Ref: 18

LIFTON

Dingles Steam Village

Dingles Steam Village, Milford, Lifton PL16 0AT   Tel: 01566 783425   Fax: 01566 783584
Email: richard@dinglesteam.co.uk   Web: www.dinglesteam.co.uk

Working heritage machinery. Road and industrial steam engines, early road signs, fairground history, vintage cars, lorries, tractors, motorcycles.

Opening Times: Jun to Sep Mon to Thu & weekends in school summer holiday 10:30-17:30.
Admission: Adult £6.00, Child/OAP £4.50, Family £19.50. Location: Rural west Devon. Map Ref: 19

OKEHAMPTON

Museum of Dartmoor Life

Museum Courtyard, 3 West Street, Okehampton EX20 1HQ
Tel: 01837 52295   Fax: 01837 659330
Email: dartmoormuseum@eclipse.co.uk
Web: museumofdartmoorlife.eclipse.co.uk

Housed on three floors in an early 19th century mill, this lively museum tells the story of how people have lived, worked and played on and around Dartmoor through the centuries. It shows how the moorland has shaped their lives just as their work has shaped the moorland. In the Cranmere Gallery, temporary exhibitions feature local history, art and crafts.

Opening Times: Easter to Oct Mon to Sat 10:00-17:00, plus Sun Jun to Sep 10:00-16:30. Winter opening please telephone 01837 52295. Admission: Adult £2.00, Child/Student £1.00, OAP £1.80, Family £5.60. Group/School rates available. Location: Centre of Okehampton, next door to The White Hart Hotel. Map Ref: 20

Devon

Elizabethan House

32 New Street, Plymouth PL1 2NA   Tel: 01752 304774

This rare survival of a sea captain's or merchant's house in the centre of Elizabethan Plymouth is 400 years old. The house retains most of its original architectural features and the rooms contain period furniture.

Opening Times: 28 Mar to 29 Sep Wed to Sun & BH 10:00-17:00. Admission: Adult £1.60, Child 60p. Location: Situated in the historic Barbican, follow brown tourism signs from city centre.

Map Ref: 21

Merchants House

33 St Andrews Street, Plymouth   Tel: 01752 304774

The largest and finest merchant's house of the 16th and 17th centuries left in Plymouth. Recently restored, it contains fascinating displays that bring the city's history to life. The exhibits include a Victorian schoolroom, a Plymouth Blitz exhibition, photographs of old Plymouth and the Park Pharmacy Shop.

Opening Times: Easter to end of Sep Tue to Fri 10:00-17:30, Sat & BH 10:00-17:00. Admission: Adult £1.10, Child 60p. Location: Off Royal Parade near St Andrew's Church. Follow signs.

Map Ref: 21

Plymouth City Museum & Art Gallery

Drake Circus, Plymouth PL4 8AJ Tel: 01752 304774

The building has been a focal point of the city since 1910, and miraculously survived the Second World War Blitz. It holds important works of art including the Cottonian Collection, featuring paintings by Joshua Reynolds, the Plymouth artist, works by the Newlyn School, Maritime Paintings, Plymouth Silver and Porcelain. Natural History is also well represented. Tales from the City is a special exhibition involving 1000 people telling the story of 20th century Plymouth in their own words.

Opening Times: Tue to Fri 10:00-17:30, Sat & BH Mon 10:00-17:00. Admission: Free. Location: Near the city centre, opposite the university. Five minutes walk from the railway station.

Map Ref: 21

Saltram House

Plympton, Plymouth PL7 1UH Tel: 01752 333500 Fax: 01752 336474 Email: dsaltr@smtp.ntrust.org.uk Web: www.nationaltrust.org.uk

Saltram contains fine period furniture, china and pictures - including many portraits by Reynolds, four rooms decorated with original Chinese wallpaper. The house starred as Norland Park in the film Sense and Sensibility.

Opening Times: 24 Mar to 30 Sep Sat to Thu (open Good Friday) 12:00-16:30, 1 Oct to 3 Nov 11:30-15:30 Sat to Thu. Admission: House & Gardens: Adult £6.00, Child £3.00, Under 5s Free, Family £15.00. Garden only £3.00. Location: Two miles west of Plympton, three and a half miles east of Plymouth City Centre, between A38 and A379.

Map Ref: 22

Smeatons Tower

The Hoe, Plymouth PL1 2PA   Tel: 01752 600608

The former Eddystone Lighthouse built in 1759 currently undergoing conservation and redisplay as the lighthouse would have been around the mid 19th century.

Opening Times: Due to open Easter 2002. Location: On Plymouth Hoe, five minutes walk from city centre.

Map Ref: 21

Devon

TAVISTOCK

Morwellham Quay Museum

🐾 ♿ 🎁 📷 ♥ 🚂 **MORWELLHAM**
— **QUAY** —
HISTORIC PORT & COPPER MINE

Morwellham, Tavistock PL19 8JL   Tel: 01822 832766   Fax: 01822 833808
Email: enquiries@morwellham-quay.co.uk
Web: www.morwellham-quay.co.uk

See, they do know how to work! Children of all ages enjoy recreating the 1860s

The greatest copper port in Queen Victoria's empire lies 23 miles inland. The Tamar ketch 'Garlandstone' is moored at the quay; original cottages, shops and hostelry. 1860s costumed staff welcome visitors and host guided tours. Explore one of the copper mines travelling by tram deep underground. In grounds extending to 150 acres enjoy carriage rides; a visit to the farm; the wildlife reserve. Live the history - wear Victorian fashion. Activities throughout the day.

Opening Times: 25 Mar to 3 Nov daily 10:00-17:30. 4 Nov to 29 Mar daily 10:00-16:30. Admission: Main Season - Adult £8.90, Child £6.20, Family £26.00, Senior £7.80. Winter - Adult £5.00, Child £3.00, Senior £4.00. Location: Valley adjacent River Tamar, approx two miles from railway, four miles from Tavistock.   Map Ref: 23

TIVERTON

Tiverton Museum of Mid-Devon Life

♿ ♥

Beck's Square, Tiverton EX16 6PJ   Tel: 01884 256295   Email: tivertonmuseum@eclipse.uk
Web: www.tivertonmuseum.org.uk

Large regional museum with collections of mid-Devon social history including agriculture, farm equipment, wagons and carts and GWR memorabilia, including Loco 1442 "Tivvy Bumper'.

Opening Times: Feb to Xmas Mon to Fri 10:30-16:30, Sat 10:00-13:00. Admission: Adult £3.50, Child £1.00, OAP £2.50, Family £8.00. Group rates available. Location: Near to the town centre and bus station.   Map Ref: 24

TORQUAY

Torquay Museum

🐾 ♿ ♥ 🎁   e*x*plorers
at Torquay Museum

529 Babbacombe Road, Torquay TQ1 1HG   Tel: 01803 293975
Fax: 01803 294186

Torquay Museum

Torquay Museum has recently re-opened after extensive lottery funded improvements. New galleries include the Devon Farmhouse, re-designed Agatha Christie Exhibition celebrating Torquay's most famous daughter and the exciting and innovative Explorers Gallery with interactives for children. See the giant replica of a Japanese man-flying kite in the entance hall. Also archaeology, including Kents Cevern material, natural history, geology, local history, Victoriana, world adornment, ancient Egyptians and wartime photography of Torquay. New local studies centre is open two days per week for local history research.

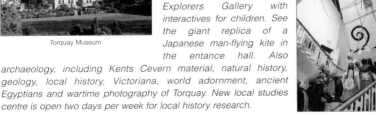

Schoolgroup viewing the Japanese man-flying kite

Opening Times: Mon to Sat 10:00-17:00, Sun (Easter to Oct) 13:30-17:00. Admission: Adult £3.00, Child £1.50, OAP £2.00, Family £7.50. Location: Six minutes walking from clocktower at bottom of Torwood Street (nr harbour). 32 bus stop outside.

Map Ref: 25

Devon

Torre Abbey Historic House & Gallery

TORRE ABBEY

The Kings Drive, Torquay TQ1 1HG   Tel: 01803 293593   Fax: 01803 215948   Email: torre-abbey@torbay.gov.uk   Web: www.torre-abbey.org.uk

Founded in a monastery in 1196, the present appearance of Torre Abbey dates from 1741-3, when it was remodelled by the Cary family. As well as nationally important monastic remains, today's visitors can see over twenty historic rooms, which contain Devon's largest art gallery together with mementoes of crime writer Agatha Christie. Teas are served in the Victorian kitchen.

Opening Times: Easter to 1 Nov daily 09:30-18:00. 2 Nov to Easter open to Groups by appointment only. Admission: Adult £3.00, Child £1.50, OAP/Student £2.50, Family £7.25.   Location: On Torquay sea front, next to the Riviera Centre.   Map Ref: 25

TOTNES

Totnes Costume Museum

Bogan House, 43 High Street, Totnes TQ9 5NP

Themed costume exhibition, changed annually. Collection holds examples of 18th to 20th century fashionable clothing, in one of the most interesting Tudor merchants' houses in Totnes.

Opening Times: 27 May to end Sep daily 11:00-17:00. Oct by appointment.   Admission: Adult £1.75, Child 75p, Concession £1.25, Family £3.50.   Location: Centre of town, opposite Market Square.   Map Ref: 26

Totnes Elizabethan Museum

70 Fore Street, Totnes TQ9 5RU   Tel / Fax: 01803 863821   Email: totnes.museum@virgin.net

Grade I Elizabethan Merchants House c1575. Collections cover local history, archaeology, crafts, industries, clocks, costumes etc. Also room devoted to computer pioneer Charles Babbage and his inventions.

Opening Times: Apr to Oct Mon to Fri 10:30-17:00. Other times by appointment. Admission: Adult £1.50, Child 50p, Accompanied Child 25p, OAP/Student/Concession £1.00, Totnes residents with proof Free.   Location: In main street, very central.   Map Ref: 26

UMBERLEIGH

Cobbaton Combat Collection

Chittlehampton, Umberleigh EX37 9RZ   Tel: 01769 540 740   Fax: 01769 540 141 Email: info@cobbatoncombat.co.uk   Web: www.cobbatoncombat.co.uk

Over 60 mainly World War II vehicles and artillery pieces, plus thousands of smaller items. All undercover, including Home Front building. Militaria and souvenir shop, NAAFI cafeteria, disabled facilities, outdoor childrens play vehicles.

Opening Times: Easter to end Oct daily 10:00-17:00 Nov to end Mar weekdays 10:00-16:00. Admission: Adult £4.25, Child £2.75, OAP £3.75.   Location: Six miles south east of Barnstaple. eight miles west of South Molton.   Map Ref: 27

Buckland Abbey

Yelverton PL20 6EY   Tel: 01822 853607   Fax: 01822 855448 Email: dbamcx@smtp.ntrust.co.uk   Web: www.nationaltrust.org.uk

Buckland Abbey, Drake's former home, from the south-west

Tucked away in its own secluded valley above the River Tavy, Buckland was originally a small but influential Cistercian monastery. The house has rich associations with Sir Francis Drake and contains much interesting memorabilia. There are exhibitions of seven centuries of history at Buckland, as well as a magnificent monastic barn, craft workshop, herb garden and delightful estate walks.

Opening Times: Nov to 22 Mar Sat & Sun 14:00-17:00 (closed Xmas to mid Feb), 23 Mar to end Oct daily except Thu 10:30-17:30.   Admission: House & Garden: Adult £4.70, Child £2.30. Garden: Adult £2.50, Child £1.20. Party: Adult £3.90, Child £1.90 (15 or more).

Location: Six miles south of Tavistock, 11 miles north of Plymouth.   Map Ref: 28

Dorset has great literary connections, there being few parts of the county that Thomas Hardy h[as]
not lovingly written about. It is renowned for its beautiful countryside, but can also lay claim [to]
some delightful seaside towns. Poole, once the haunt of pirates and smugglers, was develop[ed]
as a major port in the 13th century.

The county is rich in history and has a wonderfully wide and comprehensive selection [of]
exhibitions, displays and demonstrations portraying its diverse heritage as well as subjects fr[om]
Dinosaurs to Tutankhamun.

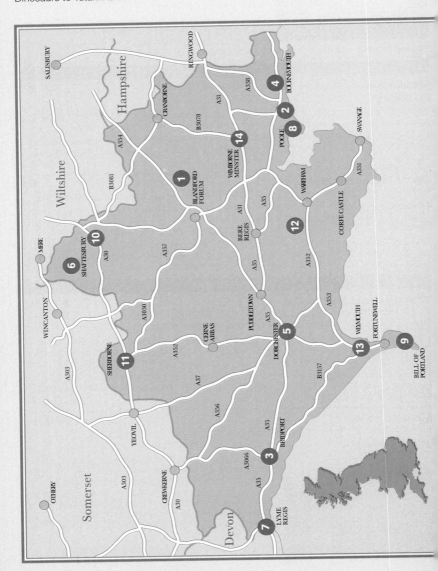

The Red Map References should be used to locate Museums etc on the pages that follow[s]

Dorset

BLANDFORD CAMP

Royal Signals Museum

Blandford Camp DT11 8RH   Tel: 01258 482248   Fax: 01258 482084   Email: royalsignals
Web: www.royalsignals.army.org.uk/museum

Interactive communications, science and technology. Plus a unique series of 'hands-on' exhibitions featuring Enigma, SOE and Elite Special Forces. Prize winning Fun and Discovery trails for children.

Opening Times: All year Mon to Fri 10:00-17:00, end of Feb to Oct also Sat & Sun 10:00-16:00. Closed 2 weeks Xmas.   Admission: Adult £4.50, Child £2.50, OAP £3.50, Family £11.00.
Location: On Blandford Camp, follow the signs from A354 Bypass and bring some form of ID.

Map Ref: 1

BOURNEMOUTH

Russell-Cotes Art Gallery & Museum

East Cliff, Bournemouth BH1 3AA   Tel: 01202 451858   Fax: 01202 451851
Email: kathy.walker@bournemouth.gov.uk   Web: www.russell-cotes.bournemouth.gov.uk

The Russell-Cotes Art Gallery & Museum

The Art Gallery and Museum is a Victorian villa, built and furnished by Sir Merton and Lady Annie Russell-Cotes and gifted to the town in 1908. The Victorian house is of architectural and historic importance with a remarkable interior, which houses a diverse collection of British fine art and ethnographic objects. Additional art galleries were built in the 1920s to house more of the founder's collections.

Opening Times: Tue to Sun 10:00-17:00. Closed Mon, Good Friday and Xmas. Admission: Free.
Location: On the cliff top overlooking the sea. Five minute walk from the town centre to the east.

Map Ref: 2

BRIDPORT

Bridport Museum

South Street, Bridport DT6 3NR   Tel: 01308 458703/422116   Fax: 01308 458704
Email: s.brien@westdorset-dc.gov.uk
Web: www.westdorset-dc.gov.uk

From Romans to ropemaking. The development of Bridport is told, from its Saxon origins to the present day. The history of the world-famous rope and net industry is covered, along with stories of local people and events. Finds from a nearby Roman hillfort are on display. Temporary exhibitions show the extensive fine art and photograph collections.

Bridport Museum

Opening Times: Apr to Oct Mon to Sat 10:00-17:00. Closed Sun.
Admission: Adult £2.00, accompanied Child Free, unaccompanied Child 50p.   Location: In town centre.

Map Ref: 3

Museums, Galleries, Historic Houses & Sites

Please let us know of any collections that are not listed in this guide that you feel should be listed. E-mail us on *editor@tomorrows.co.uk*
or return the Report Form on page 448

CHRISTCHURCH

The Red House
Museum and Gardens

Red House Museum & Gardens

 Hampshire County Council

Quay Road, Christchurch BH23 1BU   Tel: 01202 482860
Fax: 01202 481924   Email: musmjh@hants.gov.uk
Web: www.hants.gov.uk/museum/redhouse

The Red House Museum and Gardens (once a Georgian Workhouse) is the setting for outstanding displays of local social and natural history. Highlights include an interactive archaeology gallery, a display of Arthur Romney Green furniture in a 1930s room setting and a reconstruction of a local 19th century High Street taxidermist. Special exhibitions of contemporary and traditional art and an ever changing garden make every visit a new one.

Opening Times: Tue to Sat 10:00-17:00, Sun 14:00-17:00. Open spring and summer BH Mon.   Admission: Adult £1.50, Concession 80p, Family £3.50.   Location: Near town centre and Christchurch Priory, close to Quay.

Map Ref: 4

DORCHESTER

Tyrannosaurus rex

Dinosaur Museum

Icen Way, Dorchester DT1 1EW   Tel: 01305 269880   Fax: 01305 268885
Email: info@dinosaur-museum.org.uk   Web: www.dinosaur-museum.org.uk

Explore the enthralling pre-historic world of dinosaurs through actual fossils, skeletons, and life-size dinosaur reconstructions combined with hands-on, video and computer displays at this award-winning museum. The museum's innovative and friendly approach mean it was voted one of Britain's top ten Hands On Museums and make it a must for all families. It's frequently featured on national television.

Opening Times: Apr to Oct daily 09:30-17:30, Nov to Mar daily 10:00-16:30. Closed 24-26 Dec.   Admission: Adult £4.75, Child £2.95, Under 4s Free, OAP/Student £3.75, Family £13.75.   Location: In centre of town - follow pedestrian signposts from car parks.

Map Ref: 5

Dorset County Museum

High West Street, Dorchester DT1 1XA   Tel: 01305 262735

The museum reflects the life of the county of Dorset. Enjoy walking on the royal mosaic floors in the magnificent Victorian Hall. Visit the newly opened Dorchester Gallery depicting Dor-chester's history from six thousand years ago to today. Other galleries include Arch-aeology (illustrating the life of Maiden Castle), Geology, Natural History and The Dorset Writers Gallery. This houses the largest collection of Thomas Hardy memorabilia in the world, and includes a reconstruction of the Max Gate Study. There is a variety of childrens' trails and interactives, making it a museum for all the family.

Opening Times: Nov to Apr Mon to Sat 10:00-17:00, May to Oct daily 10:00-17:00. Open most BH.   Admission: Adult £3.50, Child £1.70, Concession £2.35, Family £8.70.   Location: In middle of town centre.

Map Ref: 5

Dorset Teddy Bear Museum

Antelope Walk, Dorchester DT1 1BE   Tel: 01305 263200   Fax: 01305 268885
Email: info@teddybearhouse.co.uk   Web: www.teddybearhouse.co.uk

Visit Edward Bear and his extended family of human-sized teddy bears in their Edwardian style home. Then marvel at bears from throughout the last century displayed in atmospheric settings.

Opening Times: Daily 09:30-17:00. Closed 25-26 Dec.   Admission: Adult £2.95, Child £1.50, Family £7.95.   Location: In centre of Dorchester, pedestrian sighposted from car parks.

Map Ref: 5

Dorset

The Keep Military Museum

1 Bridport Road, Dorchester DT1 1RN   Tel: 01305 264066   Fax: 01305 250373
Email: keep.museum@talk21.com   Web: www.keepmilitarymuseum.org

A military museum housing the artefacts of the army regiments of Devon and Dorset, housed in a Grade II listed building.

Opening Times: Apr to Sep Mon to Sat 09:30-17:00, Sun (Jul to Aug) 10:00-16:00, Oct to Mar Tue to Sat 09:30-17:00   Admission: Adult £3.00, Child/OAP £2.00. Group/Family rates available.   Location: On the junction of Bridport Road and High West Street at the top of the town.
Map Ref: 5

The Golden Funerary Mask

Tutankhamun Exhibition

High West Street, Dorchester DT1 1UW
Tel: 01305 269571   Fax: 01305 268885
Email: info@tutankhamun-exhibition.co.uk
Web: www.tutankhamun-exhibition.co.uk

Experience the mystery and the wonder of the world's greatest discovery of ancient treasure. Tutankhamun's tomb, treasures, jewels and mummified body are exquisitely recreated through sight, sound and smell. Be at the discovery, explore the ante-chamber and the burial chamber. Finally marvel at the superb facsimilies of Tutankhamun's greatest golden treasures including the golden Funerary Mask and the Harpooner.

Opening Times: Apr to Oct daily 09:30-17:30, Nov to Mar Mon to Fri 09:30-17:00, Sat & Sun 10:00-17:00. Closed 24-26 Dec.   Admission: Adult £4.75, Child £2.95, Under 5's Free, OAP/Student £3.75, Family £13.75.   Location: In centre of Dorchester, pedestrian signposted from car parks.
Map Ref: 5

GILLINGHAM

Gillingham Museum

Chantry Fields, Gillingham SP8 4UA   Tel: 01747 823176
Email: gillinghammuseum@waitrose.com   Web: www.brwebsites.com/gillingham.museum

Early occupations of the town and immediate parishes. The Royal Forest of Gillingham and Kings Court Palace. The coming of the railway and local industries. John Constable's visits with reproductions of his paintings of local scenes.

Opening Times: Mon, Tue, Thu, Fri 10:00-17:00, Sat 09:30-12:30. Closed Wed, Sun and BH.   Admission: Free.   Location: In public library building (opposite Waitrose). Two minutes walk from town centre.
Map Ref: 6

LYME REGIS

Lyme Regis Philpot Museum

Bridge Street, Lyme Regis DT7 3QA   Tel: 01297 443370
Email: info@lymeregismuseum.co.uk   Web: www.lymeregismuseum.co.uk

THE AWARD-WINNING
LYME REGIS MUSEUM

Philpot Museum

The museum tells the story of Lyme Regis and its landscape with award winning displays featuring; early history from prehistoric to civil war, the Cobb harbour and Lyme's involvement with the sea, fossils and geology and the importance of local personalities such as Mary Anning and Lyme's literary connections from Henry Fielding and Jane Austen to John Fowles.

Opening Times: Apr to Oct Mon to Sat 10:00-17:00, Sun 11:00-17:00. Nov to Mar Sat 10:00-17:00, Sun 11:00-17:00, weekdays in school holidays.   Admission: Adult £1.60, Child 60p, OAP £1.30.   Location: In the centre of town facing the sea and beside the Guildhall and tourist information centre.
Map Ref: 7

Dorset

POOLE

Scaplen's Court Museum

High Street, Poole BH15 1BW Tel: 01202 262600 Fax: 01202 262622
Email: museums@poole.gov.uk Web: www.poole.gov.uk

Scaplen's Court is part of the museum's education service. It is only open to the general public during the month of August or for special events, which are advertised locally.

Opening Times: Aug Mon to Sat 10:00-17:00, Sun 12:00-17:00. Admission: Adult £4.00, Child £2.85, OAP/Student £3.40, Family tickets available. Includes admission to Waterfront Museum.
Location: Adjacent to Waterfront Museum, off Poole Quay.   Map Ref: 8

Waterfront Museum

4 High Street, Poole BH15 1BW Tel: 01202 262600 Fax: 01202 262622
Email: museums@poole.gov.uk Web: www.poole.gov.uk

Waterfront Museum tells of Poole's history. Displays include a street scene, Roman occupation, trade with Newfoundland, the Studland Bay Wreck and more. Poole Local History Centre offers research facilities on the history of the town.

Opening Times: Apr to Oct Mon to Sat 10:00-17:00, Sun 12:00-17:00. Nov to Mar Mon to Sat 10:00-15:00, Sun 12:00-15:00. Admission: Adult £2.00, Child £1.35, OAP/Student £1.70, Family tickets available. August - Adult £4.00, Child £2.85, OAP/Student £3.40.
Location: Adjacent to Poole Quay   Map Ref: 8

PORTLAND

Portland Museum

217 Wakeham, Portland Tel: 01305 821804 Fax: 01305 206380

Thatched cottages and a purpose-built gallery house the natural and social history of the 'island' including smuggling, quarrying and shipwrecks. The garden has a comprehensive fossil collection.

Opening Times: Easter to Oct Fri to Tue 10:30-13:00 13:30-17:00. Admission: Adult £2.00, Child/Student Free, OAP £1.20. Location: Situated above Church Ope Cove at Wakeham, on main bus route from Weymouth.   Map Ref: 9

SHAFTESBURY

Shaftesbury Abbey Museum & Garden

Park Walk, Shaftesbury SP7 8JR Tel / Fax: 01747 852910
Email: anna@shaftesburyabbey.fsnet.co.uk Web: www.shaftesburyabbey.co.uk

In the heart of this historic hill top town, only a short distance from the famous Gold Hill, are the excavated foundations of the Abbey church, once the most important Benedictine community for women in the country.

Opening Times: Apr to Oct daily 10:00-17:00. Admission: Adult £1.50, Child 60p, OAP £1.00.
Location: Five minutes from town centre.   Map Ref: 10

Shaftesbury Town Museum

Gold Hill, Shaftesbury SP7 8JW Tel: 01747 852157

Special items reflecting life in Shaftesbury, domestically and agriculturally with some civic items. Two floors with special displays each year.

Opening Times: Easter to end Oct daily 10:30-16:30. Sat & Sun only through Nov 10:30-16:30.
Admission: Adult £1.00, Child Free. Location: Top of Gold Hill, behind Town Hall, centre of town.   Map Ref: 10

Sherborne Castle

New Road, Sherborne DT9 5NR   Tel: 01935 813182   Fax: 01935 816727
Email: enquiries@sherbornecastle.com   Web: www.sherbornecastle.com

Sherborne Castle Dorset

Historic country house built by Sir Walter Raleigh and extended by the Digby family, to whom it still belongs. Fine collections of pictures, English furniture, Oriental and European ceramics representing four hundred years of collecting. Delightful setting in parkland landscaped by Capability Brown. Walks round the lake give views of the deer park and ruined Old Castle.

Opening Times: Apr to Oct Tue to Thu, Sat, Sun & BH 11:00-17:00.   Admission: Gardens: Adult £3.00, Child Free. Castle & Gardens: Adult £5.75, Child Free, OAP £5.25.   Location: Near town centre, five minute walk from London/Waterloo to Exeter mainline railway.
Map Ref: 11

Sherborne Museum

Abbeygate House, Church Lane, Sherborne DT9 3BP   Tel: 01935 812252
Email: admin@shermus.fsnet.co.uk

Houses many items of strictly local interest, including videos of the town, abbey and countryside. Disabled people are catered for by videos showing on the ground floor what there is to see on the upper floor.

Opening Times: Easter to end Oct Tue to Sat 10:30-16:30, Sun and BH 14:30-16:30.
Admission: Adult £1.00, Child/Student Free.   Location: Near the town centre and 50 metres from Sherborne Abbey.
Map Ref: 11

WAREHAM

Tank Museum

Bovington, near Wool, Wareham BH20 6JG   Tel: 01929 405096   Fax: 01929 405360   Email: davidb@tankmuseum.co.uk   Web: www.tankmuseum.co.uk

The famous Bovington Tiger

The Tank Museum houses the world's finest international indoor collection of Armoured Fighting Vehicles; there are 150 vehicles from 26 different countries. Free audio guides available, large car park, outdoor children's play area, large specialist gift and model shop and licensed restaurant. During school holidays the exhibits are brought to life with live demonstrations and Tanks in Action displays throughout the summer.

Opening Times: Daily 10:00-17:00. Closed Xmas.
Admission: Please phone for prices.   Location: In the village of Bovington, near Wool which is a main-line station from Waterloo.
Map Ref: 12

WEYMOUTH

Nothe Fort

Barrack Road, Weymouth DT4 8UF   Tel: 01305 766626

A dramatically restored Victorian fort with ramparts, gun floors and magazines furnished as a museum of coastal defence. Seventy rooms of guns, equipment, displays, models, artefact and military memorabilia.

Opening Times: 25 Mar to 7 Apr, 1 May to 30 Sep, 27 Oct to 3 Nov. Mon to Sat 10:30-17:30, Sun 10:30-17:30.   Admission: Adult £3.50, Concessions £2.50.   Location: 15 minute walk from town centre or rowboat ferry from pavilion.
Map Ref: 13

Weymouth Museum & Exhibition Gallery

Brewers' Quay, Hope Square, Weymouth DT4 8TR   Tel: 01305 777622   Fax: 01305 761680

2002 Exhibition - Colonial Expansion - portrays exploration and expansion across the Globe in search of new lands and fortune. The story of Gabriel Steward, who went to sea as a boy. By 1763 he had completed his final voyage to Madras and China as Master of The Neptune. In 1769 he became Mayor of Weymouth. A colourful tableau and many original documents of the period are displayed.

Opening Times: Daily 10:00-17:00 except second two weeks in Jan. Admission: Free. Location: Situated at the Brewers Quay Complex. Follow brown signs.   Map Ref: 13

Statue of George III, stands on a fine Georgian Esplanade

WIMBORNE MINSTER

Priests House Museum & Garden

23/27 High Street, Wimborne Minster BH21 1HR   Tel / Fax: 01202 882533
Email: priest_house@hotmail.com

The Priest's House is an historic town house. A series of period rooms take the visitor back through the centuries. The Museum tells the story of East Dorset from ancient to modern times. With hands-on activities in the the Victorian schoolroom and Galleries of Childhood and Archaeology. There is plenty to do. The walled garden behind the house is a tranquil retreat in the centre of town.

The Victorian Kitchen

Opening Times: 29 Mar to 31 Oct Mon to Sat 10:00-16:30, Jul to Aug and BH weekends Sun 14:00-17:00. Admission: Adult £2.50, Child £1.00, OAP/Student £1.90, Family £6.50. Location: Centre of Wimborne town, opposite the Minster.   Map Ref: 14

ex is well endowed with interesting towns. Colchester, claiming to be Britain's oldest recorded
, has Europe's biggest Norman keep. Ancient Chelmsford is Essex's county town, once a
Town planned in 1199 by the Bishop of London. All of these towns have their stories to tell
plethora of splendid museums.

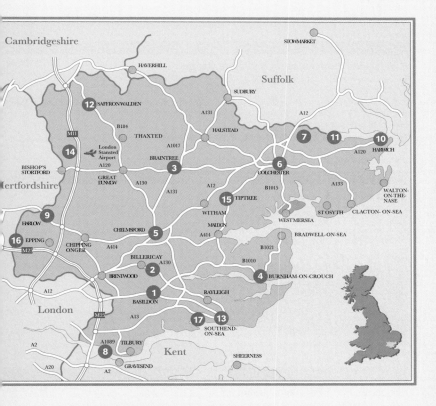

The Red Map References should be used to locate Museums etc on the pages that follow

Essex

BASILDON

The Haven Plotlands Museum

Third Avenue, Lower Dunton Road, Basildon SS16 6EB Tel: 01268 419103 Fax: 01268 546137 Email: melaniel@essexwt.org.uk Web: www.essexwt.org.uk

Original 1930s Plotland home has been restored. Fully furnished with 1930s style furnishings, memorabilia, kitchen/garden implements. The Haven offers people the chance to enjoy their memories.

Opening Times: Mar to Oct Tue to Sun 13:30-16:30. Other times by arrangement.
Admission: Free; donations appreciated. Location: On a nature reserve. Access by public transport limited.
Map Ref: 1

BILLERICAY

Barleylands Farm Museum & Visitors Centre

Barleylands Road, Billericay CM11 2UD Tel: 01268 290229/532253 Fax: 01268 290222 Email: barleyfarm@aol.com

See the collection of rural life exhibits and implements from a bygone age. The Visitor Centre includes Craft Studios, glassblowers, resident blacksmith and tearooms. Also on site is a miniature steam railway and picnic area.

Opening Times: Mar to Oct daily 10:00-17:00. Admission: Adult £3.50, Child/OAP £2.00. Groups of 10 or more less 25%. Location: Follow brown/white tourist signs off A12 & A127. We are off A129 between Billericay and Wickford.
Map Ref: 2

BRAINTREE

Braintree District Museum

Town Hall Centre, Market Square, Braintree CM7 3YG Tel: 01376 325266 Fax: 01376 344345 Email: jean@bdcmuseum.demon.co.uk

The Victorian Schoolroom

The Museum's Gallery exhibits interpret the diverse local industrial heritage of this area which has a major influence on 20th century life in England and the world, particularly in silks, man-made textiles and metal window design. The natural historian John Ray, who was born in the district, has a gallery devoted to his life and work.

Opening Times: Mon to Sat & BH 10:00-17:00, Oct to Dec Sun 13:00-16:00. Admission: District visitors: Adult £1.00, Concession 50p. All other visitors Adult £2.00, Concession £1.00. Location: Town centre, five minutes from railway station and one minute from bus station.
Map Ref: 3

BURNHAM-ON-CROUCH

Mangapps Farm Railway Museum

Mangapps Farm, Burnham-on-Crouch CM0 8QQ Tel: 01621 784898

Areas of special interest include one of the finest displays of signalling equipment on public view. A large, indoor museum containing comprehensive displays of railway memorabilia of particular East Anglian interest.

Opening Times: Sat, Sun & BH, every day Easter fortnight & Aug 13:00-17:00. Closed Xmas. Admission: Adult £4.00, Child £2.00, Under 4s Free, OAP £3.00. Location: One mile north Burnham-on-Crouch.
Map Ref: 4

CHELMSFORD

Chelmsford Museum & the Essex Regiment Museum

Oaklands Park, Moulsham Street, Chelmsford CM2 9AQ Tel: 01245 615100 Fax: 01245 611250 Email: oaklands@chelmsfordbc.gov.uk
Web: www.chelmsfordbc.gov.uk/museums/index.shtml

Local history museum featuring 'The Story of Chelmsford' exhibition, natural history, social history, costume, ceramics, early English drinking glasses, coins. The Essex Regiment Museum tells the story of the local county regiment.

Opening Times: Mon to Sat 10:00-17:00. Sun 14:00-17:00 in Summertime, 13:00-16:00 in Wintertime. Closed Good Friday & Xmas. Admission: Free Location: Three quarters of a mile from town centre.
Map Ref: 5

Essex

COLCHESTER

Castle Museum

Castle Park, Colchester CO1 1TJ   Tel: 01206 282939   Web: www.colchestermuseums.org.uk

A visit to Colchester Castle Museum takes you through 2000 years of some of the most important events in British history. The Castle is the largest keep ever built by the Normans and is constructed on the foundations of Roman Temple of Claudius. An award winning museum featuring hands-on displays and lively events programme.

Opening Times: Mon to Sat 10:00-17:00, Sun 11:00-17:00.   Admission: Adult £3.90, Child £2.60, OAP/Concession £2.60, Family £10.50.

Location: Central off high street, Castle park. 5 mins walk from bus station and town railway station.   Map Ref: 6

Colchester Castle

Hollytrees Museum

High Street, Colchester CO1 1UG   Tel: 01206 282940   Web: www.colchestermuseums.org.uk

Hollytrees Museum is in a beautiful Georgian town house built in 1718 interpreting 300 years of domestic life with fun and humour in mind. Highlights are the Childhood Gallery and interactive displays.

Opening Times: Mon to Sat 10:00-17:00, Sun 11:00-17:00.   Admission: Free.   Location: Off high street, in Castle Park five minutes from bus and railway station.   Map Ref: 6

Natural History Museum

All Saint's Church, High Street, Colchester CO1 1DN   Tel: 01206 282941   Fax: 01206 282925   Web: www.colchestermuseums.org.uk

The Natural History Museum offers an interesting perspective on the natural history of Essex from the ice age to the present day, with many hands-on displays, and summer events programme.

Opening Times: Mon to Sat 10:00-17:00, Sun 11:00-17:00.   Admission: Free.   Location: End of high street five minutes from bus and train station.   Map Ref: 6

Tymperleys Clock Museum

Trinity Street, Colchester CO1 1JN   Tel: 01206 282943   Web: www.colchestermuseums.org.uk

Tymperleys has a fine display of Colchester made clocks from the outstanding Mason collection. It is situated in a beautiful restored 15th century timber-framed house with medieval herb garden in the grounds.

Opening Times: May to Sep Tue to Sat 10:00-13:00 & 14:00-17:00.   Admission: Free.
Location: Town centre.   Map Ref: 6

DEDHAM

Sir Alfred Munnings Art Museum

Castle House, Dedham CO7 6AZ   Tel: 01206 322127

The home, studios and grounds where Sir Alfred Munnings PRA KCVO lived and worked for 40 years until his death in 1959. A large collection of his works shown in his former home. Annual special exhibition.

Opening Times: Easter Sun to 1st Sun in Oct Wed & Sun 14:00-17:00, also Aug Thu & Sat 14:00-17:00. Groups by appointment.   Admission: Adult £3.00, Child 50p, Concession £2.00.
Location: Three quarters of a mile from centre of Dedham.   Map Ref: 7

GRAYS

Thurrock Museum

Thameside Complex, Orsett Road, Grays RM17 5DX   Tel: 01375 382555   Fax: 01375 392666   Email: jeatton@thurrock.gov.uk   Web: www.thurrock.gov.uk/museum

Local history collection from archaeology to social history collections covering the history of Thurrock.

Opening Times: Mon to Sat 09:00-17:00. Closed Sun.   Admission: Free.   Location: Near town centre, five minutes walk from Grays Railway Station.   Map Ref: 8

Essex

HARLOW

The Museum of Harlow

Muskham Road, Off First Avenue, Harlow CM20 2LF   Tel: 01279 454959   Fax: 01279 626094

The museum, set within its own walled gardens, tells the story of the development of Harlow from its earliest origins 7000 years ago through to the present day.

Opening Times: Tue to Fri 09:30-17:00, Sat 10:00-12:00 13:00-16:00.   Admission: Free.
Location: Located at Muskham Road, off First Avenue. Approx one km from Harlow Mill Station.
Map Ref: 9

HARWICH

Harwich Maritime Museum

Low Lighthouse, The Green, Harwich CO12 3NL   Tel: 01255 503429

Housed in a disused lighthouse. A comprehensive display of naval and merchant ships using the port, with a commanding view of unending shipping movements in the harbour.

Opening Times: May to Aug daily 10:00-16:00.   Admission: Adult 50p, Child Free.
Location: On Harwich Green, a five minute walk from rail and bus station.   Map Ref: 10

MANNINGTREE

Essex Secret Bunker Museum

Crown Building, Shrubland Road, Mistley, Manningtree CO11 1HS   Tel: 01206 392271
Fax: 01206 393847   Email: info@essexsecretbunker.com   Web: www.essexsecretbunker.com

The award winning former Essex County Nuclear War Bunker was operational between 1951 and 1993. The site is fully interpreted by cinemas, exhibitions, sound effects and displays. Recognised by English Heritage and the Imperial War Museum.

Opening Times: 5 Jan to 24 Feb Sat & Sun 10:30-16:30. 2 Mar to 27 Oct daily 10:30-17:00 (Aug 18:00).   Admission: Adult £4.95, Child £3.75, OAP £4.45, Family £15.00.   Location: At Mistley nr Manningtree. Bus station one minute, railway station three minutes. Signposted from A120 and B1352.   Map Ref: 11

SAFFRON WALDEN

Audley End House & Gardens

Audley End, Saffron Walden CB11 4JF   Tel: 01799 522842

Audley End was one of the great wonders of the nation when it was built by the first earl of Suffolk, Lord Treasurer to James I. Some interiors were remodelled in the eighteenth century by Robert Adam, and the grounds were landscaped by Capability Brown. Picture collections, comprising family portraits and Old Master paintings, furniture, silver, mounted birds and animals, and more.

Opening Times: Please phone for details.
Admission: House & Grounds: Adult £6.75, Child £3.40, Concession £5.10, Family £16.90. Grounds only: Adult

The Chapel

£4.00, Child £2.00, Concession £3.00, Family £10.00.   Location: One mile west of Saffron Walden on B1383.   Map Ref: 12

Saffron Walden Museum

Museum Street, Saffron Walden CB10 1JL   Tel / Fax: 01799 510333
Email: museum@uttlesford.gov.uk

Friendly, family-size museum. Winner Best Museum of Social History. Good disabled access. Moccasins, mummy cases, woolly mammoths and 'Wallace The Lion' - something for all ages.

Opening Times: Mar to Oct Mon to Sat 10:00-17:00 Sun & BH 14:00-17:00. Nov to Feb Mon to Sat 10:00-16:30 Sun & BH 14:00-16:30. Closed 24-25 Dec.   Admission: Adult £1.00, Child Free, Concession 50p.   Location: Close to Parish Church, castle ruins in grounds. Map Ref: 12

Essex

Prittlewell Priory

Priory Park, Victoria Avenue, Southend-on-Sea Tel: 01702 342878 Fax: 01702 349806
Email: southendmuseum@hotmail.com Web: www.southendmuseums.co.uk

12th century Cluniac Priory with later additions, extensively restored in the 1920s, set in an attractive park. Displays focus on the history of the Priory itself, local wildlife and also on the museum's fine collection of radios and televisions (Ekco was a local firm). A fine series of recently restored panel paintings by artist Alan Sorrell are also on show.

Opening Times: Tue to Sat 10:00-13:00 and 14:00-17:00. Closed Sun, Mon and BH. Admission: Free. Location: In Priory Park, 1 kilometre north of town centre. Map Ref: 13

Prittlewell Priory from the Old World Gardens

Southchurch Hall

Southchurch Hall Close, Southchurch, Southend-on-Sea SS1 2TE Tel: 01702 467671
Fax: 01702 439806 Email: southendmuseums@hotmail.com
Web: www.southendmuseums.co.uk

A moated early 14th century timber framed manor house set in gardens. It has rooms furnished in Medieval, Tudor and Victorian styles. An exhibition room tells the story of the Hall and there are exhibits from excavations near the moat. The museum specialises in historic presentations to school children and also hosts various events, such as open days, during the year.

Opening Times: Tue to Sat 10:00-13:00 and 14:00-17:00 (mornings reserved for schools during term time). Closed Sun, Mon and BH. Admission: Free. Location: One kilometre east of town centre, five minutes walk from Southend East Railway Station. Map Ref: 13

Southchurch Hall from the South

Southend Central Museum & Planetarium

Victoria Avenue, Southend-on-Sea SS2 6EW Tel: 01702 434449 Fax: 01702 349806
Email: southendmuseums@hotmail.com Web: www.southendmuseums.co.uk

The new Discovery Centre

The museum has displays of local history, geology and wildlife with special sections on the Thames Estuary and Victorian Life. An imposing feature, dominating the main hall, is the late medieval 'Reynolds' fireplace, originally part of a building in nearby Prittlewell. The museum's Discovery Centre, opened in 2000, is an interactive centre where visitors can handle exhibits. Video microscopes allow visitors to examine a range of specimens, from London Clay fossils to coins and garden pests, in amazing detail. In addition, they can try and solve problems on topic tables and refer to SID, a rapidly growing database of historic local photographs which has a particularly fine selection of views of Southend from Victorian times to the 1960s. Upstairs, Southend Planetarium allows visitors to sit back and enjoy a forty minute tour of the Universe presented by a guide lecturer. Investigate the scale of Space, details of the Sun and the planets or take a look at the myths and legends of the skies. (Please note that under 5s are not admitted to the planetarium).

A demonstration in the Discovery Centre

Opening Times: Tue to Sat 10:00-17:00, closed Sun, Mon and BH. Planetarium open Wed to Sat at 11:00, 14:00 and 16:00. Admission: Museum Free. Planetarium Adult £2.25, Child £1.60, OAP £1.60, Group rates on request. Location: In town centre, next to Southend Victoria Railway Station. Map Ref: 13

Southend Pier Museum

Southend Pier, Marine Parade, Southend-on-Sea   Tel: 01702 611214/614553

The Pier Museum houses important collections relating to the history of the longest pleasure pier in the world. Vivid pictorial displays of the pier's entertainment, disasters, illuminations, war years, pleasure boats, railway etc.

Opening Times: May to Oct Sat, Sun, Tue, Wed and BH 11:00-17:00, 11:00-17:30 in school holidays.   Admission: Adult & (unaccompanied) Child 50p, Child under 12 (accompanied) Free. Group/School rates available.   Location: Near the town centre, three minutes from central bus station. Underneath Shore Station of Southend Pier. Access via the station.   Map Ref: 13

STANSTED

House on the Hill Museums Adventure

Stansted CM24 8SP   Tel: 01279 813237   Fax: 01279 816391   Web: www.gold.enta.net

A huge range of toys and games from later Victorian times up to the 1970s - about 75,000 exhibits in total.

Opening Times: Daily 10:00-17:00. Closed Xmas & New Year.   Admission: Adult £3.80, Child £2.80, OAP £3.50.   Location: Adjacent to Mountfitchet Castle, in the centre of Stansted village.
Map Ref: 14

TIPTREE

Tiptree Museum

Wilkin & Sons Ltd, Tiptree CO5 0RF   Tel: 01621 815407   Fax: 01621 814555   Email: tiptree@tiptree.com   Web: www.tiptree.com

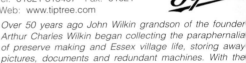

Over 50 years ago John Wilkin grandson of the founder Arthur Charles Wilkin began collecting the paraphernalia of preserve making and Essex village life, storing away pictures, documents and redundant machines. With the opening of the museum in a renovated farm building in 1995, John Wilkin's foresight was at last rewarded and visitors can now see how life was and how the art of jam making has advanced over the years.

Renovated Farm Building at Tiptree

Opening Times: Mon to Fri 10:00-17:00. During Jun, Jul & Aug also open Sun 12:00-17:00. Closed Xmas week. Admission: Free.   Location: Tiptree is 15 minutes from Colchester and the Jam Factory & Museum is along the B1023 heading towards Tollesbury.
Map Ref: 15

WALTHAM ABBEY

Epping Forest District Museum

39/41 Sun Street, Waltham Abbey EN9 1EL   Tel: 01992 716882   Fax: 01992 700427 Email: museum@efdc.fsnet.co.uk   Web: www.eppingforestdistrictmuseum.org.uk

The museum tells the story of the people who have lived and worked in this part of West Essex, from the earliest inhabitants to the present. Housed in a building dating to 1520, with a changing programme of temporary exhibitions.

Opening Times: Mon & Fri 14:00-17:00, Sun (1 May to 30 Sep) 14:00-17:00, Tue 12:00-17:00, Sat 10:00-17:00. Wed & Thu Group bookings available.   Admission: Free.   Location: Near town centre.
Map Ref: 16

Museums, Galleries, Historic Houses & Sites

Please let us know of any collections that are not listed in this guide that you feel should be listed. E-mail us on *editor@tomorrows.co.uk* or return the Report Form on page 448

Essex

Beecroft Art Gallery

Station Road, Westcliff-on-Sea, Westcliff-on-Sea SS0 7RA   Tel: 01702 347418   Fax: 01702 347681   Web: www.beecroft-art-gallery.co.uk

Edward B Seago (1910-1974).
The Doge's Palace, Venice

The gallery's fine collection of over 2,000 works includes a selection of Dutch and Flemish 17th century paintings by artists such as Molenaer, Ruisdael and Berchem. Also represented is a fair selection of 19th century artists including Rossetti, with a fine pencil drawing of model Fanny Cornforth, Constable with an early oil sketch of the Stour valley and Edward Lear with a watercolour of Egypt, 20th century works including paintings by Carel Weight, the Great Bardfield Group and a fine bronze by Jacob Epstein. The local artist Alan Sorrell is well represented by his 'Drawings of Nubia' series depicting a visit to Egypt prior to the building of the Aswan Dam. Of particular interest is the Thorpe Smith Collection of local landscape views, containing paintings, drawings and prints from as early as 1803. A selection of the finest works is always on show. There is a range of temporary exhibitions. Particularly popular are the summer 'Essex Open Exhibition', a selected show open to artists working and living in Essex, and the annual Christmas Show with a range of items suitable for presents.

Dante Gabriel Rossetti (1828-1882).
Fanny Cornforth

Opening Times: Tue to Sat 10:00-13:00 and 14:00-17:00. Closed Sun and Mon, but open at least one Sun during exhibitions.   Admission: Free.
Location: Ten minute walk from town centre, opposite Cliffs Pavilion.

Map Ref: 17

Gloucestershire

Cheltenham, the small spa village, was transformed into an elegant fashionable town in 1... through the visit of George III and the consequent patronage. Gloucester with its magnific... cathedral, the nave of which is dominated by the largest stained glass window in Britain crea... in 1349, was once a commercially important port.

The county's museums tell the story of its Arts and Crafts, its Roman occupation, its waterwa... railways, the Forest of Dean and its heritage.

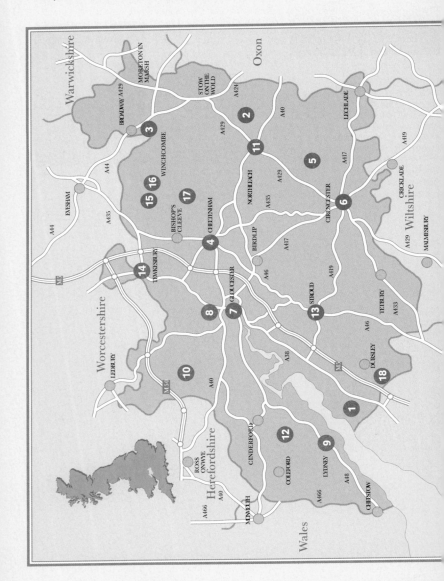

The Red Map References should be used to locate Museums etc on the pages that follow

Gloucestershire

Jenner Museum

Church Lane, Berkeley GL13 9BH   Tel: 01453 810631   Fax: 01453 811690
Email: manager@jennermuseum.com   Web: www.jennermuseum.com

Georgian country home of Edward Jenner, discoverer of vaccination against smallpox. Portraits, personal possessions and reconstruction of study, vaccination equipment and computerised display explaining modern immunology.

Opening Times: Apr to Sep Tue to Sat 12:30-17;30, Sun 13:00-17:30. Oct Sun only 13:00-17;30. Groups at other times by appointment.   Admission: Adult £2.80, Child £1.25, OAP £2.00. Group discounts available.   Location: Near Berkeley Town Centre, beside church and castle, one mile from A38 - use junction 14 or 15 of M5.

Map Ref: 1

Cotswold Motoring Museum & Childhood Toy Collection

The Old Mill, Bourton-on-the-Water GL54 2BY   Tel: 01451 821255
Email: michelle.blackmore@csma.uk.com

Full of exciting memorabilia including classic cars, motorcycles, aeroplanes, pedal cars and one of the largest collections of metal motoring signs. The museum is also home to Brum, the little yellow car from the children's TV series.

Opening Times: Mar to Oct 10:00-18:00.   Admission: Adult £2.25, Child £1.50, Family £6.90. Location: Just off High Street, a short walk from The Green.

Map Ref: 2

Snowshill Manor

Snowshill, Broadway WR12 7JU   Tel / Fax: 01386 852410
Email: snowshill@smtp.ntrust.org.uk   Web: www.ntrustsevern.org.uk

A Cotswold manor house, containing Charles Paget Wade's extraordinary collection of craftsmanship and design including Samurai armour. A delightful organic garden, shop and restaurant.

Opening Times: 29 Mar to 3 Nov Wed to Sun, BH Mon & Jubilee Mon & Tue, also Mon in Jul & Aug 12:00-17:00.   Admission: Adult £6.00, Child £3.00, Family £15.00. Garden, shop & restaurant only Adult £3.50, Child £1.75. Coach and school parties by written appointment only. Location: Two and a half miles south west Broadway off A44 bypass.

Map Ref: 3

Chinese robe and Ceramics

Cheltenham Art Gallery & Museum

Clarence Street, Cheltenham GL50 3JT   Tel: 01242 237431   Fax: 01242 262334
Email: artgallery@cheltenham.gov.uk
Web: www.cheltenhammuseum.org.uk

A world-renowned museum, the Arts and Crafts Movement collection is recognised by the government as being of national importance. Within this collection is some of the finest furniture, silver, jewellery, ceramics and textiles produced by the Arts and Crafts Movement, inspired by the ideology of William Morris. The foundation of the Art Gallery is marked by the Dutch and Flemish 17th and 19th century paintings donated by Baron de Ferrieres in 1898. Included within the 20th century paintings are works of Vanessa Bell and Stanley Spencer. The museum depicts the development of Cheltenham, including local archaeological discoveries, prehistoric flints, Roman pottery, Anglo-Saxon jewellery and medieval floor tiles. The town is explored from small market town to renowned spa in the 1800s and its development into a sporting, residential, educational and manufacturing centre.

Piano, case designed by C R Ashbee, made in oak and holly

Opening Times: Mon to Sat 10:00-17:20, Sun 14:00-16:20. Closed Easter and BH. Admission: Free.   Location: Town centre.

Map Ref: 4

111

Holst Birthplace Museum

4 Clarence Road, Pittville, Cheltenham GL52 2AY   Tel: 01242 524846   Fax: 01242 580182
Email: holstmuseum@btconnect.com   Web: www.holstmuseum.org.uk

Birthplace of the composer of The Planets, displaying personal memorabilia including his piano. Also a fine period house with rooms illustrating the 'upstairs-downstairs' way of Victorian life. Holst's music is played.

Opening Times: Tue to Sat 10:00-16:00, closed Sun, Mon and some BH. Closed Dec 2002 to Jan 2003, except for pre-booked groups.   Admission: Adult £2.50, Concessions £2.00, Family £7.00, special rate for schools.   Location: Ten minute walk from town centre. Near Portland Street car park. Opposite Gateway of Pittville Park.   Map Ref: 4

CIRENCESTER

Arlington Mill Museum

Bibury, Cirencester GL7 5NL   Tel: 01285 740368

History of Arlington Mill and artefacts relating to Victorian rural life.

Opening Times: Mar to Oct daily 10:00-18:00. Nov to Feb Thu to Tue 11:00-17:00. Admission: Adult £2.00, Child/OAP £1.20, Groups £1.00.   Map Ref: 5

Corinium Museum

Park Street, Cirencester GL7 2BX   Tel: 01285 655611   Fax: 01285 643286
Email: simone.clark@cotswold.gov.uk   Web: www.cotswold.gov.uk

A superb collection of finds from Corinium (Roman Cirencester) including spectacular mosaics and sculpture. Full scale reconstructions of a Roman dining room, garden and kitchen. Other historic displays on the Cotswolds. Events and exhibitions.

Opening Times: Mon to Sat 10:00-17:00 Sun 14:00-17:00. Closed Xmas & New Year and last Monday in March.   Admission: Adult £2.50 Child/Concession £1.00 OAP/Adult Group rate £2.00 Family £5.00.   Location: Located in central Cirencester, in Park Street between church and Bathurst Estate.   Map Ref: 6

GLOUCESTER

City Museum & Art Gallery

Brunswick Road, Gloucester GL1 1HP   Tel: 01452 396131   Fax: 01452 410898
Email: city.musuem@gloucester.gov.uk   Web: www.mylife.gloucester.gov.uk

The Museums collections include dinosaurs, fossils, unique Roman remains, stunning Birdlip mirrors, antique furniture, painting and decorative arts. Temporary exhibitions, hands-on displays, childrens holiday activities and regular special events.

Opening Times: Tue to Sat 10:00-17:00   Admission: Adults £2.00, Free for all Gloucester City Residents and under 18s.   Location: Five minutes walk from Central Bus Station, near Town Centre   Map Ref: 7

Gloucester Folk Museum

99/103 Westgate Street, Gloucester GL1 2PG   Tel: 01452 396467   Fax: 01452 330495
Email: folk.museum@gloucester.gov.uk   Web: www.mylife.gloucester.gov.uk

Grade II Listed Tudor and Jacobean timber-framed buildings with new extensions housing displays on social history, crafts, trades and industries of Gloucester City and County. Regular special exibitions, activities, crafts and an interactive ICT gallery.

Opening Times: Tue to Sat 10:00-17:00   Admission: Adults £2.00, Free for all Gloucester City Residents and under 18s.   Location: Ten minutes walk from Central Bus Station, near Town Centre   Map Ref: 7

Gloucestershire

National Waterways Museum

Llanthony Warehouse, The Docks, Gloucester GL1 2EH   Tel: 01452 318054
Fax: 01452 318066

Museum Entrance and Shop

The collection is designed as being 'of national importance' and includes many artefacts and historic floating exhibits that chart the fascinating 300 year story of our inland waterways. Interactive touch-screen computers bring history to life as does our working blacksmith forge. From Easter to October you can even take a 45 boat trip along the Gloucester and Sharpness Canal.

Opening Times: Daily 10:00-17:00. Closed Xmas Day.
Admission: Adult £5.00, Child/OAP £4.00, Family £12.00-£16.00.   Location: Situated in historic docks five miles from city centre, ten miles walk from Gloucester Bus
Station and Railway Station.   Map Ref: 7

Nature in Art

Wallsworth Hall, Twigworth, Gloucester GL2 9PA   Tel: 01452 731422   Fax: 01452 730937
Email: ninart@globalnet.co.uk   Web: www.nature-in-art.org.uk

World's first museum dedicated exclusively to art inspired by nature. Fine, decorative and applied art spanning 1500 years from 60 countries in all styles and media. Situated in a fine Georgian mansion.

Opening Times: Tue to Sun 10:00-17:00 and BH. Closed Xmas. Admission: Adult £3.35,
Child/OAP/Concession £2.85, Under 8s Free. Group rates available. Location: Two miles north of Gloucester on main A38.   Map Ref: 8

LYDNEY

Dean Forest Railway Museum

Norchard Railway Centre, Forest Road, New Mills, Lydney GL15 4ET   Tel / Fax: 01594 845840
Web: www.deanforestrailway.co.uk

General railway artefacts with emphasis on local Forest of Dean area. Also includes working telephone exchange (old restored BT system) for railway system. Story of Severn and Wye railway since 1809. Information (24 hrs) 01594 843423.

Opening Times: Summer daily 11:00-17:00. Winter Wed, Sat & Sun 11:00-16:00. Closed Xmas.
Admission: Free on non-operational days. Operational Days: Adult £5.50, Child £3.50, OAP £4.50. Group rates available. Location: Road: one mile north of Lydney Town Centre on B4234 - off A48, follow brown tourist signs. Rail: 300 yards from Lydney mainline to DFR Lydney Junction.   Map Ref: 9

NEWENT

Shambles Museum

Church Street, Newent GL18 1PP   Tel: 01531 822144

A collection set out as a Victorian town of the 1890s - houses, cottages, shops, trades around cobbled street, square and cottage garden.

Opening Times: Mid Mar to end Oct Tue to Sun 10:00-17:00. Admission: Adult £3.60, Child £1.95, OAP £2.95. Location: Centre of town.   Map Ref: 10

NORTHLEACH

Cotswold Heritage Centre

Fosse Way, Northleach GL54 3JH   Tel: 01451 860715   Fax: 01451 860091
Email: simone.clark@cotswold.gov.uk   Web: www.cotswold.gov.uk

A museum of rural life in a former 'House of Correction'. Known for the Lloyd Baker Collection of Agricultural Vehicles including several wagons made in the Cotswolds. Exhibitions and events throughout the season.

Opening Times: Apr to Oct Mon to Sat & BH 10:00-17:00 Sun 14:00-17:00. Admission: Adult £2.50 Child/Concession £1.00 OAP/Adult Group rate £2.00 Family £5.00. Location: On A429 at Northleach crossroads.   Map Ref: 11

Gloucestershire

ROYAL FOREST OF DEAN

Dean Heritage Centre

Camp Mill, Soudley, Royal Forest of Dean GL14 2UB   Tel: 01594 822170   Fax: 01594 823711
Email: deanmuse@btinternet.com

Restored mill and pond in a wooded valley. The collection covers the period from pre-history to the present day, reflecting life in the Forest of Dean and rural skills.

Opening Times: Summer: 10:00-17:30. Winter: 11:00-16:30. Admission: Adult £4.00, Child £2.50, OAP £3.50, Family £12.00. Group rates available. Location: Pretty woodland setting.

Map Ref: 12

STROUD

Museum in the Park

Museum in the Park

Stratford Park, Stratford Road, Stroud GL5 4AF
Tel: 01453 763394   Fax: 01453 752400
Email: stgcm@dial.pipex.com

New family friendly museum in historic parkland setting. Innovative and colourful displays including dinosaurs, Uley Roman Temple, the world's first lawnmower and much more! Temporary exhibition programme and fun museum trails for children of all ages.

Opening Times: Apr to Sep Tue to Fri 12:00-17:00, Sat, Sun & BH 11:00-17:00. Oct to Mar Tue to Fri 13:00-17:00, Sat & Sun 11:00-16:00. Admission: Adult £2.50, Child/OAP £1.25. Location: In Stratford Park, ten minute walk from Stroud Town Centre.

Map Ref: 13

TEWKESBURY

John Moore Countryside Museum

41 Church Street, Tewkesbury GL20 5SN   Tel: 01684 297174   Email: myecrofte@aol.com
Web: www.gloster.demon.co.uk/JMCM/index.html

A natural history collection exhibited in a 15th century house and honouring the prophetic writings on nature conservation of John Moore the writer. Displays of British woodland and wetland wildlife. The impact of people on the natural environment and the need for conservation are explored.

Opening Times: Apr to Oct & BH Tue to Sat 10:00-13:00 14:00-17:00. Nov to Mar most Sat plus special Xmas & spring half term 11:00-13:00 14:00-16:00. Admission: Adult £1.00, Child 50p, OAP 75p, Group 75p. Location: In the precincts of Tewkesbury Abbey, three minute walk from town centre.

Map Ref: 14

WINCHCOMBE

Gloucestershire Warwickshire Railway

The Railway Station, Toddington, near Winchcombe GL54 5DT   Tel: 01242 621405
Email: enquiries@gwsr.plc.uk   Web: www.gwsr.plc.uk

The 'Friendly Line in the Cotswolds' operates a round trip of 13 miles from Toddington via Winchcombe to Gotherington, including the 693 yard Greet Tunnel, one of the longest on a preserved railway. Superb views of the Cotswolds, Malverns and Vale of Evesham. Steam and diesel locomotives. Restored carriages and stations. Locomotives under restoration.

Opening Times: Jan, Feb & Nov Sun. Mar to Oct Sat & Sun. Jul & Aug BHs, selected weekdays 10:00-17:00. December weekends Santa Specials. Admission: Adult £7.00, Child £4.00, Under 5s Free, OAP £6.00, Family

Great Western autotank No.1450
at Winchcombe (Jean Hadley)

£19.00. Group rates available. Location: Ten miles east of junction 9 on M5, near the junction of B4077 and B4632.

Map Ref: 15

Gloucestershire

Hailes Abbey

Winchcombe, near Cheltenham GL54 5PB Tel: 01242 602398

This Cistercian abbey was built by Richard, Earl of Cornwall in the 13th century, in gratitude for surviving a perilous sea journey. The museum contains an important collection of floor tiles, including early inlaid tiles.

Opening Times: Apr to Sep daily 10:00-18:00, Oct daily 10:00-17:00, Nov to Mar Sat & Sun 10:00-16:00. Closed Xmas & New Year. Admission: Adult £2.60, Child £1.30, Concession £2.00, National Trust Members Free. Location: Two miles north east of Winchcombe off B4632.

Map Ref: 16

Ariel view of Sudeley Castle and Gardens

Sudeley Castle

Winchcombe GL54 5JD Tel: 01242 604357/602308
Fax: 01242 602959 Email: marketing@sudeley.org.uk
Web: www.stratford.co.uk/sudeley

Set against the beautiful backdrop of the Cotswold Hills, Sudeley Castle is steeped in history. With Royal connections spanning thousands of years, it has played an important role in the turbulent and changing times of England's past.

Opening Times: Gardens, Grounds, Shop, Exhibition & Plant Centre: 2 Mar to 27 Oct 10:30-17:30. Castle Apartments and St Mary's Church: 23 Mar to 27 Oct 11:00-17:00. Admission: Castle & Gardens: Adult £6.50, Child £3.50, Family £18.00 Concession £5.50. Gardens & Exhibition: Adult £5.00, Child £2.75, Concession £4.00. Location: Near Winchcombe, eight miles north east of Cheltenham on the B4632 (A46) or ten miles from junction 9 off the M5.

Map Ref: 17

WOTTON-UNDER-EDGE

Wotton Heritage Centre

The Chipping, Wotton-under-Edge GL12 7AD Tel: 01453 521541
Email: wottonhs@freeuk.com Web: www.conygres.co.uk

Local and family history, artefacts from Wotton's crafts and industries, with photographs, postcards, documents, maps and books. Also includes, research facilities, Tourist Information Point and a small shop.

Opening Times: Tue to Fri 10:00-13:00, 14:00-17:00 (16:00 in winter), Sat 10:00-13:00. Some Sun afternoons in summer 14:30-17:00. Admission: Free, small charge for research facilities. Location: In main car park.

Map Ref: 18

Hampshire is very much a naval county. The naval dockyard established in Portsmout
sheltered harbour in the seventeenth century developed enormously during the next century. T
county has a strong army tradition too. Winchester, the county town, was the capital of Wess
from the days of Alfred the Great and the capital of the whole of England from the tenth cent
until the Norman Conquest.

Hampshire and the Isle of Wight have a wealth of specialist museums and galleries together w
traditional art galleries.

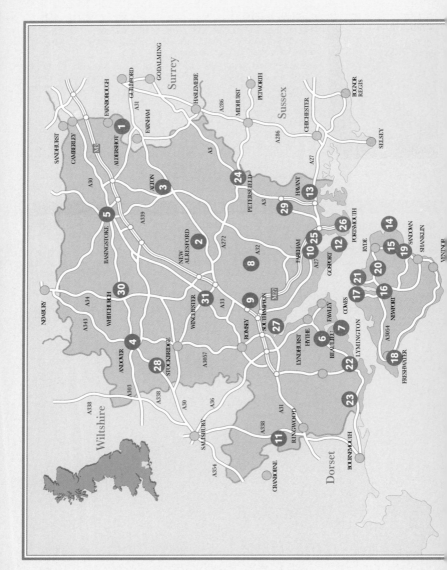

The Red Map References should be used to locate Museums etc on the pages that follow

ALDERSHOT

The Airborne Forces Museum

Browning Barracks, Aldershot GU11 2BU   Tel: 01252 349619   Fax: 01252 349203
Email: airborneforcesmuseum@army.mod.co.net

The collection covers the history of the Parachute Regiment and Airborne Forces from 1940 to the present day.

Opening Times: Daily 10:00-16:30.   Admission: Adult £3.00, Child/OAP £1.00.   Location: 15 minutes from Aldershot Railway Station.   Map Ref: 1

Aldershot Military Museum

Queens Avenue, Aldershot GU11 2LG   Tel: 01252 314598   Fax: 01252 342942
Email: musmim@hants.gov.uk   Web: www.hants.gov.uk/museum/aldshotm

Tells the story of the 'Home of the British Army'. Major new gallery refurbishment opened in October 2001 with many interactives - climb inside a Scorpion tank turret, try a Victorian soldier's bed, learn to crawl in our training tunnel and more.

Opening Times: Daily 10:00-17:00.   Admission: Adult £2.00, Concession £1.00.   Location: A short drive from junction 4 of the M3, the A331 and North Camp Railway Station.   Map Ref: 1

Army Medical Services Museum

Keogh Barracks, Ash Vale, Aldershot GU12 5RQ   Tel: 01252 868612   Fax: 01252 868832
Email: museum@keogh72.freeserve.co.uk

The Museum tells the story of medical care in the army from 1860 to the present day.

Opening Times: Mon to Fri 10:00-15:30. Closed Sat, Sun & BH.   Admission: Free.
Location: Ash Vale, 20 minute walk from Ash Vale Railway Station.   Map Ref: 1

Army Physical Training Corps Museum

Army School of Physical Training, Queen's Avenue, Aldershot GU11 2LB   Tel: 01252 347168
Fax: 01252 340785   Email: regtsec@aptc.org.uk   Web: www.aptc.org.uk

The APTC Museum was awarded full Museum Gallery Commission Registration in January 2000. The museum is an APTC and APTC Association facility and is an excellent focal and reference point for 'Corps' personnel.

Opening Times: Mon to Fri 09:30-16:00. Closed Sat, Sun & Aug.   Admission: Free. Donations welcome.   Location: On Queens Avenue, between Aldershot - North Camp entrance via Princes Avenue.   Map Ref: 1

ALRESFORD

Mid Hants Railway - Watercress Line Steam Railway

The Railway Station, Alresford SO24 9JG   Tel: 01962 733810   Fax: 01962 735448
Email: info@watercressline.co.uk   Web: www.watercressline.co.uk

Collection of railway items and archives from pre-1977.

Opening Times: Apr to Sep Sat, Sun, Tue to Thu & BH.   Admission: Adult £9.00, Child £2.00, OAP £8.00. Group rates available. Admission to Goods Shed Museum - Free.
Location: One minute walk from Alresford village.   Map Ref: 2

Museums, Galleries, Historic Houses & Sites

Please let us know of any collections that are not listed in this guide that you feel should be listed. E-mail us on *editor@tomorrows.co.uk*
or return the Report Form on page 448

Nursery Rhyme tiles in the ceramics collection

Allen Gallery

Hampshire County Council

Church Street, Alton GU34 2BW Tel: 01420 82802 Fax: 01420 84227 Email: musmtc@hants.gov.uk
Web: www.hants.gov.uk/museum/allen

The Allen Gallery houses an outstanding collection of ceramics, nearly 1900 items dating from 1250 to the present day. Highlights include the unique Elizabethan Tichborne spoons. A range of delightful watercolours and oil paintings by local artist, William Herbert Allen are also on display. There is an exciting programme of temporary exhibitions, a comfortable coffee lounge and a delightful walled garden behind the gallery.

Opening Times: Tue to Sat 10:00-17:00. Admission: Free.
Location: Town centre.   Map Ref: 3

Curtis Museum
 Hampshire County Council

High Street, Alton GU34 1BA   Tel: 01420 82802   Fax: 01420 84227
Email: musmtc@hants.gov.uk   Web: www.hants.gov.uk/museum/curtis

The renowned Anglo-Saxon Alton Buckle

One of the finest local history collections in Hampshire, exploring 100 million years of history. The wonderful array of objects includes the celebrated Roman cup found near Selborne and the impressive Anglo Saxon Alton buckle. The Gallery of Childhood is packed with toys, children's books and dolls dating back to the 18th century. Displays include prehistoric tools, local Roman pottery, Saxon burials, hop picking and brewing and local celebrities.

Opening Times: Tue to Sat 10:00-17:00.
Admission: Free. Location: Town centre.   Map Ref: 3

Jane Austen's House
Chawton, Alton GU34 1SD Tel: 01420 83262

17th century house where Jane Austen lived between 1809-17. She wrote and revised her novels here. Memorabilia of Jane Austen and her family. Donkey carriage and pretty garden.

Opening Times: Mar to Nov daily 11:00-16:30, Admission: Adult £4.00, Child 50p, Concession/Group £3.00. Location: One and a half miles south west of Alton.   Map Ref: 3

Andover Museum
 Hampshire County Council

6 Church Close, Andover SP10 1DP Tel: 01264 366283 Fax: 01264 339152 Email: musmda@hants.gov.uk Web: www.hants.gov.uk/museum/andoverm

Children's workshop in action

Flints, fossils, freshwater fish and natural habitats introduce the Andover area - detailed archaeology displays depict the rich story of human activity from the Stone Age to Saxon times. Local history episodes involve the reading of the Riot Act and an infamous Work House Scandal. The gallery has regularly changing exhibitions and the museum hosts numerous clubs and societies with a busy calendar.

Opening Times: Tue to Sat 10:00-17:00. Apr to Sep Sun and BH 14:00-17:00. Admission: Free. Location: Near St Mary's Church, three minutes walk from town centre.   Map Ref: 4

Museum of the Iron Age

6 Church Close, Andover SP10 1DP Tel: 01264 366283 Fax: 01264 339152
Email: musmda@hants.gov.uk Web: www.hants.gov.uk/museum/ironagem

Discover a way of life destroyed by the Romans. Life-sized models of weaver and warrior, reconstructed rampart and roundhouse, miniature street scene, recently excavated objects,

Hampshire & The Isle of Wight

replicas of tools, a plough, grave pits and more.

Opening Times: Tue to Sat 10:00-17:00, Apr to Sep Sun and BH 14:00-17:00.
Admission: Free. Location: Near St Mary's Church, three minutes walk from town centre.

Map Ref: 4

BASINGSTOKE

Basing House
 Hampshire County Council

Redbridge Lane, Basing, Basingstoke RG24 7HB   Tel: 01256 467294
Fax: 01256 326283   Email: musmat@hants.gov.uk
Web: www.hants.gov.uk/museum/basingho

Exploring the ruins of the Old House

Hampshire's most exciting historic ruin was once England's largest private palace, home of the Marquess of Winchester, Treasurer of Elizabeth I. His immense building covered eight acres and replaced a great Norman Castle. Civil war brought disaster to Basing which fell to the forces of Cromwell after a two year siege. Today the site, with its dovecote towers, secret tunnel, restored garden, museum and spectacular barn make an attraction of beauty and great historic interest.

Opening Times: Apr to Sep Wed to Sun and BH 14:00-16:00. Admission: Adult £1.50, Child 70p, Concessions 70p.   Location: Entrance in centre of Old Basing, short drive from Basingstoke Town Centre and junction 6 of the M3.

Map Ref: 5

The 1960s kitchen

Willis Museum
Hampshire County Council

Old Town Hall, Market Place, Basingstoke RG21 7QD   Tel: 01256 465902   Fax: 01256 471455
Email: musmst@hants.gov.uk
Web: www.hants.gov.uk/museum/willis

Discover Basingstoke's past from the rich archaeological heritage beneath our feet to a tour through the last 200 years. Meet Pickaxe, a 19th century scavenger scraping a living from the streets, and revisit the days of twin-tubs and teddy boys in the 1960s sitting room. There is always something new to see with a regularly changing programme of Special Exhibitions, children's quizzes, cafe and gifts.

Opening Times: Mon to Fri 10:00-17:00, Sat 10:0-16:00.
Admission: Free. Location: Top of town, ten minutes walk from bus/train station. Follow signs for tourist information centre.

Map Ref: 5

BEAULIEU

Beaulieu Abbey & Display of Monastic Life
Beaulieu

John Montage Building, Beaulieu SO42 7ZN   Tel: 01590 612345
Fax: 01590 612624   Email: info@beaulieu.co.uk   Web: www.beaulieu.co.uk

Palace House, once the Great Gatehouse of Beaulieu Abbey. The family home of Lord Montagu of Beaulieu, the house contains splendid rooms full of fine portraits, picture, furniture, family memorabilia and photographs. The surviving monastic buildings house an absorbing exhibition about its history and the life of worship lived there by the monks; the former refectory is now the pretty parish church.

Opening Times: May to Sep 10:00-18:00, Oct to Apr 10:00-17:00. Closed Xmas. Admission: Adult £11.95, Child £6.95, OAP £9.95, Family £33.95.

Beaulieu Abbey

Location: Beaulieu is in the heart of the New Forest.

Map Ref: 6

Bucklers Hard Village

Maritime Museum, Bucklers Hard, Beaulieu SO42 7XB   Tel: 01590 616203   Fax: 01590 616283   Email: info@bucklershard.co.uk   Web: www.bucklershard.co.uk

The historic and picturesque shipbuilding village of Bucklers Hard. After setting a course for its Maritime Museum and Historic Cottages savour the sight and sounds of the countryside on a ramble along the Riverside Walk.

Opening Times: Easter to Sep 10:30-17:00, Oct to Easter 11:00-16;00. Closed Xmas.
Admission: Adult £4.00, Child £3.00, OAP £3.00.   Location: Five minutes from the world famous National Motor Museum at Beaulieu.   Map Ref: 7

National Motor Museum

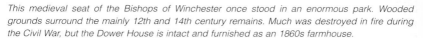

John Montagu Building, Beaulieu SO42 7ZN   Tel: 01590 612345
Fax: 01590 612624   Email: info@beaulieu.co.uk   Web: www.beaulieu.co.uk

The collection features 250 vehicles as well as memorabilia and displays. From some of the earliest examples of motoring in the 1890s to legendary World Record Breakers, 'film star' cars to family cars from the 30s, 40s and 50s. New from Easter 2002 is a stunning James Bond Boats exhibition and a sensational new Motorsport Gallery.

National Motor Museum

Opening Times: May to Sep 10:00-18:00, Oct to Apr 10:00-17:00. Closed Xmas. Admission: Adult £11.95, Child £6.95, OAP £9.95, Family £33.95.
Location: Beaulieu is in the heart of the New Forest.
Map Ref: 6

BISHOP'S WALTHAM

Bishop's Waltham Palace

Bishop's Waltham SO32 1DH   Tel: 01489 892460

This medieval seat of the Bishops of Winchester once stood in an enormous park. Wooded grounds surround the mainly 12th and 14th century remains. Much was destroyed in fire during the Civil War, but the Dower House is intact and furnished as an 1860s farmhouse.

Opening Times: Apr to Sep daily 10:00-18:00, Oct daily 10:00-17:00. Admission: Adult £2.10, Child £1.10, Concession £1.60. Location: In Bishop's Waltham, five miles from junction 8 of M27.   Map Ref: 8

EASTLEIGH

Eastleigh Museum

Hampshire County Council

The Citadel, 25 High Street, Eastleigh SO50 5LF   Tel: 023 8064 3026
Fax: 023 8065 3582   Email: musmst@hants.gov.uk
Web: www.hants.gov.uk/museum/eastlmus

Take a tour through Eastleigh's past and discover what life was like during the 1930s. Meet Mr and Mrs Brown, a local engine driver and his wife. Visit our recreation of their home, a Victorian terraced house for which Eastleigh is well known. The museum has also recreated part of the Southern Railway Locomotive Works, and a steam engine footplate. Special exhibitions, Local Studies Area, Whistle Stop Café and Gift Shop.

Local historians undertake
research for the Museum

Opening Times: Tue to Fri 10:00-17:00, Sat 10:00-16:00.
Admission: Free. Location: Town centre location, five minutes walk from bus and train station.   Map Ref: 9

Royal Armouries at Fort Nelson

Fort Nelson, Down End Road, Fareham PO17 6AN   Tel: 01329 233734
Fax: 01329 822092   Email: fnenquiries@armouries.org.uk
Web: www.armouries.org.uk

ROYAL
ARMOURIES
FORT NELSON

Wonderfully restored Victorian fortress overlooking Portsmouth harbour. Houses the National Collection of Artillery from the famous 'Gladiator' Catapult to the infamous Iraqi Supergun. Live gun firings everyday. Regular special events throughout the year, including band concert and military tattoo.

Opening Times: Apr to Oct daily 10:00-17:00, Nov to Mar 10:30-16:00. Closed 25-26 Dec. Admission: Free.
Location: Junction 11 of M27, follow brown tourist signs for Royal Armouries.   Map Ref: 10

Portisdown Artillery volunteers
with 16pr field gun.

Westbury Manor Museum

Hampshire
County Council

84 West Street, Fareham PO16 0JJ
Tel: 01329 824895 Fax: 01329 825917
Email: musmop@hants.gov.uk
Web: www.hants.gov.uk/museum/westbury

Westbury Manor Museum is housed in an impressive 18th century building in the heart of town. It unravels the history of the ancient borough of Fareham with displays on the natural, social and industrial history of the area. Highlights include The Strawberry Story, The Poor Law and the local brick industry. Exhibitions are shown in the temporary exhibitions gallery with topics ranging from contemporary art to photography and local history.

Opening Times: Mon to Fri 10:00-17:00, Sat 10:00-16:00.
Admission: Free. Location: Town centre, opposite Fareham Shopping Centre.   Map Ref: 10

The Strawberry Story

Rockbourne Roman Villa

Rockbourne, Fordingbridge SP6 3PG   Tel: 01725 518541   Email: musmjh@hants.gov.uk
Web: www.hants.gov.uk/museum/rockbourne

The remains of the largest known Roman villa in the area. Mosaics, remains of underfloor heating system and outline of forty rooms in original positions. Museum, special events and facilities for schools.

Opening Times: Apr to Sep daily 10:30-18:00. Admission: Adult £1.75, Concession 95p, Family £4.50. Location: Three miles west of Fordingbridge off the B3079.   Map Ref: 11

Gosport Museum and Gosport Gallery

Hampshire
County Council

Walpole Road, Gosport PO12 1NS   Tel: 023 9258 8035
Fax: 023 9250 1951   Email: ian.edelman@hants.gov.uk
Web: www.hants.gov.uk/museum/gosport

The Local History Gallery tells the story of the Borough from the earliest times, with fascinating objects, old photographs, archive film and life-sized costume figures. Discover more about the ground beneath your feet in the Geology Gallery, containing rare fossils and even a dinosaur footprint. The Gosport Gallery, housed in a separate building, hosts a regular programme of exhibitions from costume and textiles to photography and contemporary art.

Opening Times: Tue to Sat 10:00-17:00.
Admission: Free. Location: In town centre, a few minutes walk from ferry and bus station.   Map Ref: 12

A 200 million year old ammonite
in the Geology Gallery

Royal Navy Submarine Museum

Haslar Jetty Road, Gosport PO12 2AS   Tel: 023 92 529217/510354   Fax: 023 92 511349
Email: rnsubs@rnsubmus.co.uk   Web: www.rnsubmus.co.uk

Royal Navy Submarine Museum

Celebrate a hundred years of submarines at The Royal Navy Submarine Museum, Gosport's Premier Waterfront Tourist Attraction on Portsmouth Harbour. Step on board for a guided tour of the UK's only walk on submarine HMS Alliance. This unique attraction offers you the chance to discover stories of undersea adventure and vividly brings the heroic story of the Royal Navy's Submarine Service to life.

Opening Times: Apr to Oct 10:00-17:30, Nov to Mar 10:00-16:30. Closed Xmas & New Year. Admission: Adult £4.00, Child £2.75, OAP £2.75, Family (2 adults and 2 children) £11.00.
Location: From junction 11 on M27 follow A32. Pass the Gosport Ferry and turn left at Haslar Road. Over Haslar Bridge, the Museum is second left.   Map Ref: 12

SEARCH

50 Clarence Road, Gosport PO12 1BU   Tel: 023 9250 1957   Fax: 023 9250 1921
Email: musmjw@hants.gov.uk   Web: www.hants.gov.uk/museum/search

Hampshire Museums' hands-on education centre using real museum collections for lifelong learning. Superb facilities for schools and other groups. Open days and summer holiday workshops for families.

Opening Times: Pre-booked groups only, apart from special open days. Enquiries Mon to Fri 09:00-17:30. Admission: Special open days free, small charge for family workshops, school groups and other groups, please telephone. Location: In town centre, a few minutes walk from ferry and bus station.   Map Ref: 12

HAVANT

Havant Museum

 Hampshire County Council

56 East Street, Havant PO9 1BS   Tel: 023 9245 1155   Fax: 023 9249 8707
Email: musmcp@hants.gov.uk   Web: www.hants.gov.uk/museum/havant

The museum houses local history displays including Scalextric, Bronze Age and Roman hoards and local transport. It is the home of the nationally important Vokes Collection of Firearms. The Local Studies Collection contains an impressive range of resources and the special exhibition gallery hosts a wide range of shows from contemporary art and craft to photography and natural history.

Opening Times: Tue to Sat 10:00-17:00.
Admission: Free. Location: Short walk from town centre, next to Arts Centre.   Map Ref: 13

The contents of an old chemist's shop

ISLE OF WIGHT

Bembridge Maritime Museum & Shipwreck Centre

Providence House, Sherbourne Street, Bembridge, Isle of Wight PO35 5SB   Tel: 01983 872223
Web: www.isle-of-wight.uk.com/shipwrecks

Local history and story of Bembridge Lifeboats - past and present. Countless artefacts recovered from local shipwrecks, unique collection of ship models and much more.

Opening Times: Apr to Oct daily 10:00-17:00. Location: Centre of Bembridge village.
                                      Map Ref: 14

Brading Roman Villa

Morton Old Road, Brading, Isle of Wight PO36 0EN   Tel / Fax: 01983 406223

Large Romano British courtyard style villa, with fine mosaic floors and artefacts of Roman occupation - museum in covered west wing with large number of site finds.

Opening Times: 20 Mar to 2 Nov daily 09:30-17:00. Admission: Adult £2.95, Child/Concession £1.50, Family £7.50, Group £1.50.   Map Ref: 15

400-year-old Chamber Organ, present to Princess Beatrice

Carisbrooke Castle Museum

Newport, Isle of Wight PO30 1XY Tel: 01983 523112 Fax: 01983 536126 Email: carismus@lineone.net
Web: www.carisbrookecastlemuseum.org.uk

Accommodated inside the Castle's Great Hall, this independent museum exhibits material relating to the Castle and the history of the Isle of Wight. The Castle exhibition includes items connected with the imprisonment of King Charles I. Local history displays are changed regularly, and may feature Island places and people, and aspects of social history.

Opening Times: Apr to Sep daily 10:00-16:00, Oct 10:00-17:00, Nov to Mar 10:00-16:00. Closed Xmas & New Year.
Admission: Adult £4.60, Child £2.30, Concession £3.50, Family £11.50. Location: One mile south west of Newport. Map Ref: 16

Cowes Maritime Museum

Branch Library & Maritime Museum, Beckford Road, Cowes, Isle of Wight PO31 7SG
Tel: 01983 823433 Fax: 01983 823841 Email: tony.butler@iow.gov.uk

Ship models, photographs and real boats reflect Cowes' yachting and shipbuilding heritage. The museum holds photographs and archives from Samuel White Shipyard.

Opening Times: Mon to Wed, Fri 09:30-18:00, Sat 09:30-16:00. Admission: Free.
Location: Just off High Street, five minutes from bus and ferry terminal. Map Ref: 17

Dimbola Lodge

Terrace Lane, Freshwater Bay, Isle of Wight PO40 9QE Tel: 01983 756814 Fax: 01983 755578 Email: administrator@dimbola.co.uk Web: www.dimbola.co.uk

A permanent exhibition of Julia Margaret Cameron images together with an ongoing progress exhibition of the restoration now 4/5 complete. Revolving exhibitions of contemporary photographic art are continually staged. Original images are available for study purposes.

Opening Times: Daily 10:00-17:00 & BH. Closed Xmas. Admission: Adult £3.50, under 16 Free.
Group rates available. Location: 400 metres up from Freshwater Bay. Map Ref: 18

Dinosaur Isle

Culver Parade, Sandown, Isle of Wight PO36 8QA Tel: 01983 404344 Fax: 01983 407502
Web: www.dinosaur-isle.uk.com

Resurrects dinosaurs which lived 125 million years ago, along with their ancient habitat. Unlocks the rocky tombs of fossils and brings them together in the first ever, purpose built dinosaur attraction in Britain.

Opening Times: Apr to Oct daily 10:00-18:00, Nov to Mar daily 10:00-16:00. Admission: Adult £4.60, Child £2.60, Family £12.00. Location: Situated on the B3395 coast road at Culver Parade. Map Ref: 19

Isle of Wight Steam Railway

The Railway Station, Havenstreet, Isle of Wight PO33 4DS Tel: 01983 882204 Fax: 01983 884515 Email: hugh@iwsteamrailway.co.uk Web: www.iwsteamrailway.co.uk

A working museum of the island's railway history. A ten mile round trip in Victorian and Edwardian carriages, often hauled by a Victorian locomotive. Museum artefacts on display.

Opening Times: Apr & May Thu & Sun 10:00-16:00, Jun to Sep daily 10:00-16:00, Oct Thu, Sat & Sun 10:00-16:00. Admission: Admission & Train: Adult £7.50, Child £4.00, OAP £6.50.
Location: Havenstreet Village Station, rail served on open days. Map Ref: 20

Lilliput Antique Doll and Toy Museum

High Street, Brading, Isle of Wight PO36 0DJ Tel: 01983 407231
Email: lilliput.museum@btconnect.com Web: www.lilliputmuseum.com

One of Britain's finest and most comprehensive collections of antique dolls and toys with over 2000 exhibits dating from c.2000 BC to c.1945. All are genuine, there are no modern reproductions.

Opening Times: Daily 10:00-17:00. Closed Xmas. Admission: Adult £1.95, Child/Concession £1.00. Location: In Brading Town Centre. Map Ref: 15

Museum of Island History

The Guildhall, High Street, Newport, Isle of Wight PO30 1TY   Tel: 01983 823366   Fax: 01983 833841   Email: tony.butler@iow.gov.uk

Discover the history of the Isle of Wight from the dinosaurs to the present day, through the latest hands-on exhibits, computers and interactives. The museum also houses the Island's central Tourist Information Centre.

Admission: Adult £1.80, Child/OAP £1.00, Group £1.00.   Location: In the Guildhall, town centre of Newport. Two minute walk from bus station.   Map Ref: 16

Newport Roman Villa

c/o The Guildhall, High Street, Newport, Isle of Wight PO30 1TY   Tel: 01983 823366
Fax: 01983 823841   Email: tony.butler@iow.gov.uk

Discover the luxuries of 3rd century Roman British life. The Villa has a wonderfully preserved bath suite and reconstructed living room, kitchen and charming herb garden. Hands on activities.

Opening Times: Apr to Oct Mon to Sat 10:00-16:30, also Sun in Jul & Aug. Open for group bookings only Nov to Mar.   Admission: Adult £2.00 Child/OAP/Concession £1.20.
Location: The villa is ten minute walk from central bus station.   Map Ref: 16

Nunwell House (Aylmer Military Collection)

Brading, Isle of Wight PO36 0JQ   Tel: 01983 407240

A historic and beautifully furnished house - a family home since 1522. Special collection of one family's militaria.

Opening Times: 26 & 27 May, 1 Jul to 4 Sep Mon to Wed 13:00-17:00. Tours at 13:30, 14:30 & 15:30.   Admission: Adult £4.00, Child (under 10) £1.00, OAP £3.00.   Location: Signed on A3055. Short walk from Brading Station or bus stop.   Map Ref: 15

Osborne House

East Cowes, Isle of Wight PO32 6JY   Tel: 01983 200022

Osborne House was built for Queen Victoria and Prince Albert as a private home. The house was built by Thomas Cubitt in Italianate style and is set among terraced gardens and filled with treasured mementoes.

Opening Times: Apr to Sep 10:00-18:00, Oct daily 10:00-17:00. Please phone to check winter opening/pre-booked guided tours of house only. Closing at 16:00 21 Jul & 22 Aug
Admission: House & Grounds: Adult £7.20, Child £3.60, Concession £5.40, Family £18.00.
Grounds only: Adult £3.80, Child £1.90, Concession £2.90. Tour rates available.   Location: One mile south east of East Cowes.   Map Ref: 21

LYMINGTON

St Barbe Museum & Art Gallery

New Street, Lymington SO41 9BH   Tel: 01590 676969   Fax: 01590 679997
Email: office@stbarbe-museum.org.uk   Web: www.stbarbe-museum.org.uk

The Museum tells the story of the New Forest coastal area, with chronological and themed displays which include boat building, smuggling and the Barton Fossils. The Art Galleries feature changing art exhibitions.

Opening Times: Mon to Sat 10:00-16:00.   Admission: Adult £3.00, Concession £2.00. Group rates available.   Location: In town centre, only one minute walk from High Street.   Map Ref: 22

NEW MILTON

Sammy Miller Museum

Bashley Manor, Bashley Cross Road, New Milton BH25 5SZ   Tel: 01425 620777   Fax: 01425 619696   Web: www.sammymiller.co.uk

Sammy Miller is a legend in his own lifetime, winning competitions for 46 years. The museum houses the finest collection of fully restored motorcycles in Europe, including factory racers and exotic prototypes.

Opening Times: Daily 10:00-16:30. Closed Xmas.   Admission: Adult £3.50, Child £1.50.
Location: New Milton Hampshire off A35 at Hinton Church.   Map Ref: 23

Hampshire & The Isle of Wight

Bear Museum
38 Dragon Street, Petersfield GU31 4JJ   Tel: 01730 265108   Web: www.bearmuseum.co.uk

Established in 1984 the world's first museum of teddy bears. Housing displays of most manufacturers over the years. Also, main agent for Steiff new teddy bears. 2002 is the centenary of the teddy bear.

Opening Times: Tue to Sat 10:00-16:30. Closed Sun, Mon and BH.   Admission: Free.
Location: 100 yards south from bottom of High Street, with Tesco car park opposite. Map Ref: 24

Flora Twort Gallery

Church Path, Petersfield GU32 1HS   Tel: 01730 260756
Web: www.hants.gov.uk/museum/floratwo

A charming gallery, once the home and studio of local artist Flora Twort. It is now devoted to the display of her delightful paintings and drawings, which form a very personal record of Petersfield between the wars. The ground floor of the building has been transformed into a restaurant serving coffee, lunch and afternoon teas. It is also open for dinner on two evenings each week.

Opening Times: Tue to Sat 09:45-17:00.
Admission: Free.   Location: Town centre location.

The Flora Twort Gallery   Map Ref: 24

Portchester Castle
Castle Street, Portchester PO16 9QW   Tel: 023 9237 8291

A residence for kings, this castle has a history stretching back nearly 2000 years. Built by the Romans as a defence against barbarian attacks, Porchester became a royal castle in the medieval period. The collection includes extensive excavation material.

Opening Times: Apr to Sep daily 10:00-18:00, Oct daily 10:00-17:00, Nov to Mar daily 10:00-16:00. Closed Xmas & New Year.   Admission: Adult £3.00, Child £1.50, Concession £2.30.
Location: On south side of Portchester off A27, junction 11 on M27.   Map Ref: 25

Charles Dickens Birthplace Museum
393 Old Commercial Road, Portsmouth PO1 4QL   Tel: 023 9282 7261

Born in this modest house in 1812. Beautifully restored room settings recreate Regency life. With memorabilia, illustrations from Charles Dickens' published works, portraits of the Dickens family and the couch on which he died.

Opening Times: Apr to Sep daily 10:00-17:30, Oct daily 10:00-17:00.   Admission: Adult £2.50, Child £1.50, OAP £1.80, Family £6.50.   Location: Ten minute walk from town centre/Portsmouth & Southsea Railway Station.   Map Ref: 26

City Museum & Records Office

Museum Road, Old Portsmouth, Portsmouth PO1 2LJ   Tel: 023 9282 7261

Dedicated to local history and fine and decorative art. 'The Story of Portsmouth' displays room settings showing life in Portsmouth from the 17th century to the 1950s using modern audio-visual techniques. Experience the different life-styles of the Victorian working poor in the 'Dockyard Workers Cottage' and the affluent 'Victorian Parlour'. A 1930s kitchen with everything including the kitchen sink! A 1930s 'Art Deco' dining room and a 1950s front-room complete with flying ducks on the wall and early television showing 'Listen With Mother'. The 'Portsmouth at Play' exhibition looks at all aspects of leisure pursuits from the Victorian period to the 1970s. The museum has a fine and decorative art gallery and temporary exhibition gallery with regular changing exhibitions. The Record Office contains the official records of the City of Portsmouth from the 14th century and private and

commercial records. Collections and Exhibits of consequence: 17th Century Furniture; Art Deco Furniture - Frank Dobson Sculptures (Terracottage & Bronze), Ceri Richards Relief Work 'Le Piano', Ronald Ossory Dunlop Painting 'Still Life with Black Bottle'; JMW Turner RA watercolour 'Gosport, the Entrance to Portsmouth Harbour' c.1829. Local History: Sir Alec Rose (Round the World Yachtsman - artefacts), Verrecahias Ice Cream Parlour and artefacts.

Opening Times: Apr to Sep Daily 10:00-17:30, Oct to Mar Daily 10:00-17:00. Closed 24-26 Dec. Admission: Free. Location: Ten minute walk from the town centre/Portsmouth and Southsea Railway Station. Seven minute walk from Harbour Railway/Bus Station   Map Ref: 26

D-Day Museum and Overlord Embroidery

Clarence Esplanade, Portsmouth PO5 3NT   Tel: 023 9282 7261

Portsmouth
CITY COUNCIL

D-Day Museum Overlord Embroidery

The D-Day Museum was created to specifically commemorate the Normandy Landings on 6 June 1944 and to house the magnificent and colourful 'Overlord Embroidery' inspired by the Bayeux Tapestry. The 83 metre long embroidery depicts the moving story of 'the longest day ...' and Soundguides are available in four languages. An archive film show (in five languages) includes original footage and brings this period of the Second World War alive to the visitor. The exciting displays and exhibits recreate what it must have been like to live through this period and the events of that day. The equipment, the men who took part... its all here at the D-Day Museum. Experience life in the Anderson Shelter and the period front room of the ARP Warden. 'Listen While You Work' in the factory scene, keep vigil with the troops camped in the forest waiting their time to embark. Eavesdrop on communications in 'The Map Room', Southwick House. Board a 'Dakota' and be the first to land in a field in France and hear the story behind the crashed Horsa Glider, pass through the German pill-box and see the armada approaching the beaches and, finally, board an original landing craft of the period.

Opening Times: Apr to Sep daily 10:00-17:30, Oct to Mar daily 10:00-17:00. Closed 24-26 Dec. Admission: Adult £5.00, Child £3.00, OAP £3.75, Family £13.00. Group rates: Adult £4.25, Child £2.50, OAP £3.20, Student £2.30.   Map Ref: 26

HMS Victory

HMS Victory

Portsmouth Naval Base, Portsmouth PO1 3LJ
Tel: 023 9272 3111   Fax: 023 9272 3171
Email: enquiries@historicdockyard.co.uk
Web: www.historicdockyard.co.uk

portsmouth
HISTORIC DOCKYARD

The Royal Navy's most famous warship. She is the world's oldest commissioned ship and a proud memorial to Vice Admiral Lord Horatio Nelson, Britain's greatest Naval hero. Let loose your imagination to recreate the conditions at sea for the men and boys who lived, worked, fought and died during the battle. Follow the drama of Lord Nelson pacing the deck as battle commenced, of his fatal wounding and his death at the moment of victory. Discover how HMS Victory is being restored to her original condition prior to the Battle of Trafalgar, the bicentenary of which will be commemorated in 2005. Now experience what life was like on one of the Victory's gundecks at 'Trafalgar!' the Royal Naval Museum's explosive multi-media walk through attraction.

Opening Times: Apr to Oct 10:00-17:30, Nov to Mar 10:00-17:00. Admission: Including Royal Naval Museum - Adult £6.75, Child £5.00, OAP £6.00, Family £22.00. Location: The Historic Dockyard based at Portsmouth Harbour is five miles from junction 12 of the M27 and walking distance from Portsmouth Harbour Train/Bus Station.   Map Ref: 26

HMS Warrior 1860

Victory Gate, HM Naval Base, Portsmouth PO1
3QX Tel: 023 9277 8600

portsmouth
HISTORIC DOCKYARD

HMS Warrior 1860

HMS Warrior 1860 was launched during a period of uneasy peace between Britain and her traditional enemy, France. During her heyday she was the most formidable warship the world has ever seen. Crowds would turn up to see the new supership as she visited British ports. She never once fired a shot in anger. Her strength was her ability to keep the peace. Today she looks just as she did at the time of her first commission (1861-1864). Bigger, faster and more heavily armed than any other warship afloat, Warrior was the world's first iron hulled armoured battleship. She was powered by steam as well as sail and constructed of wrought iron. Almost overnight, Warrior had made every other warship obsolete. When you step aboard HMS Warrior 1860 you will catch a glimpse of life in a 19th century warship - as though the crew had gone ashore leaving everything ready for inspection.

Opening Times: Apr to Oct 10:00-17:30, Nov to Mar 10:00-17:00. Admission: Adult £6.25, Child £4.75, OAP £5.50, Family £20.50. Location: The Historic Dockyard based at Portsmouth Harbour is five miles from junction 12 of the M27 and walking distance from Portsmouth Harbour Train/Bus Station. Map Ref: 26

Mary Rose Museum

HM Naval Base, Portsmouth PO1 3LJ Tel: 023 9275 0521
Fax: 023 9287 0588

portsmouth
HISTORIC DOCKYARD

The Mary Rose

The Mary Rose, built between 1510-1511, lost in 1545. For many years, the Mary Rose was Henry VIIIs favourite warship, fast and successful, and yet she sank - on a fine summer day as she sailed into action against the French fleet. Amateur divers found the site and began the world's largest underwater excavation. Millions watched on television in October 1982, as she was raised to the surface and brought safely back to her home port to begin the long process of conservation. Come and see this extraordinary shipwreck being treated with polyethylene glycol - a water based wax solution - to preserve it for all time. Visit the museum and marvel not only at the cannon, longbows, gold and coins, but also at the wooden bowls, tankards and game boards that belonged to the ordinary soldiers and sailors on board. Over 1,200 objects are on display, miraculously preserved by the fine silts beneath the Solent. Together they present a unique picture of the men of the Mary Rose and the ship in which they lived, fought and died.

Opening Times: Apr to Oct 10:00-17:30, Nov to Mar 10:00-17:00. Admission: Adult £6.25, Child £4.75, OAP £5.50, Family £20.50. Location: The Historic Dockyard based at Portsmouth Harbour is five miles from junction 12 of the M27 and walking distance from Portsmouth Harbour Train/Bus Station. Map Ref: 26

Natural History Museum & Butterfly House

Cumberland House, Eastern Parade, Southsea, Portsmouth PO4 9RF Tel: 023 9282 7261

Wildlife dioramas and geology of the Portsmouth area, it has a full size reconstruction of Dinosaur 'Iguanodon' and other fossil remains. During the summer months, British and European butterflies flying free.

Opening Times: Apr to Sep daily 10:00-17:30, Oct to Mar daily 10:00-17:00. Closed 24-26 Dec. Admission: Apr to Oct: Adult £2.50, Child £1.50, OAP £1.80, Family £6.50. Nov to Mar: Adult £2.00, Child £1.20, OAP £1.50, Family £5.20. Location: Situated Canoe Lake area, nearest bus stop - Festing Road. Map Ref: 26

Royal Marines Museum

Eastney Esplanade, Southsea, Portsmouth PO4 9PX Tel: 023 9281 9385 Fax: 023 9283 8420
Email: info@royalmarinesmuseum.co.uk Web: www.royalmarinesmuseum.co.uk

An award winning museum that helps you discover the exciting 330 year story of the Royal Marines through dramatic and interactive displays. Visit the Museum at what was one of the most stately Officers' Messes in England and tour its world famous medal collection.

Opening Times: Jun to Aug daily 10:00-17:00, Sep to May daily 10:00-16:30.
Admission: Adult £4.00, Child £2.25, OAP £3.00, Family £12.00. Location: On the seafront, about one mile east of South Parade Pier. Map Ref: 26

Royal Naval Museum

HM Naval Base, Portsmouth PO1 3NH Tel: 023 9272 7562

Royal Naval Museum - Facing HMS Victory is the Royal Naval Museum. Located in magnificent Georgian storehouses, the museum contains a rich collection of artefacts including ship models, figureheads, swords, uniforms, medals and fine paintings. After a major Lottery-funded redevelopment, the Royal Naval Museum proudly presents four award-winning exhibitions. Trafalgar - the most thrilling, true to life recreation ever of the great sea battles of 1805. Learn how the Royal Navy outwitted Napoleon. Brave the sights and sounds of HMS Victory's gundeck as the fleet goes in to action. Discover a spectacular panorama of the Battle by famous Portsmouth artist, W L Wylie. The Story of HMS Victory - sail the ship and fire her cannons, meet her crew and learn about their many tasks on board. Discover the skills needed to restore a 200 year old ship of the line, plus warship figureheads and unique views over Portsmouth Harbour. Horatio Nelson: The Hero and the Man - Audio-visual presentations, interactive exhibits and some of Nelson's most personal treasures tell the story of one of Britain's greatest heroes as it has never been told before. The Sailing Navy - a thrilling interactive exhibition where the whole family can discover life aboard an 18th century warship. Climb into a leager barrel, let out the sails, weigh up a musket and fight your very own battle at the helm of a 74-gun ship.

Opening Times: Apr to Oct 10:00-17:30, Nov to Mar 10:00-17:00. Admission: Adult £3.50, Child £2.00, OAP £3.00, Family £10.50. Location: The Historic Dockyard based at Portsmouth Harbour is five miles from junction 12 of the M27 and walking distance from Portsmouth Harbour Train/Bus Station. Map Ref: 26

Southsea Castle

Clarence Esplanade, Southsea, Portsmouth PO5 3PA Tel: 023 9282 7261

Built by Henry VIII in 1544 to protect Portsmouth Harbour. Military history from Tudor times to the Victorians. 'Time Tunnel Experience' showing 'Life in the Castle', underground passages and audio-visual presentation.

Opening Times: Apr to Sep daily 10:00-17:30, Oct daily 10:00-17:00. Admission: Adult £2.50, Child £1.50, OAP £1.80, Family £6.50. Location: Situated on Southsea Seafront. Nearest bus stop - Palmerston Road. Map Ref: 26

Treadgold Industrial Heritage Museum

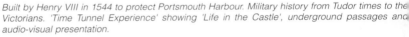

Hampshire
County Council

1 Bishop Street, Portsea, Portsmouth PO1 3DA Tel: 023 9282 4745
Fax: 023 9283 7310 Email: lawton@treadgoldm33.freeserve.co.uk
Web: www.hants.gov.uk/museum/treadgold

This 'Victorian time capsule' comprises an ironmonger's shop and storerooms, offices, stable, workshop with forges and a reconstructed tenement c.1810. A rare industrial archaeological site, it houses an entire collection of tools, machinery, office paperwork and shop stock at its original location. The listed collection of buildings dates to 1706.

Opening Times: Apr to Sep Thu to Fri 10:00-16:00. Schools and other groups, by appointment, weekdays throughout the year. Admission: Free. Location: Near Portsmouth historic dockyard, three minute walk from rail and bus station. Map Ref: 26

The forge workshop

SOUTHAMPTON

Bursledon Windmill

Windmill Lane, Bursledon, Southampton SO31 8BG Tel: 023 8040 4999
Email: musmgb@hants.gov.uk Web: www.hants.gov.uk/museum/windmill

Hampshire's only working windmill, built in 1813 and lovingly restored. Wooden machinery, traditional timber-framed barn and granary. Stoneground flour made and sold to visitors. Nature trail and special events. Teachers pack.

Opening Times: May to Sep Sat & Sun 10:00-16:00, Oct to Apr Sun 10:00-16:00.
Admission: Adult £1.50, Concession 75p, Family £3.75.   Location: Short drive from junction 8 of the M27.
Map Ref: 27

John Hansard Gallery

University of Southampton, Highfield, Southampton SO17 1BJ   Tel: 023 8059 2158   Fax: 023 8059 4192   Email: hansard@soton.ac.uk

Around six contemporary visual art exhibitions per year lasting approximately seven weeks each. University collection. Sculpture trail.

Opening Times: Tue to Fri 11:00-17:00 Sat 11:00-16:00. Please contact Gallery for Easter & Xmas closures. Admission: Free. Location: On the west side of the University of Southampton, next to the Turner Sims Concert Hall and Student Health Centre.   Map Ref: 27

Museum of Archaeology

Gods House Tower, Winkle Street, Southampton SO14 2NY   Tel: 023 8063 5904
Fax: 023 8033 9601   Email: k.wardley@southampton.gov.uk
Web: www.southampton.gov.uk/leisure/museums

One of the top designated archaeology collections in the county. The displays use finds from excavations within the city. Highlights include colourful imported pottery and glass from the medieval port, evidence of international trade and local industry from Saxon Hamwick and objects from everyday life in Roman Clausentum. Activities for children include puzzles, 'try on toga' and mosaic making.

Opening Times: First Sat of each month 13:00-16:00 or for groups by appointment. Admission: Free.

Gods House Museum, main hall

Location: In old town area, near Isle of Wight ferry terminal, five minutes walk from West Quay Shopping Centre.
Map Ref: 27

Southampton City Art Gallery

Civic Centre, Southampton SO14 7LP   Tel: 023 8083 2277   Fax: 023 8083 2153
Email: art.gallery@southampton.gov.uk   Web: www.southampton.gov.uk/leisure/arts

The most outstanding gallery in the south of England, internationally renowned for its collection of contemporary works by British artists. The collection numbers over 3500 works and spans six centuries of European art history. The gallery presents four major temporary exhibitions a year, which range from historic to contemporary art.

Opening Times: Tue to Sat 10:00-17:00, Sun 13:00-16:00. Closed Mon. Admission: Free. Location: City centre, five minute walk from railway station, opposite Watts Park, in Commercial Road.
Map Ref: 27

Galley 3, Southampton City Art Gallery

Southampton Maritime Museum

Wool House, Bugle Street, Southampton SO14 2AR
Tel: 023 8022 3941   Fax: 023 8033 9601
Email: historic.sites@southampton.gov.uk
Web: www.southampton.gov.uk/leisure/museums

The Wool House was built as a Warehouse for the medieval wool trade. It is now a museum telling the story of the port of Southampton and the great liners that sailed from here to all parts of the world. Highlights include Titanic Voices Exhibition, telling the real story of the Titanic through original artefacts and the voices of local people whose lives were affected by the tragedy.

Opening Times: Tue to Fri 10:00-13:00 & 14:00-17:00, Sat 10:00-13:00 & 14:00-16:00, Sun 14:00-17:00. Admission: Free.

Enjoy a memorable day at the Southampton Maritime Museum

Location: Corner of Bingle Street and Town Quay Road, five minutes walk from West Quay Shopping Centre.
Map Ref: 27

Tudor House Museum

Bugle Street, Southampton SO14 2AD   Tel: 023 8063 5904   Fax: 023 8033 9601
Email: historic.sites@southampton.gov.uk   Web: www.southampton.gov.uk/leisure/museums

Tudor House was built in 1495. You can find out more about the history of this fascinating building through the lives of the people who lived here. Enjoy a stroll through the reconstructed 16th century knot garden.

Opening Times: Tue to Fri 10:00-12:00 & 13:00-17:00, Sat 10;00-12:00 & 13:00-16:00, Sun 14:00-17:00. Admission: Free. Location: Bugle Street, five minutes walk from West Quay Shopping Centre.
Map Ref: 27

STOCKBRIDGE

Museum of Army Flying

Middle Wallop, Stockbridge SO20 8DY   Tel: 01980 674421   Fax: 01264 781694
Email: enquiries@flying-museum.org.uk   Web: www.flying-museum.org.uk

The collection incorporates over 100 years of army aviation from the first manned balloons and kites of the 1880s, through aircraft and artefacts of both world wars to post war helicopters.

Opening Times: Daily 10:00-16:30. Admission: Adult £4.80, Child £3.20, Concession £3.80. Group rates available. Location: On the A343 between Andover and Salisbury.   Map Ref: 28

WATERLOOVILLE

Goss & Crested China Centre

62 Murray Road, Horndean, Waterlooville PO8 9JL   Tel: 023 925 97440

A vast display of Victorian and Edwardian crested china souvenir ware made in the Staffordshire Potteries between 1860 and 1939. These include World War I, animals, miniatures, cottages, parian busts of royalty, politicians etc.

Opening Times: Mon to Sat 09:00-17:00. Closed Sun & BH. Admission: Free. Location: Nine miles from Portsmouth, nine miles from Petersfield.
Map Ref: 29

WHITCHURCH

Whitchurch Silk Mill

28 Winchester Street, Whitchurch RG28 7AL   Tel: 01256 892065
Email: silkmill@btinternet.com   Web: whitchurchsilkmill.org.uk

Traditional Silk Making at Whitchurch Silk Mill

This delightful Grade II watermill built on the river Test in 1800 has produced silk continuously since the 1820s. Now a working museum it keeps alive the art of making silk on machinery installed between 1890 and 1950. It used to produce silk for lining Burberry raincoats and for legal and academic gowns and weaves short runs for theatrical costume and historic houses.

Opening Times: Tue to Sun 10:30-17:00, also BH Mon. Last admission 16:15. Closed 24 Dec to 2 Jan. Admission: Adult £3.50, Child £1.75, OAP/Student £3.00. Location: Near town centre, 15 minute walk from rail station.
Map Ref: 30

Museums, Galleries, Historic Houses & Sites

Please let us know of any collections that are not listed in this guide that you feel should be listed. E-mail us on *editor@tomorrows.co.uk* or return the Report Form on page 448

Guildhall Gallery

Broadway, Winchester SO23 9LJ   Tel: 01962 848289   Email: museums@winchester.gov.uk
Web: www.winchester.gov.uk/heritage

Frequently changing programme of exciting exhibitions of paintings, craft, photography, ceramics and sculpture.

Opening Times: During exhibitions: Apr to Oct Mon to Sat 10:00-17:00, Sun 14:00-17:00. Nov to Mar Tue to Sat 10:00-16:00, Sun 14:00-16:00.   Admission: Free.   Location: The Broadway, situated in the Victorian Guildhall above the Tourist Information Centre.   Map Ref: 31

The Gurkha Museum

Peninsula Barracks, Romsey Road, Winchester
SO23 8TS   Tel: 01962 842832/843657
Fax: 01962 877597   Email: curator@thegurkhamuseum.co.uk
Web: www.the gurkhamuseum.co.uk

A unique commemoration of Gurkha service to the British Crown and people spanning 190 years, two world wars and numerous smaller campaigns. There is much about Nepal, its people, culture, arts and customs.

Opening Times: Mon to Sat 10:00-17:00 Sun 12:00-16:00. Closed Xmas & New Year.   Admission: Adult £1.50, Child/OAP 75p. Group 50p per person.   Location: Town centre, near Great Hall.
                                                                     Map Ref: 31

The King's Royal Hussars Museum in Winchester

Peninsula Barracks, Romsey Road, Winchester SO23 8TS   Tel: 01962 828541/828539
Fax: 01962 828538   Email: beresford@krhmuseum.freeserve.co.uk   Web: www.krh.org.uk

Story of famous cavalry regiments; 10th Royal Hussars (Prince of Wales' Own) and 11th Hussars (Prince Albert's Own) 'The Cherry Pickers' raised in 1715. The Royal Hussars 1969-1992 and today's regiment, The King's Royal Hussars from 1992. See the Charge of the Light Brigade, experience World War I trench, and see the cupboard in which Private Fowler was hidden in a French farm for three years during World War I.

The diary of The Charge of The Light Brigade by RSM Loy Smith

Opening Times: Tue to Fri 10:00-12:45 13:15-16:00 Sat, Sun, BH and half term Mon 12:00-16:00.

Admission: Free.   Location: Beside Great Hall/Law Courts.
                                                                     Map Ref: 31

Light Infantry Museum

Peninsula Barracks, Romsey Road, Winchester SO23 9PZ   Tel: 01962 828550
Fax: 01962 828534

A collection which depicts the Light Infantry Regiment, its origins, soldiers and operations. Particular displays are the Berlin Wall, Northern Ireland, Gulf War and Sir John Moore.

Opening Times: Tue to Sat and BH Mon/school holiday Mon 10:00-16:00 (closed for lunch). Sun 12:00-16:00.   Admission: Free, but donations welcome.   Location: Top of town, behind the Great Hall and five minutes from railway station.   Map Ref: 31

Royal Green Jackets

Peninsula Barracks, Romsey Road, Winchester SO23 8TS   Tel: 01962 828549   Fax: 01962 828500   Email: museum@royalgreenjackets.co.uk   Web: www.royalgreenjackets.co.uk

A unique collection of uniforms, weapons, silver, paintings, sporting and other artefacts spanning 250 years. Displays of campaigns over five continents, including a magnificent diorama of the Battle of Waterloo.

Opening Times: Mon to Sat 10:00-13:00, 14:00-17:00, Sun 12:00-16:00. Closed Xmas & New Year.   Admission: Adult £2.00, Child £1.00, OAP £1.00.   Location: North of the town centre, a five minute walk from main line railway station.   Map Ref: 31

Royal Hampshire Regiment Museum & Memorial Garden

Serle's House, Southgate Street, Winchester SO23 9EG   Tel: 01962 863658   Fax: 01962 888302

History of the regiment 1702 to 1992. Medals, uniforms, colours, weapons and many persona artefacts. Covers regulars, Volunteers, Territorials and Militia.

Opening Times: Mon to Fri 11:00-15:30. Closed 2 weeks Xmas & New Year. Weekends & BH Apr to Oct only 12:00-16:00. Admission: Free. Location: Near town centre, two minute walk from high street.   Map Ref: 3

Westgate

High Street, Winchester   Tel: 01962 848269   Email: museums@winchester.gov.uk
Web: www.winchester.gov.uk/heritage

Medieval gateway. Former debtors' prison. Contains: prisoners' graffiti, unique collection c weights & measures, armour, Tudor ceiling from Winchester College. Brass rubbing. Rooftop cit views.

Opening Times: Apr to Oct Mon to Sat 10:00-17:00, Sun 12:00-17:00. Feb to Mar Tue to Sat 10:00-16:00, Sun 12:00-16:00. Closed Nov to Jan. Admission: Free. Location: High Street, close to Great Hall.   Map Ref: 3

Winchester City Museum

The Square, Winchester   Tel: 01962 848269   Email: museums@winchester.gov.uk
Web: www.winchester.gov.uk/heritage

Tells the story of Winchester, important Roman town, and principal city of King Alfred, Anglo-Saxoi and Norman England, through to modern times with reconstructed Victorian shops.

Opening Times: Apr to Oct Mon to Sat 10:00-17:00, Sun 12:00-17:00. Nov to Mar Tue to Sat 10:00-16:00, Sun 12:00-14:00. Admission: Free. Location: The Square, between High Street and the Cathedral.   Map Ref: 3

region boasts some singularly handsome towns including Hereford, once the capital of the
verful Anglo-Saxon kingdom of Mercia and now home to the magnificent twelfth century
nedral which towers over the banks of the River Wye. Worcester too has its proud history,
ng an important centre during the Civil War. The Cotswolds in the east offer magnificent views
inspired much of the music of Sir Edward Edgar.

re are a number of excellent museums and galleries dealing with this rich region.

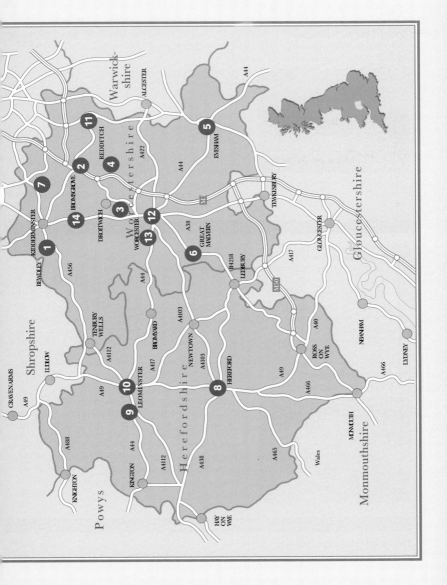

The Red Map References should be used to locate Museums etc on the pages that follow

BEWDLEY *Worcs*

Bewdley Museum   ♿ ◈

The Shambles, Load Street, Bewdley DY12 2AE   Tel: 01299 403573   Fax: 01299 404740
Email: museum-wfd@online.rednet.co.uk

Housed in the town's old Butchers Shambles, the museum provides a fascinating insight into the growth and trades of the town. Displays feature the work of basket and besom makers, charcoal burners, pewterers and brass founders. Daily craft demonstrations.

Opening Times: Apr to Sep daily 11:00-17:00, Oct 11:00-16:00.   Admission: Adult £2.00, Child Free, OAP/Concession £1.00.   Location: Bewdley - off the A456 Leominster Road, on the B4190.
Map Ref: 1

Severn Valley Railway   ✍ ♿ ◈ ▯ ♿

The Railway Station, Bewdley DY12 1BG   Tel: 01299 403816   Fax: 01299 400839   Web: www.svr.co.uk

Loco 3442 crossing
River Severn on Victoria Bridge

A standard-gauge steam railway running between Kidderminster and Bridgnorth, 16 miles. The journey provides fine views of the River Severn and visitors can alight at any of the four intermediate stations. Refreshments at main stations and on most trains. Special events throughout the year. The railway is home to one of the largest collections of pre-nationalisation locomotives, coaches and wagons.

Opening Times: Every Sat & Sun. daily 4 May to 29 Sep, Feb, Apr, Oct and local school holidays.
Admission: Adult £10.00, Child £5.00, OAP £8.00, Family £27.00.   Location: On A448 Comberton Hill. Signposted from all major roads.
Map Ref: 1

BROMSGROVE *Worcs*

Avoncroft Museum of Historic Buildings   ✍ ♿ ◈ ▯ ♿

Stoke Heath, Bromsgrove B60 4JR   Tel: 01527 831363   Fax: 01527 876934
Email: avoncrofteducation@compuserve.com   Web: www.avoncroft.org.uk

Collection of over 25 historic buildings, including windmill, prefab and church. Includes the National Telephone Kiosk collection.

Opening Times: Mar & Nov Tue to Thu, Sat & Sun 10:30-16:00. Apr to Jun, Sep to Oct Tue to Fri 10:30-16:30. Jul & Aug Mon to Fri 10:30-17:00, Sat & Sun 10:30-17:30.   Admission: Adult £5.20, Child £2.60, Concession £4.20, Family £14.00. Party rates available.   Location: Three miles north of junction 5, M5, three miles south of junction 1, M42. Off A38, south of Bromsgrove.
Map Ref: 2

Bromsgrove Museum   ✍ ◈ ♿

26 Birmingham Road, Bromsgrove B61 1DD   Tel / Fax: 01527 831809

Bromsgrove Museum gives an insight into local history with displays of past craft and industries such as nail, glass, lead, button and salt making. Also incorporated into the Museum is a street of Victorian and Edwardian shops, including a chemists, stationers and cobblers. There are also displays on The Bromsgrove Guild and AE Housman.

Opening Times: Mon to Sat 10:30-12:30 13:00-16:30.
Admission: Free.   Location: Near town centre, on Birmingham Road.
Map Ref: 2

An old workshop at the Museum

DROITWICH SPA *Worcs*

Droitwich Heritage Centre   ✍ ♿ ◈

St Richard's House, Victoria Square, Droitwich Spa WR9 8DS   Tel: 01905 774312   Fax: 01905 794226

See the fascinating history of Droitwich from prehistoric Salt Town to luxury Spa. BBC Radio room with hands-on display. Brass rubbing, Tourist Information Centre and souvenirs.

Herefordshire & Worcestershire

Opening Times: Mon to Sat 10:00-16:00. Close Sun and BH. Admission: Free. Location: Town centre location, ten minute walk from rail station. Map Ref: 3

Hanbury Hall

School Road, Hanbury, Droitwich Spa WR9 7EA   Tel: 01527 821214   Fax: 01527 821251
Email: hanbury@smtp.ntrust.org.uk   Web: www.ntrustsevern.org.uk

Beautiful English country house with tranquil reconstructed 18th century gardens and parkland. Many unusual features including outstanding staircase murals, working mushroom house and orangery, Watney Collection of fine porcelain and Dutch flower paintings.

Opening Times: 24 Mar to 30 Oct, Sun to Wed - gardens, tearoom, shop 12:00-17:30, hall 13:30-17:30. Admission: House & Garden: Adult £4.60, Child £2.30, Family £11.50, Group £4.10. Garden only: Adult £2.90, Child £1.50. Location: Junction 5 on M5, four and a half miles east of Droitwich off B4090. Map Ref: 4

EVESHAM *Worcs*

The Almonry Heritage Centre

Abbey Gate, Evesham WR11 5DY   Tel: 01386 446944   Fax: 01386 442348
Email: tic@almonry.ndo.co.uk   Web: www.evesham.uk.com

Exhibits relating to Evesham Abbey 709-1540, Battle of Evesham 1265. Agricultural and social history - Anglo Saxon treasure, archaeology, children's activities.

Opening Times: Mon to Sat 10:00-17:00, Sun 14:00-17:00. Closed Sun Nov, Dec & Jan. Admission: Adult £2.00, Child Free, OAP/Concession £1.00. Map Ref: 5

GREAT MALVERN *Worcs*

Malvern Museum

Priory Gatehouse, Abbey Road, Great Malvern WR14 3ES   Tel: 01684 567811

The museum is located in the ancient Priory Gatehouse. It takes visitors from the earliest Iron Age settlements, through to the Medieval community, the arrival of the Water Cure, Victorian enterprise and the scientific advances made by radar research.

Opening Times: Easter to Oct daily 10:30-17:00. Closed Wed in term time. Admission: Adult £1.00, Child under 7 Free, Concession 20p,. Location: In town centre, close to Tourist Office and main Post Office. Map Ref: 6

HAGLEY *Worcs*

Hagley Hall

Hagley DY9 9LG   Tel: 01562 882408   Fax: 01562 882632

Grade I Georgian House set in Grade I Park. Containing a fine collection of 18th century portraits and furniture. Hagley Hall is the home of Viscount and Viscountess Cobham.

Opening Times: 3 to 27 Jan, 4 to 24 Feb, 1 to 8 Mar, 1 to 9 Apr, 25 to 29 Aug 14:00-17:00. Closed all Sat. Admission: Adult £3.50, Child £1.50, Concession £2.50. Location: One mile from Hagley Station. Map Ref: 7

HEREFORD

Cider Museum & King Offa Distillery

21 Ryelands Street, Hereford HR4 0LW   Tel: 01432 354207   Fax: 01432 371641
Email: info@cidermuseum.co.uk   Web: www.cidermuseum.co.uk

The history of traditional cidermaking worldwide portrayed through our reconstructed farm ciderhouse, original Champagne Cider cellars, vat house, cooper's workshop and a working distillery producing King Offa Cider Brandy.

Opening Times: Apr to Oct daily 10:00-17:30, Nov to Dec daily 11:00-15:00, Jan to Mar Tue to Sun 11:00-15:00. Admission: Adult £2.60, Concession £2.10. Group rates available. Location: West side of Hereford, on A438 Brecon Road, near Sainsburys. Map Ref: 8

Hereford Museum & Art Gallery

Hereford Museum & Art Gallery   ♿

Broad Street, Hereford HR4 9AU   Tel: 01432 260692
Fax: 01432 342492   Web: www.herefordshire.gov.uk

Hereford Museum displays 'A Sense of Place', a permanent exhibition which gives an insight to the country of Herefordshire. Included are objects from collections on argriculture, landscape, folklore, schooldays and cooking. Included are community cases with changing displays, an observation beehive and hands-on displays for children. The Art Gallery houses a varied programme of temporary exhibitions on art, craft, photography and other themes.

Opening Times: Tue to Sat 10:00-17:00, Sun (Apr to Sep) 10:00-16:00, BH Mon 10:00-16:00. Closed Mon, Xmas & New Year and Good Friday.   Admission: Free.   Location: In the town centre, opposite the cathedral.   Map Ref: 8

Mappa Mundi & Chained Library

5 College Cloisters, Cathedral Close, Hereford HR1 2NG   Tel: 01432 374202
Fax: 01432 374220

The Mappa Mundi and Chained Library Exhibition is open all year round and is famous for housing both the spectacular medieval map of the world and the cathedral's unique Chained Library. Here the stories of these national treasurers are told through models, original artefacts and the latest interactive computer technology.

Opening Times: Summer: Mon to Sat 10:00-16:15, Sun 11:00-15:15. Winter: Mon to Sat 11:00-15:15, closed Sun.   Admission: Adult £4.00, Under 5s Free, Concession £3.50, Family £10.00.   Map Ref: 8

Old House

High Town, Hereford HR1 2AA   Tel: 01432 260694   Fax: 01432 342492
Web: www.herefordshire.gov.uk

Built in 1621, one of Hereford's finest timber-framed building, the last remaining from Butcher's Row. Furnished in 17th century style on three floors, the house includes a kitchen, hall and bedrooms.

Opening Times: Tue to Sat 10:00-17:00, Sun (Apr to Sep) 10:00-16:00, BH Mon 10:00-14:00. Closed Mon, Xmas & New Year and Good Friday.   Admission: Free.   Location: In the pedestrian area of the High Town at the heart of the city.   Map Ref: 8

LEOMINSTER *Herefs*

Burton Court

Eardisland, Leominster HR6 9DN   Tel: 01544 388231   Email: helenjsimpson@hotmail.com
Web: www.burtoncourt.co.uk

14th century Great Hall, European and Oriental costumes, ship models, natural history specimens, working model fairground. Archaeology dig.

Opening Times: Spring BH to end Sep Wed, Thu, Sat, Sun & BH 14:30-18:00.
Admission: Adult £3.50, Child £2.00, Groups £3.00.   Location: Near Leominster, five miles on A44.   Map Ref: 9

Leominster Folk Museum

Etnam Street, Leominster HR6 8AL   Tel: 01568 615186   Email: sallywhitfield@lineone.net

The purpose of Leominster Folk Museum is to collect, display and preserve local material for the education and enjoyment of the public.

Opening Times: Easter to Oct Mon to Fri 10:30-16:00, Sat 10:30-13:00. Open BH.
Admission: Free.   Location: Near town centre.   Map Ref: 10

Forge Mill Museum & Bordesley Abbey

Needle Mill Lane, Riverside, Redditch B98 8HY Tel: 01527 62509
Email: museum@redditch.gov.uk Web: www.redditchbc.gov.uk

Industrial museum with unique displays and collections telling the fascinating story of how needles are made. Also archaeological site museum with children's activities showing finds from the adjacent Cistercian Abbey of Bordesley.

Opening Times: Easter to Sep Mon to Fri 11:00-16:30, Sat & Sun 14:00-17:00. Feb to Easter & Oct to Nov Mon to Thu 11:00-16:00, Sun 14:00-17:00. Admission: Adult £3.50, Child 50p, OAP £2.50. Pre-booked Group rates available. Location: Off A441 Birmingham to Evesham road; junction 2 on M42. Located just north of Redditch Town Centre. Map Ref: 11

Commandery

Sidbury, Worcester WR1 2HU Tel: 01905 361821 Fax: 01905 361822
Email: thecommandery@cityofworcester.gov.uk
Web: www.worcestercitymuseums.org.uk

The commandery is the most important secular building in Worcester dating back nearly 1000 years. As well as period rooms such as the Great Hall and Painted Chamber there are exhibitions on the building's past and the English Civil War, when the building served as the Royalist Headquarters at the Battle of Worcester in 1651.

King Charles II at the
Commandery's Oak Apple Day

Opening Times: Mon to Sat 10:00-17:00, Sun 13:30-17:00. Admission: Charges apply. Location: Two minute walk from Worcester Cathedral. Map Ref: 12

The Elgar Birthplace Museum

Crown East Lane, Lower Broadheath, Worcester WR2 6H. Tel: 01905 333224 Fax: 01905 333426 Email: birthplace@elgar.org Web: www.elgar.org

A fascinating insight into the life and music, family and friends, inspirations and musical development of one of Britain's greatest composers, Sir Edward Elgar. Historic birthplace cottage in pretty garden. New exhibition and special events in the Elgar Centre, opened in 2000.

Opening Times: Daily 11:00-17:00. Closed Xmas to end Jan. Admission: Adult £3.50, Child £1.75, Concession £3.00, Family £8.75. Reduction for pre-booked groups. Location: Three miles west of Worcester, signposted off Worcester/Leominster road. Map Ref: 13

Museum of Local Life

Friar Street, Worcester WR1 2NA Tel: 01905 722349 Email: nburnett@cityofworcester.gov.uk

Small community museum depicting everyday lives of Worcester people in the past. Victorian kitchen, school room.

Opening Times: Mon to Wed, Fri & Sat 10:30-17:00. Admission: Free. Location: Five minutes from Cathedral. Map Ref: 12

Museum of Worcester Porcelain

Severn Street, Worcester WR1 2NE Tel: 01905 23221 Fax: 01905 617807
Email: museum@royal-worcester.co.uk Web: www.royal-worcester.co.uk

Travel on a design journey through time and see rare porcelain sumptuously displayed in period room settings and dining scenes in the Georgian, Victorian and 20th Century galleries.

Opening Times: Mon to Sat 09:00-17:30, Sun 11:00-17:00. Admission: Adult £3.00, Concession £2.25. Location: Two minute walk from Worcester Cathedral and town centre. Map Ref: 12

The beautiful Victorian building that
houses the collections

Worcester City Museum & Art Gallery

Foregate Street, Worcester WR1 1DT
Tel: 01905 25371   Fax: 01905 616979
Email: artgalleryandmuseum@cityofworcester.gov.uk
Web: www.worcestercitymuseums.org.uk

Housed in a beautiful Victorian building, the City Museum & Art Gallery runs a lively programme of exhibitions, activities and events for all the family. Explore the fascinating historic displays or drop in and see one of our contemporary art exhibitions. Visit our award winning café, gallery shop, children's activity area and museums of the Worcestershire Regiment and Yeomanry.

Opening Times: Mon to Fri 09:30-17:30, Sat 09:30-17:00. Closed Sun. Admission: Free. Location: Town centre, 150 yards from Foregate Street Railway Station. Map Ref: 12

Hartlebury Castle, home of the
WCM and Bishops of Worcester

Worcestershire County Museum

WORCESTERSHIRE COUNTY MUSEUM
HARTLEBURY · CASTLE

Hartlebury Castle, Hartlebury, Worcester DY11 7XZ   Tel: 01299 250416   Fax: 01299 251890
Email: museum@worcestershire.gov.uk

Housed in the sandstone home of the Bishops of Worcester for over a thousand years, the County Museum illustrates local life from the Roman period until the 20th century. Particular exhibits include reconstructed cider mill, horse-drawn transport, female costume and social history from the Victorian and Edwardian eras.

Opening Times: Feb to Nov Mon to Thu 10:00-17:00, Fri & Sun 14:00-17:00. Closed Sat & Good Friday. Other BH in season 11:00-17:00. Admission: Adult £2.50, Child/Concession £1.20, Family £6.50. Location: Four miles south of Kidderminster, signed from A449 Worcester Road. Map Ref: 14

t, the closest county to the continent, through which a host of armies poured including the
an armies of Julius Caesar, the Saxon hordes of Horsa and Hengist and on a quieter note,
sionaries from Rome on their way to Canterbury, the spiritual capital of England. Long known
e 'Garden of England', this pleasant region has always attracted the powerful and wealthy to
d their manors and mansions here.

endid and varied museums together with historic houses cover Roman occupation, naval
ory through to the Second World War, and encompass Charles Darwin to Charles Dickens

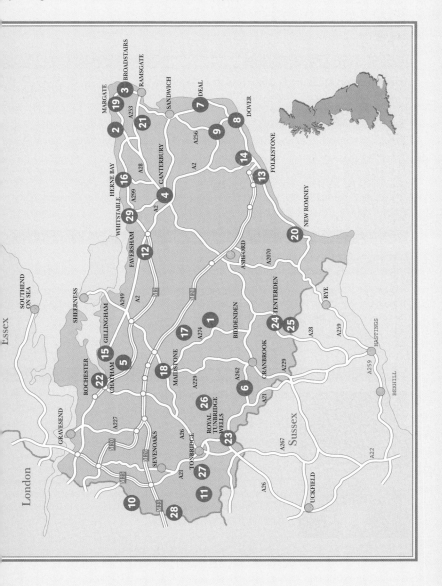

The Red Map References should be used to locate Museums etc on the pages that follow

Kent

ASHFORD

Lashenden Air Warfare Museum

Headcorn Aerodrome, Headcorn, Ashford TN27 9HX   Tel: 01622 890226/206783   Fax: 01622 206783   Email: lashairwar@aol.com

The museum preserves the aviation heritage of Kent, with particular emphasis on World War II. There is a separate building housing a First World War display, including various uniforms, tunics etc.

Opening Times: Sun & BH Easter to end Oct 10:30-18:00. Nov to Easter 10:30-15:30. Closed Xmas & New Year. Admission: Free. Location: Nine miles south of Maidstone on A274, one mile from Headcorn.   Map Ref: 1

BIRCHINGTON

Powell-Cotton Museum & Quex House & Gardens

Quex Park, Birchington CT7 0BH   Tel: 01843 842168   Fax: 01843 846661   Email: powell-cotton.museum@virgin.net   Web: www.powell-cottonmuseum.co.uk

An extraordinary collection, within a museum, stately home and garden setting of African and Asian animal displays, tribal artefacts, weapons, cannons, archeology, chinese porcelain and much more.

Opening Times: Apr to Oct Tue to Thu, Sun & BH 11:00-17:00, Nov to Mar Sun 11:00-16:00. Quex House 14:00-17:00, closed Dec, Jan and Feb. Admission: Adult £4.00, Child/OAP/Student £2.50, Family £12.00. Location: Coastal location, near town centre, 20 minute walk from railway station and beach.   Map Ref: 2

BROADSTAIRS

Dickens House Museum, Broadstairs

2 Victoria Parade, Broadstairs CT10 1QS   Tel / Fax: 01843 863453   Email: aleeault@aol.com

This lovely old house, once the home of Miss Mary Pearson Strong on whom Dickens based much of the character of Miss Betsey Trotwood ('David Copperfield'), is now a museum to commemorate the novelist's association with Broadstairs.

Opening Times: Easter to Oct daily 11;30-17:00. Admission: Adult £2.00, Child £1.00, Student £1.00, Family discount. Location: On the main seafront.   Map Ref: 3

CANTERBURY

Canterbury Heritage Museum

Poor Priests Hospital, Stour Street, Canterbury   Tel: 01227 452747   Fax: 01227 455047   Web: www.canterbury-museum.co.uk

The museum is housed in a beautiful medieval Poor Priests' Hospital built in 1373. One of the most striking features is the magnificent oak roof of the Great Hall. Many of the city's treasures are on display including the Anglo-Saxon Canterbury Cross, medieval pilgrim badges and Stephenson's very first passenger steam locomotive, the 'Invicta'. There is a special gallery for Rupert Bear whose creator was born in Canterbury.

The Magnifiicent Oak Beams
of the Great Hall

Opening Times: Mon to Sat 10:30-17:00 plus Jun to end Oct Sun 13:30-17:00. Closed Xmas & Good Friday. Admission: Adult £2.60, Concession £1.65, Family £6.80 (until 31.3.2003).

Location: In town centre, situated in the Medieval Poor Priests Hospital, just off St Margarets Street or High Street and within easy walking distance of Cathedral.   Map Ref: 4

Canterbury Roman Museum

Butchery Lane, Canterbury   Tel: 01227 785575   Fax: 01227 455047   Web: www.canterbury-museum.co.uk

Acclaimed Hands-on area

Step below today's Canterbury to discover an exciting part of the Roman town including the real remains of a house with fine mosaics. Experience everyday life in the reconstructed market place and see exquisite silver and glass. Try your skill on the touch-screen computer, and in the hands-on area with actual finds. Use the computer animation of Roman Canterbury to join the search for the lost temple.

Opening Times: Mon to Sat 10:00-17:00 plus Jun to end Oct on Sun 13:30-17:00. Closed Good Friday and Xmas. Admission: Adult £2.60, Concession £1.65, Family £6.80 (until 31.3.2003).   Location: Town centre, part of the Long Market, near the Cathedral.

Map Ref: 4

Canterbury Royal Museum & Art Gallery with Buffs Regimental Museum

18 High Street, Canterbury CT1 2RA   Tel: 01227 452747   Fax: 01227 455047
Web: www.canterbury-artgallery.co.uk

The Art Gallery

A splendid Victorian building, houses decorative arts and the city's picture collections - including a gallery for TS Cooper, England's finest cattle painter. The art gallery is the major space in the area for the visual arts with a varied exhibitions programme. Here too is the Buffs Museum, which tells the story of one of England's oldest infantry regiments and its worldwide service.

Opening Times: Mon to Sat 10:00-17:00. Closed Good Friday and Xmas. Admission: Free. Location: Situated in the Beaney Institute in the High Street, almost opposite the Post Office.

Map Ref: 4

View from the Battlements

Canterbury West Gate Towers

St Peters Street, Canterbury   Tel: 01227 452747   Fax: 01227 455047   Web: www.canterbury-museum.co.uk

Medieval West Gate is one of England's finest city gates. Built in about 1380, it has a guard chamber with its 'murder holes' and battlement cells on view. On display are arms and armours from the Civil War to the Second World War. Displays also tell the story of the city defenders. There are fine panoramic views over the city from the battlements.

Opening Times: Mon to Sat 11:00-12:30 13:30-15;30. Closed Good Friday & Xmas. Admission: Adult £1.00, Concession 65p, Family £2.50 (until 31.3.2003).   Location: The museum stands at the end of the main street beside the river.

Map Ref: 4

St Augustines Abbey

Longport, Canterbury CT1 1TF   Tel: 01227 767345

This great shrine, founded by St Augustine in 597, the year he arrived in England from Rome, marks the birthplace of Christianity in this country. St Augustine himself is buried here.

Opening Times: Apr to Sep daily 10:00-18:00, Oct daily 10:00-17:00, Nov to Mar daily 10:00-16:00. Closed Xmas & New Year. Admission: Adult £2.60, Child £1.30, Concession £2.00.
Location: In Longport, quarter of a mile east of Cathedral Close.

Map Ref: 4

CHATHAM

Amherst Heritage Park & Caverns

Dock Road, Chatham ME4 4UB   Tel: 01634 847747   Fax: 01634 830612
Email: johnloudwell@hotmail.com   Web: www.fortamherst.org.uk

A 1667 Dutch raid on Chatham Dockyard led to a review of the defences. Implemented in the

1750s was the building of defensive fortifications around the area known as the Great Lines (later called Fort Amherst).

Opening Times: Apr to Oct daily 10:30-16:00. Nov to Mar Sat & Sun 10:30-15:00. Xmas Event 14 to 24 Dec 16:00-20:00. Admission: Adult £4.50, Child £2.50. Location: A231 Chatham.

Map Ref: 5

The Historic Dockyard Chatham

The Historic Dockyard, Chatham ME4 4TZ   Tel: 01634 823800   Fax: 01634 833801
Email: info@chdt.org.uk   Web: www.chdt.org.uk

Spectacular naval heritage site with architecture and displays spanning over 400 years of naval history. Attractions include World War II destroyer HMS Cavalier, submarine Ocelot, RNLI Lifeboat exhibition, working Ropery, Wooden Walls - 18th century dockyard adventure and museum highlighting Chatham's naval past.

Opening Times: Summer daily 10:00-18:00. Feb to Mar & Nov Wed, Sat & Sun 10:00-16:00. Closed Dec & Jan. Admission: Adult £9.50, Child £6.00, Concession £7.00.
Location: Regular buses to Main Gate from Chatham Rail Station.

Map Ref: 5

Kent Police Museum

The Historic Dockyard, Dock Road, Chatham ME4 4TZ   Tel / Fax: 01634 403260
Email: kentpolmus@aol.com   Web: www.kent-police-museum.co.uk

Museum showing the history of the Kent County Constabulary from 1857 to current day. The collection consists of Police artefacts of uniform, equipment, vehicles and photographs.

Opening Times: Please phone for opening times. Admission: No entry fee to Police Museum.
Location: Within the Historic Dockyard, Chatham next to Rochester north of M2.

Map Ref: 5

The Royal National Lifeboat Collection

The Historic Dockyard, Chatham ME4 4TZ   Tel: 01634 823800   Web: www.lifeboat.org.uk

'Lifeboat!, The Royal National Lifeboat Collection'. The gallery has been created around a collection of 15 historic lifeboats.

Opening Times: Apr to Oct daily 10:00-16:00. Nov, Feb & Mar Wed, Sat & Sun 10:00-16:00.

Map Ref: 5

CRANBROOK

Finchcocks Living Museum of Music

Goudhurst, Cranbrook TN17 1HH   Tel: 01580 211702   Fax: 01580 211007
Email: katrina@finchcocks.co.uk   Web: www.finchcocks.co.uk

Celebrated collection of 100 period keyboard instruments; 40 in concert condition. Housed in fine Georgian manor in beautiful gardens. Pictures and prints on musical themes. Recitals/ Demonstrations for all visitors. Festive and many special events.

Opening Times: Open Days: Easter to Sep Sun & BH Mon, also Aug Wed & Thu 14:00-18:00. By appointment Mar to Dec most days. Admission: Open Days: Adult £7.00, Child £4.00. Group rates available. Location: One mile off A262.

Map Ref: 6

DEAL

Walmer Castle

Kingsdown Road, Walmer, Deal CT14 7LJ   Tel: 01304 364288

Walmer Castle was one of a chain of coastal artillery forts built by Henry VIII to protect the Downs. Walmer was transformed when it became the official residence of the Lords Warden of the Cinque Ports.

Opening Times: Apr to Sep daily 10:00-18:00, Oct daily 10:00-17:00, Nov to Dec & Mar Wed to Sun 10:00-16:00, Jan to Feb Sat & Sun 10:00-16:00. Closed Xmas. Admission: Adult £4.80, Child £2.40, Concession £3.60, Family £12.00. Location: On coast south of Walmer on A258. Junction 13 off M20 or from M2 to Deal.

Map Ref: 7

Kent

Dover Castle 🐾 🗅 🚜

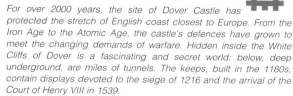

Dover CT16 1HN   Tel: 01304 201628/211067

For over 2000 years, the site of Dover Castle has protected the stretch of English coast closest to Europe. From the Iron Age to the Atomic Age, the castle's defences have grown to meet the changing demands of warfare. Hidden inside the White Cliffs of Dover is a fascinating and secret world: below, deep underground, are miles of tunnels. The keeps, built in the 1180s, contain displays devoted to the siege of 1216 and the arrival of the Court of Henry VIII in 1539.

View of the Anti-aircraft Control Room. © English Heritage

Opening Times: Apr to Sep daily 10:00-18:00, Oct daily 10:00-17:00, Nov to Mar daily 10:00-16:00. Closed Xmas & New Year. Admission: Adult £7.00, Child £3.50, Concession £5.30, Family £17.50.   Location: On east side of Dover.   Map Ref: 8

Dover Museum & The Bronze Age Boat Gallery ⌘ ♦

Market Square, Dover CT16 1PB   Tel: 01304 201066

Dover Museum tells the story of the town and port since prehistoric times, a town that for centuries has been the Gateway to England. Displays include Dover's history as a Roman port and Saxon town, Cinque Ports, Napoleonic Wars, Victorian Dover, and the two World Wars. Also on display is the world's oldest sea-going boat. Found in Dover in 1992, it is 3,550 years old, older than Tutankhamun and from the same age as Stonehenge.

Discovering archaeology, the interactive lab at Dover Museum

Opening Times: Open daily, 10:00-17:30, May to Sep 10:00-18:00. Closed Xmas & New Year Admission: Adults £1.75, Child/OAP 95p, Group discount 10% Location: In Town Centre, 3 minutes from main Bus Station, 10 minutes from Dover Priory Railway Station   Map Ref: 8

Dover Transport Museum ⌘ ♦ 🗅 🚜

White Cliffs Business Park, Honeywood Road, Whitfield, near Dover CT16 2HJ   Tel: 01304 822409   Fax: 01303 241245   Email: Dave@classicomnibus.co.uk
Web: www.dovertransportmuseum.co.uk

Bicycles to buses, model railways and tramway, Leonardo Da Vinci to the Channel Tunnel. Road, sea, air, transport. hundreds of models. replica shops, bygones.

Opening Times: Apr to Oct Wed to Sat 13:30-17:30, Sun & BH 10:30-17:00. Groups at any time by prior arrangement.   Admission: Adult £2.00, Child £1.00, OAP £1.50, Family £5.00.
Location: Just off A2 Whitfield (MacDonalds) roundabout, three miles outside Dover. Map Ref: 9

Down House 🌢 🚜

Luxted Road, Downe BR6 7JT   Tel: 01689 859119

From his study at Down House, Charles Darwin worked on the scientific theories that first scandalised and then revolutionised the Victorian world, culminating in the publication of 'On the Origin of Species by means of Natural Selection'. 3,500 objects relating to Darwin's work remain including portraits, photographs, family furniture, memorabilia from the Beagle voyage and manuscripts, including his Beagle Journal.

The Old Study, © English Heritage

Opening Times: Please telephone to check times and pre-book for the month of Aug. Groups over 11 must pre-book at all times. Admission: Adult £5.50, Child £2.80, Concession £4.10. Location: In Luxted Road, Downe, off A21 near Biggin Hill.

Map Ref: 10

Kent

EDENBRIDGE

Kent & Sharpshooters Yeomanry Museum

Hever Castle, Edenbridge TN8 7NG   Tel: 01732 865224   Email: mail@hevercastle.co.uk
Web: www.hevercastle.co.uk

*Includes pictures, uniforms, badges, medals, flags, weapons of the 4th East Kent Yeomanry, West
Kent Yeomanry, 3rd/4th County of London Yeomanry (Sharpshooters).*

Opening Times: Mar to Nov 12:00-18:00, during winter time (GMT) 12:00-16:00.
Admission: Adult £8.00, Child £4.40, OAP £6.80, Family £20.40.   Location: Three miles south
east of Edenbridge off the B2026.   Map Ref: 11

FAVERSHAM

Chart Gunpowder Mills

Choat Close, Faversham ME13 7SE   Tel: 01795 534542   Fax: 01795 533261
Email: faversham@btinternet.com   Web: www.faversham.org

*The world's oldest gunpowder mills, which made powder for Nelson at Trafalgar and Wellington at
Waterloo. Display explains how powder is made. Restored and managed by voluntary effort.*

Opening Times: Easter to Oct Sat, Sun & BH 14:00-17:00.   Admission: Free.   Location: Ten
minute walk from town centre and mainline railway station.   Map Ref: 12

Fleur de Lis Heritage Centre

13 Preston Street, Faversham ME13 8NS   Tel: 01795 534542   Fax: 01795 533261
Email: faversham@btinternet.com   Web: www.faversham.org

*Recently expanded and updated, and housed in 16th century premises, the centre's colourful
displays tell the story of 2,000 years of life in one of Britain's most historic ports.*

Opening Times: Mon to Sat 10:00-16:00, Sun 10:00-13:00.   Admission: Adult £2.00,
Child/OAP/Disabled £1.00.   Location: In town centre, four minute walk from mainline station.
                                                                      Map Ref: 12

Maison Dieu

Ospringe Street, Ospringe, Faversham ME13 8TW   Tel: 01795 534542   Fax: 01795 533261
Email: faversham@btinternet.com   Web: www.faversham.org

*Finds from a nearby Roman cemetry, and displays tracing the history of Ospringe, are housed in
the 13th century building which was once part of a Royal Lodge and pilgrims' hostel.*

Opening Times: Easter to Oct Sat, Sun & BH 14:00-17:00.   Admission: Adult £1.00, Child/OAP
50p.   Location: On main A2, 20 minute walk town centre and mainline railway station.
                                                                      Map Ref: 12

FOLKESTONE

Elham Valley Line Trust

Peene Yard, Peene, Newington, Folkestone CT18 8BA   Tel: 01303 273690

*If you like local history, artefacts and memorabilia of this the Golden Age of the Railway, pleasant
gardens, doves, ducks and trains, then this is the place to visit. The Bygone Age has been lovingly
recreated just for you.*

Opening Times: Apr to Sep, Sat, Sun & BH 10:00-17:00.   Admission: Adult £2.00, Child £1.00,
OAP £1.00.   Location: Turn off A20 for Newington and Peene.   Map Ref: 13

Folkestone Museum & Gallery

Grace Hill, Folkestone CT20 1HD   Tel / Fax: 01303 256710
Email: janet.adamson@kent.gov.uk

*Story of Folkestone, important Victorian seaside resort and Channel Port. Audio and film, hands-
on activities. Programme of events for Museum and Gallery.*

Opening Times: Mon, Tues & Thu 09:30-18:00 Fri 09:30-19:00 Wed & Sat 09:30-17:00. Closed
Sun & BH.   Admission: Free.   Location: Two minutes walk from bus station and pay car parks.
                                                                      Map Ref: 13

Kent Battle of Britain Museum

Aerodrome Road, Hawkinge, Folkestone CT18 7AG Tel: 01303 893140
Email: kentbattleofbritainmuseum@btinternet.com Web: www.kbobm.org.uk or
www.kentbattleofbritainmuseum.org.uk

Most important collection of Battle of Britain artefacts on show in the country - aircraft, vehicles, weapons, flying equipment, prints, relics from over 600 crashed Battle of Britain aircraft.

Opening Times: Good Friday to 30 Sep Tue to Sun 10:00-17:00. Closed Mon except BH. Closed Oct to Easter. Admission: Adult £3.50, Child £2.00, OAP £3.00. Group discounts available. Location: Three miles north of Folkestone. Off Aerodrome Road, Hawkinge.
Map Ref: 14

GILLINGHAM

Royal Engineers Museum

Prince Arthur Road, Gillingham ME4 4UG Tel: 01634 406397 Fax: 01634 822371
Email: remuseum.rhqre@gnet.gov.uk Web: www.royalengineers.org.uk

Displays of engineering equipment, working models, superb medal galleries with 25 VCs and the regalia of four Field Marshalls including Kitchener. Costumes and curios from around the world.

Opening Times: Mon to Thu 10:00-17:00, Sat, Sun & BH 11:30-17:00. Friday by appointment only. Closed Xmas & New Year. Admission: Adult £3.50, Child/OAP £2.00, Family £9.00. Guided Tours £5.00 per person. Location: Prince Arthur Road, Gillingham, 20 minute walk from Gillingham Station.
Map Ref: 15

HERNE BAY

Herne Bay Museum & Gallery

12 William Street, Herne Bay CT6 5EJ Tel: 01227 367368 Web: www.hernebay-museum.co.uk

Victorian seaside publicity poster

The museum highlights the history of the Victorian seaside resort of Herne Bay. Find out about the town's famous pier. See exciting finds from the nearby Roman fort and Saxon church of Reculver, as well as fossils including mammoth tusks and fossilised sharks teeth. Also on display is a famous 'bouncing bomb' from World War II. The art gallery has regularly changing temporary exhibitions.

Opening Times: Mon to Sat 10:00-16:00 plus Jul & Aug on Sun 13:00-16:00. Closed Good Friday & Xmas.
Admission: Free. Location: Town centre, 12 William Street, near the seafront at the Clock Tower end, in the same building as the Visitor Information Centre.
Map Ref: 16

MAIDSTONE

Dog Collar Museum

Leeds Castle, Maidstone ME17 1PL Tel: 01622 765400 Fax: 01622 735616
Email: enquiries@leeds-castle.co.uk Web: www.leeds-castle.com

The Dog Collar Museum at Leeds Castle is home to the world's finest collection of historic dog collars with some of the exhibits dating back over 500 years.

Opening Times: Mar to Oct 10:00-17:00, Nov to Feb 10:00-15:00. Closed Xmas, 29 Jun & 6 July. Admission: Mar to Oct Adult £11.00, Child £7.50, OAP/Student £9.50. Nov to Feb Adult £9.50, Child £6.00, OAP/Student £8.00. Location: Seven miles east of Maidstone at junction 8 of M20.
Map Ref: 17

Maidstone Museum & Bentlif Art Gallery

St Faiths Street, Maidstone ME14 1LH Tel: 01622 754497

One of the finest general collections in the south east. Galleries include Japanese art, costume and natural history. A wide selection of temporary exhibitions.

Opening Times: Mon to Sat 10:00-17:15, Sun 10:00-16:00. Closed Xmas Day.
Admission: Free. Location: Nr town centre, five minutes walk from Maidstone East Railway Station.
Map Ref: 18

Museum of Kent Life

Lock Lane, Sandling, Maidstone ME14 3AU   Tel: 01622 763936
Fax: 01622 662024   Email: enquiries@museum-kentlife.co.uk
Web: www.museum-kentlife.co.uk

Kent's award-winning open air museum is home to an outstanding collection of historical buildings which house exhibitions on life in Kent over the last 100 years. An early 20th century vintage hall and reconstruction of cottages from the 17th & 20th centuries are more recent buildings to be viewed.

Opening Times: 9 Feb to 2 Nov daily 10:00-17:30.
Admission: Adult £4.90, Child/Student £3.20, OAP £3.50.
Location: Five minutes from Maidstone.   Map Ref: 18

Oast House

Tyrwhitt-Drake Museum of Carriages

Archbishops Stables, Mill Street, Maidstone ME15 6YE   Tel: 01622 754497

Major collection of carriages, items include private and state vehicles, some items belonging to Queen Victoria. Housed in historic medieval stables.

Opening Times: Daily 10:00-15:45.   Admission: Adult £2.00, Child £1.05, Under 5s Free, Family £4.00.   Location: Town centre, two minutes walk from High Street.   Map Ref: 18

MARGATE

Margate Old Town Hall Local History Museum

Market Place, Margate CT9 1ER   Tel: 01843 231213   Fax: 01843 582359
Email: margatemuseum@bonkers16freeserve.co.uk

Margate's history from Iron Age man to modern times, collections include archaeology, maritime, war, towns silver, police and seaside resort history. All housed in the first Town Hall.

Opening Times: Easter to Oct daily 10:00-17:00, Oct to Easter Mon to Fri 09:30-16:30.
Admission: Adult £1.00, Child/OAP 50p.   Location: In the old town centre, one minute walk from harbour.   Map Ref: 19

NEW ROMNEY

Romney Hythe & Dymchurch Railway

New Romney TN28 8PL   Tel: 01797 362353   Fax: 01797 363591
Email: rhdr@dels.demon.co.uk   Web: www.rhdr.demon.co.uk

Most complete collection of one-third full size steam engines in the world (11 in all). Also toy and model museum on site.

Opening Times: Feb half term, Easter to end Sep and Oct half term daily, also weekends in Mar & Oct 09:00-18:00.   Location: Most stations within five minutes of A259. Hythe Station is three miles from junction 11 of M20.   Map Ref: 20

Museums, Galleries, Historic Houses & Sites

Please let us know of any collections that are not listed in this guide that you feel should be listed. E-mail us on *editor@tomorrows.co.uk* or return the Report Form on page 448

Kent

Spitfire & Hurricane Memorial Building

The Airfield, Manston Road, Ramsgate CT12 5DF   Tel / Fax: 01843 821940
Email: pete@spitfire752.freeserve.co.uk   Web: www.spitfire-museum.com

The Memorial Building houses wartime Spitfire & Hurricane fighter aircraft together with an ever expanding display of original and emotive memorabilia from the 1939-1945 war periods. Battle of Britain Tapestry. 'Dambusters' and 'Channel Dash' displays. The Merlin Cafeteria has superb views across London (Manston) Airport. Study/research room and Allied Air Forces Memorial Garden.

Opening Times: Apr to Sep 10:00-17:00, Oct to Mar 10:00-16:00. Closed Xmas & New Year.

Spitfiire MK XVI - TB752 on displa

Admission: Free. Location: On B2050 road, adjacent to London (Manston) Airport. Follow brown tourism signs.

Map Ref: 21

Guildhall Museum

High Street, Rochester ME1 1PY   Tel: 01634 848717   Fax: 01634 832919   Email: guildhall.museum@medway.gov.uk
Web: www.medway.gov.uk

A museum for all the family. Colourful and attractive displays in two historic buildings feature the archaeology, local and social history of the Medway towns. The 'Hulks Experience' highlights the cramped, insanitary and harsh conditions forced upon Napoleonic prisoners-of-war and convicts incarcerated on the Medway Hulks. The museum also features everyday life in Victorian and Edwardian times.

Opening Times: Daily 10:00-16:30. Closed Xmas & New Year.
Admission: Free. Location: In Rochester High Street, 15 minutes walk from Rochester Railway Station.

Reconstruction of
17th Century Militia

Map Ref: 22

Tunbridge Wells Museum and Art Gallery

Civic Centre, Mount Pleasant, Royal Tunbridge Wells TN1 1JN   Tel: 01892 554171
Web: www.tunbridgewells.gov.uk/museum

From Tunbridge ware caskets to Pantiles paintings and Minnie the LuLu terrier to an 18th century polonaise, there are displays to fascinate everyone at Tunbridge Wells Museum. The Art Gallery has varied and frequently changing art and craft exhibitions. Educational workshops and other events for all ages are held linked to the exhibit collections and Tunbridge Wells history.

Opening Times: Mon to Sat 09:30-17:00. Closed Sun & BH.
Admission: Free. Location: In the Library and Museum building, next to the Town Hall, just off the A264.

The Art Gallery

Map Ref: 23

Colonel Stephens Railway Museum

Tenterden Town Station, Station Road, Tenterden TN30 6HE   Tel: 01580 765350   Fax: 01580 765654   Email: kesroffice@aol.com   Web: www.hfstephens-museum.org.uk

Displays depicting the career of light railway promoter and engineer Lt Colonel Holman F Stephens, his pre-Raphaelite childhood, military career and involvement in 17 railways are covered with pictures, models, tableaux and relics.

Opening Times: Apr to Oct when trains run on Kent & East Sussex Railway 12:30-16:30 (hours extended for special events). Train times: tel. 01580 765155   Admission: Adult £1.00, Child 50p, Under 8s Free. Special rates for pre-booked groups of 10 or more.   Location: Adjacent to Tenterden Town Station, Station Road. 300 yards from High Street.

Map Ref: 24

Kent

Ellen Terry Memorial Museum

Smallhythe Place, Tenterden TN30 7NG   Tel / Fax: 01580 762334
Email: ksmxxx@smtp.ntrust.org.uk   Web: www.nationaltrust.org.uk

Early 16th century timber-framed house, once the home of celebrated Victorian actress Ellen Terry. Many personal and theatrical mementoes. Beautiful stage costumes from her partnership with Sir Henry Irving at Lyceum Theatre.

Opening Times: Apr to Oct Sat to Wed 11:00-17:00.   Admission: Adult £3.20, Child £1.60, Family £8.00. National Trust Members Free.   Location: Two and a half miles from Tenterden, eight miles from Rye, bus service from both towns.   Map Ref: 25

Kent & East Sussex Railway

Tenterden Town Station, Station Road, Tenterden TN30 6HE   Tel: 01580 765155   Fax: 01580 765654   Email: KESROffice@aol.com   Web: www.kesr.org.uk

You can experience the nostalgia of the days of steam and travel in the sedate pace of yesteryear over ten and a half miles of beautiful countryside.

Opening Times: Please telephone for opening times.   Admission: Adult £8.00, Child £4.00, OAP £7.50.   Location: Tenterden Town Centre.   Map Ref: 24

TONBRIDGE

The Hop Farm Country Park

Beltring, Paddock Wood, Tonbridge TN12 6PY   Tel: 01622 872068   Fax: 01622 872630
Email: info@thehopfarm.co.uk   Web: www.thehopfarm.co.uk

The Hop Farm

Set in the heart of Kent amongst the largest collection of Victorian Oast Houses in the World. There are a number of exhibitions and museums within the Oast Houses, including the Hop Story Museum, an award winning museum featuring the Story of Hop Picking and Kent Rural Heritage. The Decades Experience is an interactive walk through the 20th century, scenes including a Victorian Street, Wartime Britain and Pop Larkin's Kitchen.

Opening Times: Daily 10:00-17:00.   Admission: Adult £6.50, Child/OAP £4.50, Family (2 adults and 2 Children) £18.00.   Map Ref: 26

Penshurst Place & Gardens

Penshurst, Tonbridge TN11 8DG   Tel: 01892 870307   Fax: 01892 870866
Email: enquiries@penshurstplace.com   Web: www.penshurstplace.com

Penshurst Place is one of Kent's loveliest historic houses with 10 acres of walled Tudor gardens, set in a peaceful rural setting in the medieval village of Penshurst. The oldest part of the house is the Barons Hall, built in 1342 it is regarded as one of the best preserved examples of medieval domestic architecture in England. A series of Staterooms contain a wonderful collection of portraits, tapestries, furniture, porcelain and armour from the past five centuries. The gardens, largely unaltered since Tudor times, have been developed by generations of the Sidney family who first came to Penshurst in 1552. The walled garden is divided by yew hedging into a series of small garden 'rooms', each with its own colour and season. Today Penshurst Place remains the ancestral home of Viscount De L'Isle and his family, descendant of the famous Elizabethan poet and courtier, Sir Philip Sidney. Modern facilities include a Toy Museum, a Garden Tea Room, Gift Shop, Plant Centre, Venture Playground, and a Woodland Trail with plenty of free parking for cars and coaches. Special events at Penshurst Place include an exciting variety of shows in Home Park, drama, falconry, music, historic entertainment and storytelling in the house and grounds.

Opening Times: Weekends from 2 Mar, daily from 23 Mar to 3 Nov. House: 12:00-17:00, Grounds: 10:30-18:00.   Admission: Adult £6.50, Child £4.50, Concession £6.00.   Location: Six miles from Tunbridge Wells and Tonbridge.   Map Ref: 27

Kent

WESTERHAM

Chartwell
Westerham TN16 1PS   Tel: 01732 868381

Dining Room

The Studio

The family home where Britain's wartime prime minister lived for more than 40 years. The rooms, which are kept as they were in Sir Winston Churchill's lifetime, offer an insight into both his domestic and political life. Photographs, books and personal possessions, including his famous cigars, evoke his career, personality and family. Museum and exhibition rooms contain displays, sound recordings and collections of memorabilia including many gifts from other world leaders, uniforms and correspondence. The house contains several of Sir Winston's own paintings and more are on view in his studio, together with his easel and paint box. Many features created by Sir Winston survive in the garden including the walls he built himself, the swimming pool and lake and ponds stocked with the golden orfe he loved to feed.

Opening Times: 23 Mar to 3 Nov Wed to Sun 11:00-17:00. In addition Tue in Jul & Aug & BH Mon.   Admission: National Trust members free. Adult £5.80, Child £2.90, Family £14.50, Garden & Studio £2.90.   Location: Two miles south of Westmester (A25) on B2026 Metrobus 246 from Bromley to Gate. Sevenoaks Station six and a half miles.
                                                                                        Map Ref: 28

Squerryes Court
Westerham TN16 1SJ   Tel: 01959 562345/563118   Fax: 01959 565949
Email: squerryes.court@squerryes.co.uk   Web: www.squerryes.co.uk

17th century manor house. Paintings collected by the Warde family 1747-1774, including 17th and 18th century Italian, Dutch and English schools. 18th century Soho tapestries. Items connected with General Wolfe. Pre-booked guided tours.

Opening Times: Apr to Sep Wed, Sat, Sun and BH House: 13:30-17:30, Garden: 12:00-17:30. Admission: Adult £4.60, Child £2.50, OAP £4.10, Family £12.00. Group rates available. Garden only: Adult £3.00, Child £1.50, OAP £2.50, Family £7.00.   Location: Half a mile west of Westerham, just off A25.
                                                                                        Map Ref: 28

WHITSTABLE

Oyster dredge used to scrape the seabed for oysters

Whitstable Museum & Gallery
Oxford Street, Whitstable CT5 1DB   Tel: 01227 276998
Fax: 01227 772379   Web: www.whitstable-museum.co.uk

The museum explores Whitstable's unique coastal community and its seafaring traditions with special features on oyster fishery, diving and shipping for which the town was famous. Ship portraits, archaeology and an early piece of silent film showing the oyster fishers dredging for oysters can be seen as well as an original horse drawn fire engine. The art gallery has a range of changing exhibitions.

Opening Times: Mon to Sat 10:00-16:00 plus Jul & Aug Sun 13:00-14:00. Closed Good Friday and Xmas. Admission: Free.
Location: Town centre, in Oxford Street, close to the theatre, library and St Marys Hall. Easy walking distance of car parks and railway station.
                                                                                        Map Ref: 29

www.tomorrows.co.uk
Full information on our collection of travel guides and secure store

Lancashire

The cities and towns of the county reflect in their buildings the prosperity brought to the area the Industrial Revolution. The seaside resorts still retain their well-deserved popularity. Blackpo with its spectacular illuminations, piers and golden beaches, remains arguably Britain's m popular.

The cities of Lancashire, proud of their industrial heritage, present through their museums a galleries a quite remarkably comprehensive history of the Industrial Revolution and Lancashir rich cultural, historical and natural heritage.

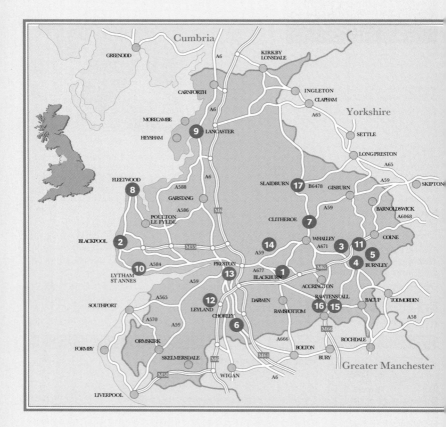

The Red Map References should be used to locate Museums etc on the pages that follow

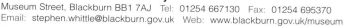

BLACKBURN

Blackburn Museum & Art Gallery

Museum Street, Blackburn BB1 7AJ Tel: 01254 667130 Fax: 01254 695370
Email: stephen.whittle@blackburn.gov.uk Web: www.blackburn.gov.uk/museum

Collections of medieval manuscripts and early printed books, large collections of coins, Japanese prints, Greek and Russian icons. Extensive collections of local social history and textile history in the adjoining Lewis Textile Museum (admission by appointment). Other attractions include Victorian paintings and sculpture, ceramics, Egyptology and contemporary art exhibitions.

Opening Times: Tue to Sat 10:00-16:45. Closed Sun, Mon & BH. Admission: Free. Location: Town centre, five minute walk from railway and central bus station.

HoKusai Lightning over Mount Fuji

Map Ref: 1

BLACKPOOL

Blackpool Lifeboat Station & Visitor Centre

The Promenade, Adjacent New Bonney Street, Blackpool FY1 5YA Tel: 01253 290816
Web: www.lifeboats.org.uk

Viewing gallery above lifeboats with displays, exhibits and videos portraying the RNLI in Blackpool.

Opening Times: All year. Admission: Free.

Map Ref: 2

Grundy Art Gallery

Queen Street, Blackpool FY1 1PX Tel: 01253 478170 Fax: 01253 478172
Email: grundyartgallery@blackpool.gov.uk

A historic and modern collection always on show. Lively temporary exhibitions. Small display of Blackpool's history, specialising in craft jewellery, some for sale at shop. Relaxing atmosphere.

Opening Times: Mon to Sat 10:00-17:00, closed Sun and BH. Admission: Free. Location: In the town centre near Talbot Road Bus Station and Blackpool North Railway Station and North Pier tramstops.

Map Ref: 2

BURNLEY

Gawthorpe Hall

Padiham, Burnley BB12 8UA Tel: 01282 771004 Fax: 01282 770178
Email: gawthorpehall@museumoflancs.org.uk Web: www.bringinghistoryalive.co.uk

A magnificent Jacobean house set in formal gardens, with many rooms remodelled in the Victorian period by Sir Charles Barry. The hall also houses the internationally important Rachel Kay-Shuttleworth textile collection.

Opening Times: Apr to Oct Tue to Thu and Sat to Sun, 13:00-17:00. Admission: Adult £3.00, Child £1.30, Concession £1.45, Family £8.00. Location: Outskirts of Padiham, frequent bus service from Burnley.

Map Ref: 3

Natural History Centre & Aquarium

Towneley Hall Art Gallery/Museums, Townley Park, off Todmorden Road, Burnley BB11 3RQ
Tel: 01282 424213 Fax: 01282 436138 Email: towneleyhall@burnley.org.uk
Web: www.towneleyhall.org.uk

Collection of local, national and international natural history specimens, fossils and geology.

Opening Times: Mon to Fri 10:00-17:00, Easter to Oct also Sun 12:00-17:00. Admission: Free. Location: One and a half miles south east of town centre, one mile from Park entrance on Todmorden Road (A671). Left from front of main hall.

Map Ref: 4

Queen Street Mill

Queen Street, Harle Syke, Burnley BB10 2HX Tel: 01282 412555 Fax: 01282 430220
Web: www.bringinghistoryalive.co.uk

The last commercial steam powered textile mill in Europe, today preserved as a museum offering *a unique experience with the sight, sound and smell of working Lancashire looms.*

Opening Times: Mar to Nov and BH during the season. Admission: Adult £2.50, Child £1.50, Concession £1.25, Family £6.00. Location: 15 minute drive from Burnley Town Centre, bus journey from Burnley approximately half an hour. Map Ref: 5

Towneley Hall Art Gallery & Museum

Towneley Holmes Road, off Todmorden Road, Burnley BB11 3RQ   Tel: 01282 424213
Fax: 01282 436138   Email: townleyhall@burnley.gov.uk   Web: www.towneleyhall.org.uk

18th and 19th century oil and watercolour paintings; studio pottery; Royal Lancastrian Pilkington Pottery; 17th and 18th century oak furniture; 18th century glass; 18th and 19th century clocks and watches.

Opening Times: Mon to Fri 10:00-17:00, Sun 12:00-17:00. Closed Sat. Admission: Free. Charge for tours. Location: One and a half miles south east of town centre, one mile from Park entrance on Todmarden Road (A671). Map Ref: 4

CHORLEY

Astley Hall Museum & Art Gallery

Astley Park, Chorley PR7 1NP   Tel: 01257 515555   Fax: 01257 515556
Email: astleyhall@lineone.net   Web: astleyhall.co.uk

A furnished house dating back to the 1580s, including fine oak furniture of the 16th and 17th centuries. Also, a collection of 18th century creamware and fine art from 17th century portraits to contemporary art.

Opening Times: Apr to Oct Tue to Sun 12:00-17:00 and BH. Nov to Mar Sat & Sun 12:00-16:00. Admission: Adult £2.95, Concession £1.95. Group rates available. Location: One mile west of Chorley, off A581 Southport Road. Map Ref: 6

CLITHEROE

Clitheroe Castle Museum

Castle Hill, Clitheroe BB7 1BA   Tel / Fax: 01200 424568
Email: hannah.chalk@mus.lancscc.gov.uk

We hold and display a range of local history and geology collections, all of which focus on Clitheroe and the surrounding areas.

Opening Times: Daily 11:00-17:00. Admission: Adult £1.55, Child £0.25, OAP £0.70, Family £3.30. Location: Near town centre, ten minute walk from bus and railway stations. Map Ref: 7

FLEETWOOD

Fleetwood Museum

Queens Terrace, Fleetwood FY7 6BT   Tel: 01253 876621   Fax: 01253 878088
Email: fleetwoodmuseum@museumoflancs.org.uk   Web: www.nettingthebay.org.uk

Situated in the Decimus Burton designed Custom House building, the museum covers the history of Fleetwood and the fishing and maritime collections of Morecambe Bay. The museum also includes a full size dolls' boarding house and an interactive gallery.

Opening Times: Apr to early Nov and BH throughout the season. Admission: Adult £2.00, Child/Concessions £1.00, Family £5.00. Location: On Queens Terrace, opposite P&O Ferry Booth - between the market and Knott End Ferry. Within easy walking distance of buses and trams. Map Ref: 8

LANCASTER

Cottage Museum

15 Castle Hill, Lancaster   Tel: 01524 64637   Fax: 01524 841692
Email: awhite@lancaster.gov.uk   Web: www.lancaster.gov.uk/council/museums

A cottage of 1739 (refitted and divided c.1820) and furnished in the style of that date.

Opening Times: Easter to Sep daily 14:00-17:00. Admission: Adult 75p, Concession 25p. Location: Near city centre, close to Castle. Map Ref: 9

Judges Lodgings Museum

Church Street, Lancaster LA1 1YS   Tel: 01524 32808
Email: judgeslodgings.lcc@btinternet.com   Web: www.bringinghistoryalive.co.uk

Lancaster's oldest town house, The Judges' Lodgings, displays an impressive collection of Gillow furniture in period rooms. Also includes porcelain, silver and paintings and a Museum of Childhood with dolls, toys and games.

Opening Times: Good Friday to end of Oct.   Admission: Adult £2.00, Child/Concessions £1.00, Family £5.00.   Location: Town centre, five minutes from bus station and ten minutes from railway station.
Map Ref: 9

Lancaster City Museum

Market Square, Lancaster LA1 1HT   Tel: 01524 64637
Fax: 01524 841692   Email: awhite@lancaster.gov.uk
Web: www.lancaster.gov.uk/council/museums

Collections illustrate history and archaeology of Lancaster and North Lancashire. Paintings, decorative arts and a series of changing exhibitions.

Opening Times: Mon to Sat 10:00-17:00. Closed Xmas.
Admission: Free.   Location: City centre, five minutes from main rail and bus stations.
Map Ref: 9

Medieval Fish Stall

Lancaster Maritime Museum

Custom House, St Georges Quay, Lancaster LA1 1RB   Tel: 01524 382264   Fax: 01524 841692   Email: awhite@lancaster.gov.uk   Web: www.lancaster.gov.uk/council/museums

Collections illustrate the history of the Port of Lancaster, fishing in Morecombe Bay, slaving and the West Indies trade. Changing exhibitions.

Opening Times: Easter to Oct daily 11:00-17:00, Nov to Easter daily 12:30-16:00.
Admission: Adult £2.00, Concession £1.00.   Location: On St George's Quay, five miles from city centre.
Map Ref: 9

Museum of The Kings Own Royal Regiment (Lancaster)

City Museum, Market Square, Lancaster LA1 1HT   Tel: 01524 64637   Fax: 01524 841692   Email: kingsownmuseum@iname.com
Web: www.lancaster.gov.uk/council/museums

Collections illustrate the history and actions of the King's Own Royal Regiment (Lancaster) (4th of Foot) from its raising in 1680 to the present day. Uniforms, medals, archives and photographs.

Opening Times: Mon to Sat 10:00-17:00. Closed Xmas.
Admission: Free.   Location: City centre, five minutes from main rail and bus station.
Map Ref: 9

Peter Scott Gallery

Lancaster University, Lancaster LA1 4YW   Tel: 01524 593057   Fax: 01524 592603
Email: m.p.gavagan@lancs.ac.uk   Web: www.lancs.ac.uk/users/peterscott/scott.htm

The Peter Scott Gallery houses Lancaster University's art collection and presents a varied series of temporary exhibitions throughout the year. The collection includes an international selection of 20th century paintings and prints. The Gallery's Royal Lancastrian Pottery Collection is displayed in the John Chambers Ceramics Room and also provides an area for temporary displays of contemporary ceramics.

Opening Times: Mon to Fri 11:00-16:00 & late Thu 18:00-20:30. During exhibitions, please telephone for details.

Peter Scott Gallery, Lancaster University

Admission: Free.   Location: On Lancaster University Campus. Accessible by road, leave junction 33 on M6; A6 to Lancaster. Public transport Lancaster Railway Station, bus to university.
Map Ref: 9

Roman Bath House

Castle Hill, Vicarage Field, Lancaster   Tel: 01524 64637

Conserved ruin forming bath wing of important Roman house just outside the fort walls. Demolished c.340 AD to build new walls and ditch, but preserved in upcast.

Opening Times: Open all daylight hours. Admission: Free. Location: Near Castle and Priory Church, two minutes from rail station.   Map Ref: 9

Ruskin Library

Lancaster University, Lancaster LA1 4YH   Tel: 01524 593587   Fax: 01524 593580
Email: ruskin.library@lancaster.ac.uk   Web: www.lancs.ac.uk/users/ruslinlib/

Largest collection of books, manuscripts and drawings by and relating to the writer and artist John Ruskin (1819-1900), in an award-winning new building. Public gallery with at least three exhibitions a year.

Opening Times: Mon to Sat 11:00-16:00, Sun 13:00-16:00. Admission: Free. Location: South of Lancaster, on A6 just off junction 33 of M6.   Map Ref: 9

LYTHAM

Lytham Heritage Centre

2 Henry Street, Lytham FY8 5LE   Tel / Fax: 01253 730767
Email: thecentre@lythamheritage.fsnet.co.uk   Web: www.lythamheritage.fsnet.co.uk

'Lytham Heritage Centre' from a Watercolour by Tom Eccles

A Grade II Listed building built in 1899, formerly the Manchester and County Bank. Acquired by Lytham Heritage Group in 1996 and converted into an exhibition centre and gallery in a Victorian style. A variety of exhibitions include Lytham Heritage and local community arts and crafts.

Opening Times: Tue to Sun & BH 10:00-16:00.
Admission: Free. Location: In Lytham Town Centre, at the corner of the Piazza.   Map Ref: 10

Lytham Windmill Museum

East Beach, Lytham FY8 4HZ   Tel / Fax: 01253 730767
Email: thecentre@lythamheritage.fsnet.co.uk   Web: www.lythamheritage.fsnet.co.uk

Lytham Windmill Museum on Lytham Green

Built in 1805 and worked as a corn mill until 1919, the Windmill Museum, housed in a restored Grade II listed building, is now a permanent heritage exhibition. Displays record the 200 years history of the mill and explanations of its machinery, with models and memorabilia. The basement includes many tableaux of Victorian life in Lytham. The museum was awarded National Museum status in 2001 and won an Award from Northwest Tourist Board as a Visitor Attraction.

Opening Times: May to Sep Tue to Thu, Sat & Sun 10:30-16:30. Admission: Free. Location: Near town centre on Lytham Green overlooking River Ribble.   Map Ref: 10

Lancashire

Pendle Heritage Centre

Barrowford, Nelson BB9 6JQ   Tel: 01282 661701/2
Fax: 01282 611718

Exhibitions on the development of the building and the history of this part of Lancashire, including the story of the Pendle Witches. The Pendle Arts Gallery holds regular exhibitions by professional artists. There is a well stocked shop and a garden tea-room serving home-cooked food, as well as a Tourist Information Centre.

Pendle Heritage Centre, rebuilt frontage

Opening Times: Daily 10:00-17:00. Closed Xmas.
Location: Five minutes from junction 13 of the M65.

Map Ref: 11

PRESTON

British Commercial Vehicle Museum

King Street, Leyland, Preston PR25 2LE   Tel: 01772 451011   Fax: 01772 623404

Britain's premier collection of fully restored commercial and passenger vehicles tracing the history of road transport over the last 100 years.

Opening Times: Apr to Sep Sun, Tue & Wed 10:00-16:30. Oct Sun 10:00-16:30. Open BH.
Admission: Adult £4.00, Child/OAP £2.00, Family £10.00.   Location: Exit M6 at junction 28, 1 mile from exit.

Map Ref: 12

Harris Museum & Art Gallery

Market Square, Preston PR1 2PP   Tel: 01722 258248   Fax: 01772 886764
Email: harris.museum@preston.gov.uk   Web: www.visitpreston.com

The Harris offers the best of Preston's heritage in a beautiful Grade I listed building, with its collections of paintings, sculpture, textiles, costume, glass and ceramics, as well as The Story of Preston Gallery. The museum shows an exciting programme of exhibitions and has a national reputation for contemporary art shows. The programme also includes local history, fine and decorative art and contemporary craft.

Harris Museum and Art Gallery, Preston

Opening Times: Mon to Sat 10:00-17:00. Closed BH.
Admission: Free.   Location: Market Square, Preston, one minute from bus station, five minutes from railway station.

Map Ref: 13

Museum of Lancashire

Stanley Street, Preston PR1 4YP   Tel: 01772 264075   Fax: 01772 264079
Web: www.bringinghistoryalive.co.uk

Housed in Preston's Old Sessions House, the museum features aspects of Lancashire's rich cultural, historical and natural heritage.

Opening Times: Daily 10:30-17:00, closed Thursdays, Sundays and BH.   Admission: Adult £2.00, Concession £1.00, Child Free.   Location: Town centre, five minutes walk from bus station.

Map Ref: 13

The National Football Museum

Sir Tom Finney Way, Deepdale, Preston PR1 6RU   Tel: 01772 908442   Fax: 01772 908433
Email: enquiries@nationalfootballmuseum.com   Web: www.nationalfootballmuseum.com

The world's largest collection of football memorabilia including the FIFA, FA, Football League and Wembley Collections. Inter-active gallery and children's education trail.

Opening Times: Tue to Sat 10:00-17:00 Sun 11:00-17:00 Midweek Match Day 10:00-19:30.
Closed Mon except BH.   Admission: Adult £6.95, Child £4.95. Full range of concessions.
Location: One mile from town centre.

Map Ref: 13

Queens Lancashire Regiment

Fulwood Barracks, Preston PR2 8AA   Tel: 01772 260362   Fax: 01772 260583

Extensive museum, archive and library, containing material relating to 30th, 40th, 47th, 59th, 81st and 82nd Regiments of Foot, The East Lancashire, South Lancashire, Loyal (North Lancashire), Lancashire and Queen's Lancashire Regiment.

Opening Times: Tue to Thu 10:00-16:00 or by appointment.   Admission: Free. Guided groups £2.00 per person.   Location: Two miles north of town centre.   Map Ref: 13

Ribchester Roman Museum

Riverside, Ribchester, Preston PR3 3XS   Tel: 01254 878261

This museum contains displays of military life at Roman Ribchester. New exhibitions include many exciting finds from the site.

Opening Times: Mon to Fri 09:00-17:00 Sat to Sun 11:00-17:30.   Admission: Adult £2.00, Child £1.00.   Location: On B6245 off A59. Bus routes from Blackburn and Preston.   Map Ref: 14

RAWTENSTALL

Holmshore Textile Museum

Holmshore Road, Holmshore, Rossendale BB4 4NP   Tel: 01706 226459   Fax: 01706 218554   Email: holmshoremuseum@museumoflancs.org.uk   Web: www.bringinghistoryalive.co.uk

Two of Lancashire's original textile mills. View international treasures including an Arkwright Water Frame and an improved Spinning Jenny. Enjoy live demonstrations of traditional textile techniques and processes.

Opening Times: Apr to Oct, closed Sat.   Admission: Adult £3.00, Child £1.50, Concession £1.50, Family £8.00.   Location: Rural location, approximately fifteen minutes from junction 5 on M65.   Map Ref: 15

Rossendale Museum

Whitaker Park, Rawtenstall, Rossendale BB4 6RE   Tel: 01706 244682   Fax: 01706 250037

19th century mill owner's residence set in a park, now a museum with varied collections, including local history, fine decorative arts, natural history. Features - William Bullock's tiger and python, small collection of late Victorian wallpapers.

Opening Times: Apr to Oct Mon to Fri 13:00-17:00, Sat 10:00-17:00, Sun 12:00-17:00. Nov to Mar Mon to Fri 13:00-17:00, Sat 10:00-16:00, Sun 12:00-16:00. Closed Xmas & New Year.   Admission: Free.   Location: Quarter of a mile from Rawtenstall centre; off A681; on main Accrington to Rochdale bus route.   Map Ref: 16

SLAIDBURN

Slaidburn Heritage Centre

25 Church Street, Slaidburn BB7 3ER   Tel / Fax: 01200 446161

Audio-visual presentation and artefacts relating to heritage of Slaidburn, including the unique 'Angel Stone Viking Carving'. Slaidburn is a conservation area in the heart of the Forest of Bowland, an area of outstanding beauty. Centre offers tourist information, morning coffee, light lunches and afternoon tea.

Opening Times: Apr to Oct Tue to Sun 11:00-17:00, Nov to Mar Thu to Sun 11:00-17:00.   Admission: Free.   Location: On the B6478 between Settle and Citheroe, near St Andrews Church. Free car park in village.   Map Ref: 17

Leicestershire is the home of the famous Quorn, Belvoir and Cottesmore hunts. However to the rest of the county many of the towns belong to the industrial east Midlands. England's smallest county, Rutland, was absorbed into Leicestershire in 1974. Nottinghamshire, lying in the low ground of the Trent basin, is the county of Robin Hood and Sherwood Forest.

The social history of these counties is preserved in some of the most comprehensive and attractive Museums in the land, catering for all interests and tastes.

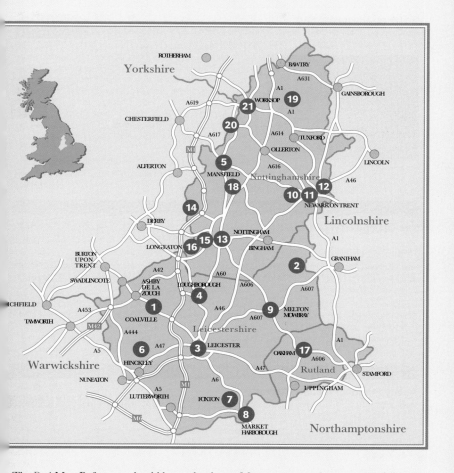

The Red Map References should be used to locate Museums etc on the pages that follow

Leicestershire & Nottinghamshire

COALVILLE *Leics*

The Manor House

Manor Road, Donnington-le-Heath, Coalville LE67 2FW   Tel / Fax: 01530 831259
Email: museums@leics.gov.uk   Web: www.leics.gov.uk

Medieval manor house dating back to 1280, with a fascinating history. The surrounding grounds have scented herb gardens, and the adjoining stone barn is home to a tempting restaurant.

Opening Times: Apr to Sep daily 11:00-17:00. Oct to Mar daily 11:00-15:00. Admission: Free.
Location: Southern outskirts of Coalville.   Map Ref: 1

Snibston Discovery Park

Ashby Road, Coalville LE67 3LN   Tel: 01530 278444   Fax: 01530 813301
Email: snibston@leics.gov.uk   Web: www.leics.gov.uk

An interactive exhibit in the Science Alive! Gallery

One of the largest and most dynamic museums in the Midlands, Snibston is Leicestershire's all-weather science and industry museum. Visitors can get their hands-on loads of fun in the popular 'Science Alive!' Gallery or explore the county's rich heritage in the Transport, Extractives, Engineering, Textiles and Fashion Galleries. Other attractions include guided colliery tours, outdoor science and water playgrounds, sculptures and nature reserve.

Opening Times: Daily 10:00-17:00. Admission: Adult £4.75, Child £2.95, Concession £3.25. Group rates available.   Map Ref: 1

GRANTHAM *Leics*

The Queens Royal Lancers

Belvoir Castle, Belvoir, Grantham NG31 7TJ   Tel: 01159 573295   Fax: 01559 573195
Email: mickholtby@deathorglorylancers.co.uk   Web: www.deathorglory.com

The museum traces the military and social history of the 16th/5th lancers, the 17th/21st lancers and The Queens Royal Lancers from their formation to present day. Weapons, uniforms, paintings, silver and personal artefacts form part of this fine collection.

Opening Times: 28 Mar to 1 Apr (Easter), 4 to 7, 14, 21 and 28 Apr, May to Sep Wed to Sun, BH and Oct Sun only, all 11:00-17:00. Admission: Adult £7.00, Child £3.50, OAP £5.50, Family (2 adults and 2 Children) £17.00.   Location: Six miles from the A1 at Grantham and 12 miles from Melton Mowbray. Nottingham and Stamford are within half an hours drive. Follow brown heritage signs.   Map Ref: 2

LEICESTER

Abbey Pumping Station Museum

Corporation Road, Off Abbey Lane, Leicester LE4 5PX   Tel: 0116 299 5111   Fax: 0116 261 3063   Web: www.leicestermuseums.ac.uk

Home to Gimson beam engines, exhibits include cinema equipment, vehicles, an interactive loo and public health and sanitation displays. The museum is also home to an impressive historic vehicle collection, including a coal-fired fish and chip van!

Opening Times: Please contact the site for seasonal opening hours. Admission: Free.
                                                                     Map Ref: 3

Belgrave Hall and Gardens

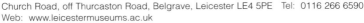

Church Road, off Thurcaston Road, Belgrave, Leicester LE4 5PE   Tel: 0116 266 6590
Web: www.leicestermuseums.ac.uk

Belgrave Hall is an 18th century Queen Anne house furnished in both Edwardian and Victorian room settings. There are several separate gardens and a new glasshouse containing permanent collections of tropical, sub-topical and alpine plants.

Opening Times: Please contact the site for seasonal opening hours. Admission: Free.
                                                                     Map Ref: 3

Guildhall

Guildhall Lane, Leicester LE1 5FQ   Tel: 0116 253 2569   Web: www.leicestermuseums.ac.uk

The Guildhall is one of Leicester's most famous buildings, dating back to the 14th century. Visitors can step back in time and see the Victorian police cells and maybe even a few ghosts!

Opening Times: Please contact the site for seasonal opening hours.   Admission: Free.

Map Ref: 3

Jewry Wall Museum

St Nicholas Circle, Leicester LE1 4LB   Tel: 0116 247 3021
Web: www.leicestermuseums.ac.uk

Local pre-historic, Roman and medieval artefacts. The museum houses several exhibitions including a series of illustrations showing street scenes from Iron Age, Roman, Saxon, Medieval and 18th century Leicester.

Opening Times: Please contact the site for seasonal opening hours.   Admission: Free.

Map Ref: 3

Leicestershire CCC Museum

County Ground, Grace Road, Leicester LE2 8AD   Tel: 0116 2832128

Collections of cricket memorabilia; bats, trophies, photographs. Themed showcases eg Ball-making, many archives from 1870 onwards, caps, blazers, medals etc.

Opening Times: Mon to Fri 09:30-15:30, winter by appointment. Admission: Free. Location: Two miles from town centre, access from M1/M69.   Map Ref: 3

Brian Davidson, a past overseas player standing in the Museum area

New Walk Museum & Art Gallery

53 New Walk, Leicester LE1 7EA   Tel: 0116 255 4100   Web: www.leicestermuseums.ac.uk

Visitors of all ages will be fascinated by the Ancient Egypt gallery with its mummies, coffins and other treasures and by the dinosaurs, rock and fossils collection in the Natural History section. The museum is a major regional Art Gallery with a notable collection of German Expressionist and European art dating from the 15th century to the present day. The Decorative Arts Gallery, in particular the ceramic collection, illustrates many aspects of social history including materials and techniques used.

The Dinosaurs at New Walk Museum

Opening Times: Please contact us for seasonal opening hours. Admission: Free. Location: Situated in the historic New Walk area of the city of Leicester. Map Ref: 3

Newarke Houses Museum

The Newarke, Leicester LE2 7BY   Tel: 0116 247 3222   Web: www.leicestermuseums.ac.uk

Newarke Houses Museum is composed of two historic houses, Wygston's Chantry House and Skeffington House. The Museum houses many fine collections including clocks, toys, greeting cards and coins.

Opening Times: Apr to Sep Mon to Sat 10:00-17:00, Sun 13:00-17:00, Oct to Mar Mon to Sat 10:00-16:00, Sun 13:00-16:00. Closed Xmas & New Year.   Admission: Free.   Map Ref: 3

LOUGHBOROUGH *Leics*

Bellfoundry Museum

Freehold Street, Loughborough LE11 1AR   Tel: 01509 233414   Fax: 01509 263305
Email: museum@taylorbells.co.uk   Web: www.taylorbells.co.uk

Exhibits showing how bells are made and tuned. Material relating to history of Taylor Family and

Company. Examples of bells, many of which can be rung by visitors. Only Bell Museum in the UK.

Opening Times: Tue to Fri & summer Sat 10:00-12:30 & 13:30-16:30. Winter Sat - please call for dates & times. Sun - Tour on first Sun in month at 14:00. Admission: Adult £1.50, Child 75p. Tour of Works (incl Museum): Adult £3.80, Child £1.90. Location: 15 minute walk from town centre, 10 minute walk from railway station. Map Ref: 4

Charnwood Museum

Queen's Hall, Granby Street, Loughborough LE11 3DU Tel: 01509 233754 Fax: 01509 268140 Email: museums@leics.gov.uk Web: www.leics.gov.uk

Charnwood Museum features a wide range of exhibits, which reflect local history and industries. Permanent exhibitions are in four areas: 'Coming to Charnwood', 'The Natural World of Charnwood', 'Living off the Land' and 'Earning a Living'.

Opening Times: Mon to Fri 10:00-16:30, Sun 14:00-17:00. Admission: Free. Location: Within town centre. Map Ref: 4

Great Central Railway Museum

Great Central Road, Loughborough LE11 1RW Tel: 01509 230726
Fax: 01509 239791 Email: booking-office@gcrailway.co.uk Web: www.gcrailway.co.uk

Main Line Steam trains - every weekend throughout the year. Recreating the experience of famous expresses of the steam age. Passenger trains also on weekdays, June to September. See one of our classic demonstration freight or parcel trains. Relax in the comfort of our classic corridor trains - steam heated in winter. Just like British Railways in the great years of steam.

Opening Times: Sat & Sun, Jun to Sep also weekdays. Admission: Free - donations welcome.
Location: Located south east of Loughborough Town Centre. 15 minute walk from Loughborough Railway Station. Map Ref: 4

'Green Arrow' on Great Central Railway

MANSFIELD *Notts*

Mansfield Museum & Art Gallery

Leeming Street, Mansfield NG18 1NG Tel: 01623 463088 Fax: 01623 412922
Email: mansfield_museum@hotmail.com

Permanent display galleries showing local, natural and social history of Mansfield and district, along with fine and decorative arts from days gone by. Always something new to see due to the varied programme of temporary exhibitions.

Opening Times: Mon to Sat 10:00-17:00. Admission: Free. Location: In the town centre. Map Ref: 5

MARKET BOSWORTH *Leics*

Bosworth Battlefield Visitor Centre & Country Park

Sutton Cheney, Market Bosworth CV13 0AD Tel: 01455 290429
Fax: 01455 292841 Email: bosworth@leics.gov.uk Web: www.leics.gov.uk

Site of the Battle of Bosworth 1485, the decisive battle of the War of the Roses where Richard III lost his life and his crown to the future Henry VII. Visitor centre with exhibitions and film theatre telling the story of this fateful battle. Battle trail (open all year), take a stroll around the trail with information boards explaining the course of the battle. Living history events throughout summer. Medieval spectacular including battle re-enactment 17/18 August 2002.

Opening Times: 27 Mar to 31 Oct Mon to Sat 11:00-17:00, Sun & BH 11:00-18:00. Nov & Dec Sun 11:00-Dusk. Mar Sat & Sun 11:00-17:00. Admission: Adult £3.00, Concession £1.90, Family £7.95. Subject to review Location: Site is bounded by A5, A444 and B585 and is clearly signposted from all these roads in the vicinity of Market Bosworth. Map Ref: 6

Leicestershire & Nottinghamshire

Foxton Canal Museum

Middle Lock, Foxton, Market Harborough LE16 7RA   Tel: 0116 279 2657
Email: mike@foxcm.freeserve.co.uk   Web: www.foxcanal.fsnet.co.uk

The story of canals, locks and boat lifts with models, interactive displays and artefacts. There is a play boat and working lock medal for younger visitors. High tech touch-screen display, and lots of artefacts.

Opening Times: Easter to Oct daily 10:00-17:00, Oct to Easter Sat to Wed 11:00-16:00.
Admission: Adult £2.00, Child Free (up to three children free with each full paying adult),
Concession £1.50.   Location: Five miles from Market Harborough at Foxton Locks. Follow
brown signs.   Map Ref: 7

Harborough Museum

Adam & Eve Street, Market Harborough LE16 7AG   Tel: 01858 821085   Fax: 01858 821086
Email: museums@leics.gov.uk   Web: www.leics.gov.uk

Displays include the Symington Collection of Corsetry and reconstruction of a local shoemaker's workshop.

Opening Times: Mon to Fri 10:00-16:30, Sun 14:00-17:00.   Admission: Free.   Location: Within
town centre.   Map Ref: 8

Melton Carnegie Museum

Thorpe End, Melton Mowbray LE13 1RB   Tel / Fax: 01664 569946
Email: museums@leics.gov.uk   Web: www.leics.gov.uk

Permanent displays feature local and natural history of the area and include work by British sporting artist John Ferneley as well as collections featuring foxhunting, the Stilton cheese and pork pie industries and the famous two-headed calf.

Opening Times: Currently closed for refurbishment and will re-open in early summer 2002.
Please phone for details.   Admission: Free.   Map Ref: 9

British Horological Institute

Upton Hall, Upton, Newark-on-Trent NG23 5TE   Tel: 01636 813795   Fax: 01636 812258

A fascinating collection of clocks, watches and tools in a fine country house with beautiful grounds. Includes some beautiful grandfather clocks and the original Speaking Clock.

Opening Times: Apr to Oct Tue to Sat 11:00-17:00, Sun 14:00-17:00. Nov to Mar Tue to Fri
13:30-16:30.   Admission: Adult £3.50, Child £2.00, OAP £3.00.   Location: In the centre of
Upton village, ten minutes drive from Newark.   Map Ref: 10

Gilstrap Heritage Centre

Castlegate, Newark-on-Trent NG24 1BG

Castle Story Exhibition featuring 1000 years of Newark Castle.

Opening Times: Oct to Mar 09:00-17:00, Apr to Sep 09:00-18:00.   Admission: Free.
Location: Situated in the grounds of Newark Castle in the town centre.   Map Ref: 11

Millgate Museum

48 Millgate, Newark-on-Trent NG24 4TS   Tel: 01636 655730   Fax: 01636 655735
Email: museums@newark-sherwooddc.gov.uk

Re-created streets, shops and rooms showing the commercial, social and domestic life of Newark. New 20th Century Gallery. Also Mezzanine Gallery displaying work of local artists.

Opening Times: Mon to Fri 10:00-17:00 Sat, Sun & BH 13:00-17:00.   Admission: Free.
Location: On the riverside walk, five minutes from Newark Town Centre.   Map Ref: 11

Leicestershire & Nottinghamshire

Newark Air Museum

Winthorpe Showground, Newark-on-Trent NG24 2NY   Tel / Fax: 01636 707170
Email: newarkair@lineone.net   Web: www.newarkairmuseum.co.uk

UK's largest volunteer managed aviation museum displaying 56 aircraft and cockpit sections from across the history of aviation. Large under cover display areas, artefact displays, souvenir shop and cafe.

Opening Times: Mar to Oct daily & BH 10:00-17:00 Nov to Feb daily 10:00-16:00.
Admission: Adult £4.25, Child £2.50, OAP £3.75.   Location: Easy access from A1, A17, A46 and A1133, follow brown/white signs.   Map Ref: 12

Newark Museum

Appletongate, Newark-on-Trent NG24 1JY   Tel: 01636 655740   Fax: 01636 655745
Email: museums@newark-sherwooddc.gov.uk

Ever wondered about Newark's early history? Find out more from the fine archaeology collections. Also look out for Newark's Civil War Heritage. Free fun trails link all the displays.

Opening Times: Mon to Sat 10:00-13:00, 14:00-17:00, closed Thu. Apr to Sep also open Sun 14:00-17:00, BH 13:00-17:00.   Admission: Free.   Location: Town centre, close to parish church.   Map Ref: 11

Newark Town Treasures & Art Gallery

Market Place, Newark-on-Trent NG24 1DU   Tel: 01636 680333   Fax: 01636 680350
Email: post@newark.gov.uk   Web: www.newark.gov.uk

Museum housed in Grade I listed Georgian Town Hall designed by John Carr in 1776. Collection consists of sumptuous civic gifts and paintings from 17th and 18th centuries. Temporary exhibitions in the Spotlight Gallery.

Opening Times: Mon to Fri 10:30-13:00 14:00-16:30 all year. Sat 13:00-16:00 (Apr to Oct). Closed Sun & BH.   Admission: Free.   Location: Town centre.   Map Ref: 11

Vina Cooke Museum of Dolls & Bygone Childhood

The Old Rectory, Cromwell, Newark-on-Trent NG23 6JE   Tel: 01636 821364

Large collection of dolls, toys, prams, dolls houses, books, games and costumes. Handmade dolls by Vina Cooke depicting royalty, stage, screen and historical characters. Also various christening robes, children's clothing and accessories. Attractively displayed in late 17th century Dower House and former rectory. An Easter Monday Extravaganza takes place every year, with Morris dancers and fascinating craft displays.

A corner of the Toy Room - 'Nanny' on duty

Opening Times: Daily except Fri 10:30-12:00, 14:00-17:00. Fri, evenings and other hours by appointment. Admission: Adult £2.50, Child £1.50, OAP £2.00.

Location: Five miles north of Newark, easy access from A1. Next to church in village of Cromwell.   Map Ref: 10

NOTTINGHAM

Angel Row Gallery

Central Library Building, 3 Angel Row, Nottingham NG1 6HP   Tel: 0115 915 2869
Email: deborah.clean@nottinghamcitygov.uk

A varied and constantly changing programme of exhibitions covers the whole range of contemporary art.

Opening Times: Mon to Sat 10:00-17:00.   Admission: Free.   Location: City centre, one minute walk from market square.   Map Ref: 13

Brewhouse Yard Museum

Castle Boulevard, Nottingham NG7 1FB   Tel: 0115 915 3600
Email: alisonb@notmusbhy.demon.co.uk

A realistic glimpse of life in Nottingham over the past 300 years.

Opening Times: Daily 10:00-17:00.   Admission: Adult £1.50, Child/Concession 80p, Family £3.80.   Location: Ten minutes walk from city centre.   Map Ref: 13

Castle Museum & Art Gallery

Nottingham NG1 6EL   Tel: 0115 915 3700   Fax: 0115 915 3653
Email: samanthah@notmusbhy.demon.co.uk   Web: www.nottinghamcity.gov.uk

Once medieval castle built on by William the Conqueror, Nottingham Castle is now a 17th century mansion building. Nottingham Castle houses and range of exciting historical and contemporary art, ceramics and silverware.

Opening Times: Daily 10:00-17:00. Admission: Free Mon to Fri. Weekends & BH - Adult £2.00, Child/Concession £1.00, Family (2 adult and 4 children) £5.00. Location: Five minutes walk from Nottingham City Centre, easy access from train and bus station.   Map Ref: 13

Djanogly Art Gallery

Lakeside Arts Centre, University Park, Nottingham NG5 1JR   Tel: 0115 951 3192   Fax: 0115 951 3194   Email: neil.walker@nottingham.ac.uk   Web: www.nottingham.ac.uk/artscentre/

Temporary exhibition galleries offering a year-round programme of contemporary and historic fine art exhibitions with education activities and events targeted at general public and schools/colleges.

Opening Times: Mon to Sat 11:00-17:00, Sun & BH 14:00-17:00. Admission: Free.
Location: One and a half miles outside city centre, on major bus route. Easy access by car from motorway.   Map Ref: 13

Durban House Heritage Centre

Mansfield Road, Eastwood, Nottingham NG16 3DZ   Tel: 01773 717353

The Heritage Centre Exhibition is now open with a host of attractions. These include a school area with blackboards and desks, clothes to try on and two walk-through coal areas.

Opening Times: Daily 09:00-17:00. Admission: Adult £2.00, Child/Concession £1.20.
Location: Signposted from A610.   Map Ref: 14

Galleries of Justice

Shire Hall, High Pavement, Nottingham NG1 1HN
Tel: 0115 952 0555   Fax: 0115 993 9828
Email: info@galleriesofjustice.org.uk
Web: www.galleriesofjustice.org.uk

GALLERIES *of* **JUSTICE**

Journey with us through 300 years of Crime and Punishment on this historic site, where your senses are bombarded with the sounds, sights and smells of justice and injustice, the guilty and the innocent. Witness a real trial in the authentic Victorian courtroom before being sentenced and 'sent down' to the original cells and medieval caves.

Opening Times: Tue to Sun & BH 10:00-17:00. Closed Xmas & New Year. Admission: Adult £6.95, Child £5.25, Concession £5.95, Family £19.95. Location: Midland Railway Station and Victoria Bus Station ten minute walk.   Map Ref: 13

Greens Mill & Centre

Windmill Lane, Sneinton, Nottingham NG2 4QB   Tel: 0115 915 6878
Email: enquiries@greensmill.org.uk   Web: www.greensmill.org.uk

A unique working windmill built at the beginning of the 19th century, once home to the mathematical genius and miller George Green. The outhouses also house a science centre.

Opening Times: Wed to Sun and BH 10:00-16:00. Admission: Free. Location: One mile outside Nottingham City Centre.   Map Ref: 13

Industrial Museum

Courtyard Buildings, Wollaton Park, Nottingham NG8 2AE   Tel: 0115 915 3910
Email: marketing@notmusbhy.demon.co.uk

The Museum is housed in the 18th century stable block for Wollaton Hall. It tells the story of the industries of Nottingham and its environs, from heavy industries such as coal mining and engineering to its famous lace.

Opening Times: Daily 11:00-17:00. Admission: Weekdays Free. Weekends and BH Adult £1.50, Child/Concession 80p, Family £3.80. Location: Four miles from Nottingham City Centre off the A6514.   Map Ref: 15

The Lace Market Centre

3/5 High Pavement, Nottingham NG1 1HF   Tel: 0115 9897365   Fax: 0115 9897301
Email: info@nottinghamlace.org.uk   Web: www.nottinghamlace.org.uk

Exhibition 'Nottingham Lace and Its People' includes machine and handmade lace demonstrations, video archives and photo story boards. Large lace shop including own brand products made on the premises.

Opening Times: Daily & BH 10:00-17:00.   Admission: Exhibition - free of charge. £1.95 hire charge audio walk of The Lace Market.   Location: City centre, ten minutes from bus and railway station.
Map Ref: 13

D H Lawrence Birthplace Museum

8A Victoria Street, Eastwood, Nottingham NG16 3AW   Tel: 01773 717353

Lawrence linked Victorian exhibits.

Opening Times: Apr to Oct daily 09:00-17:00. Nov to Mar daily 09:00-16:00.   Admission: Adult £2.00, Child/Concession £1.20.   Location: Signposted from A610.
Map Ref: 14

Long Eaton Town Hall

Derby Road, Long Eaton, Nottingham   Tel: 0115 907 1141

Temporary exhibitions of art, local and social history. Plus Howitt bequest of paintings.

Opening Times: Mon to Fri 10:00-16:00.   Admission: Free.   Location: Near town centre.
Map Ref: 16

Museum of Costume & Textiles

51 Castle Gate, Nottingham NG1 6AF   Tel: 0115 915 3500
Email: jeremyf@notmusbhy.demon.co.uk

200 years of costume displayed in a series of period room sets, finest collection of machine made and hand made lace dating from the 16th century. A collection of tapestries dating from the 17th century.

Opening Times: Wed to Sun & BH 11:00-17:00.   Admission: Free.   Location: One minute walk from the market square in the city centre.
Map Ref: 13

Natural History Museum, Wollaton Park

Wollaton Park, Nottingham NG8 2AE   Tel: 0115 915 3900
Email: carolb@notmusbhy.demon.co.uk

Nottingham's natural history collection housed in an Elizabethan mansion, set in 500 acres of natural parkland.

Opening Times: Daily 11:00-17:00.   Admission: Free, except Sat, Sun & BH Adults £1.50, Child/Concession 80p, Family £3.80.
Map Ref: 15

OAKHAM *Leics*

Normanton Church Museum

Rutland Water, Oakham LE15 8PX   Tel: 01572 653026/653022   Fax: 01572 653027

The museum shows a 30 minute video on the construction of the reservoir, together with displays of some of the archaeological finds, and the history of the church and surrounding area.

Opening Times: Easter to Sep Mon to Fri 11:00-16:00, Sat to Sun 11:00-17:00.
Admission: Small charge   Location: Near Normanton car park, South Shore, Rutland Water.
Map Ref: 17

Museums, Galleries, Historic Houses & Sites

Please let us know of any collections that are not listed in this guide that you feel should be listed. E-mail us on *editor@tomorrows.co.uk*
or return the Report Form on page 448

Oakham Castle

Market Place, Oakham   Tel: 01572 758440   Fax: 01572 758445
Email: museum@rutland.gov.uk   Web: www.rutnet.co.uk/rcc/rutlandmuseums

The 12th century Great Hall of Oakham Castle

Oakham Castle, in the town centre, was a fortified manor house. With its medieval musician sculptures and fine architecture, its Great Hall is one of the most important monuments of Norman England. Over 200 unique presentation horseshoes, forfeited by peers and royalty to the lord of the manor, hang inside. The Great Hall is a popular venue for civil marriages.

Opening Times: Late Mar to late Oct Mon to Sat 10:00-13:00 13:30-17:00, Sun 13:00-17:00. Late Oct to late Mar closes 16:00 daily. Closed Good Friday & Xmas.
Admission: Free. Location: Off Market Place. Map Ref: 17

Rutland County Museum

Catmose Street, Oakham LE15 6HW   Tel: 01572 758440   Fax: 01572 758445
Email: museum@rutland.gov.uk   Web: www.rutnet.co.uk/rcc/rutlandmuseums

*The Rutland County Museum's
1794 riding school building*

In a splendid late 18th century indoor riding school near Oakham town centre, the Rutland County Museum has extensive rural life collections. On show are rural tradesmen's tools and farming equipment of all kinds, with domestic collections, local archaeology, and a special gallery on the Volunteer Soldier in Leicestershire and Rutland. Temporary exhibitions and a Coffee Corner are additional attractions.

Opening Times: Mon to Sat 10:00-17:00, Sun 14:00-17:00. Late Oct to late Mar 14:00-16:00. Closed Good Friday & Xmas. Admission: Free. Location: On A6003 just south of town centre.   Map Ref: 17

RAVENSHEAD *Notts*

Longdale Craft Centre & Museum

Longdale Lane, Ravenshead NG15 9AH Tel / Fax: 01623 794858
Email: longdale@longdale.co.uk   Web: www.longdale.co.uk

Britains oldest and first 'real' craft centre. From its humble beginnings it has become a craft centre of international reputation, incorporating workshops, museum, gallery and a first class restaurant.

Opening Times: All day, every day.   Map Ref: 18

Newstead Abbey

Newstead Abbey Park, Ravenshead NG15 8GE   Tel: 01623 455900
Email: enquiries@newsteadabbey.og.uk   Web: www.newsteadabbey.org.uk

A beautiful historic house set in glorious landscape of gardens and parkland. Founded as a monastic house in the late 12th century, Newstead Abbey became the Byron family seat in 1540.

Opening Times: Apr to Sep daily 12:00-17:00. Admission: Adult £4.00, Child £1.50, Concession £2.00, Family £10.00. Location: 12 miles north of Nottingham on the A60, close to junction 27 of the M1.   Map Ref: 18

Papplewick Pumping Station

off Longdale Lane, Ravenshead NG15 9AJ   Tel: 0115 963 2938

Late Victorian working waterworks in landscaped grounds. One of Europe's great industrial monuments. Original engines/boilers in magnificent Temple of Steam.

Opening Times: BH and other weekends operational. Admission: Adult £3.00, Child £1.50, Concession/Group £2.50. Location: Signposted off A60/A614 seven miles north of Nottingham.
                    Map Ref: 18

Leicestershire & Nottinghamshire

Bassetlaw Museum & Percy Laws Memorial Gallery

Amcott House, Grove Street, Retford DN22 6JU   Tel / Fax: 01777 713749

Collections relating to the history and archaeology of North Nottinghamshire. Continuous programme of short-term exhibitions. Permanent display of the Retford civic plate. In restored Georgian town house setting.

Opening Times: Mon to Sat 10:00-17:00. Closed Sun & BH.   Admission: Free.   Location: 200 m from town centre (Market Square), three minutes from bus station.   Map Ref: 19

Creswell Crags Museum and Education Centre

Crags Road, Welbeck, Worksop S80 3LH   Tel: 01909 720378   Fax: 01909 724726 Email: info@creswell.crags.org.uk   Web: www.creswell-crags.org.uk

Limestone gorge with caves and lake. One of Britain's most important archaeology sites, home to Ice Age hunters 40,000 years ago. Museum displays, education centre, 'Virtually The Ice Age' website.

Opening Times: Daily Feb to Oct 10:30-16:30, Nov to Jan Sun only 10:30-16:30. Admission: Free.   Location: Half mile east of Creswell village on B6042 (off A616), 20 minutes from Creswell Railway Station.   Map Ref: 20

Harley Gallery

Welbeck, Worksop S80 3LW   Tel: 01909 501700   Email: ssherrit@harley-welbck.co.uk Web: www.harleygallery.co.uk

A changing display of contemporary arts and crafts exhibitions. Craft shop selling work from eminent British artists, a museum showing fine/decorative arts from The Portland Collection and a range of events/workshops exploring the arts.

Opening Times: Feb to Dec Tue to Sun 10:00-17:00.   Admission: Free.   Location: Situated on the A60 Mansfield Road, two miles south of Worksop.   Map Ref: 20

Mr Straw's House

7 Blyth Road, Worksop S81 0JG   Tel: 01909 482380   Web: www.nationaltrust.org

A semi-detached house offering a tantalising glimpse into the past. Letters, photos, furniture, household objects - all shown in their rightful places where the family left them.

Opening Times: Apr to Oct Tue to Sat 11:00-16:30. Due to the domestic scale of the property pre-booking is essential for all visitors.   Admission: Adult £4.20, Child £2.10, Family £10.50, National Trust Members Free.   Location: Follow signs to Bassetlaw Hospital, Blyth Grove is signposed on B6045.   Map Ref: 21

Worksop Museum

Worksop Public Library, Memorial Avenue, Worksop S80 2BP   Tel / Fax: 01777 713749

Permanent introductory exhibition to the Pilgrim Father's Story. Programme of art exhibitions. Display of the Arundel Marble statue from the frieze of the Great Altar of Pergamon in Asia Minor.

Opening Times: Mon to Wed & Fri 09:30-17:00 Thu & Sat 09:30-13:00. Closed Sun & BH. Admission: Free.   Location: Within Public Library in setting of Memorial Gardens, five minutes walk from main street.   Map Ref: 21

county town Lincoln dominates the old county of Lincolnshire, standing on the central chalk
e, the Lincolnshire Edge. The impressive triple towered cathedral overlooks the ancient
ric city with its beautiful stained glass windows and the famous Lincoln Imp. Skegness,
olnshire's seaside resort, was developed during the nineteenth century and flourished with
coming of the railway in 1873. The Holland region of drained Fen is the commercial bulb-
ving centre, ablaze with colour during the Spring months leading to Spalding's spectacular
Parade in May.

e selection of museums and historic houses encapsulate the local and social history of
olnshire.

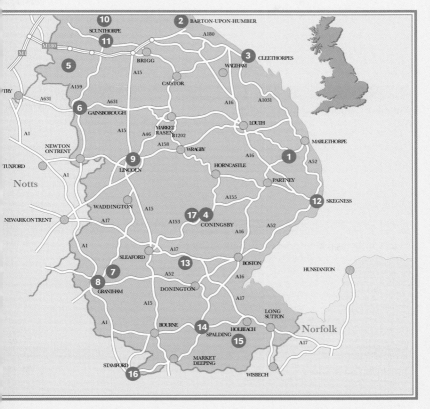

The Red Map References should be used to locate Museums etc on the pages that follow

Lincolnshire & South Humberside

ALFORD *Lincs*

Alford Manor House Museum

Alford Manor House, West Street, Alford LN13 9DJ   Tel: 01507 463073

Main attraction is the 17th century thatched manor house, with a folk museum and garden, wash house, park area. Refreshment Tuesdays, Fridays and Bank Holidays.

Opening Times: Easter to end Sep Mon to Sat 10:00-17:00 Sun 12:00-16:00.
Admission: Admission charge.   Location: Near town centre.   Map Ref: 1

BARTON-UPON-HUMBER *Humberside*

Baysgarth House Museum

Baysgarth Leisure Park, Caistor Road, Barton-upon-Humber DN18 6AH   Tel: 01652 632318

An 18th century mansion house with fine period rooms, a collection of 18th and 19th century English and Oriental pottery and an industrial museum in the stable block.

Opening Times: Tue to Sun & BH 10:00-16:00. Closed Mon and Xmas & New Year.
Admission: Free.   Location: Near town centre, 3 mins walk from Market Place.   Map Ref: 2

CLEETHORPES *Humberside*

Humber Estuary Discovery Centre

c/o The Civic Offices, Knoll Street, Cleethorpes DN35 8LN   Tel: 01472 323232   Fax: 01472 323233   Email: discovery.centre@nelincs.gov.uk   Web: www.time-discoverycentre.co.uk

Family exhibition filled with hands-on displays and activities exploring time and how Cleethorpes has changed through time. The Humber Estuary can be viewed through our high powered telescopes in the Conoco Observatory.

Opening Times: Daily 10:00-17:00. Closed Xmas & New Year.   Admission: Adult £1.95, Child/OAP £1.30, Under 3's Free.   Location: Near sea front, ten minute walk from main promenade.   Map Ref: 3

CONINGSBY *Lincs*

Battle of Britain Memorial Fight Visitor Centre

RAF Coningsby, Coningsby LN4 4SY   Tel: 01526 344041   Fax: 01526 342330
Email: bbmf@lincolnshire.gov.uk   Web: www.lincolnshire.gov.uk

Unique opportunity to view the historic aircraft of BBMF at their home base at RAF Coningsby. Visitors are shown around the hanger by knowledgeable volunteers.

Opening Times: Mon to Fri 10:00-17:00. Closed Sat, Sun, BH and two weeks at Xmas.
Admission: Adult £3.50, Child £1.50, OAP £2.00, Groups £2.00.   Location: Half mile from Coningsby Village.   Map Ref: 4

EPWORTH *Humberside*

Epworth Old Rectory

1 Rectory Street, Epworth DN9 1HX   Tel: 01427 872268
Email: epworth@oldrectory63.freeserve.co.uk   Web: www.epworthrectory.freeserve.co.uk

1709 Queen Anne House, boyhood home of John and Charles Wesley. Portraits, period furniture, prints, memorabilia, set in large grounds.

Opening Times: Mar to Oct daily. Mar, Apr & Oct 10:00-12:00 14:00-16:00. May, Jun, Jul, Aug & Sep Mon to Sat 10:00-16:30 Sun 14:00-16:30.   Admission: Adult £3.00, Child £1.00, OAP £2.50, Family £7.00.   Location: 200 yards from Epworth Town Centre.   Map Ref: 5

GAINSBOROUGH *Lincs*

Gainsborough Old Hall

Parnell Street, Gainsbrorough DN21 2NB   Tel: 01427 612669   Fax: 01427 612779
Email: gainsboroughholdhall@lincolnshire.gov.uk   Web: www.lincolnshire.gov.uk

Gainsborough's own medieval manor house. Principally a timber-framed building with a brick tower, magnificent Great Hall and one of the best preserved medieval kitchens in the country.

Opening Times: Mon to Sat 10:00-17:00 Sun 14:00-17:30. Closed Sun from end of Oct to Easter, Xmas & New Year and Good Friday.   Admission: Adult £2.50 Child £1.00 OAP £1.50.
Location: In the centre of Gainsborough.   Map Ref: 6

Lincolnshire & South Humberside

Belton House

Belton, Grantham NG32 2LS   Tel: 01476 566116   Fax: 01476 579071
Email: belton@smtp.ntrust.org.uk   Web: www.nationaltrust.org.uk

The stunning interiors of this restored country house contain exceptionally fine plasterwork and wood carving, as well as important collections of paintings, furniture, tapestries and silverware.

Opening Times: 23 Mar to 3 Nov Wed to Sun & BH Mon, Good Friday & Tue 4 Jun.   Admission: Adult £5.60, Child £2.80, Family £14.00. Group rates available if pre-booked.   Location: Three miles north east of Grantham on A607 Grantham to Lincoln Road.   Map Ref: 7

Grantham Museum

St Peters Hill, Grantham NG31 6PY   Tel: 01476 568783   Fax: 01476 592457
Email: grantham.museum@lincolnshire.gov.uk

Grantham Museum is the interpretation centre of the town with displays from its earliest archaeological remains, to displays on Isaac Newton, the Dambusters and Margaret Thatcher. Regular temporary exhibitions and events. Please contact the Museum for further details.

Opening Times: Mon to Sat 10:00-17:00 BH & Good Friday. Closed Xmas & New Year.
Admission: Free.   Location: Situated in the centre of Grantham next to the Guildhall.   Map: 8

Doddington Hall

Lincoln LN6 4RU   Tel: 01522 694308   Fax: 01522 685259
Email: fionawatson@doddingtonhall.free-online.co.uk   Web: www.doddingtonhall.free-online.co.uk

The Hall stands today exactly as it was built in 1600. The elegant Georgian interior contains a fascinating collection of pictures, textiles, porcelain and furniture that reflect four centuries of unbroken occupation.

Opening Times: Feb to May Sun, Wed & BH Gardens only. May to Sep Sun, Wed, BH House & Gardens.   Admission: Gardens: Adult £3.10, Child £1.55. House & Gardens: Adult £4.60, Child £2.30, Family £12.75.   Location: Clearly signposted off the A46 Lincoln by-pass on the B1190.
Map Ref: 9

Greyfriars

Broadgate, Lincoln LN2 1HQ   Tel: 01522 530401   Fax: 01522 530724
Email: hollandk@lincolnshire.gov.uk

Greyfriars is a beautiful 13th century building located in the lower part of Lincoln. Greyfriars is used to display annual themed exhibitions drawn from the collections of the City and County Museum, which range from pre-history to 1750. A lively programme of events throughout the year.

Opening Times: Jun to Apr Wed to Sat 10:00-13:00, 14:00-16:00. Closed 25-26 Dec and New Years Day.   Admission: Free.   Location: Located in the lower part of Lincoln between St Swithin's Church and central library.   Map Ref: 9

The Incredibly Fantastic Old Toy Show

26 Westgate, Lincoln LN1 3BD   Tel: 01522 520534

A changing themed display of toys from 1790 to 1970, with distorting mirrors, pier-end machines, buttons to push, films to watch and a unique collection of old photographs of children with toys.

Opening Times: Easter to end Sep Thu to Sat 11:00-17:00, Sun & BH 12:00-16:00. Oct to end of year Sat 11:00-17:00 Sun 12:00-16:00. Lincoln school holidays Easter to Nov.
Admission: Adult £2.20, Child £1.20, Under 5s Free, OAP/Concession £1.80.
Location: By Castle and Cathedral.   Map Ref: 9

Lincoln Castle

Castle Hill, Lincoln LN1 3AA   Tel: 01522 511068   Fax: 01522 512150

The castle was built by William the Conqueror in 1068 on a site occupied since Roman times. It is one of only two castles in Britain with two mottes.

Opening Times: Apr to Oct Mon to Sat 09:30-17:30, Sun 11:00-17:30. Nov to Mar Mon to Sat 09:30-16:30, Sun 11:00-16:30. Closed Xmas & New Year.   Admission: Admission charge.
Location: In Lincoln, 16 miles north-east of Newark-on-Trent.   Map Ref: 9

Museum of Lincolnshire Life

The Old Barracks, Burton Road, Lincoln LN1 3LY   Tel: 01522 528448   Fax: 01522 521264
Email: lincolnshire.museum@lincolnshire.gov.uk

The largest community museum in Lincolnshire boasting a nationally renowned agricultural collection; richly represented industrial and social history displays, and incorporating the newly refurbished Royal Lincolnshire Regimental Museum and an 18th century working windmill nearby.

Opening Times: May to Oct 10:00-17:30. Nov to Apr Mon to Sat 10:00-17:30 Sun 14:00-17:30. Closed Xmas & New Year.   Admission: Adult £2.00 Child 60p Family £4.50 Groups of 10 or over £1.60 per adult.   Location: Within five minutes walk of Lincoln Cathedral and Castle sites.
Map Ref: 9

Royal Lincolnshire Regiment Museum

Museum of Lincolnshire Life, Burton Road, Lincoln LN1 3LY   Tel: 01522 528448

The newly refurbished Regimental Galleries display over 300 years of the regiment's history from its inception to its amalgamation with the Royal Anglian Regiment. It uses objects and text to portray life as a soldier from 1685 to 1960.

Opening Times: May to Oct 10:00-17:00. Nov to Apr Mon to Sat 10:00-17:30 Sun 14:00-17:30. Admission: Adult £2.00 Child 60p Family £4.50 Group of 10 or more £1.60 per adult.
Location: Within five minutes walk of Lincoln Cathedral and Castle sites.   Map Ref: 9

Usher Gallery

Lindum Road, Lincoln LN2 1NN   Tel: 01522 527980   Fax: 01522 560165
Email: usher.gallery@lincolnshire.gov-uk

Major Lincolnshire venue for fine and decorative arts including the Peter de Wint Collection. A lively programme of temporary exhibitions throughout the year.

Opening Times: Tue to Sat 10:00-17:30, Sun 14:30-17:00. Closed 24-31 Dec, Mon except BH. Admission: Adult £2.00 Child/Concession 50p. Free day Fri.   Location: Situated on the slope below the Cathedral, five minutes from the town centre.   Map Ref: 9

SCUNTHORPE *Humberside*

Normanby Hall

Normanby Hall Country Park, Normanby, Scunthorpe DN15 9HU   Tel: 01724 720588
Fax: 01724 721248

Normanby Hall is a Regency country house designed by Sir Robert Smirke and furnished in period style. It also contains a costume gallery in which annually changing exhibitions are held.

Opening Times: 25 Mar to 29 Sep daily 13:00-17:00. Other times by appointment.
Admission: Adult £3.50, Concession £2.50, Family £9.50. Special Rates for North Lincolnshire residents & Groups.   Location: Four miles north of Scunthorpe off the B1430.   Map Ref: 10

Normanby Park Farming Museum

Normanby Hall Country Park, Normanby, Scunthorpe DN15 9HU   Tel: 01724 720588
Fax: 01724 721248

The Normanby Park Farming Museum shows the history of farming and rural crafts in the late 19th and early 20th centuries. Holding regular activities for children.

Opening Times: 25 Mar to 29 Sep daily 13:00-17:00. Other times by appointment.
Admission: Adult £3.50, Concession £2.50, Family £9.50. Special Rates for North Lincolnshire residents & Groups.   Location: Four miles north of Scunthorpe off the B1430.   Map Ref: 10

Lincolnshire & South Humberside

North Lincolnshire Museum

 ♿ ◆ 🚂

Oswald Road, Scunthorpe DN15 7BD   Tel: 01724 843533

The museum housed in a Victorian vicarage, depicts North Lincolnshire's early and later history, through displays of geology, archaeology and social history.

Opening Times: Tue to Sat & BH 10:00-16:00, Sun 13:00-16:00. Closed Mon and Xmas & New Year. Admission: Free. Location: Near town centre, two minute walk from railway station, bus stop outside.

Map Ref: 11

SKEGNESS *Lincs*

Church Farm Museum

 ♿ ◆ 📷 🚂

Church Road South, Skegness PE25 2HF   Tel: 01754 766658   Fax: 01754 898243
Email: walkerr@lincolnshire.gov.uk

Agricultural and country life museum 19th to 20th century. Set in original farm house and farm buildings. Lincolnshire thatched mud and stud cottage, barns and waggon hovel re-built on site.

Opening Times: Apr to Oct 10:30-17:30. Admission: Adult £1.00 Child 50p.
Location: Fifteen minutes walk from railway station.

Map Ref: 12

SLEAFORD *Lincs*

Heckington Windmill

 📷 ◆ 📷 🚂

Hale Road, Heckington, Sleaford NG34 9JJ   Tel: 01529 461919

Working 19th century windmill (major repairs expected 2002). Only eight sailed mill in Western Europe. Technical displays on history, mills and milling. Sales of stoneground flour etc.

Opening Times: Please contact. Admission: Adult £1.50 Child 75p Under 5s free.
Location: Heckington is a village in Lincolnshire between Sleaford and Boston by-passed by A17. The mill is adjacent to Heckington Railway Station.

Map Ref: 13

SPALDING *Lincs*

Ayscoughfee Hall Museum & Gardens

 📷 ♿ ◆ 📷 🚂

Churchgate, Spalding PE11 2RA   Tel: 01775 725468   Fax: 01775 762715
Email: ssladen@sholland.gov.uk   Web: www.sholland.gov.uk

 *Ayscoughfee Hall is a late Medieval (1429) wool merchants house set in five acres of walled gardens. The formal gardens were set out in 1720 and show an important 'footprint' of an early Georgian urban garden. It is home to the Museum of South Holland Life and Spalding Tourist Information*  *Centre. Tennis, putting and bowling facilities in the garden and children's play area and activities.*

Opening Times: Daily Mon to Fri 9:00-17:00, Mar to Oct Sat 10:00-17:00, Sun & BH 11:00-17:00. Admission: Free. Location: Five minutes walk from town centre, ten minutes from railway station. On east bank of River Welland.

Map Ref: 14

Museum of Entertainment

 📷 ♿ ◆ 📷 🚂

Millgate, Whaplode St Catherine, Spalding PE12 6SF   Tel: 01406 540379

This museum is a charitable trust and covers all aspects of entertainment from marionettes c.1790, music boxes, Edison phonographs, organs, The Diggola, Reed organs, radio, television, video, fairground and much more.

Opening Times: Easter four days then Sun & BH to end Jun 13:00-17:00. Jul, Aug & Sep Sun to Thu 13:00-17:00. Admission: Adult £3.00, Child £2.00, OAP £2.50.
Location: Whaplode A151, follow brown/white signs two miles.

Map Ref: 15

Lincolnshire & South Humberside

STAMFORD *Lincs*

Burghley House

Stamford PE9 3JY   Tel: 01780 752451   Fax: 01780 480125
Email: burghley@burghley.co.uk   Web: www.burghley.co.uk

Burghley House

18 state rooms including one of the most important private collections of 17th century Italian paintings, the earliest inventoried collection of Japanese ceramics in the west and wood carving by Grinling Gibbons and his followers. There are also four magnificent state beds, fine examples of English and continental furniture and important tapestries and textiles.

Opening Times: Good Friday 29 Mar to 27 Oct 11:00-17:00.   Admission: Adult £7.10, Child £3.50, OAP £6.50.   Location: One mile east of Stamford on B1443, close to A1 clearly signposted.   Map Ref: 16

Stamford Museum

Broad Street, Stamford PE9 1PJ   Tel: 01780 766317   Fax: 01780 480363
Email: crawleyt@lincolnshire.gov.uk

Displays illustrate the history of this fine stone town and include Stamford Ware pottery, the visit of Daniel Lambert and the town's more recent industrial past. Temporary exhibitions and holiday activities.

Opening Times: Apr to Sep Mon to Sat 10:00-17:00 Sun 14:00-17:00. Oct to Mar Mon to Sat 10:00-17:00. Closed 24-26 Dec & New Years Eve & Day.   Admission: Free.   Location: Town centre.   Map Ref: 16

TATTERSHALL *Lincs*

Guardhouse Museum

Tattershall Castle, Tattershall LN4 4LR   Tel: 01526 342543

Drawings and paintings of Tattershall Castle and artefacts recovered during restoration 1910-1914.

Opening Times: Apr to Oct Sat to Wed 11:00-17:30. Nov & Dec Sat & Sun 12:00-16:00.   Admission: Adult £3.20, Child £1.60.   Location: On A153, 15 miles north east of Sleaford, ten miles south west of Horncastle.   Map Ref: 17

a sense London is one enormous museum: from the first century AD when the Romans settled here ough the early medieval period of the building of the first St Paul's Cathedral, the Norman period of e construction of the White Tower, the prosperous years of the Livery Companies, through plague, fire d pestilence and the gracious years of Wren's building, to the London of today, this city has drawn to elf the nation's talent and expertise. This great city of history and pageantry has become the treasure use of Britain's skills where everything is recorded in a vast selection of the finest, and certainly the est fascinating, museums and galleries of the world.

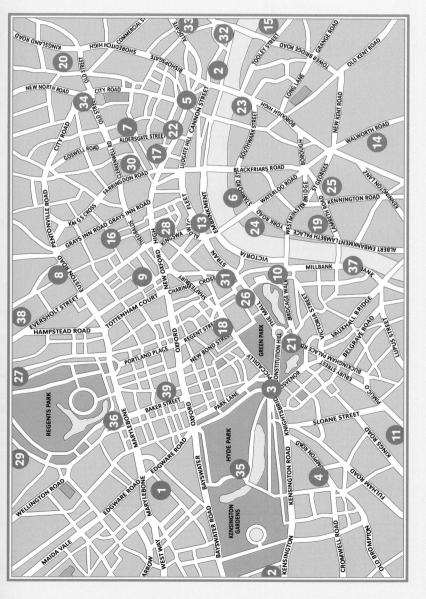

The Red Map References should be used to locate Museums etc on the pages that follow

London Underground System

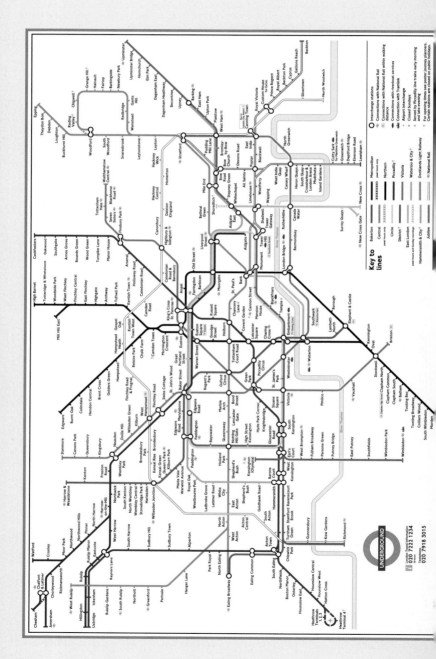

Alexander Fleming Laboratory Museum

St Marys Hospital, Praed Street, London W2 1NY   Tel: 020 7886 6528   Fax: 020 7886 6739
Email: kevin.brown@st-marys.nhs.uk

In situ reconstruction of Fleming's laboratory as it was in 1928 when he discovered penicillin there, with video and exhibition telling the story of the man, the mould and its impact on mankind.

Opening Times: Mon to Thu 10:00-13:00 (other times by appointment).   Admission: Adult
£2.00, Concession £1.00.   Location: A two minute walk from Paddington Station.   Map Ref: 1

All Hallows By The Tower Undercroft Museum

Byward Street, London EC3R 5BJ   Tel: 020 7481 2928

Undercroft museum, Roman pavement, church records, Templar altar.

Opening Times: Church: Mon to Fri 09:00-18:00, Sat & Sun 10:00-17:00. Museum: Mon to Sat
11:00-16:00, Sun 13:00-16:00.   Admission: Church: Free. Audio Tour: donation requested.
Location: Tower Hill underground five minutes walk.   Map Ref: 2

Apsley House

Hyde Park Corner, London W1J 7NT
Tel: 020 7499 5676 Fax: 020 7493 6576

Apsley House, famously known as No. 1 London, is one of the capital's finest residences. Ancestral home of the Dukes of Wellington since 1815, its sumptuous interiors house the first Duke's outstanding collection of paintings, silver, porcelain and sculpture. London Tourist Board Small Visitor Attraction of the Year 2001.

Opening Times: Tue to Sun 11:00-17:00.   Admission: Adult £4.50,
Under 18s/OAP Free, Concession £3.00, Group £2.50. Price
includes free sound guide.   Location: Hyde Park Corner. Map Ref: 3

Apsley House, The Waterloo Gallery

Baden Powell House

Suite 210, 28 Old Brompton Road, South Kensington, London SW7 3SS   Tel: 020 75847031
Fax: 020 75906902   Email: conferences.bphhostel@scout.org.uk   Web: www.scouts.org.uk

Welcomed by the only granite statue in London - Lord Robert Baden-Powell (founder of the Scouting Movement) welcomes you to a memorial to his life-time achievements. It hosts a display, which depicts his life story and boasts memorabilia given to him by world delegations. As an artist Baden-Powell produced some magnificent paintings and sketches, which are also on display.

Opening Times: 4 Jan to 21 Dec daily 07:00-23:00.
Admission: Free.   Location: Central London, South
Kensington - five minute walk from Gloucester Road and
South Kensington tube stations.   Map Ref: 4

The Granite Statue welcoming you to
Baden Powell House

Bank of England Museum

Bank of England, Threadneedle Street, London EC2R 8AH   Tel: 020 7601 4388
Fax: 020 7601 5808   Email: june.greenhalf@bankofengland.co.uk
Web: www.bankofengland.co.uk

The Museum is housed within the Bank of England itself, right at the heart of the City of London. It traces the history of the Bank from its foundation by Royal Charter in 1694 to its role today as the nation's central bank. There are gold bars dating from ancient times to the modern market bar, coins and a unique collection of bank notes.

Opening Times: Mon to Fri 10:00-17:00, also day of Lord
Mayor's Show. Closed Sat & Sun & BH.
Admission: Free.   Location: One minute walk from Bank
underground, ten minutes from Liverpool Street,
Fenchurch Street and Cannon Street.   Map Ref: 5

Visitors are invited to try to lift a
London Good Delivery Bar

Bankside Gallery

48 Hopton Street, London SE1 9JH   Tel: 020 7928 7521   Fax: 020 7928 2820
Email: bankside@freeuk.com

Bankside Gallery is home to the Royal Watercolour Society and the Royal Society of Painter-Printmakers, and stages an annual programme of exhibitions of members' work.

Opening Times: Tue 10:00-20:00, Wed to Fri 10:00-17:00, Sat, Sun & BH Mon 11:00-17:00.
Admission: Adult £3.50, Concession £2.00. Group rates available. Location: Situated on riverside, near Blackfriars Bridge and adjacent to Tate Modern.   Map Ref: 6

Barbican Art Gallery

Barbican Centre, Silk Street, London EC2Y 8DS   Tel: 020 7638 8891   Fax: 020 7382 7107   Email: jhealy@barbican.org.uk   Web: www.barbican.org.uk

Changing exhibitions of photography, art and design.

Opening Times: Mon, Tue & Thu to Sat 10:00-18:00, Wed 10:00-20:00, Sun & BH 12:00-18:00. Admission: Adult £7.00, Child/OAP/Student £5.00. Admission charges for exhibitions vary, please telepone. Location: In the heart of the city centre. The nearest underground stations are Barbican, Moorgate, St Pauls, Bank, Liverpool Street and Mansion House.   Map Ref: 7

Bernard Perlin, Orthodox Boys, 1948, copyright Bernard Perlin

---

The British Library

96 Euston Road, London NW1 2DB   Tel: 020 7412 7332   Email: visitor-services@bl.uk
Web: www.bl.uk

The British Library at St Pancras

On display are hundreds of items from the world's greatest collection of books, manuscripts, music, stamp, sound recordings and maps. The Library's collections span over three millennia and contain items from all continents of the world. The John Ritblat Gallery is home to a permanent exhibition of over 200 of the Library's Treasures. It includes documents which made and recorded history, sacred texts from the world's religions, masterpieces of illumination, landmarks of printing, great works of literature and music and major advances in science and mapmaking. Items on display include Codex Sinaiticus (c.350), Magna Carta (1215), the Gutenberg Bible (1455), Shakespeare's First Folio (1623), as well as works in the handwriting of Leonardo da Vinci, Lord Nelson, Lewis Carroll, Handel, Sir Paul McCartney and many others. It also features the Library's award winning Turning the Pages computer interactive, which allows you to turn pages or unroll a scroll simply by touching a screen. The Pearson Gallery is home to special thematic exhibitions. The Workshop of Words, Sounds and Images traces the story of book production and offers regular free demonstrations. There is also an extensive display of philatelic material, which is probably the best permanent display of stamps in the world, and National Sound Archive Jukeboxes offering a changing selection of sounds from their extensive collection of recordings. Visitors can also see the Kings Library, housed in a 17 metre glass-walled tower at the heart of the building, plus a number of other major works of art.

Early copy of The Canterbury Tales at the British Library

Opening Times: Mon 09:30-18:00, Tue 09:30-20:00, Wed to Fri 09:30-18:00, Sat 09:30-17:00, Sun & BH 11:00-17:00. Closed Xmas & New Year, 29 to 31 Mar and 15 to 18 Apr.
Admission: Free. Location: Next door to St Pancras mainline station, five minutes from both Euston and Kings Cross.   Map Ref: 8

British Museum

  THE BRITISH MUSEUM

Great Russell Street, London WC1B 3DG   Tel: 020 7323 8000
Email: information@thebritishmuseum.ac.uk
Web: www.thebritishmuseum.ac.uk

Permanent display and special exhibitions of the works of man from prehistory to the present day. Permanent displays of antiquities from Egypt, the ancient Near East, Greece and Rome as well as Prehistory, Roman Britain, Medieval, Renaissance, Modern and Oriental collection. Also the national collection of prints and drawings, coins and banknotes. The Great Court houses the Clore Education Centre, galleries and exhibition space and improved visitor facilities.

The South Facade of the British Museum, London

Opening Times: Sat to Wed 10:00-17:30, Thu & Fri 10:00-20:30. Admission: Free. Location: Nearest underground stations: Tottenham Court Road, Holborn, Russell Square.   Map Ref: 9

Cabinet War Rooms

Clive Steps, King Charles Street, London SW1A 2AQ   Tel: 020 7930 6961   Fax: 020 7839 5897   Email: cwr@iwm.org.uk   Web: www.iwm.org.uk

The secret headquarters of Winston Churchill and his Cabinet. Step back in time and view the original complex just as it was left at the end of six years of war, when the lights were finally extinguished.

Opening Times: Apr to Sep daily 09:30-18:00, Oct to Mar daily 10:00-18:00. Last admission 17:15. Closed 24-26 Dec. Admission: From 1 Apr 2002: Adult £5.80, Child Free, OAP/Student £4.20. Group rates available. Location: Two minutes from Westminster Underground Station.
Map Ref: 10

Carlyle's House

THE NATIONAL TRUST

National Trust, 24 Cheyne Row, London SW3 5HL   Tel: 020 7352 7087
Fax: 020 7352 5108   Web: www.nationaltrust.org.uk/thameschilterns

This Chelsea Queen Anne house was the home of historian, social writer, ethical thinker and powerful public speaker Thomas Carlyle for some 47 years until his death in 1881. The skilful Scottish home making of his wife Jane is much in evidence and the Victorian period decor is still in place. Their academic and domestic lives can be experienced today.

The Drawing Room - where Thomas Carlyle wrote
The French Revolution

Opening Times: 23 Mar to 3 Nov Wed to Fri 14:00-17:00, Sat, Sun and BH Mon & Tue 4 Jun 11:00-17:00.
Admission: Adult £3.60, Child £1.80, Members Free.
Location: Off Chelsea Embankment between Albert & Battersea bridges, or via Kings Road and Oakly Street tubes.   Map Ref: 11

Chelsea Physic Garden

66 Royal Hospital Road, London SW3 4HS   Tel: 0207 352 5646   Fax: 0207 376 3910
Email: sue@cpgarden.demon.co.uk   Web: www.chelseaphysicgarden.co.uk

Walled garden of 3.5 acres dating from 1674 and containing collections of medicinal plants, rare and tender species and plants linked to plant hunters. Glasshouses. 1773 rock garden and botanical order beds. Plant sale. Snowdrop opening 3-10 Feb 2002.

Opening Times: 7 Apr to 27 Oct Wed 12:00-17:00 & Sun 14:00-18:00. Special opening for Chelsea Flower Show 20 to 24 May and Chelsea Festival 17 to 21 Jun 12:00-17:00.
Admission: Adult £4.00, Child £2.00, Concession £2.00, OAP £4.00. Location: Twelve minute walk from Sloane Square tube station, on 239 bus route.   Map Ref: 11

Commonwealth Institute

Kensington High Street, London W8 6NQ   Tel: 020 7603 4535
Fax: 020 7603 4525   Email: elangham@commonwealth.org.uk
Web: www.commonwealth.org.uk

The Institute is an independent agency delivering education programmes to schools and running an exhibition programme reflecting contemporary Commonwealth arts and issues. It is home to one of the largest collections of artefacts from Commonwealth nations and regions, offering a handling collection for loan to school, community groups and business. It also houses the Commonwealth Resource Centre (library) and the Commonwealth Conference and Events Centre.

Opening Times: Mon to Sat 10:00-16:00, closed BH. Temporary exhibitions Apr to Jun & Oct to Dec daily 10:00-17:00. Admission: Free. Location: Within ten minutes walk of tube stations High Street Kensington and Holland Park, tube/mainline Olympia and one minute from bus stop serving several routes.   Map Ref: 12

Courtauld Institute Gallery

Somerset House, Strand, London WC2R 0RN   Tel: 020 7848 2526
Fax: 020 7848 2589   Email: galleryinfo@coutauld.ac.uk
Web: www.courtauld.ac.uk

The Gallery has one of the most important and best-loved small collections in the country, including world-famous Impressionist and post-Impressionist paintings. It is an integral part of the Courtauld Institute of Art, the oldest centre for the teaching of history of art in England and is housed at Somerset House, one of the finest 18th century buildings in London.

Opening Times: Daily 10:00-18:00. Admission: Adult £4.00, Concessions £3.00. Location: Central London. Nearest Undergrounds: Temple, Charing Cross, Holborn and Covent Garden.

Vincent Van Gogh, Self-Portrait with Bandaged Ear 1889

Map Ref: 13

Cuming Museum

155/157 Walworth Road, London SE17 1RS   Tel: 020 7701 1342
Fax: 020 7703 7415   Email: cuming.museum@southwark.gov.uk

Home of the rich and unusual Cuming Collection and museum of Southwark's history. Between 1780 and 1900 the Cuming family collected objects from all over the world. In 1900 the unique collection of everyday and extraordinary objects was left to the people of Southwark and the gallery was opened in 1906. The museum has an active programme of events and activities, a changing temporary exhibition space and hands-on family area.

Opening Times: Tue ot Sat 10:00-17:00. Admission: Free. Location: Near Elephant & Castle Shopping Centre, five minutes walk on the Walworth Road.   Map Ref: 14

Design Museum   & ● ☞ Desigmuseum

28 Shad Thames, London SE1 2YD   Tel: 020 7403 6933
Fax: 020 7378 6540   Web: www.designmuseum.org.uk

The Design Museum is the world's first museum of industrial design, fashion and architecture. Concerned as much with the future as the past, a changing exhibition programme captures the excitement and ingenuity of design's evolution through the 20th and 21st centuries.

Opening Times: Daily 10:00-17:45 (last entry 17:15). Admission: Adult £6.00, Concession £4.00, Family (2 adults and 2 children) £16.00. Location: London, ten minutes from Tower Hill and London Bridge Tubes.

Map Ref: 15

Design Museum, London, © Jefferson Smith

Central London

Dickens House Museum

48 Doughty Street, London WC1N 2LX   Tel: 020 7405 2127   Fax: 020 7831 5175
Email: dhmuseum@rmplc.co.uk   Web: www.dickensmuseum.com

The only surviving London home of Charles Dickens. Here, between 1837 and 1839 he completed Pickwick Papers, Oliver Twist, Nicholas Nickleby and Barnaby Rudge.

Opening Times: Mon to Sat 10:00-17:00. Admission: Adult £4.00, Child £2.00, Concession £3.00, Family £9.00.   Location: Central London, near Russell Square.   Map Ref: 16

Dr Johnsons House

17 Gough Square, London EC4A 3DE   Tel / Fax: 020 7353 3745
Email: curator@drjh.dircon.co.uk   Web: www.drjh.dircon.co.uk

This House can be described as a shrine to the English language, for it was here that Dr Samuel Johnson worked for many years to compile the first comprehensive English Dictionary which was published in 1755.

Opening Times: May to Sep Mon to Sat 11:00-17:30, Oct to Apr Mon to Sat 11:00-17:00. Closed BH. Admission: Adult £4.00, Child £1.00, Under 10s Free, Concession £3.00. Group rate £3.00.   Location: Near two underground lines (Blackfriars, Chancery Lane) and many bus routes.   Map Ref: 17

Dunhill Museum & Archive

48 Jermyn Street, London SW1Y 6DL   Tel: 020 7838 8233

A cross-section of the company's history, its products and famous customers, from motoring accessories in the 1890s, to pipes in 1910, lighters and other related products from the 1920s up to the 1950s.

Opening Times: Mon to Fri 09:30-18:00, Sat 10:00-18:00. Admission: Free. Location: Just below Piccadilly, a minutes walk from the Royal Academy.   Map Ref: 18

Florence Nightingale Museum

Gassiot House, 2 Lambeth Palace Road, London SE1 7EW   Tel: 020 7620 0374

Large collection of Florence Nightingale personal items including childhood souvenirs, her dress, furniture from her houses and Harley Street Hospital and honours awarded to Nightingale in old age. There is a small military history collection of souvenirs from the Crimean War, including military medals and military nursing uniforms from Scutari Hospital. There is also a small nursing history collection.

Lifesize reconstruction of a Crimean wardscene

Opening Times: Mon to Fri 10:00-17:00. Sat, Sun & BH 11:30-16:30. Closed Good Friday and Xmas. Admission: Adult £4.80, Child/OAP/Student £3.60, Family (2 adults and 2 children) £12.00.   Location: Car park level of St Thomas' Hospital, opposite Houses of Parliament. Nearest tube station - Westminster, Waterloo and London North.   Map Ref: 19

Geffrye Museum

GEFFRYE MUSEUM

Kingsland Road, London E2 8EA   Tel: 020 7739 9893   Fax: 020 7729 5647   Email: info@geffrye-museum.org.uk   Web: www.geffrye-museum.org.uk

The Geffrye Museum presents the changing style of the English domestic interior through a series of period rooms from 1600 to the present day. Fine collections of furniture, paintings and decorative arts. Attractive garden including a walled herb garden and a series of period gardens.

Opening Times: Tue to Sat 10:00-17:00, Sun 12:00-17:00. Closed Mon (except BH), Good Friday and Xmas & New Year. Admission: Free. Location: Liverpool Street Tube, then bus 149 or 242. Old Street Tube exit 2, then bus 243.   Map Ref: 20

Regency Room, 1800-1830

Gilbert Collection

Somerset House, Strand, London WC2R 1LA   Tel: 020 7420 9400   Fax: 020 7420 9440
Email: info@gilbert-collection.org.uk   Web: www.gilbert-collection.org.uk

The Silver Gallery

The Gilbert Collection is London's newest museum of decorative arts. The collection was formed over four decades by Sir Arthur Gilbert, a Londoner who moved to California in 1949 and made this extraordinary gift to the nation in 1996, "I felt it should return to the country of my birth." Thanks to Sir Arthur and the Heritage Lottery Fund, today this pre-eminent collection is beautifully housed in the vaulted spaces of the Embankment Building of the newly restored Somerset House, overlooking the Thames. The sequences of 17 galleries creates an impressive setting for treasure of English and Continental gold and silver, precious snuffboxes, miniature portraits in enamel and Italian cabinets and tables.

Ewer and Basin, Silver-Gilt,
Henri Auguste, Paris, 1789-90

Opening Times: Daily 10:00-18:00. Closed 24-26 Dec.
Admission: Adult £5.00, Child/Student Free, Concession £4.00.   Location: Located in the Embankment Building at Somerset House, between Covent Garden and the South Bank.   Map Ref: 13

Guide Heritage Centre

17/19 Buckingham Palace Road, London SW1W 0PT   Tel: 020 7834 6242   Fax: 020 7630 6199

The Heritage Centre is a modern, interactive visitor centre. Catering for our members from all age groups, mainly hands-on, team and individual activities.

Opening Times: Mon to Sat 10:00-17:00 (school holidays), Wed to Sat (term times).
Admission: Adult £3.80 (standard two hour visit), £5.75 (extended three hour visit).
Location: Five minute walk from Victoria Station.   Map Ref: 21

Guildhall Art Gallery

Guildhall Yard, London EC2P 2EJ   Tel: 020 7606 3030

The Corporation of London's renowned collection of works of art is now on view in a new gallery opened in 1999. The display includes Victorian art, including famous Pre-Raphaelite works, London subjects from the 17th century to the present, portraits from the 16th century onwards and one of Britain's largest oil paintings. There is also a programme of temporary exhibitions.

Opening Times: Mon to Sat 10:00-17:00, Sun 12:00-16:00.   Admission: Adult £2.50, Child Free, Concession £1.00.   Location: Follow street signs in the City of London for Guildhall Art Gallery and Guildhall.
Map Ref: 22

HMS Belfast

Morgan's Lane, Tooley Street, London SE1 2JH
Tel: 020 7940 6300 Fax: 020 7403 0719
Email: jwilson@iwm.org.uk Web: www.hmsbelfast.org.uk

HMS Belfast is a cruiser that was launched in 1938 and served throughout the Second World War, playing a leading role. After the war, she supported United Nations forces in Korea and remained in service with the Royal Navy until 1965. In 1971 she was saved for the nation as a unique and historic reminder of Britain's naval heritage in the first half of the 20th century.

Opening Times: 1 Mar to 31 Oct 10:00-18:00. 1 Nov to 28 Feb 10:00-17:00. Closed 24-26 Dec. Admission: Adult £5.40, Child Free, OAP/Student/Concession £4.00, Groups (10+) Adult £4.40, OAP/Student/Concession £3.50. Location: The ship is three minutes walk from London Bridge Station.

HMS Belfast launch 17 March 1938

Map Ref: 23

Hayward Gallery

South Bank Centre, Belvedere Road, London SE1 8XZ Tel: 020 7928 3144 Fax: 020 7401 2664 Email: visual_arts@hayward.org.uk Web: www.haywardgallery.org.uk

The Hayward Gallery acts as a fulcrum in visual culture, a bridge between the experimental and the established. It provides a prominent platform for emerging art and artists and new perspectives on internationally acclaimed artists. Challenging received opinions and crossing boundaries, the Hayward provokes critical debate and extends ideas about what art can

be. With the freedom to present work from any era and in any medium, in depth and with authority, the Hayward offers the chance to experience and enjoy the constantly changing world of art. The Hayward administers the Arts Council Collection and National Touring Exhibitions on behalf of the Arts Council of England

Opening Times: Daily 10:00-18:00, Tue & Wed until 20:00. Location: South Bank, one minute walk from Waterloo Station.

Map Ref: 24

Imperial War Museum

Lambeth Road, London SE1 6HZ Tel: 020 7416 5320

The Imperial War Museum traces the history of 20th century conflict from 1914, covering both World Wars and conflicts involving Britain and the Commonwealth post 1945. The museum has permanent exhibitions illustrating military, social, scientific and artistic aspects of war. Also a permanent exhibition dedicated to the Holocaust, art galleries, interactive displays and a changing programme of temporary exhibitions, including the 1940s House and 'Women in Uniform' opening in 2003.

Opening Times: Daily 10:00-18:00. Closed 24-26 Dec.
Admission: Free Location: Central London, 15 minute walk from Waterloo Station, five minutes from Lambeth North. Map Ref: 25

The Large Exhibits Gallery

Central London

Institute of Contemporary Arts

The Mall, London SW1Y 5AH Tel: 020 7930 0493 Fax: 020 7930 9851
Email: info@ica.org.uk Web: www.ica.org.uk

See art from contemporary artists like Damien Hirst, Steve McQueen and Tracey Emin. Watch fascinating arthouse cinema from directors like Wong Kar Wai, Jan Svankmajer and Jane Campion. Listen to talks by philosopher Anthony Grayling, Professor Stuart Hall and journalist Rosie Millard and attend dance, music and theatrical performances. The ICA houses art galleries, two cinemas, a bar and café, a new media centre, a theatre and a bookshop.

Opening Times: Mon 12:00-23:00, Tue to Sat 12:00-01:00, Sun 12:00-22:30. Admission: ICA Members Free. Annual Membership Adult £30.00, Concession £20.00. Day Membership Weekdays £1.50, Weekends £2.50. Location: Five minute walk from Trafalgar Square. Nearest tubes - Charing Cross and Piccadilly Circus. Map Ref: 26

Jewish Museum - Camden Town, London's Museum of Jewish Life

Raymond Burton House, 129/131 Albert Street,Camden Town, London NW1 7NB
Tel: 020 7284 1977 Fax: 020 7267 9008 Email: admin@jmus.org.uk
Web: www.jewmusm.ort.org

Explores the history and religious life of the Jewish community in Britain from the Norman Conquest until recent times. One of the world's finest collections of Jewish ceremonial art, awarded Designated status in recognition of their outstanding national importance. Changing exhibitions and audio-visual programmes. Highly Commended as Visitor Attraction of the Year (London Tourism Awards 2000). Group visits and educational programmes by arrangement.

Banner from London Jewish Bakers' Union

Opening Times: Mon to Thu 10:00-16:00, Sun 10:00-17:00. Closed Fri, Sat, Jewish Festivals and Public Holidays. Admission: Adult £3.50, Child £1.50, OAP £2.50, Family £8.00. Location: Three minute walk from Camden Town Underground Station. Map Ref: 27

Kensington Palace, State Apartments Ceremonial & Royal Dress Collection

London W8 4PX Tel: 020 7937 9561 Web: www.hrp.org.uk

Designed by Sir Christopher Wren for William III and Mary II, this peaceful royal retreat was the childhood home of Queen Victoria. Features include the magnificent State Apartments and 'Dressing for Royalty', a stunning presentation of royal court ceremonial dress, featuring dresses owned and worn by HM Queen Elizabeth II and Diana, Princess of Wales.

Opening Times: Mar to Oct daily 10:00-17:30. Nov to Feb 10:00-16:30. Admission: Adult £8.80, Child £6.30, OAP/Student £6.90, Family £26.80. Location: Five minutes from High Street Kensington Underground. Map Ref: 12

Kensington Palace

Leighton House Museum

12 Holland Park Road, London W14 8LZ Tel: 020 7602 3316 ext 302 Fax: 020 7371 2467
Web: www.rbkc.gov.uk/leightonhousemuseum

Leighton House was the home of Frederic, Lord Leighton (1830-1896), the great classical painter and President of The Royal Academy. The house was built between 1864-79 to designs by George Aitchison and is the expression of Leighton's vision of a private palace devoted to art.

Opening Times: 11:00-17:30 daily. Closed Tue. Admission: Free - donations welcome.
Location: Ten minutes from High Street Kensington Underground. Map Ref: 12

The Library & Museum of Freemasonry

Freemasons Hall, 60 Great Queen Street, London WC2B 5AZ Tel: 020 7395 9250 Fax: 020 7404 7418

One of the finest collections of Masonic material in the world: pottery and porcelain, glassware, silver, furniture and clocks, Masonic jewels and regalia, portraits, prints, photographs and social history items.

Opening Times: Mon to Fri 10:00-17:00.
Admission: Free. Location: Close to Covent Garden/Holborn Tube Station.

Map Ref: 28

18th Century Masonic Aprons

London's Transport Museum

Covent Garden, London WC2E 7BB Tel: 020 7379 6344 Fax: 020 7565 7253

Located in the heart of London's Covent Garden, the museum is housed in the original Victorian Flower Market. The museum is bright and airy with upper levels and a glass walkway, offering visitors a unique perspective of the historic buses, trams and trains. Complementing the display of vehicles are galleries housing originals of the famous Underground map and vibrant posters from the museum's extensive collection. Designed to appeal to Londoners and tourists alike, the museum invites visitors to take a journey through time, telling the story of interaction between transport, the capital and its people from 1800 to the present day. Hands-on exhibits, special Kidzones, working models

'Knifeboard' horse bus circa 1875

and the latest technology, including videos and touchscreen displays in several languages, contribute to the story. For visitors wanting to delve further into transport history, one innovative feature of the museum is its new Learning Centre. This drop-in information space contains a wealth of resources including books, journals, on-line databases and the museum's website. Facilities include a shop, café, baby changing and disabled toilets. A lift and ramps provide wheelchair and pushchair access throughout the museum.

West Ham Electric Tram 1910, LCC Tramways Class E1 1907/8, Metropolitan 1931

Opening Times: Sat to Thu 10:00-18:00, Fri 11:00-18:00. Closed 24-26 Dec. Admission: Adult £5.95, Child Free, Concession £4.50. Group rates available. Location: Nearest Underground: Covent Garden, Holborn, Leicester Square.

Map Ref: 28

Lord's Tour & MCC Museum

Lord's Ground, London NW8 8QN Tel: 020 7432 1033 Fax: 020 7266 3825
Email: tours@mcc.org.uk Web: www.lords.org

A fully guided tour of 'The Home of Cricket' including the Pavilion, MCC Museum and many other places of interest. The collection includes fine art, portraits, memorabilia and other items such as the world renowned Ashes urn.

Opening Times: Guided Tours Apr to Sep 10:00, 12:00 & 14:00, Oct to Mar 12:00 & 14:00. No tours on major Match Days/restrictions other Match Days. Check for Xmas opening
Admission: Adult £6.50, Child £4.50, Concession £5.00, Family £19.00. Group rates available.
Location: Located in St John's Wood in central London, 15 minute walk from St John's Wood tube station.

Map Ref: 29

Museum of Garden History

Lambeth Palace Road, London SE1 7LB Tel: 020 7401 8865 Fax: 020 7401 8869
Email: info@museumgardenhistory.org Web: www.museumgardenhistory.org

Fine collection of historic garden tools and information about the history of gardening in Britain. Replica 17th century knot garden and art exhibitions. Housed in an historic church building.

Opening Times: Feb to mid Dec daily 10:30-17:00. Admission: Voluntary admission charge £2.50, Concession £2.00. Location: Next to Lambeth Palace, at the end of Lambeth Bridge. A ten minute walk Vauxhall, Lambeth North. 15 minutes Waterloo.

Map Ref: 19

Museum of London

150 London Wall, London EC2Y 5HN   Tel: 020 7600 3699   Fax: 020 7600 1058
Email: info@museumoflondon.org.uk   Web: www.museumoflondon.org.uk

Lord Mayor's Coach

The Museum of London is the world's largest urban history museum. With a collection of more than a million objects, the museum aims to inspire a passion for London in all visitors. The collections cover every aspect of social life from pre-historic times to the present through material ranging from archaeological finds to contemporary photographs and the magnificent Lord Mayor's coach.

Opening Times: Mon to Sat 10:00-17:50, Sun 12:00-17:50. Closed 24-26 Dec, 1 Jan.   Admission: Free.
Location: Near St Paul's tube station.   Map Ref: 7

Museum of The Royal Hospital Chelsea

Royal Hospital Road, Chelsea, London SW3 4SR   Tel: 020 7881 5203   Fax: 020 7881 5463
Email: roylhospch@aol.com   Web: www.chelseapensioner.org.uk

View of The Royal Hospital from the north

The history of the Chelsea pensioners from 1692, together with a large diorama of the Royal Hospital estate in 1742. Displays of uniforms and hospital artefacts. Trophies from the Peninsula War. Large collection of medals and cap badges.

Opening Times: Mon to Sat 10:00-12:00 & 14:00-16:00, Sun 14:00-16:00 (only Apr to Sep). Closed BH.
Admission: Free.   Location: Five minutes from Sloane Square Underground.   Map Ref: 11

Museum of St Bartholomew's Hospital

St Bartholomews Hospital, West Smithfield, London EC1A 7BE   Tel: 020 76018152
Email: marion.rea@bartsandthelondon.nhs.uk

The Museum of St Bartholomew's Hospital tells the story of this renowned institution. On display are original archives dating back to the 12th century and objects including works of art, surgical instruments and medical equipment.

Opening Times: Tue to Fri 10:00-16:00. Closed BH.   Admission: Free.   Location: St Bartholomew's Hospital is near Smithfield Market, a few minutes walk from St Paul's Cathedral and the Museum of London.   Map Ref: 30

Museums of The Royal College of Surgeons of England

35/43 Lincoln's Inn Fields, London WC2A 3PE   Tel: 020 7869 6560   Fax: 020 7869 6564
Email: museums@rcseng.ac.uk   Web: www.rcseng.ac.uk/museums/default.asp

From John Hunter's specimen collection and Joseph Lister's pioneering antiseptic spray, to Charles Babbage's brain and George Stubbs' painting of The Rhinoceros, the Museums of the Royal College of Surgeons of England hold a fascinating and richly diverse range of material collected over the last three centuries.

Opening Times: Mon to Fri 10:00-17:00. Closed Sat, Sun & BH.   Admission: Free. Charges apply for guided tours. Donations welcome.   Location: Central London, ten minutes walk from Holborn Tube Station.   Map Ref: 28

Museums, Galleries, Historic Houses & Sites

Please let us know of any collections that are not listed in this guide that you feel should be listed. E-mail us on *editor@tomorrows.co.uk* or return the Report Form on page 448

National Army Museum

Royal Hospital Road, Chelsea, London SW3 4HT Tel: 020 7730 0717 Fax: 020 7823 6573
Email: info@national-army-museum.ac.uk Web: www.national-army-museum.ac.uk

Rifleman of the 95th Regiment, c1809

'Tommy' goes to War c1914

Discover the colourful story of the British Army and how the men and women who have served in it have lived and fought, from the middle ages, through two world wars, to the present day. Find out the facts behind some of the most remarkable episodes in Britain's history and the experiences of the people involved. Interactive displays enable visitors to try on helmets and kit from different eras, feel the weight of a Tudor cannonball, survey the opposing forces on a huge model of the Battle of Waterloo, explore a reproduction First World War trench and even test modern 'military' skills in exciting computer challenges. There's so much to see, from portraits by Reynolds and Gainsborough, to a lamp used by Florence Nightingale, the frostbitten fingers of Everest Conqueror Major Michael 'Bronco' Lane, and even the skeleton of Napoleon's horse. Life-like models range from an Agincourt archer to an SAS trooper, and together with videos, photos, amazing anecdotes and a host of unusual personal relics, the ordinary soldier's story is brought vividly to life. Affording your trip won't be a battle - admission is free! New this year - newly refurbished Art Gallery features paintings not previously displayed at the Museum.

Opening Times: Daily 10:00-17:30. Closed 24-26 Dec, 1 Jan, Good Friday, early May BH.
Admission: Free. Location: Ten minutes from Sloane Square Tube (Circle/District lines); 20 minutes from Victoria Station.
Map Ref: 11

National Gallery

Trafalgar Square, London WC2N 5DN Tel: 020 7747 2885 Fax: 020 7747 2423
Email: information@ng-london.org.uk Web: www.nationalgallery.org.uk

The National Gallery, London

The Maas at Dordrecht, Aelbert CUYP

The National Gallery possesses one of the greatest collections of European paintings in the world, housed in a building that is an internationally recognised landmark. Its permanent collection spans the period from about 1250 to 1900 and consists of over 2,300 works by many of the world's most famous artists. Admission to the permanent collection is free. The National Gallery also organises and hosts major temporary loan exhibitions, often in close collaboration with other national and international museums and galleries. Admission may be charged for some of these exhibitions. The gallery also offers a wide variety of free talks, guided tours and lectures. There are also courses, practical workshops and family days on the second Saturday and Sunday of each month. The National Gallery also has shops selling products inspired by the collection, Crivelli's Garden restaurant in the Sainsbury Wing and a café for light snacks and refreshments.

Opening Times: Daily 10:00-18:00, Wed until 21:00. Closed 24-26 Dec, 1 Jan and Good Friday.
Admission: Free. Location: North side of Trafalgar Square.
Map Ref: 31

National Portrait Gallery ♿ ● ▯ ◑

St Martin's Place, London WC2H 0HE Tel: 020 7306 0055 Fax: 020 7306 0056
Web: www.npg.org.uk

Early 20th Century Galleries
© Andrew Putler

The National Portrait Gallery is home to the largest collection of portraiture in the world, featuring famous British men and women who have created history from the middle ages until the present day. Over one thousand portraits are on display across three floors with sitters from Shakespeare to the Rolling Stones. The Ondaatje Wing, including new Tudor Galleries and Twentieth Century Galleries, also has a roof-top restaurant with spectacular views across London and a state-of-the-art lecture theatre. The Portrait Cafe serves a selection of refreshments and the gift/book shop offers a wide range of goods based on the Gallery's collection.

National Portrait Gallery

Opening Times: Mon to Wed, Sat & Sun 10:00-18:00. Thu & Fri 10:00-21:00. Admission: Free, although a fee is charged for some exhibitions - Adult £6.00, Concession £4.00.
Location: Nearest tube station - Leicester Square, Charing Cross. Mainline service - Charing Cross. Buses to Trafalgar Square.   Map Ref: 31

Natural History Museum ☞ ♿ ● ▯ ◑

Cromwell Road, London SW7 5BD Tel: 020 7942 5000 Fax: 020 7942 5075

Arguably the finest museum of nature in the world. Highlights include 'Dinosaurs' featuring a huge, roaring, breathing T-rex, 'The Power Within' offering an 'earthquake experience' and the beautiful 'Earths Treasury' displaying a unique collection of gems and minerals. September marks the opening of phase one of the Darwin Centre, a major new life sciences complex providing unprecedented access to the Museum's amazing specimen collections.

Opening Times: Mon to Sat 10:00-17:50, Sun 11:00-17:50.
Admission: Free. Location: Five minutes walk from South Kensington Tube Station.   Map Ref: 4

The World's most lifelike robotic T-rex

Old Operating Theatre, Museum & Herb Garret ●

9A St Thomas Street, Southwark, London SE1 9RY Tel: 020 7955 4791 Fax: 020 7378 8383
Email: curator@thegarret.org.uk Web: www.thegarret.org.uk

The museum houses a Victorian operating theatre. It has displays on surgery and herbal medicine. A secret, atmospheric space situated in the roof of a 300 year old church. Spiral staircase access.

Opening Times: Daily 10:30-17:00. Closed 15 Dec to 5 Jan. Admission: Adult £3.75, Child £2.00, Concession £2.75, Family £9.00. Group Visit Service (pre-booked) also available.
Location: Five minute walk from London Bridge station.   Map Ref: 23

Percival David Foundation of Chinese Art ☞ ●

53 Gordon Square, London WC1H 0PD Tel: 020 7387 3909 Fax: 020 7383 5163
Web: www.pdfmuseum.org.uk

The Percival David Foundation houses the finest collection of Chinese ceramics outside China. There are approximately 1700 items in the collection dating mainly to the period 10th-18th century. Guided Tours by prior arrangement only.

Opening Times: Mon to Fri 10:30-17:00. Closed Sat, Sun & BH. Admission: Free, donations welcome. Location: Ten minute walk Russell Square, Euston Square, Euston and Goodge St Underground Stations.   Map Ref: 8

Pollocks Toy Museum

1 Scala Street, London W1T 2HL   Tel: 020 7636 3452   Email: toymuseum@hotmail.com
Web: www.pollocksweb.co.uk

A delightful museum occupying adjoining Georgian and Victorian houses. Exhibits include optical toys, teddies, dolls houses, toy theatres, tin toys and dolls. Toy theatre performances are given during school holidays.

Opening Times: Mon to Sat, 10:00-17:00. Closed Sun and BH.   Admission: Adult £3.00, Child/Student £1.50.   Location: Two minutes from Goodge Street Underground Station.

Map Ref: 8

The Queen's Gallery

Buckingham Palace, London SW1A 1AA   Tel: 020 7321 2233

The Diamond Diadem, 1820.
The Royal Collection 2002

The inaugural exhibition of Royal Treasures - a Golden Jubilee Celebration will be a spectacular celebration of the individual tastes of monarchs and other members of the royal family who have shaped one of the world's greatest collections of art. Mixing the famous with the unexpected, the selection of 450 outstanding works will include paintings, drawings, watercolours, furniture, sculpture and ceramics, silver and gold, arms and armour, jewellery and miniatures, books and manuscripts.

Opening Times: Re-opens 22 May. Daily 10:00-17:30.
Admission: Adult £6.50, Child £3.00, OAP £5.00, Under 5s Free, Family (2 adults and 2 children) £16.00.   Location: Buckingham Palace Road, next to Buckingham Palace. Five minute walk from Victoria Station.

Map Ref: 21

Royal Academy of Arts

Burlington House, Piccadilly, London W1J 0BD   Tel: 020 7300 8000   Fax: 020 7300 8001   Email: webmaster@royalacademy.org.uk   Web: www.royalacademy.org.uk

Contemporary sculpture is often displayed in the courtyard

The Royal Academy of Arts is world famous for its programme of outstanding exhibitions all year round. Highlights of 2002 include Paris: Capital of the Arts 1900-1968 - a celebration of art created in Paris during seven decades; Merzbacher: The Joy of Colour - paintings from one of Europe's greatest collections of modern art and The Aztecs - a spectacular exhibition of Aztec art.

Opening Times: Daily 10:00-18:00, Fri until 22:00.
Admission: Prices vary from £6.00-£9.00, concessions available.   Location: In the centre of the West End of London. Two minutes walk from Green Park and Piccadilly Circus Underground Stations.

Map Ref: 18

Royal Fusiliers Museum

HM Tower of London, London EC3N 4AB
Tel: 020 7488 5610/5612   Fax: 020 7481 1093
Email: royalfusiliers@freeserve.co.uk

20th Battalion, Flanders 1916

The collection depicts the history of the Royal Fusiliers (the seventh regiment of foot) from 1685 when it was raised in the Tower of London. The numerous campaigns of the regiment are carried from Namur to the Gulf War and Bosnia. 11 of the 19 Victoria Crosses won are displayed, as are several fine portraits, and many items of memorabilia.

Opening Times: Mar to Oct daily 09:30-18:00, Oct to Mar daily 09:30-17:00.
Admission: Adults 50p, Child Free.   Location: Within HM Tower of London.

Map Ref: 32

Royal Fusiliers on parade.
Brantford Canada 1866

Royal Institution's Michael Faraday Museum

The Royal Institution, 21 Albemarle Street, London W1S 4BS   Tel: 020 7409 2992   Fax: 020 7629 3569   Email: ri@ri.ac.uk   Web: www.ri.ac.uk

The museum contains a reconstruction of Faraday's laboratory as it was in the 1850s with original apparatus and furniture. Also on display is the first electric transformer and electric generator both made by Faraday in 1831.

Opening Times: Weekdays only 10:00-17:00, closed BH.   Admission: Adult £1.00, Concession 50p.   Location: Close to Green Park underground station.   Map Ref: 18

Royal London Hospital Archives & Museum

Royal London Hospital, Whitechapel, London E1 1BB   Tel: 020 7377 7608
Email: r.j.evans@mds.qmul.ac.uk   Web: www.bartsandthelondon.org.uk

The London (founded 1740) became Britain's largest voluntary hospital. Its story is told in the crypt of the former hospital church. Exhibits feature surgery, nursing, children and health, x-rays, dentistry, nursing, uniforms and videos. The lives and works of individuals like Dr Barnardo, Edith Cavell, Joseph Merrick and Lord Knutsford also feature.

Opening Times: Mon to Fri 10:00-16:30. Closed Sat, Sun & BH.   Admission: Free.   Location: Three minute walk from Whitechapel Underground Station.   Map Ref: 33

The London Hospital Children's Party (detail), 1897 by Lucien Davis

The Saatchi Gallery

Top Floor, 30 Underwood Street, London N1 7JQ   Tel: 020 7336 7362   Fax: 020 7336 7364
Email: philippa@saatchi-gallery.co.uk

The Saatchi Gallery opened in March 1985. Max Gordon, a leading British architect, was commissioned by Charles Saatchi to convert 30,000 square feet of warehousing into a contemporary art museum. Its aim is to introduce new art, or art largely unseen in the UK to a wider audience. The Gallery draws from a collection of over 2000 paintings, sculptures and installations.

Opening Times: Thu to Sun 12:00-18:00. Closed Mon to Wed.   Admission: Adult £5.00, Concession £3.00.
Location: Near Old Street Station, a few minutes walk from station, off Shepherdess Road.   Map Ref: 34

The Physical Impossibility of Death in the Mind of Someone Living, by D Hirst

St John's Gate

Museum of the Order of St John, St Johns Lane, Clerkenwell, London EC1M 4DA   Tel: 020 7253 6644   Fax: 020 7336 0587

St John's Gate, Museum of the Order of St John, St John Ambulance. The Priory of Clerkenwell was built by the Knights Hospitaller in the 1140s and it is their remarkable story that lies behind the modern work of today's St John Ambulance. The Knights' surprising tale is revealed through collections including furniture, paintings, silver, armour, stained glass and other items, housed in this early 16th century gatehouse. It contains one of the country's few remaining wooden Tudor spiral staircases. Also given to Mary Tudor as her palace after the Dissolution. Royalty, authors and artist, Shakespeare, Hogarth, Edward Cave, Dr Johnson, Dickens and David Garrick were just a few of its notable visitors. Guided tours at 11:00 and 14:30 on Tuesday, Fridays and Saturdays, take visitors through upstairs rooms inside the Gate and over to the Priory Church and 12th century Crypt. The four ground floor exhibition rooms are open daily 10:00-17:00, 10:00 16:00 on Saturday (closed Sunday and bank holiday weekends). Two reference libraries are housed in the Gate, open by appointment only, one with specialist collections relating to the

Knights of St John, the Knights Templar, the Crusades and related subjects; the other, the St John Ambulance reference collection.

Opening Times: Mon to Fri 10:00-17:00, Sat 10:00-16:00. Closed Sun & BH weekend. Tours: Tue, Fri & Sat 11:00 & 14:30. Admission: Free, donations requested for tours: Adult £5.00, Concession £3.50. Location: Four minute walk from Farringdon Station. Map Ref: 30

Science Museum

Exhibition Road, London SW7 2DD   Tel: 020 7942 4000

See, touch and experience the major scientific advances of the last 300 years at the largest museum of its kind in the world with a state of the art IMAX cinema and virtual reality simulator is really something to entertain and inspire all.

Opening Times: Daily 10:00-18:00. Closed Xmas. Admission: Free. Location: Five minute walk from South Kensington tube station. Map Ref: 4

The Science Museum's Welcome Wing

Serpentine Gallery

 Serpentine Gallery

Kensington Gardens, London W2 3XA   Tel: 020 7402 6075
Fax: 020 7402 4103   Email: rosed@serpentinegallery.org
Web: www.serpentinegallery.org

The Serpentine Gallery, situated in the heart of Kensington Gardens in a 1934 tea pavilion, was founded in 1970 by the Arts Council of Great Britain. Attracting over 400,000 visitors a year it is one of London's most loved galleries for modern and contemporary arts.

Opening Times: Daily 10:00-18:00. Admission: Free.
Location: Underground: Knightsbridge, South Kensington or Lancaster Gate. Buses: 9, 10, 12, 24, 52. Map Ref: 35

Serpentine Gallery, © Peter Durant/ arcblue.com

Shakespeare's Globe Exhibition

21 New Globe Walk, Bankside, London SE1 9DT   Tel: 020 7902 1500   Fax: 020 7902 1515   Web: www.shakespeares-globe.org

Shakespeare's Globe Exhibition is the most exciting place in which to explore Shakespeare's theatre and the London in which he lived and worked. A visit to the Exhibition includes a tour into today's working theatre. Let one of our storytellers introduce you to the Globe. During the matinees, in the theatre season, exhibition storytellers will take visitors on a virtual tour of the Globe.

Opening Times: Oct to Apr 10:00-17:00, May to Sep 09:00-16:00. Closed Xmas. Admission: Adult £8.00, Child £5.00, OAP £6.00, Group £7.50. Location: On Bankside next to Tate Modern and opposite St Paul's Cathedral. Map Ref: 6

Shakespeare's Globe, copyright Richard Kalina

Sherlock Holmes Museum

221b Baker Street, London NW1 6XE   Tel: 020 7935 8866   Web: www.sherlock-holmes.co.uk

The Museum has already had over 2 million visitors since opening 12 years ago. It is very unique. It is in a Georgian building dating from 1815. It is totally unspoiled (by which is meant unmodernised!) and is identical to the lodging house described in the stories. The rooms in Mr Holmes's apartment on the first floor are maintained just as he would have left them nearly 100 years ago! The Museum has entertainment, cultural and educational value. Sherlock Holmes is very much a part of England's literary heritage and visitors flock to Baker Street to see how we are perpetuating this great legend. There

The Sherlock Holmes Museum

is a large and attractive souvenir shop on the ground floor of the Museum, containing the world's largest and most varied range of Sherlockian memorabilia, which is of tremendous interest to the collector.

Opening Times: Daily 09:30-18:00. Closed Xmas Day. Admission: Adult £6.00, Child £4.00. Groups of Under 16s one free for every 8, 10% Group Discount for over 16s. Location: One minute walk from Baker Street Underground Station. Map Ref: 36

The Sitting Room at
The Sherlock Holmes Museum

The Dome area, by Martin Charles

Sir John Soane's Museum

13 Lincolns Inn Fields, London WC2A 3BP Tel: 020 7405 2107
Fax: 020 7831 3957 Email: will.palin.soane3@ukgateway.net
Web: www.soane.org

Collection of antique fragments, sculpture, painting, models, books and drawings amassed by the architect Sir John Soane (1753-1837) in three linked houses built by him between 1793 and 1824. The interiors and collection were preserved by an Act of Parliament in 1833.

Opening Times: Tue to Sat 10:00-17:00, open late on first Tue of each month 18:00-21:00. Admission: Free. Location: Central London, two minutes from Holborn Tube Station. Map Ref: 28

Tate Britain

Millbank, London SW1P 4RG Tel: 020 7887 8008 Fax: 020 7887 8729
Web: www.tate.org.uk

Photo: Mark Heathcote

The national gallery of British art from 1500 to the present day, from the Tudors to the Turner Prize. Tate holds the greatest collection of British art in the world, including works by Blake, Constable, Epstein, Gainsborough, Hockney, Moore, Stubbs and Turner. The gallery is the world centre for understanding and enjoyment of British art and it runs an excellent programme of special exhibitions and events throughout the year.

Opening Times: Daily 10:00-17:50. Admission: Free, but charges apply for special exhibitions. Location: On the North bank of the Thames by Vauxhall Bridge, five minutes walk from Pimlico Tube Station. Map Ref: 37

Tate Modern,
Photocredit Marcus Leith

Tate Modern

Bankside, London SE1 9TG Tel: 020 7887 8000
Fax: 020 7887 8729

Tate Modern displays the Tate collection of international modern art from 1900 to present day, including major works by artists such as Bacon, Dali, Duchamp, Giacometti, Matisse, Picasso, Rothko and Warhol.

Opening Times: Sun to Thu 10:00-18:00, Fri & Sat 10:00-22:00. Admission: Free. Location: Situated opposite St Paul's Cathedral on banks of River Thames, close to both Southwark and Blackfriars Tube. Map Ref: 6

Taking Shape, an interactive exhibition by theatre-rites

Theatre Museum: National Museum of the Performing Arts

Russell Street, Covent Garden, London WC2E 7PR
Tel: 020 7943 4700   Fax: 020 7943 4777
Web: www.theatremuseum.org

The Theatre Museum, situated in the heart of London's Theatreland, celebrates performance in Britain through imaginative exhibitions, workshops and events based on the world's most exciting performing arts collections.
The galleries, charting the British stage from today back to Shakespeare's time, are brought to life by tour guides who explore the work of star performers, practitioners and their audiences using videos, photographs, costumes, designs and other memorabilia. Hands-on demonstrations reveal the secrets and skills of stage make-up and costume. Daily workshops on a variety of themes from 'My Fair Lady' to pantomime show how costume enable an actor to prepare for a role. Stage Truck - a range of activities specially designed for families to explore theatre crafts runs every Saturday and Thursday during school holidays 12:00-17:00. These are suitable for 5-16 year olds. Children under 12 must be accompanied by an adult. Kids Theatre Club also runs on Saturdays 10:00-12:00 for 8+ years. These sessions, improvising themes from West End shows, run in conjunction with the Society of London Theatre, are led by professional actors, and aim to provide a first experience of drama and acting. Booking essential 020 7943 4806.

Make-up demonstrations daily at Theatre Museum

Opening Times: Daily 10:00-18:00. Closed Mon & BH.   Admission: Free.   Location: One minute walk from Covent Garden Underground.

Map Ref: 9

Tower Bridge Experience

Tower Bridge Experience

Tower Bridge, London SE1 2UP   Tel: 020 7403 3761   Fax: 020 7357 7935
Email: enquiries@towerbridge.org.uk
Web: www.towerbridge.org.uk

See inside London's most famous landmark, with a brand new exhibition opening on 16 February 2002. Discover the history of Tower Bridge and find out how it works. Experience the breathtaking views and be amazed by the unique architecture.

Opening Times: Daily 09:30-18:00.   Admission: Adult £4.50, Child £3.00, OAP £3.00.   Location: Rail stations: London Bridge and Fenchurch Street. Underground Stations: Tower Hill and London Bridge.

Map Ref: 32

M Tower of London

Tower Hill, London EC3N 4AB   Tel: 020 7709 0765/7734 5855   Web: www.hrp.org.uk

Begun by William the Conqueror in 1078, the Tower of London has served as a royal residence, fortress, mint, armoury and more infamously as a place of execution. Now as the nation's leading historic visitor attraction, this fortress has over 900 years of British history to discover within its walls.

Opening Times: Mar to Oct Mon to Sat 09:00-17:30, Sun 10:00-17:30. Nov to Feb Tue to Sat 09:00-16:30, Sun to Mon 10:00-16:30.

Map Ref: 32

Tower of London

Veterinary Museum

The Royal Veterinary College, Royal College Street, London NW1 0TU   Tel / Fax: 020 7468 5162   Web: www.rvc.ac.uk

The Royal Veterinary College was founded at Camden Town in 1791. The museum contains thousands of books, artefacts and ephemera relating to the college, and the development of the veterinary education and science.

Opening Times: Mon to Fri 9:00-17:00 (by appointment only).   Admission: Free   Map Ref: 38

Victoria and Albert Museum

Cromwell Road, South Kensington, London SW7 2RL   Tel: 020 7942 2000
Web: www.vam.ac.uk

The V & A Dome

The V&A is one of the world's greatest museums of art and design. More than seven miles of galleries are filled with outstanding collections of objects dating from 3000BC to the present day, including glass, textiles, ceramics, photography, jewellery and fashion. Highlights include the breathtaking Cast Courts, paintings by Constable and the largest collection of Italian Renaissance sculpture outside Italy. In addition, there is an exciting programme of exhibitions, displays, activities and contemporary events. The new British Galleries tell the story of British design from 1500-1900. From Chippendale to Morris and Adam to Mackintosh, all of the top British designers of the times feature in the beautiful, newly-renovated sequence of 15 galleries. The wealth of exhibits is enhanced by computer interactives, objects to handle, video screens and audio programmes, offering an entirely new visitor experience in a stunning and innovative setting. 'A must see for your visit to London'.

The breathtaking V & A Cast Courts

Opening Times: Daily 10:00-17:45, on Wed & last Fri of month 10:00-22:00.   Admission: Free.
Location: Close to South Kensington Underground. A short walk from Harrods.   Map Ref: 4

Wallace Collection

Hertford House, Manchester Square, London W1U 3BN   Tel: 020 7563 9500

Room 3, Dining Room. © The Wallace Collection

The Wallace Collection is both a national museum and the finest private art collection ever assembled by one family. The collection was acquired principally in the 19th century by the third and fourth Marquesses of Hertford and Sir Richard Wallace, the illegitimate son of the 4th Marquess. It was bequeathed to the nation by Sir Richard's widow in 1897 and is displayed on three floors of Hertford House the family's main London residence. The 26 rooms present unsurpassed collections of French 18th century painting, furniture and porcelain together with Old Master paintings by, among others,

Titian, Canaletto, Rembrandt, Hals, Rubens, Velázquex and Gainsborough. Our magnificent collection of princely arms and armour is shown in four galleries and there are further important displays of gold boxes, miniatures, French and Italian sculpture and fine medieval and Renaissance works of art, including maiolica, glass, Limoges enamels, silver and jewellery. By the terms of Lady Wallace's bequest nothing must be added or loaned to the Collection. This provision has preserved the remarkable character of one of the greatest collections ever made by an English family.

Gallery 5, The Front State Room
© The Wallace Collection

Opening Times: Mon to Sat 10:00-17:00, Sun 12:00-17:00.   Admission: Free.   Location: On a garden square just off Oxford Street, behind Selfridges department store.   Map Ref: 3

Wesleys Chapel, Museum of Methodism & John Wesleys House

49 City Road, London EC1Y 1AU   Tel: 020 7253 2262   Fax: 020 7608 3825

John Wesley's House, Library and personal belongings. Collections relating to the history of Methodism including paintings, ceramics and manuscript letters. An 18th century Georgian House furnished with Wesley's personal belongings.

Opening Times: Mon to Sat 10:00-16:00. Sun 12:00-14:00.   Admission: Adult £4.00, Concession £2.00.   Location: One minute walk from Old Street Tube Station. Exit No.4.

Map Ref: 30

Whitechapel Art Gallery

80/82 Whitechapel High Street, London E1 7QX   Tel: 020 7522 7888   Fax: 020 7622 7887   Email: info@whitechapel.org
Web: www.whitechapel.org

Situated in London's East End, the Whitechapel has always aimed to bring the best visual arts to the widest possible public. The Gallery has no permanent collection, but mounts a diverse programme of international modern and contemporary art.

Opening Times: Tue to Sun 11:00-18:00 (Wed until 20:00).
Admission: Free, (one paying exhibition per year)
Location: Aldgate East Tube.

Map Ref: 33

Whitechapel Art Gallery

Within a bus ride or a short underground journey from Central London, there are many excepti... museums, galleries and historic houses covering subjects as diverse as Rugby, Lawn Ten... Botany, Artillery, Keats, Palaces, Clipper Ships and also housing important collection... paintings and furniture.

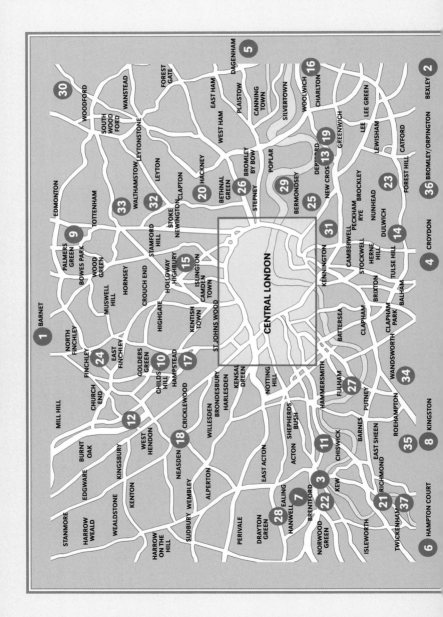

The Red Map References should be used to locate Museums etc on the pages that follow

194

Outer London

Museum of Domestic Design & Architecture (MoDA)

The Practical Householder,
Cover Oct 1957

Middlesex University, Cat Hill, Barnet EN4 8HT   Tel: 020 8362 5244   Fax: 020 8411 6639   Email: moda@mdx.ac.uk   Web: www.moda.ac.uk

The Museum of Domestic Design & Architecture (MoDA) houses one of the most important and comprehensive collections of late 19th and 20th century decorative design for the home, including the world-renowned Silver Studio Collection. Located in north London, MoDA offers a wide-ranging exhibition and events programme throughout the year alongside its permanent exhibition, 'Exploring Interiors: Decoration of the Home 1900-1960'.

Opening Times: Tue to Sat 10:00-17:00, Sun 14:00-17:00. Closed Mon, Easter, BH & Xmas. Admission: Free. Location: Tube: Piccadilly line to Oakwood or Cockfosters. Car: from junction 24 of M25 follow A111 signposed Cockfosters to MoDA.   Map Ref: 1

BEXLEY

Bexley Museum

Hall Place, Bourne Road, Bexley DA5 1PQ   Tel: 01322 526574   Fax: 01322 522921   Email: museum@bexleyheritagetrust.freeserve.co.uk

Museum collection of the London Borough of Bexley, featuring local history, art, archaeology and natural history, set in a Grade I listed Tudor and 17th century house.

Opening Times: End Oct to end Mar Tue to Sat 10:00-16:15. Closed Sun & Mon. Apr to Oct Tue to Sat 10:00-17:00, Sun 11:00-17:00. Closed Mon. Admission: Free. Location: Between Bexley and Bexley Heath, nearest railway station Bexley.   Map Ref: 2

BRENTFORD

Kew Bridge Steam Museum

Green Dragon Lane, Brentford TW8 0EN   Tel: 020 8568 4757   Fax: 020 8569 9978   Email: info@kbsm.org.uk   Web: www.kbsm.org.uk

Magnificent 19th century steam powered pumping station used to supply London's water. Also Water For Life Gallery exploring social use of water. Engines work every weekend.

Opening Times: Daily 11:00-17:00. Closed Good Friday and week prior to Xmas. Admission: Adult £4.50, Child £2.00, OAP £3.50, Family £11.50. Location: Junction 2 or M4, A205 to Kew Bridge, museum on north side of river. Two minutes from Kew Bridge Station.   Map Ref: 3

CROYDON

Croydon Clocktower

Katharine Street, Croydon CR9 1ET   Tel: 020 8253 1030   Fax: 020 8253 1032   Email: boxoffice@croydononline.gov   Web: www.croydon.gov.uk/clocktower

Lifetimes Museum is a collection of life stories which when combined help to tell the history of Croydon.

Opening Times: Mon to Sat 11:00-17:00 Sun 12:00-17:00. Admission: Lifetimes Museum: Free. Exhibition Gallery: prices vary. Location: Ten minutes from main railway station (East Croydon), two minutes from main shopping centre.   Map Ref: 4

DAGENHAM

Valence House Museum & Art Gallery

Becontree Avenue, Dagenham RM8 3HT   Tel: 020 8595 8404   Fax: 020 8227 5296   Email: valencehousemuseum@hotmail.com   Web: www.bardaglea.org.uk/4-valence/valence-menu.html

Valence House Museum is a medieval manor house and holds local history objects and archives from the London Borough of Barking and Dagenham.

Opening Times: Tue to Fri 09:00-16:30, Sat 10:00-16:00. Admission: Free.   Map Ref: 5

Outer London

Hampton Court Palace

Hampton Court Palace

East Molesey KT8 9AU   Tel: 020 8781 9500   Fax: 020 8781 9669
Web: www.hrp.org.uk

Hampton Court Palace promises a magical journey back through 500 years of royal history. Discover 60 acres of immaculately restored gardens that run alongside the River Thames, the largest and oldest vine in Europe, the William III Priory Garden and lose yourself in the world famous maze.

Opening Times: Daily Mid Mar to Mid Oct Mon 10:00-17:15, Tue to Sun 09:30-17:15. Mid Oct to Mid Mar Mon 10:15-17:45, Tue to Sun 09:30-17:45. Closed Xmas.   Admission: Adult £10.80, Child £7.20 OAP/Student £8.30, Family £32.20.   Location: Two minute walk from Hampton Court Station.   Map Ref: 6

Osterley Park House

Jersey Road, Isleworth TW7 4RB   Tel: 020 8232 5050   Fax: 020 8232 5080
Email: tosgen@smtp.ntrust.org.uk   Web: www.nationaltrust.org.uk

Robert Adam Villa, spectacular interiors contain one of Britain's most complete examples of Adam's work. Ground floor houses the Jersey Galleries which host exhibitions of contemporary art while the house is open.

Opening Times: 2 to 24 Mar, Sat & Sun, 27 Mar to 3 Nov Wed to Sun & BH. Closed Good Friday. House & Jersey Galleries 13:00-16:30, Shop 13:00-17:30, Tearoom 11:30-17:00. Admission: Adult £4.40, Child £2.20, Family £11.00, Group £3.80.   Location: Junction of Thornbury and Jersey Road off the A4. Eight miles from Central London, five miles from Heathrow, 20 minute walk from Osterley Piccadilly line underground Station.   Map Ref: 7

Kingston Museum

Wheatfield Way, Kingston upon Thames KT1 2PS   Tel: 020 8546 5386   Fax: 020 8547 6747
Email: king.mus@rbk.kingston.gov.uk

The Museum has two permanent galleries telling the story of Kingston, ancient origins and Town of Kings. The Eadweard Muybridge Gallery describes the life and work of this internationally renowned pioneer photographer.

Opening Times: 10:00-17:00, closed Wed & Sun.   Map Ref: 8

Bruce Castle Museum

Haringey Museum & Archive Service, Lordship Lane, London N17 8NU   Tel: 020 8808 8772
Fax: 020 8808 4118   Email: museum.services@haringey.gov.uk   Web: www.haringey.gov.uk

16th century manor house set in parkland. Once owned by Sir Rowland Hill, the postal reformer it houses exhibitions, collections and archives telling the history of the Borough of Haringey.

Opening Times: Wed to Sun 13:00-17:00.   Admission: Free.   Location: Underground to Seven Sisters or Wood Green, then 123 or 243 bus. Overland rail to Bruce Grove then ten minute walk.   Map Ref: 9

Camden Arts Centre

Arkwright Road, London NW3 6DG   Tel: 020 7435 2643/ 5224   Fax: 020 7794 3371
Email: info@camdenartscentre.org   Web: www.camdenartscentre.org

The centre is a venue for contemporary visual art and education. A changing programme of exhibitions, artists' residencies, offsite projects and artist-led activities offers you an opportunity to look, to make and to discuss.

Opening Times: Tue to Thu 11:00-19:00, Fri to Sun 11:00-17:30. Closed Mon and BH.
Admission: Free.   Location: On Finchley Road/Arkwright Road, ten minutes walk from Finchley Road Tube.   Map Ref: 10

Chiswick House

Burlington Lane, London W4 2RP   Tel: 020 8995 0508

Surrounded by beautiful gardens, close to the centre of London lies one of England's finest Palladian villas, designed by the third Earl of Burlington. Collections include 19 paintings from Lord Burlington's original collection.

Opening Times: Apr to Sep daily 10:00-18:00, Oct daily 10:00-17:00, Nov to Mar Wed to Sun 10:00-16:00. Closed 25 to 26 Dec and 1 to 16 Jan. Admission: Adult £3.30, Child £1.70, Concession £2.50.   Location: Burlington Lane, Chiswick Railway station half a mile, Turnham Green Tube three quarters of a mile.   Map Ref: 11

Church Farmhouse Museum

Greyhound Hill, Hendon, London NW4 4JR   Tel: 020 8203 0130   Fax: 020 8359 2885
Web: www.barnet.gov.uk/cultural_services

17th century farmhouse with reconstructed Victorian period dining room, kitchen and laundry room. Four temporary exhibitions on local and social history and the decorative arts each year. Small public garden.

Opening Times: Mon to Thu 10:00-12:30 13;30-17:00, Sat 10:00-13:00 14:00-17:30, Sun 14:00-17:30. Closed Fri. Admission: Free. Location: Next to St Mary's Church, Hendon. One minute walk from bus stop.   Map Ref: 12

Cutty Sark the world's sole surviving tea clipper

Cutty Sark Clipper Ship

King William Walk, Greenwich, London SE10 9HT
Tel: 020 8858 3445   Fax: 020 8853 3589
Email: info@cutttysark.org.uk   Web: www.cuttysark.org.uk

Cutty Sark was built in 1869 to be the fastest clipper in the annual race to bring the first of the season's crop of tea home to Britain. She is the world's sole surviving tea clipper, and since being opened to the public in 1957, has welcomed over 15 million visitors across her gangplank. Visitors 'come aboard' via an entrance to the 'Tween Deck', so called because it is between the Main Deck and the Lower Hold. This is the main museum display area telling Cutty Sark's history and details of merchant trade, together with displays of original artefacts and models. The new children's interpretive panels give the same information but in a fun and colourful way. The souvenir shop is also on deck. The Main Deck houses the crew and officers' accommodation, restored to 1870s condition - a real insight to life on board a Victorian tea

'Masters Saloon', Cutty Sark

clipper. The Gallery, Carpenter's workshop and the masts can also be seen, complete with their 11 miles of rigging. The Lower Hold houses one of the world's largest collections of colourful merchant ships' figureheads, as well as our new children's 'hands-on' activities.

Opening Times: Daily 10:00-17:00. Closed Xmas. Admission: Adult £3.90, Child/Student £2.90, OAP £2.90, Family £9.70. Location: Greenwich Town Centre, seven minutes from railway station, one minute from tube and ferry links.   Map Ref: 13

Dulwich Picture Gallery

DULWICH PICTURE GALLERY

Gallery Road, London SE21 7AD   Tel: 020 8693 5254   Fax: 020 8299 8700   Email: k.knowles@dulwichpicturegallery.org.uk
Web: www.dulwichpicturegallery.org.uk

Dulwich Picture Gallery is the greatest find in London; a magnificent collection of masterpieces by Rembrandt, Poussin, Watteau, Rubens, Canaletto, Gainsborough and many more. The critically-acclaimed international loan exhibitions and its setting in the beautiful 18th century village of Dulwich, make the Gallery a must for all art lovers. The building has been described as the most perfect small art gallery in the world.

The enfilade of galleries designed in 1811 by Sir John Soane

Opening Times: Tue to Fri 10:00-17:00, Sat, Sun & BH 11:00-17:00. Admission: Adult £4.00, OAP £3.00, Concession Free. Location: Dulwich is in south east London, 12 minutes by train from Victoria.
Map Ref: 14

Estorick Collection of Modern Italian Art

39A Canonbury Square, Islington, London N1 2AN Tel: 020 7704 9522 Fax: 020 7704 9531 Email: curator@estorickcollection.com Web: www.estorickcollection.com

The permanent collection has at its core powerful images by early 20th century Futurists housed in the intimate setting of a large Georgian villa. Also on display are works by figurative artists.

Opening Times: Wed to Sat 11:00-18:00, Sun 12:00-17:00. Closed Mon, Tue, Xmas & New Year. Admission: Adult £3.50, Concession £2.50. Location: A five minute walk from Highbury and Islington Underground Stations.
Map Ref: 15

The Fan Museum

12 Crooms Hill, Greenwich, London SE10 8ER Tel: 0208 3051441 Fax: 0208 2931889 Email: admin@fan-museum.org Web: www.fan-museum.org

The only museum in the world entirely dedicated to the history of fans and to the art and craft of fan-making. Situated within Maritime Greenwich, a World Heritage site.

Opening Times: Tue to Sat 11:00-17:00, Sun 12:00-17:00. Admission: Adult £3.50, Concession £2.50, Under 7s Free. OAP Free on Tue after 14:00. Location: Greenwich Town Centre, five minute walk from Greenwich BR and Cutty Sark DLR Station.
Map Ref: 13

Fenton House

Windmill Hill, Hampstead, London NW3 6RT Tel / Fax: 0207 435 3471 Email: tfehse@smtp.ntrust.org.uk

Charming William and Mary Merchants' House with fine collections of Georgian furniture, porcelain and needlework and the Benton Fletcher Collection of early keyboard instruments. Walled gardens include a kitchen garden and apple orchard.

Opening Times: 2 to 17 Mar Sat & Sun 14:00-17:00. 23 Mar to 3 Nov Sat, Sun & BH 11:00-17:00, Wed, Thu & Fri 14:00-17:00. Admission: Adult £4.40, Child £2.20, Family £11.00. Garden only: Adult £1.00, Child Free. National Trust Members Free. Location: Hampstead Tube 300m.
Map Ref: 10

Firepower - The Royal Artillery Museum

Royal Arsenal, Woolwich, London SE18 6ST Tel: 020 8855 7755 Fax: 020 8855 7100 Email: info@firepower.org.uk Web: www.firepower.org.uk

Visit the Monster Bits Gallery

Artillery worldwide, from earliest cannons to computer aided missile systems. In the dramatic, ground-shaking field of fire experience 20th century campaigns. As guns roar and shells whizz overhead, hear the moving stories of real gunners in their own words. See how ammunition reaches it target and appreciate its devastating effects. Use hands-on displays and interactives to discover the science and technology of gunnery.

Opening Times: Daily 10:00-17:00. Closed Christmas Day. Admission: Adult £6.50, Child £4.50, OAP £5.50, Concession £5.50, Family £18.00, Group discount available. Location: Royal Arsenal, Woolwich. Five minutes from Woolwich Arsenal Railway Station.
Map Ref: 16

Freud Museum

20 Maresfield Gardens, Hampstead, London NW3 5SX Tel: 020 7435 2002/5167 Fax: 020 7431 5452

Home of Sigmund Freud and his family when they came to London as refugees from Nazi persecution, the family recreated their Vienna home in London. Displays include his extensive library and collection of 2000 antiquities.

Opening Times: Wed to Fri 12:00-17:00. Admission: Adult £4.00, Concession £2.00.
Map Ref: 17

Outer London

Grange Museum of Community History

On the Neasden Roundabout, Neasden Lane, Neasden, London NW10 1QB   Tel: 020 8452 8311/020 8937 3600   Fax: 020 8208 4233   Email: grangemuseum@brent.gov.uk   Web: www.brent.gov.uk/grangemuseum

Brent's diverse history is brought to life through photographs, objects and spoken memories from the 1920s to the present day. Holiday activities throughout the year and a range of workshops, activities and resources for schools and adult learners.

Opening Times: Mon to Fri 11:00-17:00, Sat 10:00-17:00. Closed Sun, (except Jul & Aug Sun 14:00-17:00 and closed Mon).   Admission: Free.   Location: Located on Neasden Roundabout, five minutes walk from Neasden tube on the Jubilee Line.   Map Ref: 18

Greenwich Borough Museum

232 Plumstead High Street, London SE18 1JT   Tel: 020 8855 3240   Fax: 020 8316 5754   Email: beverley.burford@greenwich.gov.uk

Permanent displays of local history including social history, archaeology and natural history. A temporary exhibition programme, an education service for schools, a children's Saturday Club and an adult lecture and workshop programme.

Opening Times: Mon 14:00-19:00, Tue, Thu, Fri & Sat 10:00-13:00 14:00-17:00. Closed Wed, Sun & BH.   Admission: Free.   Location: First floor Plumstead Library in High Street. Ten minutes walk or five minutes by bus from Plumstead Railway Station.   Map Ref: 19

Gunnersbury Park Museum

Gunnersbury Park, London W3 8LQ   Tel: 020 8992 1612   Fax: 020 8752 0686

A beautiful nineteenth century mansion, Gunnersbury Park Museum was formerly home to the Rothschild family. It is now the community museum for Ealing and Hounslow. In contrast to the grand house, see where the servants lived and worked, in our original 19th century kitchens. View the horse drawn vehicles of Gunnersbury, including the Rothschilds' State and travelling carriages.

Opening Times: Apr to Oct Mon to Fri 13:00-17:00 Sat, Sun & BH 13:00-18:00. Nov to Mar daily 13:00-16:00. Victorian Kitchens: Apr to Oct Sat, Sun & BH 13:00-18:00.   Admission: Free.   Location: In park, on bus route (E3), near tube station (Acton Town).   Map Ref: 3

Hackney Museum

Parkside Library, Victoria Park Road, London E8 1EA   Tel: 020 8986 6914   Fax: 020 8985 7600

Discover why people have come to Hackney from all over the world for the past 1000 years, through room sets, interactives, personal stories and museum objects.

Opening Times: Open from 21 Apr 2002. Mon, Tue & Thu 09:30-20:00, Fri 10:00-20:00, Sat 09:00-18:00. Closed Wed & Sun.   Admission: Free.   Location: In the heart of Central Hackney, two minute walk from Hackney Central Railway Station.   Map Ref: 20

Ham House

Ham Street, Richmond, London TW10 7RS   Tel: 020 8940 1950

Outstanding Stuart house famous for its lavish interiors and spectacular collections of fine furniture, textiles and paintings. Also includes 17th century formal garden and an 18th century dairy.

Opening Times: House - 23 Mar to 3 Nov Sat to Wed 13:00-17:00. Garden - Sat to Wed 11:00-18:00, closed Xmas & New Year.   Admission: House & Garden - Adult £6.00, Child £3.00, Family £15.00. Garden only - Adult £2.00, Child £1.00, Family £5.00.   Location: South Bank of Thames, West of A307, at Petersham, readily accessible from M3 and M25. Bus route 65 from Kingston and 371 from Richmond Station.   Map Ref: 21

Hampstead Museum

🕊 🏛 🗂

Burgh House, New End Square, London NW3 1LT   Tel: 020 7431 0144   Fax: 020 7435 8817
Email: hampsteadmuseum@talk21.com
Queen Anne House containing a collection tracing the history of Hampstead from pre-historic times to the present day. Notable is the Helen Allingham collection and 'Isokon" furniture. Includes a permanent display about John Constable.

Opening Times: Wed to Sun 12:00-17:00, Sat by appointment. BH 14:00-17:00. Closed Good
Friday, Easter Monday, Xmas & New Year.   Admission: Free.   Location: Near central
Hampstead, a five minute walk from Hampstead Tube Station.   Map Ref: 17

Hogarth's House

🏛

Hogarth Lane, Great West Road, London W4 2QN   Tel: 020 8994 6757

Early 18th century house which was the country home of William Hogarth (1697-1764) during the last 15 years of his life. Displays of his prints, information on the life of this 'Father of English Painting', and a secluded garden containing Hogarth's mulberry tree.

Opening Times: Feb to Oct Tue to Sun 13:00-17:00. Closed Mon (except BH) and Nov, Dec &
Jan. Admission: Free. Location: On A4 (Great West Road) near Hogarth Roundabout,
Chiswick. Nearest tube station - Turnham Green (15 minutes walk).   Map Ref: 22

Horniman Museum & Gardens

♿ 🏛 🗂

100 London Road, Forest Hill, London SE23 3PQ   Tel: 020 8699
1872   Fax: 020 8291 5506
Email: enquiry@horniman.demon.co.uk
Web: www.horniman.ac.uk

Set in 16 acres of gardens, this fascinating, free museum has unique exhibitions, events and activities to delight adults and children alike. Housed in Townsend's stunning Arts and Crafts building, the museum has outstanding collections which illustrate the natural and cultural world. Discover the African Worlds gallery featuring the largest African mask, experience the Natural History Gallery with many original specimens from the Victorian age and explore marine ecology in the Living Waters Aquarium with tropical fish and seahorses. A new £13.4m

Sri Lankan Mask,
photo H Scheebeli

development will open to the public in 2002 which will dramatically transform the museum for the future. Four new galleries will be accompanied by a host of new facilities, a new entrance to link the Museum with the Gardens and greatly improved access provision. Opening Spring 2002: Treasures - stunning artefacts from every continent in a new gallery celebrating world cultures, Hands-On Base - masses of exhibits to touch and explore in a fun interactive space, Monster Creepy Crawlies - monstrously large bugs to seize the imagination of children of all ages, New shop and café

Horniman Clock Tower, photo M Harding

- overlooking the Gardens. Opening Autumn 2002: Music - a dynamic new environment for our internationally renowned collection of musical instruments incorporating sound and vision.

Opening Times: Mon to Sat 10:30-17:30, Sun 14:00-17:30. Closed 24-26 Dec.
Admission: Free. Location: South Circular Road (A205), free parking opposite. Forest Hill BR,
13 mins from London Bridge.   Map Ref: 23

Islington Museum

♿ 🏛 🚌

Islington Town Hall, Upper Street, Islington, London N1 2UD   Tel: 020 7527 3235   Fax: 020
7527 3049   Email: alison.lister@islington.gov.uk   Web: www.islington.gov.uk

Local and Social History of the London Borough of Islington. There is a programme of temporary exhibitions.

Opening Times: Wed to Sat 11:00-17:00, Sun 14:00-16:00   Admission: Free   Location: Five
minute walk from Highbury and Islington Tube.   Map Ref: 15

Jewish Museum - Finchley, London's Museum of Jewish Life

The Sternberg Centre, 80 East End Road, Finchley, London N3 2SY   Tel: 020 8349 1143
Fax: 020 8343 2162   Email: jml.finchley@lineone.net   Web: www.jewmusm.ort.org

Lively social history displays tracing Jewish immigration and settlement in London with reconstructions of tailoring and furniture workshops and hands-on activities for children. Moving exhibition on British born Holocaust survivor Leon Greenman OBE. Group visits and education programmes by arrangement.

Opening Times: Mon to Thu 10:30-17:00, Sun 10:30-16:30. Closed Fri, Sat, Jewish Festivals and Public Holidays. Also closed Sun in month of Aug and BH weekends.   Admission: Adult £2.00, Child Free, OAP £1.00.   Location: Nearest underground station Finchley Central (via Station Road and Manor View). Located on A504.   Map Ref: 24

Keats House

Keats Grove, Hampstead, London NW3 2RR   Tel: 020 7435 2062
Email: keatshouse@corpotlondon.gov.uk   Web: www.cityoflondon.gov.uk
www.keatshouse.org.uk

The Keats House Collection contains original letters from John Keats to his family and friends, manuscripts by Keats and his circle, personal possessions and a reference collection about Keats and the romantic movement.

Opening Times: Nov to Mar Tue to Sun 12:00-16:00, from April open until 17:00. Closed Xmas, New Year and Good Friday.   Admission: Adult £3.00, Child Free, Concession £1.50. Tickets are valid for one year.   Location: On the edge of Hampstead Heath close to mainline and underground stations and bus routes.   Map Ref: 17

Kenwood House

Hampstead Lane, London NW3 7JR
Tel: 020 8348 1286

Kenwood houses one of the most important collections of paintings, given to the nation by Lord Iveagh - including works by Rembrandt, Gainsborough, Turner, Van Dyck to name but a few. The house was remodelled by Robert Adam for the great judge, Lord Mansfield, and the richly decorated library is one of his masterpieces.

Opening Times: Apr to Sep daily 10:00-18:00, Oct daily 10:00-17:00, Nov to Mar daily 10:00-16:00. Closed Xmas & New Year. Admission: Free, donations welcome. Location: Hampstead Lane.

Mirrored recess in the Library © English Heritage   Map Ref: 17

Livesey Museum for Children

682 Old Kent Road, London SE15 1JF   Tel: 020 7639 5604   Fax: 020 7277 5384
Email: livesey.museum@southwark.gov.uk   Web: www.liveseymuseum.org.uk

A fully interactive museum for the under 12s showing a new hands-on exhibition every year. For 2002, new exhibition 'Shelter' and new education Resource Room.

Opening Times: Re-opens Feb 2002. Tue to Sat 10:00-17:00.   Admission: Free.   Location: On the Old Kent Road, opposite large gasworks.   Map Ref: 25

Museum of Childhood at Bethnal Green

Cambridge Heath Road, London E2 9PA   Tel: 020 8983 5200   Fax: 020 8983 5225
Email: bgmc@vam.ac.uk   Web: www.museumofchildhood.org.uk

One of the best collection of toys and games in the world, dating from the 16th century to the present day.

Opening Times: Mon to Thu, Sat & Sun 10:00-17:50. Closed Fri, Xmas & New Year.
Admission: Free.   Location: One minute walk from Bethnal Green Tube Station.   Map Ref: 26

Museum of Fulham Palace

Fulham Palace, Bishops Avenue, London SW6 6EA   Tel / Fax: 020 7736 3233

The museum within Fulham Palace tells the story of this nationally important site, home of the Bishops of London until 1973. Displays include archaeology paintings and garden history.

Opening Times: Nov to Feb Thu to Sun 13:00-16:00, Mar to Oct Wed to Sun 14:00-17:00. Open BH Mon, Closed Xmas and Good Friday.   Admission: Adult £1.00, Concession 50p, accompanied Child Free.   Location: Off Bishops Avenue. Tube Putney Bridge, District Line, ten minute walk.   Map Ref: 27

National Maritime Museum

Romney Road, Greenwich, London SE10 9NF   Tel: 020 8858 4422

20 modern public galleries at Greenwich display a fraction of the huge collections of this museum: 4,520 oil paintings; 100,000 books; 1,000 flags; 100,000 maps and charts; 70,000 prints and drawings; etc. Properties include Queen's House (Inigo Jones 1635) and the Royal Observatory Greenwich (Wren 1675). Major reference library. Web research service (www.nmm.ac.uk), maritime gateway: www.port.nmm.ac.uk and new www.portcities.org.uk.

National Maritime Museum, Stanhope entrance

Opening Times: Sep to Jun daily 10:00-17:00, Jul & Aug daily 10:00-18:00. Closed Xmas. Admission: Free, charge for special exhibitions.   Location: Near town centre, adjoining Greenwich Park.
                                                                    Map Ref: 19

Pitshanger Manor & Gallery

Walpole Park, Matlock Lane, Ealing, London W5 5EQ   Tel: 020 8567 1227   Fax: 020 8567 0595   Email: pitshanger@ealing.gov.uk   Web: www.ealing.gov.uk/pitshanger

Martinware pottery collection.

Opening Times: Tue to Sat 11:00-18:00. May to Sep Sun 13:00-17:00. Admission: Free.
Location: Eight minute walk from Ealing Broadway Station, near town centre.   Map Ref: 28

Pumphouse Educational Museum
(Rotherhithe Heritage Museum)
Lavender Pond & Nature Park, Lavender Road, Rotherhithe, London SE16 5DZ
Tel: 020 7231 2976

Artefacts from the foreshore of the River Thames dating from Roman times and exhibitions 'The Blitz Room', 'The 1950s' and '20th Century Artefacts From The Home'.

Opening Times: 09:30-15:30. Admission: Donation. School groups by arrangement.
Location: Five minutes from Rotherhithe Tube, ten minutes Canada Water Tube.   Map Ref: 29

Queen Elizabeth's Hunting Lodge

Rangers Road, Chingford, London E4 7QH   Tel: 020 8529 6681   Fax: 020 8529 8209

Historic building Grade II*. A unique timber framed building commissioned by Henry VIII as a grandstand for viewing hunting of deer. Many interesting architectural features and social history of Tudor period.

Opening Times: Wed to Sun 14:00-17:00, or dusk in winter months. Admission: Adult 50p, Child Free. Location: Chingford, London <E>4. Ten minutes from Chingford Station.
                                                                    Map Ref: 30

Ragged School Museum

46/50 Copperfield Road, Bow, London E3 4RR   Tel: 020 8980 6405   Fax: 020 8983 3481
Email: enquiries@raggedschoolmuseum.org.uk   Web: www.raggedschoolmuseum.org.uk

Displays on Tower Hamlets and its people, recreated Victorian classroom and activities for children during holiday periods.

Opening Times: Wed & Thu 10:00-17:00 and first Sun in month 14:00-17:00. Admission: Free.
Location: A ten minute walk from tube and DLR stations.   Map Ref: 26

Rangers House

Chesterfield Walk, Blackheath, London SE10 8QX   Tel: 020 8853 0035

Rangers House is home to the magnificent Suffolk collection of paintings, given to the nation by the Hon Greville and Mrs Howard, including Old Masters and the famous series of portraits by William Larkin.

Opening Times: Apr to Sep 10:00-18:00, Oct Wed to Sun 10:00-17:00.   Admission: Call 020 8853 0035 for details   Location: Chesterfield Walk, train Blackheath or Greenwich.

Map Ref: 19

Royal Air Force Museum

Grahame Park Way, Hendon, London NW9 5LL   Tel: 020 8358 4849
Fax: 020 8358 4981   Email: groupbusiness@rafmuseum.com   Web: www.rafmuseum.com

Britain's National Museum of Aviation displays over 70 historic aircraft, artefacts and exhibits telling the complete story of aviation. The spectacular, sound and light show 'Our Finest Hour' tells the story of the Battle of Britain. Try our interactive gallery, thrill on our simulator and walk through the mighty Sunderland flying boat. Gift shop, family restaurant, café and picnic area.

Opening Times: Daily 10:00-18:00. Closed Xmas & New Year. Admission: Free. Location: Colindale Tube Station, Northern line, ten minute walk from station. Thames Link, Mill Hill Broadway, Bus 303.   Map Ref: 12

The Tornado and F4 Phantom in the Main Aircraft Hall

South London Gallery

65 Peckham Road, London SE5 8UH
Tel: 020 7703 6120   Fax: 020 7252 4730
Email: mail@southlondongallery.org.uk
Web: www.southlondongallery.org.uk

Described by The Independent as 'a mecca for the art pilgrim', the SLG has a reputation for having its finger on the pulse of contemporary art. Since 1993, the Gallery has staged ground-breaking solo exhibitions including Gilbert & George, Tracey Emin and Barbara Kruger. Located in the heart of a thriving artistic community in Camberwell, the Gallery is held in great affection by the general public and artists alike.

Opening Times: Tue to Fri 11:00-18:00, Thu 11:00-19:00, Sat & Sun 14:00-18:00. Closed Mon. Admission: Free.
Location: Peckham/Camberwell border, 15 minute walk from Peckham Rye or Demark Hill railway stations.

Map Ref: 31

Sutton House

2 & 4 Homerton High Street, Hackney, London E9 6JQ   Tel: 020 8986 2264   Fax: 020 8525 9051   Email: suttonhouse@smtp.ntrust.org.uk   Web: www.nationaltrust.org.uk

Enjoy the unexpected in the oldest surviving brick house in East London. Built in 1535 Sutton House is fascinating for its visible layers of change. See the original Tudor linenfold panelling, 17th century painted staircase, Georgian parlour, Victorian study and 1980s squatter's mural.

Opening Times: 6 to 24 Feb, Wed and Sun 11:30-17:30. 1 Mar to 22 Dec, Fri and Sat 13:00-17:30. Phone for more details. Admission: Adult £2.10, Child 50p, Family £4.70. National Trust Members Free. Location: At the corner of Isabella Road and Homerton High Street. Frequent local buses. Quarter mile Hackney Central Station, half mile Hackney Downs Station.

Map Ref: 32

Vestry House Museum

Vestry Road, Walthamstow, London E17 9NH   Tel: 0208 509 1917
Email: vestry.house@al.lbwf.gov.uk

Vestry House Museum is housed in Walthamstow's original workhouse, built in 1730. The museum now serves as a centre for the collection, preservation and interpretation of the past and present story of Waltham Forest.

Opening Times: Mon to Fri 10:00-17:30, Sat 10:00-17:00. Closed Sun & BH. Admission: Free.
Location: One minute walk from Walthamstow Tube/Bus Station.   Map Ref: 33

Wandsworth Museum

The Courthouse, 11 Garratt Lane, London SW18 4AQ   Tel: 020 8871 7074/7075   Fax: 020 8871 4602   Email: wandsworthmuseum@wandsworth.gov.uk
Web: www.wandsworth.gov.uk/museum

Follow the story of Wandsworth from pre-historic times to the present. Discover how Battersea, Balham, Tooting, Putney, Roehampton, Earlsfield, Wandsworth and Southfields grew from country villages to London's biggest suburb. Interactive displays, changing exhibitions and special events.

Opening Times: Tue to Sat 10:00-17:00, Sun 14:00-17:00. Closed Mon and BH.
Admission: Free. Location: Opposite Wandsworth Shopping Centre. Ten minute walk from Wandsworth Town Station and 15 minutes walk from East Putney Tube.   Map Ref: 34

William Morris Gallery

Lloyd Park, Forest Road, London E17 4PP   Tel: 020 8527 3782   Fax: 020 8527 7070
Web: www.lbwf.gov.uk/wmg

Permanent displays of work by William Morris (1834-1896) designer, craftsman, writer and socialist, housed in his boyhood home. Work by other Arts and Crafts movement designers. Pre-Raphaelite paintings.

Opening Times: Tue to Sat & first Sun of each month 10:00-13:00 14:00-17:00.
Admission: Free. Location: 15 minute walk from Walthamstow Central Tube Station (Victoria line)   Map Ref: 33

Wimbledon Lawn Tennis Museum

Centre Court, AELTC, Church Road, Wimbledon, London SW19 5AE
Tel: 020 8946 6131   Fax: 020 8944 6497
Web: www.wimbledon.org/museum

The Home of Tennis

The Museum, located within Centre Court, tells the story of lawn tennis and explains many of the quintessentially English traditions associated with the game. It exhibits encapsulate the prestige, the glamour and the glory associated with The Championship. The Museum features views of the world-famous Centre Court, the original Championship trophies, and film and video footage of great players in action.

Opening Times: Daily 10:30-17:00. Closed Xmas & New Year. Only open to tournament visitors during Championships. Closed middle Sun of the Championships and Mon after. Location: From London take A3 to Portsmouth, turn left into A219 towards Wimbledon. 20 minute walk from Wimbledon Station, 15 minute walk from Southfields Underground   Map Ref: 35

Woodlands Art Gallery

90 Mycenae Road, Blackheath, London SE3 7SE   Tel / Fax: 020 8858 5847
Web: www.wag.co.uk

The new exhibitions each month have a variety of sources from local art groups to local school, community groups, individually grouped artists from England and abroad.

Opening Times: Mon to Sat 11:00-17:00, Sun 14:00-17:00. Closed Wed. Admission: Free.
Location: Near Blackheath Standard. Bus route, Westcombe Park. Tube, North Greenwich. Bus 108, 422 from tube. 53 from central London, 286, 202, 54.   Map Ref: 19

2 Willow Road

London NW3 1TH   Tel / Fax: 020 7435 8166

The National Trust's only modern movement house completed in 1939. Contains 20th century works of art collected by its architect Erno Goldfinger.

Opening Times: Thu to Sat 12:00-17:00. Admission: Adult £4.40, Child £2.20.
Location: Hampstead, north London, ten minutes walk from underground.   Map Ref: 17

Outer London

Bromley Museum

The Priory, Church Hill, Orpington BR6 0HH   Tel: 01689 873826
Email: bromley.museum@bromley.gov.uk   Web: www.bromley.gov.uk/museums

Archaeology of London Borough of Bromley from earliest times to Domesday. Life and work of Sir John Lubbock, First Lord of Avebury, the man responsible for giving this country its Bank Holidays. 20th century Social History displays.

Opening Times: 1 Apr to 31 Oct Sun to Fri 13:00-17:00, Sat 10:00-17:00. 1 Nov to 31 Mar Mon to Fri 13:00-17:00, Sat 10:00-17:00. Closed BH.   Admission: Free.   Location: Near town centre, 20 minutes walk from Orpington Railway Station.   Map Ref: 36

Crofton Roman Villa

Crofton Road, Orpington BR6 8AD   Tel: 01689 873826/020 8462 4737   Fax: 020 8462 4737
Web: www.bromley.gov.uk/museums

Remains of ten rooms of a Roman villa can be seen within a modern cover building. Details of the central heating system and tessellated floors. Activities for visitors.

Opening Times: 1 Apr to 31 Oct Wed, Fri & BH 10:00-13:00 14:00-17:00, Sun 14:00 -17:00.
Admission: Adult £1.00 Child/Concession 50p.   Location: Adjacent to Orpington Railway Station.   Map Ref: 36

Museum No 1 (Economic Botany)

Royal Botanic Gardens, Kew, Richmond TW9 3AE   Tel: 020 8332 5706

This fascinating and highly accessible exhibition gives visitors a glimpse into Kew's collections and emphasises their importance. It serves as a timely reminder of the close relationship between plants and people in every aspect of their lives. Discover your planet. Explore the world from rainforest to desert in vast magnificent glasshouses. Discover exotic plants in tropical surroundings or just relax in the beauty of the

The Palm House

world's most famous garden. Every season is a new experience at Kew and there is so much to enjoy: 30,000 types of plants; museum with interactive; exhibition; unique art galleries; places to eat and shop. Visit at any time of the year, in any weather.

Opening Times: Daily 09:30, closing times vary.   Admission: Adult £6.50, Child Free, Concession £4.50.   Location: Ten minute walk from Kew Bridge and Kew Gardens Station.
                                                  Map Ref: 3

The Pagoda

Museum of Richmond

Old Town Hall, Whittaker Avenue, Richmond TW9 1TP   Tel: 020 8332 1141   Fax: 020 8948 7570   Email: musrich@globalnet.co.uk   Web: www.museumofrichmond.com

The museum celebrates the unique history of Richmond with colourful displays spanning prehistoric times to the present day. Special exhibits feature Richmond Palace, the magnificent Tudor creation which gave the town its name.

Opening Times: All year Tue to Sat 11:00-17:00, May to Sep Sun 13:00-16:00. Closed Mon.
Admission: Adult £2.00, Child Free, OAP/Student/Concession £1.00.   Location: In the town centre, one minute from River Thames, five minutes from station.   Map Ref: 21

Public Record Office Museum

Ruskin Avenue, Kew, Richmond TW9 4DU   Tel: 020 8392 5202   Fax: 020 8392 5345
Email: events@pro.gov.uk   Web: pro.gov.uk

Official documents from the Domesday Book to military reports of D-Day Landings. The National Archive of the United Kingdom holds Government papers from 11th century to recent releases.

Opening Times: Mon & Wed, Fri & Sat 09:30-17:00, Tue & Thu 10:00-19:00. Closed BH.
Admission: Free.   Location: Ten minutes from tube/railway station.   Map Ref: 3

Outer London

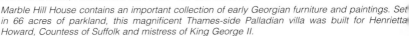
Marble Hill House
Richmond Road, Twickenham TW1 2NL   Tel: 020 8892 5115

Marble Hill House contains an important collection of early Georgian furniture and paintings. Set in 66 acres of parkland, this magnificent Thames-side Palladian villa was built for Henrietta Howard, Countess of Suffolk and mistress of King George II.

Opening Times: Apr to Sep daily 10:00-18:00, Oct daily 10:00-17:00, Nov to Mar Wed to Sun 10:00-16:00. Closed Xmas and 1 to 16 Jan.   Admission: Adult £3.30, Child £1.70, Concession £2.50.   Location: Richmond Road, frequent bus service, St Margarets Station quarter of a mile, Richmond Tube - one mile.   Map Ref: 37

Museum of Rugby
Rugby Road, Twickenham TW1 1DZ   Tel: 020 8892 8877   Fax: 020 8892 2817
Email: museum@rfu.com   Web: www.rfu.com

Children 'in action' on the Scrum Machine

The Twickenham Experience

Few would dispute that sport has an appeal that crosses gender, age and racial barriers. But few people would connect the thrills and spills of the top level competition with the standard museum environment. How can a museum compete with drama, excitement and appeal of live sport? The answer is simple: today's sports museums with their hands-on exhibits and interactive screens and sounds are more than just testaments to facts and figures, but living breathing ways of connecting with the unrivalled excitement that only sport can provide. You can find out all about rugby, its history and its star players by visiting The Museum of Rugby, Twickenham. The world's finest collection of rugby memorabilia is housed at the Museum of Rugby, which takes visitors through the history of the sport from 1823 to the present day. The Museum also offers fans a tour of Britain's most famous Rugby Stadium.

Opening Times: Tue to Sat 10:00-17:00, Sun 11:00-17:00, BH 10:00-17:00. Closed Match Day, post Match Day Sun, Mon, Good Friday and Xmas.   Admission: Museum & Tour - Adult £6.00, Concession £4.00. Museum or Tour Adult £4.00, Concession £3.00. Family £19.00.
Location: Situated inside RFU Twickenham Stadium.   Map Ref: 37

Orleans House Gallery
Riverside, Twickenham TW1 3DJ   Tel: 020 8892 0221   Fax: 020 8744 0501
Email: galleryinfo@richmond.gov.uk   Web: www.richmond.gov.uk

Borough art gallery comprising 18th century Octagon Room designed by James Gibbs, historical and contemporary exhibitions throughout the year situated in tranquil park by the River Thames.

Opening Times: Tue to Sat 13:00-17:30, Sun & BH 14:00-17:30. Oct to Mar Closes 16:30.
Admission: Free.   Location: Ten minute walk from station.   Map Ref: 37

jewel of the county is undoubtedly Norwich, the county town with its superb cathedral built in en stone and its impressive Norman Castle. To the east of Norwich are the Norfolk Broads, an a of glorious reedy lakes and meandering waterways. Norfolk, a highly efficient farming county s largely bypassed by the Industrial Revolution and its consequent urban development.

uarter of Norfolk's museums lie within the surrounds of Norwich and as one would expect in a nty with such a pastoral background there are many excellent rural life museums.

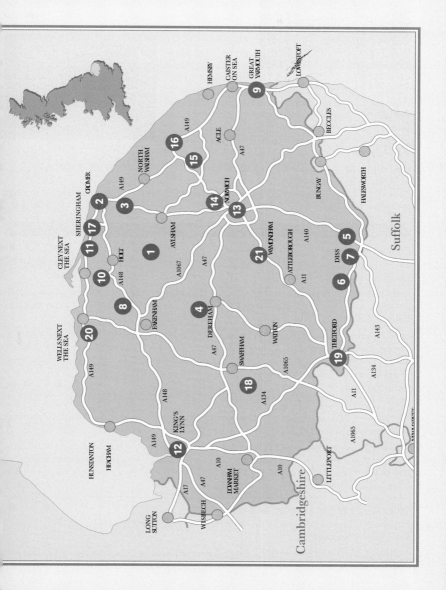

The Red Map References should be used to locate Museums etc on the pages that follow

Norfolk

Blickling Hall

Blickling, Aylsham NR11 6NF   Tel: 01263 738030   Fax: 01263 731660
Web: www.nationaltrust.org.uk

South Front of Blickling Hall, built by Sir Henry Hobart

Blickling Hall is one of the most spectacular country houses in East Anglia. The 17th century red brick house is flanked by two immense yew hedges and has an extensive colourful garden surrounded by historic park and woodland. The house contains fine furniture, pictures and tapestries set in magnificent State Rooms. The Peter the Great Room dominated by its massive tapestry of Peter the Great at the Battle of Poltawa. Close to the Hall you will find a delightful secret garden, an 18th century orangery and a dry moat with a wide range of colourful plants. To the south of the house are the great yew hedges planted in the 17th century.

North West view across the Lake

Opening Times: House - 23 Mar to 3 Nov Wed to Sun & BH 13:00-17:00. Garden, Shop & Restaurant - 23 Mar to 3 Nov Wed to Sun & BH 10:15-17:15.   Admission: House & Garden - Adult £6.70, Child £3.35. Garden only - Adult £3.80, Child £1.90.   Location: One and half miles northwest Aylsham, Norfolk.

Map Ref: 1

Cromer Museum

East Cottages, Tucker Street, Cromer NR27 9HB   Tel: 01263 513543   Fax: 01263 511651
Email: cromer.museum@norfolk.gov.uk   Web: www.norfolk.gov.uk/tourism/museums

Enter the Victorian fisherman's cottage illuminated by gaslight and imagine what it was like to live in Cromer at the end of the 19th century. Find out about Henry Blogg's famous lifeboat rescues and much more.

Opening Times: Mon to Sat 10:00-17:00, Sun 14:00-17:00.   Admission: Adult £1.80, Child 90p, Concession £1.40.   Location: In Tucker Street, opposite the East end of Cromer Parish Church.

Map Ref: 2

Felbrigg Hall

Roughton, Cromer NR11 8PR   Tel: 01263 837444

17th century hall containing original 18th century furniture and Grand Tour paintings as well as an outstanding library.

Opening Times: House: 23 Mar to 3 Nov Sat to Wed 13:00-17:00, BH Sun & Mon 11:00-17:00. Garden: 23 Mar to 3 Nov Sat to Wed 11:00-17:30.   Admission: House & Garden: Adult £5.90, Child £2.90. Garden: Adult £2.30, Child £1.00. Group rates available.   Location: Two and a half miles south of Cromer.

Map Ref: 3

RNLI Henry Blogg Lifeboat Museum

No 2 Boathouse, The Promenade, Cromer NR27 9HE   Tel: 01263 511294
Web: www.lifeboats.org.uk

Display on the life of Coxwain Henry Blogg, winner of three RNLI Gold Medals for bravery. Also displays relating to Cromer Lifeboats and the Royal National Lifeboat Institution.

Opening Times: May to Sep daily 10:00-16:00. By appointment in winter.   Admission: Free.
Location: Near town centre.

Map Ref: 2

DEREHAM

Playing the Game of Life in the
Workhouse Experience

Roots of Norfolk at Gressenhall

Gressenhall, Dereham NR20 4DR   Tel: 01362 860563
Fax: 01362 860385   Email: gressenhall.museum@norfolk.gov.uk
Web: www.norfolk.gov.uk/tourism/museums

A museum of rural life housed in a former workhouse, with displays on village and rural life and a farm worked with horses and stocked with rare breeds, all in an idyllic rural setting with farm woodland and riverside trails, gardens, a children's play area and the Mardlers Rest Café. A perfect day out for all the family, whatever the weather.

Opening Times: 22 Mar to 1 Dec daily 10:00-17:00.   Location: On B1146, three miles north west of Dereham. Follow brown signs from A47 and Dereham Town Centre.   Map Ref: 4

DISS

100th Bomb Group Memorial Museum

Common Road, Dickleburgh, Diss IP21 4PH   Tel: 01379 740708

A fine collection of USAAF uniforms, decorations, combat records, equipment, memorabilia and wartime photographs.

Opening Times: Sat, Sun & BH 10:00-17:00, May to Sep also open Wed. Also by appointment. Closed Nov, Dec & Jan.   Admission: Free.   Location: Turn off the A140 at Dickleburgh by pass (to Thorpe Abbotts), 17 miles south of Norwich, 26 miles north of Ipswich.   Map Ref: 5

Bressingham Steam Museum & Gardens

Bressingham, near Diss IP22 2AB   Tel: 01379 687386   Fax: 01379 688085
Email: info@bressingham.co.uk   Web: www.bressingham.co.uk

Where you will find majestic main-line steam locomotives; you can ride on five miles of narrow-gauge steam railway and watch clanking, hissing traction engines at work. There are also 12 acres of magnificent, world renowned colourful gardens, with blooms of Bressingham Garden Centre and a vivid re-creation of 'Dad's Army's' Walmington-on-Sea. Bressingham has something for everyone. For Special Events Listings, please phone for details.

Victorian Steam Gallopers (1900)

Opening Times: Easter to end of Oct 10:30-17:30.   Admission: Adult £10.00, Child £8.00, OAP £9.00, Family £35.00.   Location: Two and a half miles west of Diss and 14 miles east of Thetford on A1066.   Map Ref: 6

Diss Museum

11 Market Hill, Diss IP22 3JZ   Tel: 01379 650618

An award-winning museum of local history. Well researched displays about Diss and district, with something for everyone.

Opening Times: 13 Mar to 21 Dec Wed to Thu 14:00-16:00, Fri to Sat 10:30-16:30. May to Aug Sun 14:00-16:00.   Admission: Free.   Location: Middle of the Market Square.   Map Ref: 7

Thursford Collection

Thursford, Fakenham NR21 0AS   Tel: 01328 878477   Fax: 01328 878415
Email: admin@thursfordcollection.co.uk

Savages Venetian Gondola Ride

A glittering Aladdin's cave of majestic old road engines and mechanical organs of magical variety all gleaming with colour. Robert Wolfe stars live in the mighty Wurlitzer show, and there's a programme of music too from Thursford's nine very different mechanical pipe organs. Old farm buildings have been transformed into a small village with a touch of Charles Dickens' England.

Opening Times: Good Friday to mid Oct daily 12:00-17:00. Closed Sat   Admission: Adult £4.90, Child £2.40, Under 4s Free, OAP £4.60, Student £4.15. Group rates available.   Location: One mile off A148 between Fakenham and Holt.   Map Ref: 8

Elizabethan House

4 South Street, Great Yarmouth NR30 2QH   Tel: 01493 855746   Fax: 01493 745526
Web: www.norfolk.gov.uk/tourism/museums

A Tudor merchant's house hidden behind a Georgian street front, with furnished rooms and displays of home life through the ages. Visit the panelled parlour where the death of King Charles I was decided.

Opening Times: Mon 25 Mar to Thu 31 Oct. Mon to Fri 10:00-17:00, Sat & Sun 13:15-17:00.
Admission: Adult £2.00, Child £1.00, Concession £1.50, Family £4.70.   Map Ref: 9

Great Yarmouth Museums Galleries

Central Library, Tolhouse Street, Great Yarmouth NR30 2SH   Tel: 01493 745526   Fax: 01493 745459   Web: www.norfolk.gov.uk/tourism/museums

The Tolhouse was once the town courtroom and gaol. It is one of the oldest civic buildings in the country. A visit to the dungeons is a chilling experience, with their original cells and lifelike models of Victorian prisoners.

Admission: Adult 90p, Child Free, Concession 70p.   Location: In Tolhouse Street next to Great Yarmouth's Central Library.   Map Ref: 9

Maritime Museum for East Anglia

25 Marine Parade, Great Yarmouth NR30 2EN   Tel: 01493 745526   Fax: 01493 745459

Enjoy a traditional museum of sailors and the sea. Situated on Marine Parade, on the sea front. There are fascinating displays of the town's rich maritime history.

Opening Times: Mon 25 Mar to Sun 7 Apr Mon to Fri 10:00-17:00, Sat & Sun 13:15-17:00. Sun 26 May to Fri 27 Sep Mon to Fri 10:00-17:00, Sat & Sun 13:15-17:00.   Admission: Adult £1.10, Child 70p, Concession 90p, Group 90p.   Location: In Marine Parade, Great Yarmouth, opposite the Marina Centre.   Map Ref: 9

Old Merchants House & Row 111 Houses

South Quay, Great Yarmouth NR30 2RQ   Tel: 01493 857900

These two 17th century houses are a type of building unique to Great Yarmouth. They are two of the earliest surviving merchants' houses in England, and contain original fixtures and displays of local architectural fittings.   Map Ref: 9

Glandford Shell Museum

Glandford, Holt NR25 7JR   Tel: 01263 740081

A collection of shells from all corners of the world which is constantly being added to. Also a display of an evocative tapestry and many other items.

Opening Times: Easter Sat to 31 Oct Tue to Sat 10:12:30 14:00-16:30.   Admission: Adult £1.50, Child 50p, OAP £1.00.   Map Ref: 10

Muckleburgh Collection
Weybourne, Holt NR25 7EG   Tel: 01263 588210/608

The Museum is housed in the former Ack-Ack NAAFI. Since the Museum's inception 13 years ago it has carefully restored tanks and other military vehicles; to date there are 16 working tanks and other guns and vehicles.

Opening Times: Feb to Oct daily 10:00-17:00. Admission: Adult £4.95, Child £2.50, OAP £3.50. Location: Four miles west of Sheringham.   Map Ref: 11

KING'S LYNN

Lynn Museum
Market Street, King's Lynn PE30 1NL   Tel: 01553 775001   Email: lynn.museum@norfolk.gov.uk   Web: www.norfolk.gov.uk/tourism/museums

Tells the story of the people and places of King's Lynn and West Norfolk. Travel back through history and explore the changing local landscape from the earlist farmers, through Roman, Saxon and medieval times.

Opening Times: Tue to Sat 10:00-17:00. Close Xmas & New Year. Admission: Adult £1.00, Child 60p, Concession 80p. Location: Entrance off King's Lynn Bus Station, adjacent to the shopping precinct.   Map Ref: 12

Tales of the Old Gaol House
Saturday Market Place, King's Lynn PE30 5DQ   Tel: 01553 774297   Fax: 01553 772361   Email: gaolhouse@west-norfolk.gov.uk   Web: www.west-norfolk.gov.uk

Set in the town's old cells, visitors have the chance to hear the stories and experience the sights (and smells) of Lynn's criminal past. Also housed there are some of Britain's finest civic treasures, including the priceless King John Cup.

Opening Times: Easter to End Oct daily 10:00-17:00, Nov to Easter closed Wed & Thu. Admission: Adult £2.40, Concession £1.75. Location: Town centre, ten minutes walk from bus station, in the heart of the medieval part of King's Lynn.   Map Ref: 12

Town House Museum of Lynn Life
46 Queen Street, King's Lynn PE30 5DQ   Tel: 01553 773450   Email: townhouse.museum@norfolk.gov.uk   Web: www.norfolk.gov.uk/tourism/museums

Housed in a 19th century town house and former Inn. Displays focus on the everyday life of Lynn people through the ages and take you through a series of carefully reconstructed rooms.

Opening Times: May to Sep Mon to Sat 10:00-17:00, Sun 14:00-17:00. Oct to Apr Mon to Sat 10:00-16:00. Closed BH, Xmas & New Year. Admission: Adult £1.80, Child 90p, Concession £1.40. Location: Queen Street in the heart of historic 'Old Lynn' and close to the medieval Guildhall and St Margaret's Church.   Map Ref: 12

Trues Yard Fishing Heritage Centre
Trues Yard, North Street, King's Lynn PE30 1QW   Tel: 01553 770479   Fax: 01553 765100   Email: trues.yard@virgin.net   Web: http://welcome.to/truesyard

True's Yard is all that remains of the old fishing community of the north end of King's Lynn. The displays and archive rooms are housed in the original cottages which have been fully restored.

Opening Times: Daily 09:30-15:45. Admission: Adult £1.00. Location: 300 metres from Tuesday market place, opposite dock offices.   Map Ref: 12

NORWICH

Bridewell Museum of Norwich Trades & Industries
Bridewell Alley, Norwich NR2 1AQ   Tel: 01603 667228   Email: museums@norfolk.gov.uk   Web: www.norfolk.gov.uk/tourism/museums

This former merchants' house, part of which dates from 1325, became an 'open' prison for vagrants, children and women (a Bridewell), before becoming a museum focusing on Norwich life and industry.

Opening Times: Feb to 31 Oct Mon to Sat 10:00-17:00. Admission: Adult £2.00, Child £1.00, Concession £1.50, Family £5.00 Location: In city centre.   Map Ref: 13

City of Norwich Aviation Museum

🛡 📷 🚜 Aviation Museum

Old Norwich Road, Horsham St Faith, Norwich NR10 3JF
Tel: 01603 893080   Web: www.cnam.co.uk

Some of the aircraft on display

Aircraft on display include a massive Vulcan Bomber and Civil and Military aeroplanes which have flown from Norfolk over the past 40 years. Inside displays feature the achievement and sacrifces of the heroes and pioneers who have formed the aviation history of Norfolk.

Opening Times: Apr to Oct Tue to Sat 10:00-17:00, Sun & BH 12:00-17:00. Nov to Mar Wed & Sat 10:00-16:00 Sun 12:00-16:00. Closed Xmas & New Year.
Admission: Adult £2.50, Child/Concession £1.50, OAP £2.00, Family £7.00.   Location: One mile from A140 Norwich to Cromer road, follow brown tourist signs.

Map Ref: 14

Inspire Hands on Science Centre

♿ 🛡 📷

St Michaels Church, Collany Street, Norwich NR3 3DT   Tel: 01603 612612   Fax: 01603 616721   Email: inspire@science-project.org   Web: www.science-project.org

Hands-on exhibits, shows and special events. Science shop and light refreshments, perfect for families, parties and schools.

Opening Times: Daily 10:00-17:30 (last admission 16:30).   Admission: Adult £4.20, Child £3.60, Under 3s Free, Saver (2 adults and 2 children) £12.00.   Location: Norwich City Centre, five minutes walk from market.

Map Ref: 13

Norwich Castle Museum & Art Gallery

📚 ♿ 🛡 📷

Shirehall, Market Avenue, Norwich NR1 3TQ   Tel: 01603 493625   Fax: 01603 493623
Email: museum@norfolk.gov.uk   Web: www.norfolk.gov.uk/tourism/museum

Norwich Castle Museum & Art Gallery

Norwich Castle has outstanding archaeology, natural history and fine art collections and is placed with treasures as diverse as ancient gold jewellery, silver, delicate porcelain and Roman pottery. See the best collections anywhere of the Norwich School of Artists, Norwich Silver, Lowestoft Porcelain, ceramic teapots and regular exhibitions from Tate.

Opening Times: Mon to Sat 10:30-17:00, Sun 14:00-17:00. Closed Xmas.   Admission: Adult £4.70, Child £3.50, Concession £4.10.   Location: In city centre.

Map Ref: 13

Royal Air Force Air Defence Radar Museum

📚 ♿ 🛡 📷 🚜

RAF Neatishead, Norwich NR12 8YB   Tel: 01692 633309   Fax: 01692 633214
Web: www.neatishead.raf.mod.uk

History of radar and air defence from 1935 to date. Housed in original 1942 building. Features Battle of Britain, 1942 operations, Cold War Operations Room and Space Defence. Radar convoy vehicles.

Opening Times: Apr to Sep second Sat each month, BH Mon, Tue & Thu 10:00-17:00. Oct to Mar second Sat each month.   Admission: Adult £3.00, Child over 12 £1.00, Under 12s Free.   Location: Near Horning, Norfolk.

Map Ref: 15

Royal Norfolk Regimental Museum

🛡

Shirehall, Market Avenue, Norwich NR1 3JQ   Tel: 01603 493649   Fax: 01603 630214
Email: museum@norfolk.gov.uk   Web: www.norfolk.gov.uk/tourism/museums

Situated in the Shirehall, which dates from the early 1830s. The displays are themed and set out chronologically with excellent interpretative panels, designed for those with no military knowledge as well as the military historian.

Opening Times: Mon to Sat 10:00-17:00, Sun 14:00-17:00.   Admission: Adult £1.80, Child 90p, Concession £1.40.   Location: In the Shirehall buildings at the base of Norwich Castle opposite Anglia TV.

Map Ref: 13

Sainsbury Centre for Visual Arts

Sainsbury Centre for Visual Arts

University of East Anglia, Norwich NR4 7TJ
Tel: 01603 593199/592467 Fax: 01603 259401
Email: scva@uea.ac.uk Web: www.uea.ac.uk/scva

The Robert and Lisa Sainsbury Collection is housed in two distinctive buildings by Lord Foster. Combining modern Western art with fine and applied arts from Africa, the Pacific, the Americas, Asia, Egypt, medieval Europe and the ancient Mediterranean, the collection contains some 1200 objects reflecting over 5000 years of creativity. It is particularly well known for works by Francis Bacon, John Davies, Alberto Giancometti and Henry Moore.

Opening Times: Tue to Sun 11:00-17:00. Admission: Adult £2.00, Concessions £1.00.   Map Ref: 13

Free-standing male fiigure, New Zealan

Strangers Hall Museum

Charing Cross, Norwich NR2 4AL Tel: 01603 667229 Email: museums@norfolk.gov.uk
Web: www.norfolk.gov.uk/tourism/museums

One of the oldest and most fascinating buildings in Norwich. It is typical of houses occupied by the well-to-do city merchants when Norwich was in its heyday.

Opening Times: Tours Wed and Sat 11:00 and 13:00, also 15:00 Apr to Aug. Admission: Adult £2.50, Child £1.50, Concession £2.00.   Map Ref: 13

Sutton Windmill & Broads Museum

SUTTON WINDMILL BROADS MUSEUM NORFOLK

Sutton, Stalham, Norwich NR12 9RZ Tel: 01692 581195 Fax: 01692 583214 Email: broadsmuseum@btinternet.com

Windmill with nine floors. Museum has seven buildings, 1880s pharmacy, Tobacco Museum, kitchen items, animal traps, veterinary, TVs, radios, large engines, razors, banknotes, farm and trade tools, leathertrades, camera, soaps, polish, trade tricycles and coopers display.

Opening Times: Apr to Sep daily 10:00-17:30.
Admission: Child £1.50, OAP £3.50. Location: One mile off A149, nr Stalham. Brown tourism signs on A149.
Map Ref: 16

Milk Hand Cart c.1910

SHERINGHAM

North Norfolk (M & GN) Railway Museum

The Station, Station Approach, Sheringham NR26 8RA Tel: 01263 822045 Fax: 01263 820801 Email: enquiries@mandgn.co.uk Web: www.mandgn.co.uk

The Midland & Great Northern joint railway society is the support charity behind the North Norfolk Railway. The society is dedicated to preserving our railway heritage in East Anglia, especially that of the M & GN Railway. Displays of smaller artefacts are currently on view in the Sheringham Museum Coach and the model railway facilities at Weybourne and Holt. The society's collection of locomotives and rolling stock is also based on the railway.

Opening Times: Feb to Oct & Dec each day of timetable railway service. Admission: Free. Location: Museum
coach is on platform three at the North Norfolk Railway's Sheringham Station.   Map Ref: 17

Sheringham Museum

Station Road, Sheringham NR26 8RE Tel: 01263 821871 Fax: 01263 825741
Email: lattaway@globalnet.co.uk

Boat building, fishing industry, lifeboats, Roman kiln, beach finds, war years, 'The Weybourne Elephant' - one and a half million years old, photographic displays, gallery.

Opening Times: Easter week to end of Oct, two weekends immediately prior to Xmas.
Admission: Adult £1.00, Child/Concession 50p, Groups of 10+ 35p. Location: Station Road - in town centre; four minutes walk from main car park.   Map Ref: 17

SWAFFHAM

Cockley Cley Iceni Village & Museums

Estate Office, Cockley Cley, Swaffham PE37 8AG   Tel / Fax: 01760 721339

A family settlement typical of the Boadicea's Iceni Tribe of East Anglia. Farm bygones, implements and carriages, a 17th century farm cottage, St Mary's Chapel - a Saxon place of worship built in 630 AD.

Opening Times: Apr to Oct daily 11:00-17:30. Admission: Adult £4.00, Child £2.00, Concession £3.00. Location: Three miles south west of Swaffham.   Map Ref: 18

THETFORD

Ancient House Museum

White Hart Street, Thetford IP24 1AA   Tel: 01842 752599
Email: ancient.house.museum@norfolk.gov.uk   Web: www.norfolk.gov.uk/tourism/museums

This magnificent timber-framed Tudor merchant's house was built about 1490, with an extension added about 1590. The house is jetted and timber-framed, using oak with wattle and daub in-fill with fine carved ceiling and fireplace timbers.

Opening Times: Mon to Sat 10:00-12:30, 13:00-17:00. Also open 27 May to 30 Aug Sun 14:00-17:00. Admission: Sep to Jun free, Adult £1.00, Child 60p, OAP/Student/Concession 80p.
Map Ref: 19

WELLS-NEXT-THE-SEA

Bygones At Holkham

Holkham Park, Wells-next-the-Sea NR23 1AB   Tel: 01328 711163/710806   Fax: 01328 711707
Web: www.holkham.co.uk

Over 4000 items of domestic and agricultural memorabilia, carriages and vintage cars. Working steam engines, kitchen, dairy, laundry. Music and money boxes. Typewriters and sewing machines.

Opening Times: 31 Mar to 1 Apr, 5 & 6 May, 2,3 & 4 Jun, 25 & 26 Aug 11:30-17:00. 26 May to 30 Sep Sun to Thu 13:00-17:00.Holkham Country Fair 21 & 22 Sep, Hall/Museum closed.
Admission: Holkham Hall & Bygones Museum: Adult £8.00, Child £4.00. Holkham Hall or Museum: Adult £5.00, Child £2.50. Location: Two miles west of Wells-next-the-Sea, off A149 coast road.   Map Ref: 20

WYMONDHAM

Wymondham Heritage Museum

10 The Bridewell, Norwich Road, Wymondham NR18 0NS   Tel: 01953 600205
Web: www.wymondham-norfork.co.uk

Award-winning museum in 18th century model prison built 1785, later serving as a police station and courthouse. Dungeon and original cell. Displays about history of the building and town including Kett's rebellion, agriculture and brushmaking.

Opening Times: Mar to Nov Mon to Sat 10:00-16:00 Sun 14:00-16:00. Admission: Adult £2.00, Child 50p, Concession £1.50. Groups by prior arrangement. Location: Near town centre, two minutes walk from Market Cross and central car park.   Map Ref: 21

Museums, Galleries, Historic Houses & Sites

Please let us know of any collections that are not listed in this guide that you feel should be listed. E-mail us on *editor@tomorrows.co.uk*
or return the Report Form on page 448

ver was such an area blessed with so many museums, exhibitions, shows, galleries and
ivals. It is not surprising considering that this northern region (comprising Northumberland,
veland, County Durham and Tyne & Wear) is simply steeped in history, social, industrial and
tary and all minutely recorded in some of the finest museums in Britain. Added to this there are
hundred square miles of National Park telling its own story of the majestic beauty of the
reme north from Hadrian's Wall to the Cheviots and the Scottish Border. Hadrian's Wall, of
rse, boasts a string of museums telling their story of the Roman occupation of these lands,
most cities and towns of the region have their own museums.

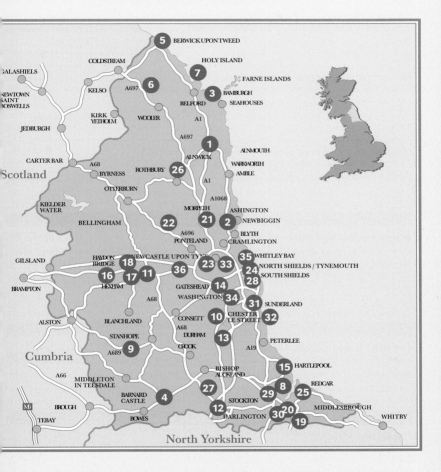

The Red Map References should be used to locate Museums etc on the pages that follow

Bondgate Gallery   ♿ ●

22 Narrowgate, Alnwick NE66 1JG   Tel: 01665 576450

Eight exhibitions per year, also craft work including wood and glass.

Opening Times: Mon to Sat 10:30-16:00.   Admission: Free.   Location: 22 Narrowgate.
     Map Ref: 1

Fusiliers Museum of Northumberland   ● ◻ ⛟

The Abbots Tower, Alnwick Castle, Alnwick NE66 1NG   Tel: 01665 602152

Exhibition tells the story of the fusiliers from 1674. Audio visual interpretation and children's activities. Life size dioramas. Guide book available.

Opening Times: 28 Mar to 25 Oct daily 11:00-17:00.   Admission: Adult £6.95, Child Free.
Group rates available.   Location: Near Alnwick Town Centre.   Map Ref: 1

Museum of Antiquities, Alnwick Castle   ● ◻ ⛟

Estates Office, Alnwick Castle, Alnwick NE66 1NQ   Tel: 01665 510777 ext 190

Displays of local archaeology from Northumberland

Opening Times: 28 Mar to 25 Oct daily 11:00-17:00.   Admission: Adult £6.95, Child Free.
Group discounts available.   Location: Near Alnwick Town Centre.   Map Ref: 1

Museum of the Percey Tenantry Volunteers 1798-1814   ● ◻ ⛟

Estate Office, Alnwick Castle, Alnwick NE66 1NQ   Tel: 01665 510777

Exhibition of artefacts and tableaux telling the story of the Percy Tenantry Volunteers 1798-1814.

Opening Times: 28 Mar to 25 Oct daily 11:00-17:00.   Admission: Adult £6.95, Child Free.
Group rates available.   Location: Near Alnwick Town Centre.   Map Ref: 1

Woodhorn Colliery Museum   ⬚ ♿ ● ◻ ⛟

Queen Elizabeth II Country Park, Ashington NE63 9YF   Tel: 01670 856968   Fax: 01670 810958

Mining and social history displays within original late 19th century pit buildings. Highlights include paintings by the Ashington Group, miners banners and a varied programme of temporary exhibitions.

Opening Times: Wed to Sun & BH 10:00-16:00 (17:00 May to Aug).   Admission: Free.
Location: Ten minute walk from Ashington Bus Station.   Map Ref: 2

The RNLI Grace Darling Museum

2 Radcliffe Road, Bamburgh NE69 7AE   Tel: 01668 214465   Web: www.lifeboats.org.uk

Items relating to the life of Grace Darling, including the original coble used for rescue.

Opening Times: Easter to Oct Mon to Sat 10:00-17:00, Sun 12:00-17:00.   Admission: Free.
     Map Ref: 3

The Bowes Museum   ⬚ ♿ ● ◻ ⛟

Barnard Castle DL12 8NP   Tel: 01833 690606   Fax: 01833 637163
Email: info@bowesmuseum.org.uk   Web: www.bowesmuseum.org.uk

The Bowes Museum has 30 public galleries. Set
in formal gardens and parkland

A world-class visitor attraction. Don't miss this unique fine art gallery, housed in a magnificent French chateau in the picturesque market town of Barnard Castle in Teesdale. Learn the romantic story of the founders, John and Josephine Bowes. See the famous silver swan musical automation. See paintings by Boudin, Canaletto and Goya. Join in the busy programme of exhibition and events.

Opening Times: Jan to Dec daily 11:00-17:00. Closed 25-26 Dec & 1 Jan.   Admission: Adult £4.00, Child/OAP/Concession £3.00, Family £12.00. Group rates available.   Location: In Barnard Castle.   Map Ref: 4

Berwick-upon-Tweed Borough Museum & Art Gallery

The Clock Block, Berwick Barracks, Ravensdowne, Berwick-upon-Tweed TD15 1DQ
Tel: 01289 330044 Fax: 01289 330540

Berwick Museum, housed within Ravensdowne Barracks, explores local social history in 'Window on Berwick'. Also on display are many of the paintings and artefacts given to the town by Sir William Burrell.

Opening Times: 1 Nov to 29 Mar Wed to Sun 10:00-16:00, 30 Mar to 31 Oct daily 10:00-18:00.
Admission: Adult £2.80, Child £1.90, Concession £2.10.   Location: Near town centre.

Map Ref: 5

Lady Waterford Gallery

Ford Village, Berwick-upon-Tweed TD15 2QA   Tel: 01890 820524

A Victorian Hall, formerly Ford village school houses the Waterford Murals created by Louisa Marchioness of Waterford from 1862 to 1883. The murals depict well known stories from the Bible, using children from the school and other local people as the subjects.

Opening Times: 23 Mar to 3 Nov, Daily 10:30-12:30 and 13:30-17:30   Admission: Adults £1.50, Children over 12 £0.50, O.A.P's and concessions £1.00   Location: Approx 12 miles south west from Berwick Upon Tweed, Signposted from the A1 and A697.

Map Ref: 6

Lindisfarne Priory

Holy Island, Berwick-upon-Tweed TD15 2RX   Tel: 01289 389200

One of the holiest sites of Anglo-Saxon England, Lindisfarne was renowned as the original burial place of St Cuthbert. Founded in 635 by St Aidan who came from Iona, it was the centre of Christianity in Scotland. Lindisfarne was a treasure house of jewels and manuscripts, including incomparable illuminated Gospels (now in British Library), and is still a holy site and place of pilgrimage today. In the award winning museum one of the most important collections of Anglo-Saxon stonework is on display.

Lindisfarne Priory copyright English Heritage

Opening Times: Apr to Sep daily 10:00-18:00, Oct daily 10:00-17:00, Nov to Mar daily 10:00-16:00. Closed Xmas & New Year. Admission: Adult £2.90, Child £1.50, Concession £2.20.   Location: On Holy Island, only reached at low tide across causeway. For details of tides telephone Berwick Tourist Information 01289 330733.   Map Ref: 7

The King's Own Scottish Borderers Regimental Museum

The Barracks, Berwick-upon-Tweed TD15 1DG   Tel: 01289 307426
Fax: 01289 331928   Email: kosbmus@milnet.uk.net
Web: www.kosb.co.uk

The history of the Regiment from 1689 to the present day is traced through displays of uniforms, badges, medals, weapons, paintings and relics from the various campaigns in which it has been involved. Tableaux and dioramas dramatically bring to life the Regiment's battles and aspects of the soldier's profession.

Opening Times: Mon to Sat 09:30-16:30. Closed certain public holidays, Xmas & New Year. Admission: Adult £2.70, Child £1.40, Under 5s Free, Concession £2.00. Members of English Heritage Free. Members of Historic Scotland and CADW Free or half price.
Location: Within Berwick Barracks, beside the town of Ramparts, two minutes walk from the town centre.

Regimental Cap Badge

Map Ref: 5

BILLINGHAM *Cleveland*

Billingham Art Gallery

Queensway, Billingham TS23 2LN   Tel: 01642 397590   Fax: 01642 397594

Offers an exciting selection of art to suit all tastes, providing a lively forum for local artists to exhibit their work.

Opening Times: Mon to Sat 09:00-17:00. Closed Sun & BH.   Admission: Free.
Location: Town centre.   Map Ref: 8

BISHOP AUCKLAND *Durham*

Killhope, the North of England Lead Mining Museum
near Cowshill, Upper Weardale, Bishop Auckland DL13 1AR   Tel: 01388 537505   Fax: 01388 537617   Email: killhope@durham.gov.uk   Web: www.durham.gov.uk/killhope

Explores the life of North Pennine lead mining families. Visitors walk down the original mine tunnel and discover the working conditions of Victorian miners. See how miners lived and worked. Woodland walk.

Opening Times: Apr to Sep 10:30-17:00 Oct Sat & Sun 10:30-17:00. Admission: Adult £3.40 Child £1.70 Family £8.50. Location: On A689, 20 minutes from Stanhope and ten minutes from Alston.   Map Ref: 9

CHESTER-LE-STREET *Durham*

Beamish, The North of England Open Air Museum

Beamish, Chester-le-Street DH9 0RG   Tel: 0191 370 4000   Fax: 0191 370 4001   Email: museum@beamish.org.uk   Web: www.beamish.org.uk

Experience the past at England's favourite open air museum - it's no ordinary museum but a vast, living and working experience of life as it was in the Great North. Buildings have been rebuilt and furnished to create a Colliery Village, Town Street, Railway Station and working Farm of 1913 and an 1825 Railway and Manor House. Photo archive and library. Designated museum.

Opening Times: Apr to Oct daily 10:00-17:00. Nov to Mar Tue to Thu, Sat & Sun 10:00-16:00. Closed Mon & Fri, Xmas & New Year. Admission: Apr to Oct Adult £12.00, Child £6.00, OAP £9.00. Group rates available. Winter

Recreation of The 1825 Railway at Beamish

months reduced operation, everyone pays £4.00.   Location: North west of Durham (12 miles), signposted from junction 63 of A1M, Chester-le-Street.   Map Ref: 10

CORBRIDGE *Northumberland*

Corbridge Roman Site Museum

Corbridge NE45 5NT   Tel: 01434 632349

Originally the site of a fort on the former patrol road, Corbridge evolved into a principal town of the Roman era, flourishing until the fifth century. The large granaries are among its most impressive remains. The museum contains a vast selection of finds from the area, illustrating the history of Hadrian's Wall.

Opening Times: Apr to Sep daily 10:00-18:00, Oct daily 10:00-17:00, Nov to Mar Wed to Sun 10:00-13:00 14:00-16:00. Closed Xmas & New Year. Admission: Adult £2.90, Child £1.50, Concession £2.20. Location: Half a mile north west of Corbridge - signed Corbridge Roman Site.   Map Ref: 11

DARLINGTON *Durham*

Darlington Railway Centre & Museum

North Road Station, Darlington DL3 6ST   Tel: 01325 460532   Fax: 01325 287746
Email: museum@darlington.gov.uk   Web: www.drcm.org.uk

Experience the atmosphere of the steam railway in the historic North Road Station of 1842. See Stephenson's "Locomotion" and explore the railway heritage of the North East through a collection of engines, carriages/wagons and railway ephemera.

Opening Times: Daily 10:00-17:00. Closed Xmas & New Year. Admission: Adult £2.10, Child £1.05, Concession £1.50. Location: 15 minute walk from town centre, frequent bus service.
Map Ref: 12

DLI - Durham Light Infantry Museum & Durham Art Gallery

Aykley Heads, Durham DH1 5TU   Tel: 0191 384 2214   Fax: 0191 386 1770
Web: www.durham.gov.uk/dli

Opening Times: Apr to Oct 10:00-17:00. Nov to Mar 10:00-16:00. Closed Xmas Day.
Admission: Adult £2.50 Concession £1.25 Family £6.25.   Location: Ten minute walk from city centre.
Map Ref: 13

Durham University Oriental Museum

Elvet Hill, Durham DH1 3TH   Tel / Fax: 0191 374 7911   Email: oriental.museum@durham.ac.uk
Web: www.dur.ac.uk/oriental.museum

The Oriental Museum is the only museum in the North East devoted solely to Oriental art and archaeology. Here you can explore cultures that range from Ancient Egypt to Imperial China and modern Japan.

Opening Times: Mon to Fri 10:00-17:00, Sat to Sun 12:00-17:00. Closed Xmas & New Year.
Admission: Adult £1.50, Concessions 75p, Family £3.50.   Location: Five minute from bus stop.
15 minute walk from town centre.
Map Ref: 13

The Monks Dormitory, Durham Cathedral

The College, Durham DH1 3EH   Tel: 0191 386 4266   Fax: 0191 386 4267
Email: enquiries@durhamcathedral.co.uk   Web: www.durhamcathedral.co.uk

Magnificent beamed roof and collection of pre-conquest stones. During August facsimile of Lindisfarne Gospels.

Opening Times: 1 Apr to 29 Sep Mon to Sat 10:00-15:30, Sun 12:30-15:15.   Admission: Adult 80p, Child 20p, Family £1.50.   Location: In cloisters of Durham Cathedral.
Map Ref: 13

Museum of Archaeology, University of Durham

The Old Fulling Mill, The Banks, Durham DH1 3EB   Tel: 0191 3743623   Fax: 0191 374 7911
Web: www.dur.ac.uk/archaeology

The Old Fulling Mill is a 16th century mill originally part of the Cathedral estates. It houses an archaeology museum tracing the history of Durham City from prehistoric to post-medieval times.

Opening Times: Apr to Oct daily 11:00-16:00. Nov to Mar Fri to Mon 11:30-15:30.
Admission: Adult £1.00, Concession 50p, Family £2.50.   Location: Five minutes from city centre on riverbank below Cathedral.
Map Ref: 13

Treasures of St Cuthbert Exhibition

The Chapter Office, The College, Durham DH1 3EH   Tel: 0191 386 4266   Fax: 0191 386 4267
Email: enquiries@durhamcathedral.co.uk   Web: www.durhamcathedral.co.uk

St Cuthbert's Coffin and Pectoral Cross, Anglo Saxon embroideries, silverware, seals, manuscripts. 'Turning the pages' electronic version of Lindisfarne Gospels.

Opening Times: Mon to Sat 10:00-16:00, Sun 14:00-16:30 (Dec & Jan 16.15). Closed Xmas & Good Friday.   Admission: Adult £2.00, Child 50p, Concession £1.50, Family £5.00.
Location: In cloisters of Durham Cathedral.
Map Ref: 13

Bowes Railway Centre

Springwell Village, Gateshead NE9 7QJ   Tel: 0191 416 1847

Rope haulage, on set days steam locomotives, Victorian workshops, colliery railway artefacts, two display exhibition areas.

Opening Times: Mon to Fri 09:00-16:00 - Static only. Set operating days.   Admission: Static: Free. Operating days: Adult £2.00, Child/Concession £1.00.   Location: Just outside Springwell village, five minutes walk from Wrekenton.
Map Ref: 14

Shipley Art Gallery

Prince Consort Road, Gateshead NE8 4JB   Tel: 0191 477 1495
Fax: 0191 478 7917   Web: www.twmuseums.org.uk

The Shipley Art Gallery combines a dazzling display of the latest glass, jewellery, ceramics, textiles and furniture alongside stunning historical artworks. The Craft Gallery features over 700 breathtaking pieces by the county's leading makers and paintings including Dutch and Flemish Old Masters. The fascinating history of the town is told in 'Made in Gateshead' and the Gallery stages superb temporary exhibitions.

Opening Times: Mon to Sat 10:00-17:00, Sun 14:00-17:00.
Admission: Free.   Location: Ten minute walk from town centre and metro station.   Map Ref: 14

HARTLEPOOL *Cleveland*

HMS Trincomalee Trust

Jackson Dock, Hartlepool TS24 0SQ   Tel: 01429 223193

HMS Trincomalee was built in 1817 and is the oldest ship afloat in Britain. This classic British frigate has been fully and sensitively restored and interpreted in an award-winning scheme. There are disabled lifts between three decks. The ship provides a unique opportunity to experience life aboard a British warship two centuries ago. There are audio guides with guided tours available for groups.

Opening Times: Apr to Oct 10:30-17:00, Nov to Mar 11:00-17:00. Closed Xmas & New Year. Admission: Adult £3.70, Concession £2.70, Family (2 + 3) £10.00. Education Groups £1.70.
Location: Located at Hartlepool Historic Quay. Follow the brown tourist signs for the Quay and look for the masts!   Map Ref: 15

HMS Trincomalee

Hartlepool Art Gallery

Church Square, Hartlepool TS24 8EQ   Tel: 01429 869706   Fax: 01429 523408   Email: arts-museums@hartlepool.gov.uk   Web: www.thisishartlepool.com

Programme of changing exhibitions feature the best of contemporary art and craft and a varied and innovative selection from Hartlepool's collection. 'The Arts and Crafts of Ancient Egypt' 9 Feb to 26 May. Also views from tower of Hartlepool (small charge).

Opening Times: Tue to Sat 10:00-17:30, Sun 14:00-17:00. Closed Mon. Admission: Free. Location: In magnificent converted Victorian Church, one minute walk from Hartlepool Railway Station.   Map Ref: 15

Museum of Hartlepool

Jackson Dock, Hartlepool   Tel: 01429 860006
Fax: 01429 867332   Email: historic.quay@hartlepool.gov.uk
Web: www.thisishartlepool.com

The museum of Hartlepool tells the story of Hartlepool from prehistoric times to the present day using many original artefacts, photo-graphs, models, hands-on and interactive displays. Fascinating archaeological finds from the stone age and the time of the Saxons give way to the engineering and shipbuilding achievements of the

Victorians. The constant presence of the sea has influenced the development of the town throughout its history and this is reflected in many of the objects on

Northumbria

display. Toys and games, sport and education provide a picture of social conditions. The paddle steamer 'Wingfield Castle' is moored alongside the museum quay and has a café on board.

Opening Times: Daily 10:00-17:00. Closed 25-26 Dec & New Year's Day. Admission: Free.
Location: At Hartlepool Marina, ten minutes walk from Hartlepool Railway Station. Map Ref: 15

HAYDON BRIDGE Northumberland

Housesteads Roman Fort & Museum
Haydon Bridge NE47 6NN   Tel: 01434 344363

Housesteads is the most complete example of a Roman fort in Britain and is one of the twelve permanent forts built by Emperor Hadrian in around 124 AD. The museum houses a range of objects found at the site, including flat-bottomed pottery and larger cooking pots which are Friesian in origin. Some of the Wall has been partially reconstructed to give one of the most vivid pictures of the Romans and their works in Britain.

Housesteads Fort © English Heritage

Opening Times: Apr to Sep daily 10:00-18:00, Oct daily 10:00-17:00, Nov to Mar daily 10:00-16:00. Closed Xmas & New Year. Admission: Adult £2.90, Child £1.50,
Concession £2.20. National Trust Members Free. Location: Nearly three miles north east of Bardon Mill on B6318. Map Ref: 16

HEXHAM Northumberland

Border History Museum
The Old Gaol, Hallgate, Hexham NE46 3NH   Tel: 01434 652349   Fax: 01434 652425
Email: museum@tynedale.gov.uk

The museum in the Old Gaol (1332) introduces the Border Reivers. They lived a violent life of raiding and stealing across the English-Scottish border. They left a legacy of dramatic stories, ballads and music.

Opening Times: Apr to Oct daily 10:00-16:30. Nov, Feb & Mar Sat, Mon & Tue 10:00-16:30.
Admission: Adult £2.00, Concession £1.00, Family £5.00. Group rates available. Location: In town centre, five minutes walk from bus and railway station and main car park. Map Ref: 17

Chesterholm Museum - Vindolanda
Bardon Mill, Hexham NE47 7JN   Tel: 01434 344 277   Fax: 01434 344 060   Email: info@vindolanda.com
Web: www.vindolanda.com

Vindolanda is a Roman Frontier military and civilian site, with archaeologists on site April to August, Sunday to Thursday, weather permitting. Vindolanda also offers an Open Air Museum featuring a Roman Temple, Shop and House, and an extensive museum housing finds from the site such as Roman boots, shoes, jewellery, textiles and special photographs of the rare ink on wood tablets written nearly 2000 years ago.

Opening Times: daily. Nov to Feb 10:00-16:00, Mar & Oct 10:00-17:00, Apr & Sep 10:00-17:30, May & Jun 10:00-18:00, Jul & Aug

Aerial View of Roman Vindolanda

10:00-18:30. Admission: Adult £3.90, Child £2.80,
OAP/Concession £3.30. Discounted joint saver tickets available with the Roman Army Museum.
Location: One mile north of the A69, near Bardon Mill, Northumberland. Map Ref: 17

HEXHAM-ON-TYNE Northumberland

Chesters Fort & Museum
Chollerford, Humshaugh, Hexham-on-Tyne NE46 4EP   Tel: 01434 681379

Chesters is one of the best-preserved examples of a cavalry fort. Many parts are still visible, including the barracks and a finely preserved bath house. The museum houses the important Clayton Collection of altars and sculptures.

Opening Times: Apr to Sep daily 09:30-18:00, Oct daily 10:00-17:00, Nov to Mar daily 10:00-16:00. Closed Xmas & New Year. Admission: Adult £2.90, Child £1.50, Concession £2.20.
Location: Quarter mile west of Chollerford on B6318. Map Ref: 18

MIDDLESBROUGH *Cleveland*

Captain Cook Birthplace Museum

Stewart Park, Marton, Middlesbrough TS7 6AS   Tel: 01642 311211   Fax: 01642 317419

Exploring the wonders of life in the 18th century, when Cook was a lad

Sailing into uncharted waters with Cook

The Museum marks the site of Cook's birthplace in Marton on the outskirts of Middlesbrough. Recently transformed, it uses computers, films, special effects and interactives to give a unique insight into Cook's early life and his seafaring career in Whitby and the Royal Navy. Life aboard ship for the officers and crew, the fascinating discoveries made by the ship's scientists and the legacy of Cook's visits are explored in detail. There are temporary exhibitions on related subjects and a varied programme of education and events. Collections - ethnography from countries visited by Cook plus maritime material, especially 18th century.

Opening Times: Mar to Oct Tue to Sun 10:00-17:30, Nov to Jan Tue to Sun 09:00-15:30, Feb Tue to Sun 09:00-16:00.
Admission: Adult £2.40, Child £1.25, OAP £1.20, Family £6.00.
Location: Within Stewart Park, Marton. Five minutes from Marton Railway Station.

Map Ref: 19

Cleveland Crafts Centre

Gilkes Street, Middlesbrough TS1 5EL   Tel: 01642 808090

Programme of craft based temporary exhibitions. Collection of studio pottery - Haile, Slee Leach etc on permanent display. A major collection of international contemporary jewellery occasionally on display.

Opening Times: Tues to Sat 10:00-17:30.   Admission: Free.   Location: In the town centre, at the rear of the bus station

Map Ref: 20

Dorman Museum

Linthorpe Road, Middlesbrough TS5 6LA   Tel: 01642 813781

Holds large natural science and social history collections. On display is the renowned Linthorpe art pottery collection. Ethnography, archaeology, ceramics, costume, ephemera, photographs, paintings, maps and archives. New display galleries, events, activities space, resource centre and discovery centre.

Opening Times: Closed for redevelopment until December 2002. Please ring for details.
Admission: Free. Some exhibitions may have a charge.   Location: One mile from the town centre, buses run along Linthorpe Road.

Map Ref: 20

Middlesbrough Art Gallery

320 Linthorpe Road, Middlesbrough TS1 3QY   Tel: 01642 358139

Mainly 20th century British art which is now considered one of the finest in the north of England. Artists in the collection include David Bomberct, Jacob Epstein, Frank Auerbach, Stanley Spencer, Dame Elizabeth Frink and Paula Rego.

Opening Times: Tues to Sat 10:00-17:30.   Admission: Free.   Location: Near the town centre, on main road and bus routes.

Map Ref: 20

Northumbria

Morpeth Chantry Bagpipe Museum
Bridge Street, Morpeth NE61 1PJ   Tel: 01670 519466   Fax: 01670 511326
Email: amoore@castlemorpeth.gov.uk

A unique museum, specialising in the Northumbrian small pipes, which are set in the context of bagpipes from around the world, from India to Inverness.

Opening Times: Jan to Dec Mon to Sat 10:00-17:00. Admission: Adult £1.50, Child/OAP 80p, Family £3.50. Location: Town centre, one minute from bus station, five minutes from railway station.
Map Ref: 21

Wallington
Cambo, Morpeth NE61 4AR   Tel: 01670 773600   Fax: 01670 774420
Email: nwaplr@smtp.ntrust.org.uk   Web: www.nationaltrust.org.uk

Magnificent plaster work and notable ceramic collection. Large collection of dolls' houses and toys. Museum of Curiosities. Famous collection of Pre-Raphaelite depictions of Northumbrian history.

Opening Times: 23 Mar to 30 Sep daily except Tue 13:00-17:00. Admission: Adult £5.70, Group £5.20.
Location: 20 minutes from Newcastle Airport. Map Ref: 22
The Central Hall at Wallington

Castle Keep Museum
The Castle Keep, Castle Garth, Newcastle upon Tyne NE1 1RQ   Tel: 0191 2327938
Email: pblue2121@aol.com   Web: thekeep-newcastle.org.uk

Built in 1168-1178 one of the finest surviving examples of a Norman keep. Panoramic views of the city, the Tyne and its bridges (overlooks central railway station and main rail lines) from its roof. Small museum with artefacts relevant to site.

Opening Times: Apr to Sep daily 09:30-17:30, Oct to Mar daily 09:30-16:30. Closed Good Friday, 25-26 Dec & New Year. Admission: Adult £1.50, Child/OAP 50p. Special rates for par-ties of 12 or more. Location: Near town centre, three minutes walk from central railway station.
Map Ref   23

Hancock Museum
Barras Bridge, Newcastle upon Tyne NE2 4PT   Tel: 0191 222 6765   Fax: 0191 222 6753
Web: www.twmuseums.org.uk

The North of England's premier Natural History Museum unravels the secrets of the natural world through sensational galleries. For more than one hundred years visitors have gained an insight into the animal kingdom and the powerful and sometimes destructive forces of Nature. From the Dinosaurs to live animals, the Hancock is home to creatures past and present and even the odd Egyptian mummy or two.

Opening Times: Mon to Sat 10:00-17:00, Sun 14:00-17:00. Admission: Adult £3.95, Child/Concession £2.95, Under 4s Free, Family (2+2) £12.50 Location: Five minutes walk from city centre.
Map Ref: 23

Hatton Gallery
The Quadrangle, University of Newcastle, Newcastle upon Tyne NE1 7RU   Tel: 0191 2226057
Fax: 0191 2226059 Email: hatton-gallery@ncl.ac.uk   Web: www.ncl.ac.uk/hatton

Permanent collections on display - African art and the Kurt Schwitters Merzbarn. In addition the gallery presents a series of prestigious and stimulating temporary exhibitions.

Opening Times: Mon to Fri 10:00-17:30, Sat 10:00-16:30. Closed Sun, BH and Xmas & New Year. Admission: Free. Location: City centre, two minutes walk from Haymarket Metro Station and Haymarket Bus Station.
Map Ref: 23

Laing Art Gallery

New Bridge Street, Newcastle upon Tyne NE1 8AG Tel: 0191 232 7734 Fax: 0191 222 0952 Web: www.twmuseums.org.uk

The North of England's premier art gallery displays a stunning array of watercolours, costume, silver, glass, pottery and sculpture alongside a striking programme of historical and contemporary exhibitions. Major works by leading Pre-Raphaelite artists including Willian Holman Hunt and Edward Burne-Jones by L S Lowry. Younger visitors can let their artistic skills run riot in the P & G Children's Gallery which includes soft play, puzzles and books. Art on Tyneside looks about the rich history of art and craft on Tyneside, including paintings, silver, ceramic, glass and textiles. Using sound, interactive games and open exhibits, the exhibitions also features a re-creation of an 18th century coffee shop, a Victorian art gallery and Tyne Bridge. The hugely popular and high profile temporary exhibition programme of both historical and contemporary art has made the Laing Art Gallery one of the most popular art galleries in the UK. The gallery also offers a café and new craft shop that sells everything from art history books to the latest contemporary craft.

Opening Times: Mon to Sat 10:00-17:00, Sun 14:00-17:00. Admission: Free. Location: One minute walk from city centre. Map Ref: 23

Military Vehicle Museum

Exhibition Park Pavillion, Newcastle upon Tyne NE2 4PZ Tel: 0191 281 7222
Email: miltmuseum@aol.com Web: www.military.museum.org.uk

Over 50 vehicles, 60 cabinets depicting a soliders life from 1900 to date. World War I trench, Anderson Shelter and Home Front display.

Opening Times: Mar to Nov daily 10:00-16:00, closed Aug BH. Nov to Mar Sat, Sun and school holidays 10:00-16:00. Closed 25-26 Dec & New Years Day. Admission: Adult £2.00, Child/Concession £1.00, Under 5s Free. Map Ref: 23

Museum of Antiquities

University of Newcastle upon Tyne, Newcastle upon Tyne NE1 7RU Tel: 0191 222 7849
Fax: 0191 222 8561 Email: l.allason-jones@ncl.ac.uk Web: www.ncl.ac.uk/antiquities

Ideal place to start visit to Hadrian's Wall. Artefacts from 8000BC to 1600AD give the visitor a unique insight into the history of the north of England.

Opening Times: Mon to Sat 10:00-17:00. Closed Sun, Xmas & New Year and Good Friday.
Admission: Free. Location: In town centre. One minute walk from Haymarket. Map Ref: 23

Newcastle Discovery Museum

Blandford Square, Newcastle upon Tyne NE1 4JA Tel: 0191 232 6789 Fax: 0191 233 1088
Web: www.twmuseums.org.uk

Explore Newcastle's past from Romans to the present day. Tyneside inventions that changed the world, a fun approach to science, a soldier's life, and take a walk through fashion. The museum is currently undergoing an exciting £12.25 million transformation to introduce spectacular new displays, including a whole floor of galleries devoted to life on the River Tyne.

Opening Times: Mon to Sat 10:00-17:00, Sun 14:00-17:00. Admission: Free. Location: Ten minutes from city centre and central station. Map Ref: 23

www.tomorrows.co.uk

Full information on our collection of travel guides and secure store

Shefton Museum of Greek Art & Archaeology

The Armstrong Building, University of Newcastle upon Tyne, Newcastle upon Tyne NE1 7RU
Tel: 0191 222 8996   Fax: 0191 222 8561   Email: l.allason-jones@ncl.ac.uk
Web: www.ncl.ac.uk/shefton-museum

The most important collection of archaeological material from the Greek world in the north of England.

Opening Times: Mon to Fri 10:00-16:00. Closed Sat, Sun and BH.   Admission: Free.
Location: In town centre, one minute walk from Haymarket.   Map Ref: 23

Stephenson Railway Museum

Middle Engine Lane, West Chirton, North Shields NE29 8DX   Tel / Fax: 0191 200 7145   Web: www.twmuseums.org.uk

Relive the glorious days of the steam railway at Stephenson Railway Museum. The Museum is home to George Stephenson's 'Billy', a forerunner of the world-famous Rocket and many other engines from the great age of steam including 'Jackie Milburn', named after the Newcastle United legend. A ride on a real steam train can be taken and the story of coal and electricity is also told.

Opening Times: Seasonal - call for details.   Admission: Free.
Map Ref: 24

REDCAR *Cleveland*

Kirkleatham Old Hall Museum

Kirkleatham, Redcar TS10 5NW   Tel: 01642 479500

Local history collection reflecting life in Redcar and Cleveland:- archaeology; social history (working and domestic life - ironstone mining; iron and steel making; fishing; shipbuilding; sea rescue); paintings; photographs. Permanent Galleries, temporary exhibitions, associated activities and events. Programme for schools and other groups. Housed in early 18th century listing building in important conservation area.

Kirkleatham Old Hall

Opening Times: Apr to Sep Tue to Sun 10:00-17:00, Oct to Mar Tue to Sun 10:00-16:00. Closed Mon (except BH) and Xmas to New Year.   Admission: Free.

Location: Kirkleatham Village, near Redcar.   Map Ref: 25

Zetland Lifeboat Museum

5 King Street, Redcar TS10 3PF   Tel: 01642 494311   Web: www.lifeboats.org.uk

Displays relating to Zetland Lifeboat, the oldest surviving lifeboat, and the Royal National Lifeboat Institution. 200th Anniversary of 'The Zetland' lifeboat in 2002.

Opening Times: Daily during summer. Closed Nov to Mar.   Admission: Free.   Map Ref: 25

ROTHBURY *Tyne & Wear*

Cragside

Rothbury NE65 7PX   Tel: 01669 620150   Fax: 01669 620066
Email: ncrvmx@smtp.ntrust.org.uk

Norman Shaw's high Victorian mansion with original furniture and fittings including William Morris stained glass and earliest wallpapers. Built for the great inventor-industrialist Lord Armstrong, who installed the world's first hydro-electric lighting.

Opening Times: House: 23 Mar to Sep 13:00-17:30, Oct to 3 Nov 13:00-16:30. Last admission one hour before closing.   Admission: Adult £6.90, Child £3.50, Family £17.30. Group rates available.   Location: Entrance one mile north of Rothbury on B6341, 15 miles north west of Morpeth, 13 miles south west of Alnwick.   Map Ref: 26

Northumbria

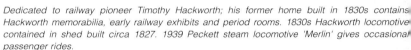

SHILDON *Durham*

Timothy Hackworth Victorian & Railway Museum

Hackworth Close, Shildon DL4 1PQ   Tel / Fax: 01388 777999
Web: www.hackworthmuseum.co.uk

Dedicated to railway pioneer Timothy Hackworth; his former home built in 1830s contains Hackworth memorabilia, early railway exhibits and period rooms. 1830s Hackworth locomotive contained in shed built circa 1827. 1939 Peckett steam locomotive 'Merlin' gives occasional passenger rides.

Opening Times: Easter to last Sun in Oct, Wed to Sun 10:00-17:00, also BH. Closed Xmas & New Year.   Admission: Adult £2.00, Child £1.00, OAP £1.00. Groups by arrangement.
Location: South east of Shildon town centre, two minutes from railway station.   Map Ref: 27

SOUTH SHIELDS *Tyne & Wear*

Arbeia Roman Fort & Museum

Baring Street, South Shields NE33 2BB   Tel: 0191 456 1369   Fax: 0191 427 6862
Web: www.twmuseum.org.uk

Situated four miles east of the end of Hadrian's Wall at South Shields, Arbeia Roman Fort guarded the entrance to the River Tyne. Built about AD160 the stone fort played an essential role in the mighty frontier system. Originally built to house a garrison Arbeia soon became the military supply base for the 17 forts along the Wall. Today, the excavated remains, stunning reconstructions of original buildings and finds from the

fort show what life was like in Roman Britain. Arbeia combines the excavated remains of this Roman military supply base with reconstructions of the fort's buildings and stunning finds unearthed from the site to show what life was like on Hadrian's Wall. The fort's West Gate has been reconstructed and work is currently under way to reconstruct the Commanding Officer's house and a soldiers' barrack block. Nowhere else on Hadrian's Wall can the sheer scale of the Romans' achievements be better understood than here at Arbeia. The museum displays feature finds excavated at Arbeia, which are amongst the most impressive found along the World Heritage Site. TimeQuest gives visitors the chance to find out what it's like to be an archaeologist.

Opening Times: Easter to Sep Mon to Sat 10:00-17:30, Sun 13:00-17:00. Oct to Easter Mon to Sat 10:00-16:00, closed Sun.   Admission: Free.   Location: Near town centre 10-15 minutes walk from metro and bus.   Map Ref: 28

South Shields Museum & Art Gallery

Ocean Road, South Shields NE33 2TA   Tel: 0191 456 8740   Fax: 0191 456 7850
Web: www.twmuseums.org.uk

Famous for its gallery dedicated to the world famous author Catherine Cookson, which features reconstructions of her childhood home and key objects from her life, from the desk on which she penned her greatest novels to her 'Big Red Book' from 'This is your Life'. The Museum also takes a look at the history of South Tyneside and how the land, sea and river have all played a part in shaping its story over the years.

Opening Times: Easter to Sep Mon to Sat 10:00-17:30, Sun 14:00-17:00. Oct to Easter Mon to Sat 10:00-16:00, closed Sun.   Admission: Free.   Location: In centre of town.   Map Ref: 28

STOCKTON-ON-TEES *Cleveland*

Green Dragon Museum   ⚅ ⬡

Theatre Yard, off High Street, Stockton-on-Tees TS18 1AT   Tel: 01642 393938
Fax: 01642 393936

Incorporating the focus at photography gallery. The museum offers a lively mix of the best in contemporary photography and history as told through photography.

Opening Times: Mon to Sat 09:00-17:00. Closed Sun & BH.   Admission: Free.
Location: Town centre off High Street.   Map Ref: 29

Preston Hall Museum   ⚅ ⬡ ⬚ ⬛

Yarm Road, Stockton-on-Tees TS18 3RH   Tel: 01642 781184

The museum illistrates Victorian social history with reconstructions of period rooms and a street with working craftsmen; collection includes costume, toys, arms, armour. There are 112 acres of parkland with riverside walks.

Opening Times: Easter to Sep daily 10:00-17:30, Oct to Easter Mon to Sat 10:00-16:30, Sun 14:00-16:30. Closed Good Friday, Xmas & New Year.   Admission: Adult £1.20, Child/Concession 60p.   Location: Set in 112 acres of parkland, between Stockton and Yarm on A135.   Map Ref: 30

SUNDERLAND *Tyne & Wear*

Monkwearmouth Station Museum   ⚅ ⬡ ⬛

North Bridge Street, Sunderland SR5 1AP   Tel: 0191 567 7075
Fax: 0191 510 9415   Web: www.twmuseum.org.uk

This splendid Victorian railway station recreates a sense of rail travel in times past. Explore the ticket office as it would have looked in Victorian times, see the guard's van and goods wagon in the railway sidings and watch today's trains zoom past Platform Gallery. The Children's Gallery has a range of toys, books and dressing-up clothes.

Opening Times: Mon 10:00-15:45, Tue to Sat 10:00-17:00, Sun 14:00-17:00.   Admission: Free.   Location: Ten minute walk from city centre.   Map Ref: 31

North East Aircraft Museum   ⬡ ⬛

Washington Road, Sunderland SR5 3HZ   Tel: 0191 5190662
Web: www.members.tripod.com/~BDaugherty/neam.html

A collection of 35 aircraft including the Vulcan Bomber and Pucara from the Falkland Islands. Aero engines, aeronautica and a large display of models from the early days of flight to the present day.

Opening Times: Apr to Sep daily 10:00-17:00, Oct to Mar 10:00-16:00. Closed Xmas & New Year.   Admission: Adult £3.00, Child/OAP £1.50. Please phone for Family and Group Concessions.   Location: Brown signposted off the A19 west of Sunderland, near to the Nissan Car Assembly Plant.   Map Ref: 31

Ryhope Engines Museum   ⬀ ⬡ ⬚ ⬛

Ryhope Pumping Station, Ryhope, Sunderland SR2 0ND   Tel: 0191 521 0235   Email: keith-bell@beeb.net   Web: www.g3wte.demon.co.uk

Based around two Woolf Compound Beam Engines of 1868 by Thomas Hawksley. Working under steam many weekends of the year by hand fired Lancashire boilers.

Opening Times: Easter to Dec Sun 14:00-16:00. BH & special event weekends 11:00-16:00 or by appointment.   Admission: Free.   Location: Three miles south of Sunderland City Centre.   Map Ref: 32

Museums, Galleries, Historic Houses & Sites

Please let us know of any collections that are not listed in this guide that you feel should be listed. E-mail us on *editor@tomorrows.co.uk*
or return the Report Form on page 448

Sunderland Museum & Winter Gardens

Mowbray Gardens, Burdon Road, Sunderland SR1 1AF   Tel: 0191 553 2323   Fax: 0191 553 7828   Web: www.twmuseums.org.uk

11 exciting hands-on exhibits and interactive displays tell the story of Sunderland from its prehistoric past through to the present day. The Art Gallery features paintings by L S Lowry alongside Victorian masterpieces and artefacts from the four corners of the world. The displays look at traditional industries including shipbuilding coal mining, pottery, glass and textile crafts through to the prehistoric, medieval and 20th century history of the City. The natural world is also explored through stunning wildlife displays and live animals. The newly refurbished museum features a striking new glazed entrance; visitor facilities such as a large shop, a brasserie, toilets and lifts to all floors form a significant part of the scheme. The stunning new Winter Gardens is home to over 1,000 of the world's most exotic flowers, plants and trees. Some of the amazing plants include an 80 year old Sicilian olive tree, a 3.5 metre-high Palm

tree and a 6.5 metre-high Yucca elaphanties from Honduras, the world's largest type of Yucca. The Gardens also feature sculptures, a waterfall, Koi carp and a stunning treetop walkway, from which visitors can look on to the displays.

Opening Times: Mon 10:00-16:00, Tue to Sat 10:00-17:00, Sun 14:00-17:00. Admission: Free. Location: In town centre.

Map Ref: 31

WALLSEND *Tyne & Wear*

Segedunum Roman Fort, Baths & Museum

Buddle Street, Wallsend NE28 8HR   Tel: 0191 236 9347   Fax: 0191 295 5858
Web: www.twmuseums.org.uk

In AD122 the Emperor Hadrian ordered a mighty frontier system to be built across Britain to defend the Roman Empire from the barbarians to the north. Segedunum Roman Fort stood on the banks of the River Tyne and was the last outpost of Hadrian's Wall. Today, Segedunum is once again the gateway to this world-famous heritage site. The excavated remains of the fort with spectacular reconstructions and exciting, hands-on museum displays show what life was like in Roman Britain. The remains represent the most extensively excavated site in the Empire and the reconstructed bath-house is the only one of its kind in Britain. No other site on Hadrian's Wall can match the views from the 100 feet-high tower. The museum features finds excavated from the fort with the latest technology to show what life was like for the soldiers who lived at the fort. The history of the fort and Wallsend after the decline of the Roman Empire is also explored.

Opening Times: 1 Apr to 31 Oct daily 10:00-17:00. 1 Nov to 31 May daily 10:00-15:30. Admission: Adult £3.50, Child/Concession £2.95. Location: One minute walk from Wallsend Metro. Map: 33

Northumbria

WASHINGTON *Tyne & Wear*

Washington Old Hall

The Avenue, District 4, Washington NE38 7LE   Tel: 0191 416 6879   Fax: 0191 419 2065

Ancestral home of George Washington, America's first President. Small 17th century manor house, with contemporary furnishings. Small very pretty garden.

Opening Times: Apr to Oct Sun to Wed 11:00-17:00 & Good Friday.   Admission: Adult £3.00, Child £1.50, Group £2.50 (15 or more).   Map Ref: 34

WHITLEY BAY *Tyne & Wear*

St Marys Lighthouse & Visitor Centre

St Marys Island, Whitley Bay   Tel: 0191 200 8650

Climb 137 steps to the top of the Lighthouse for the most spectacular views of the north east coast; these can be experienced at ground level via a video facility. Nature Reserve nearby.

Opening Times: Please telephone to check days and times as these vary.   Admission: Adult £2.00, Child/OAP £1.00, Family £4.50. Group rates available.   Location: Follow brown tourist signs from Whitley Bay turnoff on A19.   Map Ref: 35

WYLAM *Northumberland*

Wylam Railway Museum

The Falcon Centre, Falcon Terrace, Wylam NE41 8EE   Tel: 01661 852174/853520
Email: wylampc@btinternet.com

George Stephenson 'The Father of Railways' was born in Wylam and historic locomotive 'Puffing Billy' worked on Wylam Colliery waggonway. Displays in this attractive small museum illustrate Wylam's unique place in railway history.

Opening Times: Tue & Thu 14:00-17:00 17:30-19:30, Sat 09:00-12:00.   Admission: Free. Donations welcome.   Location: The Falcon Centre, off Main Street at Fox & Hounds Inn.
Map Ref: 36

Oxfordshire

The county is not renowned for its large cities and towns with Oxford, the county town, being largest. However, the city is an important commercial, residential and industrial centre domina by its university, the colleges of which, both ancient and modern, have their own partic character and treasures.

Oxford boasts museums and galleries of international fame and there are interesting collect to be found in Banbury, Henley and Woodstock.

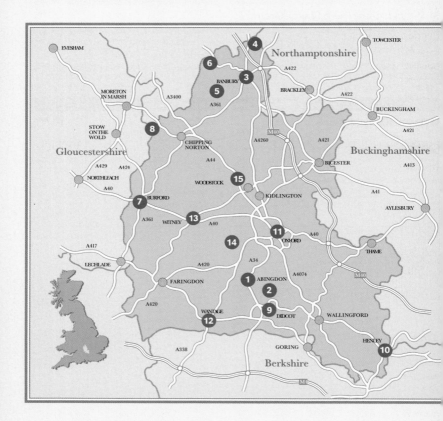

The Red Map References should be used to locate Museums etc on the pages that follow

Oxfordshire

Abingdon Museum

County Hall, Market Place, Abingdon OX14 3HG   Tel: 01235 523703   Fax: 01235 536814

The County Hall was built between 1678-1682 by Christopher Kempster, master mason who worked with Christopher Wren on St Paul's Cathedral. The museum contains local history from 'England's oldest town'.

Opening Times: Daily 10:30-16:00. Please telephone to check BH. Roof top closed during winter. Admission: Free. (Roof top £1.00). Location: In town centre.   Map Ref: 1

Pendon Museum

Long Wittenham, Abingdon OX14 4QD   Tel: 01865 407365   Web: www.pendonmuseum.com

Rural life in the Vale of the White Horse in the 1930s recreated in miniature, together with the railways that ran through the Vale.

Opening Times: Sat & Sun 14:00-17:00, also Wed during Jul & Aug. Open from 11:00 Good Friday to Easter Mon, 4 to 6 May, 1 to 4 Jun, 24 to 26 Aug. Admission: Adult £4.00, Child £2.00, Under 6 Free, OAP £3.50, Family £12.00.   Map Ref: 2

Banbury Museum

Spiceball Park Road, Banbury OX16 2PQ   Tel: 01295 259855   Fax: 01295 270556

Banbury's new canal-side museum opens summer 2002. The stunning new displays illustrate Banbury's history, beginning with some of the stories and events that have made Banbury famous, such as the nursery rhyme 'ride a cock horse to Banbury Cross'. The principal displays tell four stories: the English Civil War and how it affected Banbury; the development of the plush weaving industry (plush is a velvet like fabric); the Victorian Town; and Banbury in the 20th century. Also on display is a rare collection of costume dating from the 17th century. A separate gallery interprets the Tooley's Boatyard and the Oxford Canal. Tooley's Boatyard is a scheduled ancient monument that is attached to the museum and can be visited on a guided tour. Excellent visitor facilities are available including a canal-side café. For up to date information on the museum's opening call 01295 259855.

Opening Times: Mon to Sat 09:30-17:00, Sun 10:30-16:00. Admission: Free. Location: Town centre, main entrance Castle Quay Shopping Centre.   Map Ref: 3

Bygones Museum

Butlin Farm, Claydon, Banbury OX17 1EP   Tel: 01295 690258
Email: bygonesmuseum@yahoo.com   Web: www.bygonesmuseum.moonfruit.com

Local Banbury shops, display centre. Victorian kitchen and work shops. Traction engine, steam roller, stationary engines, tractors etc. War and craft memorabilia, typewriters, sewing machines, jars, bottles and lots more.

Opening Times: Mar to Dec Tue to Sun 10:00-17:00. Closed Mon (except BH). Admission: Adult £2.50, Child £1.75, OAP £2.00, Family £7.50. Location: In the centre of a small village, six miles north of Banbury.   Map Ref: 4

The New Visitor Information Centre

Swalcliffe Barn

Shipston Road, Swalcliffe, Banbury   Tel: 01295 788278
Fax: 01993 813239   Email: martyn.brown@oxfordshire.gov.uk
Web: www.oxfordshire.gov.uk

A magnificent 15th century barn with an original half-cruck timber roof structure. It was built in 1401 for the Rectorial Manor of Swalcliffe by New College, Oxford. The barn houses a collection of trade vehicles and agricultural machinery from Oxfordshire used in the 19th & 20th centuries.

Opening Times: Easter to Oct.   Admission: Free.
Location: In village centre.

Fletcher's House
Map Ref: 5

Upton House

Banbury OX15 6HT   Tel / Fax: 01295 670266   Email: vuplan@smtp.ntrust.org.uk
Web: www.nationaltrust.org.uk

An impressive 17th century house with fine collections and a magnificent terraced garden.

Opening Times: 23 Mar to 3 Nov Sat to Wed 13:00-17:00 (last admission 16:30). Closed Thu and Fri, but open Good Friday.   Admission: House and Garden: Adult £6.00, Child £3.00, Family (2 adults and 3 children) £15.00. Garden only: Adult £3.00, Child £1.50.   Location: On A422 seven miles from Banbury, 12 miles from Statford-on-Avon. Follow signs from junction 12 on M40.   Map Ref: 6

BURFORD

Tolsey Museum

126 High Street, Burford OX18 4QU   Tel: 01993 823196

Royal charters from 1350; wide-ranging collection illustrating Burford's industrial and social past; samplers; unusual dolls house furnished by local people in style of Jane Austen.

Opening Times: Apr to Oct Tue to Fri 14:00-17:00 Sat, Sun & BH 11:00-17:00.
Admission: Adult 75p, Child Free, OAP 50p.   Location: Centre of Burford.   Map Ref: 7

CHASTLETON

Chastleton House

Chastleton, near Stow-on-the-Wold GL56 0SU   Tel / Fax: 01608 674355
Email: tchgen@smtp.ntrust.org.uk   Web: www.nationaltrust.org.uk/regions/thameschilterns

One of England's finest and most complete Jacobean houses, filled with a mixture of rare and everyday objects, especially tapestries.

Opening Times: Apr to Sep Wed to Sat 13:00-17:00, Oct Wed to Sat 13:00-16:00.
Admission: Adult £5.40, Child £2.70, Family £13.50, Free to National Trust members.
Location: Six miles from Stow-on-the-Wold. Approach only from A436 between A44 (west of Chipping Norton) and Stow-on-the-Wold.   Map Ref: 8

DIDCOT

Didcot Railway Centre

Didcot OX11 7NJ   Tel: 01235 817200   Fax: 01235 510621   Email: didrlyc@globalnet.co.uk
Web: didcotrailwaycentre.org.uk

See the steam trains of the Great Western Railway, the original engine shed and a recreation of Brunel's broad gauge railway. Programme of Steamdays and special events including 'Day out with Thomas' during the year.

Opening Times: Apr to Sep daily 10:00-17:00, Oct to Mar Sat & Sun 10:00-16:00.
Admission: Adult £4-£7.00, Child £4.50-£6.00, OAP £3.50-£6.50, Family £12.00-£19.00.
Location: At Didcot Parkway rail station, signed from M4 junction 13 and A34.   Map Ref: 9

Oxfordshire

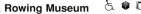

HENLEY-ON-THAMES

River & Rowing Museum

River & Rowing Museum
Henley on Thames

Mill Meadows, Henley-on-Thames RG9 1BF
Tel: 01491 415600 Fax: 01491 415601
Email: museum@rrm.co.uk Web: ww.rrm.co.uk

The Rowing Gallery

Visit the award winning River & Rowing Museum with its stunning architecture and unique interpretation of the River Thames from its source to sea, the riverside town of Henley on Thames with its famous Royal Regatta and the sport of Rowing from the days of the Ancient Greek Trireme to the recent success of the Sydney Coxless Four. History is brought to life with interactive displays and fascinating exhibits for all the family. Special exhibitions, family activities and events are held throughout the year and its Riverside Café offers excellent food in distinctive surroundings.

The River & Rowing Museum

Opening Times: Sep to Apr daily 10:00-17:00, May to Aug daily 10:00-17:30. Closed 24-25 Dec & 31 Dec-1 Jan. Admission: Adult £4.95, Concession £3.75, Family £13.95. Location: Off A4130, signposted to Mill Meadows. A short walk from Henley Town Centre, five minutes from Henley on Thames Railway Station. Map Ref: 10

OXFORD

Ashmolean Museum of Art & Archaeology

The Ashmolean

Beaumont Street, Oxford OX1 2PH Tel: 01865 278000 Fax: 01865 278018
Web: www.ashmol.ox.ac.uk

The Ashmolean Museum, Oxford

The Ashmolean houses the Oxford University's collections of art and antiquities. They range over four millennia - from Ancient Egypt, Greece and Rome to Renaissance Europe and the 20th century, plus an extensive Far Eastern collection. Sculpture, paintings, ceramics, glass, coins and musical instruments are all on show.

Opening Times: Tue to Sat 10:00-17:00, Sun 14:00-17:00. Admission: Free. Location: Town centre, five minutes walk from bus station, ten minutes walk from BR Station. Map Ref: 11

Bate Collection of Musical Instruments

Faculty of Music, St Aldate's, Oxford OX1 1DB Tel: 01865 276139 Fax: 01865 276128
Email: bate.collection@music.ox.ac.uk Web: www.ashmol.ox.ac.uk/bcmipage.html

A collection of over a thousand historic woodwind, brass and percussion instruments, a dozen historic keyboards including what may have been Handel's harpsichord; a unique bow-maker's workshop and fine collection of bows.

Opening Times: Mon to Fri 14:00-17:00, Sat 10:00-12:00. (During Oxford full term only)
Admission: Free. Location: Near town centre, opposite Christ Church College. Map Ref: 11

Christ Church Picture Gallery

Christ Church, Oxford OX1 1DP Tel: 01865 276172 Fax: 01865 202429
Email: dennis.harrington@christ-church.ox.ac.uk Web: www.chch.ox.ac.uk

Christ Church Picture Gallery was designed in 1968 by Powell and Moya and holds 300 paintings and 2000 drawings by famous artists such as Van Dyck, Leonardo and Michelangelo.

Opening Times: Oct to Mar Mon to Sat 10:30-13:00, 14:00-16:30 and Sun 14:00-16:30. Easter to Sep daily 10:30-17:30. Admission: Adult £2.00, OAP/Student/Concession £1.00. Free on Mon. Location: Near the town centre. Map Ref: 11

Museum of Modern Art

    ♿ ◉ ☕

30 Pembroke Street, Oxford OX1 1BP   Tel: 01865 722733
Fax: 01865 722573   Web: www.moma.org.uk

Located in the heart of historic Oxford, the Museum of Modern Art presents outstanding exhibitions of modern and contemporary art from all over the world. Exhibitions include painting, sculpture, photography, video, film and architecture. It's a great place to add to your 'must see' list in Oxford. Cafe Moma serves delicious, freshly cooked food and is child and baby friendly.

Opening Times: Tue to Sun 11:00-16:00, late on Thu until 21:00. Closed Mon.   Admission: Adult £2.50, Concessions £1.50, Children under 16 free.   Location: City centre, ten minutes walk from railway station, five minutes from high street.   Map Ref: 11

A Victorian Kitchen c.1880

Museum of Oxford

  ✎ ◉ **museum OfOXFORD**

St Aldates, Oxford OX1 1DZ   Tel: 01865 252761   Fax: 01865 202447   Email: museum@oxford.gov.uk
Web: www.oxford.gov.uk/museum

Discover Oxford's history by visiting the Museum of Oxford, the only museum in Oxford to tell the story of the city and its people from prehistoric times to the present day. The exhibits range from a mammoth's tooth to a 'Morris Motor' car engine. Archaeological treasures including a preserved Roman pottery kiln and a whole pavement made of cattle bones. There are six Oxford rooms recreated inside the museum from an Elizabethan Inn to a Victorian kitchen. A full programme of workshops and activities for schools and families are available - term time, school holiday and weekends.

Hythe Bridge/Oxford Castle
by Michael Angelo Rooker c.1790

Opening Times: Tue to Fri 10:00-16:00, Sat 10:00-17;00, Sun 12:00-16:00.   Admission: Adult £2.00, Child 50p, Concession £1.50.   Location: Centre of town, five minute walk from bus station, ten minutes walk from train station.   Map Ref: 11

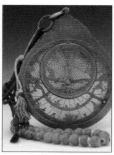

Persian Astrolabe

Museum of the History of Science

  ♿ ◉

Broad Street, Oxford OX1 3AZ   Tel: 01865 277280
Fax: 01865 277288   Email: jim.bennett@mhs.ox.ac.uk
Web: www.mhs.ox.ac.uk

Outstanding collection of early scientific instruments, astrolabes, sundials, telescopes, microscopes, etc. Displayed in Britain's first museum building includes globes, navigation, physics, chemistry and some of the earliest surviving instruments from a range of countries and cultures.

Opening Times: Tue to Sat 12:00-16:00. Closed Xmas. Admission: Free.   Location: Broad Street, next to Sheldonian Theatre.   Map Ref: 11

Oxford University Museum of Natural History

Parks Road, Oxford OX1 3PW Tel: 01865 272950 Fax: 01865 272970 Email: info@oum.ox.ac.uk Web: www.oum.ox.ac.uk

The Oxford University Museum of Natural History houses Oxford University's extensive collection of entomological, geological, mineralogical and zoological material of international importance. Current displays include the remains of Alice's Dodo Bird and a splendid display of Dinosaurs.

Opening Times: Daily 12:00-17:00. Closed Xmas and Easter.
Admission: Free. Location: Central Oxford on Parks Road
immediately opposite Keble College.   Map Ref: 11

T-rex in Victorian Court

Pitt Rivers Museum

(Museum of Natural History), Parks Road, Oxford OX1 3PP Tel: 01865 270927 Fax: 01865 270943 Web: www.prm.ox.ac.uk

This unique museum is one of Oxford's most popular attractions, famous for its period atmosphere and outstanding collections. Founded in 1884, the displays still retain much of the original layout and appearance; cases are crowded with amulets, beads, pots, masks, shrunken heads, textiles, toys and more, from many cultures around the world past and present. Many objects still carry their first tiny hand-printed label.

The Pitt Rivers Museum from the Upper Gallery

Opening Times: Mon to Sat 12:00-16:30, Sun 14:00-16:30. Admission: Free. Location: Ten minutes walk from city centre. Entrance through Oxford University Museum of Natural History.   Map Ref: 11

WANTAGE

Vale & Downland Museum

19 Church Street, Wantage OX12 8BL Tel: 01235 771447 Fax: 01235 764316 Email: museum@wantage.com Web: www.wantage.com/museum

An ideal starting-point for exploring the area. The Museum tells the story of Wantage and the Vale from earliest times to the present, through objects, films and computer interactives.

Opening Times: Mon to Sat 10:00-16:30, Sun 14:30-17:00. Please phone to check times for Xmas, New Year and BH. Admission: Adult £1.50, Child £1.00, Family £4.00. Tickets valid for one year. Location: Two minute walk from Market Place, opposite church.   Map Ref: 12

WITNEY

Bishop's Palace Site

Mount House, Church Green, Witney

The archaelogical site of the Bishop of Winchester's Palace at Witney.

Opening Times: Easter to Sep Sat & Sun 14:00-16:00. Admission: Free. Location: East of the church on the Green.   Map Ref: 13

Oxfordshire Museums Store

Witney Road, Standlake, Witney OX8 7QG

Purpose built store and collections centre for conservation and museum support services. Contains natural science, archaeology, social history, transport, agricultural, crafts, textiles, arts - all relating to Oxfordshire.

Opening Times: Mon to Fri 9:00-17:00 by appointment. Public open days in May & Sep.
Admission: Free. Location: A415 four miles south of Witney.   Map Ref: 14

Blenheim Palace, South Front

Blenheim Palace

Woodstock OX20 1PX   Tel: 01993 811325
Fax: 01993 813527   Email: administrator@blenheimpalace.com
Web: www.blenheimpalace.com

Blenheim Palace, home of the 11th Duke of Marlborough and birthplace of Sir Winston Churchill, is an English Baroque masterpiece, with fine furniture, sculpture, paintings and tapestries set in magnificent gilded state rooms overlooking sweeping lawns and formal gardens. The Palace is set in 2100 acres of parkland landscaped by 'Capability' Brown and offering walks with beautiful views over the lake and through the trees.

Opening Times: Mid Mar to end Oct 10:30-16:45.
Admission: Adult £10.00, Child £5.00, OAP/Student £7.50.
Location: A44 eight miles from Oxford.   Map Ref: 15

Oxfordshire Museum

Fletchers House, Park Street, Woodstock OX20 1SN   Tel: 01993 811456   Fax: 01993 813239
Email: oxonmuseum@oxfordshire.gov.uk   Web: www.oxfordshire.gov.uk

Located in a fine town house in the historic centre of Woodstock, the museum provides a window on Oxfordshire's rich history. Following a major Heritage Lottery funded extension and refurbishment the museum's new displays celebrate Oxfordshire in all its diversity. Featured collections reflect the archaeology, local history, landscape and wildlife of the county as well as providing an introduction to the astonishing range of ideas and technologies developed in Oxfordshire. Gallery interactives provide hands-on enjoyment for children and new computer programmes enable visitors to explore a variey of information about the objects on display. Visitors to the museum can also enjoy its peaceful garden whilst sampling a range of light refreshments in the new coffee shop.

Opening Times: Tue to Sat 10:00-17:00, Sun 14:00-17:00.   Admission: Adult £2.50, Child 50p, OAP/Concession £1.00, Family £4.50.   Location: In town centre, adjacent gates to Blenheim Palace.   Map Ref: 15

ewsbury, the county town, almost encircled by the River Severn, was from Norman times tegically important as the gateway to Wales. In the eighteenth century it became a popular tre of fashionable society and boasts a wealth of fine Georgian buildings. Despite being narily a rural agricultural county, it was here in the eighteenth century that the Industrial olution was born, in the Ironbridge Gorge of the Severn.

opshire can be justifiably proud of its first class museums concerned with the archaeology, ural history, social and industrial history of the region.

The Red Map References should be used to locate Museums etc on the pages that follow

Shropshire

BRIDGNORTH

Dudmaston

Quatt, Bridgnorth WV15 6QN   Tel: 01746 780866   Fax: 01746 780744

A late 17th century house, intimate family rooms, fine furniture, Dutch oil paintings and sculpture. 'Sir George La Bouchure' Collection of modern art. Collections of watercolours and botanical art. Nine acres garden with lakeside and Dingle Walk.

Opening Times: Apr to Sep Sun, Tue, Wed & BH Mon - House: 14:00-17:30 Garden: 12:00-18:00. Garden only Mon.   Admission: House & Garden: Adult £3.95, Child £1.30, Family £9.00. Garden: Adult £2.80.   Location: Four and a half miles south of Bridgnorth on A442 Telford to Kidderminister road.   Map Ref: 1

Northgate Museum

Burgess Hall, Northgate, Bridgnorth WV16 4ER   Tel: 01746 761859

Special features - local pictures, working 17th century turret clock, firemarks, coats-of-arms, coins, tokens, carpet loom, cameras, Victorian basinet, clay pipes, 17th century chest lock, man trap.

Opening Times: Easter to Sep Sat & Sun 14:00-16:00. School holidays Mon to Wed 14:00-16:00, extra openings.   Admission: Free.   Location: Near town centre, five minutes from car parks in 13th century gatehouse.   Map Ref: 2

CHURCH STRETTON

Acton Scott Historic Working Farm Museum

Wenlock Lodge, Acton Scott, Church Stretton SY6 6QN   Tel: 01694 781306/7   Fax: 01694 781569   Email: acton.scott.museum@shropshire-cc.gov.uk
Web: www.actonscottmuseum.co.uk

Acton Scott Historic Working Farm demonstrates farming and rural life in South Shropshire at the close of the 19th century. This is achieved not only by collecting, renovating and exhibiting implements and other agricultural items, but also by farming as it would have been farmed in the period from about 1875 to the 1920s.

Opening Times: 26 Mar to 27 Oct Tue to Sun & BH 10:00-17:00. Closed Mon except BH. Admission: Adult £3.95, Child £1.50, Under 5s Free, OAP £3.50. Groups: Adult £3.00, Child £1.25, Under 5s Free, OAP £2.50.   Location: Four miles south of Church Stretton off A49, 17 miles south of Shrewsbury of A49, 14 miles north of Ludlow off A49 at Marshbrook.   Map Ref: 3

LUDLOW

Ludlow Museum

11-13 Castle Street, Ludlow SY8 1AS   Tel: 01584 875384   Web: www.shropshire-cc.gov.uk/museum.nsf

Make a visit to Ludlow Museum and unlock the natural and social history of this fascinating planned town and the surrounding region.

Opening Times: Apr to Oct Mon to Sat 10:30-13:00 14:00-17:00. Jun, Jul & Aug also open Sun. Admission: Free.   Location: In town centre.   Map Ref: 4

MUCH WENLOCK

Much Wenlock Museum

High Street, Much Wenlock TF13 6HR   Tel: 01952 727773
Web: www.shropshire.cc.gov.uk/museum.nsf

Displays of archaeology, natural history social history Wenlock Olympian Society, Wenlock Edge Geology.

Opening Times: Apr to Sep Mon to Sat 10:30-13:00 14:00-17:00. Jun, Jul & Aug also open Sun. Admission: Free.   Location: In the centre of town.   Map Ref: 5

OSWESTRY

Oswestry Transport Museum

Oswald Road, Oswestry SY11 1RE   Tel: 01691 671749

Collection of Cambrian Railways related artefacts dating from 1880s up to present day. Small collection of bicycles and motorbikes.

Opening Times: Daily 10:00-16:00.   Admission: Adult £1.00, Concession 50p.
Location: Near town centre.   Map Ref: 6

Shropshire

SHIFNAL

Royal Air Force Museum Cosford

Cosford, Shifnal TF11 8UP   Tel: 01902 376200   Fax: 01902 376211
Email: cosford@rafmuseum.com   Web: www.cosfordairshow.co.uk

Royal Air Force Museum Cosford

From the early days of aviation through two world wars to the present day, the story of man's successes and failures in flying and missile development is told in vivid and exciting displays covering war planes, civil aviation and the development of guided missiles and jet aircraft. Displays in three wartime hangars on an active airfield.

Opening Times: Daily 10:00-18:00. Closed Xmas & New Year. Admission: Free admission. Location: On A41, less than one mile from junction 3 on M54.   Map Ref: 7

Weston Park

Weston-under-Lizard, Shifnal TF11 8LE   Tel: 01952 852100   Fax: 01952 850430
Email: enquiries@weston-park.com   Web: www.weston-park.com

Weston Park

Weston Park is a magnificent Stately Home set in 1000 acres of Parkland. Built in 1671 the house boasts a superb collection of paintings including works by Van Dyck, Constable and Stubbs, furniture and objets d'art. Outside, visitors can explore the glorious parkland, meander through the formal gardens, take a variety of woodland walks before relaxing for lunch in The Stables Restaurant.

Opening Times: Easter, Apr, May, Jun & Sep weekends, Jul & Aug daily. Admission: Adult £4.50, Child £2.50, OAP £3.50. Location: Situated on A5 at Weston-under-Lizard, three miles off junction 3 on M54 and eight miles off junction 12 on M6.   Map Ref: 8

SHREWSBURY

Shrewsbury Museum & Art Gallery

Rowley's House, Barker Street, Shrewsbury SY1 1QH   Tel: 01743 361196   Fax: 01743 358411
Email: museums@shrewsbury-atcham.gov.uk   Web: www.shrewsburymuseums.com

Major regional museum; archaeology, geology, Shropshire ceramics, costume and social history, special exhibition programme linking historic collections and contemporary artists, including national and international names.

Opening Times: May Bank Hol to End of Sep Tue to Sat 10:00-17:00, Sun to Mon 10:00-16:00. Oct to May Tue to Sat 10:00-16:00. Admission: Free. Location: Town centre, five minutes from bus and railway stations.   Map Ref: 9

Wroxeter Roman City

Wroxeter Roman Site, Wroxeter, Shrewsbury SY5 6PH   Tel: 01743 761330

Wroxeter was once the fourth largest city in Roman Britain, with an impressive bath house, the remains of which are still visible today. The museum includes a column capital carved in the shape of a hare.

Opening Times: Apr to Sep daily 10:00-18:00, Oct daily 10:00-17:00, Nov to Mar 10:00-13:00 daily 14:00-16:00. Closed Xmas & New Year. Admission: Adult £3.50, Child £1.80, Concession £2.60, Family £8.80 Location: At Wroxeter, five miles east of Shrewsbury on B4380.   Map: 10

Shropshire

TELFORD

Blists Hill Victorian Town

Legges Way, Madeley, Telford   Tel: 01952
586063/583003   Email: info@ironbridge.org.uk
Web: www.ironbridge.org.uk

*Working factories, shops and cottages in a beautiful wooded
landscape where life is lived - and demonstrated - as it was in
Victorian times. Victorian industry, crafts and traditions are brought to
life by the townsfolk who illustrate Britain's fascinating industrial
history and social life in the streets and buildings of the town.*

Opening Times: Apr to Nov daily 10:00-17:00, Nov to Mar Sat to
Wed 10:00-16:00. Admission: Passport tickets: Adult £10.00,
Child £6.00, OAP £9.00 valid for all nine Ironbridge Gorge
Museums. Group rates available. Location: Situated five miles
from Telford Central.   Map Ref: 11

Broseley Pipe Works

Duke Street, Broseley, Telford   Tel: 01952 882445
Email: info@ironbridge.org.uk   Web: www.ironbridge.org.uk

*Once home to one of the most prolific clay tobacco pipe
factories in Britain. Production ceased in the 1950s when
the works were abandoned and left untouched until
reopened as a museum in 1996. During its restoration little
has been changed since the workers left, a wonderfully
preserved 'time capsule' of an ancient local industry.*

Opening Times: Apr to Nov daily 13:00-17:00. Closed
Nov to Mar. Admission: Passport tickets: Adult £10.00,
Child £6.00, OAP £9.00 - valid for all nine Ironbridge
Gorge Museums. Groups rates available. (Prices valid
until Mar 2002) Location: Five miles from Telford Central.   Map Ref: 11

Coalport China Museum & Youth Hostel

Coalport, Telford   Tel: 01952 580650
Email: info@ironbridge.org.uk   Web: www.ironbridge.org.uk

*The national collections of Caughley and Coalport china are
displayed in the restored factory buildings and bottle kilns of the old
Coalport China Works. Galleries show the beautiful china and
explore the hardships of factory life. Enjoy the children's gallery,
workshops and speciality china shop.*

Opening Times: Daily 10:00-17:00. Closed Xmas.
Admission: Passport tickets: Adult £10.00, Child £6.00, OAP £9.00
- valid for all nine Ironbridge Gorge Museums. Group rates
available. (Prices valid until Mar 2002). Location: Five miles from
Telford Central.   Map Ref: 11

Darby Houses & Quaker Burial Ground

Darby Road, Coalbrookdale, Telford   Email: info@ironbridge.org.uk
Web: www.ironbridge.org.uk

*Rosehill and Dale House are restored Quaker Ironmasters' homes, built overlooking the Darby
Furnace in Coalbrookdale. Rosehill is fully restored as it would have been when the Darby family
lived there, housing personal belongings of the family.*

Opening Times: Apr to Nov daily 10:00-17:00. Closed Nov to Mar. Admission: Passport
tickets: Adult £10.00, Child £6.00, OAP £9.00 - valid for all nine Ironbridge Gorge Museums.
Group rates available. Location: Five miles from Telford Central.   Map Ref: 11

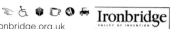

Iron Bridge & Tollhouse

Ironbridge, Telford   Tel: 01952 884391   Email: info@ironbridge.org.uk
Web: www.ironbridge.org.uk

The great symbol of success for the iron industry is the Iron Bridge, located in the heart of the designated world heritage site. The Toll House houses an exhibition about the Bridge and its fascinating history.

Opening Times: Iron Bridge - open year round. Toll House - Apr to Nov daily 10:00-17:00. Closed Nov to Mar. Admission: Passport tickets: Adult £10.00, Child £6.00, OAP £9.00 - valid for all nine Ironbridge Gorge Museums. Group rates available. (Prices valid until Mar 2002).
Location: Ironbridge Town Centre   Map Ref: 11

Jackfield Tile Museum

Jackfield, Telford   Tel: 01952 882030   Email: info@ironbridge.org.uk
Web: www.ironbridge.org.uk

Jackfield boasts magnificent displays of decorative tiles and ceramics throughout its gas-lit galleries within the restored Victorian factory buildings. Witness modern tile making combining drop-in workshops to make this a fascinating visit.

Opening Times: Daily 10:00-17:00. Closed Xmas.   Admission: Passport tickets: Adult £10.00, Child £6.00, OAP £9.00 - valid for all nine Ironbridge Gorge Museums. Group rates available. (Prices vaild until Mar 2002).   Location: Five miles from Telford Central.   Map Ref: 11

Museum of Iron & Darby Furnace

Coalbrookdale, Telford   Tel: 01952 433418
Email: info@ironbridge.org.uk   Web: www.ironbridge.org.uk

The museum interprets the beginnings of industry and the lives of those who lived and worked in Coalbrookdale. The galleries now house an exhibition dedicated to the Great Exhibition of 1851 - new for 2001! There is also a chance to see the original iron smelting furnace of Abraham Darby I.

Opening Times: Daily 10:00-17:00. Closed Xmas.
Admission: Passport tickets: Adult £10.00, Child £6.00, OAP £9.00 - valid for all nine Ironbridge Gorge Museums. Group rates available. (Prices valid until Mar 2002).   Location: Five miles from Telford Central.
          Map Ref: 11

Museum of the Gorge

Ironbridge, Telford   Tel: 01952 432405   Email: info@ironbridge.org.uk
Web: www.ironbridge.org.uk

The Old Severn Warehouse is a short walk alongside the River Severn from the Iron Bridge. Built in the 1830s it was used as a riverside warehouse. Inside is an exhibition covering the whole history of the Gorge including a scaled model of the River Valley as it was in 1796.

Opening Times: Daily 10:00-17:00. Closed Xmas.
Admission: Passport tickets: Adult £10.00, Child £6.00, OAP £9.00 - valid for all nine Ironbridge Gorge Museums. Group rates available. (Prices valid until Mar 2002).
Location: Five miles from Telford Central.   Map Ref: 11

Tar Tunnel

Coalport Road, Coalport, Telford   Tel: 01952 580627
Email: info@ironbridge.org.uk   Web: www.ironbridge.org.uk

A feature that presents the first natural source of bitumen that was discovered over 200 years ago. Visitors can don a hard hat to witness this spectacular monument.

Opening Times: Apr to Nov Daily 10:00-17:00. Closed Nov to Mar.   Admission: Passport tickets: Adult £10.00, Child £6.00, OAP £9.00 - valid for all nine Ironbridge Gorge Museums. Group rates available.   Map Ref: 11

Somerset

Taunton, the county town, has been the centre of county life since Saxon times and it was here 1685 that the Duke of Monmouth was declared King of England. Glastonbury is clos associated with the Arthurian legends and stories of the Holy Grail and the miraculous Christm flowering Glastonbury Thorn.

Somerset is an intriguing county of strange places and strange happenings, well reflected in excellent museums.

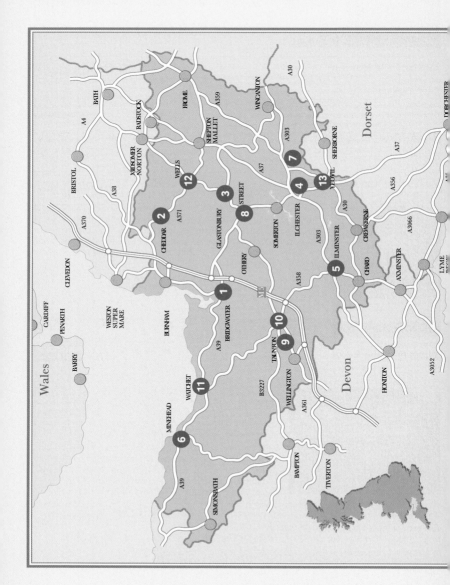

The Red Map References should be used to locate Museums etc on the pages that follow

Somerset

BRIDGWATER

Blake Museum

Blake Street, Bridgwater TA6 3NB   Tel: 01278 456127   Fax: 01278 446412
Email: museums@sedgemoor.govuk   Web: www.sedgemoor.gov.uk

Bridgwater's museum of local history and archaelogy. Special features include Robert Blake (1598-1657), The Monmouth Rebellion (1685). Bridgwater's colourful and exciting carnival, maritime history and the brick and tile industry.

Opening Times: Tue to Sat 10:00-16:00. Admission: Free. Location: In the town centre.
Map Ref: 1

Somerset Brick & Tile Museum

East Quay, Bridgwater TA6 3NB   Tel: 01278 426088

The only remaining tile kiln in Bridgwater and an impressive survivor of a major Somerset industry. Visitors can enter the kiln and see some of the many varied patterns of bricks, tiles and other wares made here.

Opening Times: Thu & Fri 09:00-16:00 or by arrangement. Admission: Free. Location: In East Quay, ten minutes from town centre.
Map Ref: 1

CHEDDAR

Cheddar Caves & Gorge

Cheddar BS27 3QF   Tel: 01934 742343   Fax: 01934 744637
Email: caves@cheddarcaves.co.uk   Web: www.cheddarcaves.co.uk

Cox's Cave

'Cheddar Man' Museum connected with show caves and other attractions. Museum features Britain's oldest complete skeleton (9000 years old) and evidence of late upper palaeolithic life in Gough's Cave. Come and see how your ancestors lived in our caves. Ticket includes entry to all attractions.

Opening Times: Daily May to mid Sep 10:00-17:00 mid Sep to Apr 10:30-16:30. Admission: Adult £7.90, Child £5.00, Under 5s Free. Location: In Britain's biggest gorge, one mile from Cheddar village centre. Map Ref: 2

GLASTONBURY

Glastonbury Abbey

Abbey Gatehouse, Magdelene Street, Glastonbury BA6 9EL   Tel / Fax: 01458 832267
Email: glastonbury.abbey@dial.pipex.com   Web: glastonburyabbey.com

The 14th century ruins viewed from the south west

This is a site museum and visitor centre for the finds and associated archives from excavations at Glastonbury Abbey. The museum preserves and interprets these finds and associated archives.

Opening Times: Mar to May & Sep to Nov 09:30-18:00 (or dusk if earlier), Dec, Jan & Feb 10:00-18:00 (or dusk if earlier), Jun, Jul & Aug 09:00-18:00. Admission: Adult £3.50, Child £1.50, OAP/Concession £3.00, Family £8.00. Group rates available. Location: Central - next to Town Hall.
Map Ref: 3

Glastonbury Lake Village Museum

The Tribunal, 9 High Street, Glastonbury BA6 9DP   Tel: 01458 832954   Fax: 01458 832949

Contains finds from one of Europe's most famous archaeological sites.

Opening Times: Apr to Sep Sun to Thu 10:00-17:00, Fri & Sat 10:00-17:30. Oct to Mar Sun to Thu 10:00-16:00, Fri & Sat 10:00-16:30. Closed Xmas. Admission: Adult £2.00, Child/OAP £1.00, Concession £1.50. Location: Town centre.
Map Ref: 3

Somerset Rural Life Museum

Abbey Farm, Chilkwell Street, Glastonbury BA6 8DB   Tel: 01458 831197

In the Abbey Farmhouse the social and domestic life of Victorian Somerset is described in reconstructed rooms and an exhibition which tells the life story of a farm worker, John Hodges. The magnificent 14th century Abbey barn is the centrepiece of the Museum. The barn and farm buildings surrounding the courtyard contain displays illustrating the tools and techniques of farming in Victorian Somerset.

Opening Times: Apr to Oct Tue to Fri & BH Mon 10:00-17:00, Sat & Sun 14:00-18:00. Nov to Mar Tue to Sat 10:00-15:00. Closed Good Friday.   Admission: Adult £2.50, Child £1.00, Under 5s Free, OAP £2.00. Parties by arrangement.   Location: In Glastonbury, follow signs to the Tor and Shepton Mallet A361.   Map Ref: 3

ILCHESTER

Fleet Air Arm Museum

Box NOS6, RNAS Yeovilton, Ilchester BA22 8HT   Tel: 01935 842614
Fax: 01935 842630   Email: info@fleetairarm.com
Web: www.fleetairarm.com

FLEET AIR ARM
MUSEUM

The Main Communications Room

The Fleet Air Arm Museum is the only British museum sited next to an operational military airfield. Using the airfield viewing galleries you may well see some of the Royal Navy's aircraft flying. The museum boasts over 40 aircraft on display within the many exhibitions throughout the museum. The Leading Edge Exhibition, just recently opened, tells the story of aircraft development from early biplanes to Concorde and the Sea Harrier. Innovative touch screen displays show you how aircraft fly and tell the stories of the aircraft and the men who flew them.

The Carrier Exhibition

Concorde 002 and the Bristol Scout are just two of the aircraft on display. Find out how it feels to be on board an 'Aircraft Carrier' of the Royal Navy. While you are on board, you can tour the Carrier's nerve centre and experience at close hand the thrills and noises of a working flight deck. Other exhibitions displayed include The Merlin Experience, World War One, World War Two, WRNS, Kamikaze, Skua & The Battle of Taranto. Disabled visitors have access to 95% of the displays and exhibitions.

Opening Times: Apr to Oct daily 10:00-17:30, Nov to Mar daily 10:00-16:30.   Admission: Adult £8.00, Child £5.50, OAP £6.50, Family (2 adults and 3 children) £25.00.   Location: On the B3151, just off the A303 near Ilchester.   Map Ref: 4

ILMINSTER

Perrys Cider Mills

Dowlish Wake, Ilminster TA19 0NY   Tel: 01460 52681   Email: info@perrycider.co.uk
Web: www.perrycider.co.uk

The old farming tools and cider presses show the country way of life in the early 1900s. Also a unique photo display of people and village events. Guided Tours for coach parties must be pre-booked.

Opening Times: Mon to Fri 09:00-17;30, Sat 09:30-16:30, Sun 10:00-13:00.   Admission: Free. Location: Ilminster - two miles. Chard - five miles.   Map Ref: 5

Somerset

MINEHEAD

West Somerset Railway

The Railway Station, Minehead TA24 5BG Tel: 01643 704996 Fax: 01643 706349 Email: info@west-somerset-railway.co.uk Web: www.west-somerset-railway.co.uk

Britain's longest Heritage Railway running 20 miles between Bishop's Lydeard (near Taunton) and Minehead, through the Quantock Hills and along the Exmoor Coast. Ten stations serving a variety of destinations.

Opening Times: Mar to Dec (selected dates) 09:30-17:30. Admission: Adult £10.00, Child £5.00, OAP £8.00. Party rates on application. Location: Four miles from Taunton (junction 25 on M5). Nearest main line railway station - Taunton. Map Ref: 6

7828 'Odney Manor' arrives at Minehead Station

West Somerset Rural Life Museum

The Old School, Allerford, Minehead TA24 8HN Tel: 01643 862529 Web: www.allerfordwebsite.ic24.net

Museum housed in the old school building with large hall, Victorian class-room, thatched roof, garden by the river. Exhibition of past local rural life. Large photographic collection.

Opening Times: Good Friday & Easter week, May to Oct Mon to Fri 10:30-13:00 14:00-16:30. BH & Sun in Aug 14:30-16:00. Admission: Adult £1.00, Child 50p, OAP 80p. Location: Off A39 between Porlock and Minehead. Map Ref: 6

SPARKFORD

Haynes Motor Museum

Sparkford BA22 7LH Tel: 01963 440804 Fax: 01963 441004 Email: recep@haynesmotormuseum.co.uk Web: www.haynesmotormuseum.co.uk

Established in 1985 from a collection of only 60 cars, today the Haynes Motor Museum is one of the largest in Europe, with a collection ranging from 1986 to the present day.

Opening Times: Mar to Oct 09:30-17:30, Nov to Feb 10:00-16:30. Open 09:30-18:30 during summer school holidays. Closed Xmas Day and New Year's Day. Admission: Adult £6.00, Child £3.50, Concession £5.00, Family from £7.50. Location: Conveniently located just off A303 mid-way between the south east and west country. Map Ref: 7

STREET

The Shoe Museum

40 High Street, Street BA16 0YA Tel: 01458 842169 Email: janet.targett@clarks.com

Contains shoes from Roman times to the present, buckles, fashion plates, machinery, hand tools and advertising material. Early history of Clarks Shoes and its role in the town.

Opening Times: Mon to Fri 10:00-16:45 Sat 10:00-17:00 Sun 11:00-17:00. Admission: Free. Location: Close to Clarks Village. Map Ref: 8

TAUNTON

Sheppy's Farm & Cider Museum

Three Bridges Farm, Bradford-on-Tone, Taunton TA4 1ER Tel: 01823 461233 Fax: 01823 461712 Email: info@sheppyscider.com Web: www.sheppyscider.com

A small private collection of agricultural and cider-making artefacts and machinery. Includes a video of the cider-maker's year.

Opening Times: Mon to Sat (all year) 08:30-18:00 Sun (Easter to Xmas) 12:00-14:00. Admission: Adult £2.00, Child £1.50, OAP £1.75. Location: A38 half way between Taunton and Wellington. Map Ref: 9

Somerset County Museum

The Castle, Castle Green, Taunton TA1 4AA   Tel: 01823 320201

There is a rich variety of objects on show at the Museum relating to the County of Somerset to intrigue and stir the imagination. There are toys and dolls, fossils, fine silver and pottery, and a rich collection of archaeological items from pre-historic and Roman Somerset. You can follow the fortunes of the Somerset Light Infantry in part of the Somerset Military Museum.

Opening Times: Apr to Oct Tue to Sat & BH Mon 10:00-17:00. Nov to Mar Tue to Sat 10:00-15:00. Closed Good Friday.   Admission: Adult £2.50, Child £1.00, Under 5s Free, OAP £2.00. Groups by arrangement.   Location: Five minute walk from Taunton Town Centre.   Map Ref: 10

Somerset Cricket Museum

7 Prior Avenue, Taunton TA1 1XX   Tel: 01823 275893

Housed in a 16th century priory barn and situated within the compounds of Somerset County Cricket Club this museum displays photographs, caps, bats etc with a good reference library.

Opening Times: Apr to Oct Mon to Fri 10:00-16:00.   Admission: Adult £1.00, Child/OAP 50p. Groups by arrangement.   Location: Situated in Somerset County Cricket Club environs within walking distance of the town, railway and bus stations.   Map Ref: 10

Somerset Military Museum

County Museum, The Castle, Taunton TA1 4AA   Tel: 01823 320201

The history of the County Regiments, especially the Somerset Light Infantry (Prince Albert's) from the 18th to the 20th century, illustrated through their uniforms, equipment, medals and memorabilia.

Opening Times: Apr to Oct Tue to Sat & BH Mon 10:00-17:00. Nov to Mar Tue to Sat 10:00-15:00. Closed Good Friday.   Admission: Adult £2.50, Child £1.00, Under 5s Free, OAP £2.00. Groups by arrangement.   Location: Within the Somerset County Museum, five minute walk from Taunton Town Centre.   Map Ref: 10

WATCHET

Watchet Market House Museum

Market Street, Watchet TA23 0AN   Tel: 01984 631345

Watchet from pre-history to present day. Fossils and Saxon Mint, iron ore mines, railways and harbour trade and industries. Maritime paintings, photographs and models.

Opening Times: Easter to Sep daily 10:30-12:30 14:30-16:30, Jul & Aug 19:00-21:00. Admission: Free.   Location: Close to harbour.   Map Ref: 11

WELLS

Wells Museum

8 Cathedral Green, Wells BA5 2UE   Tel: 01749 673477   Email: wellsmuseum@ukonline.co.uk

Wells Museum exhibits Medieval Cathedral statuary at close quarters, an insight into the social and natural history of Wells and the Mendip area and the varied artefacts excavated from the archaeological dig in the museum gardens.

Opening Times: Easter to Oct 10:00-17:30. Oct to Easter 11:00-16:00. Jul and Aug open until 20:00. Closed Tue (in winter) and Xmas Day.   Admission: Adult £2.50, Child £1.00, Concession £2.00, Family £6.00.   Location: Adjacent to Wells Cathedral.   Map Ref: 12

YEOVIL

Museum of South Somerset

Hendford, Yeovil BA20 1UN   Tel: 01935 424774

Pre-historic and Roman occupation through to agricultural and industrial revolutions, South Somerset's association with leather and glove manufacturing. You can also see the Linotype type-setting machine which was in use for newspaper production.

Opening Times: Apr to Sep Tue to Sat 10:00-16:00, Oct to Mar Tue to Fri 10:00-16:00. Admission: Free.   Location: Near town centre.   Map Ref: 13

e superb landscape of this county has been immortalised in the paintings of John Constable
o delighted in painting the lovely Stour Valley. The county is also renowned for the work of
other great painter, Thomas Gainsborough.

e Suffolk museums and galleries are mostly concerned with local history and indeed the beauty
the county but other subjects include horseracing, transport, mechanical music, historic
craft, and clocks and watches.

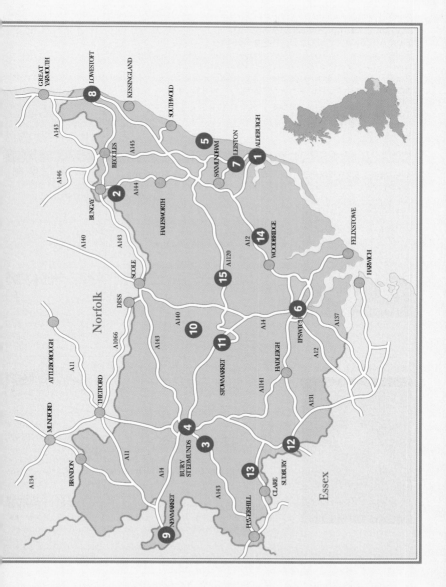

The Red Map References should be used to locate Museums etc on the pages that follow

Suffolk

Moot Hall Museum

Market Cross Place, Aldeburgh IP15 5BT   Tel: 01728 453295

Local history, Anglo Saxon urns etc. Shape Cemetery excavation 1862. Tudor building - paintings and finds from river and sea resulting from coastal erosion. Local flora and fauna, flints etc.

Opening Times: Easter to May Sat & Sun 14:30-17:00, Jun, Jul, Sep & Oct Daily 14:30-17:00, Aug 10:30-12:30 14:30-17:00. Closed Nov to Easter.   Admission: Adult 80p, Child Free.
Location: Near centre of town.   Map Ref: 1

Norfolk & Suffolk Aviation Museum: East Anglia's Aviation Heritage Centre

Buckeroo Way, The Street, Flixton, Bungay NR35 1NZ   Tel: 01986 896644
Email: nsam.flixton@virgin.net   Web: ww.aviationmuseum.net

Historic aircraft, indoor exhibitions - both civil and military, from the pioneer years through World War I to the present day. Special displays on Boulton & Paul, World War II Decoy Sites & Nature Walk.

Opening Times: Aapr to Oct Sun to Thu 10:00-17:00, Nov to Mar Sun, Tue & Wed 10:00-16:00.
Closed 15 Dec to 15 Jan.   Admission: Free.   Location: On B1062 off A143, one mile west of Bungay.   Map Ref: 2

The Pompeian Room

Ickworth House, Park & Gardens

The Rotunda, Horringer, Bury St Edmunds IP29 5QE   Tel: 01284 735270   Fax: 01284 735175   Email: aihusr@smtpntrust.org.uk
Web: www.nationaltrust.org.uk

The eccentric Earl of Bristol created this equally eccentric house, with its central rotunda and curved corridors, to house his collections. These include paintings by Titian, Gainsborough and Velasquez and a magnificent Georgian silver collection. The house is surrounded by an Italianase garden and set in a Capability Brown park with woodland walks, deer enclosure, vineyard, church, canal and lake.

Opening Times: House - 23 Mar to 3 Nov 13:00-17:00. Closed Mon (except BH) and Thu. Garden - 23 Mar to 3 Nov 10:00-17:00. Park - daily 07:00-19:00. Admission: Adult £5.95, Child £2.60, National Trust Members Free. Location: Located in the village of Horringer, two miles from the town of Bury St Edmunds.   Map Ref: 3

Manor House Museum

Honey Hill, Bury St Edmunds IP33 1RT
Tel: 01284 757076   Fax: 01284 747231

Email: saskia.stent@manorhse.stedmundsbury.gov.uk
Web: www.stedmundsbury.gov.uk/manorhse

The Manor House Museum consists of clocks, watches, paintings, furniture and costume. We are renowned for having the finest collections of clocks and watches in England. The House was built in the Georgian period of 1738, purely as an entertaining home for Lady Elizabeth Hervey, the wife of the First Earl of Bristol.

Opening Times: Sat, Sun, Tue, Wed 10:00-17:00.
Admission: Adults £3.00, Children and Senior Citizens £2.00, Free to residents of St Edmundsbury. Location: Five minutes walk from the Town Centre, through the Abbey gardens and great churchyard
                                                            Map Ref: 4

Suffolk

Moyses Hall Museum

Cornhill, Bury St Edmonds IP33 1DX   Tel: 01284 706183

Newly extended and refurbished local history museum includes Suffolk Regiment Gallery, history of Bury St Edmunds display in a wonderful 800 year old building.

Opening Times: Daily 10:00-17:00, Sun 14:00-17:00   Admission: Free for residents of Bury St Edmonds, non-residents £2.50 Adult, Concessions £2.00   Location: Town centre.   Map Ref: 4

DUNWICH

The Museum

St James Street, Dunwich IP17 3EA   Tel: 01728 648796

History of town of Dunwich from Roman times with local wildlife and social history.

Opening Times: Mar Sat & Sun 14:00-16:30, Apr to Sep daily 11:30-16:30, Oct daily 12:00-16:00. Closed Nov to Feb.   Admission: Free. Donations welcome.   Location: In centre of village.   Map Ref: 5

IPSWICH

Christchurch Mansion

Christchurch Park, Ipswich IP4 2BE   Tel: 01473 433554

Period rooms from Tudor to Victorian. Wolsey Art Gallery has contemporary art exhibitions work by Constable, Gainsborough and other Suffolk artists.

Opening Times: Tue to Sat 10:00-17:00, Sun 14:30-16:30. Closes at dusk during winter.
Admission: Free.   Location: Town centre, one mile from railway station.   Map Ref: 6

Ipswich Museum

High Street, Ipswich IP1 3QH   Tel: 01473 433550   Fax: 01473 433568

IPSWICH

Romans in Suffolk; Anglo-Saxons in Ipswich; mankind galleries; local and world geology; Victorian natural history gallery; Suffolk wildlife; British birds.

Opening Times: Tue to Sat 10:00-17:00.
Admission: Free.   Location: Town centre, one mile from railway station.   Map Ref: 6

Anglo-Saxon Gallery

Ipswich Transport Museum

Cobham Road, Ipswich IP3 9JD   Tel: 01473 715666
Web: www.ipswichtransportmuseum.co.uk

Believed the largest collection in the UK devoted to the transport and engineering heritage of one town - Ipswich. Includes bicycles, cranes, prams, fire engines, buses etc.

Opening Times: Apr to Nov Sun & BH 11:00-16:30. School holidays, Mon to Fri 13:00-16:00.
Admission: Adult £2.50, Child £1.50, Concession £2.00, Family £7.00.   Location: South east Ipswich, close to A14.   Map Ref: 6

LEISTON

Long Shop Museum

Main Street, Leiston IP16 4ES   Tel / Fax: 01728 832189   Email: longshop@care4free.net
Web: www.longshop.care4free.net

Two hundred years of the Garrett family history from the first production line to the first woman doctor. Housed in original Garrett Works buildings including Grade II* long shop.

Opening Times: Apr to Oct Mon to Sat 10:00-17:00, Sun 11:00-17:00.   Admission: Adult £3.50, Child £1.00, Under 5s Free, Concession £3.00.   Location: Near town centre.   Map Ref: 7

Suffolk

Lowestoft & East Suffolk Maritime Museum

Whapload Road, Lowestoft NR32 1XG   Tel: 01502 561963

Tells the history of the Lowestoft fishing fleet, models of boats, replica of aft cabin of steam drifter, RNLB display, collection of shipwrights tools, picture gallery and photographs.

Opening Times: Easter & 28 Apr to 6 Oct daily 10:00-16:30.   Admission: Adult 75p, Child 25p, OAP 50p.   Location: 30 minute walk from railway station, 25 minute walk from bus station.

Map Ref: 8

Lowestoft Museum

Broad House, Nicholas Everitt Park, Lowestoft NR33 9JR   Tel: 01502 511457

Third largest collection in the world of Lowestoft porcelain as well as the history of the area going back to the Stone Age and beyond.

Opening Times: 25 Mar to 6 Oct Mon to Fri 10:30-17:00 Sat/Sun 14:00-17:00 12 Oct to 3 Nov Sat/Sun 14:00-16:00. Half term week Mon to Fri 10:30-16:00.   Admission: Free.   Location: In beautiful Nicholas Everitt Park in Oulton Broad, one mile inland from town centre.   Map Ref: 8

British Sporting Art Trust

BSAT Gallery, 99 High Street, Newmarket CB8 8LU   Tel: 01264 710344   Fax: 01264 710114
Email: BSATrust@cs.com   Web: www.BSATrust.com

Annually changing exhibition of sporting paintings. Library of books relating to sporting art and field sports.

Opening Times: Easter to end Oct Tue to Sun 10:00-17:00.   Admission: Adult £3.00.
Location: Near town centre, above National Horseracing Museum, next door to Jockey Club.

Map Ref: 9

National Horseracing Museum

99 High Street, Newmarket CB8 8JL   Tel: 01638 667333   Fax: 01638 665600

The story of racing told through the museum's permanent collections, featuring the horses, people, events and scandals that made it so colourful. Six permanent galleries housing sporting paintings, bronzes, trophies and racing memorabilia historical video.

Opening Times: 29 Mar to 5 Nov Tue to Sun 11:00-17:00, also open Mon in Jul, Aug & BH. Admission: Adult £4.50, Child £2.50, Concession £3.50. Location: In town centre. Bus stop opposite, 15 minute walk from station.

Map Ref: 9

Mechanical Music Museum & Bygones

Blacksmiths Road, Cotton, Stowmarket IP14 4QN   Tel: 01449 613876

Unique collection of music-boxes, gramophones, polyphons, organettes, street pianos, barrel organs, fair organs, the Wurlitzer Theatre Pipe Organ plus many unusual items. Also large collection of teapots and memorabilia.

Opening Times: Jun to Sep Sun only 14:30-17:30. Groups by arrangement during the week. Fair Organ Enthusiasts Day 6 Oct 10:00-17:00.   Admission: Adult £4.00, Child £1.00. Location: Six miles north of Stowmarket, just off B1113 road. Nearest railway station: Stowmarket.   Map Ref: 10

Museum of East Anglian Life

Stowmarket IP14 1DL   Tel: 01449 612229   Fax: 01449 672307   Email: Pat@meal.fsnet.co.uk
Web: www.suffolkcc.gov.uk/tourism/meal

Set in 70 acres of Suffolk countryside, the museum has a fascinating collection of agricultural, industrial and social history exhibits in historic buildings. Also farm animals, gift shop, play area and tea room.

Opening Times: Apr to Oct Mon to Sat 10:00-17:00, Sun 11:00-17:00.   Admission: Adult £4.50, Child £3.00, OAP/Student £4.00, Family (2+3) £14.75.   Location: Near town centre, five minute walk from bus stop.   Map Ref: 11

SUDBURY

Gainsborough's House

46 Gainsborough Street, Sudbury CO10 2EU   Tel: 01787 372958   Fax: 01787 376991
Email: mail@gainsborough.org   Web: www.gainsborough.org

Georgian fronted townhouse, birthplace of Thomas Gainsborough RA, displaying much of his work, together with 18th century furniture and memorabilia. Varied programme of contemporary exhibitions throughout the year. Attractive walled garden.

Opening Times: Tue to Sat 10:00-17:00, Sun & BH Mon 14:00-17:00. Closing time Nov to Mar 16:00. Closed Good Friday, Xmas & New Year.   Admission: Adult £3.00, Child/Student £1.50, OAP £2.50. Group rates available.   Location: In the heart of Sudbury.   Map Ref: 12

Sue Ryder Foundation Museum

P O Box 5736, Cavendish, Sudbury CO10 8RN   Tel: 01787 282591

Includes original exhibits from Nazi Concentration Camps. Also embroidery and handicrafts made by patients in Sue Ryder homes.

Opening Times: Daily 10:00-17:30. Closed Xmas.   Admission: Adult 80p, Child/OAP 40p.
Location: On A1092 between Clare and Long Melford; Sudbury eight miles; Bury St Edmunds 16 miles; Cambridge 29 miles.   Map Ref: 13

WOODBRIDGE

Easton Farm Park

Easton, Wickham Market, Woodbridge IP13 0EQ   Tel: 01728 746475   Fax: 01728 747861
Email: easton@eastonfarmpark.co.uk   Web: www.eastonfarmpark.co.uk

Ornate Victorian dairy, built c.1870, original Victorian buildings, many old farming implements and equipment. Suffolk horses and lots of other farm animals. Gift shop, tea room, working blacksmith.

Opening Times: Mar to Oct daily 10:30-18:00, Feb & Oct half terms.   Admission: Adult £5.00, Child £3.50, OAP £4.50.   Location: Seven miles from Woodbridge, 15 miles from Ipswich. Countryside location.   Map Ref: 14

Saxstead Green Post Mill

The Mill House, Saxtead Green, Framlingham, Woodbridge IP13 9QQ   Tel: 01728 685789

This is a fine example of a post mill, where the superstructure turns on a great post to face the wind. There has been a mill here since 1287, as Framlingham was a thriving farming community.

Opening Times: Apr to Sep Mon to Sat 10:00-13:00 14:00-18:00, Oct Mon to Sat 10:00-13:00 14:00-17:00. Please check times before visiting in early part of season.   Admission: Adult £2.20, Child £1.10, Concession £1.70.   Location: Two and a half miles north west of Framlingham on A1120.   Map Ref: 15

Britain's most wooded county can still claim countryside of outstanding beauty. The magnific
North Downs cross the county from east to west and include Box Hill, a famous beauty spot
over 200 years. To the south is the fertile Surrey Weald, while to the north is the low-lying be
the Thames Valley.

The museums and galleries of Surrey are extremely varied in topics ranging from local hist
geology and archaeology, to rural life and local crafts.

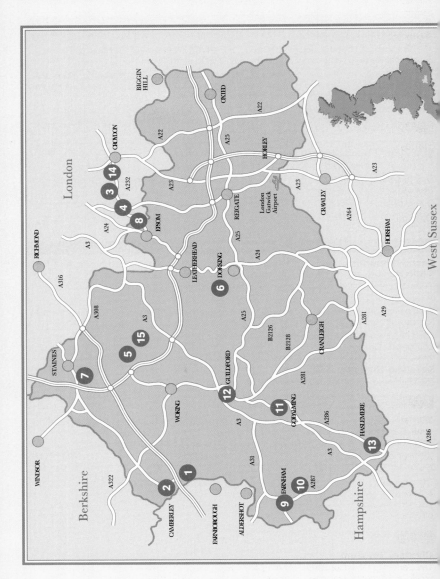

The Red Map References should be used to locate Museums etc on the pages that follow

Surrey

CAMBERLEY

Royal Logistic Corps Museum

Princess Royal Barracks, Deepcut, Camberley GU16 6RW   Tel: 01252 833371   Fax: 01252 833484   Email: query@rlcmuseum.freeserve.co.uk

Formed in 1993, the museum houses the collection of the Royal Corps of Transport, Royal Army Ordnance Corps, Royal Pioneer Corps, Army Catering Corps and Royal Engineers' Postal & Courier Service.

Opening Times: Tue to Fri 10:00-16:00. Easter to Sep Sat 12:00-16:00. Closed Sun & BH. Admission: Free.   Location: Deepcut village near Frimley Green.   Map Ref: 1

Surrey Heath Museum

Surrey Heath House, Knoll Road, Camberley GU15 3HD   Tel: 01276 707284   Fax: 01276 707183   Web: www.surreyheath.gov.uk

Small imaginatively designed museum telling the local heathland story and the development of Camberley and surrounding villages. Temporary exhibition gallery with varied programme. Schools service.

Opening Times: Tue to Sat 11:00-17:00. Closed Xmas & Good Friday.   Location: Near town centre, five minutes from railway station and bus stops. Public car park 200 yards.   Map Ref: 2

CARSHALTON

Honeywood Heritage Centre

Honeywood Walk, Carshalton SM5 3NX   Tel: 020 8770 4297   Fax: 020 8770 4777   Email: lbshoneywood@netscapeonline.co.uk   Web: www.sutton.gov.uk/lfl/heritage/honeywood

The recently restored interior of this historic building contains a wealth of period detail from the Victorian and Edwardian eras. Themed displays include Tudor life, the local River Wandle and its industries, and children's toys and games.

Opening Times: Wed to Fri 11:00-17:00, Sat, Sun & BH 10:00-17:00. Tea room open Tue to Sun 10:00-17:00.   Admission: Adult £1.20, Child 60p. Groups by prior arrangement. Location: Next to Carshalton Ponds, off A232. Four minutes walk to Carshalton Station.
Map Ref: 3

Little Holland House

40 Beeches Avenue, Carshalton SM5 3LW   Tel: 020 8770 4781   Fax: 020 8770 4777   Email: valary.murphy@sutton.gov.uk   Web: www.sutton.gov.uk/lfl/heritage/lhh

Built between 1902-04 by Frank Dickinson, an ardent devotee of the Arts & Crafts Movement, the Grade II* interior contains Dickinson's paintings, hand-made furniture, carvings and metal work in an eclectic style which is totally unique.

Opening Times: First Sun every month plus Sun & Mon of BH weekends 13:30-17:30. Closed Xmas & New Year.   Admission: Free. Group visits outside opening times by prior arrangement only - include talks and guided tour £2.50 per person.   Location: On B278 four minute walk south of Carshalton Beeches Station.   Map Ref: 3

CHEAM

Whitehall

1 Malden Road, Cheam SM3 8QD   Tel: 020 8643 1236   Fax: 020 8770 4777   Email: curators@whitehallcheam.fsnet.co.uk   Web: www.sutton.gov.uk/lfl/heritage/whitehall

A Tudor timber-framed house, built c.1500, which contains displays on various aspects of its history including the Killick family, who lived here for over 250 years.

Opening Times: Wed to Fri & Sun 14:00-17:00, Sat 10:00-17:00. BH 14:00-17:00. Closed Xmas & New Year.   Admission: Adult £1.20, Child 60p. Group rates available.   Location: On A2043 just north of junction with A232. Five minute walk from Cheam station. Pay and display car park off Park Road, opposite.   Map Ref: 4

CHERTSEY

Chertsey Museum

The Cedars, 33 Windsor Street, Chertsey KT16 8AT   Tel: 01932 565764   Fax: 01932 571118   Email: curator@chertseymuseum.org.uk   Web: www.chertseymuseum.org.uk

Collection displays explore the history of the Runnymede area and British fashion, including

Surrey

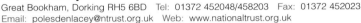

Thames Valley archaeology, clocks, social history, decorative art, Greek pottery, Chertsey Abbey and 'The Matthews Dress Collection'.

Opening Times: Tue to Fri 12:30-16:30, Sat 11:00-16:00. Closed Xmas & New Year and Good Friday. Admission: Free. Location: Near town centre, one minute walk from bus stop, 15 minute walk from train station. Map Ref: 5

DORKING

Polesden Lacey 　🚽 🏛

Great Bookham, Dorking RH5 6BD Tel: 01372 452048/458203 Fax: 01372 452023
Email: polesdenlacey@ntrust.org.uk Web: www.nationaltrust.org.uk

The Library which is decorated in neo-classical. National Trust Photo Library

In an exceptional setting on the North Downs, this originally Regency house was extensively remodelled in 1906-9 by the Hon Mrs Ronald Grenville, a well known Edwardian hostess. Her collection of fine paintings, furniture, porcelain and silver are displayed in the reception rooms and galleries, as they were at the time of her celebrated house parties.

Opening Times: House: 23 Mar to 3 Nov Wed to Sun 11:00-17:00. Open BH Mon and Tue 4 Jun. Garden: Daily 11:00-18:00 or dusk if earlier. Admission: House: Adult £7.00, Family £17.50. Garden, grounds & walks: Adult £4.00, Family £10.00. Map Ref: 6

EGHAM

Egham Museum 　🏛 🚒

Literary Institute, High Street, Egham TW20 9EW Tel: 01344 843047

Local historical collections relating to Egham, Englefield Green, Thorpe, Virginia Water and Egham Hythe. This includes Runnymede, Magna Carta, Holloway College, Lagonda Cars etc.

Opening Times: Tue, Thu & Sat 10:00-12:30 14:00-16:30. Admission: Free. Location: In town centre, near railway station and buses. Map Ref: 7

EPSOM

Bourne Hall Museum 　🚽 🏛 📷 🚒

Bourne Hall, Spring Street, Ewell, Epsom KT17 1UF Tel: 020 8394 1734

Bourne Hall Museum is set in the rambling gardens of Bourne Hall in the heart of Ewell village. The museum covers two millennia of local history.

Opening Times: Mon to Sat 09:00-17:00, Sun 09:00-13:00 Admission: Free. Map Ref: 8

FARNHAM

Museum of Farnham 　🚽 🏛

Willmer House, 38 West Street, Farnham GU9 7DX Tel / Fax: 01252 715094
Email: fmuseum@waverley.gov.uk Web: www.waverley.gov.uk

Local history collection housed in a Grade I listed Georgian town house with attractive walled garden. Audio tours, temporary exhibitions, local studies library, holiday activities for the family.

Opening Times: Tue to Sat 10:00-17:00. Admission: Free. Location: Town centre. Map Ref: 9

Rural Life Centre 　🚽 🏛 📷 🚒

Reeds Road, Tilford, Farnham GU10 2DL Tel / Fax: 01252 795571
Email: rural.life@lineone.net Web: www.surreyweb.org.uk/rural-life

Village life collection covering the last two hundred years of the 20th century set in large arboretum. Special events. Light railway, Sundays. Coaches and schools welcome by appointment.

Opening Times: Apr to Oct Wed to Sun & BH 11:00-18:00. Oct to Mar Wed 11:00-16:00. Admission: Adult £4.00, Child £2.00, OAP £3.00, Family £10.00. Location: Mid-way between Frensham and Tilford, off the A287, three miles south of Farnham. Map Ref: 10

Surry

GODALMING

Godalming Museum

109A High Street, Godalming GU7 1AQ   Tel: 01483 426510   Fax: 01483 523495
Email: museum@godalming.ndo.co.uk   Web: www.godalming-museum.org.uk

Local history and personalities including Miss Gertrude Jekyll and Sir Edwin Lutyens, Jack Phillips - wireless operator of the Titanic, General Oglethorpe - founder of the colony of Georgia and many others. Local studies library.

Opening Times: Tue to Sat 10:00-17:00 (16:00 in winter).   Admission: Free.   Location: High Street, five minutes from station.
Map Ref: 11

GUILDFORD

Guildford Cathedral Treasury

Stag Hill, Guildford GU2 7UP   Tel: 01483 565287   Fax: 01482 303350
Email: visits@guildford-cathedral.org   Web: www.guildford-cathedral.org

Out of 215 parishes, 35 Churches have lent 135 different artefacts to the Cathedral. The display represents nearly 450 years of ecclesiastical history and wonderful examples of art and craftmanship.

Opening Times: Daily 08:30-17:30.   Admission: Free - donation welcome. Small fee for Groups.   Location: Ten minute walk from mainline station.
Map Ref: 12

Guildford House Gallery

155 High Street, Guildford GU1 3AJ   Tel: 01483 444740   Fax: 01483 444742
Email: guildfordhouse@remote.guildford.gov.uk   Web: www.guildfordhouse.co.uk

Fascinating 17th century Grade I listed building. Original features include a finely carved staircase, panelled rooms, decorative plaster ceilings and wrought iron window fittings. Varied temporary exhibition programme throughout the year.

Opening Times: Tue to Sat 10:00-16:45. Closed Mon.   Admission: Free.   Location: Guildford Town Centre.
Map Ref: 12

Guildford Museum

Castle Arch, Guildford GU1 3SX   Tel: 01483 444750   Email: gfdmuseum@aol.com
Web: www.surreycc.gov.uk/guildford-museum

The Museum was founded in 1898. It now houses the largest collection of archaeology, local history and needlework in Surrey. The archaeology collection contains objects from Palaeolithic hand axes to Roman Priests' head dresses. The needlework collections include most types of sewing. Objects and pictures covering local trades and industries, social life and customs, childhood and the home. Also local characters such as Lewis Carroll and Gertrude Jekyll.

Opening Times: Mon to Sat 11:00-17:00. Closed Sun.
Admission: Free.
Map Ref: 12

Loseley Park

Guildford GU3 1HS   Tel: 01483 304440   Fax: 01483 302036   Email: enquiries@loseley-park.com   Web: www.loseley-park.com

Loseley House is a fine example of Elizabethan Architecture featuring many fine works of art including paintings, tapestries, chalk fireplace and panelling from Henry VIII's Nonsuch Palace.

Opening Times: Walled Garden: 6 May to 29 Sep Wed to Sun 11:00-17:00. Loseley House: 3 Jun to 26 Aug Wed to Sun 13:00-17:00. (Guided tours)   Admission: Garden: Adult £3.00, Child £1.50, OAP £2.50. House & Garden: Adult £6.00, Child £3.00, OAP £5.00.   Location: Three miles from Guildford Town Centre, five minutes drive from A3.
Map Ref: 12

The Watts Gallery

Down Lane, Compton, Guildford GU3 1DQ   Tel: 01483 810235
Email: wattsgallery@freeuk.com   Web: www.wattsgallery.org.uk

The studio collection of G F Watts OMRA, the famous Victorian artist, including portraits, symbolist paintings and sculpture. Nearby is the Watts Chapel, designed and built by his wife, Mary.

Opening Times: Oct to Mar Mon, Tue, Fri & Sun 14:00-16:00 Sat & Wed 11:00-13:00 14:00-16:00. Apr to Sep Mon, Tue, Fri & Sun 14:00-18:00 Sat & Wed 11:00-13:00 14:00-18:00. Admission: Free. Location: In Compton, five minutes drive from Guildford.   Map Ref: 12

HASLEMERE

Haslemere Educational Museum

78 High Street, Haslemere GU27 2LA Tel: 01428 642112   Fax: 01428 645234
Email: HaslemereMuseum@compuserve.com

Permanent exhibitions include geology, natural history, archaeology and human history. Popular features are Egyptian mummy, stuffed bear, wild flower table, and observation beehive. Attractive grounds with ha-ha, gazebo, pond and some unusual trees.

Opening Times: Tue to Sat 10:00-17:00. Admission: Free. Location: High Street location - ten minutes walk from station.   Map Ref: 13

WALLINGTON

Carew Manor Dovecote

Church Road, Beddington, Wallington SM6 7NH   Tel: 020 8770 4781   Fax: 020 8770 4777
Email: valary.murphy@sutton.gov.uk   Web: www.sutton.gov.uk/lfl/heritage/carew

The Great Hall at Carew Manor is Sutton's only Grade I listed building. Tours include the Great Hall with its arch-braced hammer-beam roof, cellars and 18th century dovecote.

Opening Times: Tours at 14:00 and 15:30 on Sun 12 May, 30 Jun & 6 Oct. Admission: Adult £3.00 per tour. Location: Just off A232 at entrance to Beddington Park.   Map Ref: 14

WEYBRIDGE

Brooklands Museum Trust Ltd

Brooklands Road, Weybridge KT13 0QN   Tel: 01932 857381   Fax: 01932 855465
Email: brooklands@dial.pipex.com   Web: www.motor-software.co.uk/brooklands

The birthplace of British motorsport and aviation, features a fine collection of historic racing and sports cars and aircraft. Including the Loch Ness Wellington bomber 'R' for 'Robert' and the Napier-Railton built for John Cobb.

Opening Times: Tue to Sun 10:00-17:00 (summer) 10:00-16:00 (winter). Admission: Adult £7.00, Child £5.00, OAP/Student £6.00, Family £18.00. NB. Extra charges may be levied on events. Location: A 20 minutes walk from Weybridge station and ten minutes from Junction 10 on A3.   Map Ref: 15

Elmbridge Museum

Library Buildings, Church Street, Weybridge KT13 8DE   Tel: 01932 843573   Fax: 01932 846552   Email: ebcmuseum@elmbridge.gov.uk   Web: www.surrey-online.co.uk/elm-mus

The collections of this interesting museum relate to the history of the Elmbridge area. With a fascinating gallery complemented by a shop, changing exhibitions and a local studies room, there is something for everyone.

Opening Times: Mon to Wed & Fri 11:00-17:00, Sat 10:00-13:00 14:00-17:00. Closed Thu, Sun & BH. Admission: Free. Location: On first floor above the library in Church Street, Weybridge.   Map Ref: 15

ch has been said and written about 'Sussex by the Sea', ever since Rudyard Kipling praised
glories Brighton, the queen of Sussex seaside towns and the largest town in East Sussex, was
ntioned in Domesday Book. The county town of West Sussex is Chichester, a Roman town
ining something of its Roman grid-iron street plan.

cream of Sussex's museums and galleries and palaces are located in the coastal towns and
e outstanding collections as well as covering the county's social and archaeological history.

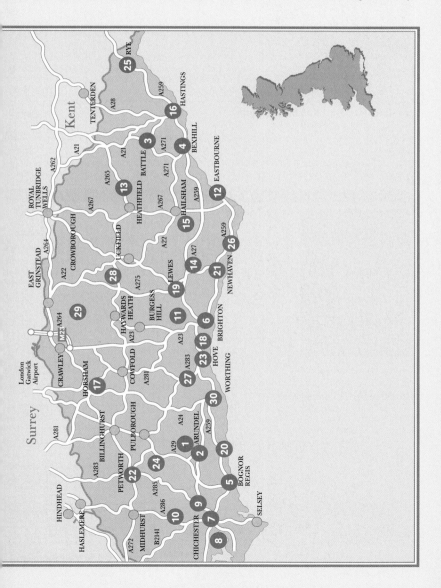

The Red Map References should be used to locate Museums etc on the pages that follow

Amberley Working Museum

  🚹 🔘 📷 🚂

Amberley, Arundel BN18 9LT   Tel: 01798 831370   Fax: 01798 831831
Email: office@amberleymuseum.co.uk   Web: www.amberleymuseum.co.uk

A 1920 Leyland bus, providing free transport around Amberley

Amberley Working Museum is a 36 acre open-air site dedicated to preserving the industrial heritage of the south-east. Exhibits include a narrow-gauge railway and vintage bus collection (both of which provide free travel around site). Besides the SEEBOARD electricity hall, a printing workshop and a roadmarker's exhibition, the museum is also home to traditional craftspeople, such as a blacksmith, potter and broom-maker.

Opening Times: 20 Mar to 3 Nov Wed to Sun 10:00-17:00. Open BH and daily through school holidays.
Admission: Adult £6.75, Child £3.75, OAP/Student £6.00, Group rates available.   Location: On the B2139, between Arundel and Storrington. Adjacent to Amberley Railway Station.

Map Ref: 1

Arundel Museum & Heritage Centre

61 High Street, Arundel BN18 9AJ   Tel: 01903 885708

The history of Arundel in pictures, artefacts, models etc, all housed in eight galleries and a courtyard.

Opening Times: Apr to Sep Mon to Sat 10:30-17:00, Sun 14:00-17:00.   Admission: Adult £1.00, Child 50p, OAP/Student 50p.   Location: In the town centre.

Map Ref: 2

Great Gatehouse from South copyright English Heritage

Battle Abbey

  🚹 🔘

Battle TN33 0AD   Tel: 01424 773792

Battle Abbey was founded around 1070 by William the Conqueror, on the site of the Battle of Hastings. The best-preserved and most impressive part of the abbey is the great gate-house, the finest of all surviving Medieval abbey entrances, which was built around 1338. There is an exhibition on the build-up to the Battle of Hastings. Collections include architectural stonework and archaeological finds.

Opening Times: Apr to Sep daily 10:00-18:00, Oct daily 10:00-17:00, Nov to Mar daily 10:00-16:00. Closed Xmas & New Year.
Admission: Adult £4.30, Child £2.20, Concession £3.20, Family £10.80.   Location: In Battle, at south end of High Street.

Map Ref: 3

Buckleys Yesterdays World

🔘 📷

Next to Battle Abbey, 89/90 High Street, Battle TN33 0AQ   Tel: 01424 775378
Fax: 01424 775174   Email: info@yesterdaysworld.co.uk
Web: www.yesterdaysworld.co.uk

Step into the world of yesterday today

Step into the world of yesterday - today at the South East's No 1 top visitor attraction. Experience the sights, sounds and smells of a by-gone age, as you journey through a hundred glorious years of shopping and social history. Discover what life was like from the 1850s onwards, and capture the charm of yesteryear as you explore over forty rooms and shop settings. Your nostalgia experience takes you along the 'high street' as you bump into many colourful life-sized characters in the various stores,

Meet colourful lifesized characters from 1850 onwards

ranging from the 1900s general store to the 1960s television shop. On the home front, the exhibition concentrates on Victorian life and you'll be thankful for today's labour saving gadgets when you see all the hard work going on in the kitchen and laundry. You'll be 'most amused' when you meet Queen Victoria in her throne room, surrounded by a host of regal memorabilia, including items belonging to Queen Victoria herself and letters written by Queen Elizabeth II. The fun continues with the Children's Play Village, Toddlers Activity Area and Miniature Golf. Indulge yourself at the Tea Terrace or Fudge Fayre overlooking the beautiful English Country Garden.

Opening Times: Daily 09:30-18:00 (17:00 in winter). Admission: Adult £4.75, Child £3.25, OAP £4.25, Family £14.75. Location: Battle Hight Street, opposite Abbey. Map Ref: 3

BEXHILL E Sussex

Bexhill Museum

Egerton Road, Bexhill TN39 3HL Tel / Fax: 01424 787950 Email: museum@rother.gov.uk
Web: bexhillmuseum.co.uk

Housed in an Edwardian Park Pavilion, collections reflect the fascinating history of Bexhill - important collections include local dinosaur remains, architect's model of De La Pavilion and much more. New access centre.

Opening Times: Feb to Dec Tue to Fri 10:00-17:00. Sat & Sun & BH 14:00-17:00.
Admission: Adult £1.00, Child Free, Concession 50p, Group 50p. School Groups Free.
Location: Just off Bexhill Seafront (B2182) by the Clock Tower, quarter mile railway station.
Map Ref: 4

BOGNOR REGIS W Sussex

Bognor Regis Museum/Bognor Regis Wireless Museum

69 High Street, Bognor Regis PO21 1RY Tel: 01243 865636

The main museum houses displays of local history, also included is an independent wireless museum.

Opening Times: Tue to Sun 10:30-16:30. Closed Mon (except BH). Admission: Free.
Location: In the town centre. Map Ref: 5

BRIGHTON E Sussex

Booth Museum of Natural History

194 Dyke Road, Brighton BN1 5AA Tel: 01273 292777 Fax: 01273 292778
Email: boothmus@pavilion.co.uk Web: www.museums.brighton-hove.gov.uk

Over half a million specimens and natural history literature and data extending back over three centuries are housed in this fascinating museum, including hundreds of British birds, butterflies, skeletons, whale and dinosaur bones.

Opening Times: Mon to Sat 10:00-17:00, Sun 14:00-17:00. Closed Thu, Good Friday, 25-26 Dec, 1 Jan. Admission: Free. Location: 15 minute bus ride from town centre, five to ten minute walk from Brighton Station. Buses 27 & 27A. Map Ref: 6

Brighton Fishing Museum

201 Kings Road Arches, Brighton BN1 1NB Tel: 01273 723064

Photographs, film starting 1896, fishing vessels (7) and daily landings by today's fishermen.

Opening Times: 10:00-17:00. Admission: Free. Location: Lower Esplanade, half way between piers.

Map Ref: 6

Brighton Museum & Art Gallery

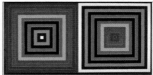

Church Street, Brighton BN1 1UE   Tel: 01273 290900   Fax: 01273 292841
Web: www.museums.brighton-hove.gov.uk

Spine Chair (des.1986) by Andre Dubreuil

Brighton Museum & Art Gallery reopens spring 2002. A £10 million redevelopment has transformed Brighton Museum into a state-of-the-art visitor's attraction. Dynamic and innovative new galleries feature exciting interactive displays appealing to all ages. Brighton Museum is famous for its collection of 20th century furniture, glass, textiles and jewellery, including examples by this century's leading designers. The extensive ceramics collection includes the famous Willett Gallery, exploring 18th and 19th century British social history through earthenware. The museum's spectacular collection of non-western arts is of national importance and it also boasts stunning collections of fashion and fascinating local history collections. The museum also has an extensive collection of fine art, ranging from the 15th to the 20th century.

Frank Stella (1936) Red Scramble, 1977, Oil on Canvas

Opening Times: Tue 10:00-19:00, Wed, Thu, Fri & Sat 10:00-17:00 .Sun 14:00-17:00. Closed Mon, 24-26 Dec & 1 Jan.   Admission: Free.   Location: Situated in town centre.   Map Ref: 6

Preston Manor

Preston Drove, Brighton BN1 6SD   Tel: 01273 292770   Fax: 01273 292771
Email: visitor.services@brighton-hove.gov.uk   Web: www.museums.brighton-hove.gov.uk

Delightful manor house, powerfully evoking the atmosphere of an Edwardian gentry home both upstairs and downstairs. Explore over 20 rooms on four floors from superbly renovated servant's quarters to the attic bedrooms.

Opening Times: Mon 13:00-17:00, Tue to Sat 10:00-17:00, Sun 14:00-17:00 and BH 10:00-17:00. Closed Mon 10:00-13:00 Good Friday, 25 & 26 Dec. Admission: Adult £3.30, Child £2.05, Group (20+) £2.80. (prices valid until 31 Mar 2002)   Location: 10-15 minute bus ride from town centre. Buses 5 & 5A   Map Ref: 6

The Royal Pavilion, Brighton

Royal Pavilion

4/5 Pavilion Buildings, Brighton BN1 1EE
Tel: 01273 290900   Fax: 01273 292871
Email: visitor.services@brighton-hove.gov.uk
Web: www.royalpavilion.brighton.co.uk

The Royal Pavilion, the famous seaside palace of King George IV, is one of the most exotically beautiful buildings in the British Isles. Originally a simple farmhouse, in 1787 architect Henry Holland created a neoclassical villa on the site. From 1815-1822, the Pavilion was transformed by John Nash into its current distinctive Indian style complete with Chinese inspired interiors. Magnificent decorations and fantastic furnishings have been re-created in an extensive restoration programme. From the opulence of the main State rooms to the charm of the first floor bedroom suites, the Royal Pavilion is filled with astonishing colours and superb craftsmanship. Witness the magnificence of the Music Room with a domed ceiling of gilded shell shapes, and the dramatic Banqueting Room lit by a huge crystal chandelier held by a silvered dragon. Visitors can discover more about life behind the scenes at the Palace during the last 200 years with an interactive multimedia visitor interpretation programme and join public guided tours daily at 11:30 and 14:30 (for a small

The Music Room at the Royal Pavilion, Brighton

extra charge). The Royal Pavilion is an ideal location for filming and photography, from fashion shoots to corporate videos. Rooms are also available for hire for corporate and private functions and civil wedding ceremonies.

Sussex

Opening Times: Daily Oct to May 10:00-17:00, Jun to Sep 10:00-18:00. Closed 25-26 Dec.
Admission: Adult £5.20, Child £3.20, Group (20+) £4.40. (prices valid until 31 Mar 2002)
Location: Situated in town centre.
Map Ref: 6

CHICHESTER W Sussex

Chichester District Museum

29 Little London, Chichester PO19 1PB   Tel: 01243 784683   Fax: 01243 776766
Email: districtmuseum@chichester.gov.uk

Find out about the archaeology and local history of the Chichester district through displays and hands-on activities. Changing exhibitions and events for all ages.

Opening Times: Tue to Sat 10:00-17:30. Closed Sun, Mon and all Public Holidays.
Admission: Free.   Location: Off East Street, Chichester. 15 minutes from Bus and Train Stations.
Map Ref: 7

Fishbourne Roman Palace & Museum

Salthill Road, Fishbourne, Chichester PO19 2QR   Tel: 01243 785859   Fax: 01243 539266   Email: pro@sussexpast.co.uk   Web: www.sussexpast.co.uk

Trajan's Column

Britain's finest collection of in situ Roman mosaics are on display at Fishbourne Roman Palace along with a museum of finds from this internationally important site, and a Roman garden replanted to its original plan. An audio-visual presentation helps bring the site back to life.

Opening Times: Jan & 16 Dec to 31 Dec Sat & Sun 10:00-16:00 Feb & Nov to 15 Dec daily 10:00-16:00 Mar to Jul & Sep to Oct daily 10:00-17:00 Aug daily 10:00-18:00   Admission: Adult £4.70 Child £2.50 Concession £4.00 Family £12.20 Disabled £3.80.   Location: Five minutes walk from Fishbourne Railway Station. North of A259 off Salthill Road in Fishbourne village. Bus services stop near end of Salthill Road.
Map Ref: 8

Guildhall Museum

Priory Park, Chichester   Tel: 01243 784683   Email: districtmuseum@chichester.gov.uk

A Grade I listed building and an ancient scheduled monument which dates from 1269 and was built as the church for the Grey Friars. Now displays large local history material.

Opening Times: Sat only Jun to Mid Sep 12:00-14:00.   Admission: Free.   Location: In Priory Park, located to the north-east of the City.
Map Ref: 7

Pallant House Gallery

9 North Pallant, Chichester PO19 1TJ   Tel: 01243 774557   Fax: 01243 536038
Email: pallant@pallant.co.uk   Web: www.pallanthousegallery.com

Predominantly British 20th century paintings. Superb collection in Queen Anne townhouse setting. Regular temporary exhibitions throughout the year.

Opening Times: Tue to Sat 10:00-17:00, Sun & BH 12:30-17:00.   Admission: Adult £4.00, Child Free, Concession £3.00, Student £2.50.   Location: Near city centre, take East Street from City Cross and turn right at Marks & Spencer.
Map Ref: 7

Royal Military Police Museum

Roussillon Barracks, Broyle Road, Chichester PO19 4BN   Tel: 01243 534225   Fax: 01243 534288   Email: museum@rhqrmp.freeserve.co.uk   Web: www.rhqrmp.freeserve.co.uk

Tracing military police history from Tudor origins, the museum displays artefacts from conflicts including World War I and World War II, Northern Ireland, the Gulf and NATO operations in the former Yugoslavia. Uniforms, badges, medals, videos.

Opening Times: Apr to Sep Tue to Fri 10:30-12:30 13:30-16:30, Sat & Sun 14:00-17:00. Oct to Mar Tue to Fri 10:30-12:30 13:30-16:30. Closed Xmas to end Jan.   Admission: Free.
Location: 15 minute walk from bus and railway station, on A286 Chichester to Midhurst road.
Map Ref: 7

Tangmere Military Aviation Museum

Tangmere, Chichester PO20 6ES   Tel: 01243 775223   Fax: 01243 789490
Email: admin@tangmere-museum.org.uk   Web: www.tangmere-museum.org.uk

The museum tells the story of military flying from the earliest days to the present time with special emphasis on the air war over southern England 1939-45.

Opening Times: Feb & Nov daily 10:00-16:30, Mar to Oct daily 10:00-17:30.   Admission: Adult £4.00, Child £1.50, OAP £3.00, Family £9.50.   Location: Three miles east of Chichester off A27.

Map Ref: 9

DITCHLING *W Sussex*

Ditchling Museum

Church Lane, Ditchling BN6 8TB   Tel / Fax: 01273 844744   Email: info@ditchling-museum.com   Web: www.ditchling-museum.com

A history of a remarkable village and its community of twentieth century artists and craftsmen, including Eric Gil - stonecarver, Edward Johnston - calligrapher, Ethel Mairet - weaver and many others. Guided tours/walks, gift shop, café, small garden.

Opening Times: Mid Feb to 24 Dec Tue to Sat & BH 10:30-17:00 Sun 14:00-17:00.
Admission: Adult £2.50, Child 50p, Concession £2.00, Group £2.00.   Location: In the heart of the village, parking in village. Hassocks Station five minute taxi ride.   Map Ref: 11

EASTBOURNE *E Sussex*

Filching Manor & Motor Museum & Karting Track Campbell Circuit

Filching Manor, Filching, Nr Polegate, Eastbourne BN26 5QA   Tel: 01323 487838

Set in 15th century Wealden Hall House. 100 top historic cars, motorcycles, boats and aircraft, including Sir Malcolm Campbell's 1937 Bluebird and many classics.

Opening Times: By prior appointment for groups of 10 or more only.   Admission: Adult £5.00, Child/OAP £3.50.   Location: One mile from A22 and A27 at Polegate. Brown tourist board signs A22 and A259 Friston.   Map Ref: 12

"How We Lived Then" Museum of Shops

20 Cornfield Terrace, Eastbourne BN21 4NS   Tel: 01323 737143

Visit the famous south coast museum of shops, see over 100,000 exhibits, collected during the past 40 years, on four floors of old shops, room-settings and displays.

Opening Times: Daily 10:00-17:00. Closed Xmas.   Admission: Adult £3.00, Child £2.00, Under 5s Free, OAP £2.50. Group rates available.   Location: Just off seafront, near town centre.

Map Ref: 12

Museum of the Royal National Lifeboat Institution

King Edward Parade, Eastbourne BN21 4BY   Tel: 01323 730717

Showing the history of Eastbourne lifeboats from 1824. Many photos of past crews and of epic rescues. Various items of lifeboat memorabilia. A small selection of lifeboat models.

Opening Times: 25 Mar to 28 Apr & 30 Sep to end Dec daily 10:00-16:00. 29 Apr to 29 Sep daily 10:00-17:00.   Admission: Free.   Location: On seafront, at The Wish Tower.   Map Ref: 12

Queens Royal Irish Hussars Museum

c/o Sussex Combined Services Msum, Redoubt Fortress,Royal Parade, Eastbourne BN22 7AQ
Tel: 01323 410300

Tracing history of cavalry regiments who took part in the Charge of the Light Brigade, up to their involvement in the Gulf War. Collections include rare uniforms.

Opening Times: Apr to 5 Nov 09:45-17:30.   Admission: £1.60.   Location: Half a mile east of pier on seafront.   Map Ref: 12

Royal Sussex Regiment Museum
c/o Sussex Combined Services Musm, Redoubt Fortress, Royal Parade, Eastbourne BN22 7AQ
Tel: 01323 410300

Collections of local infantry regiment, including uniforms, medals, regimental silver and a German General's staff car.

Opening Times: Apr to 5 Nov 09:45-17:30. Admission: £1.60. Location: Half a mile east of pier on seafront.
Map Ref: 12

Sussex Combined Services Museums & Redoubt Fortress
Royal Parade, Eastbourne BN22 7AQ Tel: 01323 410300

The history of the Army, Navy and RAF in the Sussex area. Displays include uniforms and medals, set in a Napoleonic fortress.

Opening Times: Apr to 5 Nov 09:45-17:30. Admission: £1.60.
Map Ref: 12

Towner Art Gallery & Local Museum
High Street, Old Town, Eastbourne BN20 8BB Tel: 01323 417961/info 411688 Fax: 01323 468182 Email: townergallery@eastbourne.gov.uk Web: www.eastbourne.gov.uk

Gallery: collection of mainly 19th and 20th century British art. Museum: history of Eastbourne from pre-history to the present day. Guided tours by arrangement only.

Opening Times: Nov to Mar Tue to Sat 12:00-16:00, Apr to Oct Tue to Sat 12:00-17:00, Sun & BH Mon 14:00-17:00. Closed Good Friday 24-27 Dec, New Years Day & Mon. Admission: Free (except for some special exhibitions). Location: In Old Town, Manor Gardens, approx 15 minute walk from station.
Map Ref: 12

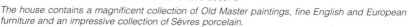
ETCHINGHAM *E Sussex*

Bateman's (Kiplings House)
Burwash, Etchingham TN19 7DS Tel: 01435 882302 Fax: 01435 882811
Email: kbaxxx@smtp.ntrust.org.uk Web: www.nationaltrust.org.uk

A 17th century Ironmaster's house, which was the former home of Rudyard Kipling. This family house with plenty of atmosphere nestles in the beautiful Sussex countryside. A working water mill, gardens and Kipling's Rolls Royce all enhance this house's appeal. Each season this house hosts concerts and events, one of the most popular being 'Last Night of the Proms', when over 4000 people gather.

Bateman's (Kiplings House)

Opening Times: 23 Mar to 29 Sep Sat to Wed 11:00-17:30. Admission: Adult £5.20, Child £2.60, Group £4.40, Family £13.00. Location: Etchingham Station three miles.
Map Ref: 13

FIRLE *E Sussex*

Firle Place
Firle BN8 6LP Tel: 01273 858567 Fax: 01273 858570

The house contains a magnificent collection of Old Master paintings, fine English and European furniture and an impressive collection of Sèvres porcelain.

Opening Times: 12 May to 29 Sep Wed, Thu, Sun & BH 13:45-16:15. Admission: Adult £5.00, Child £2.50, OAP £4.50. Location: Four miles south of Lewes.
Map Ref: 14

HAILSHAM *E Sussex*

Michelham Priory & Gardens
Upper Dicker, Hailsham BN27 3QS Tel: 01323 844224 Fax: 01323 844030
Email: pro@sussexpast.co.uk Web: www.sussexpast.co.uk

With nearly 800 years of history on display, Michelham Priory offers visitors a wealth of fascinating exhibitions inside and out. Of particular interest are the remains of a former Augustinian Priory that evolved into a splendid Tudor mansion, a 14th century gatehouse, a rope museum, a working watermill and England's longest water-filled Medieval moat.

Opening Times: 1 Mar to 31 Oct Wed to Sun 10:30 Closing times Mar & Oct 16:00, Apr to Jul & Sep 17:00, Aug 17:30. Also open daily Aug and BH. Admission: Adult £4.80 Child £2.50 Concession £4.20 Family £12.20 Disabled £2.40. Location: At Upper Dicker, approx two miles west of Hailsham and eight miles north-west of Eastbourne.
Map Ref: 15

Sussex

Fishermans Museum

Rock-a-Nore Road, Hastings TN34 3DW   Tel: 01424 461446

Model of a Hastings Lugger

Opened as a museum in 1956, the centrepiece is the 'Enterprise' one of the last Hastings sailing luggers (worked 1912-1954). Exhibits also include model ships and boats, fishing gear, historic paintings and photographs illustrating the local fishing industry. Outside are four other types of Hastings fishing boats and some examples of the unique net shops.

Opening Times: Apr to Oct daily 10:00-17:00. Nov to Mar daily 11:00-16:00. Closed Xmas. Admission: Free. Donations welcome. Location: In and around Old Fishermen's Church, on beach at eastern end of Hastings Old Town.   Map Ref: 16

Hastings Museum & Art Gallery

Bohemia Road, Hastings TN34 1ET   Tel: 01424 781155   Fax: 01424 781165
Email: vwilliams@hastings.gov.uk   Web: museum@hastings.gov.uk

Paintings, ceramics, fossils, native Americans, special features on John Logie Baird, Robert Tressell and Grey Owl, exhibitions of contemporary art. The Durbar Hall was built as part of an Indian Palace in 1886.

Opening Times: Mon to Sat 10:00-17:00, Sun 14:00-17:00. Admission: Free. Location: Ten minute walk from town centre and railway station.   Map Ref: 16

Museum of Local History

Old Town Hall, High Street, Hastings TN34 1EW   Tel: 01424 781166
Email: vwilliams@hastings.gov.uk   Web: oldtownmuseum@hastings.gov.uk

A walk back in time through the history of Hastings Old Town from the 1960s to pre-history. Subjects covered include seaside entertainment, the Napoleonic Garrison, smuggling, the Armada and the Cinque Ports.

Opening Times: Apr to Sep Mon to Sun 10:00-17:00, Oct to Mar Mon to Sun 11:00-16:00. Admission: Free.   Map Ref: 16

Shipwreck Heritage Centre

Rock-a-Nore Road, Hastings TN34 3DW   Tel / Fax: 01424 437452

Displayed are the remains of a Roman ship, the complete hull of a Victorian river barge and many relics from a 1749 Dutch merchant ship whose wreck is visible off St Leonards at low tide.

Opening Times: Mar to Oct daily 10:30-17:00, Nov to Feb daily 11:00-16:00. Admission: Suggested donation Adult £1.00. Guided Tours for Groups £1.00 per person.   Map Ref: 16

Horsham Museum

Causeway Close, 9 The Causeway, Horsham RH12 1HE   Tel: 01403 254959
Email: museum@horsham.gov.uk

Set in a timber framed Medieval house with over 20 galleries, two gardens, the museum displays costume, dinosaur bones, bicycles, toys, packaging, art and crafts as well as books by Shelley, the poet.

Opening Times: Mon to Sat (excluding BH & Sun) 10:00-17:00. Admission: Free.
Location: Near town centre, in historic street leading to Parish Church.   Map Ref: 17

Hove Museum & Art Gallery

19 New Church Road, Hove BN3 4AB   Tel: 01273 290200   Fax: 01273 292827
Web: www.museums.brighton-hove.gov.uk

Hove Museum & Art Gallery will be closed until August 2002 due to major redevelopment works. New features will include the installation of a lift, new displays of toys, film and fine art.

Opening Times: For information on opening times telephone (01273) 290200.
Admission: Free. Location: 20 minutes bus ride from town centre, five minute walk from Hove Station.   Map Ref: 18

Sussex

West Blatchington Windmill

Holmes Avenue, Hove BN3 7LE   Tel: 01273 776017   Web: www.museums.brighton-hove.gov.uk

Dating from the 1820s, this grade II listed building still has the original mill workings in place over five floors. Discover how grain is turned into flour in a traditional windmill.

Opening Times: May to Sep Sun & BH only 14:30-17:00, groups can be taken around at other times of the year by arrangement.   Admission: Adult 70p, Child 30p.   Location: Ten minute walk from Aldrington Station, 30 minutes bus ride from town centre. Buses 5A & 5B

Map Ref: 18

LEWES *E Sussex*

Anne of Cleves Museum

52 Southover High Street, Lewes BN7 1JA   Tel: 01273 474610   Email: pro@sussexpast.co.uk   Web: www.sussexpast.co.uk

The house given to Anne by Henry VIII as part of their d...rce settlement. See the old kitchen and the oak furnished main chamber, and investigate the history of the Sussex iron industry.

Opening Times: Jan & Feb, Nov & Dec Tue to Sat 10:00-17:00. Mar to Oct Mon to Sat 10:00-17:00, Sun 12:00-17:00. Closed Xmas.   Admission: Adult £2.80 Child £1.40 Concession £2.50 Family £7.00.   Location: Near town centre, about ten minutes walk from Lewes Castle and eight minutes walk from Lewes Railway Station. Bus stops nearby.   Map Ref: 19

Lewes Castle & Barbican House Museum

169 High Street, Lewes BN7 1YE   Tel: 01273 405739   Fax: 01273 486990   Email: pro@sussexpast.co.uk   Web: www.sussexpast.co.uk

Explore the Castle built soon after the Conquest of 1066 and see the spectacular views from the top. Next door Barbican House Museum displays a range of exhibitions plotting the history of the area along with a sound and light show based around a scale town model, and an interactive touch-screen computer.

Opening Times: Mon to Sat 10:00-17:30 Sun & BH 11:00-17:30. Closed Mon in Jan & Xmas.   Admission: Adult £4.20 Child £2.10 Concession £3.70 Family £11.40.   Location: In town centre, ten minutes walk from bus and railway stations.   Map Ref: 19

LITTLEHAMPTON *W Sussex*

Littlehampton Museum

Manor House, Church Street, Littlehampton BN17 5EP   Tel: 01903 738100   Fax: 01903 731690   Email: itc@arun.gov.uk

Varied collection of archaeology, social history artefacts and art relating to the Littlehampton area. Also, special displays of photographic and maritime history - over 200 ship models on show!

Opening Times: Tue to Sat 10:30-16:30.   Admission: Free.   Location: 50 metres from High Street, seven minutes walk from train.   Map Ref: 20

NEWHAVEN *E Sussex*

Newhaven Fort

Fort Road, Newhaven BN9 9DS   Tel: 01273 517622   Fax: 01273 512059   Email: enquiries@newhavenfort.org.uk   Web: www.newhavenfort.org.uk

Victorian clifftop fortress commanding superb views that really brings history to life. Experience what life was like in the First and Second World Wars, through exciting life size and interactive exhibitions.

Opening Times: 23 Mar to 3 Nov daily 10:30-18:00.   Admission: Adult £4.75, Child £3.25, OAP £4.25, Family £14.00.   Location: One mile from Newhaven Town Centre.   Map Ref: 21

Planet Earth Museum & Sussex History Trail

Paradise Park, Avis Road, Newhaven BN9 0DH Tel: 01273 512123
Fax: 01273 616005 Email: enquiries@paradisepark.co.uk Web: paradisepark.co.uk

Iguanodon Bridge

Planet Earth is one of the finest museums of its type in the country with life size moving dinosaurs, interactive displays and a spectacular collection of fossils, minerals and crystals. Handcrafted models of Sussex landmarks are the setting for the Sussex History Trail which is set in beautiful themed gardens.

Opening Times: Daily 10:00-18:00. Admission: Adult £4.99, Child £3.99, Family £16.99. Group rates available. Location: Signposted from A26 and A259. Short walk from Newhaven Railway Station and Denton Corner bus stop. Map Ref: 21

PETWORTH W Sussex

Petworth House
Petworth GU28 0AE Tel: 01798 342207

View of Petworth House taken from the Deer Park

Enjoy the National Trust's finest painting and sculpture collection including works by Van Dyck, Reynolds, Blake and Turner displayed in a magnificent 17th century mansion set in a beautiful deerpark landscaped by 'Capability' Brown. New for 2002: See the newly restored Carved Room containing Grinling Gibbons' finest limewood carvings, fine furniture, sculpture and paintings by JMW Turner including two of Petworth Park.

Opening Times: 23 Mar to 3 Nov Sat to Wed 11:00-17:30. Admission: Adult £7.00, Child £4.00, Family £18.00. National Trust Members Free.
Location: Located in the centre of Petworth. Map Ref: 22

PORTSLADE-BY-SEA E Sussex

Foredown Tower
Foredown Road, Portslade-by-Sea BN41 2EW Tel / Fax: 01273 292092
Email: foredown.tower@brighton-hove.gov.uk Web: www.museums.brighton-hove.gov.uk

A converted Edwardian water tower, home to the only operational 'camera obscura' in the south east with outstanding views over the surrounding countryside.

Opening Times: Thu to Sun & BH 10:00-17:00. Closed 24 Dec - 3 Jan (inc). Groups can visit on other days by prior arrangement. Admission: Adult £2.30, Child £1.50, Group (20+) £1.75. Prices valid until 31 Mar 2002. Location: 30 minute bus ride from town centre. Buses 6 & 6A.
Map Ref: 23

PULBOROUGH W Sussex

Bignor Roman Villa
Bignor, Pulborough RH20 1PH Tel / Fax: 01798 869259
Email: bignorromanvilla@care4free.net

All under cover. Discovered 1811. Some of the finest mosaics in Great Britain including Venus and Cupid Gladiators, Medusa and Garymere. Remains of Hypocaust system. Guided tours must be pre-booked.

Opening Times: Mar to Apr Tue to Sun & BH 10:00-17:00, May daily 10:00-17:00, Jun to Sep daily 10:00-18:00, Oct daily 10:00-17:00. Admission: Adult £3.65, Child £1.55, OAP £2.60. Group rates available. Location: Six miles north of Arundel on A29. Six miles from Petworth A285. Map Ref: 24

www.tomorrows.co.uk
Full information on our collection of travel guides and secure store

Sussex

RYE *E Sussex*

Rye Art Gallery

Ockman Lane, East Street, Rye TN31 7JY   Tel: 01797 223218/222433   Fax: 01797 225376

Two buildings linked by a courtyard. Easton Rooms holds a programme of exhibitions by contemporary artists and craftsmen. Stormant Studio holds the permanent collection of over 400 pieces shown in rotation together with in-house exhibitions.

Opening Times: Daily 10:30-13:00 14:00-17:00. Admission: Free. Location: High Street location.   Map Ref: 25

Rye Castle Museum

3 East Street, Rye TN31 7JY   Tel: 01797 226728

Rye 18th century fire engine, Rye Pottery, uniforms, smuggling items, paintings, etc. All about Rye's long and illustrious history.

Opening Times: Both sites - Apr to Oct Thu to Mon 10:30-13:00 14:00-17:00. Ypres Tower - Nov to Mar Sat & Sun 10:30-15:30. Closed 13:00-14:00 Admission: Both sites Adult £2.90, Child £1.50, Concession £2.00, Family £5.90. Single site Adult £1.90, Child £1.00, Concession £1.50, Family £4.50. Location: In town centre.   Map Ref: 25

SEAFORD *E Sussex*

Seaford Museum of Local History

c/o Tourist Information Centre, 25 Clinton Place, Seaford BN25 1NP   Tel: 01323 898222
Email: museumseaford@tinyonline.co.uk   Web: www.seafordmuseum.org

A delightful walk through recent history with tableaux of Victorian life and collections of household and office equipment.

Opening Times: Summer: Sun & BH 11:00-13:00 14:30-16:30. Wed & Sat 14:30-16:30. Winter: Sun & BH 11:00-13:00 14:00-16:00. Closed Xmas. Admission: Adult £1.00, Concession 50p. Location: On the east end of the seafront.   Map Ref: 26

STEYNING *W Sussex*

Steyning Museum

Church Street, Steyning BN44 3YB   Tel: 01903 813333

The museum charts the fluctuations in Steyning's fortunes over 2000 years. Its people, buildings, railway and 400 year old school occupy centre stage in the displays. Temporary exhibitions, displays for children and research facilities.

Opening Times: Tue, Wed, Fri, Sat & Sun PM only. Summer: 10:30-12:30 14:30-16:30, winter: 10:30-12:30 14:30-16:00. BH & other days by appointment. Admission: Free. Location: Near town centre, four minute walk.   Map Ref: 27

UCKFIELD *E Sussex*

Bluebell Railway

Sheffield Park Station, Sheffield Park, Uckfield TN22 3QL   Tel: 01825 720800
Fax: 01825 7720804   Web: www.bluebell-railway.co.uk

USA Class 0-6-0 Tank No 30064

The Bluebell Railway is a working steam heritage museum. Large collection of working locomotives travel 18 mile round trip through Sussex countryside. Small, detailed collection of railway memorabilia, stations from Victorian, 1930s and 1950s style.

Opening Times: Sheffield Park Station - Trains run daily Apr to Sep & school holidays 10:00-17:00. Closed Xmas. Admission: Adult £8.00, Child £4.00, OAP £6.40, Family £21.50. Includes all-day travel. Location: Sheffield Park Station - access from East Grinstead to Kingscote via special bus service. A275 East Grinstead / Lewes road, two miles north junction with A272   Map Ref: 28

Sussex

Priest House

North Lane, West Hoathly RH19 4PP   Tel: 01342 810479   Email: pro@sussexpast.co.uk
Web: www.sussexpast.co.uk

Built in the 15th century, The Priest House has been open as a museum since 1908. Its furnished rooms contain a fascinating array of 17th and 18th century domestic furniture, needlework and household items. Outside a formal herb garden contains over 150 culinary, medicinal and household herbs.

Opening Times: Mar to Oct Mon to Sat 11:00-17:30 Sun 14:00-17:30.   Admission: Adult £2.60 Child £1.30 Concession £2.30.   Location: In centre of village of West Hoathly.   Map Ref: 29

Worthing Museum & Art Gallery

Chapel Road, Worthing BN11 1HP   Tel: 01903 239999   Fax: 01903 236277
Email: museum@worthing.gov.uk   Web: www.worthing.gov.uk

Work by stone carver Erik Stanford

You're guaranteed a warm welcome at Worthing Museum and Art Gallery. This beautiful Edwardian building is home to a fascinating collection of toys, stunning costume, art and decorative art as well as local history and archaeology. There's so much to see that one visit just won't be enough. You'll find a Victorian nursery, wonderful treasures in the Archaeology Gallery, crinolines and platform shoes in the Costume Galleries and toys from your childhood in the foyer. If that wasn't enough the Museum staff organise a variety of temporary exhibitions throughout the year in the Art Gallery. The Studio, the Norwood Gallery and the Sculpture Garden feature work by local, national and international artists. At least one exhibition a year is based on the Museum's own collections and there are workshops, demonstrations and events for visitors of all ages planned throughout year. To help you move freely around there are ramps and a lift in the building for wheelchair and pushchairs. The Museum also has great toilets and a baby changing room. The Museum Shop is also worth a visit.

The Museum Shop is stocked with a variety of inexpensive goodies!

Opening Times: Mon to Sat 10:00-17:00. Closed Sun & some BH.   Admission: Free.
Location: In town centre, ten minute walk from Worthing Central Railway Station.   Map Ref: 30

wickshire is the quintessential English county in a region rich in history and blessed with some
he country's loveliest scenery. Warwick was rebuilt following a disastrous fire in 1694 and
sesses a wondrous castle and some fine buildings. Stratford-upon-Avon is a magnet to the
usands who flock to see Shakespeare's birthplace. Birmingham dominates the West Midlands.

re is an interesting selection of quality museums and galleries throughout the region.

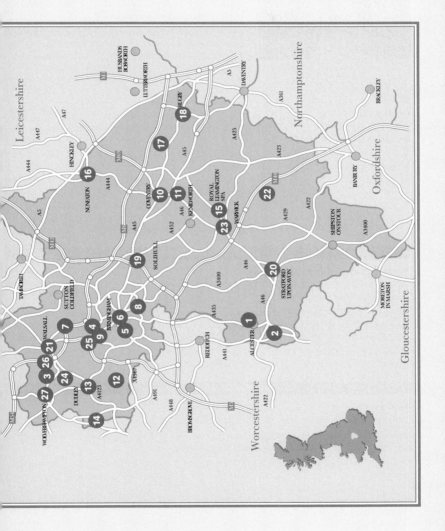

The Red Map References should be used to locate Museums etc on the pages that follow

The Red Map References should be used to locate B & B properties on the pages that follow
The Green Map References provide the location of places to visit detailed above

Warwickshire & West Midlands

Coughton Court

♿ ● 🐕 ◑ 🚌

Alcester B49 5JA Tel: 01789 400777 Fax: 01789 765544
Email: andrew@throckmortons.co.uk Web: www.coughtoncourt.co.uk

Coughton Court - The Courtyard from the East.
Tudor Gatehouse c.1530

Home of Throckmorton family since 1530. Close connections with the Gunpowder Plot. Still of Roman Catholic faith with exhibitions/material on recusancy and Catholic emancipation. Excellent collection of family portraits from Tudor times to present day plus family memorabilia, furniture, porcelain and books.

Opening Times: 23 Mar to Sep Wed to Sun, BH Mon & Tue and Tue in Jul & Aug 11:30-17:00. Oct Sat & Sun 11:30-17:00. Closed Good Friday & Sat 22 Jun & 20 Jul. Admission: House & Garden: Adult £9.45, Child £4.75, Under 5s Free. Location: Two miles north of Alcester on A435. Map Ref: 1

Ragley Hall

♿ ● 🐕 🚌

Alcester B49 5NJ Tel: 01789 762090 Fax: 01789 764791 Email: info@ragleyhall.com
Web: www.ragleyhall.com

Built in 1680 by Robert Hooke, Ragley has England's finest Baroque plasterwork by James Gibbs, 1750. Wood carvings by Grinling Gibbons, family portraits by Sir Joshua Reynolds. Sheraton and Louis XVI furniture and Minton, Copeland and Meissen china amongst others. 20th century mural by Graham Rust completed 1969-1983.

Opening Times: 28 Mar to 29 Sep Thu to Sun 12:00-17:00, Park & Gardens 10:00-18:00 (last entry at 16:30). Admission: Adult £6.00, Child £4.50, OAP £5.00, Family £22.00 (2 adults and 4 children). Location: Two miles south west of Alcester, off the A46/A435. Map Ref: 2

Bilston Craft Gallery & Museum

♿ ● 🚌

Mount Pleasant, Bilston WV14 7LU Tel: 01902 552507 Fax: 01902 552504
Web: www.wolverhamptonart.org.uk

The gallery hosts an exciting programme of contemporary craft exhibitions with workshops and events. Craftplay, an activity room for pre-school children is open for groups by appointment and in summer the sculpture gardens are a popular attraction.

Opening Times: Tue to Fri 10:00-16:00. Sat 11:00-16:00. Admission: Free. Location: Four miles from Wolverhampton and five minutes from Bilston Metro Stop. Map Ref: 3

Aston Hall

🐦 🐕 🚌

Trinity Road, Aston, Birmingham B6 6JD Tel: 0121 327 0062 Web: www.bmag.org.uk

One of the last great houses to be built in a Jacobean style, Aston Hall hosts a fine collection of paintings, textiles and furniture and a 136ft Long Gallery.

Opening Times: Apr to Oct Tue to Fri 13:00-16:00, Sat & Sun 12:00-16:00. Closed Mon except BH. Admission: Free. Location: Three miles from city centre, near junction 6 off M6.
Map Ref: 4

Barber Institute of Fine Arts

🐦 ♿ ● 🐕 🚌

University of Birmingham, Edgbaston, Birmingham B15 2TS Tel: 0121 4147333 Fax: 0121 4143370 Email: info@barber.org.uk Web: www.barber.org.uk

One of the finest small art galleries in the world housing an outstanding collection of Old Master and Modern paintings, including masterpieces by Rubens, Murillo, Rossetti, Monet and Magritte.

Opening Times: Mon to Sat 10:00-17:00, Sun 14:00-17:00. Admission: Free. Location: On University of Birmingham Campus, three miles south of city centre. Map Ref: 5

Birmingham Museum
and Art Gallery

Birmingham Museum and Art Gallery

Chamberlain Square, Birmingham B3 3DH   Tel: 0121 303 2834
Fax: 0121 303 1394   Email: bmag_enquiries@birmingham.gov.uk
Web: www.bmag.org.uk

Home to the largest collection of Pre-Raphaelite art in Europe, Birmingham Museum & Art Gallery also host a fine collection of 18th and 19th century art, silver, sculpture, ceramics and archeology. New for this year, the Waterhall Gallery of modern art and local history galleries. Gas Hall has a range of temporary exhibitions across the year.

Opening Times: Mon to Thur & Sat 10:00-17:00, Fri 10:30-17:00, Sun 12:30-17:00. Closed Xmas & New Year. Admission: Free - voluntary contribution. Location: Five minutes from New Street and Snow Hill Stations. Short walk from any city centre bus stop.
Map Ref: 6

Bishop Asbury Cottage

Newton Road, Great Barr, Birmingham B43 6HN   Tel: 0121 553 0759   Fax: 0121 525 5167

18th century furniture and artefacts connected with Bishop Frances Asbury, the first Methodist Bishop of America.

Opening Times: Open by appointment only, two open days a year. Admission: Groups £2.50 per person (min charge £25.00 per group). Location: On the A4041, Newton Road. Parking at Maltshovel Public House next door.
Map Ref: 7

Ikon Gallery

1 Oozells Square, Brindleyplace, Birmingham B1 2HS   Tel: 0121 248 0708   Fax: 0121 248 0709   Email: art@ikon-gallery.co.uk
Web: www.ikon-gallery.co.uk

Changing exhibitions of contemporary art, no collection.

Opening Times: Tue to Sun & BH Mon 11:00-18:00. Closed Mon and during installation of exhibitions. Admission: Free. Location: Central Birmingham, 15 minute walk from all railway stations.
Map Ref: 6

Ikon Gallery, photo courtesy Argent, Brindley Place

Museum of the Jewellery Quarter

75/79 Vyse Street, Hockley, Birmingham B18 6HA   Tel: 0121 554 3598
Email: 6mag_enquiries@birmingham.gov.uk   Web: www.bmag.org.uk

A perfectly preserved jewellery workshop little changed since the early part of this century. The Museum tells the story of jewellery making in Birmingham, through guided tours and demonstrations.

Opening Times: Mon to Fri 10:00-16:00, Sat 11:00-17:00. Close Sun. Admission: Adult £2.50, Concession £2.00. Location: Short bus ride from city centre. Jewellery Quarter Railway Station five minutes away.
Map Ref: 6

Sarehole Mill

Cole bank Road, Hall Green, Birmingham B13 0BD   Tel: 0121 777 6612
Email: 6mag_enquiries@birmingham.gov.uk   Web: www.bmag.org.uk

Sarehole is the only surviving example of the sixty or so watermills that once existed in Birmingham. It was also the childhood haunt of JRR Tolkien and inspiration for the mill in 'The Hobbit'.

Opening Times: Easter to Oct Tue to Fri 13:00-16:00, Sat & Sun 12:00-16:00. Closed Mon except BH. Admission: Free. Location: Five miles from city centre off A34. 15 minutes from Hall Green Station or a short walk from the 11A/11C bus stop.
Map Ref: 8

Soho House   🚻 ❂ 🗐

Soho Avenue, Handsworth, Birmingham B18 5LB   Tel: 0121 554 9122   Fax: 0121 554 5929
Email: 6mag_enquiries@birmingham.co.uk   Web: www.bmag.org.uk

Soho House was Matthew Boulton's 18th century home, restored with original items from the house. You can find out about this fascinating inventor and the great thinkers that met at the house - the Lunar Society.

Opening Times: Tue to Sat 10:00-17:00, Sun 12:00-17:00. Closes Mon except BH.
Admission: Adult £2.50, Child £2.00.   Location: Ten minutes from city centre by bus or train.
Ring for more details.   Map Ref: 9

Tyseley Locomotive Works   ❂ 🗐 🚂

670 Warwick Road, Tyseley, Birmingham B11 2HL   Tel: 0121 707 4696   Fax: 0121 764 4645
Email: office@vintagetrains.co.uk   Web: www.vintagetrains.co.uk

Tyseley Locomotive Works is the home of Vintage Trains, operating the steam-hauled Shakespeare Express between Birmingham and Stratford-upon-Avon on summer Sundays, and excursions nationwide, using restored steam locomotives and rolling stock.

Opening Times: Sat, Sun & BH 10:00-16:00.   Admission: Adult £2.50, Children Under 5s Free, Concession £1.25.   Location: Three miles south east of Birmingham City Centre, ten minutes walk from Tyseley Station.   Map Ref: 8

COVENTRY *Warwicks*

Coventry Toy Museum

Whitfriars Gate, Much Park Street, Coventry CV1 2LT   Tel: 024 7622 7560

A collection of toys of every description housed in a 14th century monastery gatehouse.

Opening Times: daily 13:00-17:00   Admission: Adult £1.50, Child/OAP £1.00.
Location: Coventry City Centre.   Map Ref: 10

Herbert Art Gallery & Museum   🚻 ❂ 🗐

Jordan Well, Coventry CV1 5QP   Tel: 024 7683 2565   Fax: 024 7683 2410
Email: artsandheritage@coventry.gov.uk   Web: www.coventrymuseum.org.uk 

Jacquard Loom dating from 1845 in Godiva City Exhibition

The Herbert Art Gallery and Museum is situated in the heart of Coventry City Centre a couple of miles walk away from Coventry Cathedral. The award winning Godiva City exhibition tells the story of the city from before Lady Godiva to the present. The rest of the Gallery is used for temporary exhibitions using objects from the museum collections and provided by other organisations and individuals. Items from the Museum's permanent collection of Lady Godiva paintings and drawings and sketches for Graham Sutherland's Cathedral tapestry are invariably on display. The collections cover visual arts, natural history, archaeology, industrial and social history.

Opening Times: Mon to Sat 10:00-17:30, Sun 12:00-17:00. Admission: Free. Location: City centre near Tourist Information Centre and Coventry Cathedral.

Coventry's 20th Century Industries in Godiva City Exhibition

Map Ref: 10

Jaguar Daimler Heritage Trust   ⌦ 🚻 ❂ 🗐 🅿 🚂

Jaguar Cars, Browns Lane, Coventry CV5 9DR   Tel: 024 76402121

Display of 30+ Jaguars, collection totals 130+ available to view if required. Archive housing original factory records and photographic collection and picture gallery.

Opening Times: Mon to Fri 08:30-16:45 and last Sun of month 10:00-16:00   Admission: Free.
Location: On bus route from city centre, good access to motorways.   Map Ref: 10

Warwickshire & West Midlands

Lunt Roman Fort

Coventry Road, Baginton, Coventry   Tel: 024 7683 2381   Fax: 024 7683 2410
Email: artsandheritage@coventry.gov.uk   Web: www.coventrymuseum.org.uk

Once inhabited by the Roman Army, this ancient site includes the Granney building which contains a museum of Roman Life with archaelogical finds.

Opening Times: 30 Mar to 27 Oct Sat, Sun & BH. 1 Jun to 9 Jun daily except Wed. 20 Jul to 1 Sep daily except Wed. All 10:00-17:00.   Admission: Adult £2.00, Concession £1.00.
Location: Baginton Village is on the south side of Coventry, just off the A45 and A46. The fort is situated off the Coventry Road.   Map Ref: 11

Museum of British Road Transport

St Agnes Lane, Hales Street, Coventry CV1 1PN   Tel: 024 7683 2425   Fax: 024 7683 2465
Email: museum@mbrt.co.uk   Web: www.mbrt.co.uk

Largest collection of British road transport in the world. Designated as a collection of National Importance with 200 cars and commercial vehicles, 200 cycles and 90 motorcycles and Thrust 2 and Thrust SSC land speed record cars.

Opening Times: Daily 10:00-17:00. Closed 24-26 Dec.   Admission: Free.   Location: Town centre, one minute walk from bus station, ten minutes from train station.   Map Ref: 10

Priory Visitor Centre

Priory Gardens, Coventry CV1 5EX   Tel: 024 7655 2242   Fax: 024 7683 2410
Email: artsandheritage@coventry.gov.uk   Web: www.coventrymuseum.org.uk

On the site of Coventry's medieval Priory and Cathedral. It tells the story of the site from the time of Lady Godiva to the Dissolution by King Henry VIII using archaeological finds from ancient excavations.

Opening Times: Mon to Sat 10:00-17:30, Sun 12:00-16:00.   Admission: Free.   Location: In city centre, near Holy Trinity Church and Coventry Cathedral.   Map Ref: 10

St Mary's Guildhall

Bayley Lane, Coventry   Tel: 024 7683 2381   Fax: 024 7683 2410
Email: artsandheritage@coventry.gov.uk   Web: www.coventrymuseum.org.uk

St Mary's Guildhall is one of the finest surviving Medieval Guildhalls in England. It dates from the 1340s and includes the imposing Great Hall with its stained glass windows and a Tournai tapestry dated 1500.

Opening Times: Easter to end Sep Sun to Thu 10:00-16:00.   Admission: Free.   Location: City centre, near Coventry Cathedral.   Map Ref: 10

CRADLEY HEATH *W Midlands*

Haden Hill House

Off Barrs Road, Cradley Heath   Tel: 01384 569444

A Victorian furnished house with a collection of social history relating to the borough of Sandwell.

Opening Times: Mon to Thu 10:00-17:00, Fri 10:00-16:30, Sat & Sun 13:00-17:00
Admission: Free   Location: Off Barrs Road, Cradley Heath near the Leisure Centre
                                                                        Map Ref: 12

Museums, Galleries, Historic Houses & Sites

Please let us know of any collections that are not listed in this guide that you feel should be listed. E-mail us on *editor@tomorrows.co.uk* or return the Report Form on page 448

Warwickshire & West Midlands

Black Country Living Museum

Tipton Road, Dudley DY1 4SQ   Tel: 0121 557 9643   Fax: 0121 557 4242
Email: info@bclm.co.uk   Web: www.bclm.co.uk

Policeman

The Black Country Museum was established in 1975 to collect, preserve research and display items relating to the social and industrial history of the Black Country. In 2002 it has a collection of well over 30,000 items, ranging from hand made nails to whole buildings. Together, the mine, the foundry and the many houses, shops and workshops rebuilt on its 26 acre site represent the Black Country when it was the heart of industrial Britain. Much of this large collection consists of the fixtures and fittings that make these buildings complete and accurate to the last detail, but in addition, Black Country products, both past and present, are continually being added to the collection. The most recent addition is a representative collection of cars and motorcycles made in Wolverhampton, an important centre of the automotive industry in the 1920s and 30s. The modern exhibition halls,

St. James's School

opened in 2000, display selections of Black Country products. The centrepiece is a permanent display of items that defined the area across the world. Chain and anchor made in Netherton for the great ocean liners, world class saddles made in Walsall, crystal glass made in Stourbridge and hardware made in Cradley Heath and exported throughout the British Empire.

Opening Times: Mar to Oct daily 10:00-17:00, Nov to Feb Wed to Sun 10:00-16:00.
Admission: Adult £8.25, Child £4.75, OAP £7.25, Family (2 adults and 3 children) £22.50.
Location: Three miles from junction 2 of the M5, six miles from junction 10 of the M6, ten miles from Birmingham City Centre.   Map Ref: 13

Dudley Museum & Art Gallery

St James's Road, Dudley DY1 1HU   Tel: 01384 815575   Fax: 01384 815576
Web: www.dudley.gov.uk

Geological gallery with definitive collection of local silurian and carboniferous fossils. Brooke Robinson museum of European paintings, furniture and ceramics. Temporary exhibitions throughout the year.

Opening Times: Mon to Sat 10:00-16:00. Closed BH Mon.   Admission: Free.   Location: Town centre.   Map Ref: 13

Broadfield House Glass Museum

Compton Drive, Kingswinford DY6 9NS   Tel: 01384 812745   Fax: 01384 812746
Email: glass.pls@mbc.dudley.gov.uk   Web: www.dudley.gov.uk

Situated in the historic glass quarter, Broadfield House celebrates the art of glassmaking. Glass artists can be watched in the studio and attractive gifts bought from the shop.

Opening Times: Tue to Sun 14:00-17:00, BH Mon 12:00-17:00.   Admission: Free.
Location: Near town centre, on main bus route.   Map Ref: 14

Leamington Spa Art Gallery & Museum, Royal Pump Rooms

The Parade, Leamington Spa CV32 4AA   Tel: 01926 742700

Award winning art gallery and museum with services on offer including: fine art collection, exhibition on the history of Royal Leamington Spa, cabinet of curiosities, gallery of interactive exhibits, Hammam (restored Turkish bathroom), changing programme of visual arts, history and local interest exhibitions and educational parties by arrangement. Fine art collection includes 16th and 17th century Dutch and Flemish, 19th and 20th century British artists, local artists, sculpture, ceramics and glass-ware.

Recent acquisitions include works of art by Mark Quinn, Mark Francis and Catherine Yass. Other key artists in the collection include Stanley Spencer, L S Lowry, Gillian Wearing, Vanessa Bell, Patrick Caulfield, Sir Terry Frost, Walter Sickert and Graham Sutherland. Facilities at The Royal Pump Rooms also include a café, library, Tourist Information Centre and assembly rooms.

Opening Times: Tue, Wed, Fri & Sat 10:30-17:00, Thu 13:30-20:00, Sun 11:00-16:00. Closed Mon. Admission: Free. Location: 500 metres from Leamington Spa Railway Station. The Royal Pump Room is situated on The Parade, two minute walk from the main shopping area.

Map Ref: 15

Museum & Art Gallery

Riversley Park, Nuneaton CV11 5TU   Tel: 024 7635 0720   Fax: 024 7634 3559
Email: museum@nuneaton-bedworthbc.gov.uk   Web: www.nuneatonandbedworth.gov.uk

The Museum and Art Gallery boasts a varied collection which includes George Eliot memorabilia, local history and paintings. As well as the permanent displays of its collections, there is a lively temporary exhibition programme showing regional artists, quality touring displays and subjects of local interest.

Opening Times: Tue to Sat 10:30-16:30 Sun 14:00-16:30. Closed Mon except BH. Admission: Free.
Location: Pleasant location in Riversley Park close to town centre.

Map Ref: 16

Recreation of George Eliot's Drawing Room

HM Prison Service Museum

Newbold Revel, Stretton under Fosse, Rugby CV23 0TH   Tel: 01788 834168/7   Fax: 01788 834186   Email: museum@breathemail.net   Web: hmprisonservice.gov.uk/prisonlife

Visit HM Prison Service Museum to find out about punishment and imprisonment from Medieval times to the present day.

Opening Times: Mon to Fri 09:00-20:00. Group visits and tours by arrangement.
Admission: Free. Location: Situated on the B4027 near Stretton under Fosse. Both the M1 and M6 pass within reasonable travelling distance.

Map Ref: 17

James Gilbert Rugby Football Museum

5 St Matthews Street, Rugby CV21 3BY   Tel: 01788 333889   Fax: 01788 540795
Email: pat@james-gilbert.com   Web: www.james-gilbert.com

Visit the museum and trace the history of the game and its evolution. Soak up the history of this noble game through memorabilia from its beginnings to the World Cup of 1999. Multi-screen show, The Rugby Experience.

Opening Times: Mon to Sat 09:00-17:00. Admission: Free. Location: Opposite Rugby School.

Map Ref: 18

Rugby Art Gallery & Museum

Little Elborow Street, Rugby CV21 3BZ   Tel: 01788 533201   Fax: 01788 533204
Email: rugbyartgallery&museum@rugby.gov.uk   Web: www.rugbygalleryandmuseum.org.uk

Tripontium collection of Roman artefacts. Rugby's social history including touchscreen kiosk about Rugby's industrial heritage. Rugby Collection of 20th and 21st century British art. Changing programme of contemporary art and craft exhibitions.

Opening Times: Tue & Thu 10:00-20:00, Wed & Fri 10:00-17:00, Sat 10:00-16:00, Sun & BH 13:00-17:00. Closed Mon.   Admission: Free.   Location: Town centre.   Map Ref: 18

Rugby School Museum

10 Little Church Street, Rugby CV21 3AW   Tel: 01788 556109

Experience over 400 years of history at Rugby School, birthplace of Rugby Football and the setting for 'Tom Brown's Schooldays'. Discover the home of Thomas Arnold and the poet Rupert Brooke.

Opening Times: Mon to Sat 10:30-12:30 & 13:30-16:30, Sun 13:30-16:30. Guided tours each day at 14:30.   Map Ref: 18

SOLIHULL W Midlands

National Motorcycle Museum

Coventry Road, Bickenhill, Solihull B92 0EJ   Tel: 01675 443311   Fax: 01675 223310
Email: sales@nationalmotorcylemuseum.co.uk   Web: nationalmotorcyclemuseum.co.uk

The National Motorcycle Museum houses a breathtaking collection of over 700 British motorcycles dating from 1898, each painstakingly restored to its original specification. Facilities at the Museum include a restaurant/snack bar, bookshop and souvenir shop.

Opening Times: Daily 10:00-18:00. Closed Xmas.
Admission: Adult £4.50, Child/OAP £3.25.
Location: The Museum is situated on the A45 junction 6 or M42. Opposite the National Exhibition Centre.

Wartime machines on view at the National Motorcycle Museum

Map Ref: 19

STRATFORD-UPON-AVON Warwicks

Royal Shakespeare Company Collection

Royal Shakespeare Theatre, Waterside, Stratford-upon-Avon CV37 6BB   Tel: 01789 296655
Fax: 01789 403413   Email: info@rsc.org.uk   Web: www.rsc.org.uk

Collection of Royal Shakespeare Company costumes, paintings, posters and theatre history.

Opening Times: Mon to Fri 13:30-18:30, Sat 10:30-18:30, Sun 12:00-16:00.   Admission: Adult £1.50, Concession £1.00.   Location: Near town centre on the banks of River Avon.   Map Ref: 20

Shakespeare Birthplace Trust

The Shakespeare Centre, Henley Street, Stratford-upon-Avon CV37 6QW   Tel: 01789 204016
Fax: 01789 263138   Email: info@shakespeare.org.uk   Web: www.shakespeare.org.uk

The Trust administers the five Shakespeare properties which house the museum collections: Shakespeare's Birthplace, Anne Hathaway's Cottage, New Place/Nash's House, Mary Arden's House and the Shakespeare Countryside Museum and Halls Croft. The collections include Elizabethan and Jacobean domestic furniture, ceramic, metal ware and textiles; Shakespeare memorabilia; archaeological and social history material relating to the Stratford-upon-Avon district; local craft and agricultural tools, vehicles and machinery; coins and medals; oil and watercolours paintings, including important portraits of Shakespeare. The Trust also administers Harvard House and the Museum of British Pewter with a large collection of pewter dating from Romano-British times. The Trust also has an important Shakespeare Library and a Records Office.

Opening Times: *Nash's House/New Place and Hall's Croft*: Nov to Mar Mon to Sat 11:00-16:00, Sun 12:00-16:00, Apr to May & Sep to Oct daily 11:00-17:00, Jun to Aug Mon to Sat 09:30-17:00, Sun 10:00-17:00.
Anne Hathaway's Cottage: Nov to Mar Mon to Sat 10:00-16:00, Sun 10:30-16:00, Apr to May & Sep to Oct Mon to Sat 10:00-17:00, Sun 10:30-17:00, Jun to Aug Mon to Sat 09:00-17:00, Sun 09:30-17:00.

Warwickshire & West Midlands

Mary Arden's House and The Shakespeare Countryside Museum Nov to Mar Mon to Sat 10:00-16:00, Sun 10:30-16:00, Apr to May & Sep to Oct Mon to Sat 10:00-17:00, Sun 10:30-17:00, Jun to Aug Mon to Sat 09:30-17:00, Sun 10:00-17:00.

Shakespeare's Birthplace: Nov to Mar Mon to Sat 10:00-16:00, Sun 10:30-16:00, Apr to May & Sep to Oct Mon to Sat 10:00-17:00, Sun 10:30-17:00, Jun to Aug Mon to Sat 09:00-17:00, Sun 09:30-17:00.

Admission: *Nash's House/New Place and Hall's Croft:* Single Ticket Adult £3.50, Child £1.70, Concession £3.00, Family £8.50.

Anne Hathaway's Cottage Single Ticket: Adult £5.00, Child £2.00, Concession £4.00, Family £11.00.

Mary Arden's House and The Shakespeare Countryside Museum Single Ticket: Adult £5.50, Child £2.50, Concession £5.00, Family £13.50.

Shakespeare's Birthplace Single Ticket: Adult £6.50, Child £2.50, Concession £5.50, Family £15.00.

Multiple House Tickets - 3 in town: Adult £8.50, Child £4.20, Concession £7.50, Family £20.00.

All 5 Houses: Adult £12.00, Child £6.00, Concession £11.00, Family £29.00. Group rates available telephone 01789 201806.
Map Ref: 20

WALSALL *W Midlands*

Birchills Canal Museum
Old Birchills, Walsall WS3 8QD   Tel: 01922 645778

This is housed in a former Boatman's Mission built in 1900. It aimed to improve the physical and spiritual lives of its visitors. The Museum contains a reconstruction of a narrowboat cabin and examples of canal decorative artwork along with other canal related objects. It provides an introduction to the history of canals in Walsall and the people who have worked on them.

Opening Times: Tue to Wed 09:30-12:30, Thur to Sun 13:00-16:00. Closed BH. Admission: Free. Location: Off A34 Green Lane.

A Boaters Gathering at Birchills Canal Museum
Map Ref: 21

Jerome K Jerome Birthplace Museum
Belsize House, Bradford Street, Walsall WS1 1PN
Tel: 01922 653116

Jerome K Jerome is Walsall's most distinguished literary figure, born here on 2 May 1859. The Museum, located on the ground floor, includes an 1850s Victorian parlour and an exhibition charting his life and times. Items on display include his World War One ambulance driver's uniform and first editions of his work.

Opening Times: Mon to Fri 09:00-17:00, Sat 12:00-14:00. Closed BH. Admission: Free. Location: Bradford Street, two minutes walk from the Bridge.

Jerone's birthplace, Belsize House
Map Ref: 21

New Art Gallery Walsall

Gallery Square, Walsall WS2 8LG   Tel: 01922 654400/info 637575
Fax: 01922 654401   Email: wilkinsonc@walsall.gov.uk
Web: www.artatwalsall.org.uk

On permanent display is The Garman Ryan Collection which was donated to the people of Walsall by Lady Kathleen Garman, widow of sculptor Sir Jacob Epstein, in 1973. The gallery is also home to a Discovery Gallery, which creates an introduction to a three storey children's house, including an artist's studio and activity room. The temporary exhibition galleries are dedicated to exhibiting the best of contemporary and historic art.

Opening Times: Tue to Sat 10:00-17:00, Sun 12:00-17:00. Open BH. Admission: Free. Location: Two minutes away from the town centre and is sign posted from all major routes into Walsall Town Centre and M6 junction 7, 8 & 10.
Map Ref: 21

Heritage Motor Centre

Banbury Road, Gaydon, Warwick CV35 0BJ Tel: 01926 641188 Fax: 01926 641555
Email: enquiries@heritagemotorcentre.org.uk Web: www.heritage.org.uk

The largest collection of historic British cars in the world with over 200 vehicles on display. The Land Rover off-road demonstration track runs everyday, with children's quad bikes and electric cars running at weekends and school holidays.

Opening Times: Daily 10:00-17:00. Closed Xmas. Admission: Adult £6.00, Child £4.00, OAP £5.00, Family (2 adults and 3 children) £17.00. Location: Two minutes from junction 12 on M40. Map Ref: 22

The Queen's Own Hussars Museum

Lord Leycester Hospital, High Street, Warwick CV34 4BH Tel / Fax: 01926 492035
Email: qohmuseum@netscapeonline.co.uk

The Collection gives a comprehensive history of the Regiment (1685-1993). Archives are held on the same site.
Opening Times: Summer: Tue to Sun 10:30-17:00. Winter Tue to Sun 10:30-16:00. Closed Xmas.
Admission: Adult £3.00, Child £2.00, OAP £2.50. No charge for Regimental Association.
Location: Housed in Lord Leycester Hospital, one minute walk from Market Square. Map Ref: 23

Royal Regiment of Fusiliers Museum (Royal Warwickshire)

St Johns House, Warwick CV34 4NF Tel: 01926 491653

Museum tells the story of the Sixth Foot (Royal Warwickshire Regiment) from its origins in 1674 to the Fusiliers of today. The displays are an exciting mix of real objects, models and activities. You can see uniforms, weapons, equipment, medals, documents, paintings and curios from all ranks of soldier - Private to Field Marshal.

Opening Times: May to Sep Mon to Sat 10:00-17:30 Sun 14:30-17:00. Admission: Free.
Location: One minute from Warwick Railway Station, near town centre. Map Ref: 23

Warwick Doll Museum

Okens House, Castle Street, Warwick CV34 4BP Tel: 01926 495546/412500 Fax: 01926 419840 Email: museum@warwickshire.gov.uk Web: www.warwickshire.gov.uk/museum

Dolls, teddies, toys and games from days gone by, displayed in Okens House - a 15th century timber-framed building. Shop catering for serious doll collectors and casual visitors.

Opening Times: Easter to Oct Mon to Sat 10:00-17:00, Sun 11:00-17:00, Nov to Easter Sat only 10:00-dusk. Admission: Adult £1.00, Child/Concession 70p, Family £3.00. Location: Near town centre, on route from Warwick Castle. Map Ref: 23

Warwickshire Museum

Market Place, Warwick CV34 4SA Tel: 01926 412500 Fax: 01926 419840
Email: museum@warwickshire.gov.uk Web: www.warwickshire.gov.uk/museum

Displays on the archaeology, geology and natural history of Warwickshire and a temporary exhibition gallery. Highlights include a huge brown bear, the Sheldon Tapestry Map of Warwickshire, live bees, fossils and ancient jewellery.

Opening Times: Mon to Sat 10:00-17:30, May to Sep also Sun 11:00-17:00. Admission: Free.
Location: Town centre, in the Market Square. Map Ref: 23

Wednesbury Museum & Art Gallery

Holyhead Road, Wednesbury WS10 7DF Tel: 0121 556 0683

Houses a Fine art collection and the world's largest public collection of Ruskin Pottery. Also has a Family fun room, changing exhibition and workshop programme.

Opening Times: Mon, Wed & Fri 10:00-17:00, Thu & Sat 10:00-13:00, closed Sun
Admission: Free Location: Off the old A41 in Wednesbury, three minute walk from bus station, five minute walk from Great Western Street Metro Station. Map Ref: 24

Oak House Museum

Oak Road, West Bromwich B70 8HJ Tel: 0121 553 0759

A Yeoman farmer's residence in pleasant grounds, housing Jacobean and Tudor furniture.

Opening Times: Apr to Sep, Mon, Tue, Wed & Fri 10:00-17:00, Sat & Sun 14:00-17:00. Oct to Mar, Mon, Tue, Wed & Fri 10:00-16:00, Sat 13:30-16:00. Closed Sun and Thu. Admission: Free
Location: Near Town Centre, Ten minutes walk from Lodge Metro Station   Map Ref: 25

WILLENHALL *W Midlands*

Willenhall Museum

Willenhall Library, Walsall Street, Willenhall   Tel: 01922 653116

Willenhall Library Building

Situated in the former Town Hall, the Museum provides a brief introduction to the history of Willenhall, showing how the community has developed from a small rural village to a large industrial centre. During the Industrial Revolution, Willenhall's traditional craft of lock making was transformed and locks were exported worldwide.

Opening Times: Mon 10:00-19:00, Tue 09:30-17:00, Thu 09:30-19:00, Fri 09:30-17:00, Sat 09:30-16:00. Closed BH.
Admission: Free. Location: Above Willenhall Library.
Map Ref: 26

WOLVERHAMPTON *W Midlands*

Bantock House & Park

Finchfield Road, Wolverhampton WV3 9LQ   Tel: 01902 552195   Fax: 01902 552196
Web: www.wolverhamptonart.org.uk

Visitors can discover the history of Wolverhampton, from market town to metropolis, as well as finding out the history of the 19th century house and park. There are activities for all ages throughout.

Opening Times: Nov to Mar Fri to Sun 12:00-16:00, Apr to Oct Tue to Sun 10:00-17:00.
Admission: Free. Location: One mile from the centre of Wolverhampton, good bus links.
Map Ref: 27

Wightwick Manor

Wightwick Bank, Wolverhampton WV6 8EE   Tel: 01902 761400   Fax: 01902 764663
Email: mwtman@smtp.ntrust.org.uk Web: www.nationaltrust.co.uk

Victorian manor house and garden owned by the Mauder family. The house is a wonderful example of the influence of William Morris and the Arts and Craft Movement. Pre-Raphaelite Art Collection, 17 acre Thomas Maswon garden with formal areas and woodland.

Opening Times: Mar to Dec Thu & Sat 13:30-17:00, BH Sun & Mon 13:30-17:00.
Admission: Adult £5.60, Child/Student £2.80, Family £13.00, National Trust Members Free.
Location: Off A454, three miles west of Wolverhampton.   Map Ref: 27

Wolverhampton Art Gallery

Lichfield Street, Wolverhampton WV1 1DU   Tel: 01902 552055   Fax: 01902 552053
Email: info.wag@dial.pipex.com   Web: www.wolverhamptonart.org.uk

Wolverhampton Art Gallery has become renowned for its innovative programme of temporary exhibitions, backed up by a lively programme of workshops and events. The contemporary collection is the finest in the region. The gallery also houses an outstanding collection of British and American Pop Art along with traditional 18th and 19th century paintings by artists such as Gainsborough, Turner and Landseer.

Opening Times: Mon to Sat 10:00-17:00.
Admission: Free. Location: Centre of city, two minute walk from bus and train stations.   Map Ref: 27

Wiltshire

Salisbury, built where the rivers Avon, Bourne and Nadder meet is arguably the most perf
cathedral city in England. Salisbury Plain contains Britain's leading concentration of ma
prehistoric sites, the main one being Stonehenge. Malmesbury in the north boasts some of
finest Roman architecture in the country and Avebury is one of the most important megali
monuments in Europe.

Wiltshire's heritage is well recorded in its museums and stately homes.

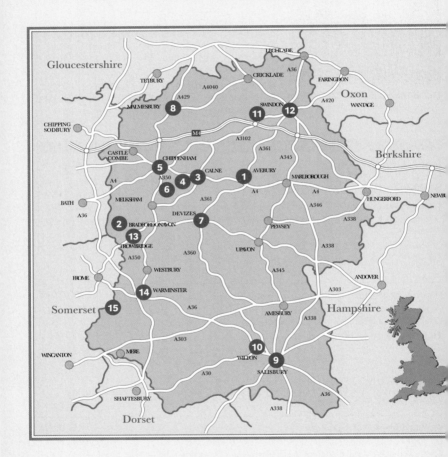

The Red Map References should be used to locate Museums etc on the pages that follow

Alexander Keiller Museum

High Street, Avebury SN8 1RF   Tel: 01672 539250   Fax: 01672 539388
Email: wavgen@smtp.ntrust.org.uk

Contains prehistoric collections from the Avebury complex of monuments, which are of similar age to Stonehenge. Admission charge also covers 'Avebury, 6000 Years of Mystery', an interactive exhibition.

Opening Times: Apr to Oct daily 10:00-18:00. Nov to Mar daily 10:00-16:00. Closed Xmas.   Admission: Adult £4.00, Child £2.00. National Trust and English Heritage Members Free.   Location: Next to prehistoric stone circles. Parking five minutes walk.   Map Ref: 1

The Alexander Keiller Museum

Bradford-on-Avon Museum

Bridge Street, Bradford-on-Avon BA15 1BY   Tel: 01225 863280

Local history of the town and surrounding villages, featuring a complete chemist shop that traded here from 1863 to 1986.

Opening Times: Easter to end Oct Wed to Sat 10:30-12:30 14:00-16:00, Sun 14:00-16:00. Nov to Easter Wed to Fri & Sun 14:00-16:00, Sat 10:30-12:30 14:00-16:00.   Admission: Free.   Location: At the centre of the town, next to the bridge.   Map Ref: 2

Atwell-Wilson Motor Museum

Downside, Stockley Lane, Calne SN11 0NF   Tel / Fax: 01249 813119   Web: www.atwell-wilson.org

The collection began in 1962 with the Buick and Singer, Vauxhall and a Model T arrived later, and wedding work commenced in 1972. The large hall was built in 1989 when the museum opened. The contents are varied with vehicles from the 1920s to the 1980s.

Opening Times: Apr to Oct Mon to Thu & Sun 11:00-17:00. Open Good Friday. Nov to Mar Mon to Thu & Sun 11:00-16:00.   Admission: Adult £2.50, Child £1.00, OAP £2.00.   Location: The site is also the location of a 17th century water meadow, which is being preserved.

Map Ref: 3

Bowood House & Gardens

Estate Office, Bowood House, Calne SN11 0LZ   Tel: 01249 812102
Fax: 01249 821757   Email: houseandgardens@bowood.org
Web: www.bowood.org

Front elevation of Bowood House

Bowood House, the family home of the Marquis and Marchioness of Lansdowne, was built during the 18th century, to the designs of Henry Keene and Robert Adam. The Chapel and famous Italianate terraced gardens were added in the 19th century. The House contains important paintings and classical and 19th century sculpture. There is a fascinating collection of Indiana (the 5th Marquis was Viceroy 1888-94). The Exhibition Rooms contain Victoriana, costume, jewellery, miniatures and fine porcelain. Among the most interesting items are the Napoleonic Collection, including Napoleon's death mask and Imperial porcelain, and one of the finest private collections of British watercolours, especially notable for works by Bonington, Roberts, Lear and Turner. Those who are interested in garden history will enjoy 'Capability' Brown's Park and the late 18th century 'picturesque' rockwork garden.

Opening Times: 23 Mar to 3 Nov daily 11:00-17:30.

The Chapel, designed by Sir Charles Cockerall, decorated for Christmas

Admission: Adult £6.05, Child £3.85, Under 4s £3.00, Under 2s Free, OAP £3.00. Group rates on request. Location: Off the A4 in Derry Hill village, midway between Calne and Chippenham. Map Ref: 4

CHIPPENHAM

Chippenham Museum & Heritage Centre

10 Market Place, Chippenham SN15 3HF   Tel: 01249 705020   Fax: 01249 705025
Email: heritage@chippenham.gov.uk

Chippenham's new museum tells the story of this historic market town. Displays focus on Saxon Chippenham, Alfred the Great, Brunel's railway, and much more.

Opening Times: Mon to Sat 10:00-16:00. Closed Sun.   Admission: Free.   Location: Near town centre, at the historic Market Place. Map Ref: 5

Fox Talbot Museum

High Street, Lacock, Chippenham SN15 2LG   Tel: 01249 730459

The Museum commemorates the achievements of a former President of Lacock Abbey, William Henry Fox Talbot (1800-77), inventor of the photographic process and whose descendants gave the Abbey and village to the Trust in 1944.

Opening Times: 16 Mar to 3 Nov daily 11:00-17:00 & winter weekends 11:00-16:00. Closed 21-29 Dec.   Admission: Adult £4.00, Child £2.40, Family £11.30.   Location: Three miles south of Chippenham off A350. Map Ref: 6

Lackham Museum of Agriculture and Rural Life

Wiltshire College - Lackham, Lacock, Chippenham SN15 2NY   Tel: 01249 466847   Fax: 01249 444474   Email: daviaj@wiltscoll.ac.uk   Web: www.lackham.co.uk

Historic thatched barn and granaries house, an intriguing range of displays depicting aspects of Wiltshire's rural life including a walk-in shepherd's hut, locally built steam engine and sound recordings.

Opening Times: May to Aug Sun & BH, also Aug Tue, Wed & Thu 10:00-17:00.
Admission: Adult £2.00, Child Free, Concession £1.50.   Location: Three miles from Chippenham on the A350 - follow signs for Wiltshire College Lackham where museum is located. Map Ref: 6

DEVIZES

Kennet & Avon Canal Museum

Canal Centre, The Wharf, Devizes SN10 1EB   Tel: 01380 721279/729489

The museum has been described as 'the best little canal museum in the country'. It tells the story of the waterway from its beginnings to the present day. There is also a shop with videos, books, maps and souvenirs.

Opening Times: Feb to Xmas daily 10:00-17:00.   Admission: Adult £1.50, Child 50p, OAP £1.00.   Location: Near town centre, situated at The Wharf, beside the canal. Map Ref: 7

Henry III, from the charter granted to Devizes Borough

Wiltshire Heritage Museum

41 Long Street, Devizes SN10 1NS   Tel: 01380 727369
Fax: 01380 722150
Email: wanhs@wiltshireheritage.org.uk
Web: www.wiltshireheritage.org.uk

The Museum is designated for its outstanding collections, which tell the story of Wiltshire from its earliest origins at the time of the dinosaurs, up to the present day. The Museum is especially strong in prehistory, and displays some of the most important artefacts from the Bronze Age, associated with Stonehenge.

Opening Times: Mon to Sat 10:00-17:00, Sun 12:00-16:00. Closed Xmas & BH.   Admission: Free Sun & Mon. Adult £3.00, Under 16s Free, Concession £2.00.   Location: Near town centre, three minute walk from Market Place. Map Ref: 7

Wiltshire

Athelstan Museum   ♿ ❂

Town Hall, Cross Hayes, Malmesbury SN16 9BZ   Tel / Fax: 01666 829258
Email: athelstanmuseum@northwilts.gov.uk

Collections include displays of archaeology, coins and tokens, maps, photographs. Malmesbury lace, costume, early bicycles and tricycles. Also an 18th century fire engine, Romano-British burial of a child, Malmesbury branch railway, the civil war and philosopher Thomas Hobbs.

Opening Times: Apr to Sep Tues to Sat 10:00-14:00. Oct to Mar Tue & Thu 10:00-14:00, Sat 10:00-12:00. Closed Sun and BH. Telephone for opening hours. Admission: Free.
Location: The museum is situated within the Town Hall, Cross Hayes, one minute walk from the Abbey and centre of Malmesbury. Buses stop opposite the museum.   Map Ref: 8

Edwin Young Gallery   ♿

Salisbury Library and Galleries, Market Place, Salisbury SP1 1BL   Tel: 01722 410614
Fax: 01722 413214   Email: peterriley@wiltshire.gov.uk

Permanent collection of Victorian watercolours by Edwin Young - shown twice per year. Other temporary exhibitions are held featuring local artists and loan exhibitions.

Opening Times: Mon, Wed & Fri 10:00-17:00, Tue 09:30-17:00, Thu 10:00-17:00, Sat 09:30-16:00. Admission: Free. Location: Near Market Place, five minutes from bus station.
    Map Ref: 9

John Creasey Museum   ♿

Salisbury Library & Galleries, Market Place, Salisbury SP1 1BL   Tel: 01722 410614
Fax: 01722 413214   Email: peterriley@wiltshire.gov.uk

Permanent collection of contemporary art by leading artists. Temporary exhibitions on various themes from the collection plus loan exhibitions.

Opening Times: Mon 12:00-17:00, Tue 09:30-19:00, Wed & Fri 12:00-19:00, Thu 10:00-14:00, Sat 09:30-16:00. Admission: Free. Location: Near Market Place, five minutes from bus station.
    Map Ref: 9

Royal Gloucestershire, Berkshire   ❂ ▱ ◎
& Wiltshire Regiment (Salisbury) Museum

The Wardrobe, 58 The Close, Salisbury SP1 2EX   Tel: 01722 414536
Web: www.thewardrobe.org.uk

Three in one attraction of historic house, lanscaped garden to River Avon and Museum of Berkshire and Wiltshire Infantry Regiments. Museum on ground floor. Licensed tea room on site.

Opening Times: Apr to Oct 10:00-17:00, Nov Tue to Sun 10:00-17:00. Admission: Adult £2.50, Child 50p, Concession £1.90, Family £5.00, Garden 50p. Location: Within Salisbury's Cathedral Close and walking distance from car parks and stations.   Map Ref: 9

Salisbury & South Wiltshire Museum   ♿ ❂ ▱

The King's House, 65 The Close, Salisbury SP1 2EN   Tel: 01722 332151
Fax: 01722 325611   Email: museum@salisburymuseum.freeserve.co.uk
Web: www.salisburymuseum.org.uk

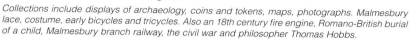

Award-winning Museum designated as having outstanding archaeology collections of national importance. Home of the re-designed Stonehenge Gallery, Warminster Jewel and Monkton Deverill gold torc. Displays of pre-history, Romans, Saxons, the Medieval history of Old Sarum and Salisbury (with the renowned Giant and Hob Nob), the Pitt Rivers collection, ceramics and costume. Pictures throughout, including Turner watercolours. Temporary exhibitions all year round.

Salisbury & South Wiltshire
Museum The King's House

Opening Times: Mon to Sat 10:00-17:00, Sun Jul & Aug 14:00-17:00. Admission: Adult £3.50, Child £1.00, Concession £2.30, Family £7.90. Location: Situated in Salisbury Cathedral Close opposite the west front of the Cathedral.   Map Ref: 9

Wiltshire

Wilton House

The Estate Office, Wilton, Salisbury SP2 0BJ   Tel: 01722 746720   Fax: 01772 744447
Email: tourism@wiltonhouse.com   Web: www.wiltonhouse.com

Inigo Jones designed house, Double Cube room arguably the finest state room in England. A very fine art collection, including many Van Dycks, important Roman, Greek and 17th century sculpture.

Opening Times: 27 Mar to 27 Oct 10:30-17:30.   Admission: Adult £9.25, Child £5.00, OAP £7.50.   Location: Three miles west of Salisbury.   Map Ref: 10

Lydiard House

Lydiard Park, Lydiard Tregoze, Swindon SN5 3PA   Tel: 01793 770401   Fax: 01793 877909
Web: www.swindon.gov.uk

Rescued from delapidation and now beautifully restored ancestral home of the Bolingbrokes. Fine furniture and family picture collection, painted glass window and 15th century Lady Diana Spencer Room. Audio guides and gift shop.

Opening Times: Mon 10:00-13:00 and 14:00-17:00, Sat 10:00-17:00, Sun 14:00-17:00. Nov to Feb closes 16:00. Closed Good Friday, Xmas & New Year.   Admission: Adult £1.40, Child/Concession 70p.   Location: From Swindon, follow signs to West Swindon and then pick up brown signs to Lydiard Park. From junction 16 on M4, follow brown signs.   Map Ref: 11

Railway Village Museum

34 Faringdon Road, Swindon SN1 5BJ   Tel: 01793 466553   Fax: 01793 466615
Email: steampostbox@swindon.gov.uk   Web: www.steam-museum.org.uk

Set in the heart of Swindon's Railway Village, the museum is a restored Victorian railway workers cottage, complete with original furnishings and fittings.

Opening Times: Apr to Oct Mon to Sat 10:00-16:00, Sun 12:00-16:00.   Admission: Free with STEAM, otherwise Adult £1.00, Child 50p.   Location: Near town centre in the Railway Village.
Map Ref: 12

Steam - Museum of the Great Western Railway

Kemble Drive, Swindon SN2 2TA   Tel: 01793 466646   Fax: 01793 466615
Email: steampostbox@swindon.gov.uk   Web: www.steam-museum.org.uk

King George V at the reconstructed Station Platform

Named the Wiltshire Family Attraction of the Year, STEAM is located in a beautifully restored railway building in the heart of Swindon works where seven generations of men and women built the great locomotives and made the Great Western Railway in its heyday, the most important employer in Swindon. STEAM - Museum of the Great Western Railway tells the story of the men and women who built, operated and travelled on 'God's Wonderful Railway'. Hands on displays, world-famous locomotives, archive film footage and the testimonies of the ex-railway workers bring the story to life. Experience the sounds, sights and smells of the Railway Works where huge locomotives were built. Walk underneath the 'Caerphilly Castle' step up on the station platform and climb aboard the famous 'King George V'. Discover the

Isambard Kingdom Brunel

romance and excitement of holiday travel by rail, explore hands on displays and computer interactives and discover what it was like to drive a train. Located next door the McArthurGlen Designer Outlet Great Western, STEAM offers a great day out for all. With excellent value group packages, special events and exhibitions, shop and café.

Opening Times: Apr to Oct Mon to Sat 10:00-17:30, Sun 11:00-17:30. Nov to Mar Mon to Sat 10:00-17:00, Sun 11:00-17:00.   Admission: Adult £5.70, Child £3.60, OAP £3.70, Family (2 Adults & 2 Children) £14.00, Groups (15+) £4.80 per person.   Location: Ten minutes walk from town centre, through Railway Village.   Map Ref: 12

Swindon Museum & Art Gallery

Bath Road, Old Town, Swindon SN1 4BA   Tel: 01793 466556   Fax: 01793 484141
Web: www.swindon.gov.uk

Situated in an elegant early 19th century house, Swindon's oldest museum contains a variety of displays on the history, archaeology and geology of Swindon and surrounding area. The Art Gallery houses an outstanding collection of 20th century British art, a selection of which is on display.

Opening Times: Mon to Sat 10:00-17:00, Sun 14:00-17:00. Closed BH.   Admission: Free.   Location: In Old Town, near town centre. Easily accessible by buses.

Map Ref: 12

TROWBRIDGE

Trowbridge Museum

The Shires, Court Street, Trowbridge BA14 8AT
Tel: 01225 751339   Fax: 01225 754608
Email: clyall@trowbridgemuseum.co.uk
Web: www.trowbridgemuseum.co.uk

Housed in a former woollen mill, museum displays tell the fascinating story of Trowbridge Town and its people. Working rooms still produce cloth, which is still sold within the museum. Other displays include reconstruction of Trowbridge Castle, a Victorian schoolroom, a weaver's cottage and a draper's shop. There are plenty of hands-on activities including a mouse-trail and history hunt.

Step back in time at
Trowbridge Museum

Opening Times: Tue to Fri 10:00-16:00, Sat 10:00-17:00. Closed Sun, Mon & BH.   Admission: Free.   Location: In the Shires Shopping Centre, five minutes from bus picking-up points and ten minutes from railway station.

Map Ref: 13

WARMINSTER

Dewey Museum

Warminster Library, Three Horseshoes Mall, Warminster BA12 9BT   Tel: 01985 216022

Mainly local history; also fossils, Victoriana and agricultural miscellaneous items.

Opening Times: Mon, Tue, Thu & Fri 10:00-17:00, Wed 10:00-13:00, Sat 09:30-12:30.
Admission: Free.   Location: Town centre, in library building.

Map Ref: 14

Longleat House

Warminster BA12 7NW   Tel: 01985 844400   Fax: 01985 844885
Email: enquiries@longleat.co.uk   Web: www.longleat.co.uk

Nestling within 900 acres of 'Capability' Brown landscaped grounds, Longleat House is widely regarded as one of the best examples of high Elizabethan architecture in Britain. Priceless collections of paintings, including works by Tintoretto and Wootton, series of magnificent ceilings by John Dibblee Crace and exquisite 17th century Flemish tapestries. Also the Safari Park, 'World's Longest Hedge Maze', Safari Boats and numerous other attractions.

Longleat House

Opening Times: Jan to 15 Mar weekends and school holidays, 16 Mar to 31 Dec 11:00-15:30, Easter to Sep 10:00-17:30. Closed Xmas Day.   Admission: Adult £15.00, Child £11.00, OAP £11.00.   Location: Just off the A36 between Bath & Sailsbury (A362 Warminster to Frome).

Map Ref: 15

Yorkshire & North Humberside

North Yorkshire is mainly rural in character, whereas South Yorkshire is industrial. West Yorksh
on the other hand, is a mixture of both and offers magnificent Pennine and moorland scen
including the dramatic Bronte Country. Dominating the Vale of York is the historic city of York. T
former East Riding now forms the northern part of Humberside.

A fine collection of museums and galleries record the achievements of the towns and industr
created by the Industrial Revolution. The artistic and cultural aspects of Yorkshire life are also w
catered for.

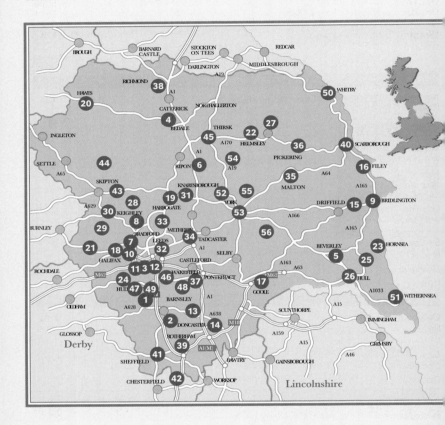

The Red Map References should be used to locate Museums etc on the pages that follow

Yorkshire & North Humberside

Cannon Hall Museum

Bark House Lane, Cawthorne, Barnsley S75 4AT   Tel: 01226 790270   Fax: 01226 792117
Email: cannonhall@barnsley.co.uk   Web: www.barnsley.co.uk

The museum has fine collections of Moorcroft Pottery, furniture and glass. It is also home to the 13th/18th Royal Hussars Military Museum and William Harvey Collection of Dutch and Flemish paintings.

Opening Times: Apr to Oct Wed to Fri 10:30-17:00, Sat & Sun 12:00-17:00. Nov/Dec/Mar Sun only 12:00-17:00. Closed Jan & Feb.   Admission: Free from April 2002.   Location: Seven miles from Barnsley Town Centre, off junction 38 on M1.
Map Ref: 1

Worsbrough Mill Museum

Worsbrough Bridge, Barnsley S70 5LJ   Tel: 01226 774527

A 17th century working water powered corn mill, milling wholemeal and white flour on sale through the mill shop.

Opening Times: Apr to Oct, Wed to Sun 10:00-17:00. Nov to Mar, Wed to Sun 10:00-16:00.
Admission: Adults 50p, all others 25p.   Location: One mile junction 36 of M2. Three miles from Barnsley Town Centre.
Map Ref: 2

Bagshaw Museum

Wilton Park, Batley WF17 0AS   Tel: 01924 326155   Fax: 01924 326164
Web: www.kirkleesmc.gov.uk

Step straight from the mystery of an Egyptian tomb into the tropical enchantment of the rainforest, taming mythical beasts on the way. With local history collections and Gothic decor.

Opening Times: Mon to Fri 11:00-17:00, Sat & Sun 12:00-17:00. Please ring for Xmas closing.
Admission: Free.
Map Ref: 3

Batley Art Gallery

Market Place, Batley WF17 5DA   Tel: 01924 326021   Web: www.kirkleesmc.gov.uk

Changing, temporary exhibitions.

Opening Times: Please ring for opening times.   Admission: Free.   Location: Town centre.
Map Ref: 3

Oakwell Hall & Country Park

Nutter Lane, Birstall, Batley WF17 9LG   Tel: 01924 326240   Fax: 01924 326249
Web: www.kirkleesmc.gov.uk

Built in 1583, the Hall is set out as a 1690s home, giving valuable insight into late 17th century life. One hundred acres of the original grounds are now managed as a country park.

Opening Times: Mon to Fri 11:00-17:00, Sat & Sun 12:00-17:00. Please call for Xmas closing.
Admission: There is a small admission charge from Mar to Oct.
Map Ref: 3

Crakehall Water Mill

Little Crakehall, Bedale DL8 1HU   Tel: 01677 423240

The Mill, on the site of a domesday mill, became Crown property in the 15th century and was sold by James I in 1624. The mill was a working mill until around 1930 and it lay derelict until 1977 when the building and machinery were restored as you see it today.

Opening Times: Easter to Sep Wed to Sun 10:00-17:00.   Admission: Adult £1.00, Child/Concession 60p.   Location: By the bridge over Crakehall Beck on A684 Bedale/Leyburn road.
Map Ref: 4

Beverley Art Gallery

Champney Road, Beverley HU17 8HE   Tel: 01482 883903   Fax: 01482 392778

The Gallery runs a lively temporary exhibition programme of art and craft. Selections from the permanent collection, which includes work by local Edwardian artists Fred and Mary Elwell, are

displayed at times during the year.

Opening Times: Wed to Fri 10:00-17:00, Sat & Sun 10:00-12:30 13:30-17:00. Closed Mon & Tue. Admission: Free. Location: Short walk from the town centre on Champney Road, above the main Beverley Library. Map Ref: 5

Museum of Army Transport

Flemingate, Beverley HU17 0NG   Tel: 01482 860445   Fax: 01482 872767
Web: www.museum-of-army-transport.co.uk

The museum covers an area of over two acres giving the history of military transport from the Boer War to modern day. The museum also houses the last remaining Blackburn Beverley aircraft.

Opening Times: Daily 10:00-17:00. Closed Xmas.   Admission: Adult £4.50, Child £3.00, OAP £3.00, Family £12.00, Under 5s Free.   Location: Near town centre, ten minute walk from central bus station, five minute walk from railway station. Map Ref: 5

BOROUGHBRIDGE *S Yorks*

Aldborough Roman Town & Museum

Main Street, Boroughbridge YO5 9EF   Tel: 01423 322768

Aldborough was once the rich Roman city Isurium Brigantum, the principal town of the Brigantes - the largest tribe in Roman Britain. The museum displays a remarkable collection of finds from the town.

Opening Times: Apr to Sep daily 10:00-13:00 14:00-18:00, Oct daily 10:00-13:00-14:00-17:00. Admission: Adult £1.80, Child 90p, Concession £1.40.   Location: In Aldborough, three quarters of a mile south east of Boroughbridge. Map Ref: 6

BRADFORD *W Yorks*

Bolling Hall

Bowling Hall Road, Bradford BD4 7LP   Tel: 01274 723057

A pleasant family home for more than five centuries, with views over the city towards the open hills and moors beyond. The oldest part has been standing before Henry VIII came to the throne and the most recent alterations are now more than two hundred years old.

Opening Times: Wed to Fri 11:00-16:00, Sat 10:00-17:00, Sun 12:00-17:00.   Admission: Free. Location: One mile south of city. Map Ref: 7

Bracken Hall Countryside Centre

Glen Road, Baildon, Bradford BD17 5EA   Tel: 01274 584140

Natural sciences and countryside walks.

Opening Times: Please ring for details.   Admission: Free.   Location: On Baildon Moor. Map Ref: 8

Bradford Industrial Museum & Horses At Work

Moorside Road, Eccleshill, Bradford BD2 3HP   Tel: 01274 631756

Norman and the Tram

Moorside mills, an original spinning mill, is alive with magnificent machinery which once converted raw wool into the world's worsted cloth. The mill yard rings to the sound of iron on stone as the shire horses give rides, pull a horse tram or haul a horse-bus. In the mill, you can experience the sounds and smells of the engines which once powered the mills throughout Yorkshire.

Opening Times: Tue to Sat 10:00-17:00, Sun 12:00-17:00. Admission: Free. Location: Signposted from the Bradford ring road and Harrogate Road (A568). Map Ref: 7

Cartwright Hall

Lister Park, Bradford BD9 4NS   Tel: 01274 751212

Our collections reflect the cultural mix that makes Bradford unique. From sumptuous Indian silks and embroideries to the challenge of contemporary art and the delights of Victorian painting. The upper galleries are reserved for display of the permanent collection of Bradford Art Galleries and Museums. Paintings, sculpture and decorative arts from the 19th and 20th centuries. The lower galleries are changing exhibitions.

Opening Times: Tue to Sat 10:00-17:00, Sun 13:00-17:00. Admission: Free.   Location: In Lister Park on the A650 Keighley Road, about one mile from city centre.   Map Ref: 7

Sitwell Museum

The Colour Museum

Perkin House, PO Box 244,1 Providence Street, Bradford BD1 2PW   Tel: 01274 390955 Fax: 01274 392888   Email: museumesdc.org.uk   Web: www.sdc.org.uk

Dedicated to the history, development and technology of colour, The Colour Museum is the only museum of its kind in Europe. A truly colourful experience for both kids and adults, it's fun, it's informative and it's well worth a visit.

Opening Times: Tue to Sat 10:00-16:00. Closed Sun, Mon, BH, Xmas & New Year. Admission: Adult £1.75, Concession £1.25, Family £4.00.   Location: In the city centre, less than ten minute walk from the Interchange Bus Station and Forster Square Railway Station.

Map Ref: 7

 BRIDLINGTON *Humberside*

Sewerby Hall Museum & Art Gallery

Sewerby Hall, Church Lane, Sewerby, Bridlington YO15 1EA   Tel: 01262 677874   Fax: 01262 674265   Email: sewerbyhall@yahoo.com   Web: www.bridlington.net/sew

East Yorkshire history and east coast maritime art. Amy Johnson collection and temporary exhibitions of regional art and photography.

Opening Times: 9 Feb to 26 Mar, 4 Nov to 22 Dec Sat to Tue 11:00-16:00. 29 Mar to 3 Nov daily 10:00-17:30.   Admission: Adult £3.10, Child £1.20, Over 60s £2.30, Groups half price. Location: Two miles north of Bridlington.   Map Ref: 9

BRIGHOUSE *W Yorks*

Smith Art Gallery

Halifax Road, Brighouse HD6 2AF   Tel / Fax: 01484 719222 Email: Karen.Belshaw@calderdale.gov.uk   Web: www.calderdale.gov.uk

Permanent displays of 19th century art works. Also has temporary exhibition space in back gallery.

Opening Times: Mon, Tue, Thu and Fri 10:00-12:30, 13:00-18:00, Sun 10:00-12;30, 13:00-16:00. Admission: Free.   Location: Two minutes walk from Brighouse Bus Station, ten minutes walk from Brighouse Railway Station.   Map Ref: 10

CLECKHEATON *W Yorks*

Red House

Oxford Road, Gomersal, Cleckheaton BD19 4JP Tel: 01274 335100 Fax: 01274 335105
Web: www.kirkleesmc.gov.uk

Home of Mary Taylor, friend of Charlotte Bronte, who featured the house as 'Briarmains' in 'Shirley'. Each room brings you closer to the 1830s and two permanent exhibitions shed light on the Brontes and life in the Spen Valley.

Opening Times: Mon to Fri 11:00-17:00, Sat & Sun 12:00-17:00. Please phone to check Xmas closing. Admission: Free.   Map Ref: 11

DEWSBURY *W Yorks*

Dewsbury Museum

Crow Nest Park, Heckmondwike Road, Dewsbury WF13 2SA   Tel: 01924 325100
Web: www.kirkleesmc.gov.uk

Remember growing up? Dedicated to the magical theme of childhood, Dewsbury Museum will not only take you back to yours, it will give you insight into the childhood of past and future generations.

Opening Times: Mon to Fri 11:00-17:00, Sat & Sun 12:00-17:00. Please ring for Xmas closing. Admission: Free.   Map Ref: 12

DONCASTER *S Yorks*

Brodsworth Hall

Brodsworth, Doncaster DN5 7XJ   Tel: 01302 722598

Brodsworth Hall has survived almost completely intact since the 1860s with an extraordinary collection of 17,000 objects. These include an important group of Italian marble sculptures, an impressive collection of paintings, silver and furniture. The gardens are spectacular including a special collection of old rose varieties.

Opening Times: Mar to Nov Tue to Sun & BH 13:00-18:00. Pre-booked guided tours in mornings Apr to Oct. Admission: Adult £5.00, Child £2.50, Concession £3.80. Location: In Brodsworth, five miles north west of Doncaster off A635 Barnsley Road, from junction 37 of A1(M).

Map Ref: 13

Cusworth Hall - The Museum of South Yorkshire Life

Cusworth Hall, Cusworth Lane, Doncaster DN5 7TU Tel / Fax: 01302 782342
Email: museum@doncaster.gov.uk Web: www.doncaster.gov.uk

The Museum illustrates the changing home, work and social life of local people and communities. Set in an imposing 18th century country house in extensive landscaped parklands.

Opening Times: Mon to Fri 10:00-17:00, Sat 11:00-17:00, Sun 13:00-17:00. Dec & Jan closing 16:00. Admission: Free. Location: Approximately two miles north from centre (off A638), nearest railway station Doncaster.   Map Ref: 14

Doncaster Museum & Art Gallery

Chequer Road, Doncaster DN1 2AE Tel: 01302 734293 Fax: 01302 735409
Email: museum@doncaster.gov.uk Web: www.doncaster.gov.uk

The Museum depicts various aspects of natural history archaeology, local history and fine and decorative art.

Opening Times: Mon to Sat 10:00-17:00, Sun 14:00-17:00. Admission: Free. Location: Near town centre, five minute walk from Southern Bus Station.   Map Ref: 14

Kings Own Yorkshire Light Infantry Regimental Museum

Doncaster Museum and Art Gallery, Chequer Road, Doncaster DN1 2AE Tel: 01302 734293
Fax: 01302 735409 Email: museum@doncaster.gov.uk Web: www.doncaster.gov.uk

Situated in the same building as Doncaster Museum & Art Gallery, in its own extension, the Museum reflects the history of this famous local regiment.

Opening Times: Mon to Sat 10:00-17:00, Sun 14:00-17:00. Admission: Free.
Location: Located as part of Doncaster Museum, near town centre.   Map Ref: 14

Yorkshire & North Humberside

Burton Agnes Hall

Estate Office, Burton Agnes, Driffield YO25 0ND   Tel: 01262 490324   Fax: 01262 490513

Elizabethan house with original carving and plasterwork. China, paintings and furniture collected over four centuries with a notable collection of modern and Impressionist paintings.

Opening Times: Apr to Oct daily 11:00-17:00.   Admission: Adult £4.80, Child £2.40, OAP £4.30.

Map Ref: 15

Filey Museum

8/10 Queen Street, Filey YO14 9EH   Tel: 01723 515013

Grade II listed building built in 1696. Seven rooms of exhibits featuring items from Filey's fishing and farming history. Garden area, replica baiting shed, extensive photographic collection. Registered museum and charity.

Opening Times: Easter to Oct Sun to Fri 11:00-17:00, Sat 14:00-17:00. Jul to Aug Tue 19:00-21:00.   Admission: Adult £1.50, Child 80p. Group rates available.   Location: About four minutes from town centre.

Map Ref: 16

Goole Museum & Art Gallery

Carlisle Street, Goole DN14 5DS   Tel: 01405 768963   Fax: 01482 392782
Email: janet.tierney@eastriding.gov.uk

History of the development of the town and port of Goole, including ship models, photographs, social history and marine paintings by Goole-born artist Reuben Chappell.

Opening Times: Mon 14:00-17:00, Tue to Fri 10:00-17:00, Sat 09:00-13:00. Closed BH and Xmas & New Year.   Admission: Free.   Location: Town centre 12 minute from bus station, five minutes from railway station.

Map Ref: 17

Waterways Museum

The Sobriety Project, Dutch Riverside, Goole DN14 5TB   Tel: 01405 768730
Fax: 01405 769868   Email: waterwaysmuseum@btinternet.com

Boats and displays illustrating the story of Goole Port and life on the Kells and Sloops of the Aire and Calder Navigation. A new Interactive Gallery where visitors can investigate boatbuilding and sailing. Raise and lower sails, lend a hand in the Boatyard and work out how to sail against the wind, then walk the Nature Trail and visit the floating Art Gallery.

Opening Times: Mon to Fri 9:30-16:00, Jun to Sep Sun & BH 12:00-17:00. Closed Sat, Xmas & New Year.

Map Ref: 17

Bankfield Museum

Boothtown Road, Halifax HX3 6HG   Tel: 01422 352334   Fax: 01422 349020
Email: Bankfield.Museum@calderdale.gov.uk   Web: www.calderdale.gov.uk

German First World War Machine Gun

Once the home of a mill owner, the magnificent Renaissance style Victorian mansion houses one of the finest collections of costumes and textiles in the country. There are also temporary exhibitions, workshops and activities.

Opening Times: Tue to Sat and BH Mon 10:00-17:00, Sun 14:00-17:00   Admission: Free   Location: 20 Minutes walk from Halifax Bus Station

Map Ref: 18

Eureka! The Museum for Children

Discovery Road, Halifax HX1 2NE   Tel: 01422 330069

Eureka! Is the interactive children's museum in Halifax, where you can touch, hear, smell, and discover hundreds of fascinating things about yourself and the world around you in the only hands-on museum in the UK designed and built especially for 3-12 year old children. With more than 400 hands-on exhibits, games and challenges, you'll be amazed at all the fun things you can do. Activities are designed to encourage the

natural curiosity of young minds. From operating TV cameras and reading the news, to saving a yacht, riding a skeleton bike, playing pinball digestion and meeting Scoot the Robot everyone will have a fun packed visit. A varied programme of special events provides different activities throughout the year from song and dance to journeys into outer space. With exciting new developments planned for 2002 exploring the familiar and more exotic environments, this popular family attraction is sure to remain a firm favourite.

Opening Times: Daily 10:00-17:00. Closed Xmas.
Admission: Adult & Child £5.50, Under 3s Free.
Location: Adjacent to train station, near town centre.

Map Ref: 18

Museum of The Duke of Wellingtons Regiment

Bankfield Museum, Boothtown Road, Halifax HX3 6HG   Tel: 01422 352334/354823
Fax: 01422 349020   Email: Bankfield.Museum@calderdale.gov.uk
Web: www.calderdale.gov.uk

The Duke of Wellingtons Regiment has nearly three hundred years of history behind them. The Regimental collection is displayed at Bankfield Museum.

Opening Times: Tue to Sat and BH Mon 10:00-17:00, Sun 14:00-17:00   Admission: Free
Location: 20 minutes walk from Halifax Bus Station   Map Ref: 18

Piece Hall Art Gallery

Piece Hall, Halifax HX1 1RE   Tel: 01422 358087   Fax: 01422 349310
Email: Karen.Belshaw@calderdale.gov.uk   Web: www.calderdale.gov.uk

Temporary exhibitions of art, crafts and local history situated in the historic Piece Hall.

Opening Times: Tue to Sun and BH 10:00-17:00   Admission: Free   Location: Two minutes
walk from Halifax Bus Station and Railway Station   Map Ref: 18

Shibden Hall

Listers Road, Halifax HX3 6XG   Tel: 01422 321455/352246   Fax: 01422 348440
Email: shibden.hall@calderdale.gov.uk

Built in 1420, Shibden Hall with its oak panelled interiors and atmospheric room settings is Halifax's Historic Home. The Folk Museum and Barn also offer you a world without electricity, where craftsmen worked in wood and iron.

Opening Times: Mar to Nov Mon to Sat 10:00-17:00, Sun 12:00-17:00. Dec to Feb Mon to Sat
10:00-16:00, Sun 12:00-16:00.   Admission: Adult £3.00, Concession £2.00, Family £7.00.

Map Ref: 18

HARROGATE *N Yorks*

Harlow Carr Museum of Gardening

Crag Lane, Harrogate HG3 1QB   Tel: 01423 565418

The Museum, which is situated within RHS Garden Harlow Carr, houses displays of gardening equipment, tools and related items such as catalogues and seed packets. It includes a 1930s 'potting shed'.

Opening Times: Daily 10:00-16:00.   Admission: Adult £4.50, Child £1.00, Under 11s Free, OAP
£3.50, RHS Members Free. NB. charge is for Gardens entrance, no extra charge for Museum.
Location: Off B6162, on the outskirts of Harrogate.   Map Ref: 19

Mercer Art Gallery

Swan Road, Harrogate HG1 2SA   Tel: 01423 566188   Fax: 01423 556130
Email: lg12@harrogate.gov.uk   Web: www.harrogate.gov.uk/museums

Originally built in 1806 as Harrogate's first spa building, 'The Promenade Room' has been restored to its former glory. The Gallery hosts a diverse programme of events and exhibitions, ranging from national touring shows of painting, photography, sculpture and crafts, to the display of work by Yorkshire artists. Also home to Harrogate's fine art collection which goes on display two or three times a year.

Opening Times: Tue to Sat 10:00-17:00, Sun & BH 14:00-17:00. Closed Mon, 24-26 Dec & New Year.

Mercer Art Gallery

Admission: Free. Location: Near town centre.

Map Ref: 19

Royal Pump Room Museum

Crown Place, Harrogate HG1 2RY   Tel: 01423 556188   Fax: 01423 556130
Email: lg12@harrogate.gov.uk   Web: www.harrogate.gov.uk/museums

Housed in Harrogate's premier Spa building and site of Europe's strongest Sulphur Well, the Royal Pump Room Museum tells the story of Harrogate as a spa. You can still see the sulphur wells, and no visit to the museum is complete without a taste of the water. For 2002 the museum will also be hosting an Ancient Egyptian Exhibition from the archaeology collection.

Opening Times: Mon to Sat 10:00-17:00 (except Nov to Mar close 16:00), Sun 14:00-17:00 (Sun in Aug open 11:00). Closed 24-26 Dec & New Year.

Royal Pump Room Museum

Admission: Adult £2.00, Child £1.25, Concession £1.50, Family £5.50. Group rates, season and combined tickets available. Location: Near town centre.

Map Ref: 19

HAWES *N Yorks*

Dales Countryside Museum

Station Yard, Hawes DL8 3NT   Tel: 01969 667494   Fax: 01969 667165
Email: dcm@yorkshiredales.org.uk

Fascinating museum telling the story of the people and landscape of the Yorkshire Dales, past, present and future. Static steam locomotive and carriages with video and displays. Interactive area. Special events, demonstrations and temporary exhibitions. Tourist information and National Park Centre.

Opening Times: Daily 10:00-17:00, except Xmas. Admission: Adult £3.00, Child £2.00, OAP £2.00, Family £8.00, Group rate available. Location: East end of town centre.   Map Ref: 20

HEBDEN BRIDGE *W Yorks*

Heptonstall Museum

Heptonstall, Hebden Bridge   Tel: 01422 843738

17th century building with original school furniture and items of local, domestic, historic and agricultural interest including a coins exhibition.

Opening Times: Easter to Oct Sat, Sun & BH 13:00-17:00. Admission: Adult £1.00, Concession 50p. Location: Buses from Hebden Bridge and Halifax. A646 to Hebden Bridge, then up to Heptonstall.

Map Ref: 21

HELMSLEY *N Yorks*

Rievaulx Abbey

Rievaulx, Helmsley YO6 5LB   Tel: 01439 798228

Founded in 1132, Rievaulx Abbey was the first Cistercian abbey in the north of England. The collection includes Medieval floor tiles, stone sculpture, late Medieval cutlery and other finds from the abbey.

Yorkshire & North Humberside

Opening Times: Apr to Sep daily 10:00-18:00 (09:30-19:00 in Aug), Oct daily 10:00-17:00, Nov to Mar daily 10:00-16:00. Closed Xmas & New Year. Admission: Adult £3.60, Child £1.80, Concession £2.70. Location: In Rievaulx, just over two miles west of Helmsley.   Map Ref: 22

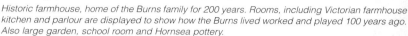

HORNSEA *Humberside*

Hornsea Museum
11 Newbegin, Hornsea HU18 1AB   Tel: 01964 533443

Historic farmhouse, home of the Burns family for 200 years. Rooms, including Victorian farmhouse kitchen and parlour are displayed to show how the Burns lived worked and played 100 years ago. Also large garden, school room and Hornsea pottery.

Opening Times: Tue to Fri 11:00-17:00, Sun 14:00-17:00. Closed Mon except School Holidays. Admission: Adult £2.00, Concession £1.50, Family Ticket £6.00. Location: Near town centre.
Map Ref: 23

HUDDERSFIELD *W Yorks*

Colne Valley Museum
Cliffe Ash, Golcar, Huddersfield HD7 4PY   Tel: 01484 659762

Experience the atmosphere of a hand weaver's home and working life c.1840-50, with working hand looms and spinning jenny, a gas lit Cloggers Shop that's fully equipped with period tools and equipment from 1910.

Opening Times: Sat, Sun & BH 14:00-17:00. Closed Xmas & New Year. Admission: Adult £1.20, Child/OAP 60p.
Map Ref: 24

Huddersfield Art Gallery
Princess Alexandra Walk, Huddersfield HD1 2SU   Tel: 01484 221964
Web: www.kirkleesmc.gov.uk

A lively programme, showcasing the best contemporary art from regional, national and international artists. In addition, the Kirklees Collection contains over 2000 items representing British art of the past 150 years.

Opening Times: Mon to Fri 10:00-17:00, Sat 10:00-16:00. Admission: Free. Location: Town centre.
Map Ref: 24

Tolson Memorial Museum
Wakefield Road, Huddersfield HD5 8DJ   Tel: 01484 223830   Fax: 01484 223843
Web: www.kirkleesmc.gov.uk

The history book of a typical Yorkshire town. Tolson Museum draws a vivid and intriguing picture of Huddersfield and its people, from the prehistoric to the present.

Opening Times: Mon to Fri 11:00-17:00, Sat & Sun 12:00-17:00. Admission: Free.
Map Ref: 24

Victoria Tower
Castle Hill, Lumb Lane, Almondbury, Victoria Tower, Huddersfield   Tel: 01484 223830
Web: www.kirkleesmc.gov.uk

Shrouded by myth, history and legend, the story of Castle Hill goes back thousands of years. Despite its castle-like appearance, the Tower is a comparative newcomer. Breathtaking panoramic views of the Pennines and Peak District.

Opening Times: Easter & May Day weekends. Every Sat & Sun from Spring Bank until early Sep 12:00-16:00. Admission: There is a small charge to the Tower.
Map Ref: 24

Museums, Galleries, Historic Houses & Sites

Please let us know of any collections that are not listed in this guide that you feel should be listed. E-mail us on *editor@tomorrows.co.uk*
or return the Report Form on page 448

Yorkshire & North Humberside

Burton Constable Hall

Burton Constable Foundation, Burton Constable, Skirlaugh, Hull HU11 4LN
Tel: 01964 562400   Fax: 01964 563229
Email: enquiries@burtonconstable.com   Web: www.burtonconstable.com

Burton Constable Hall, West Front

With nearly 30 rooms open, the public are offered a unique insight into the patronage of the Constable family, who have lived here since the house was built. Superb 18th and 19th century interiors, including a gallery, Great Hall, dining and drawing rooms, bedrooms, chapel, Chinese room and lamp room. Pictures and prints, architectural drawings, Chippendale furniture, scientific instruments, cabinet of curiosities and sporting guns.

Opening Times: Easter Sun to Oct. Closed Fri. Grounds: 12:30-17:00. Hall: 13:00-17:00. Admission: Adult £5.00, Child £2.00, OAP £4.50, Family £11.00. Grounds: Adult £1.00, Child 50p. Location: From Beverley (14 miles) follow A165 Bridlington Road. From Hull (seven miles) follow B1238 Sproatley. Follow Historic House signs.
Map Ref: 25

Ferens Art Gallery

Queen Victoria Square, Hull HU1 3RA   Tel: 01482 613902   Fax: 01482 613710
Email: museums@hullcc.gov.uk   Web: www.hullcc.gov.uk/museums

An award winning gallery, featuring Dutch Old Masters, contemporary works, an interactive children's gallery and live art space. A wide variety of workshops, exhibitions and events.

Opening Times: Mon to Sat 10:00-17:00, Sun 13:30-16:30. Admission: Free. Location: In city centre, five minutes walk from the bus and train stations.
Map Ref: 26

Hands on History

South Church Side, Market Place, Hull   Tel: 01482 613902   Fax: 01482 613710
Email: museums@hullcc.gov.uk   Web: www.hullcc.gov.uk/museums

The story of Hull and its people. Victorian and Egyptian collections, features the only replicas of King Tutenkhamun's grave goods and an Egyptian mummy.

Opening Times: Mon to Sat 10:00-17:00, Sun 13:30-16:30. Schools only - Mon-Fri term time. Admission: Free. Location: In the city centre, five minutes walk from the bus and train stations.
Map Ref: 26

Hull & East Riding Museum

36 High Street, Hull   Tel / Fax: 01482 613902   Email: museums@hullcc.gov.uk
Web: www.hullcc.gov.uk/museums

From pre-history to the Romans. Geology, archaeology and natural history collections; important Roman mosaics, the Hasholme Boat and Roos Carr figures.

Opening Times: Mon to Sat 10:00-17:00, Sun 13:30-16:30. Admission: Free. Location: In town centre, five minutes walk from the bus and train stations.
Map Ref: 26

Maritime Museum

Queen Victoria Square, Hull HU1 3DX   Tel: 01482 613902   Fax: 01482 613710
Email: museums@hullcc.gov.uk   Web: www.hullcc.gov.uk/museums

Whales and whaling, ships and shipping - a collection showcasing Hull's maritime history. Features maritime art and important Scrimshaw collection.

Opening Times: Mon to Sat 10:00-17:00, Sun 13:30-16:30. Admission: Free. Location: In town centre, five minutes walk from the bus and train stations.
Map Ref: 26

Spurn Lightship

Hull Marina, Hull   Tel: 01482 613902   Fax: 01482 613710   Email: museums@hullcc.gov.uk
Web: www.hullcc.gov.uk/museums

The Spurn Lightship - discover how the crew lived abroad, feature of the Lightship and the work of the Humber Conservancy Board.

Opening Times: Apr to Oct Mon to Sat 10:00-17:00, Sun 13:30-16:30. Admission: Free.
Location: Near town centre, moored at Hull Marina.
Map Ref: 26

Streetlife - Hull Museum of Transport

High Street, Hull   Tel: 01482 613902   Fax: 01482 613710   Email: museums@hullcc.gov.uk
Web: www.hullcc.gov.uk/museums

200 years of transport history displayed in an exciting, hands-on environment, including an innovative carriage display and street scenes.

Opening Times: Mon to Fri 10:00-17:00, Sun 13:30-16:30.   Admission: Free.   Location: In the old town, 15 minutes walk from the bus and train stations.   Map Ref: 26

University of Hull Art Collection

The University of Hull, Cottingham Road, Hull HU6 7RX   Tel: 01482 465035   Fax: 01482 465192   Web: www.hull.ac.uk/artcoll/

Includes works by Beardsley, Sickert, Steer, Lucien Pissarro, John, Spencer, Wyndham Lewis and Ben Nicholson, with sculpture by Epstein, Gill, Gaudier-Brzeska and Moore. Also two important collections of Chinese ceramics covering the period c.618-1850.

Opening Times: Mon & Tue, Thu & Fri 13:00-16:00, Wed 12:30-16:00. Closed Sat, Sun & BH.
Admission: Free.   Location: 20 minute bus ride from town centre.   Map Ref: 26

Wilberforce House Museum

25 High Street, Hull HU1 1NQ   Tel: 01482 613902   Fax: 01482 613710
Email: museums@hullcc.gov.uk   Web: www.hullcc.gov.uk/museums

Birthplace of William Wilberforce, showcases his campaign to abolish slavery, also collections of costume, Hull silver and clocks. Set in Georgian house and garden.

Opening Times: Mon to Fri 10:00-17:00, Sun 13:30-16:30.   Admission: Free.   Location: In the old town, 15 minutes walk from the bus and train stations.   Map Ref: 26

HUTTON-LE-HOLE *N Yorks*

Ryedale Folk Museum

Hutton-le-Hole YO62 6UA   Tel / Fax: 01751 417367   Email: info@ryedalefolkmuseum.co.uk
Web: www.ryedalefolkmuseum.co.uk

Rescued and restored historic buildings - manor house, cruck cottages, shops, workshops and agriculture. Regular demonstrations and events.

Opening Times: Mar to Oct daily 10:00-17:30.   Admission: Adult £3.25, Child £1.75,
OAP/Student £2.75. Group rates available.   Location: Centre of Hutton le Hole.   Map Ref: 27

ILKLEY *W Yorks*

Manor House Art Gallery & Museum

Castle Yard, Ilkley LS29 9DT   Tel: 01943 600066

A small museum specialising in a little local pre-history and Roman artefacts from the area during Roman occupation. The museum is on the site of a Roman Fort. Parts of the Manor House date back to the 15th century and the building is of architectural interest.

Opening Times: Wed to Sat 11:00-16:00, Sun 13:00-16:00. Closed Mon (except BH), Tue and Xmas.   Admission: Free.   Location: Five minutes from rail/bus station.   Map Ref: 28

KEIGHLEY *W Yorks*

Brontë Parsonage Museum

Church Street, Haworth, Keighley BD22 8DR   Tel: 01535 642323
Fax: 01535 647131   Email: bronte@bronte.org.uk
Web: www.bronte.org.uk

Charlotte, Emily and Anne Brontë, were the authors of some of the greatest books in the English language. Haworth Parsonage was their much-loved home and Jane Eyre, Wuthering Heights and The Tenant of Wildfell Hall were all written here. Set between the unique village of Haworth, and the wild moorland beyond, this homely Georgian house still retains the atmosphere of the Brontë time. The rooms they once used daily are filled with Brontës furniture, clothes and personal possessions. Here you can marvel at the handwriting in their tiny manuscript books, admire Charlotte's wedding bonnet and imagine meeting Emily's pets from her wonderful lifelike

Front entrance of the Parsonage

drawings. Gain an insight into the place and objects that inspired their work. The writing desks belonging to the three sisters are always on display, but their other personal possessions are changed on a yearly basis so you can always be sure of seeing something new. In addition to the main house, the Wade Wing houses a permanent exhibition about the whole of this remarkable creative family. Downstairs in our temporary exhibition gallery there is a changing display of manuscripts and art works from the Brontë Society collection.

Mr Bronte's Bedroom

Opening Times: Apr to Sep 10:00-17:00, Oct to Mar 11:00-16:30. Closed Xmas and Jan to 1 Feb 03. Admission: Adult £4.80, Child £1.50, Concession £3.50, Family £10.50. Location: Behind the church off Haworth Main Street.

Map Ref: 29

Cliffe Castle

Spring Gardens Lane, Keighley BD20 6LH   Tel: 01535 618230/1

Former Victorian mansion in a park housing displays of rocks, crystals, fossils, local natural hsitory, bygones, Morris stained glass, original house furniture and temporary exhibitions. Aviaries, childrens play area and education room.

Opening Times: Tue to Fri 10:00-17:00, Sun 12:00-17:00. Closed Mon except BH. Admission: Free.   Location: Ten minutes walk from town centre, surrounded by park with playground.

Map Ref: 30

East Riddlesden Hall

Bradford Road, Keighley BD20 5EL   Tel: 01535 607075   Fax: 01535 691462
Email: yorker@smtp.ntrust.org.uk   Web: www.visitbrontecountry.com

A homely 17th century merchant's house set in delightful grounds. The house has a wonderful collection of embroideries and textiles. The Great Barn with its oak frame, is one of the finest in the north of England.

Opening Times: 23 Mar to 3 Nov Sat 13:00-17:00 Sun, Tue & Wed 12;00-17:00 and BH 12:00-17:00. Additional openings school holidays.   Admission: Adult £3.60, Child £1.80, Family £9.00.   Location: One mile north east of Keighley. Bus stop 100 yards - 662 Bradford bus.

Map Ref: 30

Vintage Carriage Trust Museum of Rail Travel

Ingrow Railway Centre, Keighley BD22 8NJ   Tel: 01535 680425   Fax: 01535 610796
Email: admin@vintagecarriagestrust.org   Web: www.vintagecarriagestrust.org

Award-winning museum featuring restored railway carriages used in numerous cinema/television productions. Sit in the carriages, listen to sound presentations. Video presentations, numerous signs, posters and small exhibits.

Opening Times: Daily 11:00-16:30 or dusk if earlier. Closed Xmas.   Admission: Adult £1.00, Child/OAP 75p, Family £3.00.   Location: On A629 Keighley to Halifax road, one mile from Keighley Town Centre.

Map Ref: 30

KNARESBOROUGH *N Yorks*

Knaresborough Castle & Museum

Castle Grounds, Knaresborough HG5 8AS
Tel: 01423 556188   Fax: 01423 556130
Email: lg12@harrogate.gov.uk
Web: www.harrogate.gov.uk/museums

HARROGATE
MUSEUMS & ARTS

The home of Medieval kings, the imposing castle built by Edward III has many tales to tell. Join a guided tour and discover the mysterious underground Sallyport or explore on foot the keep and its dungeon. The castle museum houses a rare Tudor courtroom and galleries looking at Knaresborough's past, particularly the Civil War.

Opening Times: Good Friday to end Sep daily 10:30-17:00. Admission: Adult £2.00, Child £1.25, Concession £1.50, Family £5.50. Group rates and Combined and Season tickets available. Location: Town centre.

Map Ref: 31

Knaresborough Castle

Yorkshire & North Humberside

St Roberts Cave

Abbey Road, Knaresborough Tel: 01423 556188 Fax: 01423 556130
Email: lg12@harrogate.gov.uk Web: www.harrogate.gov.uk/museums

St Robert's Cave and Chapel are rare survivals of a medieval heritage. Cut out of magnesian limestone bedrock and consists of a cave, domestic area and a small chapel area which contains the grave and altar.

Opening Times: All year. Admission: Free. Location: On Abbey Road in Knaresborough, just off the Wetherby Road. Best access is to walk out of Abbey Road from Briggate, about 20 mins. Restricted access for cars.   Map Ref: 31

LEEDS W Yorks

Abbey House Museum

Abbey Walk, Abbey Road, Kirkstall, Leeds LS5 3EH Tel: 0113 230 5492 Fax: 0113 230 5499
Email: abbeyhouse.museum@virgin.net Web: www.leeds.gov.uk

Reopened to public following complete refurbishment, new displays include an interactive childhood gallery, displays devoted to Kirkstall Abbey and a gallery exploring life in Victorian Leeds. Three reconstructed streets allow visitors to immerse themselves in the sights and sounds of late 19th century, from the glamorous art furnishers shop to the impoverished widow washerwoman and the sombre workshop of the undertaker.

Opening Times: Tue to Fri 10:00-17:00, Sat 12:00-17:00, Sun 10:00-17:00. Closed Mon. Admission: Adult £3.00, Child £1.00, Concession £2.00. Group rates available. Location: Three miles west of Leeds City Centre on A65.   Map Ref: 32

Abbey House Museum

Armley Mills Industrial Museum

Canal Road, Armley, Leeds LS12 2QF Tel: 0113 263 7861
Email: armleymills.indmuseum@virgin.net Web: www.leeds.gov.uk

Formerly largest woollen mill in the world, Armley Mills now houses Leeds Industrial Museum. Located beside the River Aire, the museum explores the city's rich industrial past. Displays cover local textiles and clothing industries, printing, cinematography, photography and engineering. Working exhibits include a 1904 spinning mule and a 1920's style cinema.

Opening Times: Tue to Sat 10:00-17:00, Sun & BH 13:00-17:00. Admission: Adult £2.00, Child 50p, Concession £1.00, Family £5.00 Location: Two miles west of Leeds City Centre of A65.   Map Ref: 32

Harewood House

Harewood, Leeds LS17 9LQ Tel: 0113 218 1010 Fax: 0113 218 1002
Email: business@harewood.org Web: www.harewood.org

A stunning house with Robert Adam interiors and outstanding collections, including Renaissance masterpieces, Turner watercolours, and Chinese porcelain; furnished throughout by Thomas Chippendale including the spectacular restored State Bed; set in magnificent Capability Brown landscape and gardens, including a lakeside Bird Garden. One of the great Treasure Houses of Britain - and a Designated Museum.

Opening Times: Daily 7 Mar to 3 Nov and weekends Nov to 15 Dec. Admission: Mon - Sat Adult £9.00, Child £7.50, OAP £7.50, Family £30.00. Sun Adult £10.00,

The magnificient restored Parterre Terrace a
Harewood House

Child £5.50, OAP £8.50, Family £35.00 Location: On the A61 between Leeds and Harrogate, five mile from A1, 22 miles from York.   Map Ref: 33

Henry Moore Institute

74 The Headrow, Leeds LS1 3AH   Tel: 0113 246 7467   Fax: 0113 246 1481
Email: info@henry-moore.ac.uk   Web: www.henry-moore-fdn.ac.uk

A centre for the study of sculpture with a programme of temporary historical and contemporary exhibitions, accompanied by a series of talks, symposia and conferences.

Opening Times: Daily 10:00-17:30, Wed 10:00-21:00. Closed BH.   Admission: Free.
Location: In the centre of Leeds, a short walk from the city train station.   Map Ref: 32

Kirkstall Abbey

Abbey Walk, Kirkstall Road, Leeds LS5 3EH   Tel: 0113 230 5492   Fax: 0113 230 5499
Email: abbeyhouse.museum@virgin.net   Web: www.leeds.gov.uk

One of Britain's best preserved abbeys sits on the edge of the city by the River Aire. Founded in 1152 by a party of Cistercian monks but closed down in 1539 by Henry VIII, its buildings were given over to new use and were to become of the most spectacular, picturesque ruins, sought out by artists such as JMW Turner and Thomas Griffin.

Opening Times: Dawn to dusk all year.   Admission: Free. Guided Tours: Adult £2.00, Child 50p, Concession £1.00.   Location: Three miles west of Leeds City Centre on A65.
Map Ref: 32

Leeds City Art Gallery

The Headrow, Leeds LS1 3AA   Tel: 0113 247 8248   Web: www.leeds.gov.uk

One of the premier venues for visual arts in the north. Its nationally designated fine art collections range from early 19th to late 20th centuries. An outstanding collection of English watercolours; fine Victorian academic and pre-Raphaelite painting; late 19th century pictures as well as one of the most extensive collections of modern art. A changing exhibition programme represents reviews and explorations of 20th century art.

Opening Times: Mon to Sat 10:00-17:00, Wed 10:00-20:00, Sun 13:00-17:00. Closed BH.   Admission: Free. Location: City Centre Civil Quarter, next to the Town Hall, junction 4 on City Centre Loop.   Map Ref: 32

Lotherton Hall

Lotherton Lane, Aberford, Leeds LS25 3EB   Tel: 0113 281 3259   Fax: 0113 281 2100
Web: www.leeds.gov.uk

The interiors of the former home of the colliery-owning Gascoigne family traces a world of high Edwardian living as well as providing rich locations for collections of costume, original art and ceramics. Also bird gardens and a deer park.

Opening Times: Tue to Sat 10:00-17:00, Sun 13:00-17:00.   Admission: Adult £2.00, Child 50p, Concession £1.00, Family £5.00.   Location: 13 Miles north east of Leeds City Centre and two and a half miles east of junction 47 on A1.   Map Ref: 34

Royal Armouries Museum

Armouries Drive, Leeds LS10 1LT
Tel: 0113 220 1940/1860   Fax: 0113 220 1955
Email: debbie.jones@armouries.org.uk

3000 years of history covered by over 8000 spectacular exhibits in stunning sur-roundings make this world famous collection of arms and armour a must see attraction. Experience an exciting combination of breathtaking displays, cost-umed demonstrations and dramatic interpretations, live action events, entertaining films, interactive technology and thrilling exhibitions.

There really is something for everybody with five magnificent galleries themed on War, Tournament, the Orient, Self-defence and Hunting. You'll marvel at these priceless

displays including Henry VIII's magnificent tournament armour and the awesome 16th century Mughal elephant armour. With authentic demonstrations of jousting, falconry and pollaxe combat, you are guaranteed an unforgettable day out from start to finish.

Opening Times: Daily 10;00-17:00. Closed Xmas. Admission: Adult £4.90,
Child/OAP/Concession Free.   Map Ref: 32

Thackray Museum
Beckett Street, Leeds LS9 7LN Tel: 0113 244 4343 Fax: 0113 247 0219
Email: info@thackraymuseum.org Web: www.thackraymuseum.org

Award-winning displays bring the history of medicine to life for all ages. Walk through the slums of 1840 Leeds, visit the quack doctor, explore the giant gut in Bodyworks.

Opening Times: Tue to Sun 10:00-17:00. Closed Xmas & New Year. Admission: Adult £4.40, Child £3.30, Concession £3.60, Family £14.00. Group rates available. Location: Two miles from Leeds City Station.   Map Ref: 32

Thwaite Mills Watermill
Thwaite Lane, Stourton, Leeds LS10 1RP Tel: 0113 249 6453 Fax: 0113 277 6737
Web: www.leeds.gov.uk

Lying between river and canal, this island-based water-powered mill once sustained a small self-sufficient community. A tour of the early 19th century mill with its two giant turning waterwheels, is a journey back in time, telling of life and times of mill workers and a working partnership between nature and industry.

Opening Times: Weekends and BH. Please ring to check times. Admission: Adult £2.00, Child 50p, Concession £1.00, Family £5.00. Location: Two miles south of Leeds City Centre off A61, one and a half miles from junction 7 of M621.   Map Ref: 32

MALTON *N Yorks*

Malton Museum
Market Place, Malton YO17 7LP Tel: 01635 695136

Renowned for its splendidly displayed Roman collection, gathered from many years of local excavations. Also objects from the Wharram Percy deserted medieval village. Also a temporary exhibition in upper gallery each year.

Opening Times: Easter Sat to 31st Oct Mon to Sat 10:00-16:00. Admission: Adult £1.50, Child/OAP/Student £1.00, Family £4.00. Location: In the town centre, a five minute walk from the railway and bus stations.   Map Ref: 35

PICKERING *N Yorks*

Beck Isle Museum of Rural Life
Bridge Street, Pickering YO18 8DU Tel: 01751 473653 Fax: 01751 475653
Web: www.beckislemuseum.co.uk

The museum is housed in a Regency mansion. Twenty-four rooms containing Victorian collections, typical shops and workshops. A central yard contains farming equipment.

Opening Times: End of Mar to end of Oct daily 10:00-17:00. Admission: Adult £2.50, Child £1.20, Concession £2.00, Family £6. Group prices available. Location: Opposite Memorial Hall just around the corner from the North Yorkshire Moors Railway Station.   Map Ref: 36

North Yorkshire Moors Railway
Pickering Station, Park Street, Pickering YO18 7AJ Tel: 01751 472508/473799 Fax: 01751 476970 Email: admin@nymrpickering.fsnet.co.uk Web: www.northyorkshiremoorsrailway.com

Heritage steam locomotives/carriages and some diesel heritage.

Opening Times: 23 Mar to 3 Nov daily 10:20-17:00. Admission: Adult £10.00, Child £5.00, OAP £8.50 - all All Day Rover. Group rates available. Location: Pickering Town Centre.
                                                                                          Map Ref: 36

Yorkshire & North Humberside

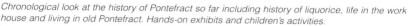

PONTEFRACT *W Yorks*

Pontefract Museum   ♿ ◆

Salter Row, Pontefract WF8 1BA   Tel: 01977 722740   Fax: 01977 722742
Web: www.wakefield.gov.uk

Chronological look at the history of Pontefract so far including history of liquorice, life in the work house and living in old Pontefract. Hands-on exhibits and children's activities.

Opening Times: Mon to Fri 10:00-16:30, Sat 10:30-16:30. Closed Xmas Day.   Admission: Free.
Location: Centre of town, next door to the library.   Map Ref: 37

RICHMOND *N Yorks*

Georgian Theatre Royal Museum   ♿ ◆

Victoria Road, Richmond DL10 4DW   Tel: 01748 823710

Theatre museum with observation window to theatre restoration. Shop and box office.

Opening Times: 4 Mar to 20 Dec 13:30-16:30.   Admission: Adult £1.50.   Location: Town centre.
    Map Ref: 38

Green Howards Museum

Trinity Church Square, Richmond DL10 4QN   Tel: 01748 822133   Fax: 01748 826561
Web: www.greenhowards.org.uk

One of the finest small military museums in the country with a unique collection of regimental uniforms, headdress, weapons, medals and silver. Display cabinets on four floors tell the story of the Green Howards in peace and war from 1688-2002. They are enhanced by touch-screen videos of WWI, WWII and the Regiment today.

Opening Times: Feb, Mar & Nov Mon to Fri 09:00-17:00, Apr to May Mon to Sat 09:00-17:00, May to Sep Mon to Sat 09:00-17:00 & Sun 14:00-17:00, Oct Mon to Sat 09:00-17:00.   Admission: Adult £2.00, Child Free, OAP £1.50, Group £1.50 per person.   Location: Situated in

Grandad explains the Crimean War (1854-56)

medieval church in centre of Richmond's cobbled market place.   Map Ref: 38

Richmondshire Museum   ♿ ◆

Ryders Wynd, Richmond DL10 4JA   Tel: 01748 825611
Email: angus.goodfellow@btinternet.com

Displays trace the history of Richmond and Richmondshire and cover leadmining, transport, domestic bygones, needlework, geology and archaeology. Features include a Dales post office, chemist shop and the vet's surgery set from television's 'All Creatures Great and Small'.

Opening Times: Apr to Oct daily 11:00-17:00.
Admission: Adult £1.50, Child/OAP £1.00, Family £4.00.
Location: Near Market Place.   Map Ref: 38

Period Chemist's Shop from Catterick Garrison

ROTHERHAM *S Yorks*

Clifton Park Museum   ♿ ◆

Clifton Lane, Rotherham S65 2AA   Tel: 01709 823635   Fax: 01709 823631
Email: Wendy.Foster@rotherham.gov.uk   Web: www.rotherham.gov.uk

The museum houses a unique collection of locally-made Rockingham pottery, glassware of South Yorkshire from 18th and 19th centuries to the present day, paintings, Victorian domestic items, local history and natural history. For the under 5s - The Lion's Den.

Opening Times: Mon to Thu & Sat 10:00-17:00, Sun 13:30-16:30 (Oct to Mar) 13:30-17:30 (Apr to Sep). Closed Fri. Closed Xmas & New Year.   Admission: Free.   Location: Near town centre, ten minute walk from central bus station.   Map Ref: 39

Rotherham Art Gallery

Rotherham Arts Centre, Walker Place, Rotherham S65 1JH   Tel: 01709 823621   Fax: 01709 823653   Email: Andy.Pollard@rotherham.gov.uk   Web: www.rotherham.gov.uk

A continuous programme of temporary exhibitions of contemporary arts and crafts.

Opening Times: Mon to Sat 09:30-17:00. Closed Sun & BH.   Admission: Free.
Location: Town centre, two minute walk from bus station.   Map Ref: 39

York & Lancaster Regimental Museum

Rotherham Arts Centre, Walker Place, Rotherham S65 1JH   Tel: 01709 323621   Fax: 01709 823653   Email: georgina.kersey@rotherham.gov.uk   Web: www.rotherham.gov.uk

The York and Lancaster Regimental Museum tells the 200 year story of the men who served in the York and Lancaster Regiment.

Opening Times: Mon to Fri 09:30-17:00, Sat 09:30-16:00. Closed Sun & BH.   Admission: Free.
Location: In town centre, three minute walk from central bus station.   Map Ref: 39

SCARBOROUGH *N Yorks*

Rotunda Museum of Archaeology & Local History

Museum Terrace, Vernon Road, Scarborough YO11 2NN   Tel: 01723 232323

Finest purpose-built museum of its age in the UK, built to a design suggested by 'Father of English Geology', William Smith. The museum displays archaeological finds from the internationally important site at Star Carr and 'Gristhorpe Man' a Bronze Age tree trunk burial. Also items of Victorian Scarborough.

Opening Times: Jun to Sep Tue to Sun 10:00-17:00. Oct to May Tue, Sat & Sun 11:00-16:00. Summer opening school holidays and BH.   Admission: Museum 'S' Pass, valid 12 months all three Scarborough museum/gallery sites. Adult £2.00, Concession £1.50, Family £5.00.
Location: On Foreshore, less than 100 yards from the South Bay beach.   Map Ref: 40

Scarborough Art Gallery

The Crescent, Scarborough YO11 2PW   Tel: 01723 232323

Displays of Scarborough's fine art collection which features seascapes and views of Scarborough including works by Grimshaw, HB Carter, Frank Mason and Ernest Dade. Lively temporary exhibitions programme featuring both contemporary work from the region and works from the permanent collection.

Opening Times: Jun to Sep Tue to Sun 10:00-17:00. Oct to May Thu, Fri & Sat 11:00-16:00. Additional opening during school holidays and BH.   Admission: Museum 'S' Pass, valud 12 months all three Scarborough museum/gallery sites. Adult £2.00, Concession £1.50, Family £5.00.   Location: Near town centre.   Map Ref: 40

Wood End Museum

The Crescent, Scarborough YO11 2PW   Tel: 01723 367326

Displays featuring local wildlife, rocks and fossils and tunny fishing. Also, 'Making Sense', four large scale artworks to stimulate the senses inspired by the natural world.

Opening Times: Jun to Sep Tue to Sun 10:00-17:00. Oct to May Wed, Sat & Sun 11:00-16:00. Summer opening for school holidays & BH.   Admission: Museum 'S' Pass, valid 12 months all three Scarborough museum/gallery sites. Adult £2.00, Concession £1.50, Family £5.00.
Location: Near town centre.   Map Ref: 40

www.tomorrows.co.uk

Full information on our collection of travel guides and secure store

Abbeydale Industrial Hamlet

Abbeydale Road South, Sheffield S7 2QW   Tel: 0114 236 7731

A water-powered scythe and steel works dating back to the 18th century. The houses, workshops, crucible steel furnaces, waterwheels, tilt hammers and machinery create a unique atmosphere of what life was like at home and work.

Opening Times: Apr to Oct Mon to Thu 10:00-16:00, Sun 11:00-16:45. Closed Fri & Sat.
Admission: Adult £3.00, Child £1.50 (under 5s Free), Concession £2.00, Family £6.00.
Location: Abbeydale Road South, Sheffield.   Map Ref: 41

Bishops' House

Norton Lees Lane, Sheffield S8 9BE   Tel: 0114 278 2600   Fax: 0114 278 2604
Email: info@sheffieldgalleries.org.uk
Web: www.sheffieldgalleries.org.uk

Bishops' House dates from around 1500 and is the oldest surviving timber-framed house in Sheffield. It retains many of its original features and gives visitors a tantalising flavour of Tudor and Stuart England. The Great Parlour is restored as a typical dining room and the first floor chamber contains the original bedroom furniture and fittings listed in a 17th century inventory of contents.

Opening Times: Sat 10:00-16:30 and Sun 11:00-16:30. Mon to Fri pre-booked groups only. Admission: Free. Location: Approx two miles from Sheffield City Centre.   Map Ref: 41

Bishops' House

Fire Police Museum

The Old Fire Station, 101/109 West Bar, Sheffield S3 8PT   Tel / Fax: 0114 249 1999

Victorian fire police station built 1900. Vintage fire and police vehicles, fire police artefacts. The only museum of its type in Britain. Private group visits available.

Opening Times: Sun & BH 11:00-17:00. Other times by appointment. Closed Xmas & New Year.
Admission: Adult £2.50, Child £1.50, Under 3s Free. Group rates available.   Location: Five minute walk from city centre, ten minute walk from bus and railway station.   Map Ref: 41

Graves Art Gallery

Surrey Street, Sheffield S1 1XZ   Tel: 0114 278 2600   Fax: 0114 273 4705
Email: info@sheffieldgalleries.org.uk   Web: www.sheffieldgalleries.org.uk

The Graves Art Gallery is home to Sheffield's outstanding collection of British and European 19th and 20th century art, including works by artists such as Stanley Spencer, Matisse, Picasso and Cezanne. The gallery also shows a superb range of touring exhibitions chosen to complement the permanent displays. Highlights of 2002 include drawings by Leonard da Vinci and photographs by Terence Donovan.

Opening Times: Mon to Sat 10:00-17:00.
Admission: Free. Location: In the town centre.

Graves Art Gallery

Map Ref: 41

Kelham Island Museum

Kelham Island, Alma Street, off Corporation St, Sheffield S3 8RY   Tel: 0114 272 2106

See the most powerful working steam engine in Europe, reconstructed workshops, major displays on Sheffield industry, its people, processes and products, scope and melting shop, interactive children's area.

Opening Times: Mon to Thu 10:00-16:00, Sun 11:00-16:45. Closed Fri & Sat. Admission: Adult £3.50, Child £2.00 (under 5s Free) , Concession £2.50, Family £8.00. Location: 15 minutes walk from Sheffield City Centre.   Map Ref: 41

Mappin Art Gallery

Weston Park, Western Bank, Sheffield S10 2TP   Tel: 0114 278 2600   Fax: 0114 275 0957   Email: info@sheffieldgalleries.org.uk   Web: www.sheffieldgalleries.org.uk

Mappin Art Gallery

The Mappin Art Gallery is situated in the grounds of Weston Park. Its magnificently restored Victorian galleries contain paintings from the City's collection dating from the 16th to 19th century, including works by Tissot, Burne-Jones, Turner and Murillo. The gallery is also a major venue for cutting-edge contemporary art and shows an exciting programme of recent and new artwork.

Opening Times: Tue to Sat 10:00-17:00, Sun 11:00-17:00 and BH Mon 10:00-17:00. Admission: Free.

Location: Five minute bus ride from city centre. Close to Children's Hospital and University of Sheffield.

Map Ref: 41

Millennium Galleries

Millennium Galleries

Arundel Gate, Sheffield S1 2PP   Tel: 0114 278 2600
Fax: 0114 278 2604
Email: info@sheffieldgalleries.org.uk
Web: www.sheffieldgalleries.org.uk

Four different galleries mean there is something to please every visitor. Enjoy blockbuster exhibitions from Britain's national galleries and museums, including the Victoria & Albert Museum and Tate. See the best craft and design, both contemporary and historical. Be dazzled by Sheffield's internationally important collection of metalwork and silverware and discover a wonderful array of treasures inside the world-renowned Ruskin Gallery.

Opening Times: Mon to Sat 10:00-17:00, Sun 11:00-17:00.
Admission: Free, apart from Special Exhibition Gallery - Adult £4.00, Child £2.00, Concession £3.00, Family £9.00.   Location: In the city centre.   Map Ref: 41

Renishaw Hall Museum, Art Gallery & Performing Art Gallery

Renishaw Hall Estate Office, Renishaw Hall, Renishaw Park, Sheffield S21 3WB   Tel: 01246 432310   Fax: 01246 430760   Email: info@renishawhall.free-online.co.uk
Web: www.sitwell.co.uk

Performing Art Gallery - this unique gallery contains pictures, gowns and personal mementoes of the stars of the silver screen and stage. John Piper Art Gallery - this gallery contains paintings by the war time artist John Piper. Costume Gallery - gowns, uniforms and staff clothing belonging to the Sitwell family, along with personal items.

Opening Times: First Fri in Apr to last Sun in Sep Fri, Sat, Sun and BH Mon 10:30-16:30. Admission: Adult £3.00, Concession £2.50. Location: Sheffield six miles, junction 30 on M1 only two miles away. Chesterfield six miles on A6135 between Eckington and Renishaw.

Map Ref: 42

Sheffield City Museum

  ♿ ⬤ ▱

Western Park, Western Bank, Sheffield S10 2TP   Tel: 0114 278 2600   Fax: 0114 275 0957   Email: info@sheffieldgalleries.org.uk   Web: www.sheffieldgalleries.org.uk

Egyptian Mummy (detail)

Sheffield City Museum contains important archaeological finds from the local region and a fine ceramics collection, which includes superb examples of Rockingham pottery. The social history collections illustrate everyday life in Sheffield from the 16th century to the present day. Many items in the geology, botany and zoology displays are of major regional significance. The museum is also the local weather centre.

Opening Times: Tue to Sat 10:00-17:00, Sun 11:00-17:00 and BH Mon 10:00-17:00. Admission: Free.

Map Ref: 41

Shepherd Wheel

Whiteley Woods, off Hangingwater Road, Sheffield S11   Tel: 0114 236 7731

A water powered grinding wheel set on a pictureque stretch of the River Porter. The site dates back to 1584. There are two restored workshops containing all the tools of the trade for cutlery grinding.

Opening Times: Please ring (0114) 236 7731 for details.   Location: Whiteley Woods, Sheffield.

Map Ref: 41

SKIPTON *N Yorks*

Embsay & Bolton Abbey Steam Railway

  ♿ ⬤ ▱ ◐ 🚂   **EMBSAY & BOLTON ABBEY STEAM RAILWAY**

Bolton Abbey Station, Bolton Abbey, Skipton BD23 6AF   Tel: 01756 710614 Fax: 01756 710720   Email: embsay.steam@btinternet.com Web: www.yorkshirenet.co.uk/embsaybasteamrailway

Travel between Embsay Station built in 1888 and the new award-winning station at Bolton Abbey. The journey takes you through picturesque Yorkshire Dales scenery. Bolton Abbey Station is the ideal stopping off point, with pleasant walks, beautiful countryside for picnics or exploring the 12th century priory.

Opening Times: For the Talking Timetable phone 01756 795189. Admission: Return fares: Adult £5.00, Child £2.50, Family £14.00.

Map Ref: 43

Upper Wharfedale Folk Museum

The Square, Grassington, Skipton BD23 5AQ

Reminders of yesteryear. Exhibits of lead mining, minerals, craft tools, farming implements, period costume, folklore and the days of the railway recorded.

Opening Times: Apr to Sep daily 14:00-16:30. Oct to Mar Sat & Sun 14:00-16:30. Admission: Adult 50p, Child/OAP 40p.   Location: Centre of village.

Map Ref: 44

THIRSK *N Yorks*

Thirsk Museum

  ✑ ♿ ⬤

14/16 Kirkgate, Thirsk YO7 1PQ   Tel: 01845 527707   Email: thirskmuseum@supanet.com Web: www.thirskmuseum.org

Local history in birthplace of Thomas Lord; life and times of James Herriot's town. Bones of the Saxon giant and finds from Castle Garth. Legend of the Busby Stoop Chair.

Opening Times: Easter to end Oct Mon to Wed, Fri & Sat 10:00-16:00. Admission: Adult £1.50, Child 75p, Family £3.50.   Location: In Kirkgate, off Market Place - free car park 100 yards.

Map Ref: 45

Yorkshire & North Humberside

Clarke Hall

Aberford Road, Wakefield WF1 4AL   Tel: 01924 302700   Fax: 01924 302701
Email: info@clarke-hall.co.uk   Web: www.clarke-hall.co.uk

Clarke Hall is completely furnished as the family home of a late 17th century gentleman, Benjamin Clarke who owned it between 1677 and 1688. It includes a knot garden, maze and herb garden.

Opening Times: Please telephone.   Admission: Open days: Adult £3.50, Child Free, Concession £2.00. Group rates available.   Location: One mile from the centre of Wakefield and three miles from junction 30 of M62. Opposite Pinderfields Hospital.   Map Ref: 46

National Coal Mining Museum For England

Caphouse Colliery, New Road, Overton, Wakefield WF4 4RH   Tel: 01924 848806   Fax: 01924 840694   Email: info@ncm.org.uk   Web: www.ncm.org.uk

A unique opportunity to go 450 feet underground, where models and machinery depict methods of mining from the 1800s to the present day. Above ground, visit the pit ponies, exhibitions, steam winder and pit head baths.

Opening Times: Daily 10:00-17:00. Closed 24-26 December & New Years Day.
Admission: Adult £5.75, Child/OAP Free, Concession/Group £4.85.   Location: On the main A642 Wakefield to Huddersfield road.   Map Ref: 47

Nostell Priory

Doncaster Road, Wakefield WF4 1QE   Tel: 01924 863892   Fax: 01924 865282

Built in 1733 the house is an architectural masterpiece by James Paine. The State Rooms were later completed by Robert Adam, and are magnificent examples of 18th century interior style and Chippendale furniture.

Opening Times: House: 31 Mar to 4 Nov Wed to Sun & BH 13:00-17:30. 10 Nov to 9 Dec Sat & Sun 12:00-16:30. Grounds: open same days as house 11:00-18:00.   Admission: House & Gardens: Adult £4.50, Child £2.20, Family £11.00. Grounds only: Adult £2.50, Child £1.20.
                    Map Ref: 48

Wakefield Art Gallery

Wentworth Terrace, Wakefield WF1 3QW   Tel: 01924 305796   Fax: 01924 305770
Web: www.wakefield.gov.uk/communitymuseumsarts

Collection of 20th century art, fine examples of work by international sculptors Henry Moore and Barbara Hepworth - both born locally. There is also an important collection of 19th and 20th century paintings.

Opening Times: Tue to Sat 10:30-16:30, Sun 14:00-16:30. Closed Mon.   Admission: Free.
Location: Approximately one mile from town centre, near to Wakefield College.   Map Ref: 46

Wakefield Museum

Wood Street, Wakefield WF1 2EW   Tel: 01924 305356
Fax: 01924 305353
Web: www.wakefield.gov.uk/community/museumsarts

Discover the world of Charles Waterton, conservationist and creator of the first nature reserve. Follow him on his journey through the rainforest of South America. Upstairs is the 'Story of Wakefield' - from ancient man through to the miners' strikes in the 1980s. 8000 photographs to view and print.

Opening Times: Mon to Sat 10:30-16:30, Sun 14:00-16:30.
Admission: Free.   Location: Close to town centre, next to Town Hall and opposite main Police Station.   Map Ref: 46

Exploring the Touchy Feely Tree in the Waterton Gallery

Museums, Galleries, Historic Houses & Sites

Please let us know of any collections that are not listed in this guide that you feel should be listed. E-mail us on *editor@tomorrows.co.uk*
or return the Report Form on page 448

Yorkshire Sculpture Park

West Bretton, Wakefield WF4 4LG   Tel: 01924 830302
Fax: 01924 830044   Email: office@ysp.co.uk
Web: www.ysp.co.uk

Set in the beautiful grounds of an 18th century country estate, it was established as this country's first permanent sculpture park. The unique outdoor setting combines stunning views and walks with exhibits of some of the best pieces of sculpture to be seen in Britain today. These include works by Henry Moore, Barbara Hepworth and Anthony Caro. It organises a number of temporary exhibitions each year, ensuring that there is always something new to see. A new visitor centre opens in Spring 2002.

Barbara Hepworth - Family of Man

Opening Times: Daily 10:00-16:00 in winter, 10:00:18:00 in summer. Closed Xmas.   Admission: Free (£1.50 car parking a day).   Location: One mile from junction 38 on the M1.   Map Ref: 49

WHITBY N Yorks

Captain Cook Memorial Museum

Grape Lane, Whitby YO22 4BA   Tel / Fax: 01947 601900
Email: captcookmuseumwhitby@ukgateway.net   Web: www.cookmuseumwhitby.co.uk

House on the harbour where the young James Cook lodged as an apprentice and learnt his seamanship. Superb collections about his explorations. Paintings, models, special exhibition. Stunning site.

Opening Times: Mar Sat & Sun 11:00-15:00. Apr to end Oct daily 09:45-17:00.
Admission: Adult £2.80, Child £1.80, OAP £2.30, Student £2.00, Family £7.80. School rate £1.50 per pupil.   Location: Town centre near swing bridge.   Map Ref: 50

Museum of Victorian Whitby

4 Sandgate, Whitby YO22 4DB   Tel: 01947 601221

Displays representing a stimulating re-creation of daily life in Victorian Whitby. Scenes including fisherman's cottage, barber's shop, cooper's yard and tallow chandlers, to mention but a few. The Bridge of the 19th Century Whaling Ship is also featured.

Opening Times: Daily 09:00-18:00.   Admission: Adult £1.50, Child £1.00.   Location: Museum is situated on first floor and basement of property.   Map Ref: 50

The RNLI Whitby Lifeboat Museum

Pier Road, Whitby YO21 3PU   Tel: 01947 602 001   Web: www.lifeboat.org.uk

Last pulling and sailing lifeboat in service on display, Robert & Ellen Robson. Models, photographs, memorabilia.

Opening Times: Easter to Oct.   Admission: Free.   Location: Pier Road.   Map Ref: 50

Whitby Abbey

Whitby YO22 4JT   Tel: 01947 603568

Whitby Abbey was founded by St Hilda in 657. The original community was destroyed by the Danes, but was refounded as a Benedictine priory in 1078. The new museum contains excavated finds and replicas.

Opening Times: Apr to Sep daily 10:00-18:00, Oct daily 10:00-17:00, Nov to Mar daily 10:00-16:00. Closed Xmas & New Year.   Admission: Adult £1.80, Child 90p, Concession £1.40.
Location: On cliff top east of Whitby. Railway station half a mile away.   Map Ref: 50

Whitby Archives & Heritage Centre

Flowergate, Whitby YO21 3BA   Tel: 01947 600170   Fax: 01947 821833

Whitby town's collection of old photographs and documents. Three exhibition areas, videos played daily, heritage shop, family history department.

Opening Times: Daily 10:00-16:00. Weekends may vary.   Admission: Free.   Location: Town centre, close to bridge.   Map Ref: 50

Whitby Museum

Pannett Park, Whitby YO21 1RE   Tel: 01947 602908   Fax: 01947 897638
Email: graham@durain.demon.co.uk   Web: www.whitby-museum.org.uk

An Edwardian/Victorian 'museum within a museum' with a very wide set of collections, relating to Whitby and the surrounding area.

Opening Times: May to Sep Mon to Fri 09:30-17:30, Sun 14:00-17:00. Oct to Apr Tue 10:00-13:00, Wed to Sat 10:00-16:00, Sun 14:00-16:00, closed Mon.   Admission: Adult £2.50, Child £1.00, Family £6.00. OAP £2.00, Group/School rates available.   Location: Near town centre.
Map Ref: 50

WITHERNSEA *Humberside*

Withernsea Lighthouse Museum

Hull Road, Withernsea HU19 2DY   Tel: 01964 613755

Maritime exhibits - RNLI and HM Coastguard, photos of shipwrecks, local history, photos of Victorian and Edwardian Withernsea including pier and promenade. Also model railway. Kay Kendall Memorial including wedding dress and excerpts of films on video.

Opening Times: Mar to Oct Sat, Sun & BH 13:00-17:00. Mid Jun to mid Sep Mon to Fri 11:00-17:00.   Admission: Adult £2.00, Child £1.00, Under 5s Free, OAP £1.50, Family £5.50.
Location: Centre of town.
Map Ref: 51

YORK *N Yorks*

Beningbrough Hall & Gardens

York YO30 1DD   Tel: 01904 470666   Fax: 01904 470002

This wonderful Georgian house is filled with 18th century treasures including portraits loaned by the National Portrait Gallery. There are beautiful gardens and parkland. All complemented by Victorian laundry, potting shed, excellent facilities for children, shop and restaurant.

Opening Times: 23 Mar to 3 Nov Sat to Wed, also Fri in Jul, Aug, 25 Oct & 1 Nov and Good Friday.
Admission: House, Garden & Exhibition - Adult £5.20, Child £2.60, Family £13.00. Garden & Exhibition - Adult £3.60, Child £1.80, Family £9.00.   Location: Eight miles northwest of York signposted off A19 & A59.

Beningbrough Hall

Map Ref: 52

Castle Museum

Eye of York, York YO1 9RY   Tel: 01904 653611   Fax: 01904 671078
Email: castle.museum@york.gov.uk   Web: www.york.gov.uk

Venture into the prison cell of notorious highwayman Dick Turpin. Wander through Victorian and Edwardian streets and experience four hundred years of fascinating social history. Famous for its collections of costume, textiles, military and social history, York Castle Museum brings history back to life. With over 100,000 items on show you'll be amazed at what's here!

Opening Times: Nov to Mar daily 09:30-16:30, Apr to Oct 09:30-17:00. Closed Xmas & New Year.
Admission: Adult £5.75, Child/Concession £3.50, Family £16.00.   Location: Centre of York, close to Clifford's Tower and the Coppergate Shopping Centre. Map Ref: 53

'Kirkgate' York Castle Museum

Yorkshire & North Humberside

Impressions Gallery of Photography

🖃 ♿ 📷

impressionsgallery

29 Castlegate, York YO1 9RN   Tel: 01904 654724   Fax: 01904 651509
Email: enquiries@impressions-gallery.com   Web: www.impression-gallery.com

Installation of Blackthorne wall paper by Diane House, photo Jerry Hardman-Jones

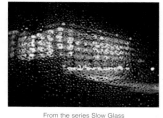

From the series Slow Glass by Naoya Hatekeyama

Impressions Gallery opened in 1972 as one of the first specialist contemporary photography galleries in Europe. Since then we have established ourselves as a leading international exhibition space for photography and digital art. We support and promote innovative and creative work that extends the boundaries of current photographic practice. Digital imagery, film and video are essential resources for the contemporary artist, and this is reflected in our programme.

Opening Times: Apr to Oct Mon to Sat 10:00-18:00 (Tue & Thu to 20:00). Nov to Mar Mon to Sat 10:00-17:30.
Admission: Free. Location: Located in the Coppergate Centre, near Clifford's Tower and the Jorvik Centre.

Map Ref: 53

Jorvik - The Viking City

♿ ♨ 📷

Coppergate, York YO1 9WT   Tel: 01904 643211   Fax: 01904 627097
Email: enquiries@vikingjorvik.com   Web: www.vikingjorvik.com

Jorvik uses archaeological evidence uncovered on the actual site to re-create the street of Coppergate in AD 975. Additionally, 800 of the original Viking Age objects are on display in the Gallery.

Opening Times: Apr to Oct daily 09:00-17:30, Nov to Mar daily 10:00-16:30. Closed Xmas Day. For full details please phone 01904 643211. Admission: Please ring for details. Location: In York City Centre, railway station and Park & Ride stops all within easy walking distance.

Map Ref: 53

Merchant Adventurers' Hall

♨

Fossgate, York YO1 9XD   Tel / Fax: 01904 654818   Email: the.clerk@mahall.york.demon.co.uk
Web: www.theyorkcompany-sagenet.co.uk

The Hall is an ancient monument of national importance. A truly unique and stunning Medieval Guildhall with timbered Great Hall, Undercroft and Chapel below. Displays of furniture from 12th century, paintings, rare silver and archaeology.

Opening Times: 2 Jan to 14 Mar & 30 Sep to 21 Dec Mon to Thu 09:00-15:30, 15 Mar to 29 Sep Mon to Thu 09:00-17:00. All year Fri & Sat 09:00-15:00. Closed Sun, Xmas & New Year
Admission: Adult £2.00, Child 70p, Under 7s Free, OAP/Student £1.70, Family £5.00. Group rates available and by prior arrangement. Location: Town centre, between Piccadilly and Fossgate, opposite Marks & Spencer Home Store.

Map Ref: 53

GREAT WESTERN RAILWAY

National Railway Museum

🖃 ♿ ♨ 📷 ◐ 🚂

Leeman Road, York YO26 4XJ   Tel: 01904 621261   Fax: 01904 631319

National Railway Museum is 'European Museum of the Year 2001'. Our collection includes 103 locomotives and 177 other items of rolling stock and tells the story of the train from Rocket to Eurostar. Permanent displays include 'Palace on Wheels' with royal saloons dating back to pre Victorian times. We also have on display the only Bullet Train outside Japan.

Opening Times: Daily 10:00-18:00. Closed Xmas.
Admission: Free, except during 'Thomas Friends' events.
Location: 540 metres from York Railway Station.   Map Ref: 53

The Regimental Museum

3 Tower Street, York YO1 9SB   Tel: 01904 662790   Fax: 01904 658824

The museum of the Royal Dragoon Guards and the Prince of Wales's Own Regiment of Yorkshire contains fascinating insight into over 300 years of military history.

Opening Times: Mon to Sat 09:30-16:30.   Admission: Adult £2.00, Child/OAP £1.00.
Location: Opposite Clifford's Tower in the centre of York.   Map Ref: 53

The Royal Dragoon Guards

3 Tower Street, York YO1 9SB   Tel / Fax: 01904 642036   Email: rdgmuseum@onetel.net.uk
Web: www.rdg.co.uk

Artefacts, standards and medals of four famous cavalry regiments covering all their battles of the past 300 years. A new six seat cinema showing 20 minute films has recently been installed.

Opening Times: Mon to Sat 09:30-16:30. Closed 22 Dec to 2 Jan.   Admission: Adult £2.00,
Child/OAP £1.00. Groups 2 for the price of 1.   Location: Centre of town, next to Cliffords Tower.
    Map Ref: 53

Shandy Hall

Coxwold, York YO61 4AD   Tel / Fax: 01347 868465   Web: www.shandy-hall.org.uk

Shandy Hall houses the world's foremost collection of editions of Laurence Sterne's novels, plus an interesting background of contemporary prints and paintings illustrating his work.

Opening Times: House: May to Sep Wed 14:00-16:30, Sun 14:30-16:30. Garden: May to Sep
Sun to Fri 11:00-16:30.   Admission: House & Garden £4.50. Garden £2.50.   Location: Above
church, last house west end of village.   Map Ref: 54

Sutton Park

Sutton-on-the-Forest, York YO61 1DP   Tel: 01347 810249   Fax: 01347 811251
Email: suttonpark@fsbd.co.uk   Web: www.statelyhome.co.uk

Rich collection of 18th century furniture and paintings. Important collection of porcelain. Plaster work by Cortese, rare Chinese wallpaper.

Opening Times: Good Friday to Easter Mon then Wed, Sun & BH Mon until 29 Sep.
Admission: Adult £5.00, Child £2.50, OAP £4.00. Group rates available.   Location: Eight miles
north of York on B1363 York to Helmsley Road.   Map Ref: 55

Treasurers House

Minster Yard, York YO1 7JL   Tel: 01904 624247   Fax: 01904 647372
Email: yorkth@smtp.ntrust.org.uk

Named after the Treasurer of York Minster and built over a Roman Road, the house is not all that it seems. Carefully restored and presented with 16th to 20th century decoration, furniture, china and glass.

Opening Times: Apr to Oct Sat to Thu 11:00-16:30.   Admission: Adult £3.80, Child £2.00,
Family £9.50. Group rates available.   Location: York City Centre, behind York Minster.
    Map Ref: 53

York City Art Gallery

Exhibition Square, York YO1 7EW   Tel: 01904 551861   Fax: 01904 551866
Email: art.gallery@york.gov.uk   Web: www.york.gov.uk/heritage/museums/art

Seven centuries of European painting from early Italian gold-ground panels to the art of the present day. Changing exhibitions of modern and contemporary art. Events for all the family.

Opening Times: Daily 10:00-17:00.   Admission: Free to
York residents; Adult £2.00, Concession £1.50.
Location: Three minutes from Minster, ten minutes from
railway station.   Map Ref: 53

William Marlow (1740-1813): Ouse Bridge, York

York Minster Undercroft Treasury & Crypt

YORK MINSTER

York Minster, Deangate, York YO1 7JF
Tel: 01904 557216

York Minster is the chief church in the Northern Province of the Church of England and is the seat of the Archbishop of York. The present building is the largest Gothic cathedral in Northern Europe, and is the setting for some of the finest 14th and 15th century stained

glass windows in existence. Whether you come to York Minster as a tourist or pilgrim, we hope that as you walk round you will understand why the cathedral has inspired people of every generation since its completion. Prayer has been offered to God on this site for nearly 1,000 years. We invite you to join us in worship and experience the real purpose for which the Minster was built. Newly refurbished, the Undercroft and Crypt uncovers the remarkable history of York Minster from its early Norman foundations to the 20th century engineering that supports the central tower. The Undercroft also contains the remains of York's Roman Legionary fortress, Viking gravestones and historic artefacts from the Minster's collection.

Opening Times: Winter 10:00-16:30. Jun, Jul & Aug 09:30-18:30. Admission: Adult £3.00, Child £1.00, OAP/Student £2.60, Family £6.50. Location: City centre. Map Ref: 53

Yorkshire Air Museum & Allied Air Forces Memorial

Halifax Way, Elvington, York YO41 4AU Tel: 01904 608595 Fax: 01904 608246
Email: museum@yorkshireairmuseum.co.uk Web: www.yorkshireairmuseum.co.uk

A fascinating museum authentically based on a former World War II Bomber Command Station. Experience the atmosphere of the original restored control tower and appreciate the interesting collections of squadron memorabilia. Other displays pay tribute to the Air Gunners, Royal Observer Corps, Airborne Forces and much more. The aircraft collection contains more than 40 historic airframes and includes the unique Halifax Bomber and the Cayley Glider.

Opening Times: Mon to Fri 10:30-16:00, Sat, Sun & BH 10:30-17:00. Times may vary in winter - please check.
Admission: Adult £4.00, Child/OAP £3.00, Family £12.00. Group rates available.
Location: Five miles south east of York, good regional road access. Map Ref: 56

Yorkshire Museum

Museum Gardens, York YO1 7FR Tel: 01904 551800 Fax: 01904 551802
Email: yorkshire.museum@york.gov.uk Web: www.york.gov.uk/heritage/museums/yorkshire

Set in ten acres of botanical gardens, the Yorkshire Museum houses some of the richest archaeological finds in Europe and covers over 1000 years of local history. Discover Roman, Anglo-Saxon, Viking and Medieval life and meet the Jurassic sea-dragons. Exciting temporary exhibitions on display throughout the year. Call for details.

Opening Times: Daily 10:00-17:00. Admission: Adult £4.50, Child/Concession £2.95. Group rates available. Location: City centre location, five minute walk from York Railway Station. Map Ref: 53

Yorkshire Museum of Farming, Murton Park

Murton Park, Murton Lane, York YO19 5UF Tel: 01904 489966 Fax: 01904 489159

Covers 200 years of agriculture, including machinery, equipment and domestic items. Land Army display, James Herriot surgery, working blacksmith's forge, paddocks with rare breeds, farm animals and poultry. Large reference library.
Opening Times: Mar to Oct 10:00-17:00, Nov to Feb 10:00-16:00. Closed Xmas & New Year.
Admission: Adult £3.60, Child £1.80, Under 5s Free, Concessions £3.00, Family £10.00. Season ticket: Adult £12.00, Family £25.00. Location: Three miles from York, just off York ring road (A64), first left from roundabout off Bridlington Road - A166. Map Ref: 56

Edinburgh, Glasgow & Southern Scotland

This is the region of Sir Walter Scott and Robert Burns, writers who did much to familiarise th[e] world with romantic Scotland. Edinburgh is a stunning city renowned for its castle and th[e] architecture of the city displayed at its best in New Town, the most impressive area of Georgia[n] architecture in the whole of Europe. Glasgow now rates as the second favourite city to visit [in] Britain, the cathedral being the central point of the oldest part of the city.

Scotland is a nation with a proud and ancient heritage, and the world-class museums an[d] galleries of Edinburgh and Glasgow provide a wonderful source of culture but there is also [a] wealth of smaller museums throughout southern Scotland each with their particular story to tell

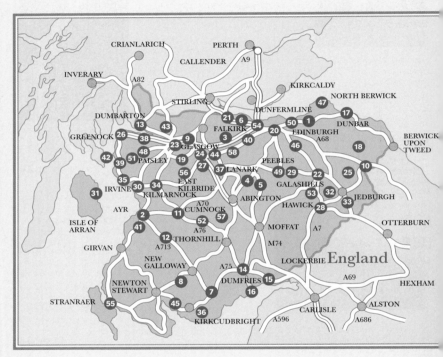

The Red Map References should be used to locate Museums etc on the pages that follow

The Red Map References should be used to locate B & B properties on the pages that follow
The Green Map References provide the location of places to visit detailed above

312

Edinburgh, Glasgow & Southern Scotland

Myreton Motor Museum

Aberlady EH32 0PZ   Tel: 01875 870288/0794 706 6666

Established in 1966, Myreton has on show cars, motorcycles, commercials from 1899 to 1969. There is also a large collection of period advertising, posters and enamel signs etc.

Opening Times: Easter to Sep daily 10:30-16:30, Oct to Easter Sun 12:00-15:00.
Admission: Adult £4.00, Child £1.00, OAP/Student £3.00.   Location: One mile from village of Aberlady, East Lothian.

Map Ref: 1

Burns Cottage & Museum

Burns Cottage, Alloway, Ayr KA7 4PY   Tel: 01292 441215   Fax: 01292 441750
Email: burnscottage@netscapeonline.co.uk   Web: www.robertburns.org

Birthplace of Robert Burns (1759-96), Scotland's National Poet. Museum contains many exhibits of Burns' songs, poems, letters and personal belongings. Original manuscripts of 'Auld Lang Syne' and 'Tam O'Shanter'.

Opening Times: Apr to Sep daily 09:00-17:30. Oct to Mar 10:00-17:00.   Admission: Adult £3.00, Child/OAP £1.50, Family £9.00.   Location: Two miles south of Ayr. One mile off A77 Glasgow to Stranraer.

Map Ref: 2

Rozelle House Gallery

Rozelle Park, Monument Road, Ayr KA7 4NQ   Tel: 01292 445447

The recently acquired Goudie Collection, an exciting series of paintings which vividly depict Burn's haunting tale of Tam O'Shanter are the focus for Rozelle Galleries. Interspersed with this will be a programme of art, craft and museum exhibitions.

Opening Times: Mon to Sat 10:00-17:00 Apr to Oct also Sun 14:00-17:00.   Admission: Free.
Location: Approximately two miles from Ayr Town Centre in Robert Burns Birthplace, Alloway.

Map Ref: 2

Bennie Museum

9/11 Mansfield Street, Bathgate EH48 4HN   Tel: 01506 634944
Email: thornton@benniemuseum.freeserve.co.uk   Web: www.benniemuseum.homestead.com

A small local history museum containing artefacts relating to the social, industrial and historic past of Bathgate.

Opening Times: Apr to Sep Mon to Sat 10:00-16:00. Oct to Mar Mon to Sat 11:00-15:30.
Admission: Free. Location: Town centre.

Map Ref: 3

Biggar Gasworks Museum

Moat Park, Biggar ML12 6DT   Tel / Fax: 01899 221050
Email: margaret@bmtrust.freeserve.co.uk   Web: www.biggar-net.co.uk

The only remaining gas works in Scotland. By 1839 Biggar had its own gasworks. A major reconstruction in 1914 brought Biggar Gasworks more or less into its present form. Closed down in 1973, but not demolished, it has been preserved for future generations.

Opening Times: May to Sep Mon to Sun 14:00-17:00.   Admission: £1.00.   Location: Near town centre.

Map Ref: 4

Gladstone Court Museum

North Back Road, Biggar ML12 6DT   Tel / Fax: 01899 221050
Email: margaret@bmtrust.freeserve.co.uk   Web: www.biggar-net.co.uk

Gladstone Court is for all the family, its small shops and offices displaying small town life as the old remember it and the young imagine it. Here is an ironmonger's store, a bank, photographers, chemist, dressmaker, watchmaker, millner, printer and bootmaker, together with a village library and schoolroom.

Opening Times: Easter to mid Oct Mon to Sat 10.30:17:00, Sun 14:00-17:00.   Admission: Adult £2.00 Child £1.00 Concessions £1.50 Family £4.00 Group discounts.   Location: Near town centre.

Map Ref: 4

Edinburgh, Glasgow & Southern Scotland

Greenhill Farmhouse Museum
Burn Braes, Biggar ML12 6DT   Tel / Fax: 01899 221050
Email: margaret@bmtrust.freeserve.co.uk   Web: www.biggar-net.co.uk

Rebuilt in the lovely Burn Braes, Biggar, stands Greenhill Farmhouse. The Museum Trust rescued it in a derelict condition and moved the house to Biggar as a home for its Covenanting Museum.

Opening Times: May to Sep 14:00-17:00 Sat & Sun or by appointment weekdays.
Admission: Adult £1.00 Child 50p Concession 75p.   Location: Near town centre, five minutes walk.
Map Ref: 4

John Buchan Centre
Broughton, Biggar ML12 6HQ   Tel / Fax: 01899 221050
Email: margaret@bmtrust.freeserve.co.uk   Web: www.biggar-net.co.uk

In the Old Free Kirk at Broughton, John Buchan, a young supply clergyman, met his wife, Helen Masterton. The Kirk now houses a display commemorating the life and work of their eldest son, John, poet, statesman and author of many popular novels. Broughton was his childhood holiday home, held in great affection by himself and his sister Anna, who also wrote under the pen name of O Douglas.

Opening Times: May to Sep daily 14:00-17:00.   Admission: Adult £1.50, Child 50p.
Location: Old Free Kirk, Broughton.
Map Ref: 5

Moat Park Heritage Centre
Moat Park, Kirkstyle, Biggar ML12 6DT   Tel / Fax: 01899 221050
Email: margaret@bmtrust.freeserve.co.uk   Web: www.biggar-net.co.uk

The Moat Park Heritage Centre was opened by HRH The Princess Royal in June 1988. One can see here how the Clyde and Tweed valleys were formed millions of years ago, rub shoulders with an Iron Age family or encounter a blood thirsty Roman soldier and other figures from our past. Splendid models display early dwellings, mottes, castles and farmhouses. There is also a magnificent Victorian patchwork.

Opening Times: Easter to mid Oct Mon to Sat 10:30-17:00, Sun 14:00-17:00.   Admission: Adult £2.00 Child £1.00 Concession £1.50 Family £4.00.   Location: Near town centre.   Map Ref: 4

BLACKRIDGE   West Lothian

Blackridge Community Museum
Craig Inn Centre, Blackridge EH48 3RJ   Tel: 01501 752396
Email: museums@westlothian.gov.uk   Web: www.wlonline.org

Display on the origins of the village as a coaching stop and its subsequent development. Programme of temporary community exhibitions.

Opening Times: Tue & Thu 14:00-18:30 Wed 09:30-12:30 13:30-16:30 alternate Sat 09:30-12:30.
Admission: Free.   Location: In centre of village, enter through library in Craig Inn Centre.
Map Ref: 3

BO'NESS   West Lothian

Scottish Railway Preservation Society
Bo'ness & Kinneil Railway, Bo'ness Station, Union Street, Bo'ness EH51 9AQ
Tel: 01506 825855   Fax: 01506 828766   Email: srps@srps.org.uk   Web: www.srps.org.uk

Caledonian Railway Locomotive CR419 at Bo'ness Station

Bo'ness & Kinneil Railway is home to an exciting collection of railway buildings, locomotives, equipment, carriages and wagons. Your journey through the Forth Valley takes you to the Caverns of Birkhill Fireclay Mine. On your return you can visit the railway exhibition depicting the history of railways in Scotland.

Opening Times: Weekends 29 Mar to 20 Oct. July & Aug Tue to Sun 11:00-16:15.   Admission: Entry to museum is free, Rail Fares - Adult £4.50, Child £2.00, Concession £3.50, Family (2 adults and 2 children) £11.00.
Location: In town of Bo'ness. From Edinburgh M9 leave junction 3, follow A904 to Bo'ness, from West leave M9 at junction 5, follow signs to Bo'ness.   Map Ref: 6

314

Edinburgh, Glasgow & Southern Scotland

CASTLE DOUGLAS *Dumfries & Galloway*

Castle Douglas Art Gallery

Market Street, Castle Douglas DG7 1BE   Tel / Fax: 01557 331643
Email: davidd@dumgal.gov.uk   Web: www.dumfriesmuseum.demon.co.uk

The Gallery plays host to an annual programme of exhibitions ranging from fine art, craft, photography. Touring exhibitions are regularly displayed at the Gallery.

Opening Times: Opening times may vary, please contact. Admission: Free. Location: Town centre.

Map Ref: 7

Clatteringshaw Visitor Centre

By New Galloway, Castle Douglas DG7 3SQ   Tel: 01671 402420   Fax: 01671 403708

See interpretive display of Galloway wildlife, touchy-feely sections. Tearoom and shop. Forest trails, cycle routes, forest drive nearby. Panoramic views of Clatteringshaw Loch to the wild Galloway Hills beyond.

Opening Times: Easter to 1 Sep daily 10:30-17:00. 2 Sep to 27 Oct daily 10:30-16:30.
Admission: Free. Location: Five miles south west of New Galloway on A712.   Map Ref: 8

COATBRIDGE *Lanarkshire*

Summerlee Heritage Park

Heritage Way, Coatbridge ML5 1QD   Tel: 01236 431261   Fax: 01236 440429

A large exhibition hall with extensive displays of social and industrial heritage. Outside is Scotland's only working electric tramway, a recreated addit mine and miners' cottages.

Opening Times: Apr to Oct daily 10:00-17:00, Nov to Mar daily 10:00-16:00. Admission: Free.
Location: To the west of Coatbridge town centre, by the central station.   Map Ref: 9

COLDSTREAM *Berwickshire*

Coldstream Museum

Market Square, Coldstream TD12 4BD   Tel: 01890 882630

Local history and Coldstream Guards.

Opening Times: Easter to Sep Mon to Sat 10:00-16:00, Sun 2-4, Oct Mon to Sat 13:00-16:00.
Admission: Free. Location: Near town centre.   Map Ref: 10

CUMNOCK *Ayrshire*

Baird Institute Museum

3 Lugar Street, Cumnock KA18 1AD   Tel / Fax: 01290 421701

A local museum featuring temporary and permanent exhibitions. Displays include Cumnock Pottery, Mauchline Boxware and Ayrshire Embroidery. A room is dedicated to Keir Hardy, founder of the Labour Party. Family history information is available.

Opening Times: Mon, Tue, Thu & Fri 10:00-13:00 & 13:30-16:30. Admission: Free.
Location: Near Cumnock Town Centre.   Map Ref: 11

DALMELLINGTON *Ayrshire*

Cathcartston Visitor Centre

Cathcartston, Dalmellington KA6 7QY   Tel: 01292 550633   Fax: 01292 550937
Email: stanley.sarsfield@east-ayrshire.gov.uk

A local history museum with a fine collection of photographs and maps showing the Doon Valley over the centuries. Local history displays combined with changing art exhibitions and a weaving tableau.

Opening Times: Mon to Fri 10:00-16:30. Admission: Free. Location: In the centre of Dalmellington, off the main square.

Map Ref: 12

Scottish Industrial Railway Centre

Minnivey Colliery, Burnton, Dalmellington KA6 7PU   Tel: 01292 531144
Email: agcthoms@aol.com   Web: www.arpg.org.uk

A live steam centre where industrial railway locomotives and rolling stock can be seen in action in an authentic setting, in the scenic Doon Valley.

Opening Times: 5, 26 & 27 May, 30 Jun, 7, 14, 21 & 28 Jul, 4, 11, 18 & 25 Aug & 1 Sep.
Admission: Adult £2.00, Child £1.50, Concession £2.00, Family £6.00.   Location: Dalmellington
one mile, Ayr 12 miles.
Map Ref: 12

DUMBARTON *Dunbartonshire*

Denny Ship Model Experimental Tank
Castle Street, Dumbarton G82 1QS   Tel: 01389 763444   Fax: 01389 743093

Step back into the world of the Victorian ship designer, fully restored and still used for testing ship designs.

Opening Times: Mon to Sat 10:00-16:00.   Admission: Adult £1.50 Child/OAP 75p Family £3.00.
Location: Near town centre, two minutes walk from railway station.
Map Ref: 13

DUMFRIES

Burns House
Burns Street, Dumfries DG1 2PS   Tel: 01387 255297   Fax: 01387 265081
Email: info@dumfriesmuseum.demon.co.uk   Web: www.dumfriesmuseum.demon.co.uk

Simple sandstone house in a quiet Dumfries street where Robert Burns, Scotland's National Poet, spent the last years of his brilliant life.

Opening Times: Apr to Sep Mon to Sat 10:00-17:00 Sun 14:00-17:00. Oct to Mar Tue to Sat
10:00-13:00 14:00-17:00.   Admission: Free.   Location: One minute walk from Broons Road car
park.
Map Ref: 14

Dumfries & Galloway Aviation Museum
Former Control Tower, Heathhall Industrial Estate, Dumfries DG1 3PH   Tel: 01387 251623
Web: www.dgam.co.uk

Based around the original control tower of RAF Dumfries, the museum is a fascinating collection of aircraft and memorabilia from the earliest days of flight to recent times.

Opening Times: Easter to Oct Sat & Sun 10:00-17:00. Jun to Aug Wed 18:00-21:00.
Admission: Adult £2.00, Child £1.00.   Location: Heathhall Industrial Estate, off A701.
Map Ref: 14

Dumfries Museum & Camera Obscura
The Observatory, Dumfries DG2 7SW   Tel: 01387 253374   Fax: 01387 265081
Email: info@dumfriesmuseum.demon.co.uk   Web: www.dumfriesmuseum.demon.co.uk

A treasure house of the history of Dumfries and Galloway telling the story of the land and people of the region.

Opening Times: Apr to Sep Mon to Sat 10:00-17:00 Sun 14:00-17:00. Oct to Mar Tue to Sat
10:00-13:00 14:00-17:00. Camera Obscura closed Oct to Mar.   Admission: Museum free.
Camera Obscura Adult £1.50 Concession 75p.   Location: Five minutes walk from Whitesands.
Map Ref: 14

Gracefield Arts Centre
29 Edinburgh Road, Dumfries DG1 1JQ   Tel: 01387 262084   Fax: 01387 255173

The Gracefield collection features paintings, drawings and prints by Scottish artists dating from the 1840s to the present day, shown in regular selected exhibitions three/four times a year.

Opening Times: Tue to Sat 10:00-17:00.   Admission: Free.   Location: Five minute walk from
train station and town centre.
Map Ref: 14

Old Bridge House
Mill Street, Dumfries DG2 7BE   Tel: 01387 256904   Fax: 01387 265081
Email: info@dumfriesmuseum.demon.co.uk   Web: www.dumfriesmuseum.demon.co.uk

Built in 1660 into the sandstone of the 15th century Devorgilla Bridge, Dumfries' oldest house is now a museum of everyday life in the town.

Opening Times: Apr to Sep Mon To Sat 10:00-17:00 Sun 14:00-17:00.   Admission: Free.
Location: One minutes walk from Whitesands.
Map Ref: 14

Robert Burns Centre

Mill Road, Dumfries DG2 7BE   Tel / Fax: 01387 264808
Email: info@dumfriesmuseum.demon.co.uk   Web: www.dumfriesmuseum.demon.co.uk
Situated in the town's 18th century watermill on the West Bank of the River Nith, The Robert Burns Centre tells the story of Robert Burns' last years spent in the bustling streets and lively atmosphere of Dumfries in the late 18th century.

Opening Times: Apr to Sep Mon to Sat 10:00-20:00 Sun 14:00-17:00. Oct to Mar Tue to Sat 10:00-13:00 14:00-17:00. Admission: Free. Location: West Bank of River Nith, opposite Whitesands.

Map Ref: 14

Savings Banks Museum

Ruthwell, Dumfries DG1 4NN   Tel: 01387 870640   Email: tsbmuseum@btinternet.com
Web: www.lloydstsb.com/savingsbanksmuseum

International collection of money boxes and savings bank memorabilia. Social and family records and information on Medieval Ruthwell Cross. History of savings banks and founder, the Rev Henry Duncan DD.

Opening Times: Daily 10:00-13:00 14:00-17:00. Closed Sun & Mon in winter. Admission: Free. Location: Six miles west of Annan on B724.

Map Ref: 15

Shambellie House Museum of Costume

New Abbey, Dumfries DG2 8HQ   Tel: 01387 850375   Fax: 01387 850461   Web: www.nms.ac.uk/custume

Step back in time and experience Victorian and Edwardian grace and refinement. Set in attractive wooded grounds, Shambellie is a beautiful Victorian country house which offers visitors the chance to see period clothes, from the 1850s to the 1950s in appropriate room settings, with accessories, furniture and decorative art.

Opening Times: Apr to Oct, 11:00-17:00. Admission: Adult £2.50, Child £1.50, Concession £1.50. Location: Seven miles south of Dumfries, on the A710.

Map Ref: 16

DUNBAR *East Lothian*

Dunbar Town House Museum

Dunbar Town House, High Street, Dunbar EH42 1ER   Tel: 01368 863734   Fax: 01620 828201
Email: elms@elothian-museums.demon.co.uk   Web: www.dunbarmuseum.org

Dunbar Town House Museum is based in a 17th century building. There is an archaeology display, a local history room and a different local history exhibition each year.

Opening Times: Apr to Sep 12:30-16:30. Admission: Free. Location: High Street.

Map Ref: 17

John Muir Birthplace

128 High Street, Dunbar EH42   Tel: 01368 860187   Fax: 01620 828201
Email: elms@elothian-museums.demon.co.uk   Web: www.muir-birthplace.org

The birthplace of the environmentalist John Muir, includes displays about Muir's life and ideas, and the conservation movement.

Opening Times: Apr to Sep 11:00-13:00 14:00-17:00. Admission: Free. Location: High Street.

Map Ref: 17

DUNS *Berwickshire*

Jim Clark Room

44 Newton Street, Duns TD11 3AU   Tel: 01361 883960
Museum dedicated to local driver Jim Clark.

Opening Times: Easter to Sep daily 10:30-13:00 14:00-16:30, Sun 14:00-16:00, Oct Mon to Sat 13:00-16:00. Admission: Adult £1.30, SBC Residents Free. Location: In main town centre.

Map Ref: 18

Calderglen Country Park

Strathaven Road, East Kilbride G75 0QZ   Tel: 01355 236644

Visitor Centre, permanent 'Hidden World' exhibit and temporary exhibitions, natural history, horticulture focus. Children's zoo, conservatory with exotic plants, and animals with activity programme.

Opening Times: Centre Apr to Sep Mon to Fri 10:30-17:00, Sat, Sun & BH 11:30-18.30. Oct to Mar 11:00-16:00. Conservatory Apr to Sep 10:00-20:30, Oct to Mar 10:00-16:30.
Admission: Free.   Location: On Strathaven Road on south edge of East Kilbride.   Map Ref: 19

Hunter House

Maxwellton Road, Calderwood, East Kilbride G74 3LU   Tel: 01355 261261

Original farmhouse home of medical pioneers John and William Hunter. Exhibits on their lives and work, interactives, audio visual, IT base.

Opening Times: Apr to Sep Mon to Fri 12:30-16:30, Sat to Sun 11:00-17:00.   Admission: Free.
Location: Near East Kilbride Town Centre.   Map Ref: 19

Museum of Scottish Country Life

Wester Kittochside, East Kilbride G76 9HR   Tel: 01355 224181   Fax: 01355 571290
Web: www.nms.ac.uk/countrylife

The new museum shows how country people lived and worked in Scotland in the past and how this has shaped the countryside of today. The site includes a new exhibition building housing the National Country Life Collections and the original Georgian farmhouse and working farm.

Opening Times: Daily 10:00-17:00.   Admission: Adult £3.00, Child Free, Concessions £1.50.
Location: Situated between East Kilbride and Glasgow.
Map Ref: 19

City Art Centre

2 Market Street, Edinburgh EH1 1DE   Tel: 0131 529 3993
Fax: 0131 529 3986   Web: www.cac.org.uk

The City Art Centre is both home to Edinburgh's outstanding collection of Scottish art and one of the United Kingdom's premier temporary exhibition spaces. Since it opened in 1980, the City Art Centre has mounted a huge range of exhibitions, from rare Egyptian antiquities to the most innovative contemporary art, from Michelangelo drawings to Star Trek. The scale and range of the exhibition programme has made the gallery one of Britain's most visited exhibition centres. The city's fine art collection consists of almost 4,000 works of Scottish art: paintings, watercolours, drawings, prints, photographs, sculpture and tapestries, including work by McTaggart, Fergusson, Peploe and Eardley. The collection reflects all of the significant influences and movements in Scottish art, ranging from early portraiture, through the Glasgow Boys, the Edinburgh School and the Colourists.

The City Art Centre

The Blue Hat

Opening Times: Mon to Sat 10:00-17:00, Sun during Jul & Aug 12:00-17:00.   Admission: Free.   Map Ref: 20

www.tomorrows.co.uk

Full information on our collection of travel guides and secure store

Dean Gallery

73 Belford Road, Edinburgh EH4 3DS   Tel: 0131 624 6200   Fax: 0131 623 7126
Email: deaninfo@nationalgalleries.org   Web: www.nationalgalleries.org

Dean Gallery

The Dean Gallery just opposite the Gallery of Modern Art, holds an extensive collection of Dada and Surrealist art including works by Dali, Ernst, Magritte, Man Ray and Miro. It is also home to an impressive collection of works by Sir Eduardo Paolozzi including a substantial number of plaster sculptures, prints and drawings. Spectacular city views and beautiful sculpture park.

Opening Times: Mon to Sat 10:00-17:00, Sun 12:00-17:00. Admission: Free to permanent collection, admission charges for special exhibitions. Location: Ten minutes walk from West End Princes Street, or catch free bus from Scottish National Portrait Gallery.   Map Ref: 20

Edinburgh Brass Rubbing Centre

Trinity Apse, Chambers Close, Royal Mile, Edinburgh EH1 1SS   Tel: 0131 556 4364
Web: www.cac.org.uk

Edinburgh Brass Rubbing Centre

The Brass Rubbing Centre occupies Trinity Apse, the sole surviving fragment of the Gothic Trinity College Church founded about 1460. It contains a fascinating collection of replicas moulded from ancient Pictish stones, and medieval church brasses. No experience is required to make a rubbing, and staff are on hand to assist. The Centre also stocks high-quality, ready-made rubbings and brass rubbing kits.

Opening Times: Apr to Sep Mon to Sat 10:00-17:00, Sun during the Edinburgh International Festival 12:00-17:00. Admission: Free.   Map Ref: 20

Edinburgh University - Historical Musical Instruments

Reid Concert Hall, Bistro Square, Edinburgh EH8 9AG   Tel: 0131 650 4367   Fax: 0131 650 2425   Email: euchmi@ed.ac.uk   Web: www.music.ed.ac.uk/euchmi

Outstanding display of over 1000 musical instruments showing 400 years of history of folk and domestic music, bands and orchestras, plus interactive devices.

Opening Times: Mon to Fri 14:00-17:00, Wed 15:00-17:00, Sat 10:00-13:00. Closed Xmas & New Year. Admission: Free. Location: Bristo Square, next to McEwan Hall   Map Ref: 20

The Fruitmarket Gallery

45 Market Street, Edinburgh EH1 1DF   Tel: 0131 225 2383   Fax: 0131 220 3130   Email: lindsay@fruitmarket.co.uk   Web: www.fruitmarket.co.uk

fruitmarket
the gallery

The Fruitmarket Gallery, Edinburgh

Situated in one of the world's most beautiful cities, Edinburgh's Fruitmarket Gallery is an acclaimed international art space which has operated as a contemporary gallery since 1974. The gallery shows a programme of exciting, thought-provoking exhibitions of Scottish, British and international contemporary art. The Fruitmarket Gallery exhibition programme is complemented by an ambient, street-level glass fronted café and innovative bookshop.

Opening Times: Mon to Sat 11:00-18:00, Sun 12:00-17:00. Admission: Most exhibitions free, small charge for festival exhibition. Location: Very central location, next to Waverley Station.   Map Ref: 20

Georgian House

7 Charlotte Square, Edinburgh EH2 4DR   Tel / Fax: 0131 226 3318

Entrance to the Georgian House
7 Charlotte Square

The Georgian House is part of Robert Adam's masterpiece of urban design, Charlotte Square. It dates from 1876, when those who could afford it began to escape the cramped, squalid conditions of Edinburgh's Old Town to settle in the fashionable New Town. The house's beautiful china, shining silver, exquisite paintings and furniture all reflect the domestic surroundings and social conditions of the times.

Opening Times: 20 Jan to 24 Mar daily 11:00-16:00, 25 Mar to 27 Oct daily 10:00-18:00, 28 Oct to 24 Dec daily 11:00-16:00. Admission: Adult £5.00, Concession £3.75, Family £13.50. Location: Two minutes from west end of Princes Street, ten minutes from Tourist Information Centre.   Map Ref: 20

The Grand Lodge of Scotland Museum

Freemasons Hall, 96 George Street, Edinburgh EH2 3DH   Tel: 0131 225 5304   Fax: 0131 225 3953   Email: grandsecretary@sol.co.uk   Web: www.grandlodgescotland.com

All objects relating to Scottish Freemasonry, including glassware, ceramics, coins, photographs and books.

Opening Times: Mon to Fri 09:30-16:30. Closed Sat, Sun & BH. Admission: Free.
Location: Town centre.   Map Ref: 20

Granton Centre

242 West Granton Road, Edinburgh EH5 1JA   Tel: 0131 247 4470   Fax: 0131 551 4106
Web: www.nms.ac.uk

Visit the major store of the National Museums of Scotland; important conservation work is carried out here, preparing thousands of objects for display, as diverse as classic motorbikes, whale bones and ancient pottery.

Opening Times: Tue, tours at 10:00 and 14:00. Admission: Adult £1.00, Child Free. Visits must be booked one day in advance. Location: Half an hour from city centre, by car, by Lothian Buses 10, 8 & 32.   Map Ref: 20

Lauriston Castle

Lauriston Castle

Cramond Road South, Davidson's Mains, Edinburgh EH4 5QD
Tel: 0131 336 2060

A 16th century tower house with later additions, Lauriston Castle stands in tranquil grounds overlooking the Forth at Cramond. The preserved Edwardian interior is an ideal backdrop to the rich collection of fine and decorative art assembled by the last private owners. The Castle and its grounds are host to a year round programme of art and craft based workshops, study days and family events.

Opening Times: Guided tours only Apr to Oct 11:20, 12:20, 14:20, 15:20 & 16:20. Closed Fri. Nov to Mar Sat & Sun 14:20 & 15:20.
Admission: Adult £4.50, Concession £3.00.   Map Ref: 20

Lothian & Borders Fire Brigade, Museum of Fire

Brigade Headquarters, Lauriston Place, Edinburgh EH3 9DE Tel: 0131 228 2401 Fax: 0131 229 8359 Email: csg@lothian.fire-uk.org Web: www.lothian.fire-uk.org

The Museum tells the history of the oldest fire brigade in the UK (formed 1824), showing the development of fire fighting, displaying a range of engines along with many other fire related items.

Opening Times: Mon to Fri 09:00-16:30. Closed Xmas & New Year also first two weeks Aug.
Admission: Free. Location: City Centre, next to Art College.   Map Ref: 20

Museum of Childhood

42 High Street, Royal Mile, Edinburgh EH1 1TG Tel: 0131 529 4142 Web: www.cac.org.uk

It is a treasure house crammed full of memories of childhood past and present. There are toys and games galore from all around the world, ranging from dolls and teddy bears to train sets and tricycles. Listen to children chanting multiplication tables in the 1930s schoolroom. Watch the street games played by Edinburgh children filmed in 1951. Find out how children were brought up, dressed and educated in decades gone by.

Opening Times: Mon to Sat 10:00-17:00, Sun during Jul & Aug 12:00-17:00. Admission: Free.   Map Ref: 20

Museum of Edinburgh

Huntly House, 142 Canongate, Royal Mile, Edinburgh EH8 8DD Tel: 0131 529 4143
Web: www.cac.org.uk

Museum of Edinburgh

Housing collections relating to the story of Edinburgh from pre-historic times to the present day, the museum's treasures include the National Covenant, the great charter demanding religious freedoms, signed in 1638. The museum also includes the feeding bowl and collar presented to 'Greyfriars Bobby', the little Skye Terrier dog that maintained a vigil by the grave of his master and won the hearts of the people of Edinburgh.

Opening Times: Mon to Sat 10:00-17:00. Sun during the Edinburgh International Festival 14:00-17:00.
Admission: Free.   Map Ref: 20

National Gallery of Scotland

The Mound, Edinburgh EH2 2EL Tel: 0131 624 6200 Fax: 0131 623 7126
Email: nginfo@nationalgalleries.org Web: www.nationalgalleries.org

National Gallery of Scotland

Scotland's greatest collection of European paintings, drawings and prints dating from the early Renaissance to the late 19th century. The collection includes works by Raphael, Titian, Velazquez, Poussin, Rembrandt, Vermeer, Rubens, Turner and the Impressionists. Also houses the national collection of Scottish art with works by Ramsay, Raeburn, Wilkie and McTaggart.

Opening Times: Mon to Sat 10:00-17:00, Sun 12:00-17:00. Admission: Free to permanent collection, charges for special exhibitions. Location: Right in the centre of Edinburgh, just off Princes Street.   Map Ref: 20

THE GORDON HIGHLANDERS

National War Museum of Scotland

♿ 🔵 🔲 🔥

Edinburgh Castle, Castlehill, Edinburgh EH1 2NG   Tel: 0131 225 7534   Fax: 0131 225 3848   Web: www.nms.ac.uk/war

Explores the Scottish experience of war and military service over the last 400 years. The lives of many thousands of Scots have been dominated by this experience - the objects in the museum and the individuals and events to which they relate make this clear. The museum also reveals the extent to which the war and military services have influenced Scotland's history, identity and reputation abroad.

Opening Times: Apr to Oct 09:45-17:30, Nov to Mar 09:45-16:30. Admission: Included in admission to Edinburgh Castle. Location: In city centre, five minutes walk from Princes Street.

Map Ref: 20

Nelson Monument

Calton Hill, Edinburgh EH7 5AA   Tel: 0131 556 2716 Web: www.cac.org.uk

High on Calton Hill, this monument to Admiral Lord Nelson and Trafalgar was built between 1807 and 1815. In 1853 a large time ball was introduced. It is lowered each day as the one o'clock gun is fired from Edinburgh Castle. The panoramic view from the monument is framed by Fife to the north, the Forth estuary to the east, the Moorfoot Hills to the south and the Forth Rail and Road Bridges to the west.

Opening Times: Apr to Sep Mon 13:00-18:00, Tue to Sat 10:00-18:00. Oct to Mar Mon to Sat 10:00-15:00.   Admission: Adult £2.00.

Map Ref: 20

Nelson Monument

Newhaven Heritage Museum

24 Pier Place, Newhaven Harbour, Edinburgh EH6 4LP   Tel: 0131 551 4165

What was it like to live in the tightly-knit fishing community of Newhaven, earning a living as a fishwife or fisherman braving the sea to bring home the catch? Discover the answer in the historic fishmarket, next to Harry Ramsden's fish and chip restaurant, overlooking picturesque Newhaven Harbour.

Opening Times: Mon to Sun 12:00-17:00. Admission: Free.

Map Ref: 20

The lively and informative Newhaven Heritage Museum

The People's Story

Canongate Tolbooth, Royal Mile, Edinburgh EH8 8BN   Tel: 0131 529 4057 Web: www.cac.org.uk

Situated in the Canongate Tolbooth, opposite the Museum of Edinburgh in the Royal Mile, The People's Story Museum uses oral history, reminiscence, written sources and reconstructed set to tell the story of the lives, work and leisure of the ordinary people of the Edinburgh from the late 18th century to the present day.

Opening Times: Mon to Sat 10:00-17:00. Sun during the Edinburgh International Festival 12:00-17:00. Admission: Free.

Map Ref: 20

The People's Story Museum

Royal Museum & Museum of Scotland

Chambers Street, Edinburgh EH1 1JF   Tel: 0131 227 4219/4422   Fax: 0131 220 4819
Email: info@nms.ac.uk   Web: www.nms.ac.uk

Royal Museum - presenting the world to Scotland. The Royal Museum houses outstanding International collections reflecting the diversity of life on earth and the ingenuity of humankind. Explore this magnificent Victorian building, distinguished by its soaring glass-topped roof, which floods the elegant main hall with natural light. Museum of Scotland - presenting Scotland to the world. A striking new landmark adjacent to the Royal Museum, in Edinburgh historic old town. This stunning building presents for the first time, the history of Scotland, its land, its people and their achievements. The series of galleries take you on a journey from Scotland's geological beginnings, through time, to the 20th century. The Royal Museum and Museum of Scotland have been awarded a five-star museum rating by the Scottish Tourist Board.

Opening Times: Mon to Fri 10:00-17:00, Tue 10:00-18:00, Sun 12:00-17:00.   Admission: Free.
Location: Near city centre, five minute walk from Princes Street and Royal Mile.   Map Ref: 20

Royal Observatory Visitor Centre

Blackford Hill, Edinburgh EH9 3HJ   Tel: 0131 668 8405   Fax: 0131 668 8429
Email: eas@roe.ac.uk   Web: www.roe.ac.uk

The Royal Observatory Visitor Centre is an interactive science centre housed in the beautiful Observatory buildings on Blackford Hill. Learn about the history of the Observatory in Edinburgh in 'Reaching for the Stars' exhibition.

Opening Times: Mon to Sat 10:00-17:00, Sun 12:00-17:00.   Admission: Adult £3.50, Child £2.50, Concession £2.00, Family £8.00.   Map Ref: 20

Royal Scots Regimental Museum

The Castle, Edinburgh EH1 2YT   Tel: 0131 310 5016/5017

The Royal Scots is the oldest Regiment in the British Army and as such is the Senior Infantry Regiment of the Line. It was raised in 1633 and through paintings, artefacts, silver and medals their fascinating story is told from formation to the present day.

Opening Times: Apr to Sep daily 09:30-17:30, Oct to Mar Mon to Fri 09:30-16:00.
Admission: Free.   Location: Edinburgh Castle.   Map Ref: 20

The Scott Monument, Edinburgh

Scott Monument

East Princes Street Gardens, Edinburgh EH2 2EJ   Tel: 0131 529 4068   Web: www.cac.org.uk

Designed by George Meikle Kemp, this monument to the great Scottish writer opened in August 1846. In the years since then millions of people have climbed the 200 foot structure to admire its commanding views of the city, the exhibition on the life of Sir Walter Scott and the statuettes of characters from his works which adorn the monument.

Opening Times: Mar to May Mon to Sun 10:00-18:00. Jun to Sep Mon to Sat 09:00-20:00, Sun 10:00-18:00. Oct Mon to Sat 10:00-18:00. Nov to Feb Mon to Sun 10:00-16:00.   Admission: Adult £2.50.   Map Ref: 20

Scottish National Gallery of Modern Art

79 Belford Road, Edinburgh EH4 3DR   Tel: 0131 624 6200
Fax: 0131 623 7126   Email: gmainfo@nationalgalleries.org
Web: www.nationalgalleries.org

Scotland's finest collection of 20th century paintings, sculpture and graphic art including works by Picasso, Matisse, Giacometti, Sickert and Hockney. Significant holdings of Surrealism and German Expressionism along with an unrivalled collection of 20th century Scottish art, from the Colourists right up to the present day. Sculptures by Moore, Hepworth and Paolozzi in surrounding grounds.

Scottish National Gallery
of Modern Art

Opening Times: Mon to Sat 10:00-17:00, Sun 12:00-17:00.
Admission: Free to permanent collection, admission charges for special exhibitions.   Location: Ten minutes walk from West End Princes Street, or catch free bus from Scottish National Portrait Gallery.   Map Ref: 20

Scottish National Portrait Gallery

1 Queen Street, Edinburgh EH2 1JD   Tel: 0131 624 6200   Fax: 0131 623 7126
Email: pginfo@nationalgalleries.org   Web: www.nationalgalleries.org

A visual history of Scotland from the 16th century to the present day, told through portraits of the people who shaped it: royals and rebels, poets and philosophers, heroes and villains. Among the most famous are Mary, Queen of Scots and Robert Burns. Also houses the National Photography Collection, including vast holdings of work by Hill and Adamson, the Scottish pioneers of photography.

Scottish National Portrait Gallery

Opening Times: Mon to Sat 10:00-17:00, Sun 12:00-17:00.   Admission: Free to permanent collection, admission charges for special exhibitions.
Location: Just a two minute walk from Princes Street (Eastend) and one minute walk from central bus station in St Andrew Square.   Map Ref: 20

Sir Jules Thorn Exhibition of the History of Surgery

Royal College Surgeons Edinburgh, 18 Nicolson Street, Edinburgh EH8 9DW   Tel: 0131 527 1649   Fax: 0131 557 6406   Email: museum@rcsed.ac.uk   Web: www.rcsed.ac.uk

The Exhibition traces the history of surgery in Edinburgh, from 1505 until the present day. Displays include descriptions of major discoveries (anaesthesia and antisepsis), as well as the story of Burke & Hare.

Opening Times: Mon to Fri 14:00-16:00. Closed Sat, Sun, BH & diploma days.
Admission: Free.   Location: Opposite Festival Theatre and University Old College (one mile from Princes Street).   Map Ref: 20

Talbot Rice Gallery

University of Edinburgh, Old College, South Bridge, Edinburgh EH8 9YL
Tel: 0131 6502211

A Georgian gallery with a collection of Italian and Dutch Old Master paintings and bronzes. The 'White Gallery' houses six contemporary exhibitions each year. The experimental 'Round Room' space has four installations each year.

The Torrie Collection

Opening Times: Tue to Sat 10:00-17:00, please phone for further details.   Admission: Free.   Location: Five minutes walk from Royal Mile, next to Royal Museum of Scotland.   Map Ref: 20

The Writers Museum

Lady Stairs House, Lady Stairs Cl, Lawnmarket, Royal Mile,
Edinburgh EH1 2PA Tel: 0131 529 4901 Web: www.cac.org.uk

The Museum is dedicated to Scotland's great literary figures: Robert Burns (1759-1796), Sir Walter Scott (1771-1832) and Robert Louis Stevenson (1850-1895). Other prominent Scottish writers are featured in the museum's temporary exhibition programme. In the adjacent Makars' Court, which takes its name from the Scots word for a writer or poet, commemorative flagstones celebrate the work of Scottish writers from the 14th century to the present day.

Opening Times: Mon to Sat 10:00-17:00. Admission: Free.
                                                                    Map Ref: 20

The Writers Museum, Edinburgh

FALKIRK

Callendar House

Callendar Estate, Falkirk FK1 1YR   Tel: 01324 503770   Fax: 01324 503771

600 years of Scottish history; costumed interpreters, working Georgian kitchen, exhibitions, Georgian gardens, gift shop, conference facilities, tea shop at the stables, the Park Gallery and maginificent grounds. Open all year.

Opening Times: Mon to Sat all year 10:00-16:00, Apr to Sep Sun 14:00-17:00. Admission: Adults £3.00, Child £1.00, OAP £1.50   Map Ref: 21

GALASHIELS *Selkirkshire*

Old Gala House

Scott Crescent, Galashiels TD1 3JS   Tel / Fax: 01896 752611

Museum and art gallery, former home of Laird of Gala.

Opening Times: Easter to Sep Tue to Sat 10:00-16:00, Jul to Aug Mon to Sat 10:00-16:00, Sun 14:00-16:00. Oct Tue to Sat 13:00-16:00. Admission: Free. Location: Five minute walk from town centre.
                                                                    Map Ref: 22

GLASGOW

Art Gallery & Museum

Kelvingrove, Glasgow G3 8AG   Tel: 0141 287 2699

Kelvingrove

Kelvingrove is home to one of the finest civic collections in Europe. The fine art displays offer old masters, including works by Filippino Lippi, Botticelli, and Rembrandt. There is also a notable collection of French 19th century paintings and of course of Scottish art, including works by Charles Rennie Mackintosh. The arms and armour displays are among the best outside London and include a set of horse armour made for the Earl of Pembroke, while other galleries feature Egyptology, Scottish archaeology and ethnography. The natural history collections range from the time of the dinosaurs to the present and feature, among other animals Sir Roger the Elephant, a popular children's favourite.

Milanese Armour

Opening Times: Mon to Sat 10:00-17:00, Fri & Sun 11:00-17:00. Admission: Free.
Location: 20 minutes from town centre.
                                                                    Map Ref: 23

Burrell Collection

2060 Pollokshaws Road, Glasgow G43 1AT   Tel: 0141 287 2550   Fax: 0141 287 2597

The Burrell Collection consists of some 9000 items of European, Near Eastern and Oriental fine and decorative art. Highlights of the collection include the spectacular medieval European stained glass, tapestries and furniture; Egyptian, Greek and Roman antiquities; 19th century French art including works by Degas and Cezanne; Islamic art and Chinese art. The collections are housed in a award winning building in the woodland surroundings of Pollak Country Park. They were a gift to the city from the great ship owner and collector Sir William Burrell.

The Warrick Vase from the Emperor
Hadrian's villa of Tivoli

Rodin, The Thinker

Opening Times: 15 Mar to 6 Jan Mon to Fri 10:00-17:00, Sat & Sun 11:00-17:00. Admission: Free.   Map Ref: 23

Clydebuilt - Scottish Maritime Museum

Kings Inch Road, Braehead, Glasgow G51 4BN   Tel: 0141 886 1013   Fax: 0141 886 1015
Email: clydebuilt@tinyworld.co.uk

The story of Glasgow, its river and people over 300 years from tobacco to shipbuilding with floating exhibits.

Opening Times: Mon to Sat 10:00-18:00 Sun 11:00-17:00. Admission: Adult £3.50 Child/OAP £1.75 Family £8.00.   Location: Next to Braehead Shopping Centre.   Map Ref: 23

Collins Gallery

University of Strathclyde, 22 Richmond Street, Glasgow G1 1XQ   Tel: 0141 548 2558
Fax: 0141 552 4053   Email: collinsgallery@strath.ac.uk

Lively, annual programme of temporary exhibitions covering contemporary Fine and Applied Art from British and International artists, both new and established. Artwork is usually for sale.

Opening Times: Mon to Fri 10:00-17:00 Sat 12:00-16:00. Closed Sun, public holidays and exhibition installations. Admission: Free. Location: City centre, 5 minute walk from railway stations and Underground.   Map Ref: 23

David Livingstone Centre

165 Station Road, Blantyre, Glasgow G72 9BT   Tel: 01698 823140

Scotland's most famous explorer and missionary was born here in Shuttlerow in 1813. Today the 18th century tenement commemorates David Livingstone's life and work.

Opening Times: 25 Mar to 24 Dec Mon to Sat 10:00-17:00, Sun 12:30-17:00. Admission: Adult £3.50, Concession £2.60, Family £9.50. Location: Just off junction 5 of M74 via A725 and A724, in Blantyre.   Map Ref: 24

Museums, Galleries, Historic Houses & Sites

Please let us know of any collections that are not listed in this guide that you feel should be listed. E-mail us on *editor@tomorrows.co.uk*
or return the Report Form on page 448

Fossil Grove

Victoria Park, Glasgow G14 1BN   Tel: 0141 950 1448

330 million year old fossilised tree stumps. The fossils represented the scale tree, which grew in swampy tropical forests during the carboniferous or coal age. Designated a Site of Special Scientific Interest by Scottish National Heritage.

Opening Times: Apr to Sep.   Admission: Free.

Fossil Grove

Map Ref: 23

Gallery of Modern Art

Queen Street, Glasgow G1 3AZ   Tel: 0141 229 1996

Opened in 1996, the gallery is housed in the elegant, neo-classical Royal Exchange Building, in the heart of Glasgow city centre. The collection consists of over 200 exhibits, mainly from living artists, including many works acquired through a specially created modern art fund. The global perspective of this collection includes contributions from artists hailing from Papua New Guinea, Australia and Mexico. The contemporary works on display include paintings, sculpture and kinetic art. Pieces featured include work by

artists, with international reputations such as Niki de Saint Phalle, David Hockney, Sebastiao Salgado and Edward Bersudsky. Some of Scotland's best known artists are also featured: Peter Howson, Steven Campbell, Adrian Wiszniewski and Alison Watt. The Gallery of Modern Art aims to widen public access to contemporary art; in particular targeting young adults aged 16-25 years. A thought-provoking programme of temporary exhibitions and workshops focuses upon contemporary social issues, often featuring groups marginalized in today's society.

Opening Times: Mon to Thu & Sat 10:00-17:00, Fri & Sun 11:00-17:00.   Admission: Free.
Location: In city centre.

Map Ref: 23

Glasgow Botanic Gardens

730 Great Western Road, Glasgow G12 0UE   Tel: 0141 334 2422
Fax: 0141 339 6964

Glasgow Botanic Gardens are best known for their tropical collections. The internationally famous Kibble Palace is home to temperate plants and white marble statuary which enhance the atmosphere of Victorian Elegance. Situated within Glasgow's west end bound on one side by the River Kelvin, the gardens have an arboretum, herbaceous borders, herb garden, unusual crops, rose and scented garden, children's play area and visitors' centre with regular sales of paintings by local artists.

Australasian tree fern

Opening Times: Glasshouse - winter daily 10:00-16:15, summer daily 10:00-16:45. Gardens - daily 07:00-dusk.
Admission: Free.   Location: Five minutes walk from Hillhead Underground Station, 15 minutes for city centre.

Map Ref: 23

The Glasgow School of Art

167 Renfrew Street, Glasgow G3 6RQ   Tel / Fax: 0141 353 4526   Email: shop@gsa.ac.uk
Web: www.gsa.ac.uk

Charles Rennie MacKintosh's architectural masterpiece. Still a working art school, the regular guided tours let visitors see inside this fascinating building that includes the breathtaking MacKintosh Library.

Opening Times: Tour times: Mon to Fri 11:00 & 14:00, Sat 10:30 & 11:30. Additional times in Jul & Aug Sat 13:00, Sun 10:30, 11:30 & 13:00. Admission: Adult £5.00, Concession £3.00. Location: City centre, 15 minute walk from Queen Street Station. Map Ref: 23

The Mackintosh House

Hunterian Art Gallery

University of Glasgow, Hillhead Street, Glasgow G12 8QQ
Tel: 0141 330 5434 Fax: 0141 330 3618
Email: hunter@museum.gla.ac.uk Web: www.hunterian.gla.ac.uk

The Hunterian Art Gallery holds a remarkable collection of European art. The founding collection of Dr William Hunter includes outstanding paintings by Rembrandt, Koninck, Chardin and Stubbs. Unrivalled holdings of work by James McNeil Whistler including paintings, pastels and prints. A popular feature of the Charles Rennie Mackintosh collection is the reconstruction of the interiors of The Mackintosh House. There are major displays of paintings by the Scottish Colourists, Fergussion, Peploe, Cadell and Hunter. The graphics collection, one of the most important in Scotland, holds some 30,000 prints. These may be seen in the Print Room by prior appointment or in the Gallery's exhibition programme. Selections from the collection can be seen in regular exhibitions drawn from the Print Room.

Red & Black: The Fan,
by J M Whistler

Opening Times: Mon to Sat 09:30-17:00. Closed Sun. Mackintosh House closes daily 12:30-13:30. Admission: Free.
Location: Located in Westend of Glasgow, 15 minutes from city centre. Map Ref: 23

Hunterian Museum

The University of Glasgow, University Avenue, Glasgow G12 8QQ Tel: 0141 330 4221
Fax: 0141 330 3617 Email: hunter@museum.gla.ac.uk Web: www.hunterian.gla.ac.uk

The Bearsden Shark: photo JK Ingham.

Scotland's first public museum was established in 1807 based on the vast collections of Dr William Hunter (1718-83). A student at Glasgow University in the 1930s, Dr Hunter later acquired fame and fortune as a physician and medical teacher in London. Many items from his valuable collections are on display. Since Dr Hunter's time, the collections have grown into one of the largest collections in the United Kingdom with new and exciting additions every year. The Hunterian Museum is located within the Gothic splendour of the University of Glasgow. It has unique exhibits of Romans in Scotland, Scottish fossils including the world famous 330

One of the largest ancient coin
collections in Britain.

million year old Bearsden shark, dinosaurs from Scotland, Scottish minerals inlcuding a large unique star sapphire, of the other treasures from around the world and beyond. The new Kelvin Gallery occasionally houses spectacular temporary exhibitions.

Opening Times: Mon to Sat 09:30-17:00. Closed Sun & BH. Admission: Free. Location: In westend of Glasgow, part of University of Glasgow, campus. Map Ref: 23

Museums, Galleries, Historic Houses & Sites

Please let us know of any collections that are not listed in this guide that you feel should be listed. E-mail us on *editor@tomorrows.co.uk* or return the Report Form on page 448

Museum of Transport

Kelvin Hall, 1 Bunhouse Road, Glasgow G3 8DP   Tel: 0141 287 2720

Fax: 0141 287 2692

The history of transport and technology in Glasgow. Horse-drawn vehicles, the world's oldest bicycle, cars, fire engines, trains, locomotives and ship models illustrating the history of Clyde shipbuilding. Kelvin Way recreates an old Glasgow street with a cinema showing films about Glasgow transport.

Opening Times: Mon to Thu & Sat 10:00-17:00, Fri & Sun 11:00-17:00. Admission: Free.   Map Ref: 23

Clyde Shipbuilding, ship models

Peoples Palace Museum

Glasgow Green, Glasgow G40 1AT   Tel: 0141 554 0223
Fax: 0141 550 0892

The historical, social and cultural history of Glasgow, especially the East End, presented through a range of displays including audio-visual clips and reconstructions including a flat, a shop and an air-raid shelter. Objects range from suffragette banners to Billy Connolly's banana boots.

Opening Times: Mon to Thu & Sat 10:00-17:00, Fri & Sun 11:00-17:00. Admission: Free.   Map Ref: 23

Billy Connelly's stage costume

Pollok House

2060 Pollokshaws Road, Glasgow G43 1AT   Tel: 0141 616 6410   Fax: 0141 616 6521

The Maxwell family is known to have been established at Pollok by 1269. The present house (c.1750) replaced three earlier structures and was extended in 1890. It is set within Pollok Country Park, also the home of the Burrell Collection. The house contains an internationally important collection of paintings, silver and ceramics, displayed as they were around 1931.

Opening Times: Daily 10:00-17:00. Closed 25-26 Dec & 1-2 Jan. Admission: Adult £5.00, Concession £3.75, Family £13.50. Location: Off junctions 1 or 2 of M77, follow signs for Burrell Collection, three miles south of Glasgow's city centre.   Map Ref: 23

Pollok House

Provands Lordship

3 Castle Street, Glasgow G4 0RB   Tel: 0141 553 2557   Fax: 0141 552 4744

The oldest house in Glasgow, built in 1471 as a manse for the St Nicholas Hospital, just opposite Glasgow Cathedral. Period display and furniture. Tranquil recreated medieval herb garden.

Opening Times: Mon to Thu & Sat 10:00-17:00, Fri & Sun 11:00-17:00. Admission: Free.   Map Ref: 23

Historic domestic interior

Royal Highland Fusiliers Regimental Museum

518 Sauchiehall Street, Glasgow G2 3LW   Tel: 0141 332 0961

The museum tells the story of three hundred and thirty years continuous service with the art of silver, weapons, artwork, medals, uniforms etc.

Opening Times: Mon to Fri 08:30-16:00. Admission: Free. Location: Charring Cross, three minutes from underground station.   Map Ref: 23

St Mungo Museum of Religious Life & Art

2 Castle Street, Glasgow G4 0RH Tel: 0141 553 2557
Fax: 0141 552 4744

The museum explores the importance of religion in people's lives across the world and through time. There are galleries of religious art, including Dali's Christ of St John of the Cross, religious life (and death) and Britain's first permanent Zen garden, symbolising the harmony between people and nature.

Opening Times: Mon to Thu & Sat 10:00-17:00, Fri & Sun 11:00-17:00. Admission: Free.   Map Ref: 23

Salvador Dali, Christ of St John of the Cross

Scotland Street School, Museum of Education

225 Scotland Street, Glasgow G5 8QB Tel: 0141 287 0500 Fax: 0141 287 0515

The building is a Glasgow Board School designed by Charles Rennie Mackintosh. The collection relates to education in the region from c.1830 to the present day, including furniture, books, photographs, documents, toys and costumes. Reconstructed period classroom and craft room.

Opening Times: Mon to Thu & Sat 10:00-17:00, Fri & Sun 11:00-17:00. Admission: Free. Location: On south side of city.   Map Ref: 23

Classroom

Tenement House

145 Buccleuch Street, Glasgow G3 6QN Tel: 0141 333 0183

Glasgow is associated with tenements. This first-floor flat is a typical late Victorian example, consisting of four rooms and retaining most of its original features such as its bed recesses, kitchen range, coal bunker and bathroom.

Opening Times: 1 Mar to 27 Oct daily 14:00-17:00. Admission: Adult £3.50, Concession £2.60, Family £9.50.
                                                                              Map Ref: 23

GORDON *Berwickshire*

Mellerstain House

Gordon TD3 6LG Tel: 01573 410225 Fax: 01573 410636
Email: mellerstein.house@virgin.net Web: www.muses.calligrafix.co.uk/mellerstain

Superb Adam Mansion. Fine interior decorations and plasterwork. Original period furniture. Art collection with portraits by Van Dyke, Ramsay, Gainsborough, Maes and Van Der Helst. Beautiful grounds, gardens and lakeside walk.

Opening Times: Easter weekend then 1 May to 30 Sep Sun to Fri 12:30-17:00. Grounds: 11:30-18:00. Oct Sat & Sun 12:30-17:00. Admission: Adult £5.50, Child £3.00, Concession £5.00. Gardens £3.00. Location: Six miles north of Kelso on A6089, 40 miles south of Edinburgh via A68.
                                                                              Map Ref: 25

GREENOCK *Inverclyde*

McLean Museum & Art Gallery

15 Kelly Street, Greenock PA16 8JX Tel: 01475 715624 Fax: 01475 715626
Email: val.boa@inverclyde.gov.uk Web: www.inverclyde.gov.uk/museum/index.htm

Permanent displays on local history, James Watt, ship and engine models, big game mounts and items from foreign lands. Temporary exhibition programme and fine art collection.

Opening Times: Mon to Sat 10:00-17:00. Closed Sun & BH. Admission: Free.
Location: West end of Greenock, close to bus station and Greenock West Railway Station.
                                                                              Map Ref: 26

Edinburgh, Glasgow & Southern Scotland

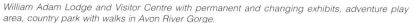

Chatelherault

🖼 ♿ 🎁 💻 🚜

Ferniegair, Hamilton ML3 7UE   Tel: 01698 426213

William Adam Lodge and Visitor Centre with permanent and changing exhibits, adventure play area, country park with walks in Avon River Gorge.

Opening Times: Visitor Centre Mon to Sat 10:00-17:00, Sun 12:00-17:00. West Lodge Mon to Thu & Sat 10:00-17:00, Sun 12:00-17:00. Admission: Free. Location: Ferniegair village, one mile south of Hamilton. Map Ref: 27

Low Parks Museums

🖼 ♿ 🎁 🚜

129 Muir Street, Hamilton ML3 6BJ   Tel: 01698 328232

Permanent exhibitions on local area and life - coal mining, textiles, farming, and Hamilton Palace Estate. Exhibition on Cameronians (Scottish rifles) Regiment. Temporary exhibitions, activities programme.

Opening Times: Mon to Sat 10:00-17:00, Sun 12:00-17:00. Admission: Free. Location: Near town centre, one mile from junction 6 M74. Map Ref: 27

Drumlanrigs Tower

🖼 ♿ 🎁

High Street, Hawick   Tel: 01450 377615   Fax: 01450 378506

Hawick's oldest building is a fortified tower enveloped inside an 18th century town house. The Tower displays the history of Hawick during Medieval times, to the industrial revolution to the present day.

Opening Times: Easter to Oct Mon to Sat 10:00-17:00, Sun 12:00-17:00. Jun & Sep closed 17:30. Jul & Aug closed 18:00. Admission: Adult £2.50, SBC Residents Free. Map Ref: 28

Hawick Museum & the Scott Gallery

🎁 🚜

Wilton Lodge Park, Hawick TD9 7JL   Tel: 01450 373457   Fax: 01450 378506
Email: fionacolton@hotmail.com

The museum and custom-built art gallery house the Jimmie Guthrie Motorcycle exhibition and the Scott Art Gallery. The Museum and Scott Gallery reflect the town's history and provide a venue for visiting exhibitions.

Opening Times: Apr to Sep Mon to Fri 10:00-12:00 13:00-17:00, Sat & Sun 14:00-17:00. Oct to Mar Mon to Fri 13:00-16:00, Sun 14:00-16:00. Admission: Free. Location: In local park, ten minute walk from town centre. Map Ref: 28

Traquair House

🎁 🅾 🚜

Innerleithen EH44 6PW   Tel: 01896 830323   Fax: 01896 830639
Email: enquiries@traquair.co.uk   Web: www.traquair.co.uk

Where Alexander I signed a charter over 800 years ago and where the 'modern wings' were completed in 1680. Once a pleasure ground for Scottish kings in times of peace, then a refuge for Catholic priests in times of terror.

Opening Times: Jun to Aug 10:30-17:30, Oct 12:30-16:30. Admission: Adult £5.50, Child £3.00, OAP £5.20, Family £16.00. Location: Innerleithen, one and a half miles from Traquair. Map Ref: 29

Scottish Maritime Museum

🖼 ♿ 🎁 💻 🚜

Laird Forge Buildings, Gottries Road, Irvine KA12 8QE   Tel: 01294 278283   Fax: 01294 313211   Email: smm@tildesley.fsbusiness.co.uk   Web: www.scottishmaritimemuseum.org

The museum holds Scotland's best collection of smaller ships and boats. Also displayed in former Alexander Stephens of Linthouse shipbuilding engine shop, shipyard machinery and tools.

Opening Times: Apr to Oct 10:00-17:00, Nov to Mar 10:00-16:00. Admission: Adult £2.50 Child/OAP £1.75 Family £5.00. Location: Near town centre, two minute walk from Irvine Railway Station. Map Ref: 30

Vennel Gallery

10 Glasgow Vennel, Irvine KA12 0BD   Tel / Fax: 01294 275059
Email: vennel@globalnet.co.uk   Web: www.northayrshiremuseums.org.uk

The Gallery has a programme of changing exhibitions of contemporary art and crafts. The gallery includes the Heckling Shop and the Lodging House where Robert Burns worked and lived in 1781.

Opening Times: Mon to Sat 10:00-13:00 14:00-17:00. Closed Wed.   Admission: Free.
Location: Just down the lane from The Porthead Tavern.   Map Ref: 30

ISLE OF ARRAN *Ayrshire*

Arran Heritage Museum

Rosaburn, Brodick, Isle of Arran KA27 8DP   Tel: 01770 302636
Email: arranmuseum@biinternet.com

The museum reflects the social history, archaeology and geology of the island.

Opening Times: Apr to Oct daily 10:30-16:30.   Admission: Adult £2.25, Child £1.00, OAP £1.50, Family £6.00.   Location: One mile from ferry terminal on main road north.   Map Ref: 31

Brodick Castle Gardens & Country Park

Brodick, Isle of Arran KA27 8HY   Tel: 01770 302202   Fax: 01770 302312

Brodick Castle - Entrance Hall

The site of this ancient seat of the Dukes of Hamilton was a fortress even in Viking times. The 13th century fortified tower was developed in the 16th century and extended by Cromwell in the 17th century. Some furniture dates from the 17th century, with superb paintings, porcelain and silver collected by the Hamiltons and William Beckford, whose daughter was married to the 10th Duke of Hamilton.

Opening Times: 25 Mar to 27 Oct 10:00-17:00. Reception centre, shop & restaurant - also open 1 Nov to 22 Dec Sat & Sun 10:00-17:00.   Admission: Adult £7.00, Concession £5.25, Family £19.00.   Location: Ferry from Ardrossan to Brodick and connecting bus to Reception Centre.   Map Ref: 31

JEDBURGH *Roxburghshire*

Harestanes Countryside Visitor Centre

Harestanes, Ancrum, Jedburgh TD8 6UQ   Tel: 01835 830306   Fax: 01835 830734

Countryside centre.

Opening Times: Easter to Oct Mon to Sun 10:00-17:00.   Admission: Free.   Location: Off main A68 road.   Map Ref: 32

Jedburgh Castle Jail & Museum

Castlegate, Jedburgh TD8 6QD   Tel: 01835 863254   Fax: 01835 864750

Comprehensive guide to Jedburgh's history. Also jail cells in two two-storey blocks. Garden and grounds for picnics and functions. Audio tours - touch screen and video.

Opening Times: Apr to Oct Mon to Sat 10:00-16:30, Sun 13:00-16:00.   Admission: Adult £1.50, Child Free, Concession £1.00.   Location: Within walking distance of the town.   Map Ref: 33

Mary Queen of Scots House

Queen Street, Jedburgh TD8 6EN   Tel / Fax: 01835 863331

Museum dedicated to Mary Queen of Scots.

Opening Times: Mar to Nov Mon to Sat 10:00-16:30, Sun 11:00-16:30.   Admission: Adult £2.50, SBC Residents Free.   Location: Five minute walk from town centre.   Map Ref: 33

KILMARNOCK *Ayrshire*

Dean Castle

Dean Road, Kilmarnock KA3 1XB   Tel: 01563 574916   Fax: 01563 554720
Email: bruce.morgan@east-ayrshire.gov.uk

Dean Castle is a magnificent collection of restored buildings dating from the 1350s. Important collections of arms and armour, musical instruments and manuscripts by Robert Burns are on

Edinburgh, Glasgow & Southern Scotland

display in public rooms.

Opening Times: Apr to Oct 12:00-17:00 Oct to Apr Sat & Sun only 12:00-16:00. Admission: Free. Location: 15 minutes walk from Kilmarnock Railway Station, set in grounds off the main road into Kilmarnock. Map Ref: 34

Dick Institute

Elmbank Avenue, Kilmarnock KA1 3BU   Tel: 01563 554343   Fax: 01563 554344
Email: jason.sutcliffe@east-ayrshire.gov.uk

Temporary and permanent exhibitions over two floors of this grand Victorian building. Fine art, social and natural history collections are upstairs, whilst downstairs galleries house temporary exhibitions.

Opening Times: Mon & Tue, Thu & Fri 09:00-20:00 Wed & Sat 09:00-17:00.   Admission: Free. Location: Near Kilmarnock town centre, ten minutes from railway station. Map Ref: 34

KILWINNING *Ayrshire*

Dalgarven Mill Museum of Ayrshire Country Life & Costume

Dalgarven Mill Trust, Dalgarven, Kilwinning KA13 6PL   Tel / Fax: 01294 552448
Email: admin@dalgarvenmill.org.uk   Web: www.dalgarvenmill.org.uk

Collection of machinery, memorabilia, furnishings and archives illustrating life in pre-industrial rural Ayrshire. Superb collection of costume spanning two centuries from 1775, beautifully displayed with changing exhibitions.

Opening Times: Easter to end Oct Tue to Sun 10:00-17:00. Nov to Easter Tue to Fri 10:00-16:00, Sat & Sun 10:00-17:00.   Admission: Admission charged.   Location: Rural situation, two miles from Kilwinning, two miles from Dalry on A737. Map Ref: 35

Kilwinning Abbey Tower

Main Street, Kilwinning   Tel: 01294 464174   Fax: 01294 275059

The tower displays the fascinating history of the Abbey and town of Kilwinning. It is also the home of the world's oldest archery competition.

Opening Times: Jun to Sep Thu & Sun 14:00-16:00, Fri & Sat 10:30-12:30 & 14:00-17:00. Admission: Free.   Location: In town centre in Abbey Grounds. Map Ref: 35

KIRKCUDBRIGHT *Dumfries & Galloway*

Broughton House & Garden

12 High Street, Kirkcudbright DG6 4JX   Tel: 01557 330437/01721 726003   Fax: 01557 330437

18th century town house of the Murrays of Broughton and Cally. Bought by E A Hornel, renowned artist, in 1901, the House still contains many of Hornel's works, paintings by other artists, an extensive collection of Scottish books and local history material.

Opening Times: 25 Mar to 28 Jun Mon to Sat 12:00-17:00, Sun 13:00-17:00, 29 Jun to 1 Sep Mon to Sat 10:00-18:00, Sun 13:00-17:00, 2 Sep to 27 Oct Mon to Sat 12:00-17:00, Sun 13:00-17:00.   Admission: Adult £3.50, Concession £2.60, Family £9.50.   Location: Off A711/A755.
Map Ref: 36

Stewartry Museum

St Mary Street, Kirkcudbright DG6 4AQ   Tel / Fax: 01557 331643
Email: DavidD@dumgal.gov.uk   Web: www.dumfriesmuseum.demon.co.uk

The Stewartry Museum was founded in 1879. As the collections grew, the present purpose-built museum was opened in 1893 and it still retains its charm as a traditional late Victorian museum. Its collections chiefly relate to the human and natural history of the Stewartry. The permanent collection includes the 'Siller Gun' - Britain's earliest surviving sporting trophy, and works by Kirkcudbrightshire artists including Jessie M King. Temporary exhibitions highlight different aspects of the collection and Museums Service activities.

Opening Times: Mon to Sat 11:00-16:00. Longer hours Jun to Sep including Sun 14:00-17:00. Admission: Adult £1.50 Child Free Concession 75p.   Location: Town Centre. Map Ref: 36

Tolbooth Art Centre

High Street, Kirkcudbright DG6 4JL   Tel: 01557 331556   Fax: 01557 331643
Email: DavidD@dumgal.gov.uk   Web: www.dumfriesmuseum.demon.co.uk

The Tolbooth Art Centre is based in Kirkcudbright's 17th century Tolbooth. Find out about

Edinburgh, Glasgow & Southern Scotland

Kirkcudbright's famous artists, such as E A Hornel, Jessie M King, E A Taylor and Charles Oppenheimer in the audio-visual shows and see their works on permanent display. The top floor of the Tolbooth, formerly the debtor's prison is now used as a gallery for ever changing contemporary art and craft exhibitions.

Opening Times: Mon to Sat 11:00-16:00. Longer hours Jun to Sep including Sun 14:00-17:00.
Admission: Adult £1.50 Child Free Concession 75p. Location: Town centre. Map Ref: 36

LANARK

New Lanark Visitor Centre

New Lanark World Heritage Village, Mill 3, Lanark ML11 9DB Tel: 01555 661345 Fax: 01555 665738 Email: development@newlanark.org Web: www.newlanark.org

Close to the Falls of Clyde, the 200 year old cotton mill village of New Lanark has been saved for future generations as a living community and lasting monument to Robert Owen, mill owner and social pioneer.

Opening Times: Daily 11:00-17:00. Admission: Adult £4.95, Concession £3.95. Location: By Lanark, signposted from all major routes (M74 and M8). Map Ref: 37

LANGBANK *Renfrewshire*

The Dolly Mixture

Finlaystone Country Estate, Langbank PA14 6XD Tel / Fax: 01475 540285
Email: info@finlaystone.co.uk Web: www.finlaystone.co.uk

All sorts of dolls from around the world, collected since 1903 by mother and daughter Clare Spurgin and Jane MacMillan. Set within a country estate with extensive gardens and woodlands.

Opening Times: Apr to Sep 12:00-17:00. Oct to Mar Sat & Sun 12:00-17:00.
Admission: Estate: Adult £3.00, Child/OAP £2.00. Museum: 50p. Location: Ten minutes west Glasgow Airport on A8. Map Ref: 38

LARGS *Ayrshire*

Largs Museum

Kirkgate House, Manse Court, Largs KA30 8AW Tel: 01475 687081

This small local history museum focuses on the unique history of Largs. The collections include Mauchline ware, costume and local antiquities, as well as an archive dealing with the written past of the area. The family of Brisbane and other Australian connections are featured.

Opening Times: Late May to early Sep Mon to Sat 14:00-17:00. Admission: Free.
Location: Off Main Street, beside 'The George'. Map Ref: 39

LINLITHGOW *West Lothian*

Canal Museum

Linlithgow Canal Centre, Canal Basin, Manse Road, Linlithgow EH49 6AJ Tel: 01506 671215
Email: info@lucs.org.uk Web: www.lucs.org.uk

Display of photographs, documents, tools and other objects illustrating the history of the Union Canal, its construction, and its working life. Video.

Opening Times: Easter to mid Oct Sat & Sun 14:00-17:00. Jul & Aug daily 14:00-17:00.
Admission: Free. Location: Five minute walk from Linlithgow Station. Map Ref: 6

House of the Binns

Linlithgow EH49 7NA Tel: 0150683 4255

The House of the Binns was built between 1612 and 1630 by Thomas Dalyell. In 1944 Eleanor Dalyell gifted the house to The National Trust for Scotland, along with a fine collection of furniture, porcelain and family portraits.

Opening Times: 1 May to 30 Sep Sat to Thu 13:30-17:00. Grounds open all year 10:00-dusk.
Admission: Adult £5.00, Child/OAP/Concession/Student £3.75, National Trust Member Free.
Location: On top of a hill, three quarters of a mile from main road, four miles east of Linlithgow and railway station. Map Ref: 6

Edinburgh, Glasgow & Southern Scotland

LIVINGSTON *West Lothian*

Almond Valley Heritage Trust

Livingston Mill, Millfield, Livingston EH54 7AR
Tel: 01506 414957   Fax: 01506 497771
Email: rac@almondvalley.co.uk
Web: www.almondvalley.co.uk

An innovative museum exploring the history and environment of West Lothian. Includes displays of Scotland's Shale Oil industry and other local manufacturing. Health, food, sanitation and hands-on environment science. Working watermill, farm, narrow-gauge railway, nature trail and play areas.

Opening Times: Daily 10:00-17:00. Admission: Adult £2.80, Child/OAP £1.60, Family (2 adult and 4 children) £8.00.
Location: Two miles from junction 3 on the M8.   Map Ref: 40

MAYBOLE *Ayrshire*

Culzean Castle & Country Park

Maybole KA19 8LE   Tel: 01655 884455   Fax: 01655 884503   Email: culzean@nts.org.uk
Web: www.culzeancastle.net

Culzean Castle

Robert Adam converted the fortified tower house into an elegant residence for David Kennedy, 10th Earl of Cassillis, between 1777 and 1792. The Castle contains a fine collection of paintings and furniture, and a display of weapons in the Armoury. The Country Park contains a wealth of natural and historical interest with garden areas including a Walled Garden and terraced Fountain Court.

Opening Times: 25 Mar to 27 Oct daily 10:00-17:00, 2 Nov to 22 Dec Sat & Sun 10:00-16:00. Admission: Adult £9.00, Concession £6.50, Family £22.00. Location: 12 miles south of Ayr on A719, 4 miles west of Maybole, off A77.   Map Ref: 41

MILLPORT *Renfrewshire*

Robertson Museum & Aquarium

Marine Parade, Millport KA28 0EG   Tel: 01475 530581   Fax: 01475 530601
Email: diane.robertson@millport.gla.ac.uk   Web: www.gla.ac.uk/Acad/Marine

Opened in 1897 the museum displays provide information on past and present planktonic life in the Clyde sea. A video illustrates how seaweed progresses to household products and the aquarium has live specimens of Clyde sealife.

Opening Times: Mon to Fri 09:00-12:15 13:45-16:15. Jun to Sep Sat 10:00-13:00 14:00-16:45. Admission: Adult £1.50, Child 75p, Under 5s Free, OAP £1.00. Location: Near town centre, with regular bus service to museum.   Map Ref: 42

MILNGAVIE

Lillie Art Gallery

East Dunbartonshire Museums, Station Road, Milngavie G62 8BZ   Tel: 0141 578 8847

20th century Scottish paintings, drawing by Joan Eardley (1921-1963), paintings, watercolours and etchings by Robert Lillie (1867-1949) and a small collection of 20th century Scottish ceramics.

Opening Times: Tue to Sat 10:00-13:00 & 14:00-17:00. Admission: Free. Location: Opposite Milngavie Railway Station. A short drive from Glasgow City Centre, off the A81.   Map Ref: 43

MOTHERWELL *Lanarkshire*

Motherwell Heritage Centre

1 High Road, Motherwell ML1 3HU   Tel: 01698 251000   Fax: 01698 268867
Email: devaneyr@northlan.gov.uk   Web: motherwellheritage.freeserve.com

The gallery features a year round programme of both in-house and touring exhibitions. Don't miss the permanent 'Technopolis' display on the area's heritage. Also local history research library.

Opening Times: Wed to Sat 10:00-17:00, Thu 10:00-19:00. Sun 12:00-17:00. Closed Mon and Tue. Admission: Free. Location: Top of Hamilton Road, by Bentley Hotel, three minutes from Motherwell Station. Map Ref: 44

NEWTON STEWART *Dumfries & Galloway*

Creetown Gem Rock Museum

Chain Road, Creetown, Newton Stewart DG8 7HJ   Tel: 01671 820357   Fax: 01671 820554
Email: gem.rock@btinternet.com   Web: www.gemrock.net

Outstanding collection and displays of crystals, gemstones, minerals and fossil. With many world class examples including British and foreign. Hand carved gemstones.

Opening Times: Good Friday to Sep daily 09:30-17:30, Oct to Nov & Mar to Good Friday daily 10:00-16:00, Dec to Feb Sat & Sun 10:00-16:00. Closed Xmas & New Year. Admission: Adult £2.90, Concession £2.40, Child 5-15 years £1.75, Family £7.55. Location: In the village of Creetown, follow signposts from village square. Map Ref: 45

NEWTONGRANGE *Midlothian*

Scottish Mining Museum

Lady Victoria Colliery, Newtongrange EH22 4QN   Tel: 0131 663 7519   Fax: 0131 654 1618
Email: enquiries@scottishminingmuseum.com   Web: www.scottishminingmuseum.com

Five star visitor attraction. Scotland's National Coal Mining Museum, historic buildings and extensive collections and archives. Retail, catering, events and hospitality venue.

Opening Times: Feb to Oct daily 10:00-17:00, Nov to Feb 10:00-16:00. Admission: Adult £4, Child/OAP £2.20, Family £10.00. Group - Adult £3.50, Concession £2.00. Location: Newtongrange, eight miles from Edinburgh on A7. Map Ref: 46

NORTH BERWICK *East Lothian*

Museum of Flight

East Fortune Airfield, North Berwick EH39 5LF   Tel: 01620 880308
Fax: 01620 880355   Web: www.nms.ac.uk/flight

Scotland's national aviation collection, some of the most extraordinary machines in the world map the development of human flight. See the oldest aircraft in Britain - an original Wright Brothers' engine, Europe's biggest rocket and some of the finest machines ever built. Based at historic East Fortune Airfield - launch site of the R34 Airship, the first aircraft to cross the Atlantic, east to west.

Opening Times: Daily 10:30-17:00, Jul & Aug 10:30-18:00. Admission: Adult £3.00, Child Free, Concessions £2.00. Location: 20 miles east of Edinburgh. Map Ref: 47

North Berwick Museum

School Road, North Berwick EH39 4JU   Tel: 01620 895457   Fax: 01620 828201
Email: elms@elothian-museums.demon.co.uk   Web: www.northberwickmuseum.org

North Berwick Museum has permanent displays of natural history, golf, seaside holidays and local history. We also have a regularly changing programme of temporary exhibitions, including displays of history and art exhibitions.

Opening Times: Apr to Sep 11:00-17:00. Admission: Free. Location: Near town centre, five minutes walk from High Street. Map Ref: 47

PAISLEY *Renfrewshire*

Coats Observatory

49 Oakshaw Street West, Paisley PA1 2DR   Tel: 0141 889 2013   Fax: 0141 889 9240
Email: museum-els@renfrewshire.gov.uk   Web: www.renfrewshire.gov.uk

Architecturally stunning, the Observatory was built by the Coats family in 1883 and is a working Victorian Observatory. Displays on astronomy, astronautics, seismology and meteorology. Meteorological and astronomical information has been recorded here since 1882. Public telescopic viewing, weather permitting on Thursday evenings in winter. Very active Renfrewshire Astronomical Society.

Opening Times: Tue to Sat 10:00-17:00 Sun 14:00-17:00. Oct to Mar Thu 19:00-21:30.
Admission: Free. Location: Access via Oakshaw Street or through Paisley Museum. Less than
ten minutes from railway station. Map Ref: 48

Paisley Museum & Art Galleries

High Street, Paisley PA1 2BA Tel: 0141 889 3151 Fax: 0141 889 9240
Email: museum.els@renfrewshire.gov.uk Web: www.renfrewshire.gov.uk

*Home to the world's largest collection of Paisley Shawls, a
selection of which are always on display. Art Galleries
show 19th century Scottish paintings and studio ceramics.
Also displays on local and natural history. Museum shop
has wide range of Paisley pattern products and exclusive
gifts. A-listed historic 1871 building.*

Opening Times: Tue to Sat 10:00-17:00, Sun 14:00-16:00,
BH 10:00-17:00. Admission: Free. Location: Less than
ten minute walk from Paisley Gilmour Street Railway
Station. Map Ref: 48

PEEBLES *Peeblesshire*

Cornice Museum of Ornamental Plasterwork

Innerleithen Road, Peebles EH45 8BA Tel / Fax: 01721 720212

*Recreation of a plasterers casting workshop from around 1900 with probably the largest collection
of plaster moulds in the country.*

Opening Times: Mon to Thu 10:00-12:00 14:00-16:00, Fri 10:00-12:00 14:00-15:30. Closed Sat,
Sun, 2 weeks at Xmas & New Year, 1 week in Apr, 1st 2 weeks of Aug. Admission: By
donation. Location: Near town centre, three minute walk from Peebles Town Centre bus stop.
Map Ref: 49

Tweeddale Museum

Chambers Institute, High Street, Peebles EH45 8AJ Tel: 01721 724820 Fax: 01721 724424
Email: rhannay@scotborders.gov.uk

Local history museum.

Opening Times: Mon to Fri 10:00-12:00 14:00-17:00, Apr to Oct also Sat 10:00-13:00 14:00-
16:00. Closed Sun. Admission: Free. Location: In town centre. Map Ref: 49

PRESTONPANS *East Lothian*

Prestongrange Industrial Heritage Museum

Morison's Haven, Prestongrange, Prestonpans EH32 9RX Tel: 0131 653 2904 Fax: 01620
828201 Email: elms@elothian-museums.demon.co.uk Web: www.prestongrangemuseum.org

*Prestongrange Museum is based in the Old Prestongrange Colliery at Morison's Haven,
Prestonpans. On the site there are steam and diesel locomotives and a Cornish Beam Engine. We
also feature an annual educational exhibition.*

Opening Times: Apr to Sep 11:00-16:00. Admission: Free. Location: Between Musselburgh
and Prestonpans, easily accessible from the A1 and on public transport. Map Ref: 50

RENFREW *Renfrewshire*

Renfrew Community Museum

The Brown Institute, 41 Canal Street, Renfrew PA4 8QA Tel: 0141 886 3149 Fax: 0141 886
2300 Email: museums.els@renfrewshire.gov.uk Web: www.renfrewshire.gov.uk

*This museum was opened for the Renfrew 600 Celebrations in 1997 in the former Brown Institute
Building, when Renfrew celebrated 600 years of Royal Burgh status. Displays of local history.*

Opening Times: Tue to Sat 10:00-13:00 14:00-17:00. Admission: Free. Location: Few
minutes walk from centre of Renfrew. Map Ref: 51

SALTCOATS *Ayrshire*

North Ayrshire Museum

Manse Street, Kirkgate, Saltcoats KA21 5AA Tel / Fax: 01294 464174
Email: namuseum@globalnet.co.uk Web: www.northayrshiremuseums.org.uk

The Museum shows the history of North Ayrshire with displays on archaeology, costume, transport and popular culture. There is a maritime history section and a reconstruction of an Ayrshire cottage interior.

Opening Times: Mon to Sat 10:00-13:00 14:00-17:00, closed Wed. Admission: Free.
Location: In church grounds between Safeways and the Post Office. Map Ref: 35

SANQUHAR *Dumfries & Galloway*

Sanquhar Tolbooth Museum
High Street, Sanquhar DG4 5BN Tel: 01659 50186 Fax: 01387 265081
Email: info@dumfriesmuseum.demon.co.uk Web: www.dumfriesmuseum.demon.co.uk

Discover Sanquhar's world famous knitting tradition and the story of the mines and miners of Sanquhar and Kirkconnel. How did the ordinary people of Upper Nithsdale live and work? All this and more can be found in the town's fine 18th century Tolbooth.

Opening Times: Apr to Sep Tue to Sat 10:00-13:00 14:00-17:00 Sun 14:00-17:00.
Admission: Free. Location: On High Street. Map Ref: 52

SELKIRK *Selkirkshire*

Bowhill House & Country Park
Bowhill, Selkirk TD7 5ET Tel / Fax: 01750 22204 Email: bht@buccleuch.com

Scottish Borders home of the Duke and Duchess of Buccleuch set in magnificent scenery. Outstanding collection of art, silverware, porcelain and French furniture. Historic relics include Monmouth's saddle and execution shirt, Sir Walter Scott's plaid and some proof editions. Queen Victoria's letters and gifts to successive Duchess of Buccleuch, her Mistress of the Robes.

Bowhill set amid magnificent scenery

Opening Times: Jul daily 13:00-16:30.
Admission: Adult £4.50, Child £2.00, OAP/Group £4.00, Under 5s/Disabled Free. Location: Three miles west of Selkirk on A708. Map Ref: 53

Halliwells House Museum
Halliwells Close, Market Place, Selkirk TD7 4BL Tel: 01750 20096/20054

Recreated ironmongers shop and local Tourist Information Centre.

Opening Times: Easter to Sep Mon to Sat 10:00-17:00, Sun 14:00-16:00, Jul & Aug 9:30-17:30 Sun 14:00-17:00. Oct Mon-Sat 10:00-16:00. Admission: Free. Location: Off Market Place.
Map Ref: 53

James Hogg Exhibition
Aikwood Tower, Ettrick Valley, Selkirk TD7 5HJ Tel: 01750 52253 Fax: 01750 52261

Collection interpreting two life and works of the Scottish writer James Hogg (the Ettrick Shepherd) 1770-1835.

Opening Times: Tue, Thu, Sun 12:00-17:00. Admission: All £1.50. Location: Four miles from Selkirk on Ettrick Valley Road (B7009). Map Ref: 53

Sir Walter Scotts Courtroom (Selkirk Town Hall)
Market Place, Selkirk TD7 4BT Tel: 01750 20096 Fax: 01750 23282
Email: dmabon@scotborders.gov.uk

Museum dedicated to local Sheriff of Selkirk - Sir Walter Scott.

Opening Times: Easter to Sep Mon to Sat 10:00-16:00, Jun to Sep also Sun 14:00-16:00, Oct Mon to Sat 13:00-16:00. Admission: Free. Location: In town centre. Map Ref: 53

SOUTH QUEENSFERRY *West Lothian*

Dalmeny House
South Queensferry EH30 9TQ Tel: 0131 331 1888 Fax: 0131 331 1788
Email: linda.edgar@dalmeny.co.uk Web: www.dalmeny.co.uk

Rothschild 18th century French furniture, tapestries and porcelain. One of the world's most important Napoleonic collections, assembled by the fifth Earl, Prime Minister, historian and owner of three Derby winners.

Opening Times: Jul & Aug Sun, Mon & Tues 14:00-17:30. Last admission 16:30.
Admission: Adult £4.00. Location: Seven miles from centre of Edinburgh. Map Ref: 54

Queensferry Museum

53 High Street, South Queensferry EH30 9HP   Tel: 0131 331 5545

Situated in the historic former Royal Burgh of Queensferry, the museum commands magnificent views of the great bridges spanning the Forth. The museum traces the history of the people of Queensferry and Dalmeny, the historic ferry passage to Fife, the construction of the rail and road bridges and takes a look at the wildlife of the Forth estuary.

Opening Times: Mon, Thu, Fri & Sat 10:00-13:00 and 14:15-17:00, Sun 12:00-17:00. Closed Tue & Wed.
Admission: Free.   Map Ref: 54

Queensferry Museum, South Queensferry

STRANRAER *Dumfries & Galloway*

Castle of St John

Castle Street, Stranraer DG9 7RT   Tel: 01776 705088   Fax: 01776 705544
Email: JohnPic@dumgal.gov.uk   Web: www.dumfriesmuseum.demon.co.uk

The Castle of St John is a Medieval tower house. Over the centuries the Castle has been used as a home, a local court, a military garrison and a prison. Videos and reconstructions are used to tell the story of the Castle. There is an activity room for families and children.

Opening Times: Easter to mid Sep Mon to Sat 10:00-13:00 14:00-17:00. Admission: Adult £1.20 Child/Concession 60p Family £3.00. Location: Town centre, within walking distance of ferry terminal.   Map Ref: 55

Stranraer Museum

The Old Town Hall, George Street, Stranraer DG9 7JP   Tel: 01776 705088   Fax: 01776 705835
Email: JohnPic@dumgal.gov.uk   Web: www.dumfriesmuseum.demon.co.uk

Displays on archaeology, local history, farming and dairying. Temporary exhibitions held throughout the year and activities for all the family.

Opening Times: Mon to Fri 10:00-17:00 Sat 10:00-13:00 14:00-17:00. Closed Xmas & New Year, Easter & May BH. Admission: Free. Location: Near town centre, a short walk from ferry terminal.   Map Ref: 55

STRATHAVEN *Lanarkshire*

John Hastie Museum

8 Threestanes Road, Strathaven ML10 6DX   Tel: 01357 521257

Local history exhibits including material from John Hastie Collections. Temporary exhibition room.

Opening Times: Apr to Sep daily 12:30-16:30. Admission: Free. Location: Off Strathaven Park in town centre.   Map Ref: 56

WANLOCKHEAD *Dumfries & Galloway*

Museum of Lead Mining

Wanlockhead ML12 6UT   Tel: 01659 74387   Fax: 01659 74481
Email: brianwmont@goldpan.co.uk   Web: www.leadminingmuseum.co.uk

Scotland's only visitor lead mine. Fabulous mineral collection. Visit 18th and 19th century miners' cottages. Scotland's second oldest miners' library.

Opening Times: Apr to end Oct daily 10:00-17:00. Admission: Adult £3.95, Child £2.50, Concession £2.75, Family £9.80. Group Adult £3.00, Group Child £2.00. Location: Situated in Wanlockhead, Scotland's highest village, signposted from junction 13 and 14 of M74 and A76.
Map Ref: 57

WHITBURN *West Lothian*

Whitburn Community Museum

Union Road, Whitburn EH47 0AR   Tel: 01501 678050   Email: museums@westlothian.gov.uk
Web: www.wlonline.org

Display on the mining history of the village and its later industrial and social development. Programme of temporary exhibitions.

Opening Times: Mon & Fri 09:30-17:30 Tue & Thu 09:30-20:00 Wed 10:00-17:30 Sat 09:30-13:00. Admission: Free. Location: In town centre, enter through library.   Map Ref: 58

There are few aspects of Scottish history, folklore and legend that cannot be examined within the great variety of museums in this central eastern region of Scotland. St Andrews, Aberdeen, Dundee, Perth and Stirling which have a variety of interesting museums, there are ancient Scottish castles with fine collections, and many smaller towns whose museums display the life, work and aspirations of their locality.

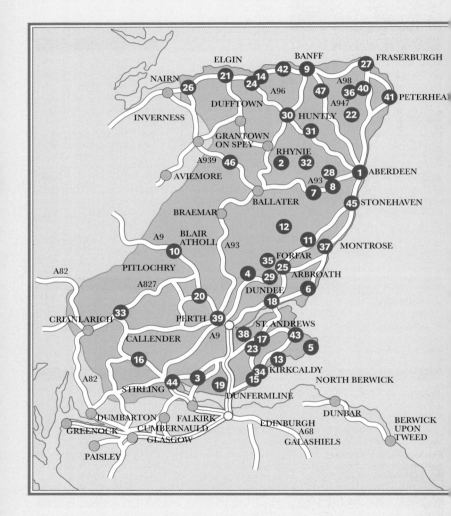

The Red Map References should be used to locate Museums etc on the pages that follow

Central, East & Northeast Scotland

Aberdeen Art Gallery

Schoolhill, Aberdeen AB10 1FQ   Tel: 01224 523700/523711
Fax: 01224 632133   Email: info@aagm.co.uk
Web: www.aberdeencity.gov.uk

One of the city's most popular tourist attractions, Aberdeen's splendid art gallery houses an important fine art collection with particularly good examples of 19th and 20th century works, a rich and diverse applied art collection and an exciting programme of special exhibitions.

Opening Times: Mon to Sat 10:00-17:00, Sun 14:00-17:00. Admission: Free. Location: Centrally located via Belmont Street, from Union Street.   Map Ref: 1

Aberdeen Art Gallery

Aberdeen Maritime Museum

Shiprow, Aberdeen AB11 5BY   Tel: 01224 337700   Fax: 01224 213066
Email: info@aagm.co.uk   Web: www.aberdeencity.gov.uk

The city's award-winning maritime museum brings the history of the North Sea to life. View multi-media displays and exciting exhibitions on the offshore oil industry, shipbuilding, fishing and clipper ships, then visit the museum shop and licensed café.

Opening Times: Mon to Sat 10:00-17:00, Sun 12:00-15:00. Admission: Free. Location: Situated facing the harbour, accessible from Union Street via Adelphi. Map: 1

Gordon Highlanders Museum

St Lukes, Viewfield Road, Aberdeen AB15 7XH   Tel: 01224 311200   Fax: 01224 319323
Email: curator@gordonhighlanders.com   Web: www.gordonhighlanders.com

Regimental collection of The Gordon Highlanders, including 12 Victoria Crosses. History of the Regiment told through audio-visual and traditional displays. Tea room, gardens and gift shop.

Opening Times: Apr to Oct Tue to Sat 10:30-16:30, Sun 13:30-16:30. Open by appointment only at all other times.   Admission: Adult £2.50, Child £1.00, OAP/Student £1.50. By appointment visits £3.50.   Location: West end of Aberdeen, just off Queens Road by Anderson Drive Roundabout.
Map Ref: 1

Marischal Museum

Marischal College, Aberdeen AB10 1YS   Tel: 01224 274301   Fax: 01224 274302
Email: museum@abdn.ac.uk   Web: www.abdn.ac.uk/marischal_museum

Major display of North-East identity from the first settlers to the present day; other gallery displays material from the rest of the world through the collections of donors - ancient Egypt with gold buddhas, African masks and Greek vases.

Opening Times: Mon to Fri 10:00-17:00, Sun 14:00-17:00.   Admission: Free.   Location: In city centre.
Map Ref: 1

Provost Skene's House

Guestrow, Aberdeen AB10 1AS   Tel: 01224 641086
Fax: 01224 632133   Email: info@aagm.co.uk
Web: www.aberdeencity.gov.uk

Dating from 1545, Provost Skene's House now houses an attractive series of period room settings recalling the elegant furnishings of earlier times. Visitors can see an intriguing series of religious paintings in the Painted Gallery, changing fashions in the Costume Gallery and enjoy displays of local interest, coins and archaeology on the top floor.

Opening Times: Mon to Sat 10:00-17:00, Sun 13:00-16:00.   Admission: Free.
Location: Guestrow is off Broad Street, opposite Marischal College.   Map Ref: 1

Central, East & Northeast Scotland

Satrosphere Ltd

The Tramsheds, 179 Constitution Street, Aberdeen AB24 5TU   Tel: 01224 640340   Fax: 01224 622211   Email: satrosphere@satrosphere.net   Web: www.satrosphere.net

Scotland's original science centre. Light up a plasma dome, make shadow photos on the flash wall, feel forces at work in the spinning chair. Aberdeen's discovery place brings science alive with hands-on fun for all ages. Exhibits, interactive shows, workshops, special events, gift shop and the Tramsheds café.

Opening Times: Mon to Sat 10:00-17:00, Sun 11:30-17:00.   Admission: Adult £5.00, Child/Concession £3.00, Family discounts available.   Location: Near Aberdeen's fun Beach, five minutes from city centre.   Map Ref: 1

Satrosphere's Plasma Dome

ALFORD *Aberdeenshire*

Grampian Transport Museum Trust

Alford AB33 8AE   Tel: 019755 62292   Fax: 019755 62180   Email: info@gtm.org.uk   Web: www.gtm.org.uk

The land travel and transport history of Aberdeenshire housed in a large road gallery and restored railway station. Road vehicles include the famous Craigievar Express, a 19th century steam tricycle and the world's oldest Sentinel Steam Waggon.

Opening Times: 31 Mar to 31 Oct daily 10:00-17:00.   Admission: Adult £4.00, Child £1.60, OAP £3.10, Family £9.60 (2 adults & up to 3 children).   Location: 25 miles west of Aberdeen, on the A944. Town centre, off free public car park.   Map Ref: 2

ALLOA *Clackmannanshire*

Clackmannanshire Council Museum & Heritage Service

Speirs Centre, 29 Primrose Street, Alloa FK10 1JJ   Tel: 01259 216913   Fax: 01259 721313   Email: smills@clacks.gov.uk   Web: www.clacksweb.org.uk

Growing collections of archaeological, social and industrial history, including large assemblage of W & J A Bailey's/Alloa Pottery and artefacts from Patons & Baldwins, Alloa wool-spinning mill, memorabilia from breweries in Alloa. Expanding art collection.

Opening Times: Tue to Fri 13:30-17:00. Closed Sat, Sun & BH. Also open by arrangement or appointment.   Admission: Free.   Location: Near town centre, two minutes walk main car park & bus station.   Map Ref: 3

ALVA *Clackmannanshire*

Mill Trail Visitor Centre

Glentana Mill, West Stirling Street, Alva FK12 5EN   Tel: 01259 769696   Fax: 01259 763100   Email: milltrailvc@aillst.ossian.net   Web: www.visitscottishheartlands.org

Follow The Mill Trail and you are guaranteed a great shopping experience. A visit to Scotland's Mill Trail Visitor Centre takes you back 150 years to discover what life was like in the mill factories of the time. Relax in the Ochil View coffee shop before discovering a variety of shops - some factory, some not; from cashmere to chocolate.

Scotland's Mill Trail Visitor Centre

Opening Times: Jan to Jun daily 10:00-17:00, Jul to Sep daily 09:00-17:00, Oct to Dec daily 10:00-17:00.   Admission: Free.   Location: Only short drive from the historic town of Stirling.

Map Ref: 3

Central, East & Northeast Scotland

Alyth Museum
Commercial Street, Alyth PH11 8AF Tel: 01738 632488 Fax: 01738 443505
Email: museum@pkc.gov.uk Web: www.pkc.gov.uk/ah

Collections relating to local history and life in and around Alyth.

Opening Times: May to Sep Wed to Sun 13:00-17:00. Admission: Free. Location: In town centre.
Map Ref: 4

Crail Museum & Heritage Centre
62/64 Marketgate, Crail, Anstruther KY10 3TL Tel: 01333 450869

Small local history museum of this ancient Royal Burgh, its Kirk, seafaring tradition, 200 year old golf club and airfield (HMS Jackdaw - FAA Station, HMS Bruce Boys Training School and JSSL).

Opening Times: Jun to Sep daily 10:00-13:00 14:00-17:00, Sun 14:00-17:00. Apr & May Sat & Sun 14:00-17:00. Admission: Free. Location: Town centre beside Tolbooth.
Map Ref: 5

Kellie Castle
Pittenweem, Anstruther KY10 2RF Tel: 01333 720271 Fax: 01333 720326

Kellie Castle is a very fine example of the domestic architecture of Lowland Scotland (dating from 1360). Sympathetically restored around 1878, it contains magnificent plaster ceilings, painted panelling and furniture designed by Sir Robert Lorimer.

Opening Times: 25 Mar to 29 Sep Thu to Mon 12:00-17:00. Admission: Adult £5.00, Concession £.375, Family £13.50. Location: On B9171, 3 miles north west of Pittenweem.
Map Ref: 5

The Scottish Fisheries Museum Trust Ltd
St Ayles, Harbourhead, Anstruther KY10 3AB Tel: 01333 310628 Fax: 01333 31068
Email: andrew@scottish-fisheries-museum.org Web: www.scottish-fisheries-museum.org

This award-winning National Museum tells the story of the Scottish fishing industry and its people from the earliest times to the present day.

Opening Times: Apr to Sep Mon to Sat 10:00-17:30 Sun 11:00-17:00. Oct to Mar Mon to Sat 10:00-16:30 Sun 12:00-16:30. Admission: Adult £3.50, Accompanied Child Free, Concession £2.50. Group rates available. Location: By Anstruther Harbour.
Map Ref: 5

Arbroath Art Gallery
Hill Terrace, Arbroath DD11 1AH Tel: 01241 875598 Fax: 01241 439263
Email: signal.tower@angus.gov.uk Web: www.angus.gov.uk/history.htm

Two galleries show temporary exhibitions of artists in the local area and from our Angus Council Collections which includes two works by 'Breughel the Younger' and works by James Watterston Herald.

Opening Times: Mon & Wed 09:30-20:00, Tues 10:00-18:00, Thu 09:30-18:00, Fri & Sat 09:30-17:00. Admission: Free. Location: Ten minute walk from bus and railway stations. Town centre location above Public Library.
Map Ref: 6

Arbroath Museum
Signal Tower, Ladyloan, Arbroath DD11 1PU Tel: 01241 875598 Fax: 01241 439263
Email: signal.tower@angus.gov.uk Web: www.angus.gov.uk/history.htm

Arbroath's fishing, flax, engineering and social history and the Bell Rock Lighthouse, the 1813 Shore Station of which is the museum building.

Opening Times: Mon to Sat 10:00-17:00 all year, Jul to Aug Sun 14:00-17:00. Admission: Free. Location: On A92 on seafront beside harbour. Seven minutes walk from bus/railway station.
Map Ref: 6

Banchory Museum

Bridge Street, Banchory AB31 5SX   Tel: 01224 664228

Exhibition on Banchory-born Scott Skinner - the 'Strathspey King'. Displays of Royal commemorative china, 19th century tartans and Deeside natural history.

Opening Times: May, Jun & Sep Mon to Sat 11:00-13:00 14:00-16:30. Jul to Aug Mon to Sat 11:00-13:00 14:00-16:30. Sun 14:00-16:30. For Apr & Oct - times 01771 622906.
Admission: Free.   Location: In Bridge Street, one minute walk from main car park in Dee Street.   Map Ref: 7

Crathes Castle - Muses Ceiling

Crathes Castle

Banchory AB31 5QJ   Tel: 01330 844525   Fax: 01330 844797

King Robert the Bruce granted the lands of Leys to the Burnett family in 1323. The ancient Horn of Leys was presented by Bruce to the family as a symbol of his gift. The castle, built in the 16th century, is an excellent example of a tower house of the period. Some rooms retain original painted ceilings and collections of family portraits and furniture.

Opening Times: 25 Mar to 30 Sep daily 10:00-17:30, 1 to 31 Oct 10:00-16:30. Restaurant & Shop: Please phone for opening times.
Admission: Adult £8.50, Concession £6.40, Family £23.00.
Location: Three miles east of Banchory.   Map Ref: 7

Drum Castle

Drumoak, Banchory AB31 5EY   Tel: 01330 811204   Fax: 01330 811962

The keep is one of the three oldest tower houses surviving in Scotland. The house contains an excellent collection of portraits and good Georgian furniture.

Opening Times: 25 Mar to 28 Jun 12:00-17:00, 29 Jun to 1 Sep 10:00-18:00, 2 Sep to 27 Oct 12:00-17:00.   Admission: Adult £7.00, Concession £5.25, Family £19.00.   Location: Off A93, three miles west of Peterculter.   Map Ref: 8

Banff Museum

High Street, Banff AB45 1AE   Tel: 01771 622884

One of Scotland's oldest museums, founded in 1828. Award-winning natural history display and the life of Thomas Edward, the 'Banff Naturalist'. Nationally important collection of Banff silver.

Opening Times: Jun to Sep Mon to Sat 14:00-16:30.   Admission: Free.   Location: In High Street, one minute walk from St Mary's car park.   Map Ref: 9

Atholl Country Life Museum

Blair Atholl PH18 5SP   Tel: 01796 481232   Email: janetcam@virgin.net
Web: www.blairatholl.org.uk

This unique and lively local museum has a wide range of information, photographs, a stuffed highland cow, magnificent horse harness, Trinafour shop and Post Office, a 1900s kitchen and much more to portray country life in Atholl. See the Caledonian Shield (Guinness record book). Children welcome.

Opening Times: End of May to mid Oct daily 13:30-17:00. Jul, Aug to mid Sep weekdays from 10:00.   Admission: Adult £3.00, Child £1.   Location: In centre of village near River Tilt.

Map Ref: 10

Blair Castle

Blair Atholl PH18 5TL   Tel: 01796 481207   Fax: 01796 481487
Email: office@blair-castle.co.uk   Web: www.blair-castle.co.uk

Blair Castle has been the ancient home and fortress of the Earls and Dukes of Atholl for over 725 years. Some 30 rooms of infinite variety display beautiful furniture, fine collections of paintings, arms and armour, china, costume, lace and embroidery, Jacobite relics and other unique treasures presenting a stirring picture of Scottish life from the 16th to 20th centuries.

Opening Times: 28 Mar to 5 Oct daily 10:00-18:00. Jul & Aug 09:30-18:00.   Admission: Adult £6.25, Child £4.00, OAP £5.25, Student £5.00, Family £18.00.   Map Ref: 10

BRECHIN *Angus*

Brechin Museum

Public Library, St Ninians Square, Brechin DD9 7AA   Tel: 01674 673232
Email: montrose.museum@angus.gov.uk   Web: www.angus.gov.uk/history.htm

Social history of this tiny Cathedral City includes local ecclesiastical, industrial history and works of art by David Waterson.

Opening Times: Mon & Wed 09:30-20:00, Tues 10:00-18:00, Thu 09:30-18:00, Fri & Sat 09:30-17:00.   Admission: Free.   Location: Close to town centre, an annexe to Brechin Public Library.
Map Ref: 11

Glenesk Folk Museum

The Retreat, Glenesk, Brechin DD9 7YT   Tel: 01356 670254

The Glenesk Folk Museum contains local archives and a wide range of artefacts depicting how life was lived in the local community over the last century - although gone, not forgotten.

Opening Times: Easter to 30 Jun Sat & Sun 12:00-18:00 1 Jul to mid Oct daily 12:00-18:00.
Admission: Adult £2.00, Child £1.00.   Location: Remote rural location, 20 miles from Brechin, 50 miles from Aberdeen and Dundee.   Map Ref: 12

BUCKHAVEN *Fife*

Buckhaven Museum

College Street, Buckhaven   Tel: 01592 412860   Fax: 01592 412870

The display features the town's history with a focus on the fishing industry. See the stained glass windows made by local people with the help of the community artist and a replica of a kitchen from the 1920s.

Opening Times: Open library hours.   Admission: Free.   Location: Above Buckhaven Library.
Map Ref: 13

BUCKIE *Moray*

The Buckie Drifter Maritime Heritage Centre

Freuchny Road, Buckie AB56 1TT   Tel: 01542 834646   Fax: 01542 835995
Email: buckie.drifter@moray.gov.uk   Web: www.moray.org/area/bdrifter/mbdrifter.html

Enter the Buckie Drifter for a journey back in time to when the herring was king, glimpse the lives of the fishing communities, recreated fishing boat and quayside display. RNLI lifeboat on display.

Opening Times: Apr to Oct Mon to Sat 10:00-17:00, Sun 12:00-17:00.   Admission: Adult £2.75, Child/OAP £1.75. Group rates available.   Location: Situated at the harbour across the road from the lifeboat station.   Map Ref: 14

Peter Anson Gallery

Town House West, Cluny Place, Buckie AB56 1HB   Tel: 01309 673701   Fax: 01309 675863
Email: museums@moray.gov.uk   Web: www.moray.gov.uk/museums/

Examples of drawings/paintings by well known and respected maritime artist Peter Anson.

Opening Times: Mon to Fri 10:00-20:00 Sat 10:00-12:00. Closed Sun.   Admission: Free.
Location: Shared building with Buckie Library near town centre.   Map Ref: 14

Central, East & Northeast Scotland

Burntisland Museum

102 High Street, Burntisland   Tel: 01592 412860   Fax: 01592 412870

Visit the exciting reproduction Edwardian fairground display and find out more about Burntisland's history.

Opening Times: Open library hours.   Admission: Free.   Map Ref: 15

Rob Roy & Trossachs Visitor Centre

Ancaster Square, Callander FK17 8ED   Tel: 01877 330342

Highland Hero; Lowland Outlaw and Hollywood Legend - Rob Roy MacGregor has inspired authors and film makers for nearly 300 years. At the Rob Roy & Trossachs Visitor Centre, Callander, learn of the daring exploits which made him a hero to his own people - and

Scotland's most notorious outlaw. Eavesdrop on Rob Roy McGregor as he plans another daring raid with one of his clansmen. Enjoy the fascinating audio visual presentation as it takes you through the life and times of Rob Roy. Walk into a farmhouse of that time, complete with byre and animals, finishing your experience with an cinematic tour of the places where Rob Roy once roamed, narrated by well known Scots personality Jimmy McGregor.

Opening Times: Mar to May & Oct to Dec daily 10:00-17:00, Jun 09:30-18:00, Jul & Aug 09:00-20:00, Sep 10:00-18:00. Jan & Feb Sat & Sun 11:00-16:00.   Admission: Adult £3.25, Child/OAP £2.25, Student £2.75, Family £9.75.   Map Ref: 16

Hill of Tarvit Mansion House

Cupar KY15 5PB   Tel: 01334 653127

Home to a notable collection including French, Chippendale-style and vernacular furniture, Dutch paintings and pictures by Raeburn and Ramsay, Flemish tapestries and Chinese porcelain and bronzes. The interior is very much in the Edwardian fashion.

Opening Times: 25 Mar to 27 Oct daily 12:00-17:00. Tearoom weekends in Oct.
Admission: Adult £5.00, Concession £3.75, Family £13.50.   Location: Off A916, two miles south of Cupar.   Map Ref: 17

Broughty Castle Museum

Castle Approach, Broughty Ferry, Dundee DD5 2TF   Tel: 01382 436916   Fax: 01382 436951
Email: broughty@dundeecity.gov.uk   Web: www.dundeecity.gov.uk/broughtycastle

15th century fort at the mouth of the Tay Estuary, housing fascinating displays on the history and natural history of the local area. Enjoy magnificent views over the river from our Observation Gallery.

Opening Times: Apr to Sep Mon to Sat 10:00-16:00, Sun 12:30-16:00. Oct to Mar Tue to Sat 10:00-16:00, Sun 12:30-16:00. Castle closed for refurbishment Apr to Jun 2002.
Admission: Free.   Location: Situated on the seafront beside Broughty Ferry harbour. Three miles from Dundee City Centre off the A930.   Map Ref: 18

McManus Galleries

Albert Square, Dundee DD1 1DA   Tel: 01382 432084   Fax: 01382 432052
Email: arts.heritage@dundeecity.gov.uk   Web: www.dundeecity.gov.uk

Gallery 4 - 'Europe and Beyond'

A remarkable gothic building housing one of Scotland's most impressive collections of fine and decorative art and award-winning displays of local history, archaeology, wildlife and the environment. There's always something new to see and do with a changing programme of exhibitions, activities, events and displays. Café serving refreshments and a gallery shop selling a variety of prints, cards, books and gifts.

Opening Times: Mon to Sat 10:30-17:00, Thu 10:30-19:00, Sun 12:30-16:00. Admission: Free.
Location: Situated in Dundee City Centre, ten minutes walk from bus and rail stations.   Map Ref: 18

Mills Observatory

Glamis Road, Balgay Park, Dundee DD2 2UB   Tel: 01382 435846   Fax: 01382 435962
Email: arts.heritage@dundeecity.gov.uk   Web: www.mills-observatory.co.uk

Mills Observatory is the UK's only full-time public observatory. See the stars and planets through an impressive Victorian telescope. Fascinating displays on astronomy and space exploration. Public planetarium shows take place monthly during the winter.

Opening Times: Apr to Sep Tue to Fri 11:00-17:00, Sat & Sun 12:30-16:00. Oct to Mar Mon to Fri 16:00-22:00, Sat & Sun 12:30-16:00. Admission: Free. Location: Balgay Park, one mile west of Dundee City Centre.   Map Ref: 18

Royal Research Ship Discovery

Discovery Point, Discovery Quay, Dundee DD1 4XA   Tel: 01382 201245   Fax: 01382 225891
Email: info@dundeeheritage.sol.co.uk   Web: www.rrsdiscovery.com

Visit Discovery Point and Royal Research Ship Discovery where you can follow in the footsteps of Captain Scott and his crew. With brand new interactives and many historic artefacts you can experience first hand this great voyage of discovery.

Opening Times: Apr to Oct Mon to Sat 10:00-17:00 Sun 11:00-17:00. Nov to Mar Mon to Sat 10:00-16:00 Sun 11:00-16:00. Admission: Adult £6.25, Child £3.85, Under 5s Free, Concession £4.70. Group rates available. Location: Near town centre, one minute walk from central railway station.   Map Ref: 18

Verdant Works

West Hendersons Wynd, Dundee DD1 5BT   Tel: 01382 225282   Fax: 01382 221612
Email: admin@dundeeheritage.col.co.uk   Web: www.verdantworks.com

Verdant Works brings the past to life using audio visual displays, computer interactives, original machinery and film show which allows you to experience what life was like in the Jute Mill.

Opening Times: Apr to Oct Mon to Sat 10:00-17:00 Sun 11:00-17:00. Nov to Mar Wed to Sat 10:30-16:30 Sun 11:00-16:30. Closed Mon & Tue. Admission: Adult £5.95, Child £3.85, Under 5s Free, Concession £4.45. Group rates available.   Map Ref: 18

DUNFERMLINE *Fife*

Andrew Carnegie Birthplace Museum

Moodie Street, Dunfermline KY12 7PL   Tel: 01383 724302

Andrew Carnegie's birthplace, cottage and memorial hall house the many treasures which he acquired during his eventful life. They include freedom caskets, keys and items from his study in Skibo Castle.

Opening Times: Apr to Oct Mon to Sat 11:00-17:00 Sun 14:00-17:00. Admission: Adult £2.00, Child (accompanied) Free, Concession £1.00. Location: Near town centre, 400 yards downhill from Dunfermline Abbey.   Map Ref: 19

Dunfermline Museum (Fife Council Museums West)

Viewfield Terrace, Dunfermline KY12 7HY   Tel: 01383 313838   Fax: 01383 313837

Linen history and Dunfermline's civic and local history. Dunfermline Museum is the headquarters for West Fife Museums Service which also includes Pittencrieff House Museum, Inverkeithing

Museum and St Margaret's Cave.

Opening Times: By appointment only. Admission: Free. Location: Five minutes walk from bus station.   Map Ref: 19

Pittencrieff House Museum

Pittencrieff Park, Dunfermline KY12 8QH   Tel: 01383 722935/313838

Temporary exhibition gallery, displays about local history and the Dunfermline Giant.

Opening Times: Good Friday to last Sun in Sep 11:00-17:00. Oct to Good Friday 11:00-16:00. Closed 14 Jan to 15 Mar 2002 for refurbishment. Admission: Free. Location: In Pittencrieff Park, western edge of Dunfermline.   Map Ref: 19

St Margaret's Cave

Dunfermline Tel: 01383 313838

No collections - a historic cave where St Margaret is reputed to have come to say her private prayers.

Opening Times: Good Friday to last Sun in Oct 11:00-16:00. Closed Nov to Good Friday. Admission: Free. Location: In town centre car park off Chalmers Street.   Map Ref: 19

DUNKELD *Perthshire*

Loch of the Lowes Visitor Centre

Scottish Wildlife Trust, Dunkeld PH8 0AW   Tel: 01350 727337   Email: abarclay@swt.org.uk

Visitor Centre and Observation Hide. Centre with wildlife displays, manned by rangers, staff and volunteers. Adjacent hide with views of breeding osprey and wildfowl. Occasional sightings of deer and otter.

Opening Times: Apr to Sep daily 10:00-17:00. Admission: Donation of Adult £1.00, Child 50p invited. Location: Two miles north east of Dunbeld, just off A923.   Map Ref: 20

ELGIN *Moray*

Elgin Museum

1 High Street, Elgin IV30 1EQ Tel / Fax: 01343 543675 Email: curator@elginmuseum.org.uk Web: www.elginmuseum.org.uk

Internationally famous fossil fish and reptiles. Also Pictish stones, archaeology, local history and wide ranging general collections. Conferences, workshops, activities and temporary exhibitions.

Opening Times: Apr to Oct Mon to Fri 10:00-17:00 Sat 11:00-16:00 Sun 14:00-17:00. Admission: Adult £2.00, Child 50p, Concession £1.00. Location: East end of High Street.
                                                                                    Map Ref: 21

ELLON *Aberdeenshire*

Haddo House

Methlick, Ellon AB41 7EQ   Tel: 01651 851440   Fax: 01651 851888

Designed by William Adam in 1732, but refurbished in the 1880s, the House elegantly blends crisp Georgian architecture with sumptuous late Victorian interiors by Wright and Mansfield. Haddo is noted for its fine furniture, paintings and objets d'art.

Opening Times: 29 Jun to 1 Sep Daily 10:00-17:00. Shop & Tearoom: 29 Mar to 29 Sep daily 10:00-17:00, weekends in Oct 10:00-17:00. Admission: Adult £7.00, Concession £5.25, Family £19.00. Location: Off B999, four miles north of Pitmedden.   Map Ref: 22

FALKLAND *Fife*

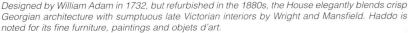

Falkland Palace & Garden

Falkland KY7 7BY Tel: 01337 857397 Fax: 01337 857980

The Royal Palace of Falkland was the country residence of Stuart kings and queens. The palace contains fine portraits of the Stuart monarchs and two sets of 17th century tapestry hangings. The garden was designed and built by Percy Cane, and contains three herbaceous borders with many varieties of shrubs and trees.

Falkland Palace - Chapel Royal

Opening Times: 1 Mar to 27 Oct Mon to Sat 10:00-18:00, Sun 13:00-17:00. Admission: Adult £7.00, Concession £5.25, Family £19.00. Location: A912, ten miles from junction 8 of M90, 11 miles north of Kirkcaldy.   Map Ref: 23

Central, East & Northeast Scotland

FOCHABERS *Moray*

Tugnet Ice House

Tugnet, Spey Bay, Fochabers IV32 7PS Tel: 01309 673701

Ice house - Scotland's largest.

Opening Times: Mar to Oct 10:30-16:30, Jul to Aug 10:30-19:00. Admission: Free.
Location: Turn north on B9104 toward Spey Bay, Tugnet one mile further, nearest town Elgin.

Map Ref: 24

FORFAR *Angus*

The Meffan, Forfar Museum & Gallery

Meffan Institute, 20 West High Street, Forfar DD8 1BB Tel: 01307 464123/467017 Fax: 01307
468451 Email: the.meffan@angus.gov.uk Web: www@angus.gov.uk/history.htm

*Stunning Pictish Stones and archaeology. A street of quaint old shops including weaver,
shoemaker, sweet shop, clock maker and baker. Art galleries with frequently changing exhibitions.
A witch's trial prior to her execution all in realistic life size displays.*

Opening Times: Mon to Sat 10:00-17:00. Admission: Free. Location: In town centre.

Map Ref: 25

FORRES *Moray*

Brodie Castle

Brodie Castle, Brodie, Forres IV36 2TE Tel: 01309 641371 Fax: 01309 641600

*The house contains fine French furniture, English, Continental and Chinese porcelain and a major
collection of paintings, including 17th century Dutch art, 19th century English watercolours,
Scottish Colourists and early 20th century works.*

Opening Times: 25 Mar to 29 Sep Thu to Mon 11:00-18:00. Admission: Adult £5.00,
Concession £3.75, Family £13.50. Location: Off A96, four and a half miles west of Forres.

Map Ref: 26

Falconer Museum

Tolbooth Street, Forres IV36 1PH Tel: 01309 673701 Fax: 01309 675863
Email: museums@moray.gov.uk Web: www.moray.gov.uk

*Information about the Royal Burgh of Forres, its people and history. Collection about the popular
folk singing duo 'The Corries'.*

Opening Times: 2 Apr to 27 Oct Mon to Sat 10:00-17:00. Closed Sun. 28 Oct to 30 Mar Mon to
Thu 11:00-12:30 13:00-15:30. Closed Fri, Sat, Sun. Admission: Free. Location: Just off the
High Street on Tolbooth Street, opposite The Tolbooth.

Map Ref: 26

Nelson Tower

c/o Falconer Museum, Tolbooth Street, Forres IV36 1PW Tel: 01309 673701 Fax: 01309
675863 Email: museums@moray.gov.uk Web: www.moray.gov.uk

*Memorabilia associated with Lord Nelson and his various battles. Pictures of Forres and
surrounding area in bygone days.*

Opening Times: May to Sep Tue to Sun 14:00-16.00. Admission: Free. Location: Around a
mile from town centre.

Map Ref: 26

FRASERBURGH *Aberdeenshire*

Museum of Scottish Lighthouses

Kinnaird Head, Fraserburgh AB43 9DU Tel: 01346 511022 Fax: 01346 511033
Web: www.lighthousemuseum.co.uk

*The new Museum of Scottish Lighthouses boasts the largest and best collection of lighthouse
lenses and equipment in the UK. Discover the unique story of the Stevenson family, lighthouse
engineers to the world.*

Opening Times: Nov to Mar daily 10:00-16:00, Sun 12:00-16:00. Apr to Oct daily 10:00-18:00,
Sun 12:00-18:00. Admission: Adult £3.90, Child £2.00, Concession £3.25, Family
£10.00/£11.00. Group rates available. Location: Fraserburgh, 15 minute walk from bus station.

Map Ref: 27

Sandhaven Meal Mill

Sandhaven, Fraserburgh AB43 4EP   Tel: 01224 664228

Restored typical 19th century Scottish meal mill. Guided tours and working demonstration model.

Opening Times: May to Sep Sat & Sun 14:00-16:30.   Admission: Free.   Location: On B9031 at eastern end of Sandhaven village.
Map Ref: 27

GARLOGIE *Aberdeenshire*

Garlogie Mill Power House Museum

Garlogie AB32 6RX   Tel: 01224 664228

Unique beam engine - only one of its type still in situ - which powered this 19th century woollen spinning mill. Award-winning AV presentation and displays on the history of textiles in the area.

Opening Times: May to Sep Sat & Sun 14:00-16:30.   Admission: Free.   Location: At west end of Garlogie village, behind Village Hall.
Map Ref: 28

GLAMIS *Angus*

Angus Folk Museum

Kirkwynd Cottage, Glamis DD8 1RT   Tel: 01307 840288   Fax: 01307 840233

Housing one of Scotland's finest folk collection, this museum presents a vivid insight into how the rural workforce used to live.

Opening Times: 25 Mar to 27 Oct Sat to Wed 12:00-17:00.   Admission: Adult £3.50, Concession £2.60, Family £9.50.   Location: Off A94 in Glamis, five miles south west of Forfar.
Map Ref: 29

Glamis Castle

Glamis DD8 1RJ   Tel: 01307 840393

Family home of the Earls of Strathmore and Kinghorne since 1372. Childhood home of Her Majesty Queen Elizabeth the Queen Mother and setting for Shakespeare's famous play 'Macbeth'.

Opening Times: 29 Mar to 27 Oct 10:30-17:30, Jul & Aug from 10:00.   Admission: Adult £6.50, Child £3.20, OAP/Student £4.80. Group rates available.
Map Ref: 29

HUNTLY *Aberdeenshire*

Brander Museum

The Square, Huntly AB54 8AE   Tel: 01224 664228

Display on Huntly-born author George Macdonald. Extensive collection of communion tokens. 19th century arms and armour from Sudan. Archaeological finds from Huntly Castle and other aspects of local history.

Opening Times: Tue to Sat 14:00-16:30. Closed BH.   Admission: Free.   Location: In The Square, town centre.
Map Ref: 30

Leith Hall

Huntly AB54 4NQ   Tel: 01464 831216   Fax: 01464 831594

Leith Hall is at the centre of a 279 acre estate which was the home of the head of the Leigh family from 1650. The house contains personal possessions of successive lairds.

Opening Times: 25 Mar to 27 Oct Wed to Sun 12:00-17:00.   Admission: Adult £7.00, Concession £5.25, Family £19.00.   Location: On B9002, one mile west of Kennethmont.
Map Ref: 30

INVERURIE *Aberdeenshire*

Carnegie Museum

The Square, Inverurie AB51 3SN   Tel: 01771 622906/01224 664228

Extensive archaeological displays, showing finds from New Stone Age to Bronze Age, as well as Early Christian carved stones. Displays on Inverurie's canal and railway history and the 19th century Volunteer Movement.

Opening Times: Mon & Wed to Fri 14:00-16:30 Sat 10:00-13:00 14:00-16:00. Closed BH.   Admission: Free.   Location: In The Square, above Inverurie Library, in town centre.   Map Ref: 31

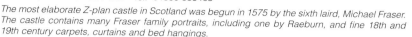

Castle Fraser

Sauchen, Inverurie AB51 7LD   Tel: 01330 833463

The most elaborate Z-plan castle in Scotland was begun in 1575 by the sixth laird, Michael Fraser. The castle contains many Fraser family portraits, including one by Raeburn, and fine 18th and 19th century carpets, curtains and bed hangings.

Opening Times: 25 Mar to 28 Jun Fri to Tue 12:00-17:00, 29 Jun to 1 Sep daily 10:00-17:00, 2 Sep to 27 Oct Fri to Tue 12:00-17:00.   Admission: Adult £7.00, Concession £5.25, Family £19.00.   Location: Off A944, four miles north of Dunecht.
Map Ref: 32

KILLIN *Perthshire*

Breadablane Folklore Centre

Falls of Dochart, Killin FK21 8XE   Tel: 01567 820214   Fax: 01567 820764

Folklore Centre, history of clans MacNab and MacGregor and area with two audio visual screens, short film and story of Saint Fillan. Sales shop and information centre.

Opening Times: Mar to May & Oct daily 10:00-17:00. Jun & Sep daily 10:00-18:00. Jul & Aug daily 09:30-18:30. Closed Nov to Feb.   Admission: Adult £2.00, Child/OAP £1.25, Student £1.50, Family £5.25. Group discounts available.   Location: At Falls of Dochart, Killin.
Map Ref: 33

KIRKALDY *Fife*

John McDouall Stuart Museum

Rectory Lane, Dysart, Kirkaldy   Tel: 01592 412860   Fax: 01592 412870

This house is the birthplace of John McDouall Stuart, the first European explorer to make a return journey across Australia in 1861-1862. Displays describe his harrowing journeys, the Australian wilderness and the Aborigines who made a life there.

Opening Times: 1 Jun to 31 Aug 14:00-17:00.   Admission: Free.   Location: In town centre.
Map Ref: 34

Kirkcaldy Museum & Art Gallery

War Memorial Gardens, Kirkcaldy KY1 1YG   Tel: 01592 412860   Fax: 01592 412870

Set in lovely grounds, Kirkcaldy Museum & Art Gallery, features superb collection of 19th and 20th century Scottish paintings, an award-winning permanent local history and a lively changing exhibition programme. Gallery shop for cards, crafts and local publications. Café incorporating Wemyss Ware Pottery displays. Enquiry and outreach service.

Opening Times: Mon to Sat 10:30-17:00, Sun 14:00-17:00. Closed Xmas & New Year.   Admission: Free.   Location: Five minute walk from town centre, adjacent to railway station.
Map Ref: 34

Blue and White Teapot by S J Peploe

KIRRIEMUIR *Angus*

Barrie's Birthplace

9 Brechin Road, Kirriemuir DD8 4BX   Tel: 01575 572646

The upper floors of this two-storeyed house are furnished as they may be been when Barrie lived here. The adjacent house contains an exhibition - 'The Genius of J M Barrie' - Barrie's literary and theatrical works.

Opening Times: 25 Mar to 27 Oct Sat to Wed 12:00-17:00.   Admission: Adult £5.00, Concession £3.75, Family £13.50.   Location: A90/A926, in Kirriemuir, six miles north west of Forfar.
Map Ref: 35

Kirriemuir Gateway to the Glens Museum

The Town House, 32 High Street, Kirriemuir DD8 4BB   Tel: 01575 575479
Email: kirriegateway@angus.gov.uk   Web: www.angus.gov.uk/history.htm

Social history of Kirriemuir and the Western Angus Glens including wildlife and archaeology.

Opening Times: Mon to Wed, Fri & Sat 10:00-17:00, Thu 13:00-17:00.   Admission: Free.   Location: In town centre.
Map Ref: 35

Central, East & Northeast Scotland

MAUD *Aberdeenshire*

Maud Railway Museum

Maud Station, Maud AB42 5LY   Tel: 01224 664228

Housed in the former Maud Railway Station buildings, this museum illustrates the history of north east railways from the GNSR period, through LNER days into the era of British Rail.

Opening Times: Easter to Sep Sat, Sun & BH 14:00-16:30.   Admission: Free.   Location: In centre of Maud Village, at old railway station site.   Map Ref: 36

METHIL *Fife*

Methil Heritage Centre

The Old Post Office Building, 272 High Street, Lower Methil, Methil KY8 3EQ   Tel: 01333 422100   Fax: 01333 422101   Web: www.methilheritage.co.uk

A lively local history museum and gallery located in the town of Methil. The museum features an exciting new permanent display 'Levenmouth Lives' as well as a temporary exhibition programme and associated events.

Opening Times: Tue to Thu 11:00-16:30, Sat 13:00-16:30.   Admission: Free.   Map Ref: 13

MONTROSE *Angus*

Montrose Museum & Art Gallery

Panmure Place, Montrose DD10 8HE   Tel: 01674 673232
Email: montrose.museum@angus.gov.uk   Web: www.angus.gov.uk/history.htm

Montrose's maritime and social history. The wildlife of Angus Gallery covering from sea to mountain top. Art Gallery with constantly changing exhibitions.

Opening Times: Mon to Sat 10:00-17:00.   Admission: Free.   Location: Two minutes walk from town centre, ten minutes walk from railway station.   Map Ref: 37

William Lamb Sculpture Studio

Market Street, Montrose DD10   Tel: 01674 673232   Email: montrose.museum@angus.gov.uk
Web: www.angus.gov.uk/history.htm

Bronze, plaster and stone sculpture, wood carvings, watercolours and etchings by William Lamb (1893-1951) who was commissioned by the Royal Family. The studio collection includes heads of the Queen Mother, and our present Queen and Princess Margaret as children.

Opening Times: Jul to early Sep Mon to Sun 14:00-17:00.   Admission: Free.   Location: In secluded close between High Street and Market Street, in town centre.   Map Ref: 37

NEWBURGH *Fife*

Laing Museum

High Street, Newburgh KY14 6DX   Tel: 01337 840223   Fax: 01334 413214
Email: museums.east@fife.gov.uk

First opened in 1896 to house Alexander Laing's Museum Collection and Reference Library, now a fascinating local history museum. It still displays Laing's material alongside the history of Newburgh.

Opening Times: Apr to Sep 11:00-17:00. Oct to Mar Wed, Sat & Sun 12:00-16:00.
Admission: Free.   Location: Town centre, High Street.   Map Ref: 38

PERTH

Black Watch Museum

Balhousie Castle, Perth PH1 5HR
Tel: 0131 310 8530   Fax: 0131 310 8525
Email: museum@theblackwatch.co.uk   Web: www.theblackwatch

Over 260 years of history of Scotland's oldest Highland Regiment: on display are paintings, uniforms, silver medals, weapons and memorabilia which brings the past alive, also displays from today. Well stocked gift shop with souvenirs, replica badges etc, on sale.

Opening Times: Oct to Apr Mon to Fri 10:00-15:30. Closed last Sat in Jun. May to Sep Mon to Sat 10:00-16:30.   Admission: Free. Donations welcome.   Location: Hay Street next to Bells Sports Centre.   Map Ref: 39

The Black Watch at Quatre Bras

Fergusson Gallery

Marshall Place, Perth PH2 8NU   Tel: 01738 441944   Fax: 01738 621152
Email: museum@pkc.gov.uk   Web: www.pkc.gov.uk/ah

Houses the most extensive collection of the work of J D Fergusson, one of the leading figures in 20th century Scottish art.

Opening Times: Mon to Sat 10:00-17:00. Closed Sun, Xmas to New Year.   Admission: Free.
Location: On southern edge of town centre, five minute walk from railway and bus stations.

Map Ref: 39

Perth Museum & Art Gallery

George Street, Perth PH1 5LB   Tel: 01738 632488   Fax: 01738 443505
Email: museum@pkc.gov.uk   Web: www.pkc.gov.uk/ah

One of Britain's oldest museums, founded in 1784, now houses wide-ranging collections of local history, archaeology, art and natural history. Changing displays throughout the year.

Opening Times: Mon to Sat 10:00-17:00. Closed Sun, Xmas to New Year.   Admission: Free.   Location: In city centre.

Perth Museum and Art Gallery

Map Ref: 39

PETERHEAD *Aberdeenshire*

Aberdeenshire Farming Museum

Aden Country Park, Mintlaw, Peterhead AB42 5FQ   Tel: 01771 622906

The main museum exhibitions cover the story of farming in north east Scotland and the life of an estate before the First World War. The working farm illustrates life in the 1950s.

Opening Times: Apr & Oct Sat, Sun & school holidays 12:00-16:30. May to Sep daily 11:00-16:30.   Admission: Free.   Location: In Aden Country Park, one mile west of A952/A950 crossroads at Mintlaw.

Map Ref: 40

Arbuthnot Museum

St Peter Street, Peterhead AB42 1QD   Tel: 01779 477778

Fishing, shipping and whaling displays. Local history, coins and Inuit art. Temporary exhibitions gallery.

Opening Times: Mon to Tue, Thu to Sat 11:00-13:00 14:00-16:30, Wed 11:00-13:00. Closed BH.
Admission: Free.   Location: In town centre, at St Peter Street/Queen Street crossroads, above Peterhead Library.

Map Ref: 41

Peterhead Maritime Heritage Visitor Centre

South Road, Lido, Peterhead AB42 0YP   Tel: 01779 473000

Award-winning building presenting aspects of Peterhead's maritime heritage. Interactive displays on fishing, whaling, navigation and the oil industry. AV presentation on maritime life.

Opening Times: Apr to Oct 10:00-17:00. Please phone 01779 473000 for winter times.
Admission: Adult £2.60, Child/Concession £1.60, Family £6.20.   Location: One mile south of Peterhead Town Centre on South Road (A952).

Map Ref: 41

PORTSOY *Aberdeenshire*

Fordyce Joiners Workshop & Visitor Centre

Fordyce, Portsoy AB45 2SL   Tel: 01224 664228

Late 19th/early 20th century rural joiner's workshop. Displays of hand tools and workshop machinery and AV presentation. See a craftsman at work and relax in a Victorian-style garden.

Opening Times: Thu to Mon 10:00-18:00.   Admission: Free.   Location: In Church Street, one minute from car park beside Fordyce Parish Church.

Map Ref: 42

British Golf Museum

Bruce Embankment, St Andrews KY16 9AB   Tel: 01334 460046   Fax: 01334 460064   Email: hwebster@randagc.org   Web: www.britishgolfmuseum.co.uk

Golf in the Inter-War period

A visit to the British Golf Museum will transport you down a pathway of surprising facts and striking feats from 500 years of golf history. Using diverse displays and exciting exhibits, the Museum traces the history of the game, both in Britain and abroad, from the middle ages to the present day. A must for golfers and non-golfers alike.

Opening Times: Apr to Oct 9:30-17:30. For winter opening times call the museum.   Admission: Adult £4.00, Child £2.00, OAP £3.00, Student £3.00, Group (10+) 50p off all charges.   Location: Ten minute walk from town centre, five minute walk from bus station. R/A Clubhouse, beside beach.   Map Ref: 43

Crawford Arts Centre

93 North Street, St Andrews KY16 9AD   Tel: 01334 474610   Fax: 01334 479880   Email: crawfordarts@crawfordarts.free-online.co.uk   Web: www.crawfordarts.free-online.co.uk

Independent arts centre with a programme of regularly changing exhibitions of all kinds of visual art and craft; also art activities organised; artist's studio; theatre.

Opening Times: Mon to Sat 10:00-17:00, Sun 14:00-17:00. Closed Xmas & New Year.   Admission: Free to galleries.   Location: Near town centre, opposite Police Station on North Street.   Map Ref: 43

St Andrews Museum

Kinburn House, Kinburn Park, Doubledykes Road, St Andrews KY16 9DP   Tel: 01334 412690   Fax: 01334 413214   Email: museums.east@fife.gov.uk

Telling the history of this ancient town, home to a university, golf and showing changing exhibitions about the local environment and Fife as a whole. This museum always has something new to see and do.

Opening Times: Apr to Sep 10:00-17:00. Oct to Mar 10:30-16:00.   Admission: Free.   Location: On western edge of town centre, near bus station.   Map Ref: 43

St Andrews Preservation Trust Museum

12 North Street, St Andrews KY16 9PW   Tel: 01334 477629   Web: www.standrewspreservationtrust.co.uk

This charming 16th century house contains a wealth of fascinating material on the history of St Andrews and its people. There are displays depicting a variety of old shops and businesses - a grocers, chemists, dentists workroom and much more.

Opening Times: May to Sep, Easter week, last week Nov daily 14:00-17:00.   Admission: Free.   Location: Near the Cathedral.   Map Ref: 43

St Andrews University Museum Collections

University of St Andrews, St Andrews KY16 9AL   Tel: 01334 462417   Fax: 01334 462401   Email: hcr1@st-andrews.ac.uk   Web: www.st-andrews.ac.uk/services/muscoll/museum.html

Founded in 1411, St Andrews is Scotland's oldest university. The University's collections date from its earliest years to the present and illustrate its history, personalities and teaching practices.

Opening Times: By appointment only.   Map Ref: 43

Scotland's Secret Bunker

Crown Buildings, Troywood, St Andrews KY16 8QH   Tel: 01333 310301   Fax: 01333 312040   Web: www.secretbunker.co.uk

Hidden beneath a Scottish Farmhouse, a tunnel leads to Scotland's Secret Bunker. 24,000 square feet of secret accommodation on two levels, 100 feet underground. Discover the twilight world of the Government Cold War, and take the opportunity to discover how they would have survived and you wouldn't!!! One of Scotland's DEEPEST and best kept secrets.

Opening Times: Apr to Oct daily 10:00-17:00.   Map Ref: 43

Central, East & Northeast Scotland

Argyll & Sutherland Highlanders Regimental Museum

Stirling Castle, Stirling FK8 1EH   Tel: 01786 475165   Fax: 01786 446038
Email: museum@argylls.co.uk   Web: www.argylls.co.uk

The Thin Red Line at Balaklava

The Museum, containing displays of silver, paintings and medals, provides visitors with tales of those who have served Britain in the ranks of the Regiment. See displays from events in the Regiment's history, from Crimea, where the Regiment formed the famous Thin Red Line, Lucknow where six Victoria Crosses were won and from both World Wars, Korea, Malaya, Cyprus, Aden and peace keeping in Northern Ireland.

Opening Times: Easter to Sep Mon to Sat 10:00-17:45, Sun 11:00-16:45. Oct to Easter daily 10:00-16:15. Admission: Free, although there is a Castle entry fee. Location: Within Stirling Castle.   Map Ref: 44

Bannockburn Heritage Centre

Glasgow Road, Stirling FK7 0LG   Tel: 01786 812664   Fax: 01786 810892

The Bannockburn Heritage Centre is situated at one of the most important historic sites in Scotland. On the battlefield nearby, in June 1314, King Robert the Bruce won freedom for the Scots.

Opening Times: 20 Jan to 24 Mar 10:30-16:00, 25 Mar to 27 Oct 10:00-18:00, 28 Oct to 24 Dec 10:30-16:00. Admission: Adult £3.50, Concession £2.60, Group £9.50. Location: Junction 9 of M80/M9, on A872 two miles south of Stirling.   Map Ref: 44

National Wallace Monument

Abbey Craig, Hillfoots Road, Stirling FK9 5LF   Tel: 01786 472140

Visit the spectacular National Wallace Monument, tribute to Scotland's national hero, Sir William Wallace's - inspiration for the Hollywood blockbuster 'Braveheart'. Learn about the turbulent events leading up to the Battle of Stirling Bridge before stepping into a recreation of Westminster Hall to become one of the observers at Wallace's trial in London. Listen to a talking head of Sir William Wallace recounting his patriotism and fight for Scotland's freedom, and wonder at the sight of Wallace's mighty two-handed broadsword. On your way to the top of *the monument visit the vaulted chamber housing the Hall of Heroes where you'll meet other great Scots sculpted in marble. The third floor of this magnificent monument gives you outstanding views of the surrounding countryside and a feeling of total 'freedom' as you learn about its history. If you feel a little wilted after all this, revive yourself in the coffee house before browsing in the souvenir gift shop for that special reminder of your visit.*

Opening Times: Jan to Feb & Nov to Dec daily 10:30-16:00, Mar to May & Oct 10:00-17:00, Jun 10:00-18:00, Jul & Aug 09:30-18:30. Admission: Adult £3.95, Child/OAP £2.75, Student £3.00, Family £10.75. Location: Ten minutes from Stirling Town Centre.   Map Ref: 44

Stirling Old Town Jail

St John Street, Stirling FK8 1EA   Tel: 01786 450050   Fax: 01786 471301
Email: otjug@aillst.ossian.net   Web: www.visitscottishheartlands.org.uk

Lock yourself into the past, explore life in a 19th century jail. Living history performances, original cells, spectacular roof top views. Meet jailors and inmates. Gift shop.

Admission: Adult £3.95, Child/OAP £2.75, Student £3.00, Family £10.75. Location: Situated in Stirling Old Town. Five minute walk from bus and railway station.   Map Ref: 44

Stirling Smith Art Gallery & Museum

Dumbarton Road, Stirling FK8 2RQ   Tel: 01786 471917   Fax: 01786 449523
Email: elspeth.king@smithartgallery.demon.co.uk
Web: www.smithartgallery.demon.co.uk

Smith Art Gallery & Museum

Founded in 1874, the Smith has a collection of Scottish and European paintings and a collection of artefacts illustrating the story of Stirling. These include the world's oldest football (c.540) and curling stone (1511), the Stirling Jug of 1457, and artefacts relating to the story of Wallace and Bruce. The Smith is an ideal place from which to explore the rest of Stirling.

Opening Times: Tue to Sat 10:30-17:00, Sun 14:00-17:00. Closed Mon. Admission: Free. Location: Dumbarton Road, 200 metres from Albert Hall and Tourist Information Centre.   Map Ref: 44

University of Stirling Art Collection

University of Stirling, Stirling FK9 4LA   Tel: 01786 466050

The Collection comprises over 300 works including paintings, prints, sketches, tapestries, sculpture and silver. There is a sculpture trail through the beautiful university grounds.

Opening Times: Daily 09:00-22:00. Closed Xmas & New Year. Admission: Free.
Location: Ten minutes from bus/railway stations.   Map Ref: 44

STONEHAVEN *Aberdeenshire*

Tolbooth Museum

The Harbour, Stonehaven AB39 2JU   Tel: 01224 664228

Stonehaven's oldest building - the Earl Marischal's 16th century storehouse which served as the County Tolbooth of Kincardineshire 1600-1767. Displays of local bygones and the building's links with the Scottish Episcopal Church.

Opening Times: Jun to Sep Wed to Mon 13:30-16:30. Please phone 01771 622906 for May & Oct times. Admission: Free. Location: On Stonehaven Harbourfront.   Map Ref: 45

TOMINTOUL *Moray*

Tomintoul Museum & Visitor Centre

The Square, Tomintoul AB37 9ET   Tel: 01309 673701   Fax: 01309 675863
Email: museum@moray.gov.uk   Web: www.moray.gov.uk/museums/

Displays on local history and wildlife.

Opening Times: 2 Apr to 1 Jun & 1 Oct to 26 Oct Mon to Fri 09:45-16:00. 2 Jun to 31 Aug Mon to Sat 09:30-16:30. 1 Sep to 29 Sep Mon to Sat 09:45-16:00. Closed 12:00-14:00 daily.
Admission: Free.   Map Ref: 46

TURRIFF *Aberdeenshire*

Fyvie Castle

Fyvie, Turriff AB53 8JS   Tel: 01651 891266   Fax: 01651 891107

Fyvie was once a royal stronghold, one of a chain of fortresses throughout Medieval Scotland. A rich portrait collection includes works by Batoni, Raeburn, Romney, Gainsborough, Opie and Hoppner. Also a fine collection of arms and armour.

Opening Times: 25 Mar to 28 Jun Sat to Wed 12:00-17:00, 29 Jun to 1 Sep daily 10:00-17:00, 2 Sep to 27 Oct Sat to Wed 12:00-17:00. Admission: Adult £7.00, Concession £5.25, Family £19.00. Location: Off A947, eight miles south east of Turriff.   Map Ref: 47

e Highlands and Islands present a back cloth of awesome mountains and majestic coastal enery. The Western Isles are a 130 mile long chain of islands rich in culture. The Orkney Islands ve the remains of a Stone Age fishing village preserved from 3000 BC.

ere are fascinating museums scattered throughout the region capturing the Highland heritage strating the local archaeology, geology, and natural, social and local history

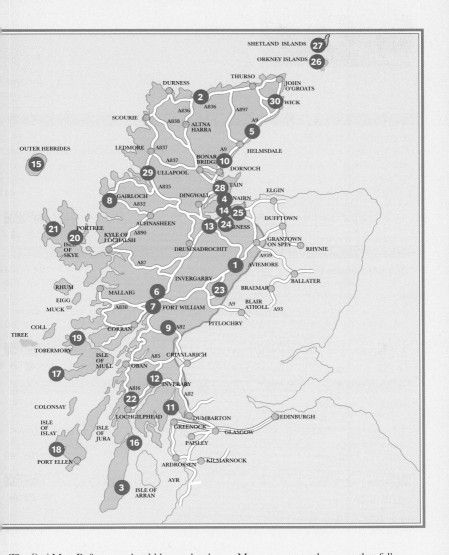

The Red Map References should be used to locate Museums etc on the pages that follow

Strathspey Railway

Aviemore Station, Dalfaber Road, Aviemore PH22 1PY   Tel: 01479 810725
Web: www.strathspeyrailway.co.uk

Boat of Garten Station

Scotland's 'Steam Railway in The Highlands', operating from Aviemore to Boat of Garten, provides splendid views of the Cairngorm Mountain range. While on board the train you can enjoy tea, coffee or something stronger, along with shortbread and/or scones. A visit to the railway will bring back many memories if you knew the days of steam or be a new thrilling experience if you do not.

Opening Times: 24 Mar to 3 Apr, Jun to Sep 09:30-17:30 Apr Sun & Wed 09:30-17:30 May & Oct Sat, Sun, Wed & Thu 09:30-17:30.   Admission: Adult £6.00, Child £3.00, OAP £4.60, Family £15.00.   Location: In centre of Aviemore and Boat of Garten.   Map Ref: 1

Strathnaver Museum

Bettyhill by Thurso KW14 7ST   Tel: 0164 521418   Email: strathnavermus@ukonline.co.uk

Strathnaver Museum is a locally run museum which first opened in 1976. It is housed in what was St Columba's Parish Church at the eastern end of Bettyhill. The Strath area abounds with archaeological sites, finds may be seen in the museum.

Opening Times: Apr to Oct Mon to Sat 10:00-13:00 14:00-17:00.   Admission: Adult £1.90, Child 50p, OAP £1.20, Student £1.00, Group £1.00 per person.   Location: Half a mile from village.   Map Ref: 2

Campbeltown Museum

Hall Street, Campbeltown PA28 6BS   Tel: 01586 552366   Fax: 01369 705797
Email: mvhelmond@abc-museums.demon.co.uk

Good display of local archaeology, geology and natural history. Programme of small temporary exhibitions in foyer of the Public Library.

Opening Times: Tue to Sat 10:00-13:00 14:00-17:00, Tue & Thu 17:30-19:30.   Admission: Free. Location: Near town centre, five minute walk from Tourist Information Centre, in the building of the Public Library.   Map Ref: 3

Cromarty Courthouse Museum

Church Street, Cromarty IV11 8XA   Tel / Fax: 01381 600418
Email: courthouse@mail.cali.co.uk   Web: www.cromarty-courthouse.org.uk

Cromarty Courthouse is a registered museum providing an enjoyable way to explore Cromarty's past.

Opening Times: Apr to Oct daily 10:00-17:00. Nov, Dec, Mar daily 12:00-16:00. Jan & Feb by arrangement. Closed Xmas.   Admission: Adult £3.00, Concession £2.00, Family £8.00.
Map Ref: 4

Hugh Millers Cottage

Church Street, Cromarty IV11 8XA   Tel: 01381 600245

Home of eminent geologist, stonemason, editor and writer Hugh Miller. The furnished thatched cottage, built c.1698 by his great-grandfather, contains an exhibition and captioned video programme on his life and work.

Opening Times: 1 May to 29 Sep daily 12:00-17:00.   Admission: Adult £2.50, Concession £1.90, Family £7.00.   Location: Via Kessock Bridge and A832 in Cromarty.   Map Ref: 4

Highlands & Islands

DUNBEATH *Caithness*

Laidhay Croft Museum
Laidhay, Dunbeath KW6 6EH   Tel: 01593 731244

Typical Caithness Rush thatched long house with separate 'Cruck' constructed barn. House incorporates dwelling accomodation with stable and byre either end. Artefacts, furniture, dairy equipment, harness and implements and machinery on view.

Opening Times: Apr to Oct daily 10:00-18:00.   Admission: Adult £1.00, Child 50p.
Location: One mile north of Dunbeath Village on A9, 20 miles south of town of Wick A99 & A9.
Map Ref: 5

FORT WILLIAM *Invernessshire*

Treasures of the Earth
Road of the Isles A830, Corpach, Fort William PH33 7JL   Tel: 01397 772283
Fax: 01397 772133

TREASURES
OF THE EARTH

A stunning collection of gemstones and crystals, displayed in fascinating simulation of cave, cavern and mining scenes. Priceless gemstones, beautiful crystals and exotic minerals light your path as they glisten and sparkle in cavities set against the scene back drop of ancient forest and tumbling waterfalls. Nuggets of gold, silver, aquamarines, rubies and opals.

Opening Times: 1 Feb to 2 Jan 10:00-17:00 (Jul, Aug & Sep 09:30-19:00).   Admission: Adult £3.00, Child £2.00, OAP £2.75.   Location: At Corpach four miles from Fort William on the A830.
Map Ref: 6

The West Highland Museum
Cameron Square, Fort William PH33 6AJ   Tel: 01397 702169   Fax: 01397 701927

Old fashioned, traditional museum, world famous for its Jacobite collections. Excellent social and local history collections including the Alexander Carmichael collection and exhibitions on charms, costume, etc. Usually there is a temporary exhibition.

Opening Times: Oct to May Mon to Sat 10:00-16:00. Jun to Sep 10:00-17:00. Sun Jul & Aug 14:00-17:00.   Admission: Adult £2.00, Child 50p, Concession £1.50.   Location: Central Square in town, next door to Tourist Office.
Map Ref: 7

GAIRLOCH *Rossshire*

Gairloch Heritage Museum
Achtercairn, Gairloch IV21 2BP   Tel: 01445 712287
Email: info@gairlochheritagemuseum.org.uk   Web: www.gairlochheritagemuseum.org.uk

Reflects the history of the parish of Gairloch: its people, their life and work, customs, the landscape, local skills such as spinning, fishing etc. Also to be seen is the light from the Rubha Reidh Light House. Children welcome.

Opening Times: Apr to Sep Mon to Sat 10:00-17:00, Oct Mon to Fri 10:00-13:30. Closed Nov to Mar. Open during winter by appointment only.   Admission: Adult £2.50, Child 50p, Under 5s Free, OAP £2.00.   Location: Situated five minutes walk from the shores of the loch, within easy reach of shops and hotels.
Map Ref: 8

GLENCOE *Argyllshire*

Glencoe & North Lorn Folk Museum
Glencoe Village, Glencoe PH49 4HS   Tel: 01855 811664

Local artefacts, clothing, weapons, Jacobite items, local history.

Opening Times: Easter week, Whitsun to end Sep Mon to Sat 10:00-17:30. Closed Sun.
Admission: Adult £2.00, Child Free, Concession £1.50.   Location: Centre of Glencoe village.
Map Ref: 9

Highlands & Islands

GOLSPIE *Sutherland*

Dunrobin Castle Museum

Dunrobin Castle, Golspie KW10 6SF   Tel: 01408 633177   Fax: 01408 634081
Email: info@dunrobincastle.net   Web: www.highlandescape.com

Pictish stones. Collection of natural history. Sutherland family artefacts.

Opening Times: Apr to 15 Oct Mon to Sat 10:30-16:30, Sun 12:00-16:30.   Admission: Adult
£6.25, Child £4.50, OAP £5.00, Family £17.00. Group rates available.   Location: One and a half
miles fro Golspie.   Map Ref: 10

HELENSBURGH *Argyllshire*

Hill House

Upper Colquhoun Street, Helensburgh G84 9AJ   Tel: 01436 673900   Fax: 01436 674685

*The finest of Charles Rennie Mackintosh's domestic creations, The Hill House sits high above the
Clyde commanding fine views of the river estuary. Walter Blackie commissioned not only the
house and garden but much of the furniture and all the interior fittings and decorative schemes.
Displays include work of new designers, demonstration of the effects of the wonderful stained
glass, and a selection of original fabrics.*

Opening Times: 25 Mar to 27 Oct daily 13:30-17:30.   Admission: Adult £7.00, Concession
£5.25, Family £19.00, Groups must book.   Location: Eastern side of Helensburgh.
                                                                                                        Map Ref: 11

INVERARAY *Argyllshire*

Inveraray Maritime Museum

The Pier, Inveraray PA32 8UY   Tel: 01499 302213   Fax: 0141 5813420

*Displays, artefacts and archive film of Clyde and West Scotland maritime history. Hands-on
activities and special displays of Highland Clearances and author Neil Munro of Para Handy fame.*

Opening Times: Apr to Sep 10:00-18:00, Oct to Mar 10:00-17:00.   Admission: Adult £3.60,
Child £2.00, OAP £2.60, Family £10.00.   Location: Near town centre at Pier.   Map Ref: 12

INVERNESS

Culloden Visitor Centre

Culloden Moor, Inverness IV2 5EU   Tel: 01463 790607   Fax: 01463 794294

*Scene of the last major battle fought on mainland Britain. The final Jacobite uprising ended here
on 16 April 1746. Turf and stone dykes which played a crucial part in the battle have been
reconstructed on their original site.*

Opening Times: 20 Jan to 24 Mar daily 10:00-16:00, 25 Mar to 27 Oct daily 09:00-18:00, 28 Oct
to 24 Dec daily 10:00-16:00.   Admission: Adult £5.00, Concession £3.75, Family £13.50.
Location: B9006, five miles east of Inverness.   Map Ref: 13

Inverness Museum & Art Gallery

Castle Wynd, Inverness IV2 3EB   Tel: 01463 237114

Archaeology Gallery

*Enjoy real Highland heritage in displays, exhibitions and events - an
extravaganza of archaeology, art, natural and local history. Discover
silver and taxidermy from Inverness, weapons and bagpipes from
the Highlands and Scottish contemporary art. The ever-changing
temporary exhibitions gallery presents a range of events and
displays which reflect the cultural activity of the city. Progamme of
talks, events and recitals. Activities for children and adults. Public
enquiry service, identifying objects and providing information. Roll
up your sleeves and discover the Highlands in the brand new
interactive discovery centre, with hundreds of interesting artefacts to
see and handle. Video macroscope to project objects onto a large
screen, computer controlled roof top camera and satellite weather
reports from around the world. Museum shop with a range of gifts,
books and Highland souvenirs.*

Opening Times: Mon to Sat 09:00-17:00. Closed Sun.   Admission: Free.   Location: In city
centre, five minutes walk from car parks, railway station and bus station.   Map Ref: 12

Highlands & Islands

Regimental Museum, Queens Own Highlanders

Fort George, Ardersier, Inverness IV2 7TD   Tel: 01463 224380

Unique collection of uniform, medals, paintings, prints, weapons of Queen's Own Highlanders, Seaforth Highlanders, The Queen's Own Cameron Highlanders, Lovat Scouts, includes regular militia, territorial battalions. Comprehensive library and archive collection, available by appointment.

Opening Times: Apr to Sep daily 10:00-18:00. Oct to Mar Mon to Fri 10:00-16:00.
Admission: Free. (Visitors to Fort George must pay entrance fee to Historic Scotland)
Location: Within Fort George, 12 miles east of Inverness.   Map Ref: 14

ISLAND OF BENBECULA

Museum Nan Eilean

Sgoil Lionacleit, Lionacleit, Island of Benbecula HS7 5PJ   Tel: 01870 602864

Artefacts, photographs illustrating archaeology, local history and way of life in the Uists. Programme of temporary exhibitions.

Opening Times: Mon, Wed & Thu 09:00-16:00. Tue, Fri & Sat 11:00-13:00 & 14:00-16:00.
Admission: Free. Location: Centrally situated on Island of Benbecula.   Map Ref: 15

ISLE OF BUTE *Argyllshire*

Bute Museum

Stuart Street, Rothesay, Isle of Bute PA20 0EP   Tel: 01700 505067

Illustrative of the natural history, archaeology and social history of the Islands of Bute and Inchmarnock.

Opening Times: Apr to Sep Mon to Sat 10:30-16:30, Sun 14:30-16:30. Oct to Mar Tue to Sat 14:30-16:30. Admission: Adult £1.20, Child 40p, OAP 70p. Location: In town centre behind castle.   Map Ref: 16

ISLE OF ISLAY *Argyllshire*

Museum of Islay Life

Daal Terrace, Port Charlotte, Isle of Islay PA48 7UA   Tel / Fax: 01496 850358
Email: imt@islaymuseum.freeserve.co.uk   Web: www.islaymuseum.freeserve.co.uk

The collection covers Islay life from earliest times, including archaeological artefacts. Domestic items are displayed in room settings. Traditional industries - whisky, joinery, crafting and fishing are well represented.

Opening Times: Apr to Oct Mon to Sat 10:00-17:00 Sun 14:00-17:00. Nov to Mar opening times advertised locally/by appointment for Groups. Admission: Adult £2.00, Child £1.00, Concession £1.20, Family £5.00. Coach reduction - 20%. Location: At edge of small village - good parking, one minute from bus stop.   Map Ref: 18

ISLE OF LEWIS

Museum Nan Eilean
Francis Street, Stornaway, Isle of Lewis HS1 2NF   Tel: 01851 703773

The collections feature local archaeology, objects and photographs relating to local history, domestic life, crofting, argriculture, crafts and fishing.

Opening Times: Apr to Sep Mon to Sat 10:00-17:30. Oct to Mar Mon to Fri 10:00-17:00, Sat 10:00-13:00. Admission: Free. Location: Short walk from town centre.   Map Ref: 15

Isle of Mull Museum

Main Street, Tobermory, Isle of Mull PA75 6NY

Historical artefacts and informative displays about the Isle of Mull from its geological beginnings to the present day.

Opening Times: Mon to Fri 10:00-16:00. Admission: Adult £1.00, Child 20p. Location: On Tobermory Main Street next to Clydesdale Bank.   Map Ref: 19

Highlands & Islands

ISLE OF SKYE

Dualchas-Skye & Lochalsh Area Museums & Heritage Service

The Highland Council, Park Lane, Portree, Isle of Skye IV51 9GP   Tel: 01478 613857
Fax: 01478 613751

The Heritage Service provides detailed information on the history and culture of the area through its varied and extensive collections including the Dualchas Collection, The Archives and the Dualchas Library.

Opening Times: Mon to Fri 10:00-17:00. Closed Sat, Sun & BH. Admission: Free.
Location: Portee, Isle of Skye.   Map Ref: 20

Dunvegan Castle

Dunvegan, Isle of Skye IV55 8WF   Tel: 01470 521206   Fax: 01470 521205
Email: info@dunvegancastle.com   Web: www.dunvegancastle.com

The stronghold of the Chiefs of MacLeod for nearly 800 years and it remains their home. Built on a rock once surrounded entirely by salt water, it is unique in Scotland as the only house of such antiquity to have retained its family and its roof throughout the centuries, surviving the extremes of feast, famine and the intermittent periods of warring with neighbouring clans.

Romantic & Historic Dunvegan Castle

Opening Times: Daily mid Mar to Oct 10:00-17:30, Nov to mid Mar 11:00-16:00. Admission: Adult £6.00, Child £3.50, OAP/Student/Group £5.50. Location: One and a half miles from village of Dunvegan, follow signposts.
                                                                                                    Map Ref: 21

KILMARTIN *Argyllshire*

Kilmartin House Museum of Ancient Culture

Kilmartin PA31 8RQ   Tel: 01546 510278   Fax: 01546 510330   Email: djam@kilmartin.org
Web: www.kilmartin.org

All-round sensory experience dedicated to the celebration and study of Scotland's richest prehistoric landscape.

Opening Times: Daily 10:00-17:30. Admission: Adult £4.50, Child £1.50, Concession £3.50, Family £10.00. Location: In Kilmartin village, next to the church.   Map Ref: 22

KINGUSSIE *Invernessshire*

Highland Folk Museum

Duke Street, Kingussie PH21 1JG   Tel: 01540 661307   Fax: 01540 661631
Email: highland.folk@highland.gov.uk   Web: www.highlandfolk.com

Award winning museum on two sites recreating the social history of the Scottish Highlands with a reconstructed 18th century farming township, Victorian water-powered sawmill, pre-war school and Isle of Lewis Blackhouse. Art Gallery features local artists.

Opening Times: Easter to Oct, please phone to confirm times. Admission: Adult £5.00, Child/OAP £3.00. Location: Kingussie Museum is five minutes from bus stop and railway station. Newtonmore Museum is 15 minutes from railway station.   Map Ref: 23

NAIRN *Invernessshire*

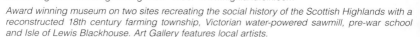

Cawdor Castle

Cawdor Castle, Nairn IV12 5RD   Tel: 01667 404615   Fax: 01667 404674   Email: info@cawdorcastle.com   www.cawdorcastle.com

Cawdor Castle, the most romantic Castle in the Highlands, has a magical name linked with Macbeth by Shakespeare. The Medieval tower and drawbridge are intact and generations of art lovers are responsible for the eclectic collections of paintings, tapestries, furniture and books in the castle. Beautiful gardens, nature trails, 9-hole golf course and putting green.

Opening Times: May to mid Oct daily 10:00-17:00.
Admission: Adult £6.10, Child £3.30, OAP £5.10, Family £18.00.
Groups of 20+ £5.30. Location: Situated between Inverness and Nairn on the B9090 off the A96.   Map Ref: 24

Nairn Museum

Viewfield House, Viewfield Drive, Nairn IV12 4EE   Tel: 01667 456791   Fax: 01667 455399
Email: manager@nairnmuseum.freeserve.co.uk   Web: www.nairnmuseum.co.uk

The two Nairn museums amalgamated in 2000. Our permanent displays cover fishermen and farmers, adventures and Nairnshire notables. Changing monthly exhibitions. Children's area. Family and local history research facilities.

Opening Times: Easter to end Oct Mon to Sat 10:00-16:30.   Admission: Adult £1.50, Child 50p, Family £2.50. Groups discount available.   Location: Near town centre, three minute walk from bus station.   Map Ref: 25

ORKNEY

Orkney Museum, Tankerness House

Broad Street, Kirkwall, Orkney KW15 1DH   Tel: 01856 873191   Fax: 01856 875160
Email: museum@orkney.gov.uk   Web: www.orkneyheritage.com

The story of Orkney, from the Stone Age to modern times. Vivid displays, including the Picts and Vikings. Internationally important artefacts housed in a historic 16th century laird's town house.

Opening Times: Oct to Apr Mon to Sat 10:30-12:30 13:30-17:00. May to Sep Mon to Sat 10:30-17:00 Sun 14:00-17:00.   Admission: Free. Location: Opposite St Magnus Cathedral. Map Ref: 26

Orkney Wireless Museum

Kiln Corner, Junction Road, Kirkwall, Orkney KW15 1ES   Tel: 01856 871400
Web: www.owm.org.uk

Wartime communications equipment from Scapa Flow, history of domestic radio, working crystal set and valve set, Gimmick transistor radios, Orkney Wartime Photographic Archive.

Opening Times: Apr to Sep Mon to Sat 10:00-16:30, Sun 14:30-16:30.   Admission: Adult £2.00, Child £1.00.   Location: Next to harbour.   Map Ref: 26

The Pier Arts Centre

Stromness, Orkney KW16 3AA   Tel: 01856 850 209   Fax: 01856 851 462

A permanent collection of 20th century British art including work by Ben Nicholson, Barbara Hepworth, Terry Frost, Roger Hilton, Alfred Wallis and Peter Lanyon and temporary exhibition programme of contemporary art by international and local artists.

Opening Times: Tue to Sat 10:30-12:30 13:30-17:00.   Admission: Free.   Location: One minute walk from bus station.   Map Ref: 26

Scapa Flow Visitor Centre & Museum

Lyness, Hoy, Orkney KW16 3NT   Tel: 01856 791300   Fax: 01856 875160
Email: museum@orkney.gov.uk   Web: www.orkneyheritage.com

The history of Scapa Flow, Britain's main naval base in both World Wars and the grave of the German High Seas Fleet. Historic buildings, photographs and artefacts.

Opening Times: Oct to May Mon to Fri 09:00-16:30. Jun to Oct daily 09:00-16:30.
Admission: Free.   Location: Lyness, Hoy.   Map Ref: 26

Stromness Museum

52 Alfred Street, Stromness, Orkney KW16 3DF   Tel: 01856 850025

Orkney maritime and natural history, including ships and fishing, Hudsons Bay log, Arctic whaling, German fleet in Scapa Flow, birds, seashells, moths and butterflies, fossils and ethnology.

Opening Times: Apr to Sep Sun to Sat 10:00-17:00. Oct to Mar Mon to Sat 11:00-15:30
Admission: Adult £2.50, Child 50p, OAP £2.00. Schools Free.   Location: 15 minute walk from town centre.   Map Ref: 26

SHETLAND

Bod of Gremista

Gremista, Lerwick, Shetland   Tel: 01595 695057   Web: www.shetland-museum.org.uk

Renovated late 18th century house and fishing booth. Three-storey, stone-roofed building. Restored rooms with period furniture. Displays on line fishing and merchant marine trade. Biography of A Anderson, local businessman.

Opening Times: Jun to mid Sep Tue to Sun 10:00-13:00, 14:00-17:00.   Admission: Free - donations welcome   Location: Outskirts of town, one mile from ferry terminal.   Map Ref: 27

Shetland Croft House Museum

Voe, Dunrossness, Shetland   Tel: 01595 695057   Fax: 01595 696729   Web: www.shetland-museum.org.uk

Restored mid-19th century steading, comprising house, byre, barn and mill. Stone walls and straw thatched traditional building with authentic contents. Locally-made furniture and agricultural implements.

Opening Times: May to Sep 10:00-13:00, 14:00-17:00.   Admission: Free - donations welcome
Location: Near Boddam, five miles from airport.   Map Ref: 27

Shetland Museum

Lower Hillhead, Lerwick, Shetland ZE1 0EL   Tel: 01595 695057   Fax: 01595 696729
Email: tommy.watt@sic.shetland.gos.uk   Web: www.shetland-museum.org.uk

Comprehensive history of Shetland, geology, archaelogy from Stone Age to Medieval, including Iron Age farm finds and Early Christian treasure. Agriculture and fisheries 18th to 20th century. Social history, textiles.

Opening Times: Mon Wed & Fri 10:00-19:00, Tue, Thu & Sat 10:00-17:00.   Admission: Free.
Location: Town centre, one minutes walk from Town Hall.   Map Ref: 27

TAIN *Rossshire*

Tain & District Museum

Tower Street, Tain IV19 1DY   Tel / Fax: 01862 894089   Email: info@tainmuseum.demon.co.uk

The highlight is an outstanding collection of Tain silver. Other important areas are costume, burgh history (archives and photographs) and Clan Ross.

Opening Times: Third Mon in Mar to end Oct daily 10:00-18:00.   Admission: Museum only:
Adult 1.50, Child 50p. Tain Through Time: Adult £3.50, Concession £2.50.   Location: In town
centre.   Map Ref: 28

ULLAPOOL *Rossshire*

Ullapool Museum & Visitor Centre

7/8 West Argyle Street, Ullapool IV26 2TY   Tel / Fax: 01854 612987
Email: ulmuseum@waverider.co.uk

Discover the Loch Broom Story! Award-winning Highland Museum, within a former Telford Parliamentary Church. Insight into a Highland parish. Audio-visual, photos, touchscreens. Local archives, records. Exhibitions.

Opening Times: Apr to Oct Mon to Sat 09:30-17:30. Nov to Feb Wed, Thu & Sat 11:00-15:00.
Mar Mon to Sat 11:00-15:00.   Admission: Adult £3.00, Child 50p, Concession & Group £2.00,
School Group Free.   Location: Near centre of village.   Map Ref: 29

WICK *Caithness*

Wick Heritage Centre

20 Bank Row, Wick KW1 5EY   Tel / Fax: 01955 605393

Contains a restored fisherman's house, tableaux of fossils, 19th century fashion, fish kiln, cooperage, complete blacksmith's shop and foundry, a working lighthouse, the famous Johnston collection of photographs of 115 years history.

Opening Times: Jun to Sep Mon to Sat 10:00-17:00.   Admission: Adult £2.00, Child 50p.
Location: Near the harbour.   Map Ref: 30

es has a strong tradition of music, literature and art, and this tradition is well represented in museums and galleries of South Wales. Cardiff and Swansea have exceptional museums and eries - Welsh heritage, the social history of coal mining, steam railways and maritime history the focus of museums throughout this region.

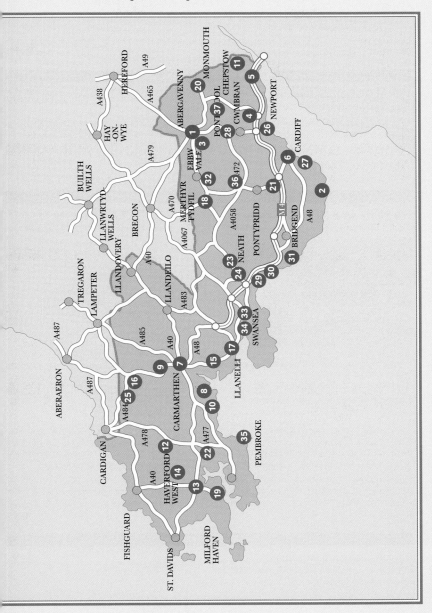

The Red Map References should be used to locate Museums etc on the pages that follow

South & Southwest Wales

ABERGAVENNY *Monmouthshire*

Abergavenny Museum & Castle

Castle Street, Abergavenny NP7 5EE   Tel: 01873 854282   Fax: 01873 736004
Email: abergavennymuseum@monmouthshire.gov.uk

The history of Abergavenny from prehistoric to present, housed in a Regency hunting lodge amid the ruins of the Norman Castle. Displays include 1950s shop interior, farm kitchen, saddlers shop. Regular exhibitions and events.

Opening Times: Open all year.   Admission: Adult £1.00 Children Free Concession 75p.
Location: Near town centre, parking nearby.   Map Ref: 1

BARRY ISLAND *Glamorgan*

Vale of Glamorgan Railway Co

The Station, Barry Island CF62 5TH   Tel: 01446 748816

Operating steam railway between Barry Island and Barry Waterfront. Museum of South Wales Railways, rolling stock viewing at Plymouth Road Depot and miniature railway rides.

Opening Times: Easter to mid Sep & Dec Sat, Sun & BH 11:00-16:00.   Admission: Adult £3.00, Child £2.00, Family £8.00.   Location: Barry Island Railway Station - one minute walk from beach.   Map Ref: 2

BLAENAVON *Torfaen*

Big Pit National Mining Museum

Big Pit, Blaenavon NP4 9XP   Tel: 01495 790311   Fax: 01495 792618   Web: www.nmgw.ac.uk

In the heart of the recently declared World Heritage Site at Blaenavon, Big Pit offers an experience unparalleled in Britain and unique to Wales. Guided by an ex-miner, you will descend 300 feet to the very depths of the mine and experience the inky blackness that the miners worked in day after day. Complete your visit on the surface and explore the colliery buildings, pit head baths and winding engine house.

Big Pit National Mining Museum

Opening Times: 5 to 18 Feb Tue to Thu 09:30-17:00, 18 Feb to 30 Nov daily 09:30-17:00.   Admission: Free.
Location: In the town of Blaenavon, approx 16 miles north of Newport. Signposted from junction 25A of M4.   Map Ref: 3

Pontypool & Blaenavon Railway

c/o Council Offices, High Street, Blaenavon NP4 9PT   Tel: 01495 792263
Email: railway@pontypoolandblaenavon.freeserve.co.uk   Web: www.pontypool-and-blaenavon.co.uk

Steam or diesel trains operate on a three quarter mile journey. Static display of locomotives and rolling stock. Stroll or picnic alongside the adjacent Garn Lakes after your train ride.

Opening Times: Easter to end Sep Sun BH Mon & Apr to Aug first Sat 11:30-16:30.
Admission: Steam Services: Adult £2.40, Child £1.20, Family £6.00. Diesel Services: Adult £2.20, Child £1.10, Family £5.50.   Location: Situated just off the B4248 Blaenavon to Brynmawr Road.   Map Ref: 3

CAERLEON *Newport*

Roman Legionary Museum

High Street, Caerleon NP18 1AE   Tel: 01633 423134   Fax: 01633 422869
Email: www.nmgw.ac.uk

Discover what made the Romans such a formidable force. See how they lived, slept and ate, how they marched and prepared for battle and which gods they worshipped.

Opening Times: Mon to Sat 10:00-17:00, Sun 14:00-17:00.   Admission: Free.   Location: On Caerleon High Street, in town centre.   Map Ref: 4

CALDICOT *Monmouthshire*

Caldicot Castle

Caldicot Castle, Church Road, Caldicot NP26 4HU   Tel: 01291 420241   Fax: 01291 435094
Email: caldicotcastle@monmouthshire.gov.uk   Web: www.caldicotcastle.co.uk

Founded by the Normans, developed in Royal hands as a Medieval stronghold and restored as a Victorian family home, the castle has a colourful and romantic history.

Opening Times: Mar to Oct daily 11:00-17:00.   Admission: Adult £3.00 Concessions and Family rates available.   Location: Five minutes from Caldicot Centre, between Chepstow and Newport.
Map Ref: 5

CARDIFF

Cardiff Castle

Cardiff Street, Cardiff CF10 3RB   Tel: 029 2087 8100   Fax: 029 2023 1417
Email: cardiffcastle@cardiff.gov.uk   Web: www.cardiff-info.com/castle

Cardiff Castle

Discover 2000 years of history in the heart of the city from the arrival of the Romans, through the Norman Conquest to lavish Victorian design - all have left their mark on the castle for you to explore. Plus traditional Welsh banquets for a great night out (booking essential).

Opening Times: Mar to Oct daily 09:30-18:00, Nov to Feb daily 09:30-17:00.   Admission: Adult £5.25, Child/Concession £3.15, Student £4.20, Family £14.75. (2001 prices)   Location: Cardiff City Centre. Quarter mile from central bus and train station.
Map Ref: 6

Museum of Welsh Life

St Fagans, Cardiff CF5 6XB   Tel: 029 2057 3500   Fax: 029 2057 3490
Web: www.nmgw.ac.uk

One of Europe's most outstanding open air museums. See how we have lived, worked, played and worshipped in over 40 buildings that have been moved from all over Wales.

Opening Times: Daily 10:00-17:00.   Admission: Free.   Location: In the village of St Fagans, approx six miles from Cardiff City Centre.
Map Ref: 6

National Museum & Gallery Cardiff

Cathays Park, Cardiff CF10 3NP   Tel: 029 2039 7951
Fax: 029 2037 3219   Web: www.nmgw.ac.uk

The National Museum & Gallery Cardiff is unique amongst British museums and galleries in its range of arts and science displays. The elegant Art Galleries house dazzling works of art by French Impressionists while the Evolution of Wales takes you on an amazing journey through 4600 million years of history. Don't miss the interactive Glanely Gallery where you can enjoy a changing programme of hands-on activities.

Opening Times: Tue to Sun 10:00-17:00, open BH Mon.   Admission: Free.   Location: In Cardiff's Civic Centre, approx five minutes walk from Cardiff City Centre.
Map Ref: 6

Regimental Museum 1st The Queens Dragoon Guards

Cardiff Castle, Cardiff CF10 2RB   Tel: 029 2022 2253   Fax: 029 2078 1384
Email: morris602@netscapeonline.co.uk   Web: www.qdg.org.uk

Uniforms, medals, accoutrements, archives of 1st King's Dragoon Guards, Queen's Bays (2nd Dragoon Guards) and 1st The Queen's Dragoon Guards.

Opening Times: Mar to Oct Sat to Thu 10:00-18:00, Nov to Feb Sat to Thu 10:00-16:30. Closed Fri.   Admission: Full tour: Adult £5.25, Child/OAP £3.15, Student £4.20. Short tour: Adult £3.15, Child/OAP £1.90.   Location: In city centre, five minute walk from railway/bus station.
Map Ref: 6

Techniquest

Stuart Street, Cardiff Bay, Cardiff CF10 5BW   Tel: 029 2047 5475   Fax: 029 2048 2517
Email: info@techniquest.org   Web: www.techniquest.org

Techniquest - the UK's most visited science centre with over 150 hands-on exhibits and puzzles, science theatre, planetarium, discovery room and The Hub.

Opening Times: Mon to Fri 09:30-16:30, Sat, Sun, BH & school holidays 10:30-17:00.
Admission: Adult £6.30, Child £4.30, Family £17.40. Group rates available.   Location: Cardiff Bay, waterfront location - five minutes from Cardiff Bay Station.   Map Ref: 6

Welch Regiment Museum (41st/69th Foot) of the Royal Regiment of Wales

The Black and Barbican Towers, Cardiff Castle, Cardiff CF10 2RB   Tel: 029 2022 9367
Web: www.rrw.org.uk

The museum commemorates the service of the Infantry of South Wales namely the Welch Regiment (41st/69th Foot), also associated militia, volunteer and territorial forces, 1719-1969. Also the Royal Regiment of Wales 24th/41st Foot 1969 to date.

Opening Times: Mar to Oct daily 10:00-18:00, closed Tue. Nov to Feb daily 10:00-16:30, closed Tue. Closed Xmas & New Year.   Admission: Museum - Free. Castle - Adult £2.60, Child/OAP £1.60, Student £2.10, Family £7.40.   Location: The Museum is situated within Cardiff Castle and is within ten minutes walking time of the main train and bus station, also City Centre multi story car parks.   Map Ref: 6

CARMARTHEN

Carmarthen Heritage Centre

The Quay, Carmarthen SA31 3AN   Tel: 01267 223788   Fax: 01267 223830
Email: cdelaney@carmarthenshire.gov.uk   Web: www.carmarthenshire.gov.uk

Exploring the history of the River Tywi and its importance for Carmarthenshire. On show are coracles made for fishing on the river and other displays.

Opening Times: Easter, May to Oct Mon to Sat 10:00-17:00. Nov to Easter Sat 11:00-16:00.
Admission: Free.   Location: Two minutes from bus station.   Map Ref: 7

Carmarthenshire County Museum

Abergwili, Carmarthen SA31 2JG   Tel: 01267 231691   Fax: 01267 223830
Email: cdelaney@carmarthenshire.gov.uk   Web: www.carmarthenshire.gov.uk

One of Wales' finest regional museums housed in the one-time Palace of the Bishop of St Davids. On show are paintings, furniture, Roman archaeology and much more. Set in own parkland with walks and picnic sites.

Opening Times: Mon to Sat 10:00-16:30. Closed Xmas & New Year.   Admission: Free.
Location: At Abergwili - one and a half miles from Carmarthen on the A40. Public transport - buses for Llandeilo.   Map Ref: 7

Dylan Thomas Boathouse

Dylans Walk, Laugharne, Carmarthen SA3 4SD   Tel: 01994 427420

The Boathouse, where Dylan and Caitlin lived with their children from 1949-1953 is now a heritage centre. The house now contains audio visual presentations, original furnishings and memborabilia, a themed bookshop, tea room, viewing platform and terrace.

Opening Times: May to Oct and Easter weekend daily 10:00-17:30, Nov to Apr daily 10:30-15:30.   Admission: Adult £1.75, Child under 7 Free.   Map Ref: 8

Gwili Steam Railway

Bronwydd Arms Station, Bronwydd, Carmarthen SA33 6HT   Tel: 01267 230666
Email: gwili@talk21.com   Web: www.gwili-railway.co.uk

A two and a half mile working standard gauge steam railway running through the Gwili Valley. Visit the working signalbox. Free miniature railway, gift shop, riverside picnic site.

Admission: Adult £4.50, Child/OAP/Concession £3.00, Under 2s Free, Family £12.50. Group rates available. Special fares for special events eg. Thomas and Santa trains.   Location: Three miles from Carmarthen on A484 road, at Bronwydd. Follow the tourist 'Steam Railway' signs.
Map Ref: 9

Museum of Speed

Pendine, Carmarthen SA33 4NY   Tel: 01994 453488   Fax: 01267 223830
Email: cdelaney@carmarthenshire.gov.uk   Web: www.carmarthenshire.gov.uk

Explores the history of Pendine's role in racing. The main exhibition in July and August, is the car 'Babs' record breaking, and fast vehicles and bikes at other times.

Opening Times: Easter to Sep daily 10:00-13:00, 13:30-17:00. Oct Fri to Mon 10:00-13:00, 13:30-17:00. Closed Nov to Easter. Admission: Free. Location: On the seafront at Pendine A4066 from the A40.
Map Ref: 10

CHEPSTOW *Monmouthshire*

Chepstow Museum

Bridge Street, Chepstow NP16 5EZ   Tel: 01291 625981

Museum reveals the rich and varied past of this ancient Wye Valley port and market centre. Wine trade, ship building and salmon fishing feature in displays which also recall Wye tourism and local social history.

Opening Times: Mon to Sat, Sun afternoon. Admission: Adult £1.00 Children Free Concession 75p. Location: In lower town, opposite Chepstow Castle.
Map Ref: 11

CLUNDERWEN *Pembrokeshire*

Penrhos Cottage

Llanycefn, Clunderwen SA66 7XT   Tel: 01437 731328   Fax: 01437 779500

Built as a 'TY UN NOS' (overnight house) at the beginning of the 19th century, Penrhos was the last occupied thatched cottage in Pembrokeshire. Three rooms containing original oak furniture.

Opening Times: By appointment. Admission: Donation. Location: Rural - Preseu Hills, near Maenclochog.
Map Ref: 12

HAVERFORDWEST *Pembrokeshire*

Haverfordwest Town Museum

Castle House, The Castle, Haverfordwest SA61 2ES   Tel: 01437 763087
Web: www.haverfordwest-town-museum.org.uk

The exterior of Haverfordwest Town Museum

The Haverfordwest Town Museum is situated in the Old Prison Governor's House in the grounds of Haverfordwest Castle. It reflects on the history of Haverfordwest from Norman times to the present day. The museum contains a wide variety of artefacts, photographs, paintings and uses multi media computer facilities with touch screen. The oldest letter box in Wales, fully restored, is in the museum. Each room in the museum reflects on a distinct theme. The castle and reception room informs visitors about the history of the castle and its use as a prison. The Civic Room has old mayoral robes, information on town development and archaeological finds. The Religion Room has finds from the excavations at Haverfordwest Priory, woodcarvings from St Mary's Church and the town stocks. The landing area has fascinating Victorian views of Haverfordwest and an oil portrait of Lord Kensington. The People Room upstairs has portraits of famous people associated with the town including Augustus John, Sir Thomas Picton and Sir John Perrot. The Trade and Industry Room has interesting artefacts like the old Llewellin churn, billheads, token coinage and old tills. The Institutions Room focuses on schools, police, fire brigade, military units and the workhouse.

A butter churn at Haverfordwest Town Museum

Opening Times: Easter to Oct Mon to Sat 10:00-16:00. Location: In the grounds of Haverfordwest Castle, in the Old Governor's House. Signposted from town centre.   Map Ref: 13

Scolton Manor Museum

Spittal, Haverfordwest SA62 5QL   Tel: 01437 731328   Fax: 01437 779500

Manor house built 1842 furnished to around 1900, also with costume and art galleries. Stable block also featuring blacksmith and carpenter's workshops. Railway area with signal box and 'Margaret' locomotive. Exhibition Hall displaying agricultural machinery and other local industries, World War II and railway galleries.

Opening Times: Apr to Oct Tue to Sun & BH 10:30-17:30.   Admission: Adult £2.00 Child £1.00 Concession £1.50.   Location: Five miles outside Haverfordwest on the B4329 (Cardigan Road).

Map Ref: 14

KIDWELLY *Carmarthenshire*

Kidwelly Industrial Museum

Broadford, Kidwelly SA17 4LW   Tel: 01554 891078   Fax: 01267 223830
Email: cdelaney@carmarthenshire.gov.uk   Web: www.carmarthenshire.gov.uk

A unique opportunity to see how tinplate was made. The museum has buildings and machinery of the tinplate industry, coal mining and much more. In a delightful rural setting.

Opening Times: Easter BH, Spring BH to 31 Aug Mon to Fri 10:00-17:00, Sat & Sun 14:00-17:00.   Admission: Free.   Location: Signposted from the A484 on the outskirts of Kidwelly.

Map Ref: 15

LLANDYSUL *Carmarthenshire*

Museum of the Welsh Woollen Industry

Dre-fach Felindre, near Carmarthen, Llandysul SA44 5UP   Tel: 01559 370929   Fax: 01559 371592   Web: www.nwgw.ac.uk

The Museum of the Welsh Woollen Industry tells the fascinating story of the most traditional of rural industries and still houses a thriving, working woollen mill, producing for the modern market.

Opening Times: Please phone for details. May be closed at certain times of the year due to re-developments.   Admission: Free.   Location: Four miles east of Newcastle Emlyn, 16 miles north west of Carmarthen, four miles off A484, in village of Dre-Fach Felindre.   Map Ref: 16

LLANELLI *Carmarthenshire*

Parc Howard Museum & Art Gallery

Felinfoel Road, Llanelli SA15 3LJ   Tel: 01554 772029   Fax: 01267 223830
Email: cdelaney@carmarthenshire.gov.uk   Web: www.carmarthenshire.gov.uk

Situated in a fine public park, Parc Howard has the largest collection of Llanelly Pottery, paintings and other items from Llanelli's past.

Opening Times: Apr to Sep Mon to Fri 11:00-13:00 14:00-18:00 Sat & Sun 14:00-18:00. Oct to Mar Mon to Fri 11:00-13:00 14:00-16:00 Sat & Sun 14:00-16:00.   Admission: Free. Location: Half a mile north of Llanelli town on the A476.

Map Ref: 17

MERTHYR TYDFIL *Rhondda*

Brecon Mountain Railway

Pant Station, Dowlais, Merthyr Tydfil CF48 2UP   Tel: 01685 722988   Fax: 01685 384854
Email: enquiries@breconmountainrailway.co.uk   Web: www.breconmountainrailway.co.uk

Travel in one of our all weather observation coaches behind a vintage steam locomotive through beautiful scenery into the Brecon Beacons National Park along the full length of the Taf Fechan Reservoir to Dol-y-Gaer on one of the most popular railways in Wales. On your return to Pant, visit our workshops where old steam locomotives are repaired.

Loco No 2 built by Baldwins of Philadelphia in 1930

Opening Times: Easter to Oct daily 09:30-17:15. Admission: Return Fares: Adult £6.80, Child £3.40, OAP £6.20.   Location: Signposted from the A470 and A465 near Merthyr Tydfil.   Map Ref: 18

South & Southwest Wales

Cyfarthfa Castle Museum & Art Gallery

Brecon Road, Merthyr Tydfil CF47 8RE Tel / Fax: 01685 723112
Email: museum@cyfarthfapark.freeserve.co.uk

Georgian castellated mansion, originally Crawshay family home, set in 160 acre park. Collection includes: local history, fine art, porcelain, costume collection, brass instruments, Egypt collection, several temporary exhibitions.

Opening Times: Apr to Sep daily 10:00-17:30. Oct to Mar Tue to Fri 10:00-16:00, Sat & Sun 12:00-16:00. Closed Mon. Admission: Free Location: Cyfarthfa Park on Brecon Road, one mile north of Merthyr Town Centre.   Map Ref: 18

Joseph Parrys Ironworkers Cottage
4 Chapel Row, Georgetown, Merthyr Tydfil CF48 1BN Tel / Fax: 01685 723112

1825 ironworkers cottage, direct contrast to Cyfarthfa Castle. Home to Parry family and birthplace of Joseph Parry, musician and composer of Myfanwy. Ground floor recreates 1841; upper floor, exhibition of Parry's life and local industry.

Opening Times: Apr to Sep Thu to Sun 14:00-17:00. Other times by appointment.
Admission: Free Location: Town centre, five minutes from bus station.   Map Ref: 18

MILFORD HAVEN *Pembrokeshire*

Milford Haven Maritime & Heritage Museum
The Old Custom House, Sybil Way, The Docks, Milford Haven SA73 3AF Tel: 01646 694496
Fax: 01646 699454

Building of Milford from early whaling to fishing, oil refining to marina. Television shows on history of town and docks. Brass rubbing, hands-on and off exhibits.

Opening Times: Mon to Sat 11:00-17:00, Sun, BH & school holidays 11:00-17:00. Also group booking in advance outside these times. Admission: Adult £1.20, Child/OAP 60p, Under 5s Free. Location: Near town centre, on Milford Haven Marina.   Map Ref: 19

MONMOUTH

Castle & Regimental Museum

The Castle, Monmouth NP25 3BS Tel: 01600 772175
Email: curator@monmouthcastlemuseum.org.uk Web: www.monmouthcastlemuseum.org.uk

The regimental museum of the Royal Monmouthshire Royal Engineers, and of the preceding Monmouthshire Militia. With some history of Monmouth Castle and Henry V. Also a small Medieval-style herb garden.

Opening Times: Apr to Oct daily 14:00-17:00, Nov to Easter Sat & Sun 14:00-16:00.
Admission: Free - donations welcome. Location: At the highest point of the town centre.
Map Ref: 20

Nelson Museum & Local History Centre

Priory Street, Monmouth NP25 3XA Tel: 01600 713519 Fax: 01600 775001
Email: nelsonmuseum@monmouthshire.gov.uk

The life, loves, death and commemoration of the famous admiral in one of Britain's major Nelson collections. In the same building, Monmouth's history is displayed, including a section on Charles Rolls, co-founder of Rolls Royce.

Opening Times: Mon to Sat 10:00-13:00, 14:00-17:00. Sun 14:00-17:00. Admission: Adult £1.00 Child Free Concession 75p Local residents Free. Location: Town centre, parking nearby.
Map Ref: 20

NANTGARW *Rhondda*

Nantgarw China Works Museum

Tyla Gwyn, Nantgarw CF15 7TB Tel: 01443 841703 Fax: 01443 841826
Email: enquiries@friendsofncwm.org Web: www.friendsofncwm.org

Dedicated to William Billingsley, the 19th century porcelain manufacturer and decorator, and the Pardoe family, domestic earthen utilityware manufacturers. Grounds contain remains of factory buildings and bottle kilns, some restored.

Opening Times: Oct to Mar Thu to Sun 10:00-16:00, Apr to Sep Tue to Sun 10:00-17:00. Closed 16 Dec to 8 Jan. Admission: Adult £1.00, Concession 50p. Location: Ten miles north of Cardiff, five miles south of Pontypridd.   Map Ref: 21

South & Southwest Wales

Wilson Museum of Narberth

13 Market Square, Narberth SA67 7AU   Tel: 01834 861719

An extensive collection illustrating many aspects of life in a typical Welsh market town over the last hundred years and more. Permanent 'Mabinogion' exhibition. Rare 'Geared Facile' bicycle. Research facilities also available.

Opening Times: Apr to Sep daily 10:30-16:30, Sat 10:30-12:30. Oct to Mar Tue to Fri 10:30-16:30, Sat 10:30-12:30.   Admission: Adult £1.00, Child/OAP 50p, Under 12s Free.
Location: Market Square.   Map Ref: 22

Cefn Coed Colliery Museum

Neath Road, Crynant, Neath SA10 8SN   Tel / Fax: 01639 750556

The museum is located on the site of the former Cefn Coed Colliery. It tells the story of life and work in the colliery.

Opening Times: Apr to Oct daily 10:30-17:00.   Admission: Free.   Location: Four miles north of Neath, south of Crynant on A4109.   Map Ref: 23

Neath Museum

Gwyn Hall, Orchard Street, Neath SA11 1DT   Tel: 01639 645741

It is a small but lively museum of local history, displaying Neath's rich history from prehistoric times through Roman, Medieval, Victorian and on. It also houses an art gallery for temporary art and photographic exhibitions.

Opening Times: Tue to Sat 10:00-16:00. Closed Sat, Sun & BH & Xmas week.
Admission: Free   Location: Centre of town, one minute walk from the Bus Station, five minutes walk from Train Station.   Map Ref: 24

The National Coracle Centre

Cenarth, Newcastle Emlyn SA38 9JL   Tel: 01239 710980   Email: martinfowler@btconnect.com
Web: coraclecentre.co.uk

A unique collection of coracles from Wales and around the world, set in the grounds of a 17th century flour mill, overlooking the salmon leap.

Opening Times: Easter to Oct Sun to Fri 10:30-17:30 and by appointment.   Admission: Adult £3.00, Child £1.00, OAP £2.50.   Location: Centre of Cenarth village, beside the river and falls.
Map Ref: 25

Newport Museum & Art Gallery

John Frost Square, Newport NP20 1PA   Tel: 01633 840064

Houses fascinating displays of the natural and human history of Newport. Archaeology displays including important material from this Roman town of Caerwent; social history displays including the chartists; natural history displays including local geology; art exhibitions of watercolours, oils and prints, John Wait teapot display and Fox collection of contemporary art. There is a temporary exhibition programme.

Opening Times: Mon to Thu 09:30-17:00, Fri 09:30-16:30, Sat 09:30-16:00.   Admission: Free.
Location: Town centre, near car parks and bus station.   Map Ref: 26

Turner House Gallery

Plymouth Road, Penarth CF64 3DN   Tel: 029 2070 8870   Web: www.nmgw.ac.uk

Elegant gallery for a changing and varied programme of visual art.

Opening Times: Tue to Sun 10:00-17:00 and BH Mon. Only during exhibition showings.
Admission: Free.   Location: Near town centre, five minutes walk from Penarth Train Station.
Map Ref: 27

PONTYPOOL *Torfaen*

Pontypool Museum

Park Buildings, Pontypool NP4 6JH   Tel: 01495 752036

The museum has a collection of different displays including art and craft, a new art gallery and a Japanware display. Telling the history of the Torfaen area - industrial and social, and is set in a Georgian stable block.

Opening Times: Mon to Fri 10:00-17:00 Sat & Sun 14:00-17:00. Closed Xmas & New Year.
Admission: Adult £1.20, Concession 60p, Family £2.40. Group bookings 10% discount.
Location: Close to town centre and Pontypool Park.   Map Ref: 28

PORT TALBOT

Margam Country Park

Margam, Port Talbot SA13 2TJ   Tel: 01639 881635   Fax: 01639 895897

850 acres of Parkland which include 12th century monastry ruins, 12th century church, 18th century orangery, 19th century country house. Largest collection of deer in Wales, 30 acres of refurbished gardens. New for 2002 - light railway attraction.

Opening Times: Daily 10:00-17:00. Admission: Free. Location: 200 yards from junction 38 of M4 west, six miles from Port Talbot.   Map Ref: 29

South Wales Miners Museum

Afan Argoed Countryside Centre, Cynonville, Port Talbot SA13 3HG   Tel: 01639 850564   Fax: 01639 850446

Set in the beautiful Afan Valley, The South Wales Miners Museum, gives information on the social history of coal mining. It tells us of the communities, family life and leisure activities.

Opening Times: Summer Mon to Fri 10:30-17:00, Sat & Sun 10:30-18:00. Winter Mon to Fri 10:30-16:00, Sat & Sun 10:30-17:00. Closed Xmas. Admission: Adult £1.20, Child/OAP 60p.
Location: Approx six miles from nearest town. The South Wales Miners Museum is in Afan Argoed in Afan Forest Park.   Map Ref: 30

PORTHCAWL

Porthcawl Museum

The Old Police Station, John Street, Porthcawl CF36 3BD   Tel: 01656 772211

Local maritime and military history, 12th century parish church, costume, Sker house, Samtampa disaster.

Opening Times: Mon to Fri 14:00-16:30, Sat 10:00-12:00 14:00-16:30. Admission: Adult 50p, Child 25p. Location: Town centre.   Map Ref: 31

RHYMNEY *Gwent*

Drenewydd Museum

26/27 Lower Row, Bute Town, Rhymney NP22 5QH   Tel: 01443 864224/ 02920 880011
Fax: 01443 864228   Email: museums@caerphilly.gov.uk   Web: www.caerphilly.gov.uk

Enter the world of a bustling Victorian household and discover what life was like over one hundred years ago.

Opening Times: Easter to Oct Sat, Sun & BH 14:00-17:00. Admission: Adult £1.00, Child/Concession 60p. Reduced group rates available. Location: Just off the A465 'Heads of the Valleys' Road.   Map Ref: 32

SWANSEA

Egypt Centre

University of Swansea, Singleton Park, Swansea SA2 8PP   Tel: 01792 295960

The largest collection of Egyptian antiquities in Wales. Includes coffins, jewellery, tools and weapons etc.

Opening Times: Tue to Sat 10:00-16:00. Closed Sun, Mon & BH. Admission: Free,
Location: On University Campus, ten minutes by car from Swansea.   Map Ref: 33

Glynn Vivian Art Gallery

Alexandra Road, Swansea SA1 5DZ   Tel: 01792 655006
Fax: 01792 651713   Email: glynn.vivian.gallery@swansea.gov.uk
Web: www.swansea.gov.uk

A changing exhibition programme of contemporary visual arts. Plus a broad spectrum of visual arts form the original bequest of Richard Glynn Vivian (1835-1910) which includes work by Old Masters as well as an international collection of porcelain and Swansea china. The 20th century is also well represented with modern painting and sculpture by Hepworth, Nicholson, Nash alongside Welsh artists such as Ceri Richards, Gwen John and Augustus John.

Opening Times: Tue to Sun 10:00-17:00. Closed Mon except BH.
Admission: Free.   Location: One minute walk from railway station.

Sculpture Court with David Nash Sculpture   Map Ref: 33

Gower Heritage Centre

Parkmill, Gower, Swansea SA3 2EH   Tel: 01792 371206   Fax: 01792 371471
Email: info@gowerheritagecentre.sagehost.co.uk
Web: www.gowerheritagecentre.sagehost.co.uk

Crafts and heritage centre based around working 12th century water-powered corn and sawmill. Daily demonstrations of wood-turning, flour making, smithing and jewellery making. Regular historical, musical and schools events throughout the year.

Opening Times: Daily 10:00-17:30.   Admission: Adult £2.95, Child/OAP £1.95, Family £8.50.
Group rates available.   Location: Eight miles west of Swansea in seaside village, on bus route.

Map Ref: 34

Mission Gallery

Gloucester Place, Maritime Quarter, Swansea SA1 1TY   Tel / Fax: 01792 652016

Converted seamen's chapel situated in the Maritime Quarter. Contemporary exhibition programme featuring artists from Great Britain plus a craft space displaying contemporary craft - a Crafts Council Selected Gallery.

Opening Times: Daily 11:00-17:00.   Admission: Free.   Location: Maritime Quarter.   Map Ref: 33

Swansea Maritime & Industrial Museum

Museum Square, Maritime Quarter, Swansea SA1 1SN   Tel: 01792 650351/470371/653004
Fax: 01792 654200   Email: swansea.maritime.museum@swansea.gov.uk

The museum features a fully functional Welsh woollen mill which demonstrates carding, spinning and weaving on a daily basis. The museum also has exhibitions which tell the stories of the town's industrialisation and the maritime trade which enabled it to happen. The museum has a collection of three ships which are open during the summer months.

Opening Times: Tue to Sun & BH 10:00-17:00. Closed Xmas & New Year.   Admission: Free.   Location: Central location close to Leisure Centre, five minutes from city centre.

Pulling & sailing lifeboat, John & Naomi Beattie.   Map Ref: 33

Swansea Museum

Victoria Road, Maritime Quarter, Swansea SA1 1SN   Tel: 01792 653763
Email: swansea.museum@swansea.gov.uk

Diverse range of collection reflecting the passions of the Victorian founders. The museum displays an exceptional collection of Swansea China. A quirky collection of artefacts provides infinite variety in the 'Cabinet of Curiosities'.

Opening Times: Tue to Sun & BH 10:00-17:00. Closed Xmas & New Year.   Admission: Free.   Location: Central location, five minutes from city centre.   Map Ref: 33

South & Southwest Wales

TENBY *Pembrokeshire*

Tenby Museum & Art Gallery

Castle Hill, Tenby SA70 7BP   Tel / Fax: 01834 842809   Email: tenbymuseum@hotmail.com

Two art galleries with regularly changing exhibitions, works by Gwen John and Augustus John. Local history, maritime, archaeology, geology and natural history. Activities for children.

Opening Times: Daily Easter to end Oct 10:00-17:00, Nov to Easter Mon to Fri 10:00-17:00. Admission: Adult £2.00, Child £1.00, Concession £1.50, Family £4.50.   Location: Near town centre.

Map Ref: 35

TREHARRIS *Caerphilly*

Llancaiach Fawr Manor

Nelson, Treharris CF46 6ER   Tel: 01443 412248   Fax: 01443 412688
Email: allens@caerphilly.gov.uk   Web: www.caerphilly.gov.uk/visiting

Costumed interpreters guide visitors around the Manor which is set in the year 1645.

Opening Times: Mon to Fri 10:00-17:00. Sat & Sun 10:00-18:00. Closed Mon in Nov to Feb. Last admission one and a half hours before closing. Admission: Adult £4.50, Child/Concession £3.00. Group rates available for over 20 persons. Location: 20 miles north of Cardiff. 11 miles south of Merthyr Tydfil.

'Meet the Servants'

Map Ref: 36

USK *Monmouthshire*

Usk Rural Life Museum

The Malt Barn, Newmarket Street, Usk NP15 1AU   Tel: 01291 673777
Email: uskrurallife.museum@virgin.net   Web: uskmuseum.members.easyspace.com

The Museum portrays life in the Welsh Borders between 1850 and the end of World War II. Exhibits include farmhouse kitchen, dairy, laundry, cider-making, Victorian shop window, agricultural equipment, bikes (Penny Farthing) and more.

Opening Times: 1 Apr or Good Friday (whichever the earliest) to end Oct, Mon to Fri 10:00-17:00, Sat & Sun 14:00-17:00. Admission: Adult £2.00, Child £1.00, OAP £1.50. Special Family and Group rates with advanced booking. Location: Within town centre.

Map Ref: 37

Glorious unspoilt border country with little traffic and described as 'one of the lost wilderness of Britain'. The Brecon Beacons National Park offers a wide variety of majestic sights including t Black Mountains.

Museums and galleries are not exactly prolific and generally focus on local history, and the a and crafts of the region.

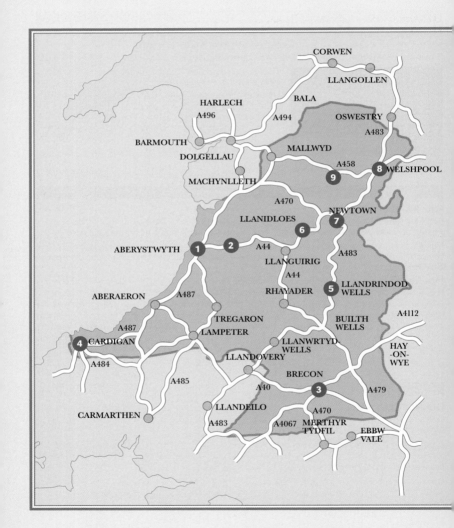

The Red Map References should be used to locate Museums etc on the pages that follow

ABERYSTWYTH *Ceredigion*

Ceredigion Museum & Gallery

Coliseum, Terrace Road, Aberystwyth SY23 2AQ Tel: 01970 633088 Fax: 01970 633084
Email: museum@ceredigion.gov.uk Web: www.ceredigion.gov.uk/coliseum

Local history museum in a restored Edwardian Theatre with exhibitions on archaeology, seafaring, agriculture, furniture etc. Changing temporary exhibition. Art Gallery.

Opening Times: Mon to Sat 10:00-17:00. Admission: Free. Location: Town centre, next to Tourist Information Centre.

Map Ref: 1

Llywernog Silver-Lead Mine Museum

Ponterwyd, Aberystwyth SY23 3AB Tel: 01970 890620 Fax: 01545 570823
Email: silverrivermine@cs.com Web: www.silverminetours.co.uk

A fascinating seven acre 'Discovery Park' based on an authentic 18th century mine in the beautiful Cambrian Mountains.

Opening Times: Mid Mar to 31 Oct 10:00-18:00. Closed Mon, except Easter, BH & Jul & Aug when open 7 days a week. Admission: Adult £4.95, Child £2.95, OAP/Student £4.25, Family £14.00. Location: Ten and a half miles drive up the A44 from Aberystwyth and the Cardigan Bay coast, 45 minutes from Aberaeron.

Map Ref: 2

School of Art Gallery & Museum : Ceramics Collection

Art Centre, Penglais, Aberystwyth SY23 3DE Tel: 01970 622460 Fax: 01970 622461
Email: mov@aber.ac.uk Web: www.aber.ac.uk/ceramics

Contemporary British, European, American and Japanese studio pottery; 18th and 19th century Welsh and English slip ware; Swansea and Nantgarw porcelain; Art Pottery and Oriental ceramics; and an outstanding collection of early 20th century British pioneer studio pottery. Changing displays.

Opening Times: Mon to Sat 09:30-17:00, also most evenings. Closed Sun, Easter & Xmas.
Admission: Free. Location: On University Campus, one mile from town centre and railway station.

Map Ref: 1

School of Art Gallery & Museum

University of Wales, Buarth Mawr, Aberystwyth SY23 1NG Tel: 01970 622460 Fax: 01970 622461 Email: neh@aber.ac.uk Web: www.aber.ac.uk/art/ or /museum

University's collection of fine and decorative art: watercolours, drawings, and European prints from 15th century to present; art in Wales since 1945; contemporary Welsh and post-war Italian photography. Changing exhibitions from the collection, touring shows and exhibitions by invited artists. Study collection by appointment. Housed in magnificent Edwardian building overlooking Cardigan Bay.

Opening Times: Mon to Fri 10:00-17:30. Closed Sat, Sun Easter & Xmas. Admission: Free.
Location: Near town centre, four minute walk from railway station and town centre. Map Ref: 1

BRECON *Powys*

Brecknock Museum & Art Gallery

Captains Walk, Brecon LD3 7DW Tel: 01874 624121 Fax: 01874 611281
Email: brecknock.museum@powys.gov.uk

Located in the centre of Brecon Beacons National Park it explores the past, natural environment and art of Brecknockshire. A Victorian Assize Court is interpreted with figures, sound and light. A lively exhibition programme features contemporary art and crafts from Wales.

Opening Times: Mon to Fri 10:00-17:00. Apr to Sep Sun 12:00-17:00, 4 Nov to Feb Sat 10:00-13:00 14:00-17:00. Admission: Adult £1.00, Child Free, Concession 50p, Residents of Powys Free. Location: Near town centre.

Map Ref: 3

Museums, Galleries, Historic Houses & Sites

Please let us know of any collections that are not listed in this guide that you feel should be listed. E-mail us on *editor@tomorrows.co.uk*
or return the Report Form on page 448

South Wales Borderers & Monmouthshire Regimental Museum

The Barracks, Brecon LD3 7EB   Tel: 01874 613310   Fax: 01874 613275
Email: sw6@rrw.org.uk   Web: www.rrw.org.uk

The Royal Regiment of Wales Museum with artefacts from the 1879 Anglo-Zulu War and equipment and war mementoes spanning 300 years.

Opening Times: Apr to Sep daily 09:00-17:00, Oct to Mar Mon to Fri 09:00-17:00.
Admission: Adult £3.00, Child Free. Group rates available.   Location: The Museum is adjacent to the Barracks in Brecon in The Walton (B4601)   Map Ref: 3

CARDIGAN *Ceredigion*

Cardigan Heritage Centre

Teifi Wharf, Castle Street, Cardigan SA43 3AA   Tel: 01239 614404

A Heritage Centre situated on the ground floor of an 18th Century warehouse on the Teifi river. There are collections on the history of Cardigan from Norman times to the present day. Also a Café, Craft Shop and riverside terrace.

Opening Times: Easter to Oct 10:00-17:00 daily   Admission: Adults £2.00, Child £1.00, Family £5.00 plus concessions   Location: On the Riverside by Cardigan Bridge   Map Ref: 4

LLANDRINDOD WELLS *Powys*

Radnorshire Museum

Temple Street, Llandrindod Wells LD1 5DL   Tel: 01597 824513   Fax: 01597 825781

An unrivalled collection of photographs of Llandrindod from Victorian times to the present day. Archaeological collections from Castal Collen (site of main defence of Roman times), Capel Maelog and a unique Sheela-na-Gig.

Opening Times: Tue to Thu 10:00-17:00, Fri 10:00-16:30, closed between 13:00-14:00. Weekends - winter Sat 10:00-13:00, summer Sat 10:00-17:00, Sun 13:00-17:00. Closed Mon. Admission: Adult £1.00, Child Free, OAP 50p, Powys Residents Free.   Location: Next to Tourist Information, two minute walk from train station.   Map Ref: 5

LLANIDLOES *Powys*

Llanidloes Museum

Great Oak Street, Llanidloes   Tel: 01686 413777

Three display areas reflecting the nature and type of the collections including local history, Victorian life and a Natural History Gallery.

Opening Times: Mon & Tue, Thu & Fri 11:00-13:00, 14:00-17:00. May to Sep Sat & Sun 11:00-13:00 14:00-17:00 Oct to Apr Sat 10:00-13:00.   Admission: Adult £1.00 Child/Residents of Powys Free, Concession 50p.   Location: In the Town Hall.   Map Ref: 6

NEWTOWN *Powys*

Newtown Textile Museum

5/7 Commercial Street, Newtown   Tel: 01686 622024

The museum is housed in a typical early 19th century weaving shop, it focuses on the history of the woollen industry in Newtown from 1790 to the beginning of the 20th century.

Opening Times: May to Sep Tue to Sat & BH 14:00-17:00.   Admission: Free.   Location: Near town centre, five minutes walk from central bus station.   Map Ref: 7

W H Smith Museum

24 High Street, Newtown SY16 2NP   Tel: 01686 626280

An engrossing collection of models and memorabilia telling how a small family business flourished over two centuries, to become one of today's biggest British companies and a household name.

Opening Times: Mon to Sat 09:00-17:30, closed Sun and BH.   Admission: Free.   Location: In town centre, three minutes walk from main car park and bus station.   Map Ref: 7

Powis Castle & Garden

Welshpool SY21 8RF   Tel: 01938 554338

Laid out under the influence of Italian and French styles, the garden retains its original lead statues, an orangery and an aviary on the terraces. In the 18th century an informal woodland wilderness was created on the opposing ridge with fine views over the Severn Valley. Perched on a rock above the garden terraces, the Medieval Castle contains one of the finest collections of paintings and furniture in Wales.

Opening Times: Castle, Garden & Museum: 23 Mar to 30 Jun, 1 Sep to 3 Nov Wed to Sun, Jul & Aug Tue to Sun & BH. Castle & Museum: 13:00-17:00, Garden 11:00-18:00. Admission: All inclusive tickets: Adult £7.50, Child £3.75, Family £18.75, Group Rates available, National Trust Members Free Location: One miles south of Welshpool, signposted off A483 . One mile from railway station.

Map Ref: 8

Powysland Museum & Montgomery Canal Centre

The Canal Wharf, Welshpool SY21 7AQ   Tel: 01938 554656

The museum is housed in a restored 19th century warehouse by the Montgomery Canal. It illustrates the history of the county from pre-historic settlers to the 21st century population.

Opening Times: Mon & Tue Thu & Fri 11:00-13:00, 14:00-17:00. May to Sep Sat & Sun 10:00-13:00, 14:00-17:00. Oct to Apr Sat 14:00-17:00. Admission: Adult £1.00 Child/Resident of Powys Free Concession 50p. Location: Near town centre, five minutes walk from railway station.

Map Ref: 8

Welshpool & Llanfair Light Railway

The Station, Llanfair Caereinion, Welshpool SY21 0SF   Tel: 01938 810441   Fax: 01938 810861 Email: info@wllr.org.uk Web: www.wllr.org.uk

The eight mile journey offers a scenic steam train ride through delightful rural Wales.

Opening Times: Apr to Oct daily & school holidays. Telephone for train times and additional services. Admission: Adult £8.50, OAP £7.50, one child with every Adult/OAP for £1.00, additional Child £4.25. Group rates available. Location: Welshpool, Raven Square Station is situated at the west end of the town on the A458.

Map Ref: 9

North Wales contains Snowdonia National Park including the highest mountains in England a[...] Wales. The north coast boasts the queen of the Welsh resorts, Llandudno, the town retain[...] much of its Victorian charm. The Isle of Anglesey is a delight with fine beaches and a remarka[...] number of Neolithic ruins.

There is a fine selection of museums and galleries throughout the region which cover both soc[...] history and local history as well as subjects as diverse as tramways, steam railways, Rom[...] remains, the style and times of David Lloyd George and Maritime history.

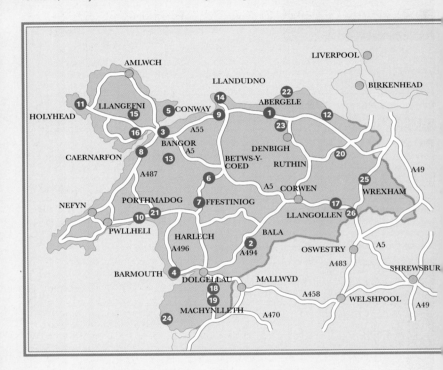

The Red Map References should be used to locate Museums etc on the pages that follow

Sir Henry Jones Museum

Y Cwm, Llangernyw, Abergele LL22 8PR   Tel: 01492 575371 01745 860661   Fax: 01492 513664   Email: ann.lloyd.williams@conwy.gov.uk

A fascinating museum of rural life with displays on Victorian life in a typical Welsh community.

Opening Times: Good Friday to Easter Mon 14:00-17:00. May to Sep Tue to Fri & BH 10:30-13:00 14:00-17:00, Sat & Sun 14:00-17:00.   Admission: Adult £1.50, Concession £1.00.
Location: On A548 Abergele to Llanrwst road in the centre of Llangernyw.   Map Ref: 1

Bala Lake Railway

The Station, Llanuwchllyn, Bala LL23 7DD   Tel: 01678 540666   Fax: 01678 540535
Web: www.bala-lake-railway.co.uk

Steam narrow gauge railway, with all steam locomotives at least 90 years old.

Opening Times: Easter to Sep. Closed some Mon & Fri.   Admission: Return journey £6.70.
Map Ref: 2

Bangor Museum & Art Gallery

Ffordd Gwynedd, Bangor LL57 1DT   Tel: 01248 353368   Email: patwest@gwynedd.gov.uk
Web: www.gwynedd.gov.uk/museums

Gwynedd's only general museum where you can learn about the ways of life led by previous generations which helps us to place our own experiences in the context of an unfolding story.

Opening Times: Tue to Fri 12:30-16:30 Sat 10:30-16:30.   Admission: Free.   Location: By the main bus stop near the town centre.   Map Ref: 3

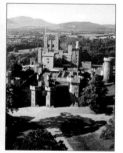

Penrhyn Castle

Bangor LL57 4HN   Tel: 01248 353084

Built on the profits of Jamaican sugar and Welsh slate, Penrhyn is a massive 19th century neo-Norman castle crammed with fascinating things including a one-ton slate bed made for Queen Victoria and a spectacular grand staircase that took ten years to build. It houses one of the best art collections in Wales, including paintings by Rembrandt, Gainsborough and Canaletto. The castle's interiors are decorated with elaborate carvings, hand-made wallpapers and stained glass, and its furniture collection includes many original pieces made of Penrhyn oak and designed by the architect Thomas Hopper. Penrhyn is

Penrhyn Castle

surrounded by 45 acres of grounds, including parkland, wooded walks and semi-tropical areas. Its Victorian walled garden contains exotic plants and shrubs from all over the world. Taking full advantage of its location, the castle offers stunning views of the mountains of Snowdonia and the Menai Strait. The stable block houses an Industrial Railway Museum with full-sized locomotives, rolling stock and track, and the Railway Model Museum. Displayed in the Doll Museum are over 500 dolls from around the world, The stable block's two exhibition galleries hold high quality temporary art exhibitions by local and internationally renowned artists.

Opening Times: 23 Mar to 3 Nov Wed to Mon Castle open 12:00-17:00 (Jul & Aug 11:00-17:00), Grounds, stable block, tearoom open one hour earlier.   Admission: National Trust Members Free. Castle ticket: Adult £6.00, Child £4.00, Family £15.00, Group (15+) £5.00. Grounds & Stable block: Adult £4.00, Child £2.00.   Location: Two miles east of Bangor at junction of A5 and A55, brown tourist signposted.   Map Ref: 3

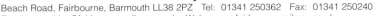

BARMOUTH *Gwynedd*

Fairbourne & Barmouth Steam Railway

Beach Road, Fairbourne, Barmouth LL38 2PZ Tel: 01341 250362 Fax: 01341 250240
Email: enquiries@fairbourne-railway.co.uk Web: www.fairbourne-railway.co.uk

Narrow gauge steam railway featuring half size models of famous narrow gauge locomotives. Runs from Fairbourne to Penrhyn Point and offers superb views of the Mawddach Estuary and Cader Idris mountain range.

Opening Times: Easter week, then May to mid Sep daily 10:30-16:30. Admission: Adult £6.10, Child £3.75, Family £16.80. Location: Directly opposite Fairbourne Mainline Station.

Map Ref: 4

Ty Gwyn & Ty Crwn & Barmouth Sailors' Institute

The Quay, Barmouth LL42 1ET Tel: 01341 241333

The presentations of photographs and pictures in all buildings portray Barmouth's maritime heritage since the Tudor period. The reading room in the Sailors' Institute dates from 1890 and is the last example of its kind in Wales.

Opening Times: Ty Gwyn & Ty Crwn - Apr to Sep daily 09:00-19:00. Barmouth Sailors' Institute - Mon to Sat 09:00-18:00. Admission: Free. Location: On the Quay, five minutes walk from town centre.

Map Ref: 4

BEAUMARIS *Anglesey*

Beaumaris Gaol & Courthouse

Beaumaris LL58 8ED Tel: 01248 810921

Crime and punishment related collections including prison and court furniture, legal robes, chains, police equipment.

Opening Times: Easter to end Sep daily 10:30-17:00. Admission: Adult £3.50, Child/OAP £2.50. Location: Court House, opposite Castle in Main Street, gaol two minute walk from Main Street.

Map Ref: 5

BETWS-Y-COED *Gwynedd*

Betws-y-Coed Motor Museum

Conwy Valley, Betws-y-Coed LL24 0AH Tel: 01690 710760

The museum was created from the private collection of the Houghton family. The varied exhibits include exotic and rare cars, and the more common cars. There are normally over 30 motor vehicles on display.

Opening Times: Easter to Oct daily 10:30:17:00. Admission: Adult £1.50, Child £1.00, Concession £1.20. Location: In main village car park.

Map Ref: 6

Conwy Valley Railway Museum

The Old Goods Yard, Betws-y-Coed LL24 0AL Tel: 01690 760568 Fax: 01690 710132

Dioramas featuring LNW Railway by the late Jack Nelson quarter full size working model 15' gauge steam locomotive 'Britannia'. Exhibits and working layouts London and North Western Railway.

Opening Times: Apr to Oct daily 10:15-17:30, Nov to Mar daily 10:00-16:00. Admission: Adult £1.00, Child/OAP 50p, Family £2.50. Location: Adjacent to railway station, four minute walk from town centre.

Map Ref: 6

CAERNARFON *Gwynedd*

Caernarfon Maritime Museum

Victoria Dock, Caernarfon Tel: 01248 752083

The museum illustrates the rich maritime and industrial history of the port and town of Caernarfon, including its seafarers. A display illustrates the operation of the dredger Seiont II through a recreation of parts of the bridge and engine room, and another the training ship HMS Conway (including an anchor outside the museum).

Opening Times: Sun to Fri 11:00-16:00. Closed Sat. Admission: Adult £1.00, Child Free. Location: Near town centre, just outside town walls on Victoria Dock. Map Ref: 8

Royal Welch Fusiliers Regimental Museum

Queens Tower, Caernarfon Castle, Caernarfon LL55 2AY   Tel: 01286 673362

Mounting the Queen's Guard in London, September, 1975

Extensive collection of uniforms, paintings, weapons and memorabilia displayed in five refurbished galleries. Outstanding collection of medals and works relating to Great War poets and authors, Siegfried Sassoon, Robert Graves, David Jones, Dr J C Dunn and Frank Richards.

Opening Times: 09:30-17:00 daily in summer. Please phone for details of winter opening.   Admission: Free, within entry to Caernarfon Castle.   Location: Town centre, five minute walk from central bus station.

Map Ref: 8

Segontium Roman Museum

Beddgelert Road, Caernarfon LL55 2LN   Tel: 01286 675625   Fax: 01286 678416
Web: www.nmgw.ac.uk

A small museum neighbouring the remains of one of Britain's most famous forts.

Opening Times: 1 Nov to Mar Mon to Sat 10:00-16:00, Sun 14:00-16:00. 1 Apr to Oct Mon to Sat 10:00-17:00, Sun 14:00-17:00.   Admission: Free.   Location: On the A4085, just out of the centre of Caernarfon.

Map Ref: 8

CONWY

Aberconwy House

2 Castle Street, Conwy LL32 8AY   Tel: 01492 592246

This 14th century house is the last remaining Medieval merchant's house in Conwy. The house has been restored and each room shows a different moment in time.

Opening Times: 23 Mar to 3 Nov Wed to Mon 11:00-17:00. Closed Tue.   Admission: Adult £2.00, Child £1.00, Family £5.00. National Trust Members Free. Group Rates available.

Map Ref: 9

Royal Cambrian Academy

Crown Lane, Conwy LL32 8AN   Tel / Fax: 01492 593413   Email: rca@rcaconwy.org
Web: www.rcaconwy.org

Nine temporary art exhibitions per year. A variety of contemporary and historical work from the best Welsh artists.

Opening Times: Tue to Sat 11:00-17:00, Sun 13:00-16:30. Closed Mon.   Admission: Adult £1.00, Child Free, Concession 50p.   Location: One minute walk from railway station and bus stop, just off Conwy High Street, behind 'Plas Mawr'.

Map Ref: 9

CRICCIETH Gwynedd

Lloyd George Museum & Highgate Cottage

Llanystumdwy, Criccieth LL52 0SH   Tel / Fax: 01766 522071
Email: nestthomas@gwynedd.gov.uk   Web: www.gwynedd.gov.uk/museums

The Museum traces the life and times of David Lloyd George featuring freedom caskets and scrolls, medals, paintings, photographs and documents such as the Treaty of Versailles. A visit to Highgate, the Victorian cottage where he lived as a child is included, which also features a Victorian garden and shoemaker's workshop.

Opening Times: Easter, Apr to May Mon to Fri 10:30-17:00. Jun Mon to Sat 10:30-17:00. Jul to Sep daily 10:30-17:00. Oct Mon to Fri 11:00-16:00.   Admission: Adult £3.00 Child/OAP/Concession £2.00 Family £7.00.   Location: Centre of the village, opposite Moriah Chapel.

Map Ref: 10

HOLYHEAD Anglesey

Holyhead Maritime Museum

8 Llainfain Estate, Llaingoch, Holyhead LL65 1NF   Tel / Fax: 01407 769745
Email: johncave4@AOL   Web: geocities.com/dickburnel

The Museum, located at the old Lifeboat House (c.1858) facing the famous breakwater, displays models, photographs and artefacts relating to the maritime history of Holyhead and district from Roman times until the present.

Opening Times: Spring to autumn daily 13:00-17:00. Closed Mon except BH.
Admission: Adult £2.00, Child 50p, OAP £1.50, Family £5.00. Location: Newry Beach, Holyhead.
Map Ref: 11

HOLYWELL Flintshire

Greenfield Valley Museum

Basingwerk House, Greenfield Valley Heritage Park, Holywell CH8 7GH Tel: 01352 714172
Fax: 01352 714791 Email: caren@GreenfieldValley.com Web: www.Greenfieldvalley.com

Museum and farm complex within a 70 acre heritage park. Period buildings including Victorian cottage, 17th century cottage, Victorian schoolroom as well as farming exhibitions, adventure playgound, small animals and weekend events.

Opening Times: Apr to Oct daily 10:00-16:30. Nov to Mar by arrangement only for Groups.
Admission: Adult £2.50, Child £1.50, Under 5s Free, Concession £2.00. Group rates available.
Location: Close to Basingwerk Abbey and St Winefride's Holy Well. Follow brown signs from A55 through Holywell or A548 coast road.
Map Ref: 12

LLANBERIS Gwynedd

Electric Mountain

Llanberis LL55 4UR Tel: 01286 870636 Fax: 01286 873002

Three galleries of local artists.

Opening Times: 15 Mar to 22 Dec daily, 4 Jan to 15 Mar Thu to Sun. Apr to Sep 09:30-17:30, Oct to Mar 10:30-16:30. Admission: Adult £5.50, Child £2.75, OAP £4.00, Family (2 adults and 2 children) £13.50. Location: Near Llanberis, five miles from Caernarfon.
Map Ref: 13

Llanberis Lake Railway

Gilfach Ddu, Llanberis LL55 4TY Tel / Fax: 01286 870549 Email: info@lake-railway.co.uk
Web: www.lake-railway.co.uk

Train services are operated by three of the original Hunslet 0-4-0 tank engines that worked here in the Dinorwic Slate Quarries, and date back to 1889.

Opening Times: Early Mar to late Oct, please phone for timetable. Admission: Adult £4.50, Child £3.00, Family saver tickets available. Location: In Padarn Country Park, next to Welsh Slate Museum.
Map Ref: 13

Welsh Slate Museum

Welsh Slate Museum, Padarn Country Park, Llanberis LL55 4TY Tel: 01286 870630
Fax: 01286 871906 Web: www.nwgw.ac.uk

A living, working piece of history, the museum tells the story of the slate industry in Wales, from nurturing traditional crafts and skills to the harsh realities of quarrying life for over 15,000 men (and boys) of Gwynedd.

Opening Times: 1 Nov to Easter Sun to Fri 10:00-16:00, Easter to End Oct daily 10:00-17:00.
Admission: Free. Location: In the middle of Padarn Country Park, Llanberis, on the A4086.
Map Ref: 13

LLANDUDNO Conwy

Great Orme Tramway

Victoria Station, Church Walks, Llandudno Tel: 01492 575275 Fax: 01492 513664
Email: enq@greatormetramway.com Web: www.greatormetramway.com

The 100 year old Great Orme Tramway is the only cable hauled tramway in Britain, an amazing way to reach the top of Llandudno's famous mountain. The tramway journey takes in the wonderful panorama of the resort, the Great Orme Country Park and a 4000 year old copper mine. From the summit, views of the Lake District mountains and the Isle of Man can be seen on a clear day.

Opening Times: Late Mar to Late Oct daily 10:00-18:00.
Admission: Adult Return £3.95, Child Return £2.80,
Family Tickets and Group discounts available.

Location: Five minutes walk from town centre, two minute walk from Pier entrance. Map Ref: 14

Llandudno Museum

17/19 Gloddaeth Street, Llandudno LL30 2DD   Tel / Fax: 01492 876517
Email: llandudno.museum@lineone.net

Painting and sculptures, objets d'art, local history from archaeology, Roman objects, town resort, war memorabilia and Welsh kitchen, etc. Temporary exhibitions from art to local history.

Opening Times: Easter to Oct Tue to Sat 10:30-13:00 14:00-17:00 Sun 14:15-17:00. Nov to Easter Tue to Sat 13:30-16:30. Open BH. Closed Xmas. Admission: Adult £1.50, Child 75p, Concession £1.20, Family £2.25/£3.50. Location: Near town centre, three minute walk from pier/promenade.   Map Ref: 14

LLANGEFNI *Anglesey*

Anglesey Heritage Gallery/Oriel Ynys Mon

Rhosmeirch, Llangefni LL77 7TQ   Tel: 01248 724444   Fax: 01248 750282

Oriel Ynys Mon comprises a museum depicting the culture and history of Anglesey, encompassing archaeology, art, history, industry and agriculture. A separate art gallery presents a changing programme of arts exhibitions by local, regional and nationally acclaimed artists. The museum's core collection includes art works by such artists as Charles Tunnicliffe and Kyffin Williams, social history and archaeology collection.

Opening Times: Tue to Sun 10:30-17:00. Closed Mon except BH. Admission: Art Gallery - Free. Museum - Adult £2.25, Child/OAP £1.25. Location: Close to town centre, on main bus route. Map Ref: 15

Plas Newydd

Plas Newydd, Llanfairpwll, Llangefni LL61 6DQ   Tel: 01248 714795   Fax: 01248 713673
Email: ppnmsn@smtp.ntrust.org.uk   Web: www.nationaltrust.org.uk

An impressive 18th century house by James Wyatt housing Rex Whistler's largest painting and an exhibition about his work. Military museum, garden, parkland, shop and tearoom.

Opening Times: House: Sat to Wed 12:00-17:00. Garden: Sat to Wed 11:00-17:30. Admission: Adult £4.60, Child £2.30, Family £11.50, Group rates available, National Trust Members Free. Location: Two miles south of Llanfairpwll and A5.   Map Ref: 16

The east front, viewed across the Menai Strait from the Faenol Estate

LLANGOLLEN *Denbighshire*

Llangollen Motor Museum

Pentrefelin, Llangollen LL20 8EE   Tel: 01978 860324
Web: www.llangollenmotormuseum.co.uk

Sixty plus vehicles from 1910 to 1970, a 50s garage village scene complete with owner's quarters, toys, tools, motor reference library and a small exhibition showing the history and development of our canal network.

Opening Times: Mar to Oct Tue to Sun 10:00-17:00. Admission: Adult £2.30, OAP £2.00, Family £5.50. Location: One mile outside Llangollen.   Map Ref: 17

Llangollen Railway PLC

The Station, Abbey Road, Llangollen LL20 8SN   Tel: 01978 860979

Preserved Heritage Railway operated principally by steam trains with some services diesel hauled through the picturesque Dee Valley in Denbighshire, North Wales.

Opening Times: Please phone for services and events in 2002. Admission: Adult £8.00, Child £3.80, Under 3s Free. Location: Heritage Railway from Llangollen (town centre) to Carrog (village 1/3 mile) route length seven and a half miles.   Map Ref: 17

Plas Newydd

Hill Street, Llangollen LL20 8AW   Tel: 01978 861314   Fax: 01824 708258
Email: archives@denbighshire.gov.uk   Web: www.denbighshire.gov.uk

The romantic home of the famous Ladies of Llangollen between 1750 and 1832. Eloping to live together in this rural retreat, their gothicisation of a once humble cottage and grounds still fascinates.

Opening Times: 1 Apr to 31 Oct daily 10:00-17:00.   Admission: Adult £2.50, Child £1.25,
Family (2 adult and 2 children) £6.00.   Location: Ten minute walk from the centre of Llangollen.
Map Ref: 17

MACHYNLLETH *Gwynedd*

Corris Railway Museum

Station Yard, Corris, Machynlleth SY20 9SH   Tel: 01654 761303   Web: www.corris.co.uk

Railway and quarry memories, including various historic relics of the villages. Engine shed at Maespoeth is also open to view rolling stock.

Opening Times: Jul/Aug daily 11:00-17:00 & all school holidays. Reduced hours (not Sat) Jun,
Sep and autumn half term.   Admission: Free.   Location: Corris car park, six miles
Machynlleth.
Map Ref: 18

Museum of Modern Art, Wales

Heol Penrallt, Machynlleth SY20 8AJ   Tel: 01654 703355   Fax: 01654 702160
Email: momawales@tabernac.dircon.co.uk   Web: www.tabernac.dircon.co.uk

Museum of Modern Art, Wales

The Museum of Modern Art, Wales has grown up alongside The Tabernacle, a former Wesleyan chapel which in 1986 reopened as a centre for the performing arts. MOMA Wales has six beautiful exhibition spaces which house, throughout the year, Showcase Wales (Wales' top artists), The Tabernacle Collection and The Brotherhood of Ruralists. Individual artists are spotlighted in a series of temporary exhibitions. In July workshops are given for adults and children, while in August expert judges and then the public choose the winners of the Tabernacle Art Competition. Many works of art in the MOMA Wales are for sale. The adjacent auditorium has perfect acoustics and pitch-pine pews to seat 400 people. It is ideal for chamber and choral music, drama, lectures and conferences. Translation booths, recording facilities and a cinema screen have been installed; the oak-beamed Foyer has a bar; and extensive access for disabled people is made possible by a lift and a ramped approach.

Augustus John: Portrait of
William McElroy

Opening Times: Mon to Sat 10:00-16:00. Closed Xmas & New Year.   Admission: Free.
Location: In town centre, five minutes walk from railway station.
Map Ref: 19

MOLD *Flintshire*

Daniel Owen Museum & Heritage Centre

Mold Library,Museum and Gallery, Earl Road, Mold CH7 1AP   Tel: 01352 754791

Displays reflect the development of the market town, the industrial heritage, the social and cultural life including the work of local poets and composers, Richard Wilson, the painter, and Daniel Owen, father of the Welsh of Novel.

Opening Times: Mon, Tue, Thu & Fri 09:30-19:00, Wed 09:30-17:30, Sat 09:30-12:30. Closed
BH.   Admission: Free.   Location: Town centre.
Map Ref: 20

PORTHMADOG *Gwynedd*

Porthmadog Maritime Museum

Oakley Wharf No 1, The Harbour, Porthmadog LL49 9LU   Tel: 01766 513736

Models, paintings, drawings, charts, navigation instruments, shipbulding tools and personal

property - all relating to shipbuilding industry and the export of slates quarried at Blaenan Ffestiniog.

Opening Times: Easter week and from May BH to end Sep daily 11:00-17:00.
Admission: Adult £1.00, Child/OAP 50p, Family £2.50. Groups by arrangement. Location: On wharf near bridge, opposite Harbour Station, behind Tourist Centre. Map Ref: 21

RHYL *Denbighshire*

Rhyl Library, Museum & Arts Centre ♿ 🅿
Church Street, Rhyl LL18 3AA Tel: 01745 353814 Fax: 01745 331438

Collection focusing on maritime history and tourism in Rhyl. Museum based on reconstruction of Rhyl Pier c.1910.

Opening Times: Mon to Fri 09:00-17:00, Sat 09:30-12:30. Admission: Free. Location: Town centre, ten minutes from railway station, two minutes from bus station. Map Ref: 22

ST ASAPH *Denbighshire*

Bodelwyddan Castle
Bodelwyddan, St Asaph LL18 5YA Tel: 01745 584060 Fax: 01745 584563
Email: enquiries@bodelwyddan-castle.co.uk Web: www.bodelwyddan-castle.co.uk

The Welsh home of the National Portrait Gallery where paintings of many famous people from the Victorian era hang in beautifully refurbished rooms. Furnishings from the Victoria and Albert Museum. Sculpture from the Royal Academy of Arts. Victorian games gallery. Free audio tour.

Opening Times: Open daily 10:30-17:00. Closed Mon & Fri Nov to Mar. Admission: Adult £4.00, Child £2.50, OAP £3.50, Family £10.00. Location: Junction 25 of A55 expressway. Map Ref: 23

Bodelwyddan Castle

TYWYN *Gwynedd*

Talyllyn Railway ♿ 🅿
Wharf Station, Tywyn LL36 9EY Tel: 01654 710472 Fax: 01654 711755 Email: enquiries@talyllyn.co.uk Web: www.talyllyn.co.uk

Narrow gauge steam trains running seven and a half miles into Snowdonia National Park. Walks from all stations, museum, cafés, shops, waterfalls, wheelchair accommodation on all trains. The first preserved railway in the world. Original 1865 train still runs on summer Sundays. Daily service varies from two to nine trains depending on season.

Opening Times: Apr to Oct daily 09:30-17:30. Admission: Fares available to all stations. Full round trip Adult £9.50, Child (accompanied) £2.00, Concession £8.50. Location: Tywyn Central Railway Station 100 yards. Map Ref: 24

WREXHAM

Bersham Ironworks & Heritage Centre
Bersham, Wrexham LL14 4HT Tel: 01978 261529 Fax: 01978 361703
Email: bershamheritage@wrexham.gov.uk Web: www.wrexham.gov.uk

Exhibitions and collections largely based on the iron, steel and coal industries, particularly John Wilkinson and nearby Bersham Ironworks. Also temporary exhibition programme.

Opening Times: Heritage Centre: Easter to Oct Mon to Fri 10:00-16:30, Sat & Sun 12:00-16:30 Oct to Mar closing 15:30. Ironworks: Easter to Aug Sat, Sun & BH 12:00-16:30.
Admission: Free. Location: Two miles from town centre. Map Ref: 25

Erddig

Wrexham LL13 0YT   Tel: 01978 355314   Fax: 01978 313333
Email: erddig@smtp.ntrust.org.uk   Web: www.nationaltrust.org.uk

Erddig is a first class example of a complete country house collection featuring fine and decorative arts. 18th century furniture and textiles, paintings/servants portraits and silver. The garden is one of the most significant surviving examples of a formal garden of the 18th century in Britain with some later features such as the Victorian Porterre, the Irish Yew Walk and a newly restored glasshouse.

Opening Times: 23 Mar to 3 Nov Sat to Wed 12:00-16:00 (Jul & Aug 12:00-16:00, 7 Oct to 3 Nov 12:00-15:00). Open Good Friday.   Admission: Adult £6.60, Child £3.30, Family £16.50, Group 15+ £5.30.   Location: Two miles south of Wrexham.   Map Ref: 25

Minera Lead Mines

Wern Road, Minera, Wrexham LL11 3DU   Tel: 01978 358916
Email: mineraleadmines@wrexham.gov.uk   Web: www.wrexham.gov.uk

Displays relating to lead mining including a small museum, reconstructed pumping engine, ore processing etc.

Opening Times: Easter to 31 Aug Sat, Sun & BH 12:00-16:30.   Admission: Free. Location: Five miles from town centre.   Map Ref: 26

Wrexham County Borough Museum

County Buildings, Regent Street, Wrexham LL11 1RB   Tel: 01978 358916   Fax: 01978 317982
Email: museum@wrexham.gov.uk   Web: www.wrexham.gov.uk

Mainly social history collections, exhibitions include 'Brymbo Man - A Bronze Age Burial', The National Football Collection and exhibitions about the town and surrounding area. Also two temporary exhibition galleries.

Opening Times: Mon to Fri 10:30-16:30, Sat 10:30-15:00.   Admission: Free.   Location: In town centre.   Map Ref: 25

ountry steeped in history with its capital city of Belfast and its beautiful sandstone castle. To
west is Londonderry encircled by a 17th century stone wall considered to be the best
served fortification in Europe. Omagh in the 'wild' county of Tyrone has an outstanding variety
andscapes - mountains, rivers and moorlands. County Fermanagh is the 'Lakeland County'
luding Devenish Island with its sixth century monastery. To the east in County Armagh the
rden of Ulster', and finally County Down with the Mourne Mountains cannot be rivalled for its
tory and wildlife.

ere are 35 interesting Museums and heritage sites depicting Northern Ireland's history, culture,
life, emigration, archaeology, geology, and natural environment.

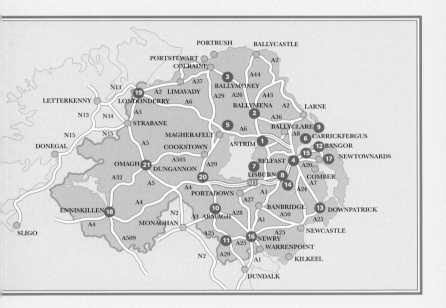

The Red Map References should be used to locate Museums etc on the pages that follow

CO ANTRIM

Clotworthy Arts Centre

Antrim Castle Gardens, Randalstown Road, Antrim BT41 4LH   Tel: 01849 428000

Arts Centre with three galleries and a small theatre. Housed in former coach yard of Antrim Castle and set within 17th century Antrim Castle gardens.

Opening Times: Mon to Fri 09:30-21:30, Sat 10:00-17:00, Sun Jul & Aug 14:00-17:00.
Admission: Free. Guided Tours £2.00 per person - must be pre-booked.   Location: Five minute walk from town centre via Market Square. By road off A6 to Randalstown, 150 metres from junction with A26 to Ballymena. Map Ref: 1

Ballymena Museum

3 Wellington Court, Ballymena, Co Antrim BT43 6EG   Tel: 028 25 642166   Fax: 028 25 638582
Email: jayneolphert@btconnect.com   Web: www.ballymena.gov.uk

Mixed social history/local collection providing an insight into the rich local cultural heritage of mid-Antrim. Temporary exhibitions and events, permanent displays, community outreach and historical enquiry service.

Opening Times: Mon to Fri 10:00-13:00 14:00-17:00, Sat 10:00-13:00. Closed Sun & BH.
Admission: Free.   Location: Town centre, between Wellington Street and Church Street.
Map Ref: 2

Royal Irish Regiment Museum

HQ The Royal Irish Regiment, St Patrick's Barracks, Ballymena, Co Antrim BT43 7NX   Tel: 028 2566 1383/1355   Fax: 028 2566 1378

Collection takes the visitor on a journey from the formation of the regiment in 1689 to the present day.

Opening Times: Wed & Sat 14:00-17:00. Also by prior arrangement.   Admission: Adult £2.00, Child/OAP £1.00.   Location: In St Patrick's Barracks. Map Ref: 2

Ballymoney Museum

33 Charlotte Street, Ballymoney, Co Antrim BT53 6AY   Tel: 028 2766 2280   Fax: 028 2766 7659   Email: keith.beattie@ballymoney.gov.uk   Web: www.1798ballymoney.org.uk

Ballymoney Museum has a collection of fascinating artefacts with local historical significance dating back to the earliest human settlements in Ireland. The museum also has a programme of temporary exhibitions.

Opening Times: Oct to Mar Mon to Fri 10:00-12:30 14:00-16:00. Apr to Sep Tue to Sat 10:00-12:30 14:00-16:00.   Admission: Free.   Location: Off Main Street, ten minutes from railway station. Map Ref: 3

Leslie Hill Open Farm

Ballymoney, Co Antrim BT53 6QL   Tel: 028 276 63109/66803

Comprehensive collection of horse-drawn farm implements, carts, mobile threshers, barn threshers and hand tools, governess cart, jaunting car and travelling coach. Household items of the past.

Opening Times: Apr & May Sun & BH 14:00-18:00. Jun Sat & Sun 14:00-18:00, Jul & Aug Mon to Sat 11:00-18:00, Sun 14:00-18:00.   Admission: Adult £2.90, Child £1.90. Group rates available.   Location: One mile north west of Ballymoney. Map Ref: 3

Fernhill House 'The Peoples Museum'

Fernhill House, Glencairn Park, Belfast, Co Antrim BT13 3PT   Tel: 028 9071 5599   Fax: 028 9071 3810

Fernhill House is a community museum which explores the history of the Greater Shankill and tells the story of the people from the early 19th century until the present day.

Opening Times: Mon to Sat 10:00-16:00, Sun 13:00-16:00.   Admission: Adult £2.00, Child £1.00, OAP 50p, Student £1.50, Family £4.00.   Location: 15 minute drive from Belfast City Centre. Map Ref: 4

Ormeau Baths Gallery

18A Ormeau Avenue, Belfast, Co Antrim BT2 8HQ   Tel: 028 9032 1402   Fax: 028 9031 2232

The Gallery is dedicated to the presentation of innovative exhibitions of contemporary visual art across a wide range of disciplines, by leading Irish and international artists.

Opening Times: Tue to Sat 10:00-18:00.   Admission: Free.   Location: Five minutes from Belfast City Hall via Bedford or Linenhall Street.   Map Ref: 4

Royal Ulster Rifles Regimental Museum

The Royal Irish Rangers Reg HQ, 5 Waring Street, Belfast, Co Antrim BT1 2EW   Tel / Fax: 028 9023 2086   Email: rurmuseum@yahoo.co.uk   Web: www.rurmuseum.tripod.com/

Over 4000 artefacts on show in the museum, including uniforms, trophies, badges, medals and other interesting items for the military historian, such as photograph albums, war diaries, pictures and muniments.

Opening Times: Daily 10:00-12:30 14:00-16:00 (Fri 15:00).   Admission: Adult £1.00, Child/OAP Free. Free to former Members of the Regiment.   Location: Town centre location, five minute walk from Laganside Bus Station. Convenient parking nearby.   Map Ref: 4

Ulster Museum

Botanic Gardens, Belfast, Co Antrim BT9 5AB   Tel: 028 9038 3000

The museum holds collections of art, history, botany and zoology, geology, antiquities and ethnography. The fine art collection of the Ulster Museum embraces a wide range of periods and schools; British painting from the 17th century to the present day, including works by Gainsborough, Reynolds and Turner; a small but significant collection of Dutch, Flemish and Italian Old Masters; an extensive holding of Irish art from the 17th century to the present; and 20th century British, European and American art.

Opening Times: Mon to Fri 10:00-17:00, Sat 13:00-17:00, Sun 14:00-17:00. Closed 12 Jul and Xmas.   Admission: Free.
Location: One mile from city centre, beside Queen's University.
                                                                                                  Map Ref: 4

Bellaghy Bawn

Castle Street, Bellaghy, Co Antrim BT45 8LA   Tel: 028 79 386812   Fax: 028 90 543111

Library of living poets of Northern Ireland including films, audio and art prints of Seamus Heaney. History displays from 17th to 19th century.

Opening Times: Daily 10:00-17:00.   Admission: Adult £1.50.   Location: At top of Castle Street.   Map Ref: 5

Flame: The Gasworks Museum of Ireland

44 Irish Quarter West, Carrickfergus, Co Antrim BT38 8AT   Tel: 028 93369575
Web: www.gasworksflame.com

The site contains one only surviving coal-gas manufacturing plant in Ireland and the largest set of horizontal retorts in western Europe. Collection of gas-related appliances and extensive research library.

Opening Times: Mar & Oct Sat & Sun 14:00-18:00, Jul & Aug daily 10:00-18:00, Apr, May, Jun & Sep daily 14:00-18:00. All other times by appointment.   Admission: Adult £2.50, Child/OAP £1.50, Under 5s Free. Groups £2.00 per person. School groups £1.00 per person. Family group £7.00.   Location: Near town centre, four minute walk from Tourist Office and Castle. (signposted)   Map Ref: 6

Ballance House

118A Lisburn Road, Glenavy, Co Antrim BT29 4NY   Tel: 02892 648492   Fax: 02892 648098
Email: ballancen3@aol.com   Web: www.johnballance.com

Artefacts relating to the life of New Zealand Prime Minister, John Ballance (1839-93) Liberal politician and welfare state reformer. Also illustrating the history of emigration from Ireland to New Zealand.

Opening Times: Apr to Sep Tue to Fri 11:00-17:00, Sat & Sun 14:00-17:00, BH 11:00-17:00. Closed Mon. Other times by appointment.   Admission: Adult £3.00, Child 50p. Group rates available.   Location: On the A30, seven miles from Lisburn, two miles from Glenavy.   Map Ref: 7

Irish Linen Centre & Lisburn Museum

Market Square, Lisburn, Co Antrim BT28 1AG   Tel: 028 9266 3377   Fax: 028 9267 2624
Email: irishlinencentre@lisburn.gov.uk

Permanent exhibition on the history of Irish linen including demonstrations of spinning and weaving. Variety of local history and cultural exhibitions.

Opening Times: Mon to Sat 09:30-17:00.   Admission: Free.   Map Ref: 8

Railway Preservation Society of Ireland

Castleview Road, Whitehead, Co Antrim BT38 9NA   Tel / Fax: 028 2826 0803
Email: rpsitrains@hotmail.com   Web: www.rpsi-online.org

Steam train rides and preserved examples of Irish main line steam locomotives and vintage carriages.

Opening Times: Jul Sun 14:00-17:00 & Xmas.   Admission: £1.50.   Location: Whitehead two minute walk from railway/bus.   Map Ref: 9

CO ARMAGH

Armagh County Museum

The Mall East, Armagh BT61 9BE   Tel: 028 375 23070

The collections of the museum reflect the lives of the people who live, work and are associated with County Armagh. The museum has an extensive reference library. A range of special exhibitions are held throughout the year. Armagh County Museum is part of the Museums & Galleries of Northern Ireland (MAGNI).

Opening Times: Mon to Fri 10:00-17:00, Sat 10:00-13:00 & 14:00-17:00. Closed Sun.   Admission: Free.   Location: On the Mall, an area of urban parkland a few minutes walk from the centre of the city.   Map Ref: 10

Armagh County Museum

Palace Stables Heritage Centre

The Palace Demesne, Armagh BT60 4EL   Tel: 028 3752 9629   Fax: 028 3752 9630

Housed in a restored Georgian stable block on the former estate of the Archbishops of Armagh (1770-1970). Guided tours explore the buildings with living history interpreters to re-enact life in 1786.

Opening Times: Mon to Sat 10:00-17:00, Sun 14:00-17:00 (Jul & Aug 13:00-17:00).
Admission: Adult £3.50, Child £2.00, OAP £2.75, Family (2 adults and 4 children) £9.50, Group £3.00, School £2.25.   Location: Near city centre, ten minute walk from city centre.   Map Ref: 10

St Patrick's Trian

40 English Street, Armagh BT61 7BA   Tel: 028 3752 1801   Fax: 028 3752 8329

The exhibition 'the least of all the faithful', examines the life and work of our patron Saint and his connections with Armagh as found in the ancient manuscript - the Book of Armagh.

Opening Times: Mon to Sat 10:00-17:00, Sun 14:00-17:00.   Admission: Adult £3.75, Child £2.00, Concession £2.75, Family £9.50.   Location: Town centre location.   Map Ref: 10

Royal Irish Fusiliers Museum

Sovereigns House, The Mall, Armagh, Co Armagh BT60 9DL   Tel / Fax: 02837 522911
Email: rylirfusiliermus@cs.com   Web: www.rirfus-museum.freeserve.co.uk

Housed in a Georgian listed building, the collection is dedicated to the history of the regiment from 1793 to 1968. An extensive medal display includes two Victoria Crosses from the Great War.

Opening Times: Mon to Fri & BH 10:00-12:30 13:30-16:00. Closed Xmas & New Year.
Admission: Free.   Location: Beside The Mall, near town centre and two minute walk from bus station.   Map Ref: 10

Cardinal Ó Fiaich Heritage Centre (Aras an Chairdimeil Ó Fiaich)

Slatequarry Road, Cullyhanna, Co Armagh BT35 0JH   Tel: 028 3086 8757
Email: info@ofiaichcentre-cullyhanna.com   Web: www.ofiaichcentre-cullyhanna.com

Exhibition includes audio-visuals of interviews and conversations, photographs, archaeological models and artefacts, personal memorabilia. The display tells the story of Tomás Ó Fiaich - student, priest, professor, scholar and Cardinal-Primate of All-Ireland.

Opening Times: Oct to Mar Mon to Fri 13:00-17:00 BH 10:00-17:00. Sat & Sun by appointment.
Apr to Oct Mon to Fri 10:00-17:00 BH 10:00-17:00. Sat & Sun by appointment.
Admission: Adult £2.50, Under 11s Free, OAP £2.00, Student & Group rates available.

Map Ref: 11

CO DOWN

North Down Heritage Centre

Town Hall, Bangor, Co Down BT20 4BT   Tel: 028 9127 1200   Fax: 028 9127 1370
Email: bangor_heritage_centre@yahoo.com   Web: www.northdown.gov.uk/heritage

Concentrates on the glorious Early Christian monastery, the heyday of seaside holidays and local archaeology. Unique collection relating to Irish entertainer Percy French.

Opening Times: Tue to Sat 10:30-16:30, Sun 14:00-16:30, Jul & Aug closed 17:30.
Admission: Free.   Location: Rear of Town Hall, Castle Park.   Map Ref: 12

Down County Museum

The Mall, Downpatrick, Co Down BT30 6AH   Tel: 028 44 615218   Fax: 028 44 615590
Email: lmckenna@downclc.gov.uk   Web: www.downcountymuseum.com

Collections relating to the history of County Down from early times to today. Museum is located in restored 18th century gaol of Down.

Opening Times: Mon to Fri 10:00-17:00, Sat & Sun 13:00-17:00.   Admission: Free.
Location: Located between Downpatrick Courthouse and Down Cathedral. Follow brown signs.

Map Ref: 13

Downpatrick Railway Museum

The Railway Station, Downpatrick, Co Down BT30 6LZ   Tel: 028 44 61 5779
Email: burkewalmae@cs.com   Web: www.downrail.icom43.net

Through the rolling drumlins of County Down, the Downpatrick Railway Museum houses and operates a unique collection of artefacts from the bygone railway golden age, the only such operating collection in Ulster and indeed Ireland.

Opening Times: Jul to Sep Sat & Sun 14:00-17:00, also 17 Mar, Easter Sun & Mon, Halloween weekend & 2nd and 3rd weekend Dec 14:00-17:00.   Admission: Tours: Adult £1.50, Child 50p. Train: Adult £4.50, Child/OAP £2.50.   Location: In Downpatrick Town Centre, adjacent to Ulsterbus Station.   Map Ref: 13

The Art Gallery

34 Lisburn Street, Hillsborough, Co Down BT26 6AB   Tel: 02892 689896   Fax: 02892 688433
Email: bill@theartgallery.freeserve.co.uk

Commercial art gallery selling contemporary work.

Opening Times: Mon to Sat 11:00-17:00 or by appointment.   Admission: Free.
Location: Centre Hillsborough Village.   Map Ref: 14

Museums, Galleries, Historic Houses & Sites

Please let us know of any collections that are not listed in this guide that you feel
should be listed. E-mail us on *editor@tomorrows.co.uk*
or return the Report Form on page 448

Ulster Folk & Transport Museum

Cultra, Holywood, Co Down BT18 0EU   Tel: 028 9042 8428

The Corner Shop

Take time to explore one of Ireland's foremost visitor attractions, recapturing a disappearing way of life, preserving traditional skills and celebrating transport history. Just minutes from Belfast the Ulster Folk & Transport Museum is situated in over 177 acres of park and grassland. At the Open Air Folk Museum 60 acres are devoted to illustrating the way of life of people in Northern Ireland in the early 1900s. Visitors can stroll through yesteryear's countryside with its farms, cottages, crops and livestock and visit a typical 1900s Ulster town with its shops, churches, and terraced housing. Indoors the Folk Gallery features a number of exhibitions. The indoor Transport Museum boasts the most comprehensive transport collection in Ireland. The Irish Railway Collection is displayed in an award-winning gallery, explaining the history and impact of both standard and narrow gauge railways in Ireland. The Road Transport Galleries boast a fine collection of vehicles ranging from cycles, motorcycles, trams, buses, fire engines and cars. The Museum also has a varied programme of major events and activities from Vehicle Days to the Rare Breeds Show and sale. Skills once commonly practised such as lace, sampler making, spinning, weaving, woodturning and forge work, and basket making are among many demonstrated and taught at the Museum.

Street Scene

Opening Times: Mar to Jun Mon to Fri 10:00-17:00, Sat 10:00-18:00, Sun 11:00-18:00. Jul to Sep Mon to Sat 10:00-18:00, Sun 11:00-18:00. Oct to Feb Mon to Fri 10:00-16:00, Sat 10:00-18:00, Sun 11:00-17:00.   Admission: Adult £4.00, Child £2.50, Under 5s Free, Concession £2.50, Family £11.00. Group Rates available.   Location: On the main Belfast to Bangor Road, just 10 minutes outside Belfast with excellent access by road, rail and bus.   Map Ref: 15

Newry Museum

1A Bank Parade, Newry, Co Down BT35 6HP   Tel: 028 3026 6232   Fax: 028 3026 6839

The museum incorporates architectural features from a now demolished Georgian house including a fully furnished panelled room. Highlights of the collection include a table reputed to have been on HMS Victory, an Order of St Patricks Robe and a Gelston Clock dating to 1770.

Opening Times: Mon to Fri 10:30-13:00 & 14:00-16:30. Closed BH.   Admission: Free. Location: Located in Newry Arts Centre. Two minute walk from bus station on the Mall. In town centre.   Map Ref: 16

The Somme Heritage Centre

233 Bangor Road, Newtownards, Co Down BT23 7PH   Tel: 028 91 823202   Fax: 028 91 823214   Email: sommeassociation@dnet.co.uk   Web: irishsoldier.org

The centre has a collection of around 5000 pieces related to Irish participation in the First World War. The centre is also starting to collect World War Two material.

Opening Times: Apr to Jun & Sep Mon to Thu 10:00-16:00 Sat 12:00-16:00 Jul to Aug Mon to Fri 10:00-17:00 Sat & Sun 12:00-17:00 Oct to Mar Mon to Thu 10:00-16:00.   Admission: Adult £3.75, Child/Concession £2.75, Family £10.00.   Map Ref: 17

Northern Ireland

CO FERMANAGH

Fermanagh County Museum

Enniskillen Castle, Castle Barracks, Enniskillen, Co Fermanagh BT74 7HL
Tel: 028 6632 5000   Fax: 028 6632 7342   Email: castle@fermanagh.gov.uk
Web: www.enniskillencastle.co.uk

Enniskillen Castle

Fermanagh County Museum collections represent Fermanagh's history, folklife, archaeology and environment. There are a variety of permanent displays relating to these topics as well as a rich and varied programme of events, education programmes and temporary exhibitions on subjects such as art, literature, music and history.

Opening Times: All year Mon 14:00-17:00, Tue to Fri 10:00-17:00. May to Sep Sat 14:00-17:00, Jul & Aug Sun 14:00-17:00. Admission: Adult £2.00, Child £1.00, OAP/Student £1.50, Family (2 adults and 2 children) £5.00. Location: Near town centre, two minute walk from Ulster Bus Station and Tourist Information Centre.
Map Ref: 18

CO LONDONDERRY

Harbour Museum

Harbour Square, Derry, Co Londonderry BT48 6AF   Tel: 02871 377331

A traditional museum, with emphasis on the city's maritime connections - temporary exhibitions are regularly displayed.

Opening Times: Mon to Fri 10:00-13:00, 14:00-16:30. Admission: Free. Location: City centre location - one minute from central bus station.
Map Ref: 19

Tower Museum

Union Hall Place, Derry, Co Londonderry BT48 6LU   Tel: 02871 372411

The Tower Museum looks at the history of Derry from its geological formation through to the present day. There are special features on the Plantation of Ulster, the Siege of Derry and the 'Troubles'.

Opening Times: Sep to Jun Tue to Sat & BH 10:00-17:00, Jul to Aug Mon to Sat 10:00-17:00, Sun 14:00-17:00. Admission: Admission charged. Location: City centre location - just inside the City Walls.
Map Ref: 19

Workhouse Museum

Glendermott Road, Waterside, Derry, Co Londonderry BT47 6BG   Tel: 028 7131 8328

First Floor - World War II display on Derry's part in protecting Atlantic convoys. Video presentations plus two rooms for temporary exhibitions. Second Floor - display on Irish and African famines. Also dormitory display.

Opening Times: Mon to Thu & Sat 10:00-16;30. Closed Fri & Sun. Jul to Aug Fri 10:00-16:00, Sun 14:00-16:30. Admission: Free. Location: One mile from city centre, on main bus route.
Map Ref: 19

CO TYRONE

US Grant Ancestral Homestead

Dergenagh Road, Dungannon, Co Tyrone BT70 1TW   Tel: 028 8776 7259/028 855 57133
Email: killymaddy@nihc.net   Web: www.dungannon.gov.uk

Explore the cottage of the Simpson family with close ties to Ulysses Simpson Grant, the Commander of the victorious Union troops in the American Civil War.

Opening Times: Apr to Sep Tue to Sat 12:00-17:00, Sun 14:00-18:00. Closed Mon.
Admission: Adult £1.50, Child/OAP 75p. Location: Off main A4, 13 miles west of Dungannon.
Map Ref: 20

Ulster American Folk Park

Mellon Road, Castletown, Omagh, Co Tyrone BT78 5QY   Tel: 028 8224 3292

A museum of Emigration and Folk Life telling the story of the floods of Emigrants who left these shores in the 18th and 19th centuries. Visit the Old and New Worlds joined by a full-sized Emigrant Sailing Ship. Explore 28, mainly original exhibit buildings from both sides of the Atlantic. Costumed interpreters tell the emigrant's story and demonstrate a wide range of traditional crafts daily. Emigrants exhibition explores related themes and the Centre for Migration Studies allows for further research. Facilities include Residential Centre, Educational programmes, shop and restaurant. Voted Visitor Attraction of The Year.

Opening Times: Apr to Sep Mon to Sat 10:30-18:00, Sun & BH 11:00-18:00. Oct to Apr Mon to Fri 10:30-17:00.   Admission: Adult £4.00, Child £2.50, OAP £3.50.   Location: A5 - three miles from Omagh on Strabane Road.   Map Ref: 21

Ulster History Park

Cullion, Lislap, Omagh, Co Tyrone BT79 7SU   Tel: 028 8164 8188   Fax: 028 8164 8011   Email: uhp@omagh.gov.uk   Web: www.omagh.gov.uk/historypark.htm

17th century Plantation Exhibit

A 35-acre outdoor museum tracing the history of settlement in Ireland through nearly 10,000 years. Full scale models of homes and monuments through the ages illustrate how people in Ireland lived from the Stone Age (8000BC) up to the 17th century Plantation period. An indoor exhibition expands the theme while an audio-visual presentation explores the legacy of the past still visable in today's lanscape.

Opening Times: Apr to Sep daily 10:00-17:30 (18:30 in Jul and Aug). Oct to Mar, Mon to Fri 10:00-17:00. Admission: Adult £3.75, Family (2 Adults & 4 Children) £12.00, Child/Student/OAP £2.50. Adult Group (15+) £3.25, Concession Group (15+) £2.00.   Location: On B48, seven miles north of Omagh. Map Ref: 21

and is a country with a unique history and is renowned for its music and literature, particularly olin with its narrow cobbled streets and the superb collections in its museums and art galleries. erever one travels in Ireland there are castles, heritage centres and sites, abbeys and in many ns museums that together provide a fascinating record of the local history and crafts, maritime ory and military history and indeed the Irish way of living and their culture.

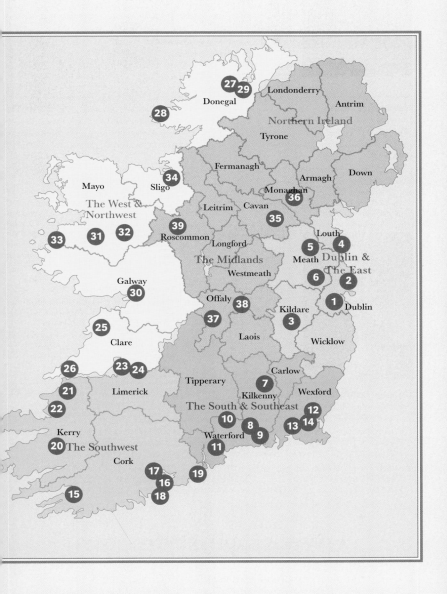

The Red Map References should be used to locate Museums etc on the pages that follow

Dalkey Castle

Dalkey Castle & Heritage Centre

HERITAGE TOWNS
of Ireland

Castle Street, Dalkey, Co Dublin   Tel: +353 (0)1 285 8366   Fax: +353 (0)1 284 3141   Email: diht@indigo.ie   Web: www.heritagetowns.com/dalkey

The castle dates from 1429 and many themes are explored in the museum: Dalkey's transport system, early Christian church and graveyard St Begnet, the Rathdown slab is on display and pre-dates the Christian era. Dalkey's many literary associations are also explored from Hugh Leonard to Maeve Binchey.

Opening Times: Apr to Oct Mon to Fri 09:30-17:00, Sat, Sun & BH 11:00-17:00. Nov to Mar Mon to Sun 11:00-17:00.   Admission: Adult €2.50, Child €1.50, OAP/Student €2.00, Family €8.00.   Location: Beside Queens Pub. Five minutes from DART Station.   Map Ref: 1

Newbridge House

Donabate, Co Dublin   Tel: +353 (0)1 843 6534   Fax: +353 (0)1 846 2537

This delightful 18th century manor has one of the finest collections of original Irish furniture in Ireland, surrounded by 350 acres of parkland, including traditional farm and children's playground.

Opening Times: Apr to Sep Tue to Sat 10:00-13:00 & 14:00-17:00, Sun & BH 14:00-18:00. Oct to Mar Sat, Sun & BH 14:00-17:00.   Admission: House: Adult €5.50, Child €3.00, Concession €5.00, Family €15.00. Farm: Adult €1.50, Child/Student €1.00, Family €3.00.   Location: 12 miles north of Dublin City on the Belfast road. Bus 33B from Eden Quay. Suburban rail from Connolly Station.   Map Ref: 2

Archaeology & History Museum

Kildare Street, Dublin 2   Tel: +353 (0)1 677 7444

Opened in 1890, the National Museum of Ireland, Kildare Street contains artefacts dating from 7000BC to the 20th century including outstanding examples of Celtic and Medieval art and the finest collection of prehistoric gold artefacts in Europe.

Opening Times: Tue to Sat 10:00-17:00, Sun 14:00-17:00. Closed Mon.   Admission: Free.   Map Ref: 1

Chester Beatty Library

Dublin Castle, Dublin 2   Tel: +353 (0)1 407 0750   Fax: +353 (0)1 407 0760   Email: info@cbl.ie   Web: www.cbl.ie

The exhibition galleries open a window on the artistic treasures of the great cultures and religions of the world. The Library's rich collection of manuscripts, prints, icons, miniature paintings, early printed books and objets d'art represent numerous cultures and countries.

Opening Times: May to Sep Mon to Fri 10:00-17:00, Oct to Apr Tue to Fri 10:00-17:00, every Sat 11:00-17:00, every Sun 13:00-17:00. Closed BH Mon, 24-26 Dec, 1 Jan & Good Friday.   Admission: Free.   Location: Ten minutes walk from Trinity College/Grafton Street.   Map Ref: 1

Decorative Arts & History Museum

Collins Barracks, Dublin 7   Tel: +353 (0)1 677 7444

The beautiful restored Collins Barracks on the banks of the River Liffey is now home to the national collection of Decorative Arts & History. On display are artefacts ranging from weaponry, furniture, folk life and costume to silver, ceramics and glassware.

Opening Times: Tue to Sat 10:00-17:00, Sun 14:00-17:00. Closed Mon. Admission: Free. Location: Nearest DART Station Pearse Street.
                                                    Map Ref: 1

The Douglas Hyde Gallery   DH9

Trinity College, Nassau Street, Dublin 2   Tel: +353 (0)1 608 1116   Fax: +353 (0)1 670 8330
Email: dhgallery@tcd.ie   Web: www.douglashydegallery.com

The Gallery has a diverse programme of exhibitions, embracing both Irish and international contemporary art. A wide range of gallery activities - tours, lectures, discussion groups - encourages audience participation and evaluation of the work on exhibition. An information leaflet accompanies every show. The Gallery has a small bookshop which stocks a wide range of art magazines, including Artforum, Frieze and Circa.

Keith Edmier mixed media exhibition installation, 1998

Opening Times: Mon to Fri 11:00-18:00, Thu 11:00-19:00, Sat 11:00-16:45. Closed Xmas, Easter and BH.
Admission: Free. Location: Trinity College, Nassau Street, Dublin 2.
                                                    Map Ref: 1

Dublin Civic Museum

City Assembly House, 58 South William Street, Dublin 2   Tel: +353 (0)1 679 4260

Experience aspects of life in Dublin through the ages. Collections include: streets and buildings of Dublin, traders, industry, transport, political history, maps and views.

Opening Times: Tue to Sat 10:00-18:00, Sun 11:0-14:00. Closed Mon. Admission: Free.
                                                    Map Ref: 1

Dublin Writers Museum

18 Parnell Square, Dublin 1   Tel: +353 (0)1 872 2077   Fax: +353 (0)1 872 2231
Email: writers@dublintourism.ie   Web: www.visitdublin.com

The collection features the lives and works of Dublin's literary celebrities over the past 200 years. Swift, Sheridan, Shaw, Wilde, Yeats, Joyce and Beckett are among those presented through their books, letters, portraits and personal items.

Opening Times: Jan to Dec Mon to Sat 10:00-17:00, Sun & BH 11:00-17:00. Late opening Jun, Jul & Aug Mon to Fri 10:00-18:00. Admission: Adult €5.50, Child €3.00, Concession €5.00, Family €15.00. Location: In Dublin City Centre, five minute walk from O'Connell Street.
                                                    Map Ref: 1

Dublin's Viking Adventure

Essex Street West, Temple Bar, Dublin 8   Tel: +353 (0)1 679 6040   Fax: +353 (0)1 679 6033
Email: viking@dublintourism.ie   Web: www.visitdublin.com

Our Viking guide takes you on a fascinating journey through a Dublin of long ago. Walk the narrow streets of the Viking town 'Dyflin' and experience the sounds and smells of the city.

Opening Times: Apr to Sep Tue to Sat 10:00-16:30. Closed Sun & Mon. Admission: Adult €7.50, Child €4.00, Concession €7.00, Family €20.00. Location: In Dublin City Centre, ten minute walk from O'Connell Bridge.
                                                    Map Ref: 1

Guinness Storehouse

St James's Gate, Dublin 8   Tel: +353 (0)1 608 4800

Set in the centre of one of the world's most famous breweries, which has been on site since Arthur Guinness founded it in 1759, the Guinness Storehouse has rapidly become Dublin's 'must see' visitor attraction. The Guinness Storehouse is a dramatic story that begins over 250 years ago and ends in Gravity, the bar in the sky, with a complimentary pint of Guinness, and an astonishing view of Dublin. Often surprising, always entertaining, the

adventure begins the moment you walk through the door and into the buildings giant, pint shaped heart of glass. As you wander up through Guinness Storehouse, you'll discover what goes into making the black stuff - the ingredients, the processes, the passion. You'll meet Arthur Guinness and find out how the drink that carries his name has been transported around the world. You'll see how Guinness has been advertised over the years and visit Guinness, at Home and Abroad. If you'd like a souvenir to remind you of your trip to the home of Guinness, there's plenty to choose from in Store, which stocks an exclusive range of merchandise.

Opening Times: 09:30-17:00. Closed Xmas & New Year, St Stephen's Day and Good Friday. Admission: Adult €12.00, Family (2 adults and 4 children) €26.00, Student over 18 €8.00, Student under 18 €5.00. Group Rates available.   Location: Bus 51B/78A from Aston Quay or 123 from O'Connell Street.   Map Ref: 1

Hugh Lane Municipal Gallery of Modern Art

Charlemont House, Parnell Square North, Dublin 1   Tel: +353 (0)1 874 1903
Fax: +353 (0)1 872 2182   Email: info@hughlane.ie   Web: www.hughlane.ie

The collection includes Impressionist masterpieces by Renoir, Monet, Degas and Morisot. A fine collection of 20th century Irish art and works by contemporary Irish and international artists. The Gallery also houses Francis Bacon's reconstructed studio accompanied by an audio visual room, a micro gallery with touch screen terminals and an exhibition gallery with works by Francis Bacon.

Opening Times: Tue to Thu 9:30-18:00, Fri & Sat 9:30-17:00, Sun 11:00-17:00. Closed Mon and Xmas. Admission: Free to permanent collection. Admission to Francis Bacon Studio - Adult €7.50, Child €2.50,

Interior Francis Bacon Studio. Photo Perry Ogden

Concession €3.50, Under 12s Free.   Location: City centre, at the end of O'Connell Street, on the north side of Parnell Square. A ten minute walk Tara Street or Connolly Street Railway Station.   Map Ref: 1

Irish Architectural Archive

73 Merrion Square, Dublin 2   Tel: +353 (0)1 676 3430

The Irish Architectural Archive collects, preserves and makes accessible records of every type on or relating to the architecture of the island of Ireland.

Opening Times: Tue to Fri 10:00-13:00 & 14:30-17:00. Closed Aug.   Admission: Free.
Location: City centre.   Map Ref: 1

James Joyce Museum

Joyce Tower, Sandycove, Co Dublin   Tel / Fax: +353 (0)1 280 9265
Email: joycetower@dublintourism.ie   Web: www.visitdublin.com

The collection includes letters, photographs, portraits and personal possessions of Joyce. There are first editions of his work including his early broadsides and the celebrated edition of 'Ulysses' illustrated by Henri Matisse.

Opening Times: Apr to Oct Mon to Sat 10:00-17:00, Sun & BH 14:00-18:00.   Admission: Adult €5.50, Child €3.00, Concession €5.00, Family €5.00.   Location: Eight miles south of Dublin City.   Map Ref: 1

Kilmainham Gaol

Inchicore Road, Dublin 8   Tel: +353 (0)1 453 5984

Access to the Gaol is by guided tour only. The tour lasts approx one hour and 15 minutes and includes the social and political history of the Gaol. In addition to the tour the public have an opportunity to visit the museum at their own convenience. The museum is on three levels is the only museum that deals with modern Irish and political history spanning from 1796-1924. Among the highlights of the collection there are artefacts from the 1798 Rebellion, the last letters of the leaders of the 1916 Rebellion, along with documents and artefacts from the Irish War of Independence and Civil War. The Gaol also plays host to a wide range of temporary exhibitions, including art and historical exhibitions etc.

Opening Times: Oct to Mar Mon to Sat 09:30-17:30, Sun 10:00-18:00, Apr to Sep Mon to Sun 09:30-18:00. Closed Xmas.   Admission: Adult €4.40, Child/Student €1.90, OAP/Group €3.10, Family €10.10.   Location: Three miles from city centre. Bus 79, 51B, 78A from Aston Quay.

Map Ref: 1

National Gallery of Ireland

Merrion Square West, Dublin 2   Tel: +353 (0)1 661 5133   Fax: +353 (0)1 661 5372
Email: artgall@eircom.net   Web: www.nationalgallery.ie

The National Gallery of Ireland has a superb collection of western European art, from the Middle Ages to the 20th century. It also holds the most important collection of Irish art in the world including the National Portrait Gallery and the Yeates Museum. Artists on display include Caravaggio, Canova, Vermeer, Rembrant, Poussin, Monet, Velazquez, Picasso, Goya, Turner, Gainsborough and all the major painters of Irish school, including the Yeates family.

Opening Times: Mon to Sat 09:30-17:30, Thur 09:30-20:30, Sun 12:00-17:30. Closed Good Friday and Xmas.

Architects Model of the New Millennium Wing opened in January 2002

Admission: Free. Location: City centre, five minutes from DART. Meter parking available.   Map Ref: 1

Natural History

Merrion Street, Dublin 2   Tel: +353 (0)1 677 7444

The Natural History Museum opened in 1857 just two years before Charles Darwin published his work 'The Origin of Species'. Packed with diverse animals from all walks of life, the museum is a place where Darwin's theories of evolution and natural selection can be studied and understood.

Opening Times: Tue to Sat 10:00-17:00, Sun 14:00-17:00. Closed Mon. Admission: Free. Location: Nearest DART Station Pearse Street.   Map Ref: 1

Natural History Museum

Royal Hibernian Academy

ROYAL
HIBERNIAN
ACADEMY
TRADITION &
INNOVATION

Gallagher Gallery, 15 Ely Place, Dublin 2
Tel: +353 (0)1 661 2558   Fax: +353 (0)1 661 0762
Email: rhagallery@eircom.net
Web: www.royalhibernianacademy.com

Established in 1823, the Royal Hibernian Academy is an artist led organisation run by artists for artists. The Academy is housed within the Gallagher Gallery, one of the largest exhibition spaces in Dublin City Centre (13,000 sq ft). It presents an innovative exhibition programme of leading Irish and international artists. Commercial shows are held at the Academy in the Ashford Gallery which represents emerging artists and Academicians.

Opening Times: Tue to Sat 11:00-17:00, Thu 11:00-20:00, Sun 14:00-17:00. Closed Mon. Admission: Free. Location: City Centre, one minute from St Stephen's Green.   Map Ref: 1

Liam Belton RHA, Herb Cutter with Five Eggs, oil on canvas

Dublin & The East

Shaw Birthplace

🦅 ⬤ 🚍

33 Synge Street, Dublin 8   Tel: +353 (0)1 475 0854   Fax: +353 (0)1 872 2231
Email: shawhouse@dublintourism.ie   Web: www.visitdublin.com

The first home of the Shaw family and the renowned playwright, restored to its Victorian elegance and charm. The house contains photographs, original documents and letters that throw light on G B Shaw's long and impressive career.

Opening Times: May to Sep Mon to Sat 10:00-17:00, Sun & BH 11:00-17:00.   Admission: Adult €5.50, Child €3.00, Concession €5.00, Family €15.00.   Location: Ten minute walk from St Stephen's Green.   Map Ref: 1

Trinity College Library

♿ ⬤

Trinity College Library, College Street, Dublin 2   Tel: +353 (0)1 677 2941   Fax: +353 (0)1 671 9003

The Old Library is home to the famous 19th gospel manuscript the Book of Kells. Also on view is The Book of Kells 'Turning Darkness into Light' Exhibition which explains the background of the Book of Kells and other related manuscripts, the Book of Armagh, the Book of Durrow, the Book of Mulling and the Book of Dimma.

Opening Times: Mon to Sat 09:30-17:00, Sun (Oct to May) 12:00-16:30, Sun (Jun to Sep) 09:30-16:30. BH Oct to May 12:00-16:30. Closed Xmas & New Year.   Admission: Adult €6.50, Child Free, Student/OAP €6.00, Family (2 adults and 4 children) €13.00. Location: City centre.   Map Ref: 1

Trinity College Library Dublin

Fry Model Railway

♿ ⬤ 📷 ◐ 🚍

Malahide Castle Demesne, Malahide, Co Dublin   Tel: +353 (0)1 846 3779   Fax: +353 (0)1 846 3723   Email: fryrailway@dublintourism.ie   Web: www.visitdublin.com

This is a unique collection of hand-made models of Irish trains, from the beginning of rail travel to modern times. One of the world's largest miniature railways. The exhibition is unique in that it is a working railway covering an area of 2500 sq ft.

Opening Times: Apr to Sep Mon to Sat 10:00-17:00, Sun & BH 14:00-18:00.   Admission: Adult €5.50, Child €3.00, Concession €5.00, Family €15.00.   Location: Eight miles north of Dublin City Centre, four miles from Dublin Airport.   Map Ref: 2

Malahide Castle

🦅 ⬤ 📷 ◐ 🚍

Malahide, Co Dublin   Tel: +353 (0)1 846 2184   Fax: +353 (0)1 846 2537
Email: malahidecastle@dublintourism.ie   Web: www.visitdublin.com

The Talbot family lived here for nearly 800 years. The Castle is furnished with beautiful Irish period furniture together with an extensive collection of Irish portrait paintings, mainly from the National Gallery of Ireland.

Opening Times: Jan to Dec Mon to Sat 10:00-17:00. Apr to Oct Sun & BH 11:00-18:00, Nov to Mar Sun & BH 11:00-17:00.   Admission: Adult €5.50, Child €3.00, Concession €5.00, Family €15.00.   Location: Eight miles north of Dublin City, four miles from Dublin Airport.   Map Ref: 2

CO KILDARE

Athy Museum

♿ ⬤ 🚍

Town Hall, Athy, Co Kildare Tel: +353 (0)507 33075 Fax: +353 (0)507 33076
Email: oriordanmargaret@eircom.net   Web www.kildare.ie/athyonline

HERITAGE TOWNS
⇒ *of Ireland* ⇐

Unique collection of artefacts belonging to famous Antarctic explorer Sir Ernest Shackleton. Audio visual/touch screen displays with photographs and historical artefacts. Learn about the Gordon Bennett Motor Race, Anglo Norman Athy etc.

Opening Times: Jan to Dec Mon to Sat 10:00-18:00, Sun & BH 14:00-18:00. Nov to Feb closed Sun.

Admission: Adult €2.00, Child €1.00, OAP/Student €1.50, Family (2 adults and 2 children) €5.00.   Map Ref: 3
Athy Heritage Town

Dublin & The East

Millmount Museum & Tower

Millmount, Drogheda, Co Louth   Tel: +353 (0)41 983 3097   Fax: +353 (0)41 984 1599
Email: info@millmount.net   Web: www.millmount.net

Exhibits include unique 18th century guild banners, Geology Collection with over 300 examples of granite and marble, and an authentic folk kitchen. The Martello Tower provides magnificent views of the town and Boyne Valley.

Opening Times: Mon to Sat 10:00-18:00, Sun & BH 14:30-17:30.   Admission: Adult €4.50, Child/OAP €2.50, Family €11.50. Group rates available.   Location: Five minute walk from town centre.   Map Ref: 4

Kells Heritage Centre

HERITAGE TOWNS
◦≡ of Ireland ≡◦

The Courthouse, Headfort Place, Kells, Co Meath   Tel / Fax: +353 (0)46 47840   Email: info@meathtourism.ie
Web: www.meathtourism.ie/kellsheritagecentre

This is the home of the Book of Kells - an exhibition entitled 'The Splendour of Ireland' gives an insight into the crafts and culture of monastic Ireland. Relics of St Columcille and a facsimile copy of the Book of Kells.

Opening Times: May to Sep Mon to Sat 10:00-18:00, Sun & BH 13:30-18:00. Oct to Apr Tue to Sat 10:00-18:00.   Admission: Adult €3.00, Child/OAP/Student €1.50, Family (2 adults and 2 children) €8.00.   Location: On Navan Road N3.   Map Ref: 5
Photo Caption:

Trim Visitor Centre

HERITAGE TOWNS
◦≡ of Ireland ≡◦

Mill Street, Trim, Co Meath   Tel: +353 (0)46 37227   Fax: +353 (0)46 38053
Email: info@meathtourism.ie   Web: www.meathtourism.ie

An exciting multimedia exhibition which paints a vivid picture of the Medieval ruins of Trim. The 'Power and Glory' gives the visitor a great insight into Norman Ireland.

Opening Times: Mon to Sat 10:00-17:00, Sun & BH 12:00-17:30. Closed 12:30-13:30 for lunch.
Admission: Adult €2.00, Child €1.00, OAP/Student €1.25, Family €5.00. Group Rates on request.   Location: Mill Street, close to town centre, five minutes from Castle.

Map Ref: 6

The South & Southeast

Butler Gallery

The Castle, Kilkenny   Tel: +353 (0)56 61106

Public funded gallery. Exhibitions include Tony Cragg, Bill Woodrow, Sol le Wit, James Turrell, Petah Coyne, Jean Scully and Roman Signer. Collection contains contemporary sculpture, paintings and photography.

Opening Times: Oct to Mar daily 10:30-17:00, Apr to Sep daily 10:00-19:00.   Admission: Free.
                                                                                                Map Ref: 7

Rothe House Museum

Parliament Street, Kilkenny   Tel: +353 (0)56 22893

Rothe House was built by prosperous merchant John Rothe in 1594. The Kilkenny Archaeological Society bought and restored the house. Within the house are various exhibitions from folk to costume and accessories.

Opening Times: Mon to Sat 10:30-17:00 Sun 15:00-17:00. Opening hours may vary off-season.
Location: City centre - five minutes from rail/bus station.   Map Ref: 7

Bolton Library

GPA Building, John Street, Cashel, Co Tipperary   Tel / Fax: +353 (0)62 61944
Email: boltonlibrary@oceanfree.net
Web: www.heritagetowns.com/cashel

A unique collection of two Archbishops over 12,000 volumes. Manuscript collections, early printing from 12th century. 20 titles prior to 1500, spectacular copy of Nuremburg Chronicle (1493) and many more. Visit the Georgian Cathedral in grounds and Cashel City walls 14th century.

Opening Times: Mar to Oct Tue to Sat 09:30-17:30, Oct to Feb Mon to Fri 09:30-17:30.   Admission: Adult €1.50, Child €0.50, OAP/Student €1.00.   Map Ref: 8

Bolton Library

Tipperary S R County Museum

The Borstal, Emmet Street, Clonmel, Co Tipperary   Tel: +353 (0)52 34551   Fax: +353 (0)52 80390   Email: museum@southtippcoco.ie
Local history and fine art illustrating the history of the county and its people.
Opening Times: Tue to Sat 10:00-17:00.   Admission: Free.   Location: Five minutes from railway and bus station.   Map Ref: 9

Excel Heritage Centre & Art Gallery

Mitchell Street, Tipperary   Tel: +353 (0)62 33466   Fax: +353 (0)62 31067
Email: info@tipperary-excel.com   Web: www.tipperary-excel.com

This multicultural centre houses an art gallery, heritage centre, tourism office, cinema, coffee shop and craft shop. Multimedia exhibition explores Tipperary today, sport, the land, the town and hear about the song 'Its a long way to Tipperary'.

Opening Times: Daily 09:00-18:00. Closed Good Friday, Xmas & New Year.   Admission: Adults €3.00.   Location: Beside town car park, Market Square.

Excel Heritage Centre & Art Gallery   Map Ref: 10

The Lismore Experience

The Courthouse, Lismore, Co Waterford
Tel: +353 (0)58 54975   Fax: +353 (0)58 53009
Email: lismoreheritage@eircom.net   Web: www.lismore-ireland.eom

A 30 minute Lismore Experience will transport you through 1400 years of history. Guided tours of the town can be arranged, learn about Sir Robert Boyle 'Father of Modern Chemistry', Boyles Law - from Lismore, artefacts and new exhibition.

Opening Times: Apr to May Mon to Sat 09:30-17:30, Sun 10:00-17:30. Jun to Aug Mon to Sat 09:30-18:00, Sun 10:00-17:30. Sep to Oct Mon to Sun 09:30-17:30. Nov to Jan Mon to Fri 10:00-17:30.
Admission: Adult €3.00, Child/OAP €2.00, Student €2.50, Family €6.00, Group €2.50.   Location: In town centre.   Map Ref: 11

The Lismore Experience

www.tomorrows.co.uk

Full information on our collection of travel guides and secure store

The South & Southeast

Wexford County Museum

The Castle, Enniscorthy, Co Wexford Tel / Fax: +353 (0)54 35926
Email: wexmus@iol.ie

The County Museum is in four main sections which illustrate in a dramatic way the stories and history of County Wexford through the centuries - military, agriculture, writing, crafts, industrial and ecclesiastical. The museum is a veritable treasure house of information for anyone interested in Irish ways of living, culture and heritage.

Opening Times: Mar to Sep 10:00-17:30, Sun 14:00-17:30.
Admission: Adult €3.80, Student/Senior €2.50, Child €0.60, Family €9.50 Location: Town centre.   Map Ref: 12

Wexford County Museum

Irish National Heritage Park

Ferrycarrig, Co Wexford Tel: +353 (0)53 20733 Fax: +353 (0)53 20911
Email: info@inhp.com Web: www.inhp.com

HERITAGE TOWNS
→ of Ireland ←

This park depicts mans' settlement in Ireland from 7000BC to the arrival of the Normans in 12th century. Stroll through the park with its homesteads, places of ritual, burial mounds and long forgotten remains.

Opening Times: Mar to Oct daily 09:30-18:30.
Admission: Adult €5.00, OAP/Student €4.00, Family (2 adults and 3 children) €12.50. Location: Off N25 to Waterford.   Map Ref: 13

Irish Agricultural Museum

Johnstown Castle Old Farmyard, Wexford Tel: +353 (0)53 42888 Fax: +353 (0)53 42213

Extensive displays on rural transport, farming and the activities of the farmyard and the farmhouse. Nationally important collection of Irish country furniture - over 100 pieces. Also Famine Exhibition and Ferguson System display.

Opening Times: Mon to Fri 09:00-17:00, Apr to Nov also Sat & Sun 14:00-17:00.
Admission: Adult €4.00, Child €2.50, Family €13.00. Group rates available. Location: Four miles south west of Wexford Town.   Map Ref: 14

The Southwest

Bantry House

Bantry, Co Cork Tel: +353 (0)27 50047 Fax: +353 (0)27 50795 Email: info@bantryhouse.ie
Web: www.bantryhouse.ie

Bantry House and Gardens has been home to the White family since 1739, and is one of the finest stately homes in Ireland. The house contains a unique collection of tapestries, furniture, carpets and art treasures, collected mainly by the second Earl in the 19th century. These include Russian icons, 18th century French, Flemish and Irish furniture, Gobelin tapestries and Aubusson carpets.

Opening Times: Mid Mar to end Oct daily 09:00-17:00.
Location: Near town centre on N71, ten minute walk.
                                              Map Ref: 15

Cobh Museum

Scots Church, High Road, Cobh, Co Cork   Tel: +353 (0)21 481 4240   Fax: +353 (0)21 481 1018   Email: cobhmuseum@eircom.net

The museum is housed in the former Scots Presbyterian Church. Exhibitions reflect the social and cultural history of the town of Cobh (Queenstown), the Great Island and the harbour.

Opening Times: Easter to Oct Mon to Sat 11:00-13:00 14:00-18:00, Sun 15:00-18:00.
Admission: Adult €1.50, Child/OAP €0.75, Family €3.75.   Location: Five minutes walk from town centre, near Tourist Office and station.   Map Ref: 16

Cobh - The Queenstown Story

Cobh Railway Station, Deepwater Quay, Cobh, Co Cork   Tel: +353 (0)21 481 3591   Fax: +353 (0)21 481 3595   Email: info@cobhheritage.com   Web: www.cobhheritage.com

Discover Cobh's maritime history and connections with the Lusitania, Titanic and Irish emigration. Collection of memorabilia including letters, menus and personal belongings.

Opening Times: Mar-Dec 10:00-18:00 (last admission 17:00) Dec-Mar 10:00-17:00 (last admission 16:00)   Admission: Adult €3.95, Child €2.00, OAP €3.20.   Location: Adjacent to Cobh Railway Station in Cobh Town.   Map Ref: 16

Cork Public Museum

Fitzgerald Park, Mardyke, Cork   Tel: +353 (0)21 427 0679   Fax: +353 (0)21 427 0931   Email: museum@corkcorp.ie

General collection outlining the history of Cork from earliest times to present day, includes archaeology, geology, history - social and political. Cork silver and glass.

Opening Times: Mon to Fri 11:00-13:00 and 14:15-17:00 (Jun & Aug to 18:00), Sun 15:00-17:00. Closed Sat and BH weekends. Admission: Free Mon to Fri. Sun - Adult €1.50, Family/Group €3.00.   Location: Ten minute walk from town centre, two minute walk from number 8 bus stop on Western Road.   Map Ref: 17

Crawford Municipal Art Gallery

Emmet Place, Cork   Tel: +353 (0)21 427 3377   Fax: +353 (0)21 480 5043   Email: crawfordgallery@eircom.net   Web: www.crawfordgallery.com

In a collection of (mostly) Irish art from the last three centuries, highlights include works by James Barry, Daniel Maclise, Walter Osborne, Sean Keating, Jack B Yeats, Louis le Brocquy, Paul Seawright and Kathy Prendergast.

Opening Times: Mon to Sat 10:00-17:00. Closed Sun & BH.   Admission: Free.   Location: City centre.   Map Ref: 17

International Museum of Wine

Desmond Castle, Cork Street, Kinsale, Co Cork   Tel: +353 (0)21 477 4853   Email: info@heritageireland.ie   Web: www.heritageireland.ie

HERITAGE TOWNS
of Ireland

International Museum of Wine

Exhibition which documents the intriguing story of Irelands wine links with Europe and under world from early modern period to present day.

Opening Times: Mid Apr to mid Jun Tue to Sun 10:00-18:00, open BH. Mid Jun to late Oct daily 10:00-18:00. Admission: Adult €2.00, Child/Student €1.00, Group/OAP €1.50, Family €5.00.   Location: 600 metres from Guard Well along Cork Street.   Map Ref: 18

The Southwest

Youghal Heritage Centre

Tourism House, Youghal, Co Cork Tel: +353 (0)24 20170
Fax: +353 (0)24 20171 Email: youghal@eircom.net

A visit to this centre is essential. Walking tours of the town depart at 11:00 each day during summer period. Learn about Sir Walter Raleigh who was based in Youghal.

Opening Times: Oct to May Mon to Fri 09:30-17:30. Jun to Sep daily 09:00-19:00. Admission: Adult €2.50, Child/Student €2.00, Group €1.00. Location: On N25, beside Quays/Clock Tower.

Youghal Heritage Centre

Map Ref: 19

CO KERRY

Listowel Literary Museum

24 The Square, Listowel, Co Kerry Tel: +353 (0)68 22212 Fax: +353 (0)68 22217 Email: info@seanchai-klcc.com Web: www.seanchai-klcc.com

This is a literary museum dedicated to five internationally known Kerry writers; Dr John B Keane, Dr Bryan MacMahon, Brendan Kennelly, Maurice Walsh and George Fitzmaurice. Kerry Film Centre Archival Library also is a cultural centre and illustrates the history of Listowel Writers Week.

Opening Times: Mar to Oct daily 10:00-18:00. Nov to Feb by appointment. Admission: Adult €4.00, Child/OAP/Student €2.00, Family (2 adults and 3 children)

Listowel Literary Museum

€10.00. Location: Located in town square. Map Ref: 21

Kerry County Museum

Ashe Memorial Hall, Denny Street, Tralee, Co Kerry Tel: +353 (0)66 712 7475/712 7777

Kerry County Museum, Tralee is Ireland's most visited regional museum. Located in the splendidly restored Ashe Memorial Hall in Tralee Town Centre it traces the history and archaeology of Kerry from earliest times. The Museum comprises four elements: Kerry in Colour - a widescreen audio-visual presentation on Kerry's spectacular scenery, its heritage sites and traditions. Permanent Museum Galleries - with the Treasures of Kerry divided into ten sections chronologically from the Stone Age to the Present Day. The majority of the artefacts on display are on loan from the National Museum of Ireland. There are special sections on Daniel O'Connell (1775-1847), called The Liberator, after whom O'Connell Street in Dublin is named, on Gaelic Football - Ireland's premier sporting passion, and a fascinating newsreel collection on life and political developments in Ireland from 1916-66. Geraldine Tralee Medieval Experience - a reconstruction of Tralee in 1451 when it was headquarters of the Munster Geraldines. Visitors sit in time cars and are transported back in time and experience a day in the life of an Irish Medieval town complete with sounds and smells. Commentaries are

provided in a choice of seven languages. Temporary Exhibition Area - that houses major international temporary exhibitions in conjunction with overseas institutions.

Opening Times: Daily 17 Mar to 21 Dec. Mar to Oct 09:30-17:30, Nov to Dec 11:30-16:30. Admission: Adult €8.00, Child €5.00, OAP/Student €6.00, Family €22.00. Location: In town centre.

Map Ref: 22

The Southwest

CO LIMERICK

The Hunt Museum

🖼 ♿ 🖊 💼 ❂

The Custom House, Rutland Street, Limerick   Tel: +353 (0)61 312833   Fax: +353 (0)61 312834   Email: info@huntmuseum.com   Web: www.ul.ie/~hunt

A magnificent collection of art and antiquity - donated to the 'people of Ireland' by John and Gertrude Hunt. Exhibited in an 18th century Custom House, with gift shop and a riverside restaurant.

Opening Times: 1 Jan to 28 Feb, 1 Mar to 31 Dec, Mon to Sat 10:00-17:00, Sun 14:00-17:00.
Admission: Jan to Feb, Adult €5.30, Child €2.50, Family €12.70. Mar to Dec, Adult €5.70, Child €2.70, Family €14.00.   Location: Two minute walk from Limerick Tourist Information Office.

Map Ref: 23

Limerick City Gallery of Art

🖼

Carnegie Building, Pery Square, Limerick   Tel: +353 (0)61 310633

The permanent collection consists of some 600 works in a wide variety of media and styles dating from the 18th century to contemporary practice, it is mostly Irish or Irish related in origin with exceptional examples of work by leading Irish artists of all periods. The permanent collection also houses the National Collection of Contemporary Drawing with a published catalogue and the Michael O'Connor Poster Collection, which consists of 3,800 works of international design.

Opening Times: Mon to Wed & Fri 10:00-18:00, Thu 10:00-19:00, Sat 10:00-13:00.
Admission: Free.   Location: One minute walk from train and bus station.   Map Ref: 23

Limerick Museum

♿ 🚂

Castle Lane, Nicholas Street, Limerick   Tel: +353 (0)61 417826   Fax: +353 (0)61 415266
Email: lwalsh@limerickcorp.ie   Web: www.limerickcorp.ie

Regional museum covering all aspects of the past of Limerick City and the region. Principal themes include archaeology, Limerick silver, Limerick lace, numismatics, printing, labour history, manufacturers, national independence movements, topographical paintings, prints, old photographs, postcards, etc.

Opening Times: Tue to Sat 10:00-13:00 14:15-17:00. Closed Sun, Mon and BH. Admission: Free.
Location: Limerick City, beside King John's Castle.
A Section of the Display Galleries   Map Ref: 23

The West & Northwest

CO CLARE

Bunratty Castle & Folk Park

🖼 ♿ 🖊 💼 ❂ 🚂

Bunratty, Co Clare   Tel: +353 (0)61 360788   Fax: +353 (0)61 361020
Email: horganj@shannondev.ie   Web: www.shannonheritagetrade.com

Bunratty Castle was built in 1425 by the McNamara family. During the 16th and 17th centuries it was an important stronghold of the O'Briens - Kings and later Earls of Thomond. The folk park contains typical 19th century rural and urban dwellings.

Opening Times: Jun to Aug 09:00-18:30, Sep to May 09:30-17:30. Location: 16km from Limerick City. 3km from Shannon Airport.   Map Ref: 24

Museums, Galleries, Historic Houses & Sites

Please let us know of any collections that are not listed in this guide that you feel should be listed. E-mail us on *editor@tomorrows.co.uk* or return the Report Form on page 448

Burren Centre

Kilfenora, Co Clare   Tel: +353 (0)65 708 8030   Fax: +353 (0)65 708 8102

'A walk through time' is a multi dimensional exhibition. Beautifully displayed artefacts, original works of art enthralling audio visual and interactive experiences together with dramatic life like reproductions of human activity all combine to provide insight into heritage of the Burren.

Opening Times: 10 Mar to Jun daily 10:00-17:00, Jun to Sep daily 09:30-18:00, Oct daily 10:00-17:00.   Admission: Adult €5.00, OAP €3.00, Student €3.00, Group €4.00.   Location: From Galway via Ballyvaughan and Lisdoonvarna. From Limerick via Ennis to Corofin or Ennistyon to Kilfenoro.   Map Ref: 25

Kilrush Heritage Centre

Town Hall, Kilrush, Co Clare   Tel: +353 (0)65 905 1047   Fax: +353 (0)65 905 2821   Email: icleary@clarecoco.ie   Web: www.westclare.com

This exhibition illustrates 'Kilrush in landlord times'. Learn about the importance of the towns port in the Napoleonic era, the impact of the 1847 famine and the Vandelur landlords.

Opening Times: May to Sep Mon to Sat 10:00-18:00, Sun 12:00-18:00. Oct to Apr Mon to Fri 11:00-16:00.

Admission: Adult €2.00, Child/OAP/Student €1.00.
Location: Town centre.

Kilrush Heritage Centre   Map Ref: 26

CO DONEGAL

Glebe House & Gallery

Church Hill, Co Donegal   Tel: +353 (0)74 37071

Regency house, 1828, set in woodland gardens, decorated with William Morris textiles, Islamic and Japanese art. Collection includes works by leading 20th century artists - Picasso, Kokoshka as well as Irish and Italian artists.

Opening Times: Mid May to end Sep Sat to Thu 11:00-18:30.   Admission: Adult €2.50, Child €1.20, OAP/Group €1.90, Family €6.30.   Map Ref: 27

Fr McDyers Folk Village Museum

Dooey, Glencolmcille, Co Donegal   Tel: +353 (0)73 30017   Fax: +353 (0)73 30334
Email: folkmus@indigo.ie   Web: www.infowing.ie/donegal/Ad/Fr.htm

The museum offers an excellent guided tour where you will get the chance to experience life as it was in the 1700s, 1800s and 1900s. The thatched cottages are exact replicas of those belonging to that era and are furnished accordingly. See how our ancestors lived, cooked, the beds they lay on, the tools they used, their means of lighting and heat etc.

Opening Times: Easter Sat to last Fri in Sep Mon to Sat 10:00-18:00, Sun 12:00-18:00. Admission: Admission charged. Location: Ten minute walk from village.
                                                                        Map Ref: 28

Donegal County Museum

High Road, Letterkenny, Co Donegal   Tel: +353 (0)74 24613   Fax: +353 (0)74 26522
Email: jmccarthy@donegalcoco.ie

The museum is housed in a stone building which was once part of Letterkenny Workhouse built in 1846. The museum houses and displays a fascinating range of artefacts covering all aspects of the history of County Donegal.

Opening Times: Mon to Fri 10:00-12:30 13:00-16:30, Sat 13:00-16:30.   Admission: Free.
Location: Signposted in Letterkenny, five minute walk from town centre.   Map Ref: 29

CO GALWAY

Athenry Medieval Museum

St Marys Heritage & Art Centre, Athenry, Co
Galway   Tel: +353 (0)91 844661
Email: info@athenryheritagetown.com
Web: www.athenryheritagetown.com

HERITAGE TOWNS
of Ireland

*A variety of interactive media - visual and audio model of Athenry.
See the Mace of Athenry - original artefacts. Special children's
programmes.*

Opening Times: Apr to Sep daily 10:00-18:00.   Admission: Adult
€2.00, Child/OAP/Student €1.50, Groups on request.

Athenry Medieval Museum   Map Ref: 30

CO MAYO

Irish Folklife

Turlough Park, Castlebar, Co Mayo

*Turlough Park is the only branch of the Museum outside the
capital. It tells the story of people in rural Ireland,
emphasising the continuity of traditions of lifestyles,
established for several hundred years and lasting well into
the 20th century.*

Opening Times: Tue to Sat 10:00-17:00, Sun 14:00-17:00.
Closed Mon.   Admission: Free.   Map Ref: 31

Westport Heritage Centre

The Quay, Clew Bay, Westport, Co Mayo
Tel: +353 (0)98 26852   Email: royce@anu.ie
Web: www.anu.ie/westport/

HERITAGE TOWNS
of Ireland

*A unique folk museum giving an insight to the history of Westport and
surrounding areas. Large collection of artefacts on display and
guided tours of the town.*

Opening Times: May to Aug daily 10:00-17:00.   Admission: Adult
€2.00, Child/OAP/Student €1.00, Group rate on request.
Location: On the Quay - Clew Bay. Ten minutes from town centre.

Westport Heritage Centre   Map Ref: 33

CO SLIGO

Sligo County Museum

Stephen Street, Sligo   Tel: +353 (0)71 47190   Fax: +353 (0)71 46798   Email: sligolib@iol.ie
Web: www.sligococo.ie

*There is a Yeats Collection and an accumulation of local artefacts. Yeats Collection comprises
photographs, prints, letters, drawings and medals awarded to W B Yeats as Nobel Prize for
Literature 1923.*

Opening Times: Oct to May Tue to Sat 14:00-16:00. Jun to Sep Tue to Sat 10:00-12:00 14:00-
16:00.   Admission: Free.   Location: Near town centre.   Map Ref: 34

The Midlands

CO CAVAN

Cavan County Museum

Virginia Road, Ballyjamesduff, Co Cavan   Tel: +353 (0)49 854 4070   Fax: +353 (0)49 854 4332   Email: ccmuseum@eircom.net   Web: www.cavanmuseum.ie

Cavan County Museum, a magnificent 19th century building, which is beautifully situated amid extensive grounds, houses the material culture of County Cavan and is an ideal starting point for a relaxing family day out.

Opening Times: Tue to Sat 10:00-17:00, also May to Oct Sun & BH 14:00-18:00.
Location: Five minute walk from town centre.   Map Ref: 35

CO MONAGHAN

Monaghan County Museum

1/2 Hill Street, Monaghan   Tel: +353 (0)47 82928   Fax: +353 (0)47 71189
Email: comuseum@monaghancoco.ie

The extensive and rapidly growing collections at Monaghan County Museum range from ancient Stone Age right up to modern times. A purpose built gallery houses temporary exhibitions.

Opening Times: Tue to Fri 10:00-13:00 14:00-17:00, Sat 11:00-13:00 14:00-17:00. Closed Sun & Mon. Admission: Free. Location: Town centre.   Map Ref: 36

CO OFFALY

Birr Castle Science Museum

Birr Castle, Birr, Co Offaly   Tel: +353 (0)509 20336   Fax: +353 (0)509 21583   Email: info@birrcastle.com   Web: www.birrcastle.com

HERITAGE TOWNS ⟶ of Ireland ⟵

Discover the largest telescope in the world constructed in the 1840s. Travel through the evolution of astronomy from 17th century with Gallileo, Newton and Hershell. Amazing collection of original artefacts, photographs, drawings and letters can be found in the galleries.

Opening Times: Daily 09:00-18:00.   Location: Near town centre.

Giant Telescope, Birr Castle Science Museum   Map Ref: 37

Tullamore Dew Whiskey Museum

Bury Street, Tullamore, Co Offaly   Tel: +353 (0)506 25015   Fax: +353 (0)506 25016   Email: tullamoredhc@eircom.net   www.tullamore-dew.org

HERITAGE TOWNS ⟶ of Ireland ⟵

The centre uses a combination of artefacts, story panels, recordings and slide shows, with a tasting of the world famous whiskey Tullamore Dew or Irish Mist liqueur.

Opening Times: May to Sep Mon to Sat 09:00-18:00, Sun 12:00-17:00. Oct to Apr Mon to Sat 10:00-17:00, Sun 12:00-17:00. Admission: Adult €3.50, Child €2.25, OAP/Student €2.75, Family €9.00, Group €3.00.
Location: Along Canalside in restored warehouse.

Tullamore Dew Whiskey Museum   Map Ref: 38

CO ROSCOMMON

National Irish Famine Museum

Strokestown, Co Roscommon
Tel: +353 (0)78 33013   Fax: +353 (0)78 33712   Email: info@strokestownpark.ie
Web: www.strokestownpark.ie

HERITAGE TOWNS ⟶ of Ireland ⟵

Famine museum uses original documents from the house estate. The history of the Irish famine is explained and draws parallels to the occurrence of famine today.
Opening Times: Apr to Oct daily 11:00-17:30.
Admission: Adult House/Museum/Gardens €9.00, House only/Museum only €3.50, Gardens only €4.50. OAP/ Student/Group discounts.. Location: In town on N5 main Dublin/Ballina road.   Map Ref: 39

ISLE OF MAN

Rushen Abbey

Ballasalla Tel: 01624 648000 Fax: 01624 648001
Email: enquiries@mnh.gov.im Web: www.gov.im/mnh

Rushen Abbey is the most substantial and important medieval religious site in the Isle of Man. Discover what life was like for the Cistercian community, walk through the remains of substantial medieval buildings and see where archaeology research has revealed traces of buildings below ground. This is a highlight of a 'Christian Heritage' route around the Island.

Opening Times: Easter to Oct daily 10:00-17:00.

Rushen Abbey, Ballasalla

Calf Sound

Calf Sound Tel: 01624 648000 Fax: 01624 648001 Email: enquiries@mnh.gov.im
Web: www.gov.im/mnh

Visitor centre sited and styled to address this unique setting of beautiful landscape, sea and the Calf. Information and audio visual presentations about history and wildlife in this area.

Opening Times: Due to open summer 2002. Admission: Free. Location: One and a half miles from Cregneash.

Castle Rushen

Castletown Tel: 01624 648000 Fax: 01624 648001
Email: enquiries@mnh.gov.im Web: www.gov.im/mnh

One of Britains best preserved 12th century medieval castles, Castle Rushen is a limestone fortress rising out of the heart of the old capital of the Island, Castletown. Once the fortress of the Kings and Lords of Mann, Rushen is brought alive with rich decorations, sounds and smells of a bygone era.

Opening Times: Easter to Oct daily 10:00-17:00.
Location: In the town centre.

Castle Rushen, Castletown

Nautical Museum

10 Bridge Street, Castletown Tel: 01624 648000 Fax: 01624 648001
Email: enquiries@mnh.gov.im Web: www.gov.im/mnh

Set at the mouth of Castletown harbour, this museum is home to an 18th century armed yacht. A replica sailmaker's loft, ship model and photographs bring alive Manx maritime life and trade in the days of sail.

Opening Times: Easter to Oct daily 10:00-17:00.

Old Grammar School

Castletown Tel: 01624 648000 Fax: 01624 648001 Email: enquiries@mnh.gov.im
Web: www.gov.im/mnh

The former capital's first church was built around 1200AD and was a school from 1570 to 1930. The main wing is the oldest roofed structure in the Island.

Opening Times: Easter to Oct daily 10:00-17:00. Admission: Free.

Old House of Keys

Parliament Square, Castletown   Tel: 01624 648000   Fax: 01624 648001
Email: enquiries@mnh.gov.im   Web: www.gov.im/mnh

Manx
National
Heritage

The history of the Old House of Keys building is one chapter in the long, and often turbulent, history of Manx politics which stretches back to the ninth and tenth centuries when the Viking Kings ruled the Isle of Man. It has been restored to its appearance in 1866 and provides an insight into the political life and times of the Island through interactive audio presentations.

Opening Times: Easter to Oct daily 10:00-17:00.
Location: Opposite Castle Rushen in the town centre.

Old House of Keys, Castletown

Manx Museum

Kingswood Grove, Douglas IM1 3LY   Tel: 01624 648000   Fax: 01624 648001
Email: enquiries@mnh.gov.im   Web: www.gov.im/mnh

Manx
National
Heritage

The natural point to begin your exploration of the Island and the fascinating 10,000 year old 'Story of Mann'. Displays of Manx archaeology, history, folk life and natural science. Also houses the National Art Gallery and the Island's national archive and reference library. In a matter of hours you'll discover all kinds of facts and intriguing features that bring the past to life.

Opening Times: Mon-Sat 10:00-17:00. Closed Xmas & New Year. Admission: Free.

Manx Museum, Douglas

Manx National Heritage

Manx Museum, Kingswood Grove, Douglas IM1 3LY   Tel: 01624 648000   Fax: 01624 648001
Email: enquiries@mnh.gov.im   Web: www.gov.im/mnh

Manx National Heritage is a major award winning and unique organisation in Europe. The portfolio of Heritage responsibilities include:- The National Museum Service, The National Monuments Service, The National Trust Service, The National Archives and The National Art Gallery.

The Great Laxey Wheel & Mines Trail

Laxey   Tel: 01624 648000   Fax: 01624 648001   Email: enquiries@mnh.gov.im
Web: www.gov.im/mnh

Manx
National
Heritage

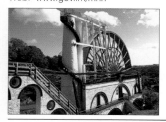

Built in 1854 and 22 metres in diameter, the Great Laxey Wheel - christened 'Lady Isabella' after the wife of the then Lieutenant Governor of the Isle of Man, is the largest working water wheel in Europe, and has remained one of the Island's most dramatic tourist attractions. It was designed to pump water from the lead and zinc mines and is an acknowledged masterpiece of Victorian engineering.

Opening Times: Easter to Oct daily 10:00-17:00.

The Great Laxey Wheel, Laxey

House of Manannan

East Quay, Peel   Tel: 01624 648000   Fax: 01624 648001
Email: enquiries@mnh.gov.im   Web: www.gov.im/mnh

Manx
National
Heritage

Using reconstructions, interactive displays, audio visual presentations and original material, the House of Manannan explores the Celtic, Viking and Maritime traditions of the Isle of Man. It brings to life themes which are both ancient and modern. Experience two hours of drama, colour and excitement by the harbour in the City of Peel.

Opening Times: Daily 10:00-17:00. Closed Xmas & New
House of Manannan, Peel   Year. Location: By Peel Harbour.

Isle of Man

Peel Castle

Peel   Tel: 01624 648000   Fax: 01624 648001   Email: enquiries@mnh.gov.im
Web: www.gov.im/mnh

In the 11th century the Castle was the ruling seat of the Norse Kingdom of Mann. Stoll through the remains of the Round Tower, 13th century Cathedral and site of the 90ft long giant's grave.

Opening Times: Easter to Oct daily 10:00-17:00.

Cregneash Village Folk Museum

Cregneash, Port St Mary   Tel: 01624 648000   Fax: 01624 648001
Email: enquiries@mnh.gov.im   Web: www.gov.im/mnh

Experience what life was really like in a Manx crofting village during the early 19th century. Stroll around this attractive village set in beautiful countryside, call into Harry Kelly's Cottage, The Turner's Shed, a Weaver's House and the Blacksmith's Smithy. Grazing nearby will be the Manx four horned Loghtan sheep along with other animals from the village farm. Home baked refreshments in the village café will complete your visit.

Opening Times: Easter to Oct daily 10:00-17:00.

Cregneash Village Folk Museum, Cregneash

The Grove Rural Life Museum

Andreas Road, Ramsey   Tel: 01624 648000   Fax: 01624 648001
Email: enquiries@mnh.gov.im   Web: www.gov.im/mnh

Victorian time capsule, a country house built as a summer retreat for a Liverpool shipping merchant. Rooms are filled with period and often original furnishings and outbuildings house 19th century vehicles and farming tools.

Opening Times: Easter to Oct daily 10:00-17:00.

Channel Islands

ALDERNEY

Alderney Society Museum

The Old School, Alderney GY9 3TG   Tel: 01481 823222   Fax: 01481 824979
Email: alderney.museum@virgin.net   Web: www.alderneymuseum.org

A museum of local interest. Special features - Iron Age pottery, Elizabethan shipwreck, German occupation and fortifications, 19th century harbour and fortifications.

Opening Times: Easter to end Oct Mon to Fri 10:00-12:00 14:00-16:00, Sat & Sun 10:00-12:00.
Admission: Adult £2.00, Child Free.   Location: High Street.

GUERNSEY

Guernsey Folk Museum

Saumarez Park, Castel GY5 7UJ   Tel / Fax: 01481 255384   Web: www.nationaltrust-gsy.org.gg

Social/agricultural history of Guernsey from Victorian period. Recreated rooms and displays set in old farm complex around central farm courtyard. Original and reproduction period costumes on display.

Opening Times: 25 Mar to 31 Oct daily 10:00-17:30.   Admission: Adult £3.00,
Child/Concession £1.00. Group rates available.   Location: Set in Saumarez Park, public park.
On regular bus route.

German Occupation Museum

Forest GY8 0BG   Tel: 01481 238205

Unique collection of German occupation items recreated street scene, restored fortifications audio-visual experience. Tearoom and garden.

Opening Times: Apr to Oct daily 10:00-16:30. Nov to Mar daily 10:00-13:00.   Admission: Adult £9.00, Child £1.50, Groups £2.50.   Location: 15 minutes from town centre.

414

Castle Cornet

St Peter Port Tel: 01481 721657 Fax: 01481 740719 Email: admin@museum.guernsey.net
Web: www.museum.guernsey.net

Maritime Museum, Royal Guernsey Militia Museum, 'The Story of Castle Cornet', 201 Squadron RAF Museum and a summer season of outdoor theatre.

Opening Times: Apr to Oct daily 10:00-17:00. Admission: Adult £5.00, Child Free, OAP £3.00.
Location: St Peter Port, five minute walk from bus station.

Guernsey Museum & Art Gallery

Candie, St Peter Port GY1 1UG Tel: 01481 726518 Fax: 01481 715177
Email: admin@museum.guernsey.net Web: www.museum.guernsey.net

Museum - 'The Story of Guernsey'. Art Gallery - exhibitions Feb to Dec.

Opening Times: Feb to Dec daily 10:00-17:00. Winter closing 16:00. Admission: Adult £3.00, Child Free, OAP £2.00. Location: Candie Gardens, four minute walk from centre of St Peter Port.

Fort Grey Shipwreck Museum

Rocquaine, St Peters GY7 9BY Tel: 01481 65036 Email: admin@museum.guernsey.net
Web: www.museum.guernsey.net

Objects recovered from the many wrecks off Guernsey's west coast, dating from 1777 to 1973.

Opening Times: Apr to Oct daily 10:00-17:00. Admission: Adult £2.00, Child Free, OAP £1.00.
Location: South west coast of Guernsey - Rocquaine Bay.

JERSEY

La Hougue Bie Museum

Grouville Tel: 01534 353823

A loft neolithic mound dominates this site that also includes an extensive geology and archaeology museum, neolithic encampment and memorial bunker to the slave workers of the occupation years.

Opening Times: Apr to Nov daily 10:00-17:00. Closed winter. Admission: Adult £4.70, Concession £3.95, Under 10s Free, 15% Group Discount available. Location: On major bus route from St Helier.

Noirmont Command Bunker

Noirmont Point, St Brelade Tel: 01534 482089

The bunker has been restored to a very high standard and provides a unique insight into the sheer scale and thoroughness of German military engineering.

Opening Times: Please contact for details. Admission: Free.

Elizabeth Castle

St Helier Tel: 01534 723971

A magnificent fortress that host a number of fine exhibitions detailing its past and those who have been stationed there. Noon-day gun fired daily.

Opening Times: Apr to Nov daily 10:00-18:00. Closed winter. Admission: Adult £4.70, Concession £3.95, Under 10s Free, 15% Group Discount available. Location: Located in the Bay of St Aubin.

Jersey Museum

The Weighbridge, St Helier JE2 3NF Tel: 01534 633300

The start point to any visit to Jersey. This award winning museum traces Jersey's past from the Ice Age to the present day. Also includes a fine art gallery and three floors of restored Victorian merchant's house.

Opening Times: Apr to Nov daily 10:00-17:00, winter 10:00-16:00. Admission: Adult £4.70, Concession £3.95, Under 10s Free, 15% Group Discount available. Location: Located next to bus station.

Maritime Museum & Occupation Tapestry Gallery

New North Quay, St Helier   Tel: 01534 811043

Interactive fun, discovery and art commissions this museum is ideal for the maritime enthusiast and family alike. The 12 panels of the tapestry movingly record the privation and suffering of occupied people.

Opening Times: Apr to Nov daily 10:00-17:00, Winter 10:00-16:00.   Admission: Adult £5.50, Concession £4.70, Under 10s Free, 15% Group Discount available.   Location: One minute walk from Jersey Tourism Visitor Centre.

Hamptonne Country Life Museum

Rue de la Patente, St Lawrence   Tel: 01534 863955

A unique collection of restored farm houses and buildings tracing 600 years of Jersey's rural past.

Opening Times: Apr to Nov daily 10:00-17:00. Closed winter.   Admission: Adult £4.70, Concession £3.95, Under 10s Free, 15% Group Discount available.   Location: Centre of Jersey.

Mont Orgueil Castle

Gorey, St Martin   Tel: 01534 853292

A mediaeval castle built in the 13th century, Mont Orgueil dominates the Royal Bay of Granville. It remains one of the most complete castles of its type and commmands some of Jersey's finest views.

Opening Times: Apr to Nov daily 10:00-18:00, winter times available on request.
Admission: Adult £4.70, Concession £3.95, Under 10s Free, 15% Group Discount available.
Location: South east coast of Jersey.

Channel Islands Military Museum

The Five Mile Road, St Ouen   Tel: 01534 723136

The islands finest collection of original military and civilian occupation items to be seen on the island, housed in a restored bunker which formed part of Hitler's Atlantic wall defence.

Opening Times: 25 Mar to 31 Oct daily 10:00-17:00.   Admission: Adult £3.00, Child £1.00.
Location: At the rear of Jersey Woollen Mills and across from Jersey Pearl.

Jersey Battle of the Flowers Museum

La Robeline, Mont des Corvees, St Ouen JE3 2ES   Tel: 01534 482408

The Battle of Flowers Museum presents the show of the year, so why not come on safari and see a wonderland of animals, meet the zebras, lions, and the 101 dalmations and lots of other interesting animals.

Opening Times: Daily 10:00-17:00.   Admission: Adult £3.00, Child £1.00, OAP £2.75.
Location: West of island, seven miles from town.

Jersey Motor Museum

St Peter's Village, St Peter JE3 7AG   Tel: 01534 482966

A fascinating and priceless collection of motoring history. Each year the museum adds to its collection of historic veteran and vintage cars including the Rolls Royce Phantom III used by General Montgomery. The museum also includes a fascinating insight on the Jersey Steam Railways housed in an actual railway carriage from the Jersey Railway and Tramways Company.

Opening Times: End Mar to end Oct daily 10:00-17:00.
Admission: Adult £3.00, Child £1.50, Group £2.00.
Location: Centre of St Peters Village, bus route 9.

1926 Austin Seven

Sir Francis Cook Gallery

Augres, Trinity   Tel: 01534 863333

Hosting Jersey artists, this venue holds regular exhibitions of their work.

Opening Times: Dependent on exhibitions, please phone for details.   Location: Main bus route to north of Jersey.

Classifications Index

see Classifications List on page 11

Anthropology

Horniman Museum & Gardens, London 200
Hunterian Museum, Glasgow. 328
Liverpool Museum, Liverpool 47
Marischal Museum, Aberdeen 341
Museum of Witchcraft, Boscastle 61
Peoples History Museum, Manchester 53
Pitt Rivers Museum, Oxford 235
St Andrews University, St Andrews 354
Scott Polar Research, Cambridge 34
University Museum, Cambridge 34

Archaeological

Abbey House Museum, Leeds 298
Abergavenny Museum, Abergavenny 366
Abingdon Museum, Abingdon 231
Alderney Society Museum, Alderney 414
Alexander Keiller Museum, Avebury 281
Andover Museum, Andover 118
Arbeia Roman Fort Museum, South Shields 226
Archaeology & History, Dublin 398
Armagh County Museum, Armagh 392
Armitt Library & Museum, Ambleside 70
Arran Heritage Museum, Isle of Arran 332
Art Gallery & Museum, Glasgow 325
Ashmolean Museum of Art, Oxford 233
Athelstan Museum, Malmesbury 283
Avoncroft Museum, Bromsgrove 134
Bangor Museum, Bangor 381
Basing House, Basingstoke 119
Bassetlaw Museum, Retford 166
Beamish, Chester-le-Street 218
Bedford Museum, Bedford 20
Bersham Ironworks, Wrexham 387
Bexhill Museum, Bexhill 259
Bexley Museum, Bexley 195
Birmingham Museum, Birmingham 271
Bishop's Palace Site, Witney 235
Blake Museum, Bridgwater 243
Bodmin Town Museum, Bodmin 61
Bowes Museum, Barnard Castle 216
Brading Roman Villa, Isle of Wight 122
Brander Museum, Huntly 350
Brecknock Museum, Brecon 377
Bridport Museum, Bridport 97
Bristol City Museum, Bristol 16
British Museum, London 177
Bromley Museum, Orpington 205
Buckinghamshire Museum, Aylesbury 20
Burren Centre, Kilfenora 409
Burton Court, Leominster 136
Bute Museum, Isle of Bute 361
Buxton Museum, Buxton 78
Calleva Museum, Silchester 29
Camborne Public Library, Camborne 61
Campbeltown Museum, Campbeltown 358
Canterbury Heritage, Canterbury 140
Canterbury Roman Museum, Canterbury 141
Cardinal ‡ Fiaich Centre, Cullyhanna 393
Carmarthenshire Museum, Carmarthen 368
Carnegie Museum, Inverurie 350
Castle Keep Museum, Newcastle upon Tyne 223
Castle Museum, Colchester 105
Cavan County Museum, Ballyjamesduff 411
Chart Gunpowder Mills, Faversham 144
Cheddar Showcaves & Gorge, Cheddar 243
Chelmsford Museum, Chelmsford 104
Chertsey Museum, Chertsey 253
Chesterholm Museum, Hexham 221

Chesters Fort & Museum, Hexham-on-Tyne 221
Chichester Museum, Chichester 261
City Museum & Art Gallery, Gloucester 112
Clackmannanshire Museum, Alloa 342
Corinium Museum, Cirencester 112
Cork Public Museum, Cork 406
Creswell Crags Museum, Worksop 166
Crofton Roman Villa, Orpington 205
Daventry Museum, Daventry 35
Dean Heritage Centre, Royal Forest of Dean 114
Derby Museum, Derby 79
Dewa Roman Experience, Chester 44
Doncaster Museum, Doncaster 290
Dorman Museum, Middlesbrough 222
Dorset County Museum, Dorchester 98
Dover Museum, Dover 143
Droitwich Heritage Centre, Droitwich Spa 134
Dublin's Viking Adventure, Dublin 399
Dumfries Museum & Camera, Dumfries 316
Dunbar Town House Museum, Dunbar 317
Durham University, Durham 219
Egypt Centre, Swansea 373
Elgin Museum, Elgin 348
Ely Museum, Ely 35
Epping Forest District, Waltham Abbey 108
Eyam Museum, Hope Valley 81
Fermanagh County Museum, Enniskillen 395
Fishbourne Roman Palace, Chichester 261
Folkestone Museum, Folkestone 144
Fordyce Joiners Workshop, Portsoy 353
Forge Mill Museum, Redditch 137
Fr McDyers Folk Village, Glencolmcille 409
Freud Museum, London 198
Gairloch Heritage Museum, Gairloch 359
Garlogie Mill Power House, Garlogie 350
Geevor Tin Mine, Penzance 65
Gillingham Museum, Gillingham 99
Gilstrap Heritage Centre, Newark-on-Trent 161
Glastonbury Abbey, Glastonbury 243
Glastonbury Lake Village, Glastonbury 243
Grantham Museum, Grantham 169
Greenwich Borough Museum, London 199
Greyfriars, Lincoln 169
Grosvenor Museum, Chester 44
Guildford Museum, Guildford 255
Guildhall Museum, Rochester 147
Haverfordwest Town Museum, Haverfordwest 369
Helston Folk Museum, Helston 63
Herbert Art Gallery, Coventry 272
Herne Bay Museum, Herne Bay 145
Hull & East Riding Museum, Hull 295
Hunterian Museum, Glasgow 328
Inverness Museum, Inverness 360
Ipswich Museum, Ipswich 249
Isle of Mull Museum, Isle of Mull 361
Isles of Scilly Museum, Isles of Scilly 63
Jorvik - The Viking City, York 309
Kendal Museum, Kendal 74
Kerry County Museum, Tralee 407
Kilmartin House Museum, Kilmartin 362
Kirkstall Abbey, Leeds 299
Kirriemuir Gateway Museum, Kirriemuir 351
Knaresborough Castle, Knaresborough 297
La Hougue Bie Museum, Grouville 415
Lancaster City Museum, Lancaster 153
Leamington Spa Museum, Leamington Spa 275
Letchworth Museum, Letchworth 25
Limerick Museum, Limerick 408
Littlehampton Museum, Littlehampton 265
Liverpool Museum, Liverpool 47

Classifications Index

Lowestoft Museum, Lowestoft 250
Ludlow Museum, Ludlow. 238
Lunt Roman Fort, Coventry 273
Luton Museum Art Gallery, Luton 25
McManus Galleries, Dundee 347
Maidstone Museum, Maidstone 145
Maison Dieu, Faversham 144
Malton Museum, Malton 300
Manchester Museum, Manchester 51
Manor House Art Gallery, Ilkley 296
Manx Museum, Douglas 413
Margam Country Park, Port Talbot 373
Marischal Museum, Aberdeen 341
Meffan, Forfar Museum, Forfar 349
Mill Green Museum & Mill, Hatfield 22
Millmount Museum & Tower, Drogheda 403
Minera Lead Mines, Wrexham 388
Moot Hall Museum, Aldeburgh 248
Moyses Hall Museum, Bury St Edmunds 249
Much Wenlock Museum, Much Wenlock 238
Museum Nan Eilean, Island of Benbecula. 361
Museum Nan Eilean, Isle of Lewis 361
Museum of Antiquities, Alnwick 216
Museum of Antiquities, Newcastle upon Tyne 224
Museum of Archaeology, Durham 219
Museum of Archaeology, Southampton 129
Museum of Barnstaple, Barnstaple 88
Museum of East Anglia, Stowmarket 251
Museum of Fulham Palace, London 202
Museum of Harlow, Harlow 106
Museum of Hartlepool, Hartlepool 220
Museum of Island History, Isle of Wight 124
Museum of Islay Life, Isle of Islay. 361
Museum of Reading, Reading 27
Museum of South Somerset, Yeovil. 246
Museum of the Iron Age, Andover 118
National Museum & Gallery, Cardiff 367
Neath Museum, Neath 372
Newark Museum, Newark-on-Trent. 162
Newport Museum, Newport 372
Newport Roman Villa, Isle of Wight 124
Normanton Church Museum, Oakham 164
Norris Museum, St Ives 38
North Ayrshire Museum, Saltcoats 337
North Berwick Museum, North Berwick 336
North Down Heritage, Bangor 393
North Somerset Museum, Weston-super-Mare 18
Northampton Museum, Northampton 37
Norton Priory Museum, Runcorn. 54
Norwich Castle Museum, Norwich 212
Old Merchants House, Great Yarmouth 210
Orkney Museum, Tankerness, Orkney 363
Otterton Mill Centre, Budleigh Salterton. 89
Oxfordshire Museum, Woodstock. 236
Oxfordshire Museums Store, Witney. 235
Peel Castle, Peel 414
Perth Museum, Perth 353
Peterborough Museum, Peterborough. 38
Plymouth City Museum, Plymouth. 93
Potteries Museum, Stoke-on-Trent. 85
Powell-Cotton Museum, Birchington. 140
Powysland Museum, Welshpool. 379
Priest's House Museum, Wimborne Minster 102
Priory Visitor Centre, Coventry 273
Radnorshire Museum, Llandrindod Wells 378
Red House Museum, Christchurch 98
Ribchester Roman Museum, Preston 156
Richmondshire Museum, Richmond. 301

Rockbourne Roman Villa, Fordingbridge 121
Roman Bath House, Lancaster 154
Roman Baths, Bath 15
Roman Legionary Museum, Caerleon. 366
Roman Theatre, St Albans 29
Rotunda Museum, Scarborough 302
Royal Albert Memorial, Exeter 90
Royal Museum, Edinburgh 323
Royal Pump Room Museum, Harrogate 293
Royston & District Museum, Royston. 28
Rugby Art Gallery, Rugby 276
Rushen Abbey, Ballasalla 412
Rutland County Museum, Oakham 165
Ryhope Engines Museum, Sunderland. 227
Saffron Walden Museum, Saffron Walden 106
St Andrews University, St Andrews. 354
Salisbury & South Wilts, Salisbury 283
Sandhaven Meal Mill, Fraserburgh. 350
Scolton Manor Museum, Haverfordwest 370
Segedunum Roman Fort, Wallsend 228
Segontium Roman Museum, Caernarfon 383
Sewerby Hall Museum, Bridlington. 289
Shaftesbury Abbey Museum, Shaftesbury 100
Shakespeare Birthplace, Stratford-upon-Avon. . . . 276
Sheffield City Museum, Sheffield 305
Shefton Museum of Greek, Newcastle upon Tyne . 225
Sherborne Museum, Sherborne 101
Shetland Museum, Shetland 364
Shipwreck Heritage Centre, Hastings. 264
Shrewsbury Museum, Shrewsbury 239
Somerset County Museum, Taunton 246
Southend Central Museum, Southend-on-Sea. . . . 107
Stafford Castle, Stafford 85
Stamford Museum, Stamford 172
Stranraer Museum, Stranraer. 339
Strathnaver Museum, Bettyhill 358
Sunderland Museum, Sunderland 228
Swalcliffe Barn, Banbury. 232
Swansea Museum, Swansea. 374
Swindon Museum, Swindon. 285
Tenby Museum, Tenby 375
Threlkeld Quarry Museum, Keswick 75
Thurrock Museum, Grays 105
Tipperary S R Museum, Clonmel 404
Tolbooth Art Centre, Kirkcudbright 333
Torquay Museum, Torquay 94
Torre Abbey House, Torquay 95
Torrington Museum, Great Torrington 91
Totnes Elizabethan Museum, Totnes 95
Tunbridge Wells Museum, Royal Tunbridge Wells . 147
Tutankhamun Exhibition, Dorchester 99
University Museum, Cambridge 34
Vale & Downland Museum, Wantage 235
Ware Museum, Ware 30
Warwickshire Museum, Warwick 278
Wells Museum, Wells 246
Welwyn Roman Baths, Welwyn. 30
West Berkshire Museum, Newbury 26
Whitby Museum, Whitby 308
Willis Museum, Basingstoke 119
Wiltshire Heritage Museum, Devizes 282
Wisbech & Fenland Museum, Wisbech 39
Woodhorn Colliery Museum, Ashington 216
Worcestershire Museum, Worcester 138
Worthing Museum, Worthing 268
Wrexham County Museum, Wrexham. 388
Wymondham Heritage Museum, Wymondham . . . 214
York Minster Undercroft, York. 311
Yorkshire Museum, York 311

Classifications Index

Art, Crafts & Textiles

Abingdon Museum, Abingdon 231
Allhallows Museum, Honiton 91
American Museum, Bath 13
Andrew Carnegie Museum, Dunfermline 347
Arbroath Museum, Arbroath 343
Armagh County Museum, Armagh 392
Armitt Library & Museum, Ambleside 70
Ascott House, Leighton Buzzard 24
Astley Hall Museum, Chorley 152
Aston Hall, Birmingham 270
Bangor Museum, Bangor 381
Bankfield Museum, Halifax 291
Bantry House, Bantry 405
Barbican Art Gallery, London 176
Basildon Park, Reading 27
Belton House, Grantham 169
Beningbrough Hall, York 308
Beverley Art Gallery, Beverley 287
Bilston Craft Gallery, Bilston 270
Birmingham Museum, Birmingham 271
Blackburn Museum, Blackburn 151
Blackwell - Arts & Crafts, Bowness-on-Windermere 71
Blair Castle, Blair Atholl 345
Blenheim Palace, Woodstock 236
Bodelwyddan Castle, St Asaph 387
Bodmin Town Museum, Bodmin 61
Bondgate Gallery, Alnwick 216
Borough Museum, Newcastle-under-Lyme 83
Braintree District Museum, Braintree 104
Brantwood, Coniston 73
Brecknock Museum, Brecon 377
Bridport Museum, Bridport 97
Brighton Museum, Brighton 260
Buckinghamshire Museum, Aylesbury 20
Buckland Abbey, Yelverton 95
Building of Bath Museum, Bath 13
Burghley House, Stamford 172
Bygones Museum, Banbury 231
Carmarthenshire Museum, Carmarthen 368
Castle Douglas Gallery, Castle Douglas 315
Castle Museum, York 308
Cathcartston Visitor, Dalmellington 315
Cavan County Museum, Ballyjamesduff 411
Cawdor Castle, Nairn 362
Cecil Higgins Art Gallery, Bedford 21
Central Art Gallery, Ashton-under-Lyne 41
Cheddleton Flint Mill, Leek 81
Cheltenham Art Gallery, Cheltenham 111
Chertsey Museum, Chertsey 253
Clackmannanshire Museum, Alloa 342
Colne Valley Museum, Huddersfield 294
Colour Museum, Bradford 289
Conservation Centre, Liverpool 46
Cowper Memorial Museum, Olney 26
Crawford Arts Centre, St Andrews 354
Dalmeny House, South Queensferry 338
Decorative Arts & History, Dublin 399
Derby Industrial Museum, Derby 79
Design Museum, London 178
Devon Guild of Craftsmen, Bovey Tracey 88
Ditchling Museum, Ditchling 262
Doddington Hall, Lincoln 169
Dorset County Museum, Dorchester 98
East Riddlesden Hall, Keighley 297
Edwin Young Gallery, Salisbury 283
Elgin Museum, Elgin 348
Elstow Moot Hall, Bedford 21
Fan Museum, London 198

Ford Green Hall, Stoke-on-Trent 85
Fordyce Joiners Workshop, Portsoy 353
Forge Museum, Much Hadham 26
Gairloch Heritage Museum, Gairloch 359
Garlogie Mill Power House, Garlogie 350
Gawthorpe Hall, Burnley 151
Geffrye Museum, London 179
Gilbert Collection, London 180
Gladstone Pottery Museum, Stoke-on-Trent 85
Glandford Shell Museum, Holt 210
Gloucester Folk Museum, Gloucester 112
Gower Heritage Centre, Swansea 374
Grundy Art Gallery, Blackpool 151
Guildford Museum, Guildford 255
Guildhall Gallery, Winchester 131
Ham House, London 199
Hanbury Hall, Droitwich Spa 135
Harestanes Countryside, Jedburgh 332
Harewood House, Leeds 298
Harley Gallery, Worksop 166
Harris Museum, Preston 155
Hill House, Helensburgh 360
Hogarth's House, London 200
Holburne Museum of Art, Bath 14
Holmshore Textile Museum, Rawtenstall 156
Hove Museum & Art Gallery, Hove 264
Hunterian Art Gallery, Glasgow 328
Irish Linen Centre, Lisburn 392
Jewish Museum - Camden, London 182
John Creasey Museum, Salisbury 283
Judges Lodgings Museum, Lancaster 153
Kirkcaldy Museum, Kirkcaldy 351
Lace Market Centre, Nottingham 164
Lauriston Castle, Edinburgh 320
Leamington Spa Museum, Leamington Spa 275
Little Holland House, Carshalton 253
Lloyd George Museum, Criccieth 383
Longdale Craft Centre, Ravenshead 165
Low Parks Museums, Hamilton 331
Lowestoft Maritime Museum, Lowestoft 250
Lowestoft Museum, Lowestoft 250
McManus Galleries, Dundee 347
Macclesfield Silk Museum, Macclesfield 49
Millennium Galleries, Sheffield 304
Mission Gallery, Swansea 374
Museum of Costume, Nottingham 164
Museum of Fulham Palace, London 202
Museum of Modern Art, Oxford 234
Museum of Reading, Reading 27
Museum of South Somerset, Yeovil 246
Museum of St Albans, St Albans 28
Newtown Textile Museum, Newtown 378
Normanby Hall, Scunthorpe 170
Normanby Park Farming, Scunthorpe 170
Norris Museum, St Ives 38
North Cornwall Museum, Camelford 62
Oxfordshire Museum, Woodstock 236
Oxfordshire Museums Store, Witney 235
Paradise Mill, Macclesfield 49
Peacock Heritage Centre, Chesterfield 79
Peoples History Museum, Manchester 53
Peter Scott Gallery, Lancaster 153
Pickfords House Museum, Derby 80
Piece Hall Art Gallery, Halifax 292
Pitt Rivers Museum, Oxford 235
Pittencrieff House Museum, Dunfermline 348
Pontypool Heritage Centre, Pontypool 373
Quarry Bank Mill, Wilmslow 59
Red House Museum, Christchurch 98
Richmondshire Museum, Richmond 301

Classifications Index

Royal Cornwall Museum, Truro 68
Rugby Art Gallery, Rugby 276
Ruskin Museum, Coniston 73
St Andrews University, St Andrews 354
Salford Museum, Salford 55
Sally Lunns House, Bath 15
Saltram House, Plymouth 93
Sanquhar Tolbooth Museum, Sanquhar 338
School of Art Gallery, Aberystwyth 377
School of Art Gallery, Aberystwyth 377
Shaftesbury Town Museum, Shaftesbury 100
Shakespeare Birthplace, Stratford-upon-Avon. . . . 276
Shambellie House Museum, Dumfries 317
Shetland Museum, Shetland 364
Shipley Art Gallery, Gateshead 220
Shire Hall Gallery, Stafford 84
Shrewsbury Museum, Shrewsbury 239
Shugborough Estate, Stafford. 84
Stained Glass Museum, Ely 36
Stewartry Museum, Kirkcudbright 333
Sue Ryder Foundation, Sudbury 251
Sunderland Museum, Sunderland 228
Sutton Park, York 310
Swansea Museum, Swansea 374
Totnes Elizabethan Museum, Totnes 95
Turton Tower, Turton. 57
Vennel Gallery, Irvine 332
Victoria Albert Museum, London 192
Walker, Liverpool. 48
West Park Museum, Macclesfield 49
Whitby Museum, Whitby 308
Whitchurch Silk Mill, Whitchurch 130
Whitworth Art Gallery, Manchester 53
Wightwick Manor, Wolverhampton 279
William Morris Gallery, London. 204
Wisbech & Fenland Museum, Wisbech 39
Woodhorn Colliery Museum, Ashington 216
Worthing Museum, Worthing 268
Wymondham Heritage Museum, Wymondham . . . 214

China & Glass

Allen Gallery, Alton 118
Ascott House, Leighton Buzzard. 24
Banchory Museum, Banchory 344
Bassetlaw Museum, Retford 166
Baysgarth House Museum, Barton-upon-Humber . 168
Birmingham Museum, Birmingham 271
Blackburn Museum, Blackburn 151
Blair Castle, Blair Atholl. 345
Bowood House & Gardens, Calne 281
Brighton Museum, Brighton 260
Bristol City Museum, Bristol 16
British Museum, London 177
Broadfield House Museum, Kingswinford 274
Brodick Castle Gardens, Isle of Arran 332
Burghley House, Stamford. 172
Burton Art Gallery, Bideford 88
Bury Art Gallery & Museum, Bury 43
Cannon Hall Museum, Barnsley. 287
Castle Museum & Gallery, Nottingham 163
Cecil Higgins Art Gallery, Bedford 21
Chelmsford Museum, Chelmsford 104
Cheltenham Art Gallery, Cheltenham 111
Clackmannanshire Museum, Alloa 342
Cleveland Crafts Centre, Middlesbrough 222
Clifton Park Museum, Rotherham 301
Coalport China Museum, Telford 240
Conservation Centre, Liverpool. 46

Coughton Court, Alcester 270
Cyfarthfa Castle Museum, Merthyr Tydfil. 371
Dalmeny House, South Queensferry. 338
Dartington Crystal, Great Torrington 91
Decorative Arts & History, Dublin 399
Derby Museum, Derby 79
Devon Guild of Craftsmen, Bovey Tracey 88
Doddington Hall, Lincoln. 169
Dorman Museum, Middlesbrough 222
Fenton House, London 198
Firle Place, Firle 263
Ford Green Hall, Stoke-on-Trent 85
Georgian House, Edinburgh 320
Gilbert Collection, London. 180
Goss & Crested China, Waterlooville 130
Grand Lodge of Scotland, Edinburgh. 320
Guildhall Gallery, Winchester 131
Hanbury Hall, Droitwich Spa 135
Harewood House, Leeds. 298
Hill House, Helensburgh 360
Holburne Museum of Art, Bath 14
Jackfield Tile Museum, Telford. 241
Judges Lodgings Museum, Lancaster 153
Leamington Spa Museum, Leamington Spa 275
Library of Freemasonry, London. 183
Lotherton Hall, Leeds 299
Lowestoft Museum, Lowestoft 250
Mansfield Museum, Mansfield 160
Museum of Worcester, Worcester. 137
Nantgarw China Works, Nantgarw 371
Norwich Castle Museum, Norwich 212
Old Guildhall Museum, Looe 64
Parc Howard Museum, Llanelli. 370
Percival David Foundation, London 186
Peter Scott Gallery, Lancaster 153
Petworth House, Petworth 266
Pitt Rivers Museum, Oxford 235
Pollok House, Glasgow 329
Potteries Museum, Stoke-on-Trent. 85
Powderham Castle, Exeter. 90
Powell-Cotton Museum, Birchington 140
Ragley Hall, Alcester 270
Royal Cornwall Museum, Truro 68
Royal Crown Derby Visitor, Derby 80
Royston & District Museum, Royston. 28
Rye Castle Museum, Rye 267
Saffron Walden Museum, Saffron Walden 106
Salisbury & South Wilts, Salisbury 283
Saltram House, Plymouth 93
School of Art Gallery, Aberystwyth 377
Shakespeare Birthplace, Stratford-upon-Avon. . . . 276
Sheffield City Museum, Sheffield 305
Shipley Art Gallery, Gateshead 220
Shrewsbury Museum, Shrewsbury 239
Somerset County Museum, Taunton 246
Spode Museum, Stoke-on-Trent 86
Stained Glass Museum, Ely 36
Stamford Museum, Stamford 172
Sutton Park, York 310
Swansea Museum, Swansea 374
Torre Abbey House, Torquay 95
Towneley Hall Art Gallery, Burnley 152
Treasures House, York 310
Treasures of the Earth, Fort William 359
Victoria Art Gallery, Bath 15
Victoria Albert Museum, London 192
Woburn Abbey, Woburn 31
World of Glass, St Helens 55
Worthing Museum, Worthing 268

Classifications Index

Communications

Bath Postal Museum, Bath 13
Bletchley Park, Milton Keynes 25
Bognor Regis Museum, Bognor Regis 259
Ilfracombe Museum, Ilfracombe 92
The Museum of Science, Manchester 52
Orkney Wireless Museum, Orkney 363
Prittlewell Priory, Southend-on-Sea 107
Scapa Flow Visitor Centre, Orkney 363

Egyptian

Ashmolean Museum of Art, Oxford 233
Bagshaw Museum, Batley 287
Bexhill Museum, Bexhill 259
Blackburn Museum, Blackburn 151
Bolton Museum, Bolton 43
Bristol City Museum, Bristol 16
British Museum, London 177
Burrell Collection, Glasgow 326
Cyfarthfa Castle Museum, Merthyr Tydfil 371
Egypt Centre, Swansea 373
Fitzwilliam Museum, Cambridge 33
Hands on History, Hull 295
Hunterian Museum, Glasgow 328
Liverpool Museum, Liverpool 47
Manchester Museum, Manchester 51
Marischal Museum, Aberdeen 341
New Walk Museum & Gallery, Leicester 159
Saffron Walden Museum, Saffron Walden 106
Sainsbury Centre, Norwich 213
Swansea Museum, Swansea 374
Tutankhamun Exhibition, Dorchester 99
Warrington Museum, Warrington 58
Wisbech & Fenland Museum, Wisbech 39

Fashion

Abington Museum, Northampton 36
Allhallows Museum, Honiton 91
Arlington Court, Barnstaple 88
Athelstan Museum, Malmesbury 283
Banbury Museum, Banbury 231
Bangor Museum, Bangor 381
Blair Castle, Blair Atholl 345
Bowood House & Gardens, Calne 281
Bridport Museum, Bridport 97
Brighton Museum, Brighton 260
British Empire Museum, Bristol 17
Burton Court, Leominster 136
Castle Museum, York 308
Cavan County Museum, Ballyjamesduff 411
Chertsey Museum, Chertsey 253
Chesterholm Museum, Hexham 221
Clackmannanshire Museum, Alloa 342
Claydon House, Buckingham 21
Cyfarthfa Castle Museum, Merthyr Tydfil 371
Dalgarven Mill Museum, Kilwinning 333
Decorative Arts & History, Dublin 399
Design Museum, London 178
Dumfries Museum & Camera, Dumfries 316
Flambards, Helston 63
Gallery of Costume, Manchester 49
Gawthorpe Hall, Burnley 151
Harborough Museum, Market Harborough 161
Hat Works, Stockport 56
Hitchin Museum, Hitchin 23
Kensington Palace, London 182
Killerton House, Exeter 90
Leominster Folk Museum, Leominster 136
Lotherton Hall, Leeds 299

Manor House Museum, Bury St Edmunds 248
Museum of Costume, Bath 14
Museum of Costume, Nottingham 164
Museum of the Manchesters, Ashton-under-Lyne . . 41
Normanby Hall, Scunthorpe 170
North Ayrshire Museum, Saltcoats 337
Northampton Museum, Northampton 37
Pickfords House Museum, Derby 80
Potteries Museum, Stoke-on-Trent 85
Provost Skene's House, Aberdeen 341
Renishaw Hall Museum, Sheffield 304
Rothe House Museum, Kilkenny 403
Rye Castle Museum, Rye 267
Saffron Walden Museum, Saffron Walden 106
Salisbury & South Wilts, Salisbury 283
Scolton Manor Museum, Haverfordwest 370
Shambellie House Museum, Dumfries 317
Sherborne Museum, Sherborne 101
Shoe Museum, Street 245
Shrewsbury Museum, Shrewsbury 239
Tain & District Museum, Tain 364
Totnes Costume Museum, Totnes 95
Totnes Elizabethan Museum, Totnes 95
Tunbridge Wells Museum, Royal Tunbridge Wells . 147
Victoria Albert Museum, London 192
Vina Cooke Museum, Newark-on-Trent 162
West Berkshire Museum, Newbury 26
Worcestershire Museum, Worcester 138
Worthing Museum, Worthing 268

Geology

Andover Museum, Andover 118
Armitt Library & Museum, Ambleside 70
Arran Heritage Museum, Isle of Arran 332
Art Gallery & Museum, Glasgow 325
Bexhill Museum, Bexhill 259
Bexley Museum, Bexley 195
Bodmin Town Museum, Bodmin 61
Bolton Museum, Bolton 43
Brantwood, Coniston 73
Bridport Museum, Bridport 97
Bristol City Museum, Bristol 16
Buxton Museum, Buxton 78
Camborne School of Mines, Redruth 66
Campbeltown Museum, Campbeltown 358
Chelmsford Museum, Chelmsford 104
City Museum & Art Gallery, Gloucester 112
Clackmannanshire Museum, Alloa 342
Cliffe Castle, Keighley 297
Cork Public Museum, Cork 406
Creetown Gem Rock Museum, Newton Stewart . . 336
Dinosaur Museum, Dorchester 98
Dorset County Museum, Dorchester 98
Dudley Museum & Art, Dudley 274
Eyam Museum, Hope Valley 81
Florence Mine Heritage, Egremont 73
Gairloch Heritage Museum, Gairloch 359
Gillingham Museum, Gillingham 99
Gosport Museum, Gosport 121
Helston Folk Museum, Helston 63
Hugh Millers Cottage, Cromarty 358
Hull & East Riding Museum, Hull 295
Hunterian Museum, Glasgow 328
Ipswich Museum, Ipswich 249
Isle of Mull Museum, Isle of Mull 361
Keswick Museum, Keswick 75
Ludlow Museum, Ludlow 238
Lyme Regis Philpot Museum, Lyme Regis 99
Manchester Museum, Manchester 51
Millmount Museum & Tower, Drogheda 403

Classifications Index

Much Wenlock Museum, Much Wenlock. 238
Museum of Barnstaple, Barnstaple 88
National Museum & Gallery, Cardiff 367
Natural History Centre, Burnley 151
North Lincolnshire Museum, Scunthorpe 171
Peterborough Museum, Peterborough. 38
Radstock Museum, Radstock 18
Red House Museum, Christchurch 98
Richmondshire Museum, Richmond 301
Rotunda Museum, Scarborough 302
Royal Albert Memorial, Exeter 90
Ruskin Museum, Coniston 73
St Andrews University, St Andrews. 354
Sedgwick Museum, Cambridge 34
Somerset County Museum, Taunton 246
Sunderland Museum, Sunderland 228
Threlkeld Quarry Museum, Keswick 75
Torquay Museum, Torquay 94
Ulster Museum, Belfast 391
Warwickshire Museum, Warwick 278
Wiltshire Heritage Museum, Devizes 282
Wisbech & Fenland Museum, Wisbech 39
Wood End Museum, Scarborough 302

Health & Medicine

Alexander Fleming, London. 175
Almond Valley Heritage, Livingston 335
Army Medical Services, Aldershot 117
Hunter House, East Kilbride 318
Jenner Museum, Berkeley 111
Leamington Spa Museum, Leamington Spa 275
Museum of Liverpool Life, Liverpool 47
Museum of St Barts Hosptl, London 184
Royal College of Surgeons, London. 184
Old Operating Theatre, London 186
Royal London Hospital, London 188
St Andrews University, St Andrews. 354
St John's Gate, London. 188
Sir Jules Thorn Exhibit, Edinburgh 324
Thackray Museum, Leeds 300
Veterinary Museum, London 192

Horticultural

Arlington Court, Barnstaple 88
Ashton Court Visitor, Bristol 16
Bicton Park, Budleigh Salterton 89
Blenheim Palace, Woodstock 236
Buckland Abbey, Yelverton. 95
Calderglen Country Park, East Kilbride. 318
Callendar House, Falkirk 325
Chelsea Physic Garden, London 177
Eden Project, St Austell 67
Fenton House, London 198
Geffrye Museum, London 179
Glasgow Botanic Gardens, Glasgow 327
Ham House, London. 199
Hampton Court Palace, East Molesey 196
Harlow Carr Museum, Harrogate 292
Jersey Battle of Flowers, St Ouen 416
Loseley Park, Guildford. 255
Museum No 1, Richmond 205
Museum of Fulham Palace, London 202
Museum of Garden History, London 183
Oxfordshire Museum, Woodstock. 236
Priest House, West Hoathly 268
Renishaw Hall Museum, Sheffield 304
Royal Glos, Berks & Wilts, Salisbury 283
Upton House, Banbury 232
Wightwick Manor, Wolverhampton 279

Jewellery

Bowood House & Gardens, Calne 281
Brighton Museum, Brighton 260
Cheltenham Art Gallery, Cheltenham 111
Chesterholm Museum, Hexham 221
Cleveland Crafts Centre, Middlesbrough 222
Gilbert Collection, London. 180
Grundy Art Gallery, Blackpool 151
Hunt Museum, Limerick 408
Library of Freemasonry, London. 183
Shipley Art Gallery, Gateshead 220
Shire Hall Gallery, Stafford 84
Victoria Art Gallery, Bath 15
Victoria Albert Museum, London 192
Worthing Museum, Worthing 268

Literature & Libraries

Armitt Library & Museum, Ambleside 70
Barrie's Birthplace, Kirriemuir 351
Beatrix Potter Gallery, Ambleside 70
Bellaghy Bawn, Bellaghy. 391
Bolton Library, Cashel. 404
Booth Museum, Brighton 259
British Library, London 176
British Sporting Trust, Newmarket 250
Brontä Parsonage Museum, Keighley. 296
Building of Bath Museum, Bath 13
Burns Cottage & Museum, Ayr. 313
Burns House, Dumfries 316
Chester Beatty Library, Dublin 398
Commonwealth Institute, London 178
Coughton Court, Alcester 270
Cowper Memorial Museum, Olney 26
Daphne Du Maurier's, Launceston 64
Dickens House Museum, Broadstairs 140
Dickens House Museum, London 179
Dorset County Museum, Dorchester 98
Dove Cottage, Grasmere 73
Dr Johnsons House, London 179
Dublin Writers Museum, Dublin 399
Elstow Moot Hall, Bedford 21
Felbrigg Hall, Cromer 208
Grand Lodge of Scotland, Edinburgh. 320
Hagley Hall, Hagley 135
James Hogg Exhibition, Selkirk 338
James Joyce Museum, Dublin. 400
Jane Austen's House, Alton 118
Jerome K Jerome, Walsall 277
John Buchan Centre, Biggar 314
John Bunyan Museum, Bedford 21
John Rylands Library, Manchester 50
Kells Heritage Centre, Kells. 403
Keswick Museum, Keswick 75
Listowel Literary Museum, Listowel 407
Liverpool Central Library, Liverpool. 46
Lloyd George Museum, Criccieth. 383
Lyme Regis Philpot Museum, Lyme Regis 99
Manx Museum, Douglas 413
Mappa Mundi, Hereford 136
Milton's Cottage, Chalfont St Giles 22
Mirehouse, Keswick. 75
Museum of Harlow, Harlow 106
Museum of Lead Mining, Wanlockhead 339
National Maritime Museum, Falmouth 62
Robert Burns Centre, Dumfries 317
Ruskin Library, Lancaster 154
Shandy Hall, York 310
Shaw Birthplace, Dublin 402
Sligo County Museum, Sligo 410

Classifications Index

Somerset Cricket Museum, Taunton 246
Trinity College Library, Dublin 402
Wiltshire Heritage Museum, Devizes 282

Maritime

Aberdeen Maritime Museum, Aberdeen 341
Alderney Society Museum, Alderney 414
Arbroath Museum, Arbroath 343
Arbuthnot Museum, Peterhead 353
Bembridge Maritime Museum, Isle of Wight 122
Blackpool Lifeboat, Blackpool 151
Blake Museum, Bridgwater 243
Bod of Gremista, Shetland 363
Braunton Museum, Braunton 88
Brighton Fishing Museum, Brighton 259
Brixham Heritage Museum, Brixham 89
Buckie Drifter Maritime, Buckie 345
Bucklers Hard Village, Beaulieu 120
Burton Court, Leominster 136
Caernarfon Maritime, Caernarfon 382
Captain Cook Birthplace, Middlesbrough 222
Captain Cook Museum, Whitby 307
Castle Cornet, St Peter Port 415
Chepstow Museum, Chepstow 369
Clydebuilt, Glasgow 326
Cobh The Queenstown Story, Cobh 406
Cowes Maritime Museum, Isle of Wight 123
Cromer Museum, Cromer 208
Dartmouth Museum, Dartmouth 90
Decorative Arts & History, Dublin 399
Denny Ship Model, Dumbarton 316
Dock Museum, Barrow-in-Furness 70
Fishermans Museum, Hastings 264
Fleetwood Museum, Fleetwood 152
Fort Grey Shipwreck, St Peters 415
Gairloch Heritage Museum, Gairloch 359
Golden Hind Museum Ship, Brixham 89
HMS Belfast, London 181
HMS Trincomalee Trust, Hartlepool 220
HMS Victory, Portsmouth 126
HMS Warrior 1860, Portsmouth 127
Harbour Museum, Derry 395
Harwich Maritime Museum, Harwich 106
Helston Folk Museum, Helston 63
Historic Dockyard, Chatham 142
Holyhead Maritime Museum, Holyhead 383
House of Manannan, Peel 413
Inveraray Maritime Museum, Inveraray 360
Isle of Mull Museum, Isle of Mull 361
Isles of Scilly Museum, Isles of Scilly 63
Lancaster Maritime Museum, Lancaster 153
Littlehampton Museum, Littlehampton 265
Maritime Museum, Hull 295
Maritime Museum, St Helier 416
Maritime Museum, Great Yarmouth 210
Mary Rose Museum, Portsmouth 127
Merseyside Maritime, Liverpool 47
Milford Haven Maritime, Milford Haven 371
Montrose Museum, Montrose 352
Museum of Hartlepool, Hartlepool 220
Museum of Islay Life, Isle of Islay 361
Museum of Submarine, Penzance 65
Museum of the RNLI, Eastbourne 262
Nairn Museum, Nairn 363
National Maritime Museum, Falmouth 62
National Maritime Museum, London 202
Nautical Museum, Castletown 412
Newcastle Discovery, Newcastle upon Tyne 224
North Ayrshire Museum, Saltcoats 337
Old Guildhall Museum, Looe 64

Pendeen Lighthouse, Penzance 65
Peterhead Maritime Centre, Peterhead 353
Pilchard Works, Penzance 66
Porthcawl Museum, Porthcawl 373
Porthmadog Maritime, Porthmadog 386
RNLI Henry Blogg Lifeboat, Cromer 208
RNLI Grace Darling Museum, Bamburgh 216
RNLI Whitby Lifeboat, Whitby 307
Rhyl Library, Museum, Rhyl 387
Robertson Museum, Millport 335
Royal Marines Museum, Portsmouth 127
Royal National Lifeboat, Chatham 142
Royal Navy Submarine, Gosport 122
Royal Research Ship, Dundee 347
SS Great Britain, Bristol 17
St Marys Lighthouse, Whitley Bay 229
Scapa Flow Visitor Centre, Orkney 363
Scott Polar Research, Cambridge 34
Scottish Fisheries Museum, Anstruther 343
Scottish Maritime Museum, Irvine 331
Shetland Museum, Shetland 364
Shipwreck Heritage Centre, Hastings 264
Southampton Maritime, Southampton 129
Stromness Museum, Orkney 363
Swansea Maritime Museum, Swansea 374
Tenby Museum, Tenby 375
Topsham Museum, Exeter 91
Trinity House, Penzance 66
Ty Gwyn, Ty Crwn Barmouth, Barmouth 382
Watchet Market House, Watchet 246
Weymouth Museum, Weymouth 102
Whitstable Museum, Whitstable 149
Williamson Art Gallery, Birkenhead 42
Withernsea Lighthouse, Withernsea 308
Youghal Heritage Centre, Youghal 407
Zetland Lifeboat Museum, Redcar 225

Military & Defence

100th Bomb Group Memorial, Diss 209
Abington Museum, Northampton 36
Airborne Forces Museum, Aldershot 117
Alderney Society Museum, Alderney 414
Aldershot Military Museum, Aldershot 117
Amherst Heritage Park, Chatham 141
Argyll & Sutherland, Stirling 355
Armagh County Museum, Armagh 392
Army Medical Services, Aldershot 117
Army Physical Training, Aldershot 117
Battle of Britain Centre, Coningsby 168
Black Watch Museum, Perth 352
Borough Museum, Newcastle-under-Lyme 83
Broughty Castle Museum, Dundee 346
Cabinet War Rooms, London 177
Cannon Hall Museum, Barnsley 287
Canterbury Royal Museum, Canterbury 141
Canterbury West Gate, Canterbury 141
Captain Cook Birthplace, Middlesbrough 222
Castle & Regiment Museum, Monmouth 371
Castle Cornet, St Peter Port 415
Castle Museum, York 308
Cavan County Museum, Ballyjamesduff 411
Channel Islands Military, St Ouen 416
Chelmsford Museum, Chelmsford 104
Cheshire Military Museum, Chester 44
Clackmannanshire Museum, Alloa 342
Claydon House, Buckingham 21
Cobbaton Combat, Umberleigh 95
Culzean Castle, Maybole 335
DLI - Durham Light, Durham 219
D-Day Museum and Overlord, Portsmouth 126

Classifications Index

Dean Castle, Kilmarnock. 332
Derby Museum, Derby. 79
Dover Castle, Dover 143
Duke of Cornwalls Museum, Bodmin. 61
Firepower, London 198
Fleet Air Arm Museum, Ilchester 244
Florence Nightingale, London 179
Fusiliers Museum, Bury 43
Fusiliers Museum, Alnwick. 216
Gordon Highlanders Museum, Aberdeen 341
Green Howards Museum, Richmond 301
Gurkha Museum, Winchester. 131
HMS Belfast, London 181
HMS Victory, Portsmouth 126
HMS Warrior 1860, Portsmouth 127
Hitchin Museum, Hitchin 23
Imperial War Museum, Cambridge 33
Imperial War Museum, London 181
Imperial War Museum North, Manchester 50
Keep Military Museum, Dorchester 99
Kent Battle of Britain, Folkestone 145
Kent & Sharpshooters, Edenbridge 144
Kings Own Yorkshire, Doncaster 290
King's Royal Hussars, Winchester 131
Lashenden Air Warfare, Ashford 140
Leamington Spa Museum, Leamington Spa 275
Light Infantry Museum, Winchester 131
Llandudno Museum, Llandudno. 385
Lloyd George Museum, Criccieth. 383
Low Parks Museums, Hamilton 331
Luton Museum Art Gallery, Luton 25
Military Vehicle Museum, Newcastle upon Tyne . . 224
Muckleburgh Collection, Holt. 211
Museum of Army Transport, Beverley. 288
Museum Duke of Wellington, Halifax 292
Museum of The Kings Own, Lancaster 153
Museum of Lancashire, Preston. 155
Museum of Lincolnshire, Lincoln 170
Museum of Liverpool Life, Liverpool 47
Museum - Royal Hospital, London 184
Museum of the Border Reg, Carlisle 72
Museum of the Manchesters, Ashton-under-Lyne. . 41
Museum of Percey Tenantry, Alnwick 216
National Army Museum, London 185
National War Museum, Edinburgh 322
Nelson Museum, Monmouth 371
Nelson Tower, Forres. 349
Newcastle Discovery, Newcastle upon Tyne 224
Newhaven Fort, Newhaven 265
Noirmont Command Bunker, St Brelade 415
Nothe Fort, Weymouth 101
Nunwell House, Isle of Wight 124
Plas Newydd, Llangefni 385
Preston Hall Museum, Stockton-on-Tees. 227
Queens Lancashire Reg, Preston. 156
The Queen's Own Hussars, Warwick 278
Queens Royal Irish Hussar, Eastbourne 262
Queens Royal Lancers, Grantham 158
REME Museum of Technology, Reading 27
Regimental Museum, York. 310
Regimental Museum, Cardiff 367
Regimental Museum, Inverness 361
Regimental Museum, Derby. 80
Royal Air Force Museum, Norwich 212
Royal Air Force Museum, London 203
Royal Air Force Museum, Shifnal 239
Royal Armouries Museum, Leeds. 299
Royal Armouries, Fareham 121
Royal Dragoon Guards, York 310
Royal Engineers Museum, Gillingham 145

Royal Fusiliers Museum, London 187
Royal Glos, Berks & Wilts, Salisbury. 283
Royal Green Jackets, Winchester. 131
Royal Hampshire Regiment, Winchester. 132
Royal Highland Fusiliers, Glasgow 329
Royal Irish Fusiliers, Armargh 392
Royal Irish Regiment, Ballymena 390
Royal Lincs Reg Museum, Lincoln 170
Royal Logistic Corps, Camberley. 253
Royal Marines Museum, Portsmouth 127
Royal Military Police, Chichester 261
Royal Naval Museum, Portsmouth 128
Royal Norfolk Regimental, Norwich 212
Royal Regiment Fusiliers, Warwick 278
Royal Scots Reg Museum, Edinburgh 323
Royal Signals Museum, Blandford Camp. 97
Royal Sussex Regiment, Eastbourne 263
Royal Ulster Rifles, Belfast. 391
Royal Welch Fusiliers, Caernarfon 383
St John's Gate, London. 188
Scapa Flow Visitor Centre, Orkney 363
Scotland's Secret Bunker, St Andrews 354
Somerset Military Museum, Taunton 246
Somme Heritage Centre, Newtownards 394
South Wales Borderers, Brecon 378
Southsea Castle, Portsmouth. 128
Spitfire & Hurricane, Ramsgate 147
Staffordshire Regiment, Lichfield 81
Stondon Museum, Henlow 23
Sussex Combined Services, Eastbourne 263
Tangmere Military Museum, Chichester 262
Tank Museum, Wareham. 101
The King's Own Scottish, Berwick-upon-Tweed. . . 217
Welch Regiment Museum, Cardiff 368
Wexford County Museum, Enniscorthy 405
Whitby Museum, Whitby 308
York & Lancaster Regiment, Rotherham 302
Yorkshire Air Museum, York 311
Youghal Heritage Centre, Youghal 407

Mills - Water & Wind

Almond Valley Heritage, Livingston 335
Bradford Industrial, Bradford 288
Bursledon Windmill, Southampton 128
Canal Museum, Towcester 39
Caudwell's Mill, Matlock. 82
Cheddleton Flint Mill, Leek 81
Crakehall Water Mill, Bedale 287
Dean Heritage Centre, Royal Forest of Dean. . . . 114
Derby Industrial Museum, Derby 79
Ford End Watermill, Ivinghoe 24
Gower Heritage Centre, Swansea 374
Greens Mill & Centre, Nottingham 163
Heckington Windmill, Sleaford 171
Highland Folk Museum, Kingussie 362
Holmshore Textile Museum, Rawtenstall 156
Kingsbury Watermill, St Albans. 28
Michelham Priory, Hailsham. 263
Mill Green Museum & Mill, Hatfield 22
Museum of Welsh Wool, Llandysul 370
New Mills Heritage, High Peak 80
Queen Street Mill, Burnley. 151
Sarehole Mill, Birmingham. 271
Saxstead Green Post Mill, Woodbridge 251
Sir Richard Arkwrights, Matlock 82
Swansea Maritime Museum, Swansea 374
Thwaite Mills Watermill, Leeds. 300
West Blatchington, Hove. 265
Whitchurch Silk Mill, Whitchurch 130

Classifications Index

Multicultural

Brighton Museum, Brighton 260
Burrell Collection, Glasgow 326
Chester Beatty Library, Dublin 398
Durham University, Durham 219
Elgin Museum, Elgin 348
Fitzwilliam Museum, Cambridge 33
Hastings Museum, Hastings 264
Hatton Gallery, Newcastle upon Tyne 223
Horniman Museum & Gardens, London 200
Ilfracombe Museum, Ilfracombe 92
Jewish Museum - Camden, London 182
Jewish Museum - Finchley, London 201
Liverpool Museum, Liverpool 47
McLean Museum, Greenock 330
Marischal Museum, Aberdeen 341
Museum of East Asian Art, Bath 14
Museum of Liverpool Life, Liverpool 47
Museum of Modern Art, Oxford 234
Nature in Art, Gloucester 113
Pitt Rivers Museum, Oxford 235
Powell-Cotton Museum, Birchington 140
Sainsbury Centre, Norwich 213
University Museum, Cambridge 34
West Park Museum, Macclesfield 49

Music & Theatre

Bate Collection, Oxford 233
Claydon House, Buckingham 21
Cyfarthfa Castle Museum, Merthyr Tydfil 371
Dean Castle, Kilmarnock 332
Edinburgh University, Edinburgh 319
Elgar Birthplace Museum, Worcester 137
Ellen Terry Memorial, Tenterden 148
Fenton House, London 198
Finchcocks Living Museum, Cranbrook 142
Georgian Theatre Royal, Richmond 301
Holst Birthplace Museum, Cheltenham 112
Horniman Museum & Gardens, London 200
House on the Hill Museum, Stansted 108
Inst of Contemporary Arts, London 182
Joseph Parrys Ironworkers, Merthyr Tydfil 371
Mechanical Music Museum, Stowmarket 250
Morpeth Chantry Bagpipes, Morpeth 223
Museum of Entertainment, Spalding 171
Museum of Liverpool Life, Liverpool 47
Royal Shakespeare Company, Stratford-upon-Avon 189
Shakespeare's Globe Exhib, London 189
Theatre Museum, London 191
Thursford Collection, Fakenham 210
William Herschel Museum, Bath 15

Oriental

Ashmolean Museum of Art, Oxford 233
Bagshaw Museum, Batley 287
Baysgarth House Museum, Barton-upon-Humber . 168
British Museum, London 177
Burrell Collection, Glasgow 326
Burton Court, Leominster 136
Durham University, Durham 219
Liverpool Museum, Liverpool 47
Museum of East Asian Art, Bath 14
Percival David Foundation, London 186
Pontypool Museum, Pontypool 373
Royal Pavilion, Brighton 260
Victoria Albert Museum, London 192

Palaces

Basing House, Basingstoke 119
Bishop's Palace Site, Witney 235
Blenheim Palace, Woodstock 236
Falkland Palace & Garden, Falkland 348
Hampton Court Palace, East Molesey 196
Museum of Fulham Palace, London 202
Royal Pavilion, Brighton 260

Police, Prisons & Dungeons

Beaumaris Gaol, Beaumaris 382
Bodmin Town Museum, Bodmin 61
Ely Museum, Ely 35
Fire Police Museum, Sheffield 303
Galleries of Justice, Nottingham 163
Great Yarmouth Museums, Great Yarmouth 210
HM Prison Service Museum, Rugby 275
Jedburgh Castle Jail, Jedburgh 332
Kent Police Museum, Chatham 142
Old Guildhall Museum, Looe 64
Royal Military Police, Chichester 261
Stirling Old Town Jail, Stirling 355
Westgate, Winchester 132
Wymondham Heritage Museum, Wymondham . . . 214

Railways

Almond Valley Heritage, Livingston 335
Amberley Working Museum, Arundel 258
Armley Mills Museum, Leeds 298
Bala Lake Railway, Bala 381
Beamish, Chester-le-Street 218
Bluebell Railway, Uckfield 267
Bowes Railway Centre, Gateshead 219
Brecon Mountain Railway, Merthyr Tydfil 370
Bressingham Steam Museum, Diss 209
Buckinghamshire Railway, Aylesbury 20
Colonel Stephens Railway, Tenterden 147
Conwy Valley Railway, Betws-y-Coed 382
Corris Railway Museum, Machynlleth 386
Dales Countryside Museum, Hawes 293
Darlington Railway Centre, Darlington 218
Dean Forest Rail Museum, Lydney 113
Derby Industrial Museum, Derby 79
Didcot Railway Centre, Didcot 232
Downpatrick Railway, Downpatrick 393
Elham Valley Line Trust, Folkestone 144
Embsay & Bolton Abbey, Skipton 305
Fairbourne & Barmouth, Barmouth 382
Fry Model Railway, Malahide 402
Gillingham Museum, Gillingham 99
Glos Warwick Railway, Winchcombe 114
Great Central Railway, Loughborough 160
Gwili Steam Railway, Carmarthen 368
Ilfracombe Museum, Ilfracombe 92
Irchester Narrow Gauge, Wellingborough 39
Isle of Wight Steam Rail, Isle of Wight 123
Kent & East Sussex Rail, Tenterden 148
Launceston Steam Museum, Launceston 64
Leighton Buzzard Railway, Leighton Buzzard 24
Llanberis Lake Railway, Llanberis 384
Llangollen Railway PLC, Llangollen 385
Mangapps Farm Railway, Burnham-on-Crouch . . . 104
Margam Country Park, Port Talbot 373
Maud Railway Museum, Maud 352
Mid Hants Railway, Alresford 117
Midland Railway Centre, Ripley 83
Monkwearmouth Station, Sunderland 227
The Museum of Science, Manchester 52
National Railway Museum, York 309

Classifications Index

National Waterways Museum, Gloucester 113
Nene Valley Railway, Peterborough 37
North Norfolk (M & GN), Sheringham 213
North Yorkshire Moors, Pickering 300
Northampton & Lamport, Chapel Brampton 35
Oswestry Transport Museum, Oswestry 238
Pendon Museum, Abingdon 231
Penrhyn Castle, Bangor 381
Pontypool & Blaenavon, Blaenavon 366
Prestongrange Museum, Prestonpans 337
Princess Royal Locomotive, Ripley 83
Railway Preservation, Whitehead 392
Railworld, Peterborough 38
Ravenglass Railway Museum, Ravenglass 76
Romney Hythe & Dymchurch, New Romney 146
Rural Life Centre, Farnham 254
Scolton Manor Museum, Haverfordwest 370
Scottish Industrial Rail, Dalmellington 315
Scottish Railway Society, Bo'ness 314
Severn Valley Railway, Bewdley 134
Shore Road Station, Birkenhead 42
Snibston Discovery Park, Coalville 158
South Tynedale Railway, Alston 70
Southend Pier Museum, Southend-on-Sea 108
Stephenson Railway Museum, North Shields 225
Strathspey Railway, Aviemore 358
Talyllyn Railway, Tywyn 387
Timothy Hackworth, Shildon 226
Tiverton Museum, Tiverton 94
Torrington Museum, Great Torrington 91
Tyseley Locomotive Works, Birmingham 272
Vale of Glamorgan Railway, Barry Island 366
Vintage Carriage Trust, Keighley 297
Welshpool & Llanfair Rail, Welshpool 379
West Somerset Railway, Minehead 245
Wylam Railway Museum, Wylam 229

Religion

All Hallows By The Tower, London 175
Beaulieu Abbey, Beaulieu 119
British Museum, London 177
Carlisle Cathedral, Carlisle 71
Cavan County Museum, Ballyjamesduff 411
Chertsey Museum, Chertsey 253
Chester Beatty Library, Dublin 398
Coughton Court, Alcester 270
Dalkey Castle & Heritage, Dalkey 398
Guildford Cathedral, Guildford 255
Haverfordwest Town Museum, Haverfordwest 369
Jewish Museum - Camden, London 182
Jewish Museum - Finchley, London 201
John Buchan Centre, Biggar 314
John Bunyan Museum, Bedford 21
Kells Heritage Centre, Kells 403
Monks Dormitory, Durham, Durham 219
Museum of Fulham Palace, London 202
Museum of Liverpool Life, Liverpool 47
Museum of Witchcraft, Boscastle 61
Old Grammar School, Castletown 412
Rushen Abbey, Ballasalla 412
St Margaret's Cave, Dunfermline 348
St Mungo Museum, Glasgow 330
Shetland Museum, Shetland 364
Torre Abbey House, Torquay 95
Treasures of St Cuthbert, Durham 219
Wesleys Chapel, London 193
York Minster Undercroft, York 311

Roman

Aldborough Roman Town, Boroughbridge 288
All Hallows By The Tower, London 175
Armitt Library & Museum, Ambleside 70
Ashmolean Museum of Art, Oxford 233
Bignor Roman Villa, Pulborough 266
Borough Museum, Newcastle-under-Lyme 83
Brading Roman Villa, Isle of Wight 122
Bridport Museum, Bridport 97
British Museum, London 177
Burrell Collection, Glasgow 326
Calleva Museum, Silchester 29
Camborne Public Library, Camborne 61
Canterbury Roman Museum, Canterbury 141
Chesterholm Museum, Hexham 221
Chesters Fort & Museum, Hexham-on-Tyne 221
Corbridge Roman Site, Corbridge 218
Corinium Museum, Cirencester 112
Crofton Roman Villa, Orpington 205
Curtis Museum, Alton 118
Dewa Roman Experience, Chester 44
Ely Museum, Ely 35
Fishbourne Roman Palace, Chichester 261
Havant Museum, Havant 122
Honeywood Heritage Centre, Carshalton 253
Housesteads Roman Fort, Haydon Bridge 221
Hull & East Riding Museum, Hull 295
Hunterian Museum, Glasgow 328
Hypocaust, St Albans 28
Jewry Wall Museum, Leicester 159
Llandudno Museum, Llandudno 385
Malton Museum, Malton 300
Museum of Archaeology, Durham 219
Museum of Reading, Reading 27
Museum of the Iron Age, Andover 118
Newport Roman Villa, Isle of Wight 124
Ribchester Roman Museum, Preston 156
Rockbourne Roman Villa, Fordingbridge 121
Roman Baths, Bath 15
Roman Legionary Museum, Caerleon 366
Roman Theatre, St Albans 29
Rugby Art Gallery, Rugby 276
Saffron Walden Museum, Saffron Walden 106
Segontium Roman Museum, Caernarfon 383
Senhouse Roman Museum, Maryport 75
Verulamium Museum, St Albans 29
Wall Roman Site & Museum, Lichfield 82
Ware Museum, Ware 30
Welwyn Roman Baths, Welwyn 30
Winchester City Museum, Winchester 132
Wroxeter Roman City, Shrewsbury 239

Science - Earth & Planetary

At-Bristol Ltd, Bristol 16
Birr Castle Museum, Birr 411
Catalyst, Widnes 58
Coats Observatory, Paisley 336
Dumfries Museum & Camera, Dumfries 316
Elgin Museum, Elgin 348
Foredown Tower, Portslade-by-Sea 266
Greens Mill & Centre, Nottingham 163
Hunterian Museum, Glasgow 328
Inspire Hands on Science, Norwich 212
Jodrell Bank, Macclesfield 48
Liverpool Museum, Liverpool 47
Mills Observatory, Dundee 347
The Museum of Science, Manchester 52
Museum History of Science, Oxford 234
National Maritime Museum, London 202

Classifications Index

Newcastle Discovery, Newcastle upon Tyne 224
Oxfordshire Museums Store, Witney 235
Michael Faraday Museum, London 188
Royal Museum, Edinburgh 323
Royal Observatory Visitor, Edinburgh 323
St Andrews University, St Andrews 354
Satrosphere Ltd, Aberdeen 342
Science Museum, London 189
Snibston Discovery Park, Coalville 158
Techniquest, Cardiff 368
Torquay Museum, Torquay 94
Whipple Museum, Cambridge 34
William Herschel Museum, Bath 15

Sculpture
Ashmolean Museum of Art, Oxford 233
Bowood House & Gardens, Calne 281
Butler Gallery, Kilkenny 403
Devon Guild of Craftsmen, Bovey Tracey 88
Guildhall Gallery, Winchester 131
Henry Moore Institute, Leeds 299
Leamington Spa Museum, Leamington Spa 275
New Walk Museum & Gallery, Leicester 159
Peter Scott Gallery, Lancaster 153
Petworth House, Petworth 266
Saatchi Gallery, London 188
Talbot Rice Gallery, Edinburgh 324
Torre Abbey House, Torquay 95
Victoria Albert Museum, London 192

Sporting History
British Golf Museum, St Andrews 354
Donington Grand Prix, Derby 80
James Gilbert Museum, Rugby 275
Leicestershire CCC Museum, Leicester 159
Lord's Tour & MCC Museum, London 183
Manchester United Museum, Manchester 52
Museum of Liverpool Life, Liverpool 47
Museum of Rugby, Twickenham 206
National Football Museum, Preston 155
National Horseracing, Newmarket 250
North Berwick Museum, North Berwick 336
Peoples History Museum, Manchester 53
River & Rowing Museum, Henley-on-Thames 233
Rugby School Museum, Rugby 276
St Andrews Museum, St Andrews 354
Stewartry Museum, Kirkcudbright 333
Wimbledon Lawn Tennis, London 204
Wrexham County Museum, Wrexham 388

Toy & Childhood
Bear Museum, Petersfield 125
Beatrix Potter Gallery, Ambleside 70
Blaise Castle House, Bristol 16
Borough Museum, Newcastle-under-Lyme 83
Corgi Heritage Centre, Heywood 44
Cotswold Motoring Museum, Bourton-on-the-Water 111
Coventry Toy Museum, Coventry 272
Cumberland Toy Museum, Cockermouth 72
Curtis Museum, Alton 118
Dewsbury Museum, Dewsbury 290
Dolly Mixture, Langbank 334
Eureka! The Museum, Halifax 292
Fleetwood Museum, Fleetwood 152
Hollytrees Museum, Colchester 105
Honeywood Heritage Centre, Carshalton 253
House on the Hill Museum, Stansted 108
Hove Museum & Art Gallery, Hove 264
Ilfracombe Museum, Ilfracombe 92
Incredibly Old Toy Show, Lincoln 169

Judges Lodgings Museum, Lancaster 153
Leamington Spa Museum, Leamington Spa 275
Lilliput Antique Doll, Isle of Wight 123
Livesey Museum, London 201
Museum of Childhood, Edinburgh 321
Museum of Childhood, London 201
Penshurst Place & Gardens, Tonbridge 148
Pitt Rivers Museum, Oxford 235
Pollocks Toy Museum, London 187
Preston Hall Museum, Stockton-on-Tees 227
Romney Hythe & Dymchurch, New Romney 146
Saffron Walden Museum, Saffron Walden 106
Scotland Street School, Glasgow 330
Tunbridge Wells Museum, Royal Tunbridge Wells . 147
Vina Cooke Museum, Newark-on-Trent 162
Wallington, Morpeth 223
Warwick Doll Museum, Warwick 278
Worthing Museum, Worthing 268

Transport
Amberley Working Museum, Arundel 258
Athelstan Museum, Malmesbury 283
Atwell-Wilson Museum, Calne 281
Bass Museum, Burton upon Trent 78
Battle of Britain Centre, Coningsby 168
Beamish, Chester-le-Street 218
Betws-y-Coed Motor Museum, Betws-y-Coed 382
Birchills Canal Museum, Walsall 277
Black Country Museum, Dudley 274
Blaise Castle House, Bristol 16
Blists Hill, Telford 240
Bodmin Town Museum, Bodmin 61
Bressingham Steam Museum, Diss 209
Bristol Industrial Museum, Bristol 17
British Vehicle Museum, Preston 155
British Cycling Museum, Camelford 62
Bromsgrove Museum, Bromsgrove 134
Brooklands Museum Trust, Weybridge 256
Bygones Museum, Banbury 231
Canterbury Heritage, Canterbury 140
Cars of The Stars Museum, Keswick 74
City of Norwich Aviation, Norwich 212
Cobh The Queenstown Story, Cobh 406
Cotswold Heritage Centre, Northleach 113
Cotswold Motoring Museum, Bourton-on-the-Water 111
Crich Tramway Village, Matlock 82
Dalkey Castle & Heritage, Dalkey 398
De Havilland Aircraft, St Albans 28
Dickens House Museum, Broadstairs 140
Donington Grand Prix, Derby 80
Dover Transport Museum, Dover 143
Dumfries & G'way Aviation, Dumfries 316
Eastleigh Museum, Eastleigh 120
Filching Manor, Eastbourne 262
Fleet Air Arm Museum, Ilchester 244
Foxton Canal Museum, Market Harborough 161
Grampian Transport Museum, Alford 342
Granton Centre, Edinburgh 320
Great Orme Tramway, Llandudno 384
Havant Museum, Havant 122
Haynes Motor Museum, Sparkford 245
Helicopter Museum, Weston-super-Mare 18
Heritage Motor Centre, Warwick 278
Ipswich Transport Museum, Ipswich 249
Jaguar Daimler Heritage, Coventry 272
Jersey Motor Museum, St Peter 416
Lakeland Motor Museum, Cark-in-Cartmel 71
Launceston Steam Museum, Launceston 64
Llangollen Motor Museum, Llangollen 385
London's Transport Museum, London 183

Classifications Index

McLean Museum, Greenock 330
Military Vehicle Museum, Newcastle upon Tyne . . 224
Milton Keynes Museum, Milton Keynes 26
Museum of Army Flying, Stockbridge 130
Museum of Army Transport, Beverley 288
Museum of British Road, Coventry 273
Museum of Flight, North Berwick 336
Museum of Liverpool Life, Liverpool 47
The Museum of Science, Manchester 52
Museum of Speed, Carmarthen 369
Museum of Transport, Glasgow 329
Museum of Transport, Manchester 52
Myreton Motor Museum, Aberlady 313
National Coracle Centre, Newcastle Emlyn 372
National Maritime Museum, Falmouth 62
National Motor Museum, Beaulieu 120
National Motorcycle, Solihull 276
Nelson Museum, Monmouth 371
Newark Air Museum, Newark-on-Trent 162
Norfolk & Suffolk Museum, Bungay 248
North Ayrshire Museum, Saltcoats 337
North East Aircraft, Sunderland 227
Oxfordshire Museums Store, Witney 235
Prestongrange Museum, Prestonpans 337
Railway Preservation, Whitehead 392
Railway Village Museum, Swindon 284
Railworld, Peterborough 38
Royal Air Force Museum, London 203
Royal Air Force Museum, Shifnal 239
Royal Logistic Corps, Camberley 253
Sammy Miller Museum, New Milton 124
Shakespeare Birthplace, Stratford-upon-Avon 276
Shetland Museum, Shetland 364
Shuttleworth Collection, Biggleswade 21
Spitfire & Hurricane, Ramsgate 147
Spurn Lightship, Hull 295
Steam - Museum of GWR, Swindon 284
Stockwood Craft Museum, Luton 25
Stondon Museum, Henlow 23
Streetlife - Hull Museum, Hull 296
Swalcliffe Barn, Banbury 232
Swansea Maritime Museum, Swansea 374
Torrington Museum, Great Torrington 91
Tyrwhitt-Drake Museum, Maidstone 146
Ulster Folk Museum, Holywood 394
Waterways Museum, Goole 291
Whitby Museum, Whitby 308
Windermere Steamboat, Windermere 76
Worcestershire Museum, Worcester 138
World of Country Life, Exmouth 91

Victoriana

Banbury Museum, Banbury 231
Beck Isle Museum, Pickering 300
Belgrave Hall and Gardens, Leicester 158
Bodelwyddan Castle, St Asaph 387
Bodmin Town Museum, Bodmin 61
Borough Museum, Newcastle-under-Lyme 83
Botanic Gardens Museum, Southport 55
Bowes Railway Centre, Gateshead 219
Brodsworth Hall, Doncaster 290
Bury Art Gallery & Museum, Bury 43
Bygones Museum, Banbury 231
Caldicot Castle, Caldicot 367
Cardiff Castle, Cardiff 367
Carlyle's House, London 177
Cecil Higgins Art Gallery, Bedford 21

Christchurch Mansion, Ipswich 249
Church Farmhouse Museum, London 197
Clifton Park Museum, Rotherham 301
Coldharbour Mill, Cullompton 90
Cookworthy Museum, Kingsbridge 92
Cragside, Rothbury 225
Dewey Museum, Warminster 285
Dimbola Lodge, Isle of Wight 123
Eastleigh Museum, Eastleigh 120
Easton Farm Park, Woodbridge 251
Ely Museum, Ely 35
Fire Police Museum, Sheffield 303
Flambards, Helston 63
Gladstone Court Museum, Biggar 313
Gladstone Pottery Museum, Stoke-on-Trent 85
Great Yarmouth Museums, Great Yarmouth 210
Greenfield Valley Museum, Holywell 384
Grove Rural Life Museum, Ramsey 414
Hands on History, Hull 295
Haverfordwest Town Museum, Haverfordwest 369
Hitchin Museum, Hitchin 23
Holst Birthplace Museum, Cheltenham 112
Honeywood Heritage Centre, Carshalton 253
Ilfracombe Museum, Ilfracombe 92
Jersey Museum St Helier 415
Killhope, Bishop Auckland 218
D H Lawrence Birthplace, Nottingham 164
Llanidloes Museum, Llanidloes 378
Lloyd George Museum, Criccieth 383
Lord's Tour & MCC Museum, London 183
Mill Green Museum & Mill, Hatfield 22
Milton Keynes Museum, Milton Keynes 26
Morwellham Quay Museum, Tavistock 94
Museum of Local Life, Worcester 137
Museum of Victorian, Whitby 307
Museum of the Jewellery, Birmingham 271
North Somerset Museum, Weston-super-Mare 18
Old Operating Theatre, London 186
Potters Museum, Launceston 64
Radnorshire Museum, Llandrindod Wells 378
Railway Village Museum, Swindon 284
Rossendale Museum, Rawtenstall 156
Rotunda Museum, Scarborough 302
Royal Museum, Edinburgh 323
Salford Museum, Salford 55
Scolton Manor Museum, Haverfordwest 370
Seaford Museum, Seaford 267
Shambellie House Museum, Dumfries 317
Shambles Museum, Newent 113
Shaw Birthplace, Dublin 402
Sherlock Holmes Museum, London 189
Sir Henry Jones Museum, Abergele 381
Somerset Rural Life, Glastonbury 244
Sudley House, Liverpool 47
Sutton House, London 203
Tenement House, Glasgow 330
Torre Abbey House, Torquay 95
Trowbridge Museum, Trowbridge 285
Trues Yard Fishing, King's Lynn 211
Turton Tower, Turton 57
Uttoxeter Heritage Centre, Uttoxeter 86
Victoria Albert Museum, London 192
West Somerset Rural Life, Minehead 245
Wigan Pier, Wigan 58
Wightwick Manor, Wolverhampton 279
Winchester City Museum, Winchester 132
Wisbech & Fenland Museum, Wisbech 39
World of Country Life, Exmouth 91
Worthing Museum, Worthing 268

Museum/Gallery Name Index

2 Willow Road, London 204
100th Bomb Group Memorial, Diss 209

A

Abbey House Museum, Leeds 298
Abbey Pumping Station, Leicester 158
Abbeydale Industrial, Sheffield 303
Abbot Hall Art Gallery, Kendal 74
Aberconwy House, Conwy 383
Aberdeen Art Gallery, Aberdeen 341
Aberdeen Maritime Museum, Aberdeen 341
Aberdeenshire Farming, Peterhead 353
Abergavenny Museum, Abergavenny 366
Abingdon Museum, Abingdon 231
Abington Museum, Northampton 36
Acton Scott, Church Stretton 238
Airborne Forces Museum, Aldershot 117
Aldborough Roman Town, Boroughbridge 288
Alderney Society Museum, Alderney 414
Aldershot Military Museum, Aldershot 117
Alexander Fleming, London 175
Alexander Keiller Museum, Avebury 281
Alford Manor House Museum, Alford 168
Alfred East Gallery, Kettering 36
All Hallows By The Tower, London 175
Allen Gallery, Alton 118
Allhallows Museum, Honiton 91
Almond Valley Heritage, Livingston 335
Almonry Heritage Centre, Evesham 135
Althorp, Northampton 37
Alyth Museum, Alyth 343
Amberley Working Museum, Arundel 258
American Museum, Bath 13
Amersham Museum, Amersham 20
Amherst Heritage Park, Chatham 141
Ancient High House, Stafford 84
Ancient House Museum, Thetford 214
Andover Museum, Andover 118
Andrew Carnegie Museum, Dunfermline 347
Angel Row Gallery, Nottingham 162
Anglesey Heritage Gallery, Llangefni 385
Angus Folk Museum, Glamis 350
Anne of Cleves Museum, Lewes 265
Apsley House, London 175
Arbeia Roman Fort Museum, South Shields 226
Arbroath Art Gallery, Arbroath 343
Arbroath Museum, Arbroath 343
Arbuthnot Museum, Peterhead 353
Archaeology & History, Dublin 398
Argyll & Sutherland, Stirling 355
Arlington Court, Barnstaple 88
Arlington Mill Museum, Cirencester 112
Armagh County Museum, Armagh 392
Armitt Library & Museum, Ambleside 70
Armley Mills Museum, Leeds 298
Army Medical Services, Aldershot 117
Army Physical Training, Aldershot 117
Arnolfini, Bristol 16
Arran Heritage Museum, Isle of Arran 332
Art Gallery, Hillsborough 393
Art Gallery & Museum, Glasgow 325
Arundel Museum & Heritage, Arundel 258
Ascott House, Leighton Buzzard 24
Ashmolean Museum of Art, Oxford 233
Ashton Court Visitor, Bristol 16
Ashwell Village Museum, Ashwell 20
Astley Cheetham Art, Stalybridge 306
Astley Hall Museum, Chorley 152
Aston Hall, Birmingham 270
At-Bristol Ltd, Bristol 16
Athelstan Museum, Malmesbury 283
Athenry Medieval Museum, Athenry 410
Atholl Country Museum, Blair Atholl 344

Athy Museum, Athy 402
Atkinson Art Gallery, Southport 55
Atwell-Wilson Museum, Calne 281
Audley End House, Saffron Walden 106
Avoncroft Museum, Bromsgrove 134
Ayscoughfee Hall Museum, Spalding 171

B

Baden Powell House, London 175
Bagshaw Museum, Batley 287
Baird Institute Museum, Cumnock 315
Bala Lake Railway, Bala 381
Ballance House, Glenavy 391
Ballymena Museum, Ballymena 390
Ballymoney Museum, Ballymoney 390
Banbury Museum, Banbury 231
Banchory Museum, Banchory 344
Banff Museum, Banff 344
Bangor Museum, Bangor 381
Bank of England Museum, London 175
Bankfield Museum, Halifax 291
Bankside Gallery, London 176
Bannockburn Heritage, Stirling 355
Bantock House & Park, Wolverhampton 279
Bantry House, Bantry 405
Barber Institute Fine Art, Birmingham 270
Barbican Art Gallery, London 176
Barleylands Farm Museum, Billericay 104
Barrie's Birthplace, Kirriemuir 351
Basildon Park, Reading 27
Basing House, Basingstoke 119
Bass Museum, Burton upon Trent 78
Bassetlaw Museum, Retford 166
Bate Collection, Oxford 233
Bateman's Kiplings House, Etchingham 263
Bath Abbey Heritage Vault, Bath 13
Bath Postal Museum, Bath 13
Batley Art Gallery, Batley 287
Battle Abbey, Battle 258
Battle of Britain Centre, Coningsby 168
Baysgarth House Museum, Barton-upon-Humber . . 168
Beacon, Whitehaven 76
Beamish, Chester-le-Street 218
Bear Museum, Petersfield 125
Beatrix Potter Gallery, Ambleside 70
Beaulieu Abbey, Beaulieu 119
Beaumaris Gaol, Beaumaris 382
Beck Isle Museum, Pickering 300
Beckford's Tower & Museum, Bath 13
Bedford Museum, Bedford 20
Beecroft Art Gallery, Westcliff-on-Sea 109
Belgrave Hall and Gardens, Leicester 158
Bellaghy Bawn, Bellaghy 391
Bellfoundry Museum, Loughborough 159
Belton House, Grantham 169
Bembridge Maritime Museum, Isle of Wight 122
Beningbrough Hall, York 308
Bennie Museum, Bathgate 313
Bersham Ironworks, Wrexham 387
Berwick-upon-Tweed Museum, Berwick-upon-Tweed 217
Betws-y-Coed Motor Museum, Betws-y-Coed 382
Beverley Art Gallery, Beverley 287
Bewdley Museum, Bewdley 134
Bexhill Museum, Bexhill 259
Bexley Museum, Bexley 195
Bicton Park, Budleigh Salterton 89
Big Pit Mining Museum, Blaenavon 366
Biggar Gasworks Museum, Biggar 313
Bignor Roman Villa, Pulborough 266
Billingham Art Gallery, Billingham 218
Bilston Craft Gallery, Bilston 270
Birchills Canal Museum, Walsall 277
Birkenhead Priory, Birkenhead 42

Museum/Gallery Name Index

Birmingham Museum, Birmingham 271
Birr Castle Museum, Birr 411
Bishop Asbury Cottage, Birmingham 271
Bishops' House, Sheffield 303
Bishop's Palace Site, Witney 235
Bishop's Waltham Palace, Bishop's Waltham 120
Black Country Museum, Dudley 274
Black Watch Museum, Perth 352
Blackburn Museum, Blackburn 151
Blackpool Lifeboat, Blackpool 151
Blackridge Museum, Blackridge 314
Blackwell - Arts & Crafts, Bowness-on-Windermere 71
Blair Castle, Blair Atholl 345
Blaise Castle House, Bristol 16
Blake Museum, Bridgwater 243
Blenheim Palace, Woodstock 236
Bletchley Park, Milton Keynes. 25
Blickling Hall, Aylsham 208
Blists Hill, Telford 240
Bluebell Railway, Uckfield 267
Boat Museum, Ellesmere Port. 44
Bod of Gremista, Shetland 363
Bodelwyddan Castle, St Asaph 387
Bodmin Town Museum, Bodmin 61
Bognor Regis Museum, Bognor Regis 259
Bolling Hall, Bradford 288
Bolton Library, Cashel. 404
Bolton Museum, Bolton 43
Bondgate Gallery, Alnwick. 216
Booth Museum, Brighton 259
Border History Museum, Hexham 221
Borough Museum, Newcastle-under-Lyme. 83
Boscobel House, Bishop's Wood 78
Bosworth Battlefield, Market Bosworth 160
Botanic Gardens Museum, Southport 55
Boughton House, Kettering 36
Bourne Hall Museum, Epsom 254
Bowes Museum, Barnard Castle 216
Bowes Railway Centre, Gateshead 219
Bowhill House & Park, Selkirk 338
Bowood House & Gardens, Calne 281
Bracken Hall Countryside, Bradford 288
Bradford Industrial, Bradford 288
Bradford-on-Avon Museum, Bradford-on-Avon . . . 281
Brading Roman Villa, Isle of Wight 122
Braintree District Museum, Braintree 104
Bramall Hall, Stockport 56
Brander Museum, Huntly. 350
Brantwood, Coniston 73
Braunton Museum, Braunton 88
Breadalbane Folklore, Killin 351
Brechin Museum, Brechin 345
Brecknock Museum, Brecon 377
Brecon Mountain Railway, Merthyr Tydfil 370
Bressingham Steam Museum, Diss 209
Brewhouse Yard Museum, Nottingham 162
Bridewell Museum, Norwich 211
Bridport Museum, Bridport 97
Brighton Fishing Museum, Brighton 259
Brighton Museum, Brighton 260
Bristol City Museum, Bristol 16
Bristol Industrial Museum, Bristol 17
British Vehicle Museum, Preston 155
British Cycling Museum, Camelford 62
British Empire Museum, Bristol 17
British Golf Museum, St Andrews 354
British Horological, Newark-on-Trent. 161
British Library, London 176
British Museum, London 177
British Sporting Trust, Newmarket 250
Brixham Heritage Museum, Brixham 89
Broadfield House Museum, Kingswinford 274
Brodick Castle Gardens, Isle of Arran 332
Brodie Castle, Forres 349
Brodsworth Hall, Doncaster. 290
Bromley Museum, Orpington 205
Bromsgrove Museum, Bromsgrove 134
Brontá Parsonage Museum, Keighley. 296
Brooklands Museum Trust, Weybridge 256
Broseley Pipe Works, Telford 240
Broughton House & Garden, Kirkcudbright. 333
Broughty Castle Museum, Dundee. 346
Bruce Castle Museum, London 196
Buckhaven Museum, Buckhaven 345
Buckie Drifter Maritime, Buckie 345
Buckinghamshire Museum, Aylesbury. 20
Buckinghamshire Railway, Aylesbury 20
Buckland Abbey, Yelverton 95
Bucklers Hard Village, Beaulieu. 120
Buckleys Yesterdays World, Battle 258
Bude-Stratton Museum, Bude. 61
Building of Bath Museum, Bath 13
Bunratty Castle, Bunratty. 408
Burghley House, Stamford 172
Burns Cottage & Museum, Ayr. 313
Burns House, Dumfries 316
Burntisland Museum, Burntisland. 346
Burrell Collection, Glasgow 326
Burren Centre, Kilfenora 409
Bursledon Windmill, Southampton 128
Burton Agnes Hall, Driffield 291
Burton Art Gallery, Bideford 88
Burton Constable Hall, Hull 295
Burton Court, Leominster 136
Bury Art Gallery & Museum, Bury 43
Bushey Museum, Bushey. 22
Bute Museum, Isle of Bute. 361
Butler Gallery, Kilkenny 403
Buxton Museum, Buxton 78
Bygones At Holkham, Wells-next-the-Sea 214
Bygones Museum, Banbury 231

C

Cabinet War Rooms, London. 177
Caernarfon Maritime, Caernarfon. 382
Calderglen Country Park, East Kilbride. 318
Caldicot Castle, Caldicot. 367
Calf Sound, Calf Sound. 412
Callendar House, Falkirk 325
Calleva Museum, Silchester 29
Camborne Public Library, Camborne 61
Camborne School of Mines, Redruth. 66
Cambridge & County Museum, Cambridge 33
Camden Arts Centre, London 196
Campbeltown Museum, Campbeltown 358
Canal Museum, Linlithgow. 334
Canal Museum, Towcester 39
Cannon Hall Museum, Barnsley 287
Canterbury Heritage, Canterbury. 140
Canterbury Roman Museum, Canterbury 141
Canterbury Royal Museum, Canterbury 141
Canterbury West Gate, Canterbury 141
Captain Cook Birthplace, Middlesbrough 222
Captain Cook Museum, Whitby 307
Cardiff Castle, Cardiff. 367
Cardigan Heritage Centre, Cardigan 378
Cardinal ‡ Fiaich Centre, Cullyhanna 393
Carew Manor Dovecote, Wallington 256
Carisbrooke Castle Museum, Isle of Wight 123
Carlisle Cathedral, Carlisle. 71
Carlyle's House, London 177
Carmarthen Heritage, Carmarthen 368
Carmarthenshire Museum, Carmarthen 368
Carnegie Museum, Inverurie 350
Cars of The Stars Museum, Keswick 74
Cartwright Hall, Bradford. 289

Museum/Gallery Name Index

Castle & Regiment Museum, Monmouth 371
Castle Cornet, St Peter Port 415
Castle Douglas Gallery, Castle Douglas 315
Castle Fraser, Inverurie 351
Castle Keep Museum, Newcastle upon Tyne . . . 223
Castle Museum, Colchester 105
Castle Museum, York 308
Castle Museum & Gallery, Nottingham 163
Castle Rushen, Castletown 412
Castle of St John, Stranraer 339
Catalyst, Widnes 58
Cathcartston Visitor, Dalmellington 315
Caudwell's Mill, Matlock 82
Cavan County Museum, Ballyjamesduff 411
Cawdor Castle, Nairn 362
Cecil Higgins Art Gallery, Bedford 21
Cefn Coed Colliery Museum, Neath 372
Central Art Gallery, Ashton-under-Lyne 41
Ceredigion Museum, Aberystwyth 377
Chadkirk Chapel, Stockport 56
Channel Islands Military, St Ouen 416
Charles Dickens Museum, Portsmouth 125
Charnwood Museum, Loughborough 160
Chart Gunpowder Mills, Faversham 144
Chartwell, Westerham 149
Chastleton House, Chastleton 232
Chatelherault, Hamilton 331
Cheddar Showcaves & Gorge, Cheddar 243
Cheddleton Flint Mill, Leek 81
Chelmsford Museum, Chelmsford 104
Chelsea Physic Garden, London 177
Cheltenham Art Gallery, Cheltenham 111
Chepstow Museum, Chepstow 369
Chertsey Museum, Chertsey 253
Cheshire Military Museum, Chester 44
Chester Beatty Library, Dublin 398
Chesterfield Museum, Chesterfield 78
Chesterholm Museum, Hexham 221
Chesters Fort & Museum, Hexham-on-Tyne 221
Chichester Museum, Chichester 261
Chiltern Open Air Museum, Chalfont St Giles 22
China Clay Museum, St Austell 67
Chippenham Museum, Chippenham 282
Chiswick House, London 197
Christ Church Picture, Oxford 233
Christchurch Mansion, Ipswich 249
Church Farm Museum, Skegness 171
Church Farmhouse Museum, London 197
Cider Museum & King Offa, Hereford 135
City Art Centre, Edinburgh 318
City Museum & Art Gallery, Gloucester 112
City Museum & Records, Portsmouth 125
City of Norwich Aviation, Norwich 212
Clackmannanshire Museum, Alloa 342
Clarke Hall, Wakefield 306
Clatteringshaw Visitor, Castle Douglas 315
Claydon House, Buckingham 21
Cleveland Crafts Centre, Middlesbrough 222
Cliffe Castle, Keighley 297
Clifton Park Museum, Rotherham 301
Clitheroe Castle Museum, Clitheroe 152
Clock Tower, St Albans 28
Clotworthy Arts Centre, Antrim 390
Clydebuilt, Glasgow 326
Coalport China Museum, Telford 240
Coats Observatory, Paisley 336
Cobbaton Combat, Umberleigh 95
Cobh Museum, Cobh 406
Cobh The Queenstown Story, Cobh 406
Cockley Cley Iceni, Swaffham 214
Coldharbour Mill, Cullompton 90
Coldstream Museum, Coldstream 315
Collins Gallery, Glasgow 326

Colne Valley Museum, Huddersfield 294
Colonel Stephens Railway, Tenterden 147
Colour Museum, Bradford 289
Commandery, Worcester 137
Commonwealth Institute, London 178
Conservation Centre, Liverpool 46
Conwy Valley Railway, Betws-y-Coed 382
Cookworthy Museum, Kingsbridge 92
Corbridge Roman Site, Corbridge 218
Corgi Heritage Centre, Heywood 44
Corinium Museum, Cirencester 112
Cork Public Museum, Cork 406
Cornice Museum, Peebles 337
Cornish Mines & Engines, Redruth 66
Corris Railway Museum, Machynlleth 386
Cotswold Heritage Centre, Northleach 113
Cotswold Motoring Museum, Bourton-on-the-Water 111
Cottage Museum, Lancaster 152
Coughton Court, Alcester 270
Courtauld Gallery, London 178
Coventry Toy Museum, Coventry 272
Cowes Maritime Museum, Isle of Wight 123
Cowper Memorial Museum, Olney 26
Cragside, Rothbury 225
Crail Museum, Anstruther 343
Crakehall Water Mill, Bedale 287
Crathes Castle, Banchory 344
Crawford Arts Centre, St Andrews 354
Crawford Municipal Art, Cork 406
Creetown Gem Rock Museum, Newton Stewart . . 336
Cregneash Village Folk, Port St Mary 414
Creswell Crags Museum, Worksop 166
Crich Tramway Village, Matlock 82
Crofton Roman Villa, Orpington 205
Cromarty Courthouse, Cromarty 358
Cromer Museum, Cromer 208
Cromwell Museum, Huntingdon 36
Croxteth Hall, Liverpool 46
Croydon Clocktower, Croydon 195
Culloden Visitor Centre, Inverness 360
Culzean Castle, Maybole 335
Cumberland Pencil Museum, Keswick 74
Cumberland Toy Museum, Cockermouth 72
Cuming Museum, London 178
Curtis Museum, Alton 118
Cusworth Hall, Doncaster 290
Cutty Sark Clipper Ship, London 197
Cyfarthfa Castle Museum, Merthyr Tydfil 371

D

DLI - Durham Light, Durham 219
D-Day Museum and Overlord, Portsmouth 126
Dales Countryside Museum, Hawes 293
Dalgarven Mill Museum, Kilwinning 333
Dalkey Castle & Heritage, Dalkey 398
Dalmeny House, South Queensferry 338
Daniel Owen Museum, Mold 386
Daphne Du Maurier's, Launceston 64
Darby Houses & Quaker, Telford 240
Darlington Railway Centre, Darlington 218
Dartington Crystal, Great Torrington 91
Dartmouth Museum, Dartmouth 90
Daventry Museum, Daventry 35
David Livingstone Centre, Glasgow 326
De Havilland Aircraft, St Albans 28
Dean Castle, Kilmarnock 332
Dean Forest Rail Museum, Lydney 113
Dean Gallery, Edinburgh 319
Dean Heritage Centre, Royal Forest of Dean 114
Decorative Arts & History, Dublin 399
Denny Ship Model, Dumbarton 316
Derby Industrial Museum, Derby 79
Derby Museum, Derby 79

Museum/Gallery Name Index

Design Museum, London 178
Devon Guild of Craftsmen, Bovey Tracey 88
Dewa Roman Experience, Chester 44
Dewey Museum, Warminster 285
Dewsbury Museum, Dewsbury 290
Dick Institute, Kilmarnock 333
Dickens House Museum, Broadstairs 140
Dickens House Museum, London 179
Didcot Railway Centre, Didcot 232
Dimbola Lodge, Isle of Wight 123
Dingles Steam Village, Lifton 92
Dinosaur Isle, Isle of Wight 123
Dinosaur Museum, Dorchester 98
Diss Museum, Diss 209
Ditchling Museum, Ditchling 262
Djanogly Art Gallery, Nottingham 163
Dock Museum, Barrow-in-Furness 70
Doddington Hall, Lincoln 169
Dog Collar Museum, Maidstone 145
Dolly Mixture, Langbank 334
Doncaster Museum, Doncaster 290
Donegal County Museum, Letterkenny 409
Donington Grand Prix, Derby 80
Dorman Museum, Middlesbrough 222
Dorset County Museum, Dorchester 98
Dorset Teddy Bear Museum, Dorchester 98
Douglas Hyde Gallery, Dublin 399
Dove Cottage, Grasmere 73
Dover Castle, Dover 143
Dover Museum, Dover 143
Dover Transport Museum, Dover 143
Down County Museum, Downpatrick 393
Down House, Downe 143
Downpatrick Railway, Downpatrick 393
Dr Johnsons House, London 179
Drenewydd Museum, Rhymney 373
Droitwich Heritage Centre, Droitwich Spa 134
Drum Castle, Banchory 344
Drumlanrigs Tower, Hawick 331
Dualchas-Skye & Lochalsh, Isle of Skye 362
Dublin Civic Museum, Dublin 399
Dublin Writers Museum, Dublin 399
Dublin's Viking Adventure, Dublin 399
Dudley Museum & Art, Dudley 274
Dudmaston, Bridgnorth 238
Duke of Cornwalls Museum, Bodmin 61
Dulwich Picture Gallery, London 197
Dumfries & G'way Aviation, Dumfries 316
Dumfries Museum & Camera, Dumfries 316
Dunbar Town House Museum, Dunbar 317
Dunfermline Museum, Dunfermline 347
Dunham Massey Hall, Altrincham 41
Dunhill Museum, London 179
Dunrobin Castle Museum, Golspie 360
Dunvegan Castle, Isle of Skye 362
Durban House Heritage, Nottingham 163
Durham University, Durham 219
Dylan Thomas Boathouse, Carmarthen 368

E

East Carlton Steel Centre, East Carlton 35
East Riddlesden Hall, Keighley 297
Eastleigh Museum, Eastleigh 120
Easton Farm Park, Woodbridge 251
Eden Project, St Austell 67
Edinburgh Brass Rubbing, Edinburgh 319
Edinburgh University, Edinburgh 319
Edwin Young Gallery, Salisbury 283
Egerton Bridge, Birkenhead 42
Egham Museum, Egham 254
Egypt Centre, Swansea 373
Electric Mountain, Llanberis 384
Elgar Birthplace Museum, Worcester 137

Elgin Museum, Elgin 348
Elham Valley Line Trust, Folkestone 144
Elizabeth Castle, St Helier 415
Elizabethan House, Great Yarmouth 210
Elizabethan House, Plymouth 93
Ellen Terry Memorial, Tenterden 148
Elmbridge Museum, Weybridge 256
Elstow Moot Hall, Bedford 21
Ely Museum, Ely 35
Embsay & Bolton Abbey, Skipton 305
Epping Forest District, Waltham Abbey 108
Epworth Old Rectory, Epworth 168
Erddig, Wrexham 388
Erewash Museum, Ilkeston 81
Essex Secret Bunker, Manningtree 106
Estorick Collection, London 198
Eureka! The Museum, Halifax 292
Excel Heritage Centre, Tipperary 404
Eyam Museum, Hope Valley 81

F

Fairbourne & Barmouth, Barmouth 382
Falconer Museum, Forres 349
Falkland Palace & Garden, Falkland 348
Falmouth Art Gallery, Falmouth 62
Fan Museum, London 198
Farmland Museum, Cambridge 33
Felbrigg Hall, Cromer 208
Fenton House, London 198
Ferens Art Gallery, Hull 295
Fergusson Gallery, Perth 353
Fermanagh County Museum, Enniskillen 395
Fernhill House, Belfast 390
Filching Manor, Eastbourne 262
Filey Museum, Filey 291
Finchcocks Living Museum, Cranbrook 142
Fire Police Museum, Sheffield 303
Firepower, London 198
Firle Place, Firle 263
First Garden City Museum, Letchworth 24
Fishbourne Roman Palace, Chichester 261
Fishermans Museum, Hastings 264
Fitzwilliam Museum, Cambridge 33
Flambards, Helston 63
Flame, Carrickfergus 391
Fleet Air Arm Museum, Ilchester 244
Fleetwood Museum, Fleetwood 152
Fleur de Lis Heritage, Faversham 144
Flora Twort Gallery, Petersfield 125
Florence Mine Heritage, Egremont 73
Florence Nightingale, London 179
Folkestone Museum, Folkestone 144
Ford End Watermill, Ivinghoe 24
Ford Green Hall, Stoke-on-Trent 85
Fordyce Joiners Workshop, Portsoy 353
Foredown Tower, Portslade-by-Sea 266
Forge Mill Museum, Redditch 137
Forge Museum, Much Hadham 26
Fort Grey Shipwreck, St Peters 415
Fossil Grove, Glasgow 327
Fox Talbot Museum, Chippenham 282
Foxton Canal Museum, Market Harborough 161
Fr McDyers Folk Village, Glencolmcille 409
Freud Museum, London 198
Fruitmarket Gallery, Edinburgh 319
Fry Model Railway, Malahide 402
Furness Abbey, Barrow-in-Furness 71
Fusiliers Museum, Bury 43
Fusiliers Museum, Alnwick 216
Fyvie Castle, Turriff 356

G

Gainsborough Old Hall, Gainsborough 168
Gainsborough's House, Sudbury 251

Museum/Gallery Name Index

Gairloch Heritage Museum, Gairloch 359
Galleries of Justice, Nottingham 163
Gallery Oldham, Oldham 54
Gallery of Costume, Manchester 49
Gallery of Modern Art, Glasgow 327
Garlogie Mill Power House, Garlogie 350
Gawthorpe Hall, Burnley 151
Geevor Tin Mine, Penzance 65
Geffrye Museum, London 179
Georgian House, Bristol 17
Georgian House, Edinburgh 320
Georgian Theatre Royal, Richmond 301
German Occupation Museum, Forest 414
Gilbert Collection, London 180
Gillingham Museum, Gillingham 99
Gilstrap Heritage Centre, Newark-on-Trent 161
Gladstone Court Museum, Biggar 313
Gladstone Pottery Museum, Stoke-on-Trent 85
Glamis Castle, Glamis 350
Glandford Shell Museum, Holt 210
Glasgow Botanic Gardens, Glasgow 327
Glasgow School of Art, Glasgow 327
Glastonbury Abbey, Glastonbury 243
Glastonbury Lake Village, Glastonbury 243
Glebe House & Gallery, Church Hill 409
Glencoe & North Lorn Folk, Glencoe 359
Glenesk Folk Museum, Brechin 345
Gloucester Folk Museum, Gloucester 112
Glos Warwick Railway, Winchcombe 114
Glynn Vivian Art Gallery, Swansea 374
Godalming Museum, Godalming 255
Golden Hind Museum Ship, Brixham 89
Goole Museum, Goole 291
Gordon Highlanders Museum, Aberdeen 341
Gosport Museum, Gosport 121
Goss & Crested China, Waterlooville 130
Gower Heritage Centre, Swansea 374
Gracefield Arts Centre, Dumfries 316
Grampian Transport Museum, Alford 342
Grand Lodge of Scotland, Edinburgh 320
Grange Museum, London 199
Grantham Museum, Grantham 169
Granton Centre, Edinburgh 320
Graves Art Gallery, Sheffield 303
Great Central Railway, Loughborough 160
Great Laxey Wheel & Mines, Laxey 413
Great Orme Tramway, Llandudno 384
Great Yarmouth Museums, Great Yarmouth 210
Green Dragon Museum, Stockton-on-Tees 227
Green Howards Museum, Richmond 301
Greenfield Valley Museum, Holywell 384
Greenhill Farmhouse, Biggar 314
Greens Mill & Centre, Nottingham 163
Greenwich Borough Museum, London 199
Greyfriars, Lincoln 169
Grosvenor Museum, Chester 44
Grove Rural Life Museum, Ramsey 414
Grundy Art Gallery, Blackpool 151
Guardhouse Museum, Tattershall 172
Guernsey Folk Museum, Castel 414
Guernsey Museum, St Peter Port 415
Guide Heritage Centre, London 180
Guildford Cathedral, Guildford 255
Guildford House Gallery, Guildford 255
Guildford Museum, Guildford 255
Guildhall, Leicester 159
Guildhall Art Gallery, London 180
Guildhall Gallery, Winchester 131
Guildhall Museum, Carlisle 71
Guildhall Museum, Chichester 261
Guildhall Museum, Rochester 147
Guinness Storehouse, Dublin 400
Gunnersbury Park Museum, London 199

Gurkha Museum, Winchester 131
Gwili Steam Railway, Carmarthen 368

H

HM Customs & Excise, Liverpool 46
HM Prison Service Museum, Rugby 275
HMS Belfast, London 181
HMS Trincomalee Trust, Hartlepool 220
HMS Victory, Portsmouth 126
HMS Warrior 1860, Portsmouth 127
Hackney Museum, London 199
Haddo House, Ellon 348
Haden Hill House, Cradley Heath 273
Hagley Hall, Hagley 135
Hailes Abbey, Winchcombe 115
Halliwells House Museum, Selkirk 338
Ham House, London 199
Hampstead Museum, London 200
Hampton Court Palace, East Molesey 196
Hamptonne Country Museum, St Lawrence 416
Hanbury Hall, Droitwich Spa 135
Hancock Museum, Newcastle upon Tyne 223
Hands on History, Hull 295
Harborough Museum, Market Harborough 161
Harbour Museum, Derry 395
Hardwick Hall, Chesterfield 79
Harestanes Countryside, Jedburgh 332
Harewood House, Leeds 298
Harley Gallery, Worksop 166
Harlow Carr Museum, Harrogate 292
Harris Museum, Preston 155
Hartlepool Art Gallery, Hartlepool 220
Harwich Maritime Museum, Harwich 106
Haslemere Educational, Haslemere 256
Hastings Museum, Hastings 264
Hat Works, Stockport 56
Hatton Gallery, Newcastle upon Tyne 223
Havant Museum, Havant 122
Haven Plotlands Museum, Basildon 104
Haverfordwest Town Museum, Haverfordwest 369
Hawick Museum & Gallery, Hawick 331
Haynes Motor Museum, Sparkford 245
Hayward Gallery, London 181
Heaton Hall, Manchester 49
Heckington Windmill, Sleaford 171
Helicopter Museum, Weston-super-Mare 18
Helston Folk Museum, Helston 63
Henry Moore Institute, Leeds 299
Heptonstall Museum, Hebden Bridge 293
Herbert Art Gallery, Coventry 272
Hereford Museum & Gallery, Hereford 136
Heritage Motor Centre, Warwick 278
Herne Bay Museum, Herne Bay 145
Hertford Museum, Hertford 23
Highland Folk Museum, Kingussie 362
Hill House, Helensburgh 360
Hill Top, Ambleside 70
Hill of Tarvit Mansion, Cupar 346
Historic Dockyard, Chatham 142
History Shop, Wigan 58
Hitchin Museum, Hitchin 23
Hogarth's House, London 200
Holburne Museum of Art, Bath 14
Hollytrees Museum, Colchester 105
Holmshore Textile Museum, Rawtenstall 156
Holst Birthplace Museum, Cheltenham 112
Holyhead Maritime Museum, Holyhead 383
Honeywood Heritage Centre, Carshalton 253
Hop Farm Country Park, Tonbridge 148
Horniman Museum & Gardens, London 200
Hornsea Museum, Hornsea 294
Horsham Museum, Horsham 264
House of Manannan, Peel 413

Museum/Gallery Name Index

House of the Binns, Linlithgow.............. 334
House on the Hill Museum, Stansted 108
Housesteads Roman Fort, Haydon Bridge 221
Hove Museum & Art Gallery, Hove............ 264
How We Lived Then","Eastbourne, ... 262
Huddersfield Art Gallery, Huddersfield 294
Hugh Lane Municipal, Dublin 400
Hugh Millers Cottage, Cromarty.............. 358
Hughenden Manor, High Wycombe 23
Hull & East Riding Museum, Hull 295
Humber Estuary Discovery, Cleethorpes........ 168
Hunt Museum, Limerick 408
Hunter House, East Kilbride 318
Hunterian Art Gallery, Glasgow 328
Hunterian Museum, Glasgow 328
Hypocaust, St Albans 28

I

Ickworth House, Bury St Edmunds............ 248
Ikon Gallery, Birmingham 271
Ilfracombe Museum, Ilfracombe 92
Imperial War Museum, Cambridge 33
Imperial War Museum, London 181
Imperial War Museum North, Manchester 50
Impressions Gallery, York 309
Incredibly Old Toy Show, Lincoln 169
Industrial Museum, Nottingham 163
Inspire Hands on Science, Norwich 212
Inst of Contemporary Arts, London 182
International Museum Wine, Kinsale........... 406
Inveraray Maritime Museum, Inveraray 360
Inverness Museum, Inverness 360
Ipswich Museum, Ipswich 249
Ipswich Transport Museum, Ipswich.......... 249
Irchester Narrow Gauge, Wellingborough 39
Irish Agricultural Museum, Wexford 405
Irish Architectural Museum, Dublin 400
Irish Folklife, Castlebar 410
Irish Linen Centre, Lisburn 392
Irish National Heritage, Ferrycarrig.......... 405
Iron Bridge & Tollhouse, Telford 241
Isle of Mull Museum, Isle of Mull 361
Isle of Wight Steam Rail, Isle of Wight 123
Isles of Scilly Museum, Isles of Scilly 63
Islington Museum, London 200
Izaak Walton's Cottage, Stone 86

J

Jackfield Tile Museum, Telford............... 241
Jaguar Daimler Heritage, Coventry 272
James Gilbert Museum, Rugby 275
James Hogg Exhibition, Selkirk 338
James Joyce Museum, Dublin............... 400
Jane Austen's House, Alton................. 118
Jedburgh Castle Jail, Jedburgh.............. 332
Jenner Museum, Berkeley 111
Jerome K Jerome, Walsall.................. 277
Jersey Battle of Flowers, St Ouen 416
Jersey Motor Museum, St Peter............. 416
Jersey Museum, St Helier 415
Jewish Museum - Camden, London........... 182
Jewish Museum - Finchley, London 201
Jewry Wall Museum, Leicester.............. 159
Jim Clarke Room, Duns.................... 317
Jodrell Bank, Macclesfield 48
John Buchan Centre, Biggar 314
John Bunyan Museum, Bedford 21
John Creasey Museum, Salisbury 283
John Hansard Gallery, Southampton 129
John Hastie Museum, Strathaven............ 339
John McDouall Stuart, Kirkcaldy 351
John Moore Countryside, Tewkesbury 114
John Muir Birthplace, Dunbar 317

John Rylands Library, Manchester 50
John Southern Wildlife, Liskeard............. 64
Jorvik - The Viking City, York............... 309
Joseph Parrys Ironworkers, Merthyr Tydfil...... 371
Judges Lodgings Museum, Lancaster 153

K

Keats House, London 201
Keep Military Museum, Dorchester 99
Kelham Island Museum, Sheffield 303
Kellie Castle, Anstruther 343
Kells Heritage Centre, Kells................. 403
Kendal Museum, Kendal 74
Kennet & Avon Canal, Devizes 282
Kensington Palace, London................. 182
Kent Battle of Britain, Folkestone 145
Kent & East Sussex Rail, Tenterden 148
Kent Police Museum, Chatham 142
Kent & Sharpshooters, Edenbridge 144
Kenwood House, London 201
Kerry County Museum, Tralee............... 407
Keswick Museum, Keswick 75
Kettle's Yard, Cambridge 34
Kew Bridge Steam Museum, Brentford 195
Kidwelly Ind Museum, Kidwelly 370
Killerton House, Exeter.................... 90
Killhope, Bishop Auckland.................. 218
Kilmainham Gaol, Dublin................... 401
Kilmartin House Museum, Kilmartin 362
Kilrush Heritage Centre, Kilrush 409
Kilwinning Abbey Tower, Kilwinning 333
King's Own Scottish, Berwick-upon-Tweed 217
Kings Own Yorkshire, Doncaster 290
King's Royal Hussars, Winchester 131
Kingsbury Watermill, St Albans.............. 28
Kingston Museum, Kingston upon Thames...... 196
Kirkcaldy Museum, Kirkaldy 351
Kirkleatham Old Hall, Redcar 225
Kirkstall Abbey, Leeds 299
Kirriemuir Gateway Museum, Kirriemuir 351
Knaresborough Castle, Knaresborough 297
Knutsford Heritage Centre, Knutsford 45

L

La Hougue Bie Museum, Grouville............ 415
Lace Market Centre, Nottingham 164
Lackham Museum, Chippenham 282
Lady Lever Art Gallery, Bebington 41
Lady Waterford Gallery, Berwick-upon-Tweed.... 217
Laidhay Croft Museum, Dunbeath 359
Laing Art Gallery, Newcastle upon Tyne 224
Laing Museum, Newburgh 352
Lakeland Motor Museum, Cark-in-Cartmel...... 71
Lancaster City Museum, Lancaster 153
Lancaster Maritime Museum, Lancaster 153
Largs Museum, Largs 334
Lashenden Air Warfare, Ashford 140
Launceston Steam Museum, Launceston 64
Lauriston Castle, Edinburgh 320
D H Lawrence Birthplace, Nottingham 164
Lawrence House Museum, Launceston........ 64
Leamington Spa Museum, Leamington Spa 275
Leeds City Art Gallery, Leeds 299
Leicestershire CCC Museum, Leicester 159
Leighton Buzzard Railway, Leighton Buzzard.... 24
Leighton House Museum, London 182
Leith Hall, Huntly 350
Leominster Folk Museum, Leominster 136
Leslie Hill Open Farm, Ballymoney........... 390
Letchworth Museum, Letchworth 25
Lewes Castle & Barbican, Lewes 265
Library of Freemasonry, London............. 183
Lichfield Heritage Centre, Lichfield........... 81

Museum/Gallery Name Index

Light Infantry Museum, Winchester 131
Lillie Art Gallery, Milngavie 335
Lilliput Antique Doll, Isle of Wight. 123
Limerick City Gallery, Limerick. 408
Limerick Museum, Limerick 408
Lincoln Castle, Lincoln 170
Lindisfarne Priory, Berwick-upon-Tweed 217
Lismore Experience, Lismore 404
Listowel Literary Museum, Listowel 407
Little Holland House, Carshalton 253
Littlehampton Museum, Littlehampton 265
Liverpool Central Library, Liverpool 46
Liverpool Museum, Liverpool 47
Livesey Museum, London 201
Llanberis Lake Railway, Llanberis 384
Llancaiach Fawr Manor, Treharris. 375
Llandudno Museum, Llandudno. 385
Llangollen Motor Museum, Llangollen 385
Llangollen Railway PLC, Llangollen 385
Llanidloes Museum, Llanidloes 378
Lloyd George Museum, Criccieth. 383
Llywernog Silver-Lead, Aberystwyth. 377
Loch of the Lowes, Dunkeld 348
London's Transport Museum, London. 183
Long Eaton Town Hall, Nottingham. 164
Long Shop Museum, Leiston 249
Longdale Craft Centre, Ravenshead 165
Longleat House, Warminster 285
Lord's Tour & MCC Museum, London 183
Loseley Park, Guildford. 255
Lotherton Hall, Leeds 299
Lothian & Borders Fire, Edinburgh 321
Low Parks Museums, Hamilton 331
Lowestoft Maritime Museum, Lowestoft 250
Lowestoft Museum, Lowestoft 250
Lowewood Museum, Hoddesdon 24
Lowry, Manchester 50
Ludlow Museum, Ludlow 238
Lunt Roman Fort, Coventry 273
Luton Museum Art Gallery, Luton 25
Lydiard House, Swindon 284
Lyme Park, Stockport. 56
Lyme Regis Philpot Museum, Lyme Regis 99
Lynn Museum, King's Lynn 211
Lytham Heritage Centre, Lytham 154
Lytham Windmill Museum, Lytham 154

M

McLean Museum, Greenock 330
McManus Galleries, Dundee 347
Macclesfield Silk Museum, Macclesfield 49
Maidstone Museum, Maidstone 145
Maison Dieu, Faversham. 144
Malahide Castle, Malahide 402
Malton Museum, Malton 300
Malvern Museum, Great Malvern 135
Manchester Art Gallery, Manchester 51
Manchester Jewish Museum, Manchester 51
Manchester Museum, Manchester 51
Manchester United Museum, Manchester 52
Mangapps Farm Railway, Burnham-on-Crouch . . . 104
Manor House, Coalville 158
Manor House Art Gallery, Ilkley 296
Manor House Museum, Bury St Edmunds 248
Manor House Museum, Kettering 36
Mansfield Museum, Mansfield 160
Manx Museum, Douglas 413
Manx National Heritage, Douglas. 413
Mappa Mundi, Hereford 136
Mappin Art Gallery, Sheffield 304
Marble Hill House, Twickenham 206
Margam Country Park, Port Talbot 373
Margate Old Town Hall, Margate 146

Marischal Museum, Aberdeen. 341
Maritime Museum, Hull 295
Maritime Museum, St Helier. 416
Maritime Museum, Great Yarmouth 210
Mary Queen of Scots House, Jedburgh 332
Mary Rose Museum, Portsmouth 127
Maud Railway Museum, Maud. 352
Mechanical Music Museum, Stowmarket 250
Meffan, Forfar Museum, Forfar. 349
Mellerstain House, Gordon 330
Melton Carnegie Museum, Melton Mowbray 161
Mercer Art Gallery, Harrogate 293
Merchant Adventurers Hall, York 309
Merchants House, Plymouth. 93
Merseyside Maritime, Liverpool 47
Methil Heritage Centre, Methil 352
Mevagissey Folk Museum, Mevagissey. 65
Michael Faraday Museum, London 188
Michelham Priory, Hailsham. 263
Mid Hants Railway, Alresford 117
Middlesbrough Art Gallery, Middlesbrough 222
Midland Railway Centre, Ripley 83
Milford Haven Maritime, Milford Haven 371
Military Vehicle Museum, Newcastle upon Tyne . . 224
Mill Green Museum & Mill, Hatfield 22
Mill Trail Visitor Centre, Alva. 342
Millennium Galleries, Sheffield 304
Millgate Museum, Newark-on-Trent 161
Millmount Museum & Tower, Drogheda. 403
Mills Observatory, Dundee 347
Milton Keynes Gallery, Milton Keynes 26
Milton Keynes Museum, Milton Keynes 26
Milton's Cottage, Chalfont St Giles 22
Minera Lead Mines, Wrexham 388
Mirehouse, Keswick. 75
Mission Gallery, Swansea 374
Moat Park Heritage Centre, Biggar 314
Monaghan County Museum, Monaghan 411
Monks Dormitory, Durham, Durham 219
Monkwearmouth Station, Sunderland 227
Mont Orgueil Castle, St Martin 416
Montrose Museum, Montrose. 352
Moot Hall Museum, Aldeburgh 248
Morpeth Chantry Bagpipes, Morpeth 223
Morwellham Quay Museum, Tavistock. 94
Motherwell Heritage, Motherwell 335
Mount Edgcumbe House, Torpoint 68
Moyses Hall Museum, Bury St Edmunds 249
Mr Straw's House, Worksop. 166
Much Wenlock Museum, Much Wenlock. 238
Muckleburgh Collection, Holt. 211
Muncaster Castle Gardens, Ravenglass 75
Museum, Dunwich 249
Museum & Art Gallery, Nuneaton 275
Museum Nan Eilean, Island of Benbecula. 361
Museum Nan Eilean, Isle of Lewis 361
Museum No 1, Richmond 205
Museum in the Park, Stroud. 114
Museum of Antiquities, Alnwick 216
Museum of Antiquities, Newcastle upon Tyne 224
Museum of Archaeology, Durham 219
Museum of Archaeology, Southampton 129
Museum of Army Flying, Stockbridge 130
Museum of Army Transport, Beverley. 288
Museum of Barnstaple, Barnstaple 88
Museum of Bath at Work, Bath 14
Museum of British Road, Coventry 273
Museum of Cannock Chase, Cannock 78
Museum of Childhood, Edinburgh 321
Museum of Childhood, London 201
Museum of Costume, Bath 14
Museum of Costume, Nottingham 164
Museum of Dartmoor Life, Okehampton 92

Museum/Gallery Name Index

Museum of Domestic Design, Barnet 195
Museum Duke of Wellington, Halifax 292
Museum of East Anglia, Stowmarket 251
Museum of East Asian Art, Bath 14
Museum of Edinburgh, Edinburgh 321
Museum of Entertainment, Spalding 171
Museum of Eton Life, Windsor 31
Museum of Farnham, Farnham 254
Museum of Flight, North Berwick 336
Museum of Fulham Palace, London 202
Museum of Garden History, London 183
Museum of Harlow, Harlow 106
Museum of Hartlepool, Hartlepool 220
Museum of Iron, Telford 241
Museum of Island History, Isle of Wight 124
Museum of Islay Life, Isle of Islay 361
Museum of Kent Life, Maidstone 146
Museum of The Kings Own, Lancaster 153
Museum of Lakeland Life, Kendal 74
Museum of Lancashire, Preston 155
Museum of Lead Mining, Wanlockhead 339
Museum of Lincolnshire, Lincoln 170
Museum of Liverpool Life, Liverpool 47
Museum of Local History, Hastings 264
Museum of Local Life, Worcester 137
Museum of London, London 184
Museum of Modern Art, Machynlleth 386
Museum of Modern Art, Oxford 234
Museum of Oxford, Oxford 234
Museum of Reading, Reading 27
Museum of Richmond, Richmond 205
Museum - Royal Hospital, London 184
Museum of Rugby, Twickenham 206
Museum of Science, Manchester 52
Museum of Scottish Life, East Kilbride 318
Museum of Scot' L'houses, Fraserburgh 349
Museum of South Somerset, Yeovil 246
Museum of Speed, Carmarthen 369
Museum of St Albans, St Albans 28
Museum of St Barts Hosptl, London 184
Museum of Submarine, Penzance 65
Museum of Transport, Glasgow 329
Museum of Transport, Manchester 52
Museum of Victorian, Whitby 307
Museum of Welsh Life, Cardiff 367
Museum of Witchcraft, Boscastle 61
Museum of Worcester, Worcester 137
Museum of the Border Reg, Carlisle 72
Museum of the Gorge, Telford 241
Museum History of Science, Oxford 234
Museum of the Iron Age, Andover 118
Museum of the Jewellery, Birmingham 271
Museum of the Manchesters, Ashton-under-Lyne . . 41
Museum of Percey Tenantry, Alnwick 216
Museum of the RNLI, Eastbourne 262
Museum of Welsh Wool, Llandysul 370
Myreton Motor Museum, Aberlady 313

N

Nairn Museum, Nairn 363
Nantgarw China Works, Nantgarw 371
Nantwich Museum, Nantwich 54
National Army Museum, London 185
National Coal Mining, Wakefield 306
National Coracle Centre, Newcastle Emlyn 372
National Football Museum, Preston 155
National Gallery, London 185
National Gallery, Dublin 401
National Gallery Scotland, Edinburgh 321
National Horseracing, Newmarket 250
National Irish Famine, Strokestown 411
National Maritime Museum, Falmouth 62
National Maritime Museum, London 202

National Motor Museum, Beaulieu 120
National Motorcycle, Solihull 276
National Museum & Gallery, Cardiff 367
National Portrait Gallery, London 186
National Railway Museum, York 309
National Wallace Monument, Stirling 355
National War Museum, Edinburgh 322
National Waterways Museum, Gloucester 113
Natural History, Dublin 401
Natural History Centre, Burnley 151
Natural History Museum, Colchester 105
Natural History Museum, London 186
Natural History Museum, Nottingham 164
Natural History Museum, Portsmouth 127
Nature in Art, Gloucester 113
Nautical Museum, Castletown 412
Neath Museum, Neath 372
Nelson Monument, Edinburgh 322
Nelson Museum, Monmouth 371
Nelson Tower, Forres 349
Nene Valley Railway, Peterborough 37
New Art Gallery Walsall, Walsall 277
New Lanark Visitor Centre, Lanark 334
New Mills Heritage, High Peak 80
New Walk Museum & Gallery, Leicester 159
Newark Air Museum, Newark-on-Trent 162
Newark Museum, Newark-on-Trent 162
Newark Town Treasures, Newark-on-Trent 162
Newarke Houses Museum, Leicester 159
Newbridge House, Donabate 398
Newcastle Discovery, Newcastle upon Tyne 224
Newhaven Fort, Newhaven 265
Newhaven Heritage Museum, Edinburgh 322
Newlyn Art Gallery, Penzance 65
Newport Museum, Newport 372
Newport Roman Villa, Isle of Wight 124
Newry Museum, Newry 394
Newstead Abbey, Ravenshead 165
Newtown Textile Museum, Newtown 378
No 1 Royal Crescent, Bath 15
Noirmont Command Bunker, St Brelade 415
Norfolk & Suffolk Museum, Bungay 248
Normanby Hall, Scunthorpe 170
Normanby Park Farming, Scunthorpe 170
Normanton Church Museum, Oakham 164
Norris Museum, St Ives 38
North Ayrshire Museum, Saltcoats 337
North Berwick Museum, North Berwick 336
North Cornwall Museum, Camelford 62
North Down Heritage, Bangor 393
North East Aircraft, Sunderland 227
North Lincolnshire Museum, Scunthorpe 171
North Norfolk (M & GN), Sheringham 213
North Somerset Museum, Weston-super-Mare 18
North Yorkshire Moors, Pickering 300
Northampton Museum, Northampton 37
Northampton & Lamport, Chapel Brampton 35
Northgate Museum, Bridgnorth 238
Norton Priory Museum, Runcorn 54
Norwich Castle Museum, Norwich 212
Nostell Priory, Wakefield 306
Nothe Fort, Weymouth 101
Nunwell House, Isle of Wight 124

O

Oak House Museum, West Bromwich 278
Oakham Castle, Oakham 165
Oakwell Hall, Batley 287
Old Bridge House, Dumfries 316
Old Gala House, Galashiels 325
Old Gaol Museum, Buckingham 22
Old Grammar School, Castletown 412
Old Guildhall Museum, Looe 64

Museum/Gallery Name Index

Old House, Hereford. 136
Old House of Keys, Castletown 413
Old Merchants House, Great Yarmouth 210
Old Operating Theatre, London 186
Oliver Cromwell's House, Ely 35
Ordsall Hall Museum, Salford 55
Orkney Museum, Tankerness, Orkney 363
Orkney Wireless Museum, Orkney 363
Orleans House Gallery, Twickenham 206
Ormeau Baths Gallery, Belfast. 391
Osborne House, Isle of Wight 124
Osterley Park House, Isleworth 196
Oswestry Transport Museum, Oswestry 238
Otterton Mill Centre, Budleigh Salterton. 89
Oxford University Museum, Oxford. 235
Oxfordshire Museum, Woodstock. 236
Oxfordshire Museums Store, Witney. 235

P

Paisley Museum, Paisley 337
Palace Stables Centre, Armagh 392
Pallant House Gallery, Chichester 261
Pankhurst Centre, Manchester 53
Papplewick Pumping Stn, Ravenshead 165
Paradise Mill, Macclesfield 49
Parc Howard Museum, Llanelli. 370
Peacock Heritage Centre, Chesterfield 79
Peak District Mining, Matlock 82
Peel Castle, Peel 414
Pendeen Lighthouse, Penzance 65
Pendennis Castle, Falmouth. 63
Pendle Heritage Centre, Nelson. 155
Pendon Museum, Abingdon 231
Penlee House Gallery, Penzance 66
Penrhos Cottage, Clunderwen 369
Penrhyn Castle, Bangor 381
Penshurst Place & Gardens, Tonbridge 148
Penwith Galleries, St Ives 67
Peoples History Museum, Manchester 53
Peoples Palace Museum, Glasgow 329
People's Story, Edinburgh 322
Percival David Foundation, London 186
Perrys Cider Mills, Ilminster. 244
Perth Museum, Perth 353
Peter Anson Gallery, Buckie 345
Peter Scott Gallery, Lancaster 153
Peterborough Museum, Peterborough. 38
Peterborough Sculpture, Peterborough 38
Peterhead Maritime Centre, Peterhead. 353
Petworth House, Petworth 266
Pickfords House Museum, Derby 80
Piece Hall Art Gallery, Halifax 292
Pier Arts Centre, Orkney 363
Pilchard Works, Penzance 66
Pitshanger Manor, London. 202
Pitt Rivers Museum, Oxford. 235
Pittencrieff House Museum, Dunfermline 348
Planet Earth Museum, Newhaven. 266
Plas Newydd, Llangefni 385
Plas Newydd, Llangollen 386
Plymouth City Museum, Plymouth 93
Poldark Mine & Heritage, Helston 63
Polesden Lacey, Dorking. 254
Pollocks Toy Museum, London. 187
Pollok House, Glasgow. 329
Pontefract Museum, Pontefract 301
Pontypool & Blaenavon, Blaenavon 366
Pontypool Museum, Pontypool. 373
Port Sunlight Heritage, Bebington. 41
Portchester Castle, Portchester 125
Porthcawl Museum, Porthcawl. 373
Porthmadog Maritime, Porthmadog 386
Portland Basin Museum, Ashton-under-Lyne 41

Portland Museum, Portland 100
Potteries Museum, Stoke-on-Trent. 85
Potters Museum, Launceston 64
Powderham Castle, Exeter 90
Powell-Cotton Museum, Birchington. 140
Powis Castle & Garden, Welshpool 379
Powysland Museum, Welshpool 379
Prescot Museum, Prescot. 54
Preston Hall Museum, Stockton-on-Tees. 227
Preston Manor, Brighton 260
Prestongrange Museum, Prestonpans 337
Priest House, West Hoathly 268
Priest's House Museum, Wimborne Minster 102
Princess Royal Locomotive, Ripley 83
Priory Visitor Centre, Coventry 273
Prittlewell Priory, Southend-on-Sea 107
Provands Lordship, Glasgow. 329
Provost Skene's House, Aberdeen 341
Public Record Office, Richmond 205
Pumphouse Museum, London 202

Q

Quarry Bank Mill, Wilmslow 59
Q E Hunting Lodge, London 202
Queen Street Mill, Burnley. 151
Queen's Gallery, London. 187
Queens Lancashire Reg, Preston. 156
The Queen's Own Hussars, Warwick 278
Queens Royal Irish Hussar, Eastbourne 262
Queens Royal Lancers, Grantham 158
Queensferry Museum, South Queensferry 339

R

REME Museum of Technology, Reading 27
RNLI Henry Blogg Lifeboat, Cromer 208
RNLI Grace Darling Museum, Bamburgh 216
RNLI Whitby Lifeboat, Whitby 307
Radnorshire Museum, Llandrindod Wells 378
Radstock Museum, Radstock. 18
Ragged School Museum, London 202
Ragley Hall, Alcester 270
Railway Preservation, Whitehead 392
Railway Village Museum, Swindon 284
Railworld, Peterborough. 38
Rangers House, London 203
Ravenglass Railway Museum, Ravenglass 76
Red House, Cleckheaton 290
Red House Museum, Christchurch 98
Red Lodge, Bristol. 17
Regimental Museum, York 310
Regimental Museum, Cardiff 367
Regimental Museum, Inverness. 361
Regimental Museum, Derby 80
Renfrew Community Museum, Renfew 337
Renishaw Hall Museum, Sheffield 304
Rhyl Library, Museum, Rhyl 387
Ribchester Roman Museum, Preston 156
Richmondshire Museum, Richmond 301
Rievaulx Abbey, Helmsley 293
Ripley Castle, Ripley 83
River & Rowing Museum, Henley-on-Thames 233
Rob Roy & Trossachs, Callander 346
Robert Burns Centre, Dumfries 317
Robertson Museum, Millport 335
Rochdale Pioneers Museum, Rochdale 54
Rockbourne Roman Villa, Fordingbridge 121
Roman Bath House, Lancaster 154
Roman Baths, Bath 15
Roman Legionary Museum, Caerleon. 366
Roman Theatre, St Albans 29
Romney Hythe & Dymchurch, New Romney 146
Roots of Norfolk, Dereham 209
Rossendale Museum, Rawtenstall 156

Museum/Gallery Name Index

Rothe House Museum, Kilkenny 403
Rotherham Art Gallery, Rotherham 302
Rotunda Museum, Scarborough 302
Royal Academy of Arts, London 187
Royal Air Force Museum, Norwich 212
Royal Air Force Museum, London 203
Royal Air Force Museum, Shifnal 239
Royal Albert Memorial, Exeter 90
Royal Armouries Museum, Leeds. 299
Royal Armouries, Fareham 121
Royal Cambrian Academy, Conwy 383
Royal College of Surgeons, London 184
Royal Cornwall Museum, Truro 68
Royal Crown Derby Visitor, Derby 80
Royal Dragoon Guards, York 310
Royal Engineers Museum, Gillingham 145
Royal Fusiliers Museum, London 187
Royal Glos, Berks & Wilts, Salisbury. 283
Royal Green Jackets, Winchester. 131
Royal Hampshire Regiment, Winchester. 132
Royal Hibernian Academy, Dublin 401
Royal Highland Fusiliers, Glasgow 329
Royal Irish Fusiliers, Armargh 392
Royal Irish Regiment, Ballymena 390
Royal Lincs Reg Museum, Lincoln 170
Royal Logistic Corps, Camberley. 253
Royal London Hospital, London 188
Royal Marines Museum, Portsmouth 127
Royal Military Police, Chichester 261
Royal Museum, Edinburgh 323
Royal National Lifeboat, Chatham 142
Royal Naval Museum, Portsmouth 128
Royal Navy Submarine, Gosport 122
Royal Norfolk Regimental, Norwich 212
Royal Observatory Visitor, Edinburgh 323
Royal Pavilion, Brighton 260
Royal Pump Room Museum, Harrogate 293
Royal Regiment Fusiliers, Warwick 278
Royal Research Ship, Dundee 347
Royal Scots Reg Museum, Edinburgh 323
Royal Shakespeare Company, Stratford-upon-Avon 276
Royal Signals Museum, Blandford Camp. 97
Royal Sussex Regiment, Eastbourne 263
Royal Ulster Rifles, Belfast. 391
Royal Welch Fusiliers, Caernarfon 383
Royston & District Museum, Royston. 28
Rozelle House Gallery, Ayr 313
Rugby Art Gallery, Rugby 276
Rugby School Museum, Rugby 276
Rural History Centre, Reading 27
Rural Life Centre, Farnham 254
Rushen Abbey, Ballasalla 412
Ruskin Library, Lancaster 154
Ruskin Museum, Coniston 73
Russell-Cotes Art Gallery, Bournemouth 97
Rutland County Museum, Oakham. 165
Rye Art Gallery, Rye 267
Rye Castle Museum, Rye 267
Ryedale Folk Museum, Hutton-le-Hole 296
Ryhope Engines Museum, Sunderland. 227

S

SS Great Britain, Bristol 17
SEARCH, Gosport 122
Saatchi Gallery, London 188
Saddleworth Museum, Oldham. 54
Saffron Walden Museum, Saffron Walden 106
Sainsbury Centre, Norwich 213
St Andrews Museum, St Andrews 354
St Andrews Preservation, St Andrews. 354
St Andrews University, St Andrews. 354
St Augustines Abbey, Canterbury 141
St Barbe Museum, Lymington 124

St Ives Museum, St Ives. 67
St Ives Society of Artist, St Ives 68
St John's Gate, London. 188
St Margaret's Cave, Dunfermline 348
St Mary's Guildhall, Coventry. 273
St Marys Lighthouse, Whitley Bay 229
St Mungo Museum, Glasgow. 330
St Patrick's Trian, Armagh 392
St Roberts Cave, Knaresborough. 298
Salford Museum, Salford 55
Salisbury & South Wilts, Salisbury 283
Sally Lunns House, Bath 15
Saltram House, Plymouth. 93
Sammy Miller Museum, New Milton 124
Samuel Johnson Birthplace, Lichfield 81
Sandhaven Meal Mill, Fraserburgh. 350
Sanquhar Tolbooth Museum, Sanquhar 338
Sarehole Mill, Birmingham. 271
Satrosphere Ltd, Aberdeen 342
Savings Banks Museum, Dumfries 317
Saxstead Green Post Mill, Woodbridge 251
Scapa Flow Visitor Centre, Orkney. 363
Scaplen's Court Museum, Poole 100
Scarborough Art Gallery, Scarborough 302
School of Art Gallery, Aberystwyth 377
School of Art Gallery, Aberystwyth 377
Science Museum, London 189
Scolton Manor Museum, Haverfordwest 370
Scotland Street School, Glasgow 330
Scotland's Secret Bunker, St Andrews 354
Scott Monument, Edinburgh 323
Scott Polar Research, Cambridge. 34
Scottish Fisheries Museum, Anstruther. 343
Scottish Industrial Rail, Dalmellington. 315
Scottish Maritime Museum, Irvine 331
Scottish Mining Museum, Newtongrange 336
Scottish National Gallery, Edinburgh 324
Scottish Nat'l Portrait, Edinburgh 324
Scottish Railway Society, Bo'ness 314
Seaford Museum, Seaford. 267
Sedgwick Museum, Cambridge 34
Segedunum Roman Fort, Wallsend 228
Segontium Roman Museum, Caernarfon 383
Senhouse Roman Museum, Maryport 75
Serpentine Gallery, London. 189
Severn Valley Railway, Bewdley. 134
Sewerby Hall Museum, Bridlington. 289
Shaftesbury Abbey Museum, Shaftesbury 100
Shaftesbury Town Museum, Shaftesbury 100
Shakespeare Birthplace, Stratford-upon-Avon. . . . 276
Shakespeare's Globe Exhib, London 189
Shambellie House Museum, Dumfries 317
Shambles Museum, Newent 113
Shandy Hall, York 310
Shaw Birthplace, Dublin 402
Shaw's Corner, Welwyn 30
Sheffield City Museum, Sheffield 305
Shefton Museum of Greek, Newcastle upon Tyne . 225
Shepherd Wheel, Sheffield 305
Sheppy's Farm & Museum, Taunton 245
Sherborne Castle, Sherborne 101
Sherborne Museum, Sherborne 101
Sheringham Museum, Sheringham. 213
Sherlock Holmes Museum, London 189
Shetland Croft House, Shetland. 364
Shetland Museum, Shetland 364
Shibden Hall, Halifax 292
Shipley Art Gallery, Gateshead 220
Shipwreck Heritage Centre, Hastings 264
Shire Hall Gallery, Stafford 84
Shoe Museum, Street 245
Shore Road Station, Birkenhead. 42
Shrewsbury Museum, Shrewsbury 239

Museum/Gallery Name Index

Shugborough Estate, Stafford 84
Shuttleworth Collection, Biggleswade 21
Sir Alfred Munnings Art, Dedham 105
Sir Francis Cook Gallery, Trinity 416
Sir Henry Jones Museum, Abergele 381
Sir John Soane's Museum, London 190
Sir Jules Thorn Exhibit, Edinburgh 324
Sir Richard Arkwrights, Matlock 82
Sir Walter Scotts Court, Selkirk 338
Slaidburn Heritage Centre, Slaidburn 156
Sligo County Museum, Sligo 410
Slough Museum, Slough 29
Smeatons Tower, Plymouth 93
Smith Art Gallery, Brighouse 289
Snibston Discovery Park, Coalville 158
Snowshill Manor, Broadway 111
Soho House, Birmingham 272
Somerset Brick & Tile, Bridgwater 243
Somerset County Museum, Taunton 246
Somerset Cricket Museum, Taunton 246
Somerset Military Museum, Taunton 246
Somerset Rural Life, Glastonbury 244
Somme Heritage Centre, Newtownards 394
South London Gallery, London 203
South Shields Museum, South Shields 226
South Tynedale Railway, Alston 70
South Wales Borderers, Brecon 378
South Wales Miners Museum, Port Talbot 373
Southampton City Gallery, Southampton 129
Southampton Maritime, Southampton 129
Southchurch Hall, Southend-on-Sea 107
Southend Central Museum, Southend-on-Sea 107
Southend Pier Museum, Southend-on-Sea 108
Southsea Castle, Portsmouth 128
Spitfire & Hurricane, Ramsgate 147
Spode Museum, Stoke-on-Trent 86
Spurn Lightship, Hull 295
Squerryes Court, Westerham 149
Stafford Castle, Stafford 85
Staffordshire Regiment, Lichfield 81
Stained Glass Museum, Ely 36
Stamford Museum, Stamford 172
Steam - Museum of GWR, Swindon 284
Stephenson Railway Museum, North Shields 225
Stevenage Museum, Stevenage 29
Stewartry Museum, Kirkcudbright 333
Steyning Museum, Steyning 267
Stirling Old Town Jail, Stirling 355
Stirling Smith Art Gall'y, Stirling 356
Stockport Air Raid, Stockport 57
Stockport Art Gallery, Stockport 57
Stockport Museum, Stockport 57
Stockwood Craft Museum, Luton 25
Stondon Museum, Henlow 23
Strangers Hall Museum, Norwich 213
Stranraer Museum, Stranraer 339
Strathnaver Museum, Bettyhill 358
Strathspey Railway, Aviemore 358
Streetlife - Hull Museum, Hull 296
Stromness Museum, Orkney 363
Sudeley Castle, Winchcombe 115
Sudley House, Liverpool 47
Sue Ryder Foundation, Sudbury 251
Sulgrave Manor, Sulgrave 39
Summerlee Heritage Park, Coatbridge 315
Sunderland Museum, Sunderland 228
Surrey Heath Museum, Camberley 253
Sussex Combined Services, Eastbourne 263
Sutton House, London 203
Sutton Park, York 310
Sutton Windmill, Norwich 213

Swalcliffe Barn, Banbury 232
Swansea Maritime Museum, Swansea 374
Swansea Museum, Swansea 374
Swindon Museum, Swindon 285

T

Tabley House Stately Home, Knutsford 45
Tain & District Museum, Tain 364
Talbot Rice Gallery, Edinburgh 324
Tales of the Old Gaol, King's Lynn 211
Talyllyn Railway, Tywyn 387
Tamworth Castle & Museum, Tamworth 86
Tangmere Military Museum, Chichester 262
Tank Museum, Wareham 101
Tar Tunnel, Telford 241
Tate Britain, London 190
Tate Liverpool, Liverpool 48
Tate Modern, London 190
Tate St Ives, St Ives 68
Tatton Park, Knutsford 45
Techniquest, Cardiff 368
Tenby Museum, Tenby 375
Tenement Museum, Glasgow 330
Thackray Museum, Leeds 300
Theatre Museum, London 191
Thirsk Museum, Thirsk 305
Thornbury & District, Thornbury 18
Three Rivers Museum, Rickmansworth 27
Threlkeld Quarry Museum, Keswick 75
Thurrock Museum, Grays 105
Thursford Collection, Fakenham 210
Thwaite Mills Watermill, Leeds 300
Timothy Hackworth, Shildon 226
Tipperary S R Museum, Clonmel 404
Tiptree Museum, Tiptree 108
Tiverton Museum, Tiverton 94
Tolbooth Art Centre, Kirkcudbright 333
Tolbooth Museum, Stonehaven 356
Tolgus Tin, Redruth 66
Tolsey Museum, Burford 232
Tolson Memorial Museum, Huddersfield 294
Tomintoul Museum, Tomintoul 356
Topsham Museum, Exeter 91
Torquay Museum, Torquay 94
Torre Abbey House, Torquay 95
Torrington Museum, Great Torrington 91
Totnes Costume Museum, Totnes 95
Totnes Elizabethan Museum, Totnes 95
Tower Bridge Experience, London 191
Tower Museum, Derry 395
H M Tower of London, London 191
Town House Museum, King's Lynn 211
Towneley Hall Art Gallery, Burnley 152
Towner Art Gallery, Eastbourne 263
Traquair House, Innerleithen 331
Treadgold Industrial, Portsmouth 128
Treasurers House, York 310
Treasures of St Cuthbert, Durham 219
Treasures of the Earth, Fort William 359
Trevithick Cottage, Camborne 61
Trim Visitor Centre, Trim 403
Trinity College Library, Dublin 402
Trinity House, Penzance 66
Trowbridge Museum, Trowbridge 285
Trues Yard Fishing, King's Lynn 211
Tudor House Museum, Southampton 130
Tugnet Ice House, Fochabers 349
Tullamore Dew Museum, Tullamore 411
Tullie House Museum, Carlisle 72
Tunbridge Wells Museum, Royal Tunbridge Wells . 147
Turner House Gallery, Penarth 372
Turnpike Gallery, Leigh 45
Turton Tower, Turton 57

Museum/Gallery Name Index

Tutankhamun Exhibition, Dorchester 99
Tweeddale Museum, Peebles 337
Ty Gwyn, Ty Crwn Barmouth, Barmouth 382
Tymperleys Clock Museum, Colchester 105
Tyrwhitt-Drake Museum, Maidstone 146
Tyseley Locomotive Works, Birmingham 272

U

US Grant Ancestral, Dungannon 395
Ullapool Museum, Ullapool 364
Ulster American Folk Park, Omagh 396
Ulster Folk Museum, Holywood 394
Ulster History Park, Omagh 396
Ulster Museum, Belfast 391
University Museum, Cambridge 34
University of Hull Art, Hull 296
University of Liverpool, Liverpool 48
University of Stirling, Stirling 356
Upper Wharfedale Folk, Skipton 305
Upton House, Banbury 232
Usher Gallery, Lincoln 170
Usk Rural Life Museum, Usk 375
Uttoxeter Heritage Centre, Uttoxeter 86

V

Vale & Downland Museum, Wantage 235
Vale of Glamorgan Railway, Barry Island 366
Valence House Museum, Dagenham 195
Vennel Gallery, Irvine 332
Verdant Works, Dundee 347
Verulamium Museum, St Albans 29
Vestry House Museum, London 203
Veterinary Museum, London 192
Victoria Art Gallery, Bath 15
Victoria Tower, Huddersfield 294
Victoria Albert Museum, London 192
Vina Cooke Museum, Newark-on-Trent 162
Vintage Carriage Trust, Keighley 297

W

W H Smith Museum, Newtown 378
Waddesdon Manor, Aylesbury 20
Wakefield Art Gallery, Wakefield 306
Wakefield Museum, Wakefield 306
Walker, Liverpool 48
Wall Roman Site & Museum, Lichfield 82
Wallace Collection, London 192
Wallington, Morpeth 223
Walmer Castle, Deal 142
Walter Rothschild, Tring 30
Wandsworth Museum, London 204
Ware Museum, Ware 30
Warrington Museum, Warrington 58
Warwick Doll Museum, Warwick 278
Warwickshire Museum, Warwick 278
Washington Old Hall, Washington 229
Watchet Market House, Watchet 246
Waterfront Museum, Poole 100
Waterways Museum, Goole 291
Watford Museum, Watford 30
Watts Gallery, Guildford 256
Wednesbury Museum, Wednesbury 278
Welch Regiment Museum, Cardiff 368
Wells Museum, Wells 246
Welsh Slate Museum, Llanberis 384
Welshpool & Llanfair Rail, Welshpool 379
Welwyn Roman Baths, Welwyn 30
Wesleys Chapel, London 193
West Berkshire Museum, Newbury 26
West Blatchington, Hove 265
West Highland Museum, Fort William 359
West Park Museum, Macclesfield 49
West Somerset Railway, Minehead 245

West Somerset Rural Life, Minehead 245
Westbury Manor Museum, Fareham 121
Westgate, Winchester 132
Weston Park, Shifnal 239
Westport Heritage Centre, Westport 410
Wexford County Museum, Enniscorthy 405
Weymouth Museum, Weymouth 102
Whipple Museum, Cambridge 34
Whitburn Community Museum, Whitburn 339
Whitby Abbey, Whitby 307
Whitby Archives, Whitby 307
Whitby Museum, Whitby 308
Whitchurch Silk Mill, Whitchurch 130
Whitechapel Art Gallery, London 193
Whitehall, Cheam 253
Whitstable Museum, Whitstable 149
Whitworth Art Gallery, Manchester 53
Wick Heritage Centre, Wick 364
Wigan Pier, Wigan 58
Wightwick Manor, Wolverhampton 279
Wilberforce House Museum, Hull 296
Willenhall Museum, Willenhall 279
William Herschel Museum, Bath 15
William Lamb Sculpture, Montrose 352
William Morris Gallery, London 204
Williamson Art Gallery, Birkenhead 42
Willis Museum, Basingstoke 119
Wilson Museum of Narberth, Narberth 372
Wilton House, Salisbury 284
Wiltshire Heritage Museum, Devizes 282
Wimbledon Lawn Tennis, London 204
Wimpole Hall & Home Farm, Royston 38
Winchester City Museum, Winchester 132
Windermere Steamboat, Windermere 76
Wirral Museum, Birkenhead 42
Wisbech & Fenland Museum, Wisbech 39
Withernsea Lighthouse, Withernsea 308
Woburn Abbey, Woburn 31
Wolverhampton Art Gallery, Wolverhampton 279
Wood End Museum, Scarborough 302
Woodhorn Colliery Museum, Ashington 216
Woodlands Art Gallery, London 204
Worcester City Museum, Worcester 138
Worcestershire Museum, Worcester 138
Workhouse Museum, Derry 395
Worksop Museum, Worksop 166
World of Country Life, Exmouth 91
World of Glass, St Helens 55
Worsbrough Mill Museum, Barnsley 287
Worthing Museum, Worthing 268
Wotton Heritage Centre, Wotton-under-Edge . . . 115
Wrexham County Museum, Wrexham 388
Writers Museum, Edinburgh 325
Wroxeter Roman City, Shrewsbury 239
Wycombe Museum, High Wycombe 23
Wylam Railway Museum, Wylam 229
Wymondham Heritage Museum, Wymondham . . . 214
Wythenshawe Hall, Manchester 53

Y

York City Art Gallery, York 310
York & Lancaster Regiment, Rotherham 302
York Minster Undercroft, York 311
Yorkshire Air Museum, York 311
Yorkshire Museum, York 311
Yorkshire Museum Farming, York 311
Yorkshire Sculpture Park, Wakefield 307
Youghal Heritage Centre, Youghal 407

Z

Zetland Lifeboat Museum, Redcar 225